D1743661

FAITH LIFE and THEOLOGY

A Reorientation

FAITH LIFE and THEOLOGY

A Reorientation

John C. Vander Stelt

PAIDEIA PRESS

2020

Faith Life and Theology: A Reorientation
by J. C. Vander Stelt

© 2020 Paideia Press

Published 2020 by Paideia Press
P.O. Box 1000, Jordan Station, Ontario, Canada L0R 1S0
and
The Reformational Publishing Project
www.reformationalpublishingproject.com

Manufactured in the United States of America

ISBN 978-0-88815-267-1

Dedications

To Sandy Vander Stelt, the love of my life for 60 years, mother of four wonderful children, soulmate, confidant, caretaker, grace-giver, joy-giver, green thumb with many plants and flowers, and the one whom God has used to keep me grounded far more than many will ever know or understand—thank you! Your prayers, patience, love and encouragement have carried me and this project towards completion.

And to these friends, contemporaries, colleagues whom I respect, honor and stand humbly with in seeking His Shalom:

JAMES SKILLEN (1944–)

A man who has humbly provided a revolutionary, Reformed voice for Biblical justice across all spheres of life, but with great emphasis in politics. From classrooms, to the halls of local, state and national government buildings, talking to policy makers in their offices and speaking in public, he has always issued a clarion call.

GORDON SPYKMAN (1926–1993)

A man who has been too often marginalized, yet stands head and shoulders above his critics for writing and speaking with profound clarity, simplicity, yet important depth on weighty matters within the Christian Reformed Church, and the global church at large, in Reformed thinking and praxis.

Gerald VandeZande (1923–2011)

A man whose charismatic character was effectively used to fight for justice for the common laborers across Canada. He led and others followed, as he gave voice to the voiceless, pressed against the status quo, stood strong in the midst of formidable resistance and exemplified courageous servant leadership.

Contents

Foreword

As a son of John C. Vander Stelt, I'm humbled by the privilege to write this introduction to his magnum opus.

During my growing-up years, Dad's study was filled with hundreds of theology and philosophy books, magazines, journals and articles in English, Dutch and German. His library included Calvin's *Institutes*, a large collection of Abraham Kuyper books, correspondence from various organizations—Christian Labor Association, Institute for Christian Studies, Center for Public Justice, etc.—several century-old Bibles, course notes, lectures, sermons, student papers, and much more.

Dad knew many of the authors by name; some of them were colleagues of his both near and far. Those he didn't know personally were nonetheless active past and present dialogue partners in his heart and mind who offered questions, ideas, and thoughts in ongoing conversations regarding how to live and act before the triune God.

Not all of these scholars agreed with Dad, nor did Dad agree with them. He pressed on with relentless intensity and passion to engage in many deep conversations that seemed too abstract and theoretical to some people, yet others found great clarity, encouragement and focus in their lives as they prayerfully pondered how to respond to the Gospel call to follow Jesus Christ.

One of Dad's main work tools in the early years was his manual typewriter. Long before today's computers, with their auto-correcting and shared-editing capabilities across vast networks, Dad used his old-fashioned typewriter to write and correspond. There was a rhythmic "tap-tap-tap" as he stroked the keys, a "ding" with each manual return, and an occasional "clunk" of the metal cabinet drawer as he took out a new bottle of white-out to retype a word or sentence that needed correction. My brother and I remember all this well because we shared a bedroom right next to Dad's study. My sisters, just a room away, could also hear them. We all often fell asleep to the familiar sounds of the typewriter as Dad toiled late into the night or got up early in the morning to pick up his work. Indeed, his work rarely left him, as there was always another lecture to write, a letter to respond to, an idea to unpack or a fresh question to ask.

Born in the Netherlands in 1934, Dad grew up on a family farm where faith was very important. Family, church, and Christian schools were a solid tripod of life. Raised with a strong Dutch work ethic, Dad and his siblings put in very long days between school and chores. Dad's family also lived through the horrors of World War II, and the ravages of Hitler's regime of terror, domination, death, and destruction left deep impressions on him. There were tense exchanges between Allied troops and Nazi soldiers right on my father's Dutch farmstead; many told and untold stories highlight the impact of these wartime experiences on him.

When Dad's family immigrated in 1951 to Ontario, Canada, they established a new family farm there. But Dad eventually turned in his work boots and gloves and swapped them for books. Though the smell of potatoes and horseradish fields still puts a smile on his face today, back then Dad plunged earnestly into God's Word and a massive amount of books as he began to tackle important questions that seemingly only a small group of people in Reformed circles dared to ask or address.

Dad's overriding calling all along has been to contribute to unpacking what it means to have a Kingdom-focused world-and-life view that proclaims the Lordship of Jesus Christ in every sphere of life. For him, God's sovereignty and shalom were not just concepts to be relegated to the classroom or the pulpit but, rather, *realities* to be *lived out* in everyday life. Faith was not merely something that pertained to Sundays for two hours (morning and evening services). Having a biblically grounded world-and-life view meant that choices had to be made regarding what to pray for, what to think about, how to act, and how to engage the secular culture all around us.

In all kinds of situations—conversations in the living room with students and colleagues, lectures in the classroom, preaching from pulpits, or taking long walks with bankers, farmers and businessmen—Dad constantly sought to recognize that all of life was redeemed, and he encouraged everybody to live daily with that in mind.

Admittedly, the questions that he typically raised seemed foreign to many in Sioux Center, Iowa, where he taught. For some, his conversations seemed counterintuitive and countercultural—and at times even unbiblical. Yet Dad was not dissuaded by either mild or abrasive opposition that came his way. He pressed forward, relentlessly endeavoring to add clarity and focus to real-life issues. This he saw as his primary calling and task in life.

In 1999, Dad retired from teaching theology and philosophy at Dordt College (now University). Though he stepped away from the classroom, he embarked on a journey to write a book that would synthesize key thoughts, conversations and observations that engaged him throughout his career. In this way, he *refired*, spending most of his time diving deeper into his books, and he methodically began to write. Even as he moved with Mom to Grand Rapids, Michigan, in 2006 to be closer geographically to family members, he had a relentless drive to write this book.

I, my mom, and my siblings would agree that this book arguably should have been finished several years ago. But unbeknownst to us until recently, Dad took to heart a mentor's advice, given to him many decades ago, that a book is not truly ready for publishing until one has written it three or four times. Agree or disagree, this is what Dad has been doing for the past twenty-one years. Worth noting is that very few people have been invited to read, provide feedback, ask clarifying questions, or comment on the full content of what is written in this book.

Also worth noting is that Dad has been dealing with the progression of dementia for the past several years, so the final parts of this journey towards completion have been significantly hampered. Ideally, a peer or colleague of Dad's might have been more suited than I to write this introduction. Nonetheless, due to timing and logistics, it's an honor for me to do it. My hope is that these personal reflections will give readers additional insight for understanding the context and the content of *Faith Life and Theology: A Reorientation.*

Those of us close to Dad have done our very best to bring this book to completion. We acknowledge that portions of these pages could be more clearly and more succinctly written. But we've deliberately chosen to minimize changing the content and writing style in order to honor Dad and his work. We've also chosen to include in the back a comprehensive bibliography. More than just a bibliography, however, it catalogs Dad's "LifeWorks"— all the books, articles, and sources that have served as his ecosystems in print to help shape his views. Please excuse any inaccuracies and/or omissions, as we have not been able to verify every last detail.

I want to acknowledge and thank these people for their time and work in helping to complete this book:

- Editors: Chris Gousmett and Joel Niewenhuis
- Project Assistance: Michael and Eleanor (Vander Stelt) Romijn, Kris Vander Stelt, Lydia Vander Stelt
- Book Cover design by Matter, Design + Marketing
- Cover drawing by Renee van der Stelt
- Cover design: Matter, Design + Marketing, in consultation with Renee van der Stelt.
- Interior layout/design: Klaas Wolterstorff
- Bibliography and Lifeworks: Michael and Eleanor (Vander Stelt) Romijn, Marcella Vander Stelt, Renee van der Stelt (McConville)
- Book advisor: Kerry Hollingsworth
- Publishing/promoting: John Hultink

Two special acknowledgments:

- John Hultink—longtime friend of Dad, businessman, generous under-writer of this book, and firm champion of a holistic Reformed world-and-life view.
- Kerry Hollingsworth—advisor to all of us, a great source of encourage-ment, and an advocate to see this book come to completion.

This book is a labor of love and has been a team effort. Our prayer-filled hope is that it will provide further clarity to crucial questions asked, greater understanding through answers provided, and encouragement to all to live humbly yet courageously, thoughtfully and faithfully, before the One in whom we live and breathe and have our being firmly grounded.

Finally, two Latin phrases come to mind that I believe aptly encapsulate Dad's life and work: *Ora et labora,* "Pray and work," and *Soli Deo gloria,* "Glory to God alone."

NATHAN (NATE) VANDER STELT

On the occasion of celebrating his and Sandy's 60th wedding anniversary (September 16, 1960), and while enjoying being with his children David, Nathan, Renee (via video) and Rachelle, along with their spouses, Dr. John C. Vander Stelt, age 86, passed away of a sudden heart attack on Saturday, September 19, 2020.

Prior to his passing, there was much joy, good food, reminiscing about years gone by, and the sharing of the news that this book was completed and ready for print. Within an hour after hearing this news, surrounded by his family, and with a heart full of joy, John breathed his last breath on earth.

He was preceded in death by his parents; siblings, Case Vander Stelt, Elizabeth Verhagen, and Walter Vander Stelt; and is survived by Agnes Huls, William (Vander Stelt) Steele and Joe Vander Stelt. He will be lovingly remembered by his wife, Sandy; children and grandchildren, David and Marcella Vander Stelt (Kyle, Riley, Spencer), Nathan and Kris Vander Stelt (Nicholas and Tori, Lydia, Joshua), Renee van der Stelt and husband Matt McConville (Helen), Rachelle (Vander Stelt) and Tom Knapper (Megan and Monte DeKam, Aaron Knapper).

Preface

God created humans to take care of his creation in a covenant-centered way. Rejection of His "covenant" with the world He created is evident in the "religious" conflict of major Greek thinkers as Socrates (c. 470–399 BC), Plato (428–348 BC), and Aristotle (384–322 BC) in their probing into the nature of such basic terms as reality, truth, certainty, philosophy, epistemology and even theology.

After Christ's life, death, resurrection and the Spirit's outpouring, joy-filled preachers, caring neighbors, eager missionaries, etc., talked joyfully about God's love-filled grace and celebrated a "freedom" they experienced day and night in response to his overwhelming presence.

A culture shaped by pagan thinkers is not totally void of certain "truth, certainty and reality" features that are treated as being absolutes, like gods. Restless humans have not been totally unaware of the triad of "ontology, anthropology and logic" in their restless and endless philosophical and theological inquiries. This is evident also in at least five forms of "scholastic" thinking. (i) St. Augustine (354–430) thought of "truth, faith, reality, good and evil," etc., in terms of both Scripture and Platonic thinking. (ii) T. Aquinas (1125–205) stated that all "theology" students, male and female, must take an introductory course (prolegomena) in Aristotle's philosophy and epistemology. (iii) T. Beza (1519–1605), a friend and coworker of J. Calvin, taught both philosophy and theology for three decades in his famous course called "dogmatics." In his famous lecture in 1559—at the official opening of John Calvin's Academy in Geneva in 1559—he used Aristotle's "logical method" to explain the difference between his "deductive theology" and the view of J. Arminius (1560–1609), his former student, who disagreed with Beza's view and stressed "inductive theology" until his death in the Netherlands in 1609. This difference caused a severe, even bloody, clash between Beza's "supra-natural" theology and Arminius's "infra-natural" theology in God's election. (iv) T. Reid (1710–1796), the founder of Scottish "Common Sense" philosophy, was a lifelong advocate of scholastic theology and its view of election. (v) The Roman Catholic Church declared in 1878 and 1950 that scholastic thinking is not an option, but a necessity, and declared in 1998 that all church leaders, priests, authors, teachers, scholars, etc., must think, teach and write according to T. Aquinas's medieval view of "faith and reason."

The sixteenth-century Protestant Reformation focused on God's grace and redemption in Christ and through the Spirit. The Protestant Reformation continued the Roman Catholic custom of requiring all theology students and church leaders to be familiar with the main features of Platonic and Aristotelian thinking in their anthropology and epistemology, including logic, truth, virtue, society, church and state, religion and politics, etc., which were all perpetuated in most Reformed, and all Presbyterian, Episcopalian, even evangelical, traditions in their theological and educational views.

One year after Hitler invaded the Netherlands, one of my elementary Christian grade-school teachers, Mr. J. Klop, tactfully taught me/us about especially (a) Hitler's evil worldview and brutal invasion of our land, and (b) A. Kuyper's (1937–1920) emphasis on the importance of Christ-centered and Spirit-directed thinking and living. He told us in class that in 1880 A. Kuyper founded the Free University in Amsterdam, wrote many articles for school-children and their teachers, young and old people, citizens and laborers, pastors and parishioners, social and medical leaders, national and international issues, and was a Prime Minister of the Netherlands.

With my parents, I emigrated in 1950 to Ontario, Canada. Four years later, I met Rev. Frans Guillaume, who had migrated from Amsterdam and was serving a congregation in Toronto. In 1944/5 he had been captured in Amsterdam by a pro-German Dutchman immediately after he had preached an anti-Hitler sermon, and he was shipped to a harsh concentration camp in Germany. I wondered how he had "walked with God" as a prisoner. His answer I still remember: that horrific experience convinced him, and his fellow prisoners, that in such a horrific situation one cannot "live without God" and become a victim of brutal power and cruelty.

In 1952, as an international and culturally sensitive Christian, Guillaume welcomed H. Evan Runner's appointment to teach philosophy at Calvin College, Grand Rapids, MI, USA. In 1939–1940 Runner studied for a half year at the reputable Reformed Seminary, in Kampen, the Netherlands—where, since 1882, H. Bavinck, a close friend of A. Kuyper, had taught "systematic theology." Runner returned to the USA, however, in February 1940, three months before Hitler invaded the Netherlands. Only after Hitler's defeat in 1945 did Runner return in 1946 to the Netherlands, this time to study (not theology in Kampen, but) philosophy at the Free University in Amsterdam. He wanted to benefit from a graduate education that was both broader and deeper than traditional thinking in theology.

He focused on the perspectives of several talented students working in Kuyper's line, especially H. Dooyeweerd, professor of jurisprudence, and his friend (and brother-in-law) D. Vollenhoven, a former pastor, who had become an historian of principled "reformational" thinking in philosophy. Runner focused on Dooyeweerd's view of issues related to especially the history and structure of society, and on Vollenhoven's awareness of the complex history of Western thinking about philosophical issues. Both thinkers were interested in, for example, the meaning of being human, the structure of society, the role of history, the essence of justice, the importance of industry, and the place of labor unions, medical care, etc. Crucial in all humans is not so much whether, but how, they "walk with God" in everything they do. Genuine human living calls for a covenant-centered way of reacting to God's all-encompassing love-command, not just intermittently at special times of a day, week, year, event, celebration, catastrophe, etc., but wholeheartedly in whatever humans do in all levels/phases of education, factories, markets, banks, hospitals, retreats, research centers, armies, sport centers, farms, etc.

Direly needed are Christ-centered and Spirit-filled educators, who in a simple, yet radical, way train future servants to love justice, help the needy and avoid the idols of, for instance, socialism, capitalism, militarism, nationalism, sexism, scientism and fame. Any speculative theology and philosophical arrogance about our immensely intricate universe—with its many Western and non-Western cultures—and about God and his stunning creation calls for a careful tip-toeing through his garden—His creation. Such a daily walking with the Creator provides, in principle, true freedom in all of life, also in both our philosophy and our theology.

A grant in 2001 from a foundation of the Free University in Amsterdam enabled me to explore the nature and impact of scholastic thinking in Western philosophy and theology, so as to find perhaps a better way to think about such basic terms as "religion", "faith life", and "theology." In short, how does God's "love command" enable humans as his "image-bearers" to walk with him in their daily life?

It is impossible for humans to live without religion. To be human is not an option, but a necessity, not a luxury, but unavoidable. To be religious reveals the basic direction in which humans live, behave day and night in whatever they do, including their reflecting on life, thinking about it, celebrating it and reflecting on it, etc.

Scholastic thinking has affected not only theology and philosophy but also the way humans act as citizens, politicians, bankers, doctors/nurses, parents, pilots, families, teachers, soldiers, street cleaners, entertainers, contractors, etc. In three major encyclicals, the Roman Catholic Church stated in 1879, 1950 and 1998 that proper thinking, preaching, organizing, shaping society and culture, etc., are impossible without complex scholastic (integrated) ways of thinking.

Religion is not restricted to intentional, or organized, faith life. Rather, it points to how humans behave in all their daily responsibilities. It is evident in how they raise children, welcome strangers, pay taxes, play games, cast a ballot in a voting booth, protect the environment, treat animals, and act privately and publicly.

Shortly before graduating from Calvin College, I benefited greatly from three two-day study conferences organized on a farm in Unionville, a town near Toronto. Eleven lectures, followed by extensive discussions, were given by two speakers from Canada, three from the Netherlands, one from South Africa, and one from the USA. These probing experiences helped me immensely in my six-year graduate study of theology and philosophy at the Free University.

In 1974 Dordt College asked me to attend an International "Conference of Reformed Colleges, Seminaries, Universities and Educational Institutions." When I attended this conference in 1975 in South Africa, the problem of apartheid caused considerable tension. Two hours after the conference opened, I co-signed a protest document of delegates shocked by a statement of the South African conference president.

Between 1975 and 1987, several successful regional conferences were held. The fifth conference, in Lusaka, Zambia, adopted the name still used today: International Association for the Promotion of Christian Higher Education (IAPCHE). The sixth conference, held at Dordt College, was carefully organized by J. B. Hulst, who retired in 1997 as Dordt College's second President. Since 1995, he was the Executive Secretary of IAPCHE. To stress IAPCHE's distinct vision, he suggested that the Conference Committee ask Harry J. Fernhout to be the keynote speaker and focus on the importance of a renewal in Christian higher education.

As a Canadian student, Fernhout graduated from Dordt College in 1971, studied several years at the Institute of Christian Studies (ICS) in Toronto, and was for two decades the professor of education there. After he moved from Toronto to The King's University, in Edmonton, Alberta, he continued to teach graduate education and serve as its President. As the chief speaker at IAPCHE's sixth International Conference, at Dordt College in 2000, he gave a riveting lecture focused on family dynamics and issues in integral Christian higher education in North America.[1]

After I became the Christian Reformed pastor in New Market, ON, Canada, the Christian Labor Association of Canada (CLAC) asked me to speak at its national and annual event on the meaning of "Jubilee," and to discuss the nature and influence of secular USA labor unions in Canada. One week after that "Jubilee" event, the Institute for Christian Studies (ICS) asked me to work two years to expedite the opening of ICS in Toronto by meeting with several student clubs at three universities in Ontario regarding, among other things, "secular" and "compromising" thinking, and the importance of wholehearted Christian thinking and living.

In 1967, the president of Dordt College called me to be interviewed about something I had not thought about, viz., teach two or three years in two independent, though often conflicting, departments, viz., theology and philosophy. Reluctantly, I accepted this unexpected, and unusual, request.

I sensed that such a position would enable me to study, teach, and debate with USA, Canadian, and foreign students about issues related to, for instance, religion, covenant, walking with God, truth, reality, justice, thinking, teaching, living responsibly as his image-bearing caretakers. I could also think about what it meant to see God in terms of Greek ideas of, for instance, reality, truth and virtue, as well as accommodated Western understandings of church and society, special and common grace, private and public faith, free will, and an anthropology focused on feeling, willing, thinking, along with an ontology based on what is physical, ethical, spiritual, and the suchlike.

My intent in this study is to explore a way to live in the One who arose from death, through the Spirit's power, and to respond to God's call to "love" him, by tiptoeing through his stunning garden through his power-filled love for all creation—to Satan's chagrin and fury!

---

1. Harry Fernhout, "Family Dynamics: Issues in Integral Christian Higher Education in North America," pages 251–274, published in *Christian Higher Education*. Special Issue: *Challenges for Christian Higher Education in the 21st Century*, ed., J. B. Hulst, Vol 1, No 2–3, 2002.

PART I

ORIENTATION

Introduction

F OR HUMANS TO BE RELIGIOUS IS NOT AN OPTION, but a necessity. It reveals who we are, not something we have. It is not what positivist educators believe to be outdated in our modern culture, nor can it be equated with the Western belief that religion is personal, limited to praying, expressed in worship, and that it consists of visiting those who are lonely and sick, feeding the hungry, helping humans locked up in prison, etc. But according to this view it is not essential in, for example, science, scholarship, agriculture, politics, government, labor unions, industry, stock-markets, communication, sports, etc.

What a rudder does to direct a boat (or ship), religion does to direct all humans in activities and the course of history. What is unique about humans is that they are responsible beings, a fact that can be seen in the way adults behave as spouses, how they raise their children, how they function as members of a community, how they act in a responsible way, serve as soldiers and police to protect a country, how they are care-givers and gifted doctors, etc. God's basic law of love expects humans to behave as His garden-keepers. The focus of this chapter centers on four intertwined issues: the nature of "faith life and theology," the method and terms used, certain pressing issues, and the structure and content of this study.

Three Experiences

Since the 1950s, I have wondered about the nature of terms associated with human faith life and how to study it. This interest was triggered by personal experiences in three countries: the Netherlands, Canada and the USA. This interest deepened and broadened when, in 1975, I became involved in Christian higher education (not primarily limited to theology and philosophy), and in non-Western, even global issues.[1]

Ever since the 1950s, I have wondered about various practical implications of being a Christian grounded in God's love. What is the secret and the effect of God's good news for rebelling humans who live in broken societies and cultures within one world? Three experiences in local and global Christian higher education compelled me to rethink certain often-used but little-understood terms: *religion, faith* and *theology*.

First, in 1940, when I was only six years old, I watched, while holding my father's hand, dozens of cavalry, followed by hundreds of infantry, invade our small town of Nieuwendijk (cf. the "new dyke" which Napoleon had built around 1810), heard them shout "Heil Hitler!" as they raised their right hands in salute and clicked the heels of their war boots. Until May 5, 1945, I saw the words "Gott mit uns" (God with us) on the polished belt-buckles of high-ranking officers.

What made it possible, I wondered as a lad in Holland, as a teenager in Canada and as a resident-alien in the USA, for Germany, the country where Martin Luther (d. 1546) started the Protestant Reformation, to give rise to the horrors of Nazi-fascism?[2] How could this country eventually terrorize not only Europe but also Russia, North Africa, and even England, the USA and Canada?

Any society and culture has the potential to misdirect the course of history. Blinded by an evil religion, or spirit, any faith in wealth, race, power, deception, etc., is inherently destructive. When a distorted religion becomes the basis for freedom, the essence of truth, or the structure of society, etc., it affects the course of history. Such a distorted faith is possible also in Hinduism and Buddhism, Islam and Zionistic Judaism, Russian and Chinese

---

1. Through consultations, conferences and presentations from 1975 to 2008 hosted by an organization known since 1989 as IAPCHE (International Association for the Promotion of Christian Higher Education) with its central office located at Dordt College, Sioux Center, IA, and, since 2012, at Calvin College, Grand Rapids, MI.

2. Resulting in the death of considerably more than 100 million humans, including six million Jews and thousands of Roma, or Romani, and homosexuals.

communism, modern colonialism and rationalism, capitalism and socialism, pragmatism and nihilism.

Christian faith is not restricted to what is "personal, private and organized." To be a follower of Christ Jesus, one must be God-centered and Spirit-directed. To be Christian is not the same as to belong to some organized church. As a student in 1952–1954 at the Brantford Collegiate Institute (BCI) in Ontario, Canada, I already rejected Western rationalism, including the secular distinction between science and faith, "objectivity" and "neutrality."[3]

Second, as students in my Christian[4] elementary school, we were taught to reflect God's holy presence in how we behaved in class, at home, on the farm, with friends, with German soldiers and fellow citizens, and we were encouraged to be interested in other countries and cultures. At a two-year Dutch vocational (ambacht) school and in Canada, at BCI,[5] I pursued (in a Greek course) the question about thinking in a Christian, versus a neutral or secular, way.

Third, as an apprentice in 1951, I was puzzled by the owner of a small experimental farm implement factory in Hespeler, ON, Canada. He turned out to be a fervent Baptist who held a dispensationalist view of "Scripture" and a secular view of "Reality." He required his twenty-two employees to meet on Monday mornings for a half-hour devotion and prayer in the lunchroom of his factory. After reading Scripture, he meditated briefly, thanked God for giving us a job, asked us to evangelize, and thus prepare for Christ's return to establish the Kingdom. In his office, he encouraged me to read several books about Christ's return and suggested that I not waste my time reading newspapers, especially editorials in major newspapers about Canada's history, culture and future.[6]

This way of thinking and living was something a friendly and gifted classmate at BCI three years later encouraged me to do in a dualistic way,

---

3. This explains why I was attracted in 1954 to the worldview of H. Evan Runner, one of my philosophy professors at Calvin College.

4. A result of Abraham Kuyper's insight that societal freedom and justice implies that Christian schools are also public and, therefore, entitled to proportional tax-based state support—a policy still in place today, also for humanists, Jews and Muslims.

5. At BCI, I studied English, History, Physical Education, Mathematics, French, Greek and German.

6. After doing as he suggested for some three months, I became confused by countless sensational "signs of the times," especially the many changing dates of Christ's return. My pastor, Rev. Adam Persenaire, warned me about the frenzy-feeding speculations of Hal Lindsey's *The Late Great Planet Earth* (1970), and Tim LeHaye and Jerry B. Jenkins's popular *Left Behind* books, conferences, videos and Armageddon movies.

i.e., thinking of "faith" as something private, personal and optional, and thinking of business, industry, politics, farming, education, art, sports, etc., as things which were not "religious," or faith-dependent, but necessary and cultural. In a candy store across the street from BCI, a kind classmate told me that "Christian faith" was optional, an "add-on," something irrelevant for studying classic liberal arts, natural science, athletics and mathematics.[7]

Thirteen years later, a gifted graduate student at a major Canadian university stated hesitantly, after I had given a short lecture, that she had begun to doubt Christ's origin and birth. In response to my question about what she meant by "science," she replied that she had started to doubt not just the origin of Christ but also the nature of human "faith life" and God's revelation. Her faith in the truth of "natural science" had deprived her of sleep. Her problem was not a conflict between "faith" and "science," but a conflict between two faiths: Christian or biblical faith and secular or positivist faith.[8]

Two additional experiences deepend my interest in the nature of "religion" and "faith life": being a member of the departments of "Theology" and "Philosophy," and secondly, my doctoral dissertation (published in the USA as *Philosophy & Scripture: A Study in Old Princeton and Westminster Theology*, 1978[9]) under G. C. Berkouwer and his successor, J. Veenhof at the Free University.

Stance, Method, Terms, Definition of Topic

As to God's revelation and my response to it, my basic stance[10] is neo-Kuyperian. Abraham Kuyper's reformation focused on ecclesiastical, social, economic, educational, political, ethical and aesthetic issues. His unique

7. My mathematics teacher at BCI talked in class about how an infinite series of numbers ultimately leads to an "infinite number, infinity or God," after which he added, "John Vander Stelt intends to become a theologian." After class, several classmates wondered, Why was I more interested in "eternal" matters" and not in "factual" issues?

8. This struggle affected numerous Christian students when they encountered this kind of "secularized" faith in (Western) scholarship and education.

9. For details, see Vander Stelt 1978. Lefferts A. Loetscher, professor at PTS, informed me about his growing interest in the major impact of Scottish "Common Sense" philosophy on Presbyterian theology in especially the USA.

10. To acknowledge one's confessional stance is in postmodern culture not as strange as it used to be. In contrast to traditional Enlightenment thinking about "subjective" and "objective," postmodernism stresses a knowledge that involves both a "subjective" element and an "objectivity" that calls for careful listening to the views of others.

worldview became known in North America in mainly two ways: his famous L. P. Stone "Lectures on Calvinism," delivered at Princeton University in the USA in 1898, and since 1949 through a major emigration of thousands of Dutch citizens, shaped by his significant reformation, who emigrated mainly to Canada but also to the USA.

The effect of these two migrations was a desire to continue Kuyper's simple, yet profound, worldview. It enabled them to act in a Christian manner during the week what they celebrated on Sunday, especially to help poor, lonely and handicapped people. In principle, they wanted to continue to "walk with God" in a Spirit-directed and Christ-centered way also in a new world with its own customs and culture.

In the spirit of John Calvin (1509–1564), a French reformer and refugee in Switzerland, who founded the Academy of Geneva in 1559, Kuyper (1837–1920) founded the Free University in 1880, in order to recover, deepen, and broaden what, three centuries earlier, Calvin had believed about the need for an ongoing spiritual renewal.

Six years after Kuyper's death in 1920, the Free University appointed two professors who in their elementary, secondary and graduate education had been trained in the reforming tradition of Calvin, G. Groen van Prinsterer, Kuyper and others—two young professors, viz., Herman Dooyeweerd (1894–1977) in "Jurisprudence" and (his brother-in-law) D. H. T. Vollenhoven (1892–1978) in "Philosophy." In the tradition of their parents and other mentors, notably Kuyper, they thought and taught in a culturally different and religiously more liberating and radical way. They reformulated various ideas found in the writings of their mentors, and even in their own thinking, about created reality and the unique task of humans in it.

Their restless probing about created reality was not centered on theology, but rather on God's covenant and kingdom. After I had studied two years at BCI in Canada, I majored in English, Latin and Philosophy at Calvin College in Grand Rapids, MI, USA, and for six years studied "theology and philosophy" at the Free University in Amsterdam. During the last three years I often preached in various Dutch provinces.

These various and interrelated experiences helped me in six ways: (i) as a pastor in the Christian Reformed Church in Ontario, Canada; (ii) promoting ICS for a year in Eastern Canada/Eastern USA; (iii) writing my doctoral dissertation in 1978 (republished in 2018) about North American Presbyterian "philosophy and theology"; (iv) teaching Theology and Philosophy at Dordt College; (v) since 1975, my involvement in life-changing experiences in IAPCHE; and (vi) writing this challenging study since 2001.

The intent of this study is to encourage those who seek to be faithful to God as the Creator of "heaven and earth," who calls humanity to be aware of the mystery and power of His love, to be freed from misleading debates about, for instance, conservatism and liberalism, communism and capitalism, humanism and socialism, etc. The world created and maintained by God reveals His powerful love and loving power through the Word Incarnate and through the Holy Spirit.

God's revelation is the condition for whatever is, including human denial of it. "Reality" is the sine qua non, the actual basis, or foundation, for what is, including humans' denial of it. To deny God's power is to ignore what the redeeming work the Lord has done for those who are persecuted, imprisoned, tortured and killed.

Covenant-centered living does not complicate what is simple, but actually simplifies what is religiously complex. To be positive, i.e., loving, caring, serving, honest, etc., in a sinful world is very difficult. A proper study of human faith life calls for distinguishing between what human beings have in common, or share structurally, but disagree about directionally, or religiously. Comments will be made about humans who rejected Western rationalism and explored a way of thinking in philosophy and theology that avoids the danger of biblicism and presses for a Christ-centered, Spirit-driven and God-honoring way of daily living, also in our thinking. Our deeply troubled world direly needs a heart-centered religion, not some abstract theory of God's incarnated Word and powerful Spirit of true love and freedom.

All our thinking, learning and teaching about God's awesome presence is central to all our living, including our thinking about, for instance, such interrelated topics as created reality (ontology), being human (anthropology), knowing and knowledge (epistemology), structure of a curriculum (encyclopedia) and human faith life (pisteology).

To be a blessing for others,[11] our thinking about human faith life may call for a kind of faith so important and strong that we are willing to be persecuted, even to die, for it. This is true for both Christians and non-Christians. One cannot be truly human without relying on something ultimate, perhaps oneself, someone else, or some major human or natural event.

Unique to Western rationalism is the idea that Christian faith is impossible without some form of divine revelation. Based on Greek thinking, especially that of Plato and Aristotle, human knowledge is basically logical, intellectual and atheistic. God did not create everything nor did He make

11. Cf. Genesis 12:2b and 3b, and 9:9–17, notably 14–16.

a covenant with humans as His image-bearers. For classic Greek thinkers, truth and certainty are human ways to think, to remove intellectual insecurity and to anchor truth, reality and order in a certain way.

The secret of being human can be summarized in the short phrase "life is religion."[12] It points to the essence of being human, i.e., to walk with God, act in His presence, live within His covenant, bear His image, reflect His glory. This is basic to all human behavior, also in studies of ontology, anthropology, epistemology, history, etc., and of such disciplines as mathematics, physics, biology, psychology, logic, linguistics, technology, sociology, economics, jurisprudence, etc. A study focused on discovering and describing[13] the structure of all human experiences is crucial also in the study of Christian and non-Christian "faith life," in this study called "pisteology" (study of human faith), not "theology" (study of God).

An important feature of this study is (a) its use of such terms as discipline, Wissenschaft, science, pisteology and (b) the relations within, and between, all human studies of human faith life. It focuses on how diverse features affect Christian and non-Christian[14] faith traditions and their relations to faith life and other forms of human life. Such a reforming way of thinking is not something imposed on reality, but important for every discipline, including the study of pisteology.

Method

The stance described above calls for a new way of thinking. It refuses to turn earlier forms of thinking into theories, or utopias, of Baconian empiricism, Reformed scholasticism, Kantian idealism, Hegelian dialectics, positivist logic-chopping, analytic hair-splitting and postmodern relativism.

---

12. H. Evan Runner (1916–2002), a student of both Vollenhoven and Dooyeweerd at the Free University, taught philosophy at Calvin College in Grand Rapids, MI, and was a chief mentor of those who started the Institute for Christian Studies (ICS) in Toronto in 1965. He adopted this phrase as a motto for the curriculum and teaching at ICS.

13. In distinction from "creating," or "projecting," as Edmund Husserl proposed with his phenomenological theory of "intentionality of human consciousness," a theory which does not acknowledge the *revelatory* character of created reality. See Mulder 1985: 3–15.

14. Since God's creational revelation impinges on all humans, Christians can learn from non-Christians. It happens despite the latter's *religious* ignorance and even their *rejection* of the Gospel as well.

In a positive way, it looks for a way to think in terms of a distinct religious stance. In addition to specific structural features in every discipline, Christian thinking acknowledges the presence of a religious conflict about the origin and structure of a reality into which Christians were born and of which they have become a part[15] and about which they are compelled to reflect and theorize. Scholarship consists of three parts: an investigator, an area to be studied and a specific relation between these two. How one views reality influences not just what one studies but also the relation between these two.

Christian scholarship presupposes a world God created, in which humans, as His image-bearers, realize that His revelation is not restricted to a book.[16] God's revelation assumes a broken society and culture that need to be renewed. To deal with major economic, political and cultural clashes, respond to critical health issues, remove debilitating personal conflicts, etc., is not an option, but a necessity.

Any biblicism, or "book religion," misuses Scripture: it thinks of it as an "almanac of truths." It denies that the Old and New Testaments were written as God's call to humans to live within the boundaries of His covenant with them. To use Scripture as a textbook does injustice to human knowledge, the nature of theory, the character of science and Scripture itself.

Despite human rejection of it, God's revelation remained intact and human responses to it did not cease. It is impossible for humans to suppress His revelation "in unrighteousness" without assuming the reality of revelation.[17] God's promise also to humans who rejected His faithfulness did not stop his ongoing revelation. On the contrary, He remained sovereign and maintained His covenant even with humans who refused to bear His image.[18] He reveals this in the promise, birth, life, death and resurrection

---

15. To do this is not easy (Matthew 7:21–22); it calls for vigilance and boldness (Hebrews 10:39). Proper dialogue presupposes awareness of the religious commitment of all parties involved. Cf. Griffioen (1982): 50–68.

16. Furthermore, to think of the Incarnate-Word in a moralistic way, and, worse, to think of the Incarnated One as a *second* source from which Christians can get knowledge about how to live fosters a form of "imitation" thinking: e.g., Christians must live as Christ did, avoid what he avoided, etc. They ignore that the Anointed Savior is unique, cannot be imitated—cf. the fad of WWJD (What Would Jesus Do) used in North American evangelical circles in the 1990s. For details, see Vander Stelt, (1978): 271–302.

17. See Romans 1:18–20.

18. For details, see Kuyper (1902–1904) and (1911–1912); Veenhof (1968): 345–365; Wolters (1985).

of the Word-made-flesh.[19] With their hearts turned back to their Creator, Christians seek to serve God in everything they do.[20]

In distinction from their "heart-centered" trusting in their Creator, the human act of "theorizing" focuses on understanding created differences in their proper context. Within the context of these two distinct, yet interrelated, activities, humans express their responsibilities and gain proper insights. Both are human and concrete, as they are in their acts of eating, voting, playing, buying, selling, building, etc. In all these ways, humans reveal concretely what they are committed to.

Religious[21] secularization is not restricted to one's faith life, something personal and isolated from the way one behaves in one's society and culture. Secularization is not neutral but religious, something negative, and affects the central thrust of one's whole life. It reveals a "basic stance" (*pou sto*), a defying of God's life-giving Word and of life in a covenant-anchored world.[22]

Terms

Each philosophical tradition has its own distinct vocabulary. This is true also of leading neo-Calvinist and -Kuyperian thinkers such as Vollenhoven and Dooyeweerd since the 1920s and many other reformational thinkers in diverse disciplines in the Netherlands and several other countries.[23]

Reformational thinkers have been accused of undermining, even ig-

---

19. Cf. John 1, Romans 1, Colossians 1, Ephesians 1 and Revelation 1.

20. Though Stroh errs in placing *theoretical* knowledge before *practical* knowledge, his *distinction* between these two in John Dewey's thinking is correct. See Stroh (1968): 249ff.

21. This religious secularization differs from structural secularization, i.e., a structure of society which rejects the control of any institutional church, organized faith community, or national religion that controls the rest of society. For details, see Mouw and Griffioen (1993): especially 1–19.

22. See L. Zuidervaart's Inaugural Address, Senior Member in Philosophy, Toronto, Ontario, Canada, (November 21, 2003).

23. Netherlands: J. Mekkes, K. Popma, S. Zuidema, H. Van Riesen. A. Troost, H. Geertsema, S. Griffioen, E. Schuurman, J. Klapwijk, A. Tol, K. Brill, J. Dengerink, J. Stellingwerff, M. C. Smit, A. Bos, G. Puchinger, H. Rookmaker, and others; North America: H. Evan Runner, C. Seerveld, B. Zylstra, H. Hart, J. H. Olthuis, A. Wolters, R. Clouser, J. Skillen, John Witte, Jr, Johan van der Vijver, J. Kok, J. Van Dyk, R. Sweetman, L. Zuidervaart; Japan: Haruna; S. Korea: Bong Ho Son, Sung So Kim; S. Africa: H. Stoker, B. J. van der Walt, D. Strauss, T. Van der Merwe; Australia: K. Sewell, B. Wearne; England-Scotland.

noring, "rational, intellectual and logical" clarity especially in two areas: (i) their distinction between, for example, heart and function, structure and direction, sphere sovereignty and universality, modalities and entities, anticipations and retrocipations, subject-functions and object-functions, founding and qualifying functions, naive and theoretic knowing, laws and norms; and (ii) their using terms like covenant, revelation, religion, reality, creatures, time, meaning, history, law, function, aspect, dualism, synthesis and antithesis.[24] Unlike what happened in Roman Catholic, Anglican-Episcopalian, diverse Protestant traditions, both neo-Calvinist and Kuyperian leaders developed their own way to resist both secular and accommodational thinking and to develop a way of thinking and living that was simpler and more life-encompassing.

Since the early 1920s, both Dooyeweerd and Vollenhoven sensed the debilitating effects of scholastic thinking at the Free University, in both "jurisprudence" and "theology." The well-intentioned but questionable, even debilitating, scholastic use of such terms as "truth," "reality," "law," "justice" and "order" calls for a response, which Dooyeweerd and Vollenhoven developed in their biblically directed (but anti-biblicist) thinking. Our thinking must be "simple in a radical way," Vollenhoven told me (during an afternoon walk in Amsterdam's Central Park), i.e., one must "walk with God, also in philosophy" (*wandelen met God, ook in filosophie*).

Critics of reformational thinking tend to minimize, if not ignore, the fact that every philosophy has its own nomenclature. This is evident in, for example, scholasticism,[25] rationalism,[26] existentialism, phenomenology,[27]

24. In addition to these terms and distinctions, developed chiefly by Vollenhoven, Dooyeweerd distinguished between "law-side and subject-side" "supra-temporal and temporal," "transcendent and transcendental," and used expressions like "meaning of being," "enkaptic relationships," "temporal horizon of experience" and process of "opening-up," "differentiation" and "disclosure."

25. Since the Middle Ages, in Roman Catholic culture, and since the Reformation, also in Protestant traditions—terms and distinctions like substance, essence, intellect, hierarchy, proofs, four causes, faith seeking understanding, form and matter, means and end, nature and grace, faith and reason, substantial and accidental, natural and supra-natural.

26. From around 1600 to 1900—terms and ideas like self-evident, autonomy, certainty, verification, a priori notions, innate ideas, scientific method, reason as basis and norm for both faith and religion, the distinctions between natural and rational, subjective and objective, clear and distinct, fact and value.

27. Such terms as situation, subjective, search, care, Angst, Sorge, passion, historical, existential, event, freedom, authentic, estrangement, alienation, orientation, absurd, horizon, epoche, intentionality, decision, consciousness, moment, dialectic.

pragmatism,[28] analytic philosophy[29] and postmodernism.[30] For philosophy to have its own terminology is not a liability but an asset. It enhances dialogue in a conflict-riddled culture. A scripturally directed philosophy has its own terminology to convey "reformational" thinking,"[31] reduce confusion, and encourage dialogue.

Integral—not "integrated" or "scholastic"—thinking refuses to deal with complex issues in a simplistic biblicist way. It is critical, but not belligerent, and avoids both non- and anti-Christian thinking. It wants, and needs, a simpler and practical way to study human faith life.

Delineation of Topic

In addition to physical, psychic, social, economic, political and other experiences, human faith life is also important in daily life. The human ability to trust, or have faith in something or someone, is not an option but a built-in created feature, a condition of being human. According to positivism, however, it is a form of superstition, being immature.[32] But for humans to trust or have faith in something or someone is not a personal option but a universal necessity. It cannot be removed from a country, culture, academy, or laboratory.

28. For example, change, operation, function, relative, practical, useful, context, probability, development, experimentation, process, and words with the prefix "re-": reconstruct, review, renew, revive, research, reconsider, readjust, rearrange, reflect, retry and retest.

29. Such terms and things as propositions, logic, ordinary language, language-games, picture-theory, warrant, coherence, logical consistency, plausibility, contingency, method, if-then reasoning, illocutionary, symbolic, clarifying, elucidating, defining, refereeing, 'doing' philosophy, stories about points of view, describing relationships, contexts, usages.

30. For example, individual, unique, deconstruction, interpretation, freedom, responsibility, hermeneutics, otherness, the other, "difference," power or control, contingency, relational, community, tradition, communication, openness, spirit(uality), text(uality), "subjective" order.

31. At the Synod of the North American Christian Reformed Church held at Dordt College in Iowa in 1996, Richard Muller, a newly appointed professor of Historical Theology at Calvin Theological Seminary, Grand Rapids, responded to a question by G. J. Spykman, a synodical advisor, about his view of "reformational philosophy." Muller said he did not know there was a sixteenth-century reformer in philosophy. When Spykman indicated that reformational thinking had to do with thinkers like Vollenhoven, Dooyeweerd and others after the 1920s, Muller said he was unaware of such philosophers in this century (for details, see Chapters 14 and 15 below).

32. Cf. A. Comte's philosophy of positivism in his classic *Course in Positive Philosophy, I-V* (1830–1842) and his *Positive Catechism* (1854).

Faith life is reflected in the actions, priorities and aspirations of all humans—Christians, Jews, Muslims, Buddhists, etc. It is evident in the priorities of countless Western humanists, rationalists, pragmatists and postmodernists, and in the idols of humanism, communism, capitalism, individualism, eroticism, mysticism, militarism, etc. It is evident in the Qur'an, the Book of Mormon, etc., and reflected in various liturgies, synagogues, mosques, temples, reading rooms, near large trees, at spiritual retreats, and all monasteries. It is present in large ecumenical events and the way "spiritual" leaders dress and meditate.

Neither is Christian faith life isolated from a person's daily routine, biotic needs, psychic preferences, economic situations, political contacts, environmental conditions, sexual behavior, preferred collars, etc.[33] My elementary education in two high schools in two countries, "liberal arts" training at Calvin College, my six years of graduate studies in Theology and Philosophy at the Free University in Amsterdam, and, after 1975, many global experiences in higher education convinced me, when I retired from Dordt College in 1999, to focus my reading and reflecting on the issue of human faith-life in our rapidly changing and shrinking world.[34]

Neither liberalism nor pietism deals properly with countless personal, public, cultural and global issues in our shrinking world shaped by a privatized and moralistic faith that fosters what it opposes, i.e., a lifestyle that restricts the essence, scope and power of God's redeeming Word in our restless world.[35]

After preaching and lecturing about central issues especially in theology and philosophy and being involved in many issues in different regions of the world, I decided in 2001 to center my studies on the nature of, and relation between, such issues as preaching and theology, catechism and education, poverty and wealth, church membership and national citizenship.

33. During German and Canadian bombardments in 1944, one of our neighbors left the Gereformeerde Kerk for "theological" reasons, joined a new denomination and ended his contact with my family. When, in 1994, after fifty years, I met this old, now widowed, neighbor, he embraced me at the door, wept and asked me to forgive him for what he had done to my parents and us as children. Never will I forget our long conversation about the power of the Gospel and the danger of "speculative theology and philosophy."

34. Of course, also experiences related to World War II, marrying Sandy, parenting four children, unforgettable experience in *International Christian Higher Education* since 1975.

35. The basis for this awareness was one of my elementary school teachers who understood H. Bavinck's comment that Christians experience two kinds of conversions: (1) a turning away from rebelling against God and back to Him in joy, and (2) a turning away from pietism and back to the world.

Lecturing for three decades on worldview-related issues especially in philosophy and theology, and interacting with inquisitive students and several gifted colleagues, I was compelled (as a Canadian in the USA) during the Vietnam War in the late 1960s to reflect on the nature of such pressing issues as faith, religion, freedom, justice, theology, worldview, war and peace, life and death. Can a (male) pre-seminary student avoid the draft for a long and brutal war between the USA and Vietnam? Can, or should, a (male) student be (or become) a student of "theology" as way to avoid killing, or being killed by, others? Is the faith life of pre-seminary students, pastors, priests, monks, etc., authentic, i.e., different from that of the faith life of a factory worker, banker, lawyer, doctor, garbage collector, etc.? What is God's kingdom, the nature of discipleship, the difference between studying theology and philosophy—is the former more important than the latter?

Being a member of the Purpose Committee and the Curriculum Committee, I wondered about the meaning of such often-used but little-understood expressions as "liberal arts," "biblically directed education," "reformed theology" and "doing things to God's glory." As chairman of a Task Force on "Global and Cross-Cultural Education," I developed and, for my last three years at DC, taught a mandatory course named "Calling, Task and Culture" (CTC) for all upper-level students. More than any other course, this privilege compelled me to reflect on the relation between our faith life and "Christian higher education" in our ever-shrinking and expanding world.

As executive secretary, board member and advisor of IAPCHE,[36] I looked for some clarity about the meaning of such much-used but little-understood terms as faith, religion, being biblical, Word of God, theology[37] and God's kingdom.[38] This compelled me to explore the role of the classic "liberal arts education" in Western colleges, universities and theological seminaries, and their use of terms like religion, study, discipline, analysis, anthropology,

---

36. As a participant in (i) seven international conferences (South Africa, 1975; USA, 1978 and 1981; the Netherlands, 1984; Zambia, 1987; USA, 2000, and Nicaragua, 2006); (ii) four regional conferences: Hungary, 1993; Russia, 1995; Philippines, 1998; Costa Rica, 2003; (iii) as executive secretary, 1981–1987; (iv) board member, 1989–2000; and (v) North American Advisor, 2000–2012.

37. I discussed in some detail with G. C. Berkouwer, my main mentor at the Free University, the role of "theology" in connection with faith life and the specific discipline of philosophy. These discussions deepened my awareness of the kingdom importance of anthropology within the context of God's liberating kingdom.

38. In the spirit of Gordon J. Spykman's remarks, at the end of his Commencement Address at Dordt College in 1988: ". . . nothing matters but the King, but because of the Kingdom, everything, literally everything, matters." Spykman (1988): 4.

science, theology, and philosophy. Needed in this connection is an integrally Christian way of thinking in every discipline, also in traditional Western philosophy and theology. In this way scholastic theology (study of God) can be replaced with, for instance, pisteology (study of human faith life). Such a reformulation sheds light on (i) the role of human faith life in all higher education; and (ii) how such "faith" life, and study of it (pisteology), influences both the religious direction and the structure of society in all academic, social, economic, technical, political and other kinds of human behavior.

This study is primarily intended for educators, researchers and students in colleges, seminaries, universities and vocational institutions. Urgently needed in our intricate but troubled world are God's caretakers, or servant-leaders,[39] who tiptoe through His huge garden filled with food, animals, parks, water, air, shelter, etc. His image-bearing creatures are called to reflect Him in whatever they do, also in their faith life. To be broad-minded in a narrow-hearted way is a temptation for humans in a rapidly changing but shrinking world. This is especially true for traditional philosophers and theologians, whose views tend to be myopic and dangerous.

Part I: Orientation (Chapters 1–6)

Chapter 1

This chapter focuses on certain experiences in my faith life and my involvement in studying and teaching both theology and philosophy. To start with an abstract discussion about faith life and theology may prevent inquiring readers from thinking about dangerous undertows and fatal rip-currents.[40] To help Christians and non-Christians sense the importance of faith in diverse cultures and traditions, I wrote this directionally simple, but structurally complex, study to deepen our self-knowledge and enhance our dialogue with fellow humans about the nature and role of our faith life.

We live in a world filled with immense suffering, obscene wealth, inde-

---

39. E.g., principals, educational supervisors, curricular and pedagogical experts, recruiters, book publishers, research foundations and media specialists.

40. The depth and scope of modern skepticism resemble two earlier forms of doubt, i.e., Hellenism in the early centuries and skepticism during the 14th–16th centuries. In response to the first, early Christianity arose, in response to the second, a clash between humanism and Reformation developed. One wonders about what our response to contemporary postmodern skepticism will be?

scribable poverty, broken promises, "stones-for-bread" preaching, profitable pop-theologies, and simple superficial philosophies. In 1999, I reduced my regular preaching, in order to look back, around, ahead, and up, encourage college, seminary and university students and teachers, challenge students and professors in vocational schools to focus on God's "love of life" and "life of love" for all His human image-bearers.

Chapter 2

This chapter focuses on a Western problem about the object of religion and the object of theology. Is God, Scripture, revelation, the church, Jesus Christ, the creed, or the Spirit, etc., the object? What is the relation between theology and curriculum, the essence of elementary, secondary and tertiary Christian education, the difference between theological seminaries and a divinity school, etc. Seven reputable national and international theologians spoke at an annual plenary session of the American Academy of Religion (AAR), attended by more than six thousand "theologically educated" scholars and teachers who tried to understand the academic significance of theology in carefully organized workshops and surrounded by large bookstalls.

Chapter 3

This chapter centers on the traditional scholastic tradition in philosophy (logic, proper reasoning, classic anthropology, ethics) and theology for more than four hundred years in Lutheran and Calvinist circles, especially in dogmatics, apologetics and truth.

Chapters 4–5

These two chapters indicate that both Bavinck and Kuyper were basically Christ-centered and Spirit-directed followers of "the Way" in what they did personally and publicly in their teaching and scholarship. However, by the end of the nineteenth century, Kuyper at the Free University had become less scholastic in his thinking than Bavinck at the Seminary in Kampen, with particular respect to his view of society, culture and history. In this regard he was more idealistic in his view of society, religion, faith life, scholarship and even theology.[41]

What united these two "reformers" was their rejection of both flight from the world (pietism) and worldliness (humanism), but they disagreed about how to do this. As professor of dogmatics at the Reformed (Gereformeerde) Seminary in Kampen for more than twenty years (1880–1902), Bavinck developed a scholastic view of reality, including the nature of being human and of knowing. In 1902, Bavinck left Kampen and joined Kuyper at the Free University in Amsterdam. His main interest shifted from traditional theology whose emphasis was on dogmatics and apologetics, and focused on more pressing societal and cultural issues. This shift indicated Bavinck's deepening interest in more practical, especially ecumenical, and other global issues.

Chapter 6

This chapter focuses on the immense influence of Plato's and Aristotle's dualistic anthropology and the immense impact of Greek "faculty psychology" theory with its emphasis on the tripod of "thinking, willing and feeling" about what is "true, moral and beautiful." These three Greek abilities or capacities guide humans in their view of laws or norms, to be thought and taught in all liberal arts disciplines. The influence of this classic idea of human faith life and studies of philosophy and theology in especially Western—even global—culture and thinking has been enormous.[42]

Part II: Reform(ul)ation (Chapters 7–13)

Chapters 7–11

These five chapters focus on a clearer understanding of three issues: (i) human faith life; (ii) replacing scholastic theology (study of God) with

41. Foppe M. Ten Hoor, from 1900–1924, professor of dogmatics at CTS, advocated Bavinck's view of theology and warned against Kuyper's ideas. For details, see Chapter 15 below.

42. This chapter is an edited and expanded version of "Faculty Psychology and Theology," presented at the 1998 international Quadrilateral Conference of the Free University, Institute for Christian Studies, Calvin College, and Dordt College, and was published by the Dordt Press. See Vander Stelt (2005): 45–59.

covenant-centered pisteology (study of human faith); and (iii) acknowledging the presence of a religious conflict.

Chapters 7 and 8 stress the need for an ongoing religious reformation also in diverse Reformed and Presbyterian traditions since the rise in fifteenth-century Protestant Reformation of scholastic thinking about human faith life and the role of theology. In these two issues, both Bavinck and Kuyper were still traditional in their thinking regarding the essence and role of "theology," as indicated in Chapters 4–5 above.

Despite this limitation in his theological thinking, Kuyper sensed the need to be religiously simpler, and culturally more relevant, for God's people immersed in Christ and moved by the Spirit. It calls for an ongoing renewal in how Spirit-directed followers of Jesus Christ act personally and publicly in their society, culture and world. He founded the Free University, lectured for four decades, preached regularly, wrote many major studies, books and articles about education, politics, culture, church life, industry, justice, national issues, etc., served as Prime Minister of the Netherlands, and visited and lectured in Indonesia, South Africa, the USA and Canada. For four decades, he was the foremost leader in Christian Higher Education. Two of the gifted students at the Free University were H. Dooyeweerd and D. H. T. Vollenhoven.

In 1926, six years after Kuyper died, both Dooyeweerd and Vollenhoven, who had studied at the Free University—the school at which their parents had encouraged their sons to study—were appointed to the staff. Dooyeweerd was appointed to teach Jurisprudence (not philosophy) and Vollenhoven to teach Philosophy (not theology). There, they focused their studies on basically two things: developing biblically directed self-knowledge and avoiding a traditional accommodating way of thinking and daily living triggered by scholastic theology and philosophy.

Their common view of religion affected their ontology, anthropology and epistemology. With respect to problems in faith and theology,[43] Vollenhoven's approach helped me more in my study of faith life than Dooyeweerd's view of it. It is more specific and practical, although not necessarily in conflict with Dooyeweerd's approach.[44] Thinking about theology in terms of pisteology, Vollenhoven addressed a major philosophical, anthropological

---

43. Dooyeweerd was never a pastor, nor a theologian. As an expert in political theory and jurisprudence, he discussed a wide range of complex philosophical issues.

44. Vollenhoven was a pastor and a theologian for several years before his appointment in 1926 as professor of philosophy at the Free University in Amsterdam.

and epistemological problem in all scholastic thinking. His ideas about the structure of human faith life are dealt in some detail in Chapters 9 and 10.

Chapter 11

This chapter indicates the nature of religious, or directional, conflict in human faith life. Although they disagreed in some respects about the religious thrust of what humans do in society, culture and history, Vollenhoven and Dooyeweerd moved in the same direction that Bavinck and Kuyper, as their predecessors, had done at the Free University, i.e., a religious conflict in our broken world.

Though this struggle is not inherent or integral to the structure of created reality, it is unavoidable for humans who refuse to honor God as their Creator. The mystery of iniquity is the source of all misery. This conflict may not be denied, ignored or celebrated. It must be recognized and countered by relying on God's promises and appealing to His covenant, sealed in the truth of the Savior. The latter is not just a concept of the "human mind," but inherent in God's covenant, sealed in the Son and through the Spirit at the core of created reality. To make a distinction between church and world, Christ and culture, faith and philosophy, Scripture and science, religion and politics, etc., denies that Christians are disciples of the risen One, who is "the way, the truth and the life."[45]

Chapter 12

This chapter focuses on the difference between faith life and pisteology, focuses on different faith traditions and warns against persecutors, those who outlaw or even kill those who believe differently.

Chapter 13

This chapter consists of various observations about hermeneutical issues, discerning God's revelation, the work of the Holy Spirit, reading God's covenant love-letter and relying on His promises.

45. John 14:6.

Part III: Accommodation (Chapters 14–18)

Chapter 14

This long chapter was written last, in response to a suggestion of Jacob Klap-wijk, a colleague in theology and philosophy at the Free University[46], to provide some historical depth and cultural context for issues discussed in Chapters 15–18 by calling attention to three crucial encyclicals published by the Roman Catholic Church (RCC) in 1879, 1950 and 1998, about how Thomas Aquinas had become the chief architect of a scholastic view of both faith and reason and theology and philosophy.

Chapters 15–18

These four chapters focus on scholastic features in (a) theology at Calvin Theological Seminary (CTS) at the end of the nineteenth century and beginning of the twentieth, during which period theologians arose, such as F. M. Ten Hoor, S. Volbeda, L. Berkhof and even H. J. Stob, who tended to favor Augustinian thinking (Chapters 15–16); and (b) philosophy at Calvin College since the 1930s in such thinkers as especially W. Harry Jellema and, after 1970, Jellema's gifted students Nicholas Wolterstorff and Alvin Plantinga (Chapters 17–18).

The co-founder of Reformed Epistemology (RE) was Wolterstorff, who wrote his doctoral dissertation on the Common Sense philosophy in Thomas Reid (1710–1796), a major Scottish philosopher and theologian (cf. Chapter 15). The main founder of RE, Plantinga, focused his thinking on the method of Thomas Aquinas (1225–1274), as a major synthesis thinker in both philosophy and theology about "reality, certainty, logic, knowing, education," and the tripod of "true, good, beautiful," especially after the RCC published two encyclicals in 1879 and 1950, which declared the thinking of Thomas Aquinas not to be optional, but required, for all priests, professors, educators and teachers at all levels of education (cf. Chapter 16).

---

46. Since 1960 as a fellow student and for several decades philosopher at the Free University.

Part IV: Reorientation (Chapters 19–20)

Chapter 19

H. Evan Runner, a philosophy professor at Calvin College, stressed the importance of God's covenant-centered revelation about the human heart, faith, truth, covenant-walking with God in everything we do, through God's Spirit, as followers of Jesus Christ, our Savior.

To teach at Calvin College, one had to be a member of the Christian Reformed Church in North America. As a Presbyterian, Runner studied at Westminster Theological Seminary (WTS) in Philadelphia, and theology for a half year at Reformed (Gereformeerd) Seminary in Kampen, the Netherlands, where, since 1880, Bavinck had taught a scholastic dogmatics, something Theodore Beza had become famous for almost three centuries earlier at Calvin's Academy in Geneva.

Fearing Hitler's fury, Runner suddenly returned to the USA a few months before the Nazi invasion of the Netherlands. After studying Greek and Latin at Harvard University, he returned in 1946 to the Netherlands, not to study theology in Kampen, but to immerse himself in philosophy at the Free University, to understand more clearly Kuyper's unique worldview, the notable new insights of H. Dooyeweerd and D. Vollenhoven, and where he received his doctorate (*cum lauda*) in the philosophy of Aristotle (384–322 BC).

After teaching philosophy for one year, Runner became the main sponsor of the Groen van Prinsterer Club at Calvin College and Calvin Theological Seminary. At three summer conferences on a farm in Unionville, east of Toronto, he played a crucial role in starting what a few years later became the Institute for Christian Studies (ICS) in Toronto. He stressed the need for Christian Labor Unions, Christian thinking about civic and political responsibilities, and translated S. G. De Graaf's *Verbondsgeschiedenis*, I-II, into English and got it published in Canada, with financial support from a former classmate in the USA as the four-volume work *Promise and Deliverance*.

Chapter 20

To think about philosophy, theology, anthropology, epistemology, etc., in a world filled with rebellious thinking about "truth, morality and religion,"[47] may be well-intentioned, but it does not reflect God's wide and deep covenant of love in Christ Jesus. It calls for daily renewal, something Runner stressed to consist of a life-encompassing and Spirit-filled religion.

This latter condition challenges every human to reform what they do day and night, wherever they live in this world. At the dawn of creation, humans were told to actively bear God's image. Because of a negative human response to God's command to love Him, God urged humans to serve Him as their Maker by renewing the way they need to walk with Him in their private and public faith life. Hence humans must learn what to live for, the difference between what is responsible and irresponsible, etc.

47. For details, see Chapter 6 below on "Faculty Psychology."

CHAPTER TWO

The Object of Theology

To indicate precisely what the study of theology consists of at seminaries, divinity schools, Christian colleges and universities is not easy—on the contrary, it is quite difficult. Is it only about what Christians believe? Does it focus on what is generally considered to be "religious" or "spiritual"? Exactly what does the nebulous term *theology* refer to in countless local and global faith traditions and related educational and academic institutions?

This issue needs to be dealt with before we explore the feasibility of thinking of theology as a study of not only Christian but also non-Christian faith life, and, for that reason, as will be proposed below, replace theology (study of God) with pisteology (study of faith life).

The traditional place of theology in an academy, society or culture assumes that faith life is inherent in both Christian and non-Christian faith traditions. Faith life precedes one's study of it. The reverse is not true: a study of theology is not basic to any actual faith life—that would place the cart before the horse, and reflect a form of projection-thinking, according to which a biblically directed faith life depends on some prior human action.

To place one's faith in something considered to be most important in life is not an example of theological thinking. The difference between these two activities is comparable to teaching and thinking about teaching, being a citizen and studying citizenship, etc. To believe in an Ultimate is not the same as to speculate about such a belief. All humans, including skeptics, believe that something provides the key to reality, even when that key is constantly changing. Although human acts of believing, and thinking about it, are closely interrelated, they are not the same. To live one's faith and think about it are not the same. It fosters the distorted idea that believing God and reading Scripture enables one to be a "theologian."[1]

To cope with increasing conflicts in human faith life, a better, or at least a clearer, view of "faith life" and "theology" is direly needed. To meet this challenge may not remove unnecessary conflicts in Christian faith life, but it will reduce them. It may enable pastors and theologians not to be misled themselves, nor to mislead others, with speculative ideas and actions that threaten the peace and power of fellow humans in a fractured and groaning world. A question one of my non-theological colleagues asked in 1985 in a short article which he aptly titled "Theology: Molder of a Graven Image?" is not a cynical hyperbole, but something significant which ought to be taken seriously:

> It seems to me that the issues of the nature, place, and task of theology in the Reformed community remains a question of utmost importance. There can be no doubt that a good deal of disagreement present among us is to be attributed to a diversity of silent assumptions regarding the nature of both theology and philosophy and the relation between them. In a recent issue of the Reformed Ecumenical Synod Theological Forum, there appeared a discussion about the uniqueness of Reformed theology. There was no unanimity about what makes theology Reformed. Striking, however, was the conspicuous absence of some formulation or definition of what theology is in the first place. Can we assume that it is clear to us what we are talking about when we refer to 'theology'?

Four Views

One way to respond to such a probing question is to indicate the wide range of views in Christian circles about the much-used but little-understood word *theology*. What is really the object of this discipline, its field of investigation? Among the many answers given to this crucial question, the four prominent ones are "God," "Scripture," "revelation" and "churches and their creeds." A few comments about these four views will highlight the main issues.

---

1. For details about this view and its implications, see Chapters 9 and 10 below, as well as Chapter 15 about F. M. ten Hoor at Calvin Theological Seminary from 1900 to 1934. See also Klaas Schilder (1909–1952) in the Netherlands, Karl Barth (1886–1968) in Germany/Switzerland, and most Evangelical theologians in North America.

God as Object

The notion that the object of Theology is the study of God (θεος)[2] reflects a compromising Greek way of abstract thinking about God, as though He were not the Creator, but part of what He created, in distinction from what numbers and space are in Mathematics, natural things in Physics, plants in Botany, animals in Zoology, emotions in Psychology, logic in Epistemology, interaction in Sociology, justice in Jurisprudence, and loyalty in ethics.[3]

Scripture as Object

Generally speaking, Christian traditions, including Reformed and Evangelical, stress this approach. For historical reasons, this emphasis is understandable,[4] though in a systematic sense it is riddled with problems. It raises questions as to whether theologians read Scripture incorrectly. Must non-theologians depend on theologians? What is the role of Scripture for all who read it in their distinct disciplines, including theology? Do introductory theology courses at Christian colleges and seminaries deal with issues not dealt with in Scripture concerning, for example, philosophy, epistemology, language, logic, environment, culture and pedagogy? Do liberal arts, social science, natural science, etc., influence one's reading of Scripture, especially the relevance of God in one's daily life?

Revelation as Object

In this case, a distinction between Scripture and revelation is assumed and the latter is considered to be broader than the former. God's revelation is not limited to a book. His revelation is not just Scriptural, but also creational and incarnational. This response is a significant improvement over the view that

2. This term is a Greek compound of logos (study) and theos (god). About its use in Plato and Aristotle, see chapter 8 below.

3. Used here in a reformational anthropology, not a Greek or scholastic one. For details, see especially Chapters 6–9 below.

4. Especially during the sixteenth century when Protestants, rejecting Roman Catholicism, stressed sola Scriptura, and during the last two centuries when Evangelicals emphasized biblicism in their opposition to humanism and materialism.

God and Scripture are the focus of theology. Though less speculative than the first response, it is broader than the second one.

Despite this improvement, this view is still contestable in that the object of theology is now too broad. It opens the gate to a subtle and lethal form of subjectivism and liberalism. Given its inclusive nature, this kind of theology turns, sooner or later, into an all-encompassing study of all created reality. It invites theologians to reach for the pinnacle of power by pontificating to non-theologians about how to live and (mis)direct a culture and civilization.[5] This form of theology is guilty of two dangerous evils: it overestimates the importance of theologians and underestimates the role of experts in non-theological disciplines.[6]

Churches and Creeds as Object

If organized faith communities, each with its own distinct creedal statements, are the object of theology, the nature and role of theology becomes even more nebulous and problematic. Are there as many theologies as there are organized churches?

Those who believe Scripture to be the object of theology reject this approach because it stresses too much the subjective human response to God's revelation in Scripture and does not put enough emphasis on Scripture as God's revelation to humans in their personal faith life. A more important critique of such a view of the object of theology is that it does not fully realize that it includes issues not directly, but only indirectly, ecclesiastical in nature. These four views about the object of theology share a misleading idea about the relation between theology, as a specific discipline, and all the other disciplines in a traditional liberal arts curriculum. That kind of relation can be any one of the following three: isolation, culmination and contrast.

---

5. This approach has been practiced in both Christian and non-Christian traditions, as is evident in theocratic state-church views of society in Western culture and, especially, in Islamic countries and traditions.

6. To reject this view of theology, I declined to lecture as a theologian on Genesis.

Isolation

To isolate theology from non-theological disciplines is to impoverish both theology and the other disciplines. It violates the unity of created reality and the distinct nature of every discipline. While it claims that the content of theology differs from that of the other disciplines, it assumes that the method used in theology resembles that of all other disciplines. It ignores the issue of what is distinct about the content and method within each discipline. The same is true with respect to the correlation between content and method in all disciplines. The impact on scholarship, including theology, of Greek thinking about, for example, "truth" and "method" in Western culture, about "knowledge" and "certainty," and of non-Western habits and beliefs has given rise to numerous problems in our Western culture.[7]

Culmination

Another way to think about the relation between theology and other disciplines has been the classic Augustinian idea that theology is the culmination or epitome of all knowledge and scholarship. This general view permeated the mind and method of Thomas Aquinas (1225–1274). In a neo-Platonic and neo-Aristotelian way, he believed that, unlike all other disciplines, theology is a basically an Aristotelian lifelong arduous and sacred endeavor. As "study of God," theology epitomizes all knowledge, and it is the queen of all science, the apex of all insight.[8]

Contrast

The third way to think of the relation between theology and all other disciplines is neither isolation nor culmination. The encyclopedic relation between theology and all other disciplines is an elusive and complicated one. It

---

7. E.g., the influence of medieval scholasticism on Roman Catholicism, post-reformation scholasticism on Lutheran and Calvinist scholarship and faith life, existentialism on Barthian neo-orthodoxy, and linguistic-analytical methods on Anglo-American scholarship and theology. For details, see Chapters 3–6 below.

8. This view of theology presupposes the notion of super-natural revelation in relation to (Christian) faith. Thomas Aquinas referred to this theology as natural theology based on natural reason.

is basic to the (soft-Lutheran and hard-Kierkegaardian) struggle between (a) being God-directed and self-centered living, (b) heaven-bound and world-centered thinking, and (c) the paradoxes in humans between grace and sin, submission and defiance, good and evil.

Theology and Curriculum

Implied in these four questionable views about the object of theology and three wrong ideas about the relation between theology and all other disciplines are several unavoidable problems about the name and role of theology in traditional Christian liberal arts colleges and universities. At least four names have been given to the department responsible for courses in human faith life and their related values, i.e., Bible, Theology, Divinity and Religion, or some combination of these four. Encyclopedic or curricular problems associated with such a department have been both unavoidable and unresolvable.

Bible Department

This concept stresses God's revelation recorded in some sixty-six books in Scripture. To adopt the notion that Scripture is the object of theology tends to restrict God's revelation to Christ Jesus as the incarnated One. It calls insufficient attention to God's *creational revelation* because it focuses primarily on human faith activities. Such courses and programs perpetuate a faith instruction provided at home, taught in the catechism classes of local faith communities, etc. The teachers or professors of Bible Departments are often graduates of a Bible College or of a Seminary that uses Scripture as a textbook.

Methodists, Evangelicals and Pentecostals are generally fundamentalist in their view of the Bible Department. They tend to personalize and privatize faith life, associate religion with something in which they are engaged for only part of their time, but not as something that is truly radical, life-encompassing, the central thrust of everything humans do in their daily life.

In such a Department, the religious thrust of one's Christian living is reduced to, or equated with, faith life alone. Its desire to be biblical is laudable, but to call that "Bible Department" is not helpful. It claims too much for itself. To think that Scripture is the "object" of theology is not only unhelpful, but even unbiblical. It does injustice to the depth and scope of God's reve-lation. Human life is religious in that it responds to God's all-encompassing revelation.[9] A personalized and privatized faith life fails to acknowledge His impinging revelation in a world rife with educational, societal, and cultural problems, the role of government in a global world filled with poverty,[10] terror and obscene wealth.

Religion Department

This term is used in public state-controlled colleges and universities.[11] It is not characteristic of Bible schools, liberal arts colleges and theological seminaries. The reason for using "Religion" is to avoid denominational, sectarian and intolerant thinking in higher education. It tries to minimize Scripture, not to avoid it, thereby calling attention to the role humans play in ascertaining God's revelation. Whereas "Bible Department" stresses the objective content of faith, "Religion Department" focuses more on the sub-jective projections of human faith.[12] Since it encompasses more than "Bible Department," to replace it with "Religion Department" is an improvement. However, it still involves, in Western thinking, the idea that religion calls for rational human faith acts expressed in the rationalist myth of, for example, John Locke, Adam Smith, Thomas Jefferson, Benjamin Franklin, Auguste Comte, etc. As a result, academic life relates to faith life in the same way that public life relates to private life, a political party and a religion. A human not involved in faith life is not really religious, i.e., he or she has no religion. One can be human without being religious. Pervasive in Western culture, especially in higher education and scholarship, is a deepening commitment to the conundrum of—irony of ironies—a religious secularism.

This Enlightenment faith is clear in the positivism of Comte (1798–

9. For the reformational idea of "human life as religion," see Chapters 11 and 16 below.

10. In a discussion in 1982 with members of a "Bible Department" at a theological sem-inary in a non-Western country, I was told that in two of their economic courses (Economic Theories and Christian Economics) the principles and practices of the capitalism of the Chicago Friedman School of Economics were taught as being compatible with Scriptural revelation.

11. And in most Western countries, although not the Netherlands after Kuyper's under-standing of citizenship altered the structure of society with regard to the role of education. For details, see Chapter 5 below.

12. For details, see Chapters 8–10 below.

1857). In fact, he believed that religion arose during an early phase in history, when humans were still primitive and superstitious, believed in supernatural forces, practiced magic, and were not able to explain reality in a scientific way.

With regard to religion, this view of history has been severely criticized. Despite positivism's denial of the enduring role of religion and Karl Marx's crusade against any religion, there is today a growing sense that religion must be recognized as an inherent feature of being human. Though they do so tacitly and reluctantly, studies in psychology, art, cultural anthropology, sociology, history, ethics, political theory and medicine acknowledge that there is something unexplainable in being human. Despite this awareness, the notion that religion is a lingering residue of primitive living limited to an isolated part of life continues to bewitch Christian educators and scholars in Bible and Religion Departments; they agree and disagree with this idea.

Faculty of Divinity

This term has been used in Roman Catholic and Anglican, or Episcopalian, faith traditions.[13] It claims that what is studied, taught and learned in such a faculty focuses on what is sacred, in distinction from secular, on what is "spiritual" or above, not on what is "natural or rational" below.

Theology Department

It indicates a Greek mind-set, especially about knowledge, truth and metaphysics. According to Plato (c. 427–348 BC) and Aristotle (384–322 BC), divine knowledge assumes an ability to know what is higher and deeper than common or ordinary knowledge. It is an inquiry into the first principles of philosophy (study of wisdom), metaphysics (what is beyond physics), and called theology (study of God). Philosophy needs theology as its most significant part of knowing and determines everything in philosophy.

The medieval theologian and philosopher Thomas Aquinas (1225–1275) called this knowledge natural theology. It is based on nature and reason, in distinction from supernatural theology, which is based on God's revelation in

---

13. Used also in such (initially semi-Calvinist) institutions as Harvard University and Yale University.

Scripture and Christ. Since the Protestant Reformation, Lutheran, Calvinist and Anglican theological seminaries and divinity schools found ways to synthesize Aristotle's theology and philosophy and incorporate them into their own accommodationist thinking. To make this natural or rational theology more useful in their own thinking, Protestant theologians, even more than the Roman Catholic Church had done, also conceived of theology in terms of Scripture understood as supra-natural revelation.

This well-intentioned but questionable accommodation resulted in an inability to distinguish clearly between, for instance, faith and theology, pulpit and lectern, practice and theory, dogmas and dogmatics, creeds and symbols, etc.[14] At the center of this compromise, with its inherent problems, are two major forms of religious compromise, or forms of synthesis, i.e., an Augustinian one and a Thomist one. In the former case, thinking moves from pulpit to lectern, believing to understanding and faith to theology, and in the latter case, thinking moves essentially from lectern to pulpit, understanding to believing and theology to faith.

In both cases, the often-used but little-understood phrase *fides quaerens intellectum* (faith seeking understanding) became a shibboleth in theological circles. Its complicated meaning continues to be vigorously debated. In a neo-Platonic way, Augustine emphasized practical living, stressed the human will, and thought about intellect more in terms of a large creedal context. In a neo-Aristotelian way, Aquinas focused more on philosophical knowing and on the role of human intellect, and reflected on human will more in terms of human intellect or reason.

Assumed in scholastic thinking is a fundamental religious dualism. The basic aim of Christians is to perform their daily tasks, reflect on both the structure of society and the nature of culture and develop a curriculum that reflects the unity and diversity of all human behavior. A religious conflict, however, has undermined this laudable intent of humans, disrupted the unity of their life, fostered tensions and deprived humans of joy in their daily living. Any half-hearted thinking and teaching stymies renewal in human behavior, as well as in their views about faith life and theology.

The possibilities of religious synthesis in how we think and live as Christians are numerous. This is evident in questionable ways of thinking about, for instance, special and general revelation, special and common grace, grace and nature, eternal and temporal, church and society, sacred and secular, calling and job, value and fact, holy and profane, Christ and Caesar, theon-

---

14. For details, see Chapters 9 and 10 below.

omy and autonomy, seminary and university, faith and reason, revelation and nature, theology and anthropology, theology and philosophy.

In a religiously dualistic world, with all its educational and curricular challenges, theology assumes supernatural revelation and combines it with general revelation. It tries to Christianize natural scholarship by directing it back to God as "First Cause." Christians appeal to theology to provide some Christian perspective on, for example, education, farming, sexuality, environment, citizenship, government, business, economics, communication, technology, sports, entertainment, etc.

Christian educators and scholars know that, as in any other discipline, theology also has its own kind of analysis. Especially in a secularized culture, for theologians to think they play a mediating role in Christianizing an existing curriculum is well-meant but actually rather presumptuous. It reflects a wrong view of their role in society and misconstrues what they are up against. It underestimates what they are really up against in their academic centers, especially in an intellect-oriented and liberal arts centered Western culture.

The central academic and educational challenges in our local and global world are exciting, complex and troubling. A major challenge, which is perhaps the most important one, is the enormous diversity in Christians and non-Christian faith traditions in our rapidly shrinking world. There is, according to Scripture, only one God, Word-made-flesh and guiding Spirit, but there are countless theologians and theologies. In such a world, it is a necessity, not an option, to reflect once more on the meaning of a renewal in faith life and on the related study of what could be called reformational pisteology.

For a better, at least more helpful, understanding of faith life, two issues are important: (i) the influence of society, culture and history on faith life; and, (ii) the structure of faith, pedagogical issues in catechetical instruction, psychological insights in pastoral care, principles of communication in preaching, cultural trends in forms of worship, and logic in dogmatics and apologetics.

American Academy of Religion

After the turbulent 1960s and 1970s, various theologians reflected anew on the meaning of such fundamental terms as *religion, faith* and *theology*. National and international political, economic and social changes affected the

33

general spirit and main direction of Western culture. In North America (the USA, Canada and Mexico) the teaching and researching of religion and faith were traditionally considered to be chiefly the duty of state colleges and universities, to be paid for by national tax dollars. Theology, however, was traditionally considered to be private, done in theological schools or at special events, and paid for privately and/or denominationally.

For Christian, Jewish, Islamic and other faith traditions, this understandable but dubious[15] arrangement presupposes two crucial assumptions: (i) religious studies are natural and rational, based on human wishes, projections, myths, or idols; (ii) theology focuses on God's supernatural revelation to humans. The distinction between religious studies and theology indicates that the former focuses on the subjective acts of human faith (e.g., meditating, chanting, worshiping, praying, confessing) and the latter on what God through his supernatural revelation reveals about the objective content of what humans believe.

A main reason for distinguishing between studies in religion and theology is a major shift in nineteenth-century academic circles. The intent and effect of Enlightenment thinking had intensified and become a culturally significant assumption. Talented philosophers and liberal theologians abandoned the idea of ultimate dependence on something transcendent. They replaced the latter with the immanence-based belief of human self-sufficiency. In the radical tradition of Ludwig Andreas von Feuerbach (1804–1872),[16] the focus shifted from what is divine to what is human, i.e., from revelation to projection, what is objective to what is subjective. This shift was reinforced by a concomitant[17] change, especially in academic circles, in what could simplistically but accurately be described as a move from theory to practice, intellect to will, thought to experience, system to phenomena, dogma to method, and content to activity.

This significant nineteenth-century shift—away from a generally Lutheran and Calvinist way of living and from a post-Reformation scholastic way of thinking—to twentieth-century thinking was the effect of a deepening religious crisis in Western culture. It subverted the traditional view

---

15. About why this arrangement is unjust and undemocratic, see A. Kuyper (1898); H. Dooyeweerd (1979); B. Zylstra (1982); J. Skillen (1974, 1990, 1994); D. Van Heemst (1993); P. J. Heslam (1998) and J. Bratt (1998).

16. For details about the essence and scope of Feuerbach's revolution, see his major books of 1841, 1844 and 1845.

17. Though concomitant, this shift was more philosophical than cultural and religious. In that regard, it differed from Feuerbach's shift.

of the relation between God and humanity and, as a result, the meaning of theology and religious studies and their interrelationship.

After describing what seven North American[18] Christian thinkers said about this crisis, this chapter will end with a brief summary about several practical, academic, and pedagogical problems related to the object of theology as discipline.

Charles S. Rooks

In his article "Theological Reflection in an Uncertain Age" C. S. Rooks spoke about a crisis that took place between World War II and the 1960s in the discipline of theology.[19] He characterized this period as a "golden era" of preaching and of homiletics, i.e., study of preaching. Its chief theological centers were Union Theological Seminary, Yale University and Wheaton College, and its most famous preachers were Fulton J. Sheen, Billy Graham, and the brothers Richard and Reinhold Niebuhr.

The dominant cultural spirit during those fifteen years was hampered by the twin threats of conservatism and spiritual inertia. The deep and widespread identity crisis of the 1960s resulted mainly from the spiritual shallowness of materialism and the trauma of the Vietnam War. During the 1970s an attempt was made to reform institutions from within, in contrast to what had been tried a decade earlier when anti-establishment forces sought to destroy institutions from without. The crisis of this insecure period became so desperate that it triggered "serious theological reflection" by churches, not merely by widespread protestations at state colleges and universities.

What Rooks meant by "theological reflection," in the title of his article, was not clear. Does it call for a return to what is truly basic in life? Does it refer to some Ultimate one must bow to, if there is going to be any hope? Is there an original principle, comparable to an axiom in metaphysics, which needs no proof but is the basis for certainty? In that case, is "theology" then something Aristotle had in mind when he equated philosophy with a study of first principles?

From Rooks's lecture and discussion it is unclear what he meant by the term "theological." Formally, it was comparable to the Western notion of

---

18. That all seven persons spoke in 1979 does not detract from the importance of their message for today.

19. Rooks, *Theology Today*, (1979): 220–227.

rational agreement. It did not point to something distinctively Christian in one's view of God and created reality. A problem in Rooks's thinking is his belief that denominational theological seminaries and divinity schools must deal with this issue and, by means of the churches, press for an answer in their daily living in a deeply troubled culture.

In such a restless world, Rooks looks to theology to provide an answer to a problem of which he is not fully aware, and for which he is unable to propose an alternative; in fact, traditional theology is part of the problem Rooks addresses. That discipline does not deal with the basic principles and practical implications of, for example, how political issues, societal structures, economic systems and environmental challenges affect, and are affected by, faith life.

Three other factors have contributed to uncertainty in the modern world and the need for theological reflection. First, the loss of prestigious seminaries as places for creative theological thinking; second, the rise of theological diversity based on difference in skin color (black, white, red), ethnic origin (European, Hispanic, American) and other theologies (poor, political); third, the use by European theologians of positivism's highly "technical language" and complex "methods" that most Christians do not understand. The great challenge of "theological reflection" is, in Rooks's opinion, to turn the uncertainties of modern culture into opportunities for advancing Christianity. Only such a response will result in a modicum of meaning and stability in a restless world.

Robert B. Griffiths

Concerning the relation between theology and science in general, the approach of R. B. Griffiths, an evangelical physicist at Carnegie-Mellon University in Pittsburgh, reflects a dominant view in all higher education. In his article "Is Theology a Science?" he writes that science is "any systematic investigation" interested in "discovering the nature of the world" and for that purpose uses "empirical methods for investigation."[20]

In distinction from the term "science" used in mathematical and quantitative natural studies, theology, although still a scholarly discipline, explores "God's nature, his relationship to the physical world, and his relationship to

---

20. For details, see Griffiths (1980): 169–173.

mankind." In traditional Baconian and Anglo-American fashion,[21] he states that Christian theology is scientific only to the extent it uses the method of acquiring knowledge through critical investigation of empirical evidence. Characteristics "unique to theology do not place it in a separate category... but are merely a reflection of its special subject matter."[22]

Given their relevance for issues touched on in this chapter and throughout this book, a few quotations from Griffiths's comments about encyclopedic issues related to theology highlight his understanding of, and problems with, the discipline of theology.

[T]he scientific theologian can say: "The reason for believing this to be true is as follows . . ." and what follows is tied to empirical evidence which the critic can investigate, and for which he is free to suggest alternative interpretations.

If the theologian, for example, considers his primary task to be one of making up myths to comfort the distressed, or of providing an ideological basis to further (or to counter) the goals of a social reform movement, or of constructing a formal philosophical system whose validity cannot byesubjected to any empirical test, then the label 'scientific'. . . is, of course, inappropriate. . . . It is undeniable that theological study employs certain methods that are distinctively different from those used in the other sciences. . . . The real question of interest is whether the methods employed in theology are appropriate ones in view of the nature of the subject matter.[23]

[Theology must] apply a methodology appropriate to the nature of God if it is to make progress . . . If God is the source of moral authority and the proper object of men's worship and honor, as theology indicates, then the theologian has a moral obligation to worship and obey God who is the subject of his study. This state of affairs is unique to theology and raises an important question as to the possibility of theology as a scientific discipline. Can the theologian be both a trusting, obedient servant of God and, at the same time, a critical scientist who objectively examines evidence about the nature of God, including evidence which might indicate that he (the theologian) is mistaken in his belief that God exists?[24]

21. For the impact of empiricism on Presbyterian ideas about Scripture at Princeton Theological Seminary and Westminster Theological Seminary in Philadelphia, see VanderStelt (1978; reprint 2014).

22. Griffiths (1980): 169.

23. Griffiths (1980): 171.

24. "There are two extreme positions concerning the relationship of theology and the

If "science" includes "experimental and historical sciences," then it is possible for theology to appeal to "empirical evidence subjected to critical analysis" as the basis for its "conclusions."

Theology's "distinctive" appeal to the "authority of revelation" indicates the "nature of its subject matter" and does not thereby display a "non-scientific approach." In treating "subjects in common with other sciences, such as history and psychology," theology can be "scientific" in that its provides a "check on its methods and its consistency."[25]

To assume that other disciplines by themselves can provide a proper picture of humans without referring to "God or god," or theology, is really "superfluous." The inability of "non-theistic systems" to provide a scientific view of the "basis of normative ethics" proves that theology plays "an irreducible role in our understanding of man."[26]

Griffiths's comments about "theology" reflect a general Evangelical ambiguity-filled understanding of, for example, science and theology, evidence and faith, sciences of theology and ethics, and misguided theism-atheism thinking.

Jacob Neusner

Unlike Rooks and Griffiths, who focused on a crisis in culture and theology's reaction to it, Neusner dealt with a crisis in religious studies in his "General Education Programs" at liberal arts colleges and state universities. In his inaugural lecture, in the Department of Religious Studies at Arizona State University, titled "Strangers at Home: The Task of Religious Studies," Neusner stated that religious studies do not seek to reshape, or kindle, faith in students, but attempt to interpret religious phenomena as a formidable force in human life.[27]

To understand a daily newspaper calls for a modicum of familiarity with faith issues related to the role of Islam in Iran, Judaism in Israel, Protestant-

---

sciences. One claims that all aspects of human experience for which theology provides some explanation are better explained, or soon will be, in terms of other sciences (e.g., psychology). The other claims that theology is in a privileged position and need not concern itself with developments in other sciences. Neither of these positions is correct; theology is related to other sciences in much the same way the latter are related to one another" (Griffiths 1980: 172).

25. Griffiths (1980): 173.

26. Griffiths mistakenly equates "normative ethics" with "theology."

27. Neusner (1979): 1–13.

ism in Northern Ireland, Roman Catholicism in Quebec, Poland, and Latin America, Christianity in Lebanon, and cult in Jonestown, Guyana. "Religion" is not a waning bias held over from another era, but a powerful force in life and society. "The world as we know it is shaped by the formation of society and culture around religious belief, by the way in which people refer to religions to make their choices how they will live."[28]

Religion is the "transcendent side of human imagination and of society and culture." It is a "protein" and "ubiquitous" force which integrates our humanness. Religious studies cast a "net over land" and make life whole again. They require interdisciplinary and cross-cultural ways of thinking. They presuppose the work of historians, philosophers, social scientists, psychologists, artists and anthropologists. To study and teach "religion" properly is a complicated and demanding undertaking.

Regrettably, those who are engaged in religious studies are often superficial and incompetent. They readily succumb to a Western preoccupation with various literary features of religion (e.g., teaching Scripture only as literature) or with pointing out merely formal similarities between religions in different cultures. Their introductory courses often succumb to "theological faddism" and "academic consumerism." As generalists, they use "technical gibberish," resort to "insufferable banality" and chatter in "Intellectual Esperanto."[29]

To help theologically opinionated students who fear what is unfamiliar, Neusner suggests they learn to welcome differences in faith, discover for themselves the immense diversity of religions, and enter with sympathy into the alien beliefs of, for example, Judaism, Islam, and Buddhism. General education courses at state colleges and universities must teach all students to be tolerant not just at home, but also in the often strange world of unfamiliar religions. Such liberating teaching and learning is essential in our colleges and universities in our restless culture, argues Neusner.

Langdon Gilkey

Whereas Rooks, Griffiths and Neusner focused on theology as a discipline and the need for introductory courses in religious studies, Langdon Gilkey reflected on the relation between "religion" and "culture." In the same year as

---

28. Neusner (1979): 4.
29. Neusner (1979): 8.

the three speakers mentioned above and the three speakers to be highlighted below, Gilkey spoke as president of the AAR on the urgent topic of "AAR and Anxiety of our Non-Being: An Analysis of our Modern Culture."

Unlike theology as a prescriptive study centered on what ought to be believed, the "study of religion" is a descriptive discipline focused on what is believed. Both disciplines are, in our modern culture, epiphenomenal. Along with art and philosophy, they are relegated to the spiritual superstructure of life. Our culture is dominated by a profound concern for what is technological and managerial, the craft of economic and political control, and whatever is quantitative and statistical. Religious studies are now combined with history, psychology, sociology and literature, i.e., with disciplines that were stowaways when churches were isolated from culture and controlled by theological thinking.

Modern society and culture display four main traits: (i) technology permeated by Comtean rationality; (ii) widespread interest in what is esoteric or manifested in new questions about life, nature, communities, religion, and demons; (iii) growing stress on the role of ideology in integrating communities by means of symbols and rituals; (iv) belief that all world cultures are equal and all truth is relative. The last trait has given rise to such profound and complex issues in our postmodern world related to, for example, the question of whether there is such a thing as truth in a world in which my truth is not necessarily the truth.[30]

Catherine L. Albanese

Catherine Albanese expressed another approach to the study of religion. In "Research Needs in American Religious History,"[31] she talks about new materials, methods and models in the study of religion in American colleges and universities and distinguishes between "outer" and "inner" history of religion. While the former focuses on "religious" leaders, activities, institutions and societies, and involves, for charting purposes, the disciplines of social history, psychology, anthropology, and structural and quantitative history, the latter centers on the language of myths and the experience of rituals.

30. Is truth specific, general, relative, valid? What is its personal/local and universal/global nature? For details, see Gilkey (1979).

31. Published in Bulletin of the Council on the Study of Religion. For details, see Albanese (1979): 101–105.

Traditional approaches to religious studies and theology are no longer adequate. They put too much emphasis on ecclesiastical institutions, church order, leadership in society, mastery over nature, discursive systems, imposing values on society, the role of elite positions, and the importance of political orientation (cf. "chosen nation," "destiny of new Israel"). Instead of studying external matters, the focus should be on the role of contemplation, intuition, metaphors, inner experience, long-range developments, cultural boundaries, popular religions, religious pluralism, tolerating other religions, and the importance of secularized religious symbols.

She appreciates[32] the stance of Whole Earth Catalog and Mother Earth News, especially its "creed" of correspondence between man and nature, its "code" about the harmony of natural rhythms, and the place it gives to "cultic action" in nature religions. Humans live with and from nature, not apart from or over it. Because all creeds and codes reflect what is unique in religious experiences, religious phenomena cannot be forced into one preconceived rigid mold.

John F. Wilson

In "Recent Historical Studies in Western Religion," John F. Wilson provides a different approach to the study of religion. General history used to be written almost exclusively from the perspective of ecclesiastical and political ideas and institutions. Today, however, attempts are made to go beyond the traditional models of doctrinal and political issues, i.e., those that concern church and state.[33]

Influenced by the views of Emil Durkheim and Max Weber, Wilson stressed the importance of social theories to develop a proper understanding of the "religious" aspect of culture. There is a growing awareness today of a close correlation between cosmology, social structure, and coherence of human behavior and beliefs. "Speaking in very general terms it seems to me [that] religion has come to be understood as the 'directionality' a culture pos-

32. In the spirit of stressing such common features of, for example, the pragmatism of C. S. Pierce, W. James and J. Dewey about evolutionism, the role of process, the nature of experience, the relationship between humans and nature, the importance of toleration, and the role of symbols.

33. Wilson (1979): 105–107. According to Wilson, S. Ahlstrom, C. L. Albanese, and W. Clebsch state that ". . . recent history study of Western religions has moved decisively beyond the theological formalities . . ." Wilson (1979): 107.

sesses."[34] The "religious aspects of culture" are linked to political, social and economic issues. To a large extent, the latter determine the nature and role of religion in any culture. In short, today a "newer set of interests is a commitment to the serious academic study of religious materials in their own rights, under the formality of religion as a significant aspect of culture."[35]

James B. Wiggins

Finally, James Wiggins's view of religion and religious studies illustrates the complexity, and confusion, about the object, or field of inquiry, of the discipline of theology and its curricular and pedagogical implications for higher education. The expressed and implied theoretical and practical issues in the six thinkers mentioned above with respect to religion and theological studies are all somehow present in the views of Wiggins.

He reviewed the history of the Religion Department at Syracuse University,[36] which was owned and operated by Methodists from 1870 to 1920. This university established in 1895 a Department of Semitics and Archeology. In 1959, this Department was changed to "Department of Bible and Religion" (and changed again in 1979 to "Department of Religion"). Until 1960, it offered all students a course in only Judaism and Christianity. Because of a growing interest in non-Western cultures and religious pluralism, both Western and non-Western religions were added to a mandatory course in General Education.

During the 1970s, this mandatory course was revamped in a major way on both the undergraduate and graduate levels. On the undergraduate level, it was subdivided into two tiers. Tier One consisted of three components: (i) expressions of religion: Scripture, rituals and communities; (ii) issues of religion: belief, death, eschaton and suffering; and (iii) methodology of religion: psychology, philosophy and history. Tier Two consisted of a variety of discretely chosen three-hour courses focused on specific religious traditions and subjects.

On the graduate level, the course combined a study of religion with various cultural disciplines. It focused on symbol systems and the need for her-

---

34. Wilson (1979): 107. For a similarity between his views and those of the Southwest, or Heidelberg, School of Philosophy, especially Wilhelm Dilthey's, see Chapter 13.

35. Wilson (1979): 107.

36. Wiggens (1979): 170–111.

meneutic sensitivity. Requisites for this part of General Education were such (non-logical) disciplines as linguistics, aesthetics, ethics, and psychology.

Because they seek to serve faith, Wiggins thinks that—in distinction from any theological seminary—state universities do not teach theology. They provide only objective descriptions of religious phenomena. They do not presuppose any faith commitment on the part of instructor or student. The discipline of theology is private, the study of religion is public.

As to the basic and all-pervasive distinction between "private" and "public," theology and religion, church and state, and Christian and secular, Wiggins commented, in a so-called neutral North American way, about the pragmatic, and financial, benefit derived from the important distinction between theology and religion, as follows:

> Seminaries, theological schools, divinity faculties exist to theologize, but religion studies aim at objective description. No faith commitments may legitimately be presumed on the part of either faculty persons or students. The community of scholars differs markedly from the community of faith. . . . Furthermore, as a political strategy to help justify the constitutionality of religion studies in tax-supported colleges and universities it was an important move [to exclude faith commitment and the study of theology] to have made.[37]

Summary

The ideas mentioned above about the discipline of theology, especially with respect to the meaning of faith and religion, are complex and crucial. They involve various systematic issues, have encyclopedic implications, and are culturally relevant. They are not speculative but concrete, not a luxury but a necessity. They affect the aspirations, hopes, joys and fears of all humans in a world filled with God's unavoidable presence and human positive and negative responses to it.

As always, culture and curriculum are interdependent. This close interdependence reveals the priorities of any culture and the (primary, secondary and tertiary) forms of education. They reinforce each other's goals and activities. When that interdependence is imperiled, culture and curriculum,

37. Wiggins (1979): 110.

as well as (by implication) society and education, are compelled to reform(u-late) their structure and direction.

Given our interest in the nature and role of faith life and theology, the reason for this chapter (and the next eighteen chapters) is to obtain a better awareness of what is of ultimate importance in our culture and how that is addressed, particularly in higher education. The intent of this entire study is to review human faith traditions in, not and, people's responsibilities as family members, citizens, bankers, academics, teachers, preachers, doctors, athletes, caregivers, or whatever.

In short, what is the relation between, on the one hand, faith life, the shape of society and direction of culture, and, on the other hand, formal education, academic endeavor, and curriculum, especially the traditional study of theology? What is the relation between Christian and non-Christian faith life and the powerful, often confused and conflicted, educational world we live in? For a brief overview of what happened in this regard in Western culture at the time of the Reformation, and for the two and a half centuries thereafter in Calvinist/Reformed circles with respect to the nature of faith life and discipline of theology, we turn to our next chapter. The basic issues raised in it will provide helpful insight into some religiously fundamental and structurally systematic issues hinted at already in this chapter.

CHAPTER THREE

"Theology" in Reformed Higher Education

Theology played a significant role in Reformed and Presbyterian faith traditions shaped by J. Calvin, a second-generation reformer, in Reformed and Presbyterian higher education in European and Anglo-American countries. This chapter focuses primarily on Reformed thinking about faith, especially an ambiguity about the nature of the study called theology.

While the intent of theology in this tradition was to be biblical, its content and role resulted in an accompanying reformation of "theology" as an established academic discipline focused on thinking about redirected faith life. Unintentionally, the reformers' perpetuated the traditional encyclopedic nature and role of "theology" in higher education. The detrimental effects of traditional "theology" on the reformers' passion to be biblically simpler and truly radical in their "faith" will be highlighted in this chapter.

Ambiguity about the encyclopedic role of "theology" has undermined the need for a transforming heart-centered religion in all of life, including one's intentional faith life. To address this problem of a better and more vibrant faith tradition requires taking another look at what has been thought to be the "object" of theology in a systematic (cf. Chapter 2) and historical way (cf. Chapter 3).

To trace this development from the sixteenth-century Reformation to the present calls for a reorientation in our thinking about "theology" as a discipline and about "faith life" as something preceding and anchored in, not equated with, religion in the sense of a heart-centered and -directed way of living in God's presence. Close attention will be given to the relation between faith life and theology and their relevance for all other human activities and correlated studies.

A brief survey of this problem during the last four centuries of "Reformed" higher education focuses on both the nature, and interrelations, of terms like "faith," "religion," "worldview," "anthropology," "philosophy" and "theology." Special attention will be given to two second-generation reformers: J. Calvin, as preacher and pastor, and his colleague, T. Beza, as scholar and educator.[1] Their understanding of "faith" and "theology" will be stressed in relation to the views of two first-generation reformers—Luther and his friend P. Melanchthon—on "philosophy" and "education."[2]

Sixteenth Century

Martin Luther (1483–1546)

For four years (1501–1505), Luther taught nominalistic logic[3] at the University of Erfurt. He lived as a monk for three years in a monastery, and in 1508 he joined the Philosophy Department at the University of Wittenberg, where for three years he taught the nominalistic views of William of Ockham (d. 1349), which centered on doubt and skepticism.

In 1511, he moved to the Theology Department at that university. In his study of the Book of Psalms for two years (1513–1515), he rejected two central, and interrelated, assumptions that soon proved to be basic for the Reformation. The first assumption focused on the four classic medieval hermeneutical principles of "literal," "allegorical," "moral" and "anagogical" levels of meaning about, respectively, "facts," "what to believe," "what to do" and "what to hope for." The second assumption centered on being fixated on conscience, and emphasized contrition as condition and preparation for obtaining some certainty about truth and salvation.

His rediscovery of salvation and certainty through the Spirit, in Jesus Christ, did not result in a non-dualistic worldview, however. He perpetuated the medieval two-realm theory. He slightly modified the nature of the two

---

1. And, briefly, Peter Ramus in mainly logic, and extensively J. Arminius in philosophy and theology.

2. Much of what follows is based on D. Vollenhoven's study in 1933 on Calvinism and reformational philosophy.

3. In the tradition of William of Ockham (c. 1300–1349), Peter d'Ailly (1350–1420), John Gerson (1363–1429) and Gabriel Biel (c. 1425–1495).

realms and their interrelation,[4] but retained the idea of a higher world of faith, grace and church, as an invisible communion of saints, and the idea of a lower world of reason, law and state. In 1520, he rejected curialism when, defiantly, he threw the Papal Bull of Excommunication into a campus bonfire, while students, who stood around him, sang "Te Deum laudamus" (We praise you, O Lord). In 1524, he penned his classic *De servo arbitrio* (On the enslaved will), in response to Erasmus's classic writing *De libero arbitrio* (On the free will).

Despite these and many other changes that he introduced, as a reformer, into the tradition of a fossilized faith, Luther did not abandon his two-realm worldview about, for example, Gospel and law, church and state, supernatural and natural, private and public life. His rejection of faith-undermining "nominalism" and faith-choking "scholasticism" was commendable. However, it did not prevent him from advocating—because of Melanchthon's influence on him, I surmise—the enfeebling, and controversial, Aristotelian idea of "substance" in his traditional view of the Lord's Supper.[5]

Philip Melanchthon (1497–1560)

Like Luther, Melanchthon abandoned the certainty-debilitating philosophy of late-medieval nominalism. But, unlike Luther, he advocated an Aristotelian view of "reality" and "knowledge," as reflected in his "inaugural" lecture of 1517 on "Artes Liberales" (Liberal Arts) at the University of Tübingen. In his "opening" lecture, in 1518, as professor of Greek at the University of Wittenberg,[6] he indicated his intent to revive classical learning, oppose certain cumbersome forms of medieval scholasticism, revamp the entire educational program, and publish a new edition of Aristotle's works. Since it deals with worldly wisdom, or human dignity and power, it is the duty of philosophy to provide, among other things, the basis for the study of theology.

Melanchthon has justifiedly been called the *Praeceptor Germaniae*.[7] He wrote curricula and textbooks for the Universities of Marburg, Königsberg and Jena. In his famous Instruction for the Visitation (1528), he described his

4. E.g., in a Platonizing-Aristotelian way of considering God as invisible and unknown.

5. Disagreements about the Lord's Supper at that time in Europe caused endless debates, and at times even deadly conflicts between five Christian faith traditions: Roman Catholic, Lutheran, Anglican, Calvinist and Anabaptist.

6. With an enrollment of 200 students in 1518 and 602 in 1520.

7. For details, see Beck 1969: 101–102.

educational philosophy, provided detailed guidelines for higher education, and stated that philosophy is propaedeutic, i.e., introductory, to theology, and helps students become aware of, and resist, the prominent trilogy of three major dangers: confusion, skepticism and heresy.[8]

Although he questioned certain features of Aristotle's view of metaphysics, eternal world and tripartite soul, Melanchthon accepted his three views on the nature of (i) free will, (ii) natural virtue, and (iii) natural theology, as study of first principles in philosophy. In the first edition of his *Loci Communes* (1521), he emphasized—because of Luther's influence on him at that time—the inability of humans to believe and their need for biblical faith. However, in the second edition (1535), and especially in the third (1542) and fourth (1555) editions, he started to move away in his philosophical and theological thinking from the central thrust of the Reformation.

Abandoning Luther's idea of "enslaved will," Melanchthon stressed more and more, in a synergistic way, three things: (i) an impeded but partly free will, still able to be contrite and take the first step toward salvation; (ii) need for courses in natural theology and philosophical ethics, based on the innate ability of reason to know "God," "substance," and "world-order"; (iii) two-fold truth, according to which supernatural grace strengthens the innate judgments and virtues humans can know through experience.[9]

The four main sources of human knowledge are "innate ideas," "experience," "logical inferences" and "revelation." Ultimately, the combination of "innate ideas" and "logical inferences" determines the basic method and structure of theology. In his *Loci Communes*, he replaced a Ciceronian rhetoric, which stresses "probability" and "notion," with an Aristotelian dialectic, which emphasizes "logic" and "certainty."[10]

8. The impact of this curricular policy (of requiring a course in introductory philosophy) on departments of theology and theological seminaries has been huge. It permitted central philosophical ideas to influence theology, especially basic assumptions in apologetics, dogmatics, exegesis, preaching, catechetical instruction and even pastoral care.

9. For details, see Breen 1986: 82–84, especially Melanchthon's statement: "The reader should be advised to inquire as to what distinguishes political from evangelical doctrine. To clarify the matter, we use this comparison: . . . medicine is far removed from the Gospel; and just as medicine contains a doctrine which is founded in reason, so politics is founded in reason, and no more pertains to the Gospel than does medicine. It is desirable for a physician to be a pious man; so it is desirable for one who governs a commonwealth to be a pious man. Nevertheless *the arts have as such no relationship with the Gospel*" (emphasis added).

10. I am indebted to D. Sinnema for his pertinent comment to me (in November 2012) in this connection: "The structure of studying in the Arts faculty (philosophy and other subjects) before moving to the higher faculties of theology, law, and medicine was inherited from the

Against the background of this thought-pattern in Melanchthon's enormously influential *Loci Communes,* and given much subsequent Protestant theology, it is not surprising that eventually in Reformed circles "doctrines" were viewed in an objective, intellectual, propositional and abstract way, and "faith" life was thought of in a primarily subjective, affective, emotional and imaginative practical way.

John Calvin (1509–1564)

In "Blessed Are the Poor in Spirit," an inaugural lecture—believed to be one he wrote for Nicolas Cop in 1533—Calvin distinguished between, one could say, what is creationally good and what is religiously sinful. This distinction is present also in what he wrote in 1536 in his "Letter to Amateurs of Jesus Christ":

> For he [Adam] has been formed in his image and likeness in such a way that the light of His glory is clearly reflected in him. What made him exist in this state is that in humility he always humbled himself before God's majesty. . . . But wretched man, desiring to be something in himself . . . has his image and likeness effaced by this.[11]

Contrary to a widespread view in popular non-academic and in Reformed/Presbyterian academic circles, Calvin was not a professional theologian. Living as he did at a precarious and dangerous time, filled with many conflicts, he was (compelled to be) primarily a practical reformer. Formally, he was trained in jurisprudence, not theology. As a refugee and still quite young, he was suddenly forced into a situation of helping fellow French refugees in Geneva, Switzerland, and Strasbourg, Germany. In his extensive correspondence, he advised and encouraged fellow believers in England, Scotland, Poland, Hungary, France and the Netherlands to be faithful followers of Jesus Christ.[12]

---

medieval universities, and this structure was not changed by the Reformation, or in Post-Reformation Protestant universities."

11. Olivetan used this letter as the *Introduction* to his French translation of the New Testament. Vollenhoven commented in a class in 1963 that Calvin wrote in a Scriptural, i.e., non-speculative, way about issues like immortal life, eternal death, truth and certainty.

12. For examples of his practical letters, see Beveridge and Bonnet 1983: Vols 4–7, Parts 1–4.

Being a refugee himself, he searched for a homeland, a place where he, with fellow humans, could live privately and publicly in liberty.[13] In a self-effacing way, he shared with others, living in similar precarious situations, God's presence in their dire circumstances, and urged them to live in a Spirit-filled, childlike way. Calvin's simple but powerful faith enabled him to endure the difficulties he experienced as a refugee who, with fellow displaced exiles, confessed God's perpetual nearness. His motto in all circumstances, especially dangerous and difficult ones, indicates the secret of being a Christian, viz., to live *coram Deo* (in God's presence).

Caught up in the whirlwind of a heart-centered renewal in his faith life and thinking about society and culture, Calvin turned to Scripture as a compass, not a blueprint, for his orientation. According to Scripture, God is the Creator, who is above the law[14] and faithful to his Word for creation, including humans. Sin is not some neo-Platonic absence of something,[15] nor is it the opposite of God's grace. Rather, it is human heart-centered rebellion against God's basic law of love for the world he created, including humans as his image-bearers.

It is human is to have different tasks and responsibilities. For those who are Spirit-led and Christ-engrafted, human tasks are not removed but, on the contrary, maintained. The problem does not lie in God's law(s) for humans, but it lies in humans who refuse to love, i.e., to live in gratitude, and, for no reason, opted for self-centeredness. Given this basic stance and life-encompassing view, Calvin sensed something missing, or wrong, in the mind-set of, for example, Plato, Aristotle, Intellectualism, Nominalism, Humanism, Renaissance and Anabaptism.[16]

13. For details, see Oberman 1983, 1986, 1988 and 1992. In teaching a General Education course at Dordt College on Calvin's *Institutes of the Christian Religion*, I reminded students for fifteen years to thank God we don't know where J. Calvin was buried— it prevented Calvinists from turning his grave into an idol for (profitable?) pilgrimages, and prevented grave robbers, who reject his stress on depravity, from hooliganism. Calvin focused on God's kingdom in Christ through the Spirit, not on himself.

14. Rejecting the nominalist notion that God is outside the law (*Deus ex lex*), Calvin stressed God being above the law (*Deus legibus solutus*).

15. For a description, and critique, of this subtle neo-Platonic view of sin, see T. Plantinga 1980.

16. Concerning remnants of Luther's view of "two-kingdoms," D. Sinnema informed me about his "Luther and Calvin on Christianity and Politics" in *Tydskrif vir Christelike Wetenschap*, 16 (1980) 1–24, and reprinted in B. J. van der Walt, *Confessing Christ in Doing Politics* (1995) 72–103. For details about other neo-Platonic tendencies in Calvin's thinking, see Chapters 7 and 8 below, especially D. Vollenhoven as professor of philosophy at the Free University.

Despite his new religious stance and interest in a more Scripturally directed way of thinking, Calvin's work as "reformer" was limited. He was a child of his day and age. He did not escape the effect of certain ideas in influential traditions of his day and age. Uncritically, he accepted several ideas that prevented him from applying new insights in all his thinking.[17] With respect to his neo-Platonic leaning in his anthropology, he (i) associated human depravity more with the human will than with the human intellect, (ii) thought about soul and body as two distinct substances, (iii) considered the human body to be a prison of the human soul, (iv) accepted the Greek principle of "'faculty' psychology,"[18] (v) arranged human sense, reason, imagination and intellect hierarchically, (vi) tended to relate "image of God" to the human mind, or intellect, and (vi) interpreted John 1:4–5, 9 (about Christ as Word-incarnate) in a semi-scholastic way.[19]

These lingering elements contributed to his historically understandable, but systematically regrettable, perpetuation of semi-medieval ideas about "natural" and "supernatural" revelation, and about *Logos* as mediator in "creation" and Christ as mediator in "salvation."[20] He was, understandably, insufficiently critical of remnants of Greek and medieval scholastic thinking, in the areas of anthropology and theology. Pertinent in this connection are William P. Armstrong's remarks about Calvin's importance and limitations as a reformer:

> The Reformation at its very beginning found itself in the presence of problems and exigencies of indefinite range, first of all, conflicts of purely religious and theological character—doctrinal, liturgical, and constitutional conflicts. What an amount of spiritual strength was consumed even on these conflicts! How much there was which went wrong! What unrest, what losses these conflicts produced! And yet the problems which then appeared could be settled by reference to the fundamental religious principle of Protestantism, and on the whole were in fact settled in a truly Protestant way. Much more difficult and dangerous, however, was a second adjustment, which lay more on the periphery of religious truth and yet was no less necessary,

---

17. Cf. T. van der Merwe 1982: 69–84, S. Fowler 1984: 339–352, and B. J. van der Walt 1984: 300–308, 1985: 135–137.

18. About "intellect, will, and feeling," see Chapter 6 below.

19. The phrase "coming into the world" Calvin associated not to Christ's birth, but to the birth of every human.

20. Cf. Richard Muller, Chapter 3, pp. 123–170, in The Study of Theology: From Biblical Interpretation to Contemporary Formulation, 1991.

namely, the adjustment to the general ethical, political and social problems, to science and art. This adjustment, I say, was unavoidable, for if Protestantism, over against the medieval-Catholic world, involves a new world-view, then there must necessarily be a Protestant science of politics, a Protestant philosophy and science, a Protestant art. . . .

For such an adjustment, however, in the very nature of things, time is required; it cannot be accomplished by one man or by one generation. It was, indeed, a thank-worthy undertaking, when Calvin in his *Institutio* did not entirely ignore politics, but the results were of such a kind that they did not give satisfaction. . . . But now the tasks and problems of culture came upon the young evangelical church in a storm. Not so much upon the Lutherans . . .[21]

Theodore Beza (1519–1609)

As Calvin's successor in Geneva and the head of the Academy of Geneva for forty years, T. Beza respected Calvin as a reformer of faith life. As scholar and educator, he had a huge impact on higher education, especially theology,[22] and on the international community that appreciated and supported Calvin's work and views.

In his opening address of the Academy of Geneva in 1559, Beza talked about "The Origin, Value, Necessity, and Use of Schools." That Calvin founded the Academy and Beza opened it indicates a keen awareness in Reformed higher education of the strategic importance of a distinctly Christian form of higher education. However, what was taught in this Academy, and later in Reformed/Presbyterian circles of higher education, was philosophically and theologically not always distinct. Regrettably, first slowly and tacitly, then subtly and pervasively and, finally, rapidly and destructively, the worm of scholastic thinking wriggled into significant curricular and pedagogical issues in especially philosophy and theology.

The effect of this accommodation was multi faceted. It undermined, and

21. Lang 1890: 56–57 (emphasis added), as cited also by H. Evan Runner. For details, see Chapter 19 below.

22. Beza's relation to Calvin and Calvinism resembles Melanchthon's relation to Luther and Lutheranism. About Beza's influence on Zacharias Ursinus (1534–1583), author of the Heidelberg Catechism (1563), and the impact of Aristotle's logic on his views, see D. Sinnema 1990: 124–134.

eventually eliminated, the distinctive Christian character of higher education about the structure of society, direction of culture and course of history. The implied religious accommodation restricted the liberating power of God's impinging revelation and leavening force of Christian faith.

Like Melanchthon at the time of Luther, also Beza uncritically accepted cardinal principles in Aristotelian thinking and fused them with some emphases in Calvin's notions about preaching and teaching. To consolidate and systematize Christian faith at a time of much confusion triggered by the Reformation, Beza adopted a method of thinking and teaching that was shaped by Aristotle's famous theory of "four-fold causality."

To develop an understandable, logically coherent and rationally lucid set of beliefs for the purpose of defending truth and refuting error, Beza thought it helpful to think in a logically deductive way about crucial tenets of Christian faith. He used this method in his understanding of, for example, primary and secondary causes, means and ends, God's eternal decrees before creation, predestination, God's all-determinative sovereignty, evil in relation to God's will, and "clay" and "lump" (Romans 9:21) as implying "shaped substances."[23]

Inasmuch as Beza developed and taught at the Academy of Geneva this scholastic method, it affected the faith life of Christians because it restricted the full power of reformation. Slowly and subtly, Scripture came to be read as a book of truths, doctrines as a system of beliefs, creeds as products of systematic theology, and dialogues among Christians as a forum for theological discussions and (potential) conflicts. The relation between Scripture, contemporary context and a person's faith life began to be explained, and endlessly debated, in terms of something logical, e.g., major premise, minor premise and conclusion.

This form of synthesis thinking fostered a tendency in many Reformed

---

23. In the later editions of *Institutes of the Christian Religion*, even Calvin adopted this Aristotelian view of "material," "formal," "efficient" and "final" causes (cf. Calvin 1960: III, xiv, 17, 21). This method gave rise to interminable theological speculations and, consequent, energy-sapping and joy-robbing schisms. A basic flaw in this theology is that "election" (which in Scripture is a comfort for Christians in their faith) becomes a theological problem and robs faith of its vibrancy. For details, see D. Sinnema about: (i) Beza's reliance on "primary-secondary causality" thinking in connection with "God's Eternal Decree and its Temporal Execution: The Role of this Distinction in Theodore Beza's Theology," in *Adaptations of Calvinism in Reformation Europe*, ed. in Holt (2007), 55–78; (ii) "Calvin and Beza: The Role of the Decree-Execution Distinction in Their Theologies," in *Calvinus Evangelii Propugnator*, ed. D. Wright (2006) 191–207; and (iii) "Beza's View of Predestination in Historical Perspective," in *Theodore de Beza, (1519–1605) (2007), 219–239.

traditions to think about "religion" in terms of one's faith life and beliefs in oversimplified ways in which rhetoric depended on logic, preaching on dogmatics, truth on the first principles of philosophy, emotions on reason, subjective experiences on objective truths, pastors on theologians and denominations on theological schools.[24]

Peter Ramus (1515–1572)

In reaction to this Aristotelian form of scholastic thinking and believing, P. Ramus, an internationally renowned French logician,[25] advocated a more Platonizing approach. He rejected esoteric Aristotelian thinking, renowned for its abstract reasoning and deductive-hypothetical argumentation. Its effects are detrimental to a person's faith life. With great passion and flare, he developed a much simpler and more natural "method of disputing well" (*ars bene disserendi*), an ability to be practical, i.e., make concrete, not abstract, judgments.

Already at the age of twenty-one, he publicly attacked Aristotelian thinking. "When I came to Paris," he said, "I fell into the subtleties of the sophists, and they taught me the liberal arts through questions and disputes, without ever showing me a single thing of profit or service. All that has been said about Aristotle is forged."[26] Despite his vehement opposition to any "scholastic curriculum" based on Aristotle's causality-thinking, his own method of thinking was, however, actually "more a simplification and revision of the Aristotelian system than an abandonment of it."[27] Nevertheless, the impact of his philosophy on the academic community, especially in theology, in France, Switzerland, Germany, Holland, England, Scotland, Sweden and North America, was phenomenal and profound.[28]

24. For details, see Sinnema 1986: 467–506; for a different view, see Hesselink 1983: 31–38.

25. As professor of logic at the Royal College of Paris, Ramus lectured sometimes for up to two thousand, mostly foreign, students in just a single session. For his anti-Aristotelian stance, two French kings, Francis I and Henry II, initially blocked his appointment as professor of philosophy; but after learning to appreciate his novel ideas about logic, they permitted his appointment at the Royal College.

26. Cf. Miller 1961: 123.

27. See Sinnema 1990: 123; also, "Ramist logic, though outwardly antithetical, was actually a simplified restructuration of the Aristotelian system motivated more by humanist pedagogical concerns than any concern for biblical reformation." (143).

28. E.g., Ramus's influence on J. Ursinus, German theologian and author of the Heidelberg Catechism, on Sir W. Temple and J. Milton in England, and on R. Snellius and W. Snellius,

Given Beza's philosophical stance and prominent role in Calvin's Academy in Geneva, it is revealing that Ramus would not have been appointed as professor of philosophy, even if the Academy's budget had permitted it. One reason why Ramus's wish to teach in Geneva did not materialize was his rejection of Aristotelian philosophy. About this historically significant philosophical disagreement, C. Bangs commented:

> His religious views were essentially Calvinistic, but with certain deviations (related to his humanistic sympathies) which brought him into conflict with the Calvinistic leader, Beza. The first and broadest point of conflict was over the matter of Aristotelian logic itself. In 1570, during one of the periods when Ramus was in exile from Paris, he appears to have wanted a position as professor at Geneva under Beza. Beza wrote a reply in which Ramus' overture is turned down for an ostensibly financial reason, but in which the real philosophical differences are brought to light. . . . As [Beza wrote] "The second obstacle lies in our determination to follow the position of Aristotle, without deviating a line, be it in logic or in the rest of our studies. I tell you this frankly, as the old adage goes: 'Between men of good will there must be good deeds.'"[29]

Jacobus Arminius (1559–1609)

One of the students at the Academy of Geneva in 1586 was J. Arminius. He was the first student to receive a doctorate in theology at the University of Leyden (est. 1575), the first Calvinist University in the Netherlands. As a graduate of the two first Calvinist institutions of higher education in Europe, he was appointed in 1603 as professor of theology at the University of Leyden, his alma mater. After he started to teach there, he gave three private disputations on theology[30] at this university on the important and sensitive issue of the nature and method of theology.

In these three inaugural orations on theology, he discussed, in great detail, the pressing question of the "extent, dignity, and excellence of theology." For his views on theology, non-theological disciplines and their interrela-

---

professors at the University of Franeker, where many Hungarians studied theology and from which some graduates went to North America to study at Harvard University.

    29. See Bangs 1971: 60–61; also Sinnema 1990: 129.

    30. These three private disputations on theology must be distinguished from his three public orations on theology.

tionship, he received an enthusiastic endorsement from his theological colleague, F. Gomarus (1563–1641)[31] and all the students attending his orations.

Two principles that influenced his (non-Ramist and non-Platonizing) "method" were Aristotle's theory of causality and his own distinction between legal and evangelical. The four-fold causality principle provided him with a general thought-pattern he shared with his chief mentor, T. Beza, at the Academy of Geneva and his colleague Gomarus at the University of Leyden. Within the parameters of this common method, i.e., scholastic framework, he started to probe, and raise questions, about how two prominent scholars in his own academic tradition perceived the basic and all-pervasive God-human relationship.

The "legal-evangelical" distinction he used in his attempt to find a better understanding of theology as discipline. He stressed the importance for theology of three causes in Aristotle's thinking: the "object" of theology as material cause (*causa materia*), the "author" of theology as efficient cause (*causa efficiens*) and the "end" of theology as final cause (*causa finalis*).

Earlier, in a commentary on the Heidelberg Catechism, Z. Ursinus (1534–1583) had used the distinction between "legal" and "evangelical" for the purpose of indicating the difference between "law" and "gospel." Also, Guido de Brès (1522–1567), author of the Belgic Confession, had correlated the "legal-evangelical" distinction with the situation "before the fall" and "after the fall." After Arminius died in 1609, J. Coccejus (1603–1669) used this, by that time, widely known "legal-evangelical" distinction to indicate the difference between "covenant of works" and "covenant of grace."[32]

Comparable to what earlier P. Ramus, and later W. Amesius, had done, also Arminius—although not for ostensibly Platonizing reasons—had become critical of the rigid Aristotelian method, which earlier T. Beza and later (at the time of the Synod of Dordrecht in 1618/9) F. Gomarus and J. Maccovius had used. He wanted a less abstract and a more practical method. He

---

31. Gomarus attended the Synod of Dort (1618/9), ten years after Arminius' death in 1609. His Aristotelian view of "causality" in relation to "election" and "reprobation" was brought against him and other "conservative" pastors and theologians. For details, see "Conclusions," added to the Five Points of the Canons of Dordrecht, and aimed at such theologians, including T. Beza and F. Gomarus, who favored a logic that went beyond the bounds of Scripture.

32. This way of thinking was later used to distinguish between "common grace" and "special grace," to the detriment of integral Christian scholarship and higher education, when "common grace" was associated with philosophy in state universities and "special grace" with theology in denominational schools and universities. About implications for Christian scholarship and education, see footnote 29 and end of Chapter 20 below.

did not want a logical method that moved from divine decrees to human faith, God's glory to man's blessedness, what is universal to what is individual. As a result, he ascribed priority to what is individual, thought of covenant in terms of a contract, believed that adopting creeds threatens a person's freedom, and emphasized the role of freedom and toleration.[33]

Noteworthy in this connection is what J. Arminius did while an undergraduate student at the Academy of Geneva. He absconded from Calvin's Academy and enrolled at the University of Padua in Italy. This departure angered the national Dutch Reformed Church, which through Classis Amsterdam had given him a stipend to study in Geneva, not in Padua, and urged him to return to the Academy without delay. The reason Arminius secretly ran away from Geneva to Padua was his desire to study logic under Jacopo Zabarella (1533–1589).

Zabarella was an internationally renowned logician, an expert on the role of "method and order" in thinking and scholarship. In *On Method* (*De Methodis*), he had developed a novel, simpler and exciting pedagogical method. Central in his view of "method" was his conviction that logically humans move from what is known to what is unknown, what is practical to what is abstract, what is analytical to what is synthetical. When this method is used in theology, one moves from Scripture to dogmatics, not from dogmatics to Scripture.

This view of Zabarella fascinated Arminius. It provided him with an alternative to the way T. Beza, his teacher at the Academy, thought and taught. It attracted the attention of many other (second-generation) theologians, who had become dissatisfied with traditional abstract Aristotelian thinking. They wanted an easier and more practical way of thinking and reading Scripture, a simpler understanding of human life, especially faith life.[34]

To understand what Arminius was up against, what he and his followers, especially ten years after his death in 1609, did not like in hyper-scholastic theologians and preachers, one must sense the relevance for theology of Aristotle's notion of formal cause (*causa formalis*). He associated "cause" with "certainty"[35] and "formal cause" with "method" of thinking. As was the case in all non-theological disciplines, "formal cause" (focused on method

---

33. See R. Muller's article "The Scholastic Arminius." (Sinnema)

34. For details, see Sinnema 1974: 1–41, especially 31–33 about Zabarella. Soon after 1582, and along with Aristotle's *Organon*, "the commentaries of Zabarella became the fundamental text in logic" at the University of Leyden, the alma mater of Arminius. See Sinnema 1990: 122.

35. Arminius associated Aristotle's "material," "efficient" and "final" causes with, respectively, the "object," "author" and "end" of faith life and theology.

and certainty) received much attention in Reformed churches and higher education.

Unique to "formal cause" is its laser-like focus in all studies, also in theology, on "certainty." Implied in this pivotal assumption is that the distinction between "legal" and "evangelical" is no longer necessary, but irrelevant. It is replaced with what is true in a "general" and a "particular" way. Certainty is essentially intellectual.

General certainty consists of two things: sense-based experience and reason-based knowledge. It is presupposed in every particular certainty. This is true also in one's faith life and related revelation. Proper logical "method" assumes and points to certainty and truth, even apart from whether one is Christian or not.[36] For many Protestant theologians, this 'novel' idea of "method" and implied "certainty" perpetuates, in a different historical context, the medieval scholastic idea that natural theology precedes Christian theology. In terms of "method," the former provides the basis, and opportunity, for the latter.

Arminius associated the "certainty" of methodology with the relevance of "theology" for all disciplines, including Christian higher education. In his three inaugural lectures in 1603, he placed theology at top of the curriculum when he stated: "For to every kind of study in the most noble theatre of the sciences, I assign, as it becomes me, its due place, and that an honorable one; and each being content with its subordinate station, all of them with the greatest willingness concede the president's throne to that science of which I am now treating". Theology is the "gate to heaven," "door to paradise," "ladder of Jacob" or "golden chain connecting heaven and earth." The task of theology is to urge humans to work "together with Him in manifesting the Gospel."

Although the method of reasoning is essentially the same in all academic disciplines, there is something unique about theology. As to their "object," "author," "end" and "certainty," the difference between theology and all other disciplines is that in theology God as "object" coincides with God as "author," but God as "end" transcends present life with its boundaries. By way of contrast, in all non-theological disciplines, including philosophy, the "object" consists of only derived, and hence inferior, created things.[37]

36. This misleading idea gave rise to the misguided scholastic belief at Calvin Theological Seminary and Calvin College (for details, see Chapter 15 below) that issues related to "intellect," "reason," "philosophy," "logic" and "method" are neutral, preserved by "common grace."

37. Herein lies the reason for the religious secularization in Western culture of non-theological disciplines, and eventually even theology.

In short, in this latter view the relation between philosophy and theology is harmonious only when right reason is used, true philosophy challenges wrong philosophy, and philosophy accepts natural and Christian theology as the ultimate science and final norm within the academy and the rest of life.

Seventeenth and Eighteenth Centuries

The scholastic method affected also the Synod of Dort (1618–1619), as D. Sinnema has shown. F. Gomarus, professor of theology at the University of Leyden and colleague of J. Arminius, used the "scholastic method" (*theologia scholastica*) to teach truth and defend it against falsehood. The distinctive characteristics of this method, according to Sinnema, are as follows:

> . . . the widespread use of the formal disputation, with its defendants and objectors; the introduction of metaphysics into Protestant universities at the turn of the seventeenth century and the resultant use of many metaphysical distinctions; the commonplace approach; analysis by definition and division, the division proceeding according to the four Aristotelian causes, their sub-causes, effects, adjuncts, and so on; rational demonstration of truth and rebuttal of error especially by means of the formal syllogism; teaching by the analytical and synthetical methods. . . .[38]

Its purpose was to "present the Christian faith as a logically coherent and rationally defensible system of belief," and its method reinforced the "role given to reason and logic in presenting and defending religious truth." The method was interested in "metaphysical and speculative questions, and a non-historical view of Scripture as a self-consistent account that can be reduced to a creedal statement."[39]

The term "scholastic" (*scholasticus*) was used in three senses: (i) "school"

38. Sinnema 1986: 472. For helpful details, see 467–506, especially 487ff. about "hard phrases" (phrases duriores) of Maccovius, another scholastic delegate at the Synod, and 495–497 about the difference between, on the one hand, the synthetic method (move from cause to effects) used by Paul in Ephesians and scholars in the academy, and, on the other hand, the analytic method (move from effects to cause) used by Paul in Romans and common people in churches as faith communities.

39. Sinnema 1990: 119. (This description, derived from B. Armstrong, Sinnema informed me in 2012, is somewhat dated and needs refining.) On 114, endnotes 1 and 2, Sinnema refers to detailed studies about the Aristotelian renaissance in Europe from approximately 1500 to

matters, (ii) medieval "scholastics," and (iii) "teaching style and methods" and "method or way of treating any subject," even theology. During the post-Reformation era, Reformed theologians used "scholastic interpretation" in distinction from "popular interpretation." Although Calvin never explicitly used this distinction in his *Institutes*, A. Hyperius (1511–1564), an avid advocate of his views, did between 1546 and 1552.[40]

The distinction between "scholastic" and "popular" is important not so much to explain our "understanding" of Scripture as to explain its "meaning." "Scholastic" interpretation is appropriate for learned men and young students in academic halls, but "popular" interpretation is significant for common, uneducated and illiterate people in large sanctuaries of worship. While the former is concise, compact and rigorous, interested in intellectual proofs, arguments and knowledge of truth, the latter is diffuse, expansive, rhetorically free and focused on arousing "goodwill," moving the "emotions" and providing comfort.[41] Near the end of his "Aristotle and Early Reformed Orthodoxy: Moments of Accommodation and Antithesis" Sinnema writes,

> It is evident that the classics and especially Aristotelianism in various forms pervaded the theological environment of early Reformed Orthodoxy. This was particularly true in the arts faculty of universities where theological students were taught the classics, even by theologians, before proceeding to specialize in theology. . . . Since it was thought that logic, as a gift of God, does not influence theological content, it was easy to assume that Aristotelian logic was neutral with respect to Christian faith. . . . The tendency to accommodate Aristotle to the Reformed faith was a significant factor in the late-sixteenth-century emergence of Reformed scholasticism, a movement that would become an important source of rationalist theology a century later.[42]

1650 by P. O. Kristeller, F. E. Cranz, C. Lohr, C. Smith and, more recently, B. Armstrong, J. Bray, and J. P. Donnelly.

40. See Sinnema 1999: 127–128; note 3 on 128 regarding W. van't Spyker, Principe, Methode en Functie van de Theologie bij Andreas Hyperius (Kampen: Kok, 1990).

41. See Sinnema 1994: 128–143, especially 128–133. For details about Greek anthropology in the "scholastic-popular" distinction, see Chapter 6 below on "Faculty Psychology."

42. Sinnema 1999: 143. For the importance of Antoine de Chandieu (1534–1591), a French Reformed theologian, who in *De Verbo Dei Scripto* (1580) "for the first time in the Reformed tradition," made "an explicit and urgent call for a 'scholastic method'" see Sinnema's detailed study in 1994: 159–190. See also his review of Willem Van Asselt and Eef Dekker, eds., *Reformation and Scholasticism: An Ecumenical Enterprise*, published in Calvin Theological Journal, 2002 (37): 157–160.

The demise of a European culture, which for centuries had been dominated by a Roman Catholic form of Christianity and is now coping with the shock-wave effects of classical Humanism, Renaissance, Reformation and spreading nationalism, greatly affected the importance and cultural power of institutions of higher education. Furthermore, Western Europe experienced the ravages of the Thirty Year Religious Wars (1618–1648), which resulted in the death of about thirty percent of the population in certain parts of Europe.

Faced with a major crisis in their culture, various scholars and educators sensed the great need for a new understanding of being human and the structure of society. In this turbulent and historically formative period, they worked feverishly to develop and, at least educationally, implement new insights into such matters as truth, order, freedom and justice.[43] Two such proactive and probing thinkers in a broadly conceived Reformed faith and thought tradition were J. Althusius and H. Grotius.

Johannes Althusius (1557–1638)

As professor of jurisprudence at the Academy of Herborn in Germany from 1584 to 1604, J. Althusius introduced a novel view of societal and political principles and their relation to Christian discipleship. After turning down a teaching position at the University of Leyden and University of Franeker in the Netherlands, he worked from 1614 until his death in 1638 as a council member in Emden, Germany, sometimes called "the Geneva of the North."

In *Politica*, his major study, he described his understanding of the structure of society, in reaction to the horrific "religious" wars that raged in Europe at that time. He reflected on the sensitive and complex issue of the relation between "church" and "state," i.e., membership in a faith community

---

43. For example, while many Reformed church leaders and theologians from different West European countries met at the Synod of Dort (1618–19) in The Netherlands, in an attempt to remove confusion and unrest caused by scholastic disputes, Rene Descartes (1596–1650), a young and gifted Roman Catholic thinker, visited a local school principal in Dordrecht. They discussed, among other things, the need for a new view of man, society, curriculum and pedagogy. From 1628 to 1648, while living in Amsterdam, he developed ideas about man, certainty, truth, proof, and method. Later, Spinoza (1632–1677), who, like Descartes, lived in Amsterdam, developed a view of society which, though different in structure, shared the spirit of Descartes's rationalism. Whereas the views of these two (and other) prominent thinkers were eagerly and widely studied in prominent universities, the views of pastors and theologians with a Synod of Dort mind-set were studied by only a small number of persons.

and in a national state, or one's general role in society.[44] Fundamental to his view of society and culture was his idea of "consociation," an elemental building block for the principle of "societal sphere sovereignty" Abraham Kuyper introduced two hundred and fifty years later and which Dooyeweerd and Vollenhoven deepened and broadened in an ontological, anthropological, epistemological and encyclopedic-curricular way.[45]

As a Dutch affluent international lumber trader, H. Bos (1881–1970) secretly collected for nearly fifty years sixteenth- and seventeenth-century books, pamphlets and articles of chiefly Calvinist Reformed thinkers about all sorts of confessional, political, societal and cultural issues.[46] Late in life, Bos abandoned his plans to write a doctoral dissertation on the salient ideas of J. Althusius. Three years before he died in 1970, he donated his massive book collection (the largest ever of one person in Dutch history) to Kuyper's Free University in Amsterdam. A condition for his donation was that in each publication a logo be printed with a picture of Johannes Althusius at its center, together with the dates 1557–1638.[47]

Hugo Grotius (1583–1645)

Another influential thinker at this time was H. Grotius. His views about man, natural law, freedom, contract, society and state are expressed in his classic *Concerning Just War and Peace* (1625).[48] His ideas were in spirit more Arminian than Reformed. The significance and scope of his understanding of all human life, not just faith life, is evident in his ideas about "war" and "peace" during three-decades-long bloody clashes between disagreeing faith and theology traditions.

For their role in Reformed higher education four more thinkers about chiefly "faith" and "theology" related matters are noteworthy: W. Amesius, J. Alsted, G. Voetius and (about education) J. Comenius.

44. See J. Althusius, Politics. 1964
45. About Kuyper, Dooyeweerd and Vollenhoven, see Chapters 5, 7 and 8 below. For details about "sphere sovereignty," see J. Dengerink 1948; its advocates in North America include H. Evan Runner (cf. Chapter 19 below), Bernard Zylstra, John Witte, Jr., and J. W. Skillen 1974: 191–217.
46. For twenty years between 1917 and 1961, he was Director of the Free University and served as president, secretary and treasurer of the Board of Governors.
47. For details, see Stellingwerff 1971: 9–57.
48. See Grotius 1925 and Curtis 1961.

William Amesius (1576–1633)

For his Puritan and anti-Anglican stance, W. Amesius, or Ames, a graduate of Christ College in England, fled in 1620 to the Netherlands, where he joined fellow refugees in Rotterdam, The Hague and Franeker. His dream to establish a Puritan college somewhere in Europe did not materialize. After he died in the Netherlands, his family emigrated to New England, where two of his sons studied at Harvard University in 1643.

In *The Marrow of Sacred Divinity* (*Medulla Theologiae*), his most important theological publication, Ames used the philosophical "method" P. Ramus had developed earlier. About this method, Keith L. Sprunger commented:

> The leading seventeenth-century English exponent of Ramist theology was William Ames. . . . The Marrow, one of the most frequently printed Protestant theological treatises of the seventeenth century, was renowned among English Puritans and continental Calvinists. The popularity of the Marrow stemmed apparently from two factors: the emphasis on method and the emphasis on practical divinity. Ramus provided Ames with method and organization.

> The end result of applying Ramism to theology, to all appearances, was a textbook of theology very suitable for student use. Ames, in fact, originally prepared the Marrow for teaching young theology students in Leiden. . . . For many years the Marrow also served as a textbook at Harvard and Yale and in the dissenting academies in England. It was the catechism writ large. What the catechisms had done for instructing young minds, the Marrow was designed to do for more mature students.[49]

In *Technometria*, his most significant philosophical publication, Ames extended the Ciceronian principle of "systematic treatment of grammar" in his attempt to include the whole curriculum and all the relationships between the sciences. While practical logic is the first link in the chain of the arts to obtain knowledge, theology is the last link, and also the queen, of the whole curriculum. Theology is not one of the regular "sciences," however. It does not arise out of nature and human inquiry, but centers on "doctrine" that rises out of God's revelation. About Ames's general philosophy of reality,

---

49. See Sprunger 1966: 141, 146.

structure of the curriculum, unique place of theology and logic, Sprunger states,

> All knowledge, emanating as it did from God, arranged itself into a cosmic pattern of the arts, and within this scheme, theology, the chief of the arts, had its assigned place as did the arts of logic, rhetoric, grammar, mathematics, and physics. To know the overall patterns and then the specifics of each of the individual arts was the beginning of knowledge.[50]

Johann H. Alsted (1588–1638)

As professor of philosophy and theology at the Academy of Herborn—where earlier J. Althusius had taught for two decades—Alsted became famous in circles of Reformed higher education for his three most important publications: *Scholastic Theology* (1618), *Course in Encyclopedia of Philosophy* (1620), and *Triumph of Sacred Scriptures or Biblical Encyclopedia* (1625).

The second work consisted of twenty-seven volumes of methodically arranged summaries of all available scientific knowledge.[51] Its impact on Protestant theology and philosophy was enormous. This is especially true of his extensive use of medieval dualism between "natural theology" and "revealed theology" and his uncritical acceptance of the all-pervasive "nature-grace" distinction.

The third book stressed the inadequacy of the natural realm and the superiority of the supernatural one. He used Scripture as a source book for all kinds of encyclopedic matters. In biblicistic fashion, he thought that Scripture provided, in addition to revelation about God's faithfulness to his promises and about humanity's need for salvation, all sorts of useful data for "cultural" and "natural" sciences.

---

50. For details, see Ames 1979; Parker 1975: "Before the student could embark on theology, medicine, or law . . . , he had to pass through the arts faculty . . . (which consisted entirely of philosophy . . .), and here theology was still *regina scientiarum*, the crown of education, for which all arts and sciences were a preparation. Students were trained, not to get degrees or lucrative employment, but so they might serve God as preachers of the Gospel or as godly magistrates" (29).

51. In content, not length, this publication was not surpassed until Abraham Kuyper published his massive *Encyclopedie der Heilige Godgeleerdheid*, I-III, 1894.

Gisbertus Voetius (1589–1676)

Perhaps the most influential seventeenth-century Reformed thinker was Gisbert Voetius, the first theology professor at the University of Utrecht in the Netherlands. During the Thirty-Year Religion Wars (1618–1648), as an ardent polemicist he fought against five evils: ecclesiastical disorders, Roman Catholic beliefs and practices, national sins, Arminian liberalism and Cartesian rationalism. To fight the last two forms of evil, i.e., the views of J. Arminius and R. Descartes, he used, ironically, apologetic methods based on the validity of various traditional scholastic and contemporary rationalistic arguments.

In *On Piety Combined with Science (De Pietate cum Scientia Coniugenda)*, his inaugural address at the University of Utrecht, he stressed the need for a "piety" based on a practical godliness that included some form of asceticism and precision in a person's daily spiritual exercises. Despite the title of his address, he did not talk about nature and role of "scientia," a topic which, he claimed, had already been dealt with by his colleagues in the four (non-theological) disciplines of jurisprudence, history, literature and philosophy

Speaking as a "theologian," he focused on the necessity and nature of simple piety (*pietas*) in one's faith life and academic endeavors. The ultimate source, and norm, for *scientia* is revealed in Scripture. It is the task of theology to call attention to Scripture, help uncover its revelation, and apply it to all of life, including academic and political life. Non-theological disciplines must give priority to the supernatural world and the study of theology.

> Also you, medics, belong to the race of philosophers. . . . You will agree with me that there is not a single part of your study which does not elevate the mind via the steps of created things to the supernatural, which does not by means of an investigation of causes arrive at the first cause of all things, the first Mover of Aristotle, the center of the universe, the maker and final goal of all things—"whether they may touch and find him, even though He is not far removed from each one of us. Because in Him we live and move and are," as the Apostle in Athens explained in the presence of philosophers with words derived from philosophy. In general, one described philosophy as "the knowledge of divine and human matters;" Plato as "a meditation on death"; others again in a different way. No one is so narrow in his understanding as to notice that already through the name but even much more through the study of philosophy . . . he is aroused to a denigrating of the

world, a meditating on heavenly things, a reverencing of divinity, an observing of sacred things.[52]

As a delegate to the Synod of Dort, Voetius opposed certain unbiblical tenets in the faith life of Christians. But philosophically and theologically, he was in his views and teaching quite traditional, even conservative. He did not see the need for any inner renewal in philosophy and science as such. While stressing piety, he perpetuated a tradition in higher education that incorporated Aristotelian thinking about such crucial terms as "substance," "intellect," "logic," "method" and "truth." In this regard, he continued in theology, higher education and the pulpit to promote a restricted vision and reduced witness in a world groping, even screaming, for peace.[53]

Johann Amos Comenius (1592–1670)

J. Comenius, a pedagogue and philosopher in Czechoslovakia, studied at the University of Herborn in Germany (cf. J. Althusius and J. Alsted above). His influence was huge: Poland, Hungary, France, Sweden, Germany, England, the Netherlands and even the Arab world.[54]

He rejected most of the pedagogical methods in vogue at that time in leading universities in Europe. He incorporated many ideas gleaned from J. Alsted's colossal *Course in Encyclopedia of Philosophy* (1620). These insights he combined with new ideas about "method" based on the empiricist and inductive philosophy of Francis Bacon (1561–1626). Eclectically, he fused these ideas with traditional views about sense and reason, and advocated a Christian faith which denied total depravity and believed humans can resist God's grace.

52. See Voetius 1634: 41 and 43.

53. As a student and a young pastor, even A. Kuyper was much attracted to Voetius's stress on piety (cf. Chapter 5 below).

54. See Comenius, *The Great Didactic*, I-IV, published in 39 books. For details, see Vladimir Jelinek, *The Analytic Didactic of Comenius* (Chicago: Chicago University Press, 1953); S.S. Laurie, *J. A. Comenius* (New York: Burt Franklin Reprints, 1972); J. E. Sadler, *Comenius* (London: McMillan Company, 1969) and *Comenius and the Concept of Universal Education* (New York: Barnes and Nobles, 1976). At the turn of this century, the International Institute for Christian Studies (IICS) established The Comenius Institute of Prague in the spirit of Comenius's ideas that (a) "as the whole world is a school for the human race . . . so every individual's lifetime is a school from cradle to the grave" and (b) "the goal of education is the acquisition of wisdom, comprised of learning, morality, and the Christian faith." (cf. www.IICS.org.)

Education enables people to improve themselves and society. Because it is rational, reality is coherent. At all four levels of education (1–6, 7–12, 13–18 and 19–24) nine different areas of nature and culture are studied, viz., physical things, plants, animals, humans, arts, natural philosophy, moral philosophy, politics/war and religion.

As a significant educational reformer directly in elementary and secondary, and indirectly in tertiary, i.e., all higher, education, Comenius was only marginally Reformed in his faith life. Basically, he went beyond, at times even against, the faith tradition of such reformers as M. Luther and J. Calvin. His little known, although significant, Pansophy deepened the "religious" character of Western secularism in higher education, philosophy and even theology.

Nineteenth and Twentieth Centuries

The religious secularization of European society and culture deepened in the philosophies of formidable thinkers like I. Kant (1724–1804), G. W. F. Hegel (1770–1831), A. Comte (1789–1857), L. Feuerbach (1804–1872), C. Darwin (1809–1882) and K. Marx (1818–1883). They all believed that enlightened teachers and scientists are the "high priests" of civilization and redeemers of society. The best way to resist, and ultimately eliminate, evil is to provide proper education for all citizens (cf. "by building schools one can tear down jails"). An apt slogan of this mind-set is "Ni Dieu, Ni Maître" (No God, No Master).

Various Dutch Reformed Christians sensed something of the depth, scope and practical consequences of this religiously misguided spirit and culturally powerful faith. In their response, they began to take a Scripturally more prophetic stance on various central issues not only, or primarily, in their personal and institutional faith life, but also in all their societal concerns and educational endeavors. Five visionary persons who took such a prophetic stance were G. Groen van Prinsterer, A. Kuyper, H. Bavinck, H. Dooyeweerd and D. Vollenhoven.

G. Groen van Prinsterer (1801–1876)

To arouse the Christian community to rediscover the power and scope of God's Word and respond to growing crises resulting from a religious secularization sweeping across especially Europe, G. Groen van Prinsterer, a perceptive historian and gifted lawyer, published *Unbelief and Revolution* (*Ongeloof en Revolutie*) in 1847,[55] one year before K. Marx published his *Communist Manifesto*. In 1854, he opened the first Christian elementary day school. In 1866, he started a Christian political party, and urged Abraham Kuyper in 1878 to assist him in developing a politically meaningful alternative to a deepening and spreading apostasy in Western Europe, especially the Netherlands.

When truth is replaced by opinion, revelation by subjectivity and faith by unbelief, then Christians have no choice but to alert the younger generation and future leaders to the importance of God's Word for life-renewing truth, justice and peace. At the center of human history, also in Western society and culture, rages a "spiritual" battle between a life-encompassing non-Christian faith, which nurtures revolutions, and a Christian faith that calls for reforming life through love-driven obedience in everything Christians think, say and do as citizens.

This central and life-encompassing conflict is culturally so pervasive that to begin to address it seriously and tactfully, it is necessary to begin to establish liberating parent-controlled Christian elementary schools.[56] Although van Prinsterer was not an educator and his marriage had remained childless, with great insight and passion he saw the need for Christian elementary schools and, through it eventually, a new view of history, faith life, politics and society. His commitment as a full-time disciple of Jesus Christ in "all of life" compelled him to encourage fellow Christians to join him, and others, in this small but important endeavor. It was mysteriously rewarded when G. van Prinsterer, weary and lonely, met a young, visionary preacher, A. Kuyper, who shared his emphasis on a radical, all-encompassing renewal.

55. In his doctoral dissertation at the Free University in Amsterdam, H. Van Dyke provided a detailed study and superb translation of this book—which for two decades played a crucial role in the "Groen Club" attended by interested students of Calvin College and Calvin Seminary. For details, see H. Van Dyke 1989 and Chapter 19 below about H. Evan Runner.

56. This founder of Christian elementary day schools was not an isolationist. The goal of such education was integral to his faith life, something practical for children and their parents, and for the benefit of society and culture in general.

Abraham Kuyper (1837–1920)

In a sudden and surprising way, A. Kuyper woke up from his "dogmatic slumbers" when he became aware of the vicious attacks of liberalism, dangers of evolutionism, problems of industrial revolution, and effects of "higher criticism" on a proper understanding of Scripture. For more than a century, Protestant Christianity focused too much, at times almost exclusively, on faith-related issues as debated by scholastic and liberal speculative theologians and preachers.

Kuyper sensed that by the end of the nineteenth century Protestant and Roman Catholic Christians had become too "pietistic," or too "liberal," to deal properly with pressing political, social, economic, industrial and educational revolutions that had swept across Europe. His negative response to rationalism's relentless onslaught on dwindling vestiges of Christian faith had deepened and broadened significantly within the span of only a few years. He saw the error of restricting Christian faith to ecclesiastical life. Christian faith is inherently pertinent also for all non-ecclesiastical changes and challenges in his day and age. This is particularly true in higher education, especially in philosophy.

In response to the threats of deepening secularism and skepticism, the Roman Catholic Church adopted in 1869 the doctrine of "papal infallibility," and it established in 1872 the Thomas Aquinas Academy in Rome. In 1879 Pope Leo XIII published *Aeterni Patris*, an encyclical, or pastoral letter, to inform all Roman Catholic philosophers, theologians and educators that they must "esteem" Aquinas as their "angelic teacher" by using his philosophy in all their research and teaching.

As a Protestant Christian, Kuyper also reacted to the growing crises in eighteenth- and nineteenth-century mainly European culture. His response was religiously deeper and more pertinent than that of Pope Leo XIII. Kuyper did not return first of all to Calvin, but to God's Spirit-filled powerful Word for all of life. He attempted to avoid the dangers of (i) "conforming" to the world, (ii) "escaping" from it, and (iii) "compromising" with it. Instead, he advocated a world-"reforming" approach—by focusing on the "heart" in the sense of an ongoing "reformation" of the heart. In terms of this biblical idea of heart-centered renewal, he scanned the sense of right and wrong in his day and age and stressed the need for a non-theocratic response to God's Good News for everything humans do anytime and anywhere.

In terms of this novel approach and inherent strategy, Kuyper's most significant contribution as a "reformer" was establishing the Free University in Amsterdam in 1880. With this strategically major move, he ventured into a culturally crucial area outside faith life in organized churches and theological schools. However, as a "theologian," he continued to read Calvin's sixteenth-century writings through the colored lenses of seventeenth-century Protestant scholastic thinking. In his new edition of Voetius's *Commentary on the Heidelberg Catechism*, he still appreciated Voetius's scholastic way of thinking and stress on "method."

A careful study of Kuyper as a "reformer" reveals an inconsistency between the main thrust of his new religious stance and remnants of traditional Reformed scholasticism, plus a leaning in the direction of modern romanticism and idealism. This inconsistency is evident in his *Encyclopaedie der Heilige Godgeleerdheid,* I-III (1893–1894)[57] and his famous lectures on Calvinism, his Stone Lectures at Princeton University in 1898.[58] In his *Encyclopedia of Sacred Theology*, he dealt in great detail with all sorts of historical and systematic issues related to the nature of theology and its role in the curriculum of a university. The impact of his ideas described in this massive study on Reformed higher education in, for example, the Netherlands, South Africa, Indonesia, USA, Canada, South Korea, and Japan has been formidable with regard to the essence of theology and its relation to all other studies or sciences.

Herman Bavinck (1854–1921)

In 1880, after Bavinck received his doctorate in theology at the University of Leyden, Kuyper was not successful in convincing him to join him to be his colleague in theology at the Free University he opened that year in Amsterdam. Kuyper's third attempt, in 1902, to have Bavinck join him (and, by that time, several other professors) at the Free University, was successful.

In his inaugural, in 1882, at the Reformed Theological Seminary in Kampen, Bavinck talked about "The Science of Sacred Theology," and in his second inaugural twenty years later, in 1902, at the Free University, he lectured on the broad topic of "Religion and Theology." After preparing for and completing his magnum opus—the *Gereformeerde Dogmatiek*, I-IV (1895–1901)—his interest shifted from the traditional (scholastic) Reformed

---

57. For an English translation of the first part of Vol. I and all of Vol. II, see A. Kuyper 1954.

58. For a detailed and perceptive study ,see Heslam 1998, which Shin Toyakawa, in Tokyo, translated into Japanese and published by Inter-Varsity Press of Japan in 2001.

dogmatics to newer and broader issues related to society, culture, history, philosophy and ecumenism. In 1908, a decade after Kuyper had delivered his Stone Lectures on Calvinism at Princeton University in the USA, Bavinck gave his Stone Lectures at Princeton University on the important topic of Philosophy and Revelation.[59]

For his ideas of "revelation," "cosmos," "knowledge," "society" and "culture," he turned to the tradition of St. Augustine and Calvin. He railed against "a-cosmic pietism" in Anabaptism, used some philosophical ideas of T. Aquinas,[60] disagreed about some features in Kuyper's view of revelation and reality, and developed his own ideas about the nature and place of theology and philosophy.

A difference between Bavinck and Kuyper about certain philosophical issues later played an important, though initially seemingly small but actually major, role in a disagreement later between D. Vollenhoven in Amsterdam and H. J. Stoker in Potchefstroom, South Africa, about "Christian scholarship" generally and the specific relation between "theology" and "philosophy."

Bavinck agreed with Kuyper that (a) practical everyday life precedes abstract, or theoretical, philosophy, and that (b) general revelation is presupposed in special revelation. In his epistemology, he rejected nominalism and conceptualism, as well as empiricism and idealism. In opposition to these two one-sided views, he advocated a form of "critical realism," together with the implied notion of a correspondence theory anchored in the Logos.[61]

Herman Dooyeweerd (1894–1977) and Dirk H. T. Vollenhoven (1892–1978)

Influenced by their parents' great respect for A. Kuyper and H. Bavinck as Reformed leaders, already as young gifted thinkers, H. Dooyeweerd and D. Vollenhoven sensed the need for an ongoing reformation in one's faith life and one's public life in society, the academy and culture. That keen sense deepened when they, as graduate students, discovered various implications

59. See Bavinck 1953 (reprint). For details, see Bavinck 1908: 529–543 and the H. Bavinck centennial International Conference in 2008, at Calvin Theological Seminary in Grand Rapids.

60. For a helpful study of philosophical, especially Aristotelian, ideas in Bavinck's theology, see Bremmer 1961; also Veenhof 1977: 345–365 (translated by A. Wolters in 1994).

61. For details, see Chapters 4 and 15–18 below.

of this for philosophy as a general discipline (*wetenschap*) and for such special disciplines as jurisprudence, natural science, logic and theology.

As to the nature and role of "faith life" and "theology," they reflected on certain traditional basic assumptions about human behavior, including human thinking within the academy. They reflected critically on dominant patterns of thinking and living in Western culture and history. They pressed themselves, each other, and friends around them to look for more helpful ideas and insights within the scope and power of God's Word of love for a hurting humanity.

In the spirit of a new consorting, reflected in such reformers as Calvin, Bavinck and Kuyper, and with a clearer awareness of lingering problematic, possibly untenable, elements in their own views, Vollenhoven and Dooyeweerd, along with others in the Netherlands and elsewhere, continued on their arduous, though liberating, task of rethinking basic philosophical, anthropological and epistemological problems. They focused on diverse disciplines, including the ambiguities and inescapable problems of the meaning and role of "theology," the study of, or about, God the Creator and His covenant love for His creation and its human caretakers.

Summary

In view of work done by some reformers in the Netherlands[62] and in other countries,[63] the aim of this study of "faith life" and "theology" is to sense where we are presently, reflect some more on basic assumptions, and explore a biblically better attuned, educationally more relevant, and cross-culturally more meaningful understanding of faith life, study of theology and the relation between these two. The brief survey given above about faith, theology and theological education, from the sixteenth-century Reformation to the present, has provided six helpful insights.

1. Reformed higher education has incorporated various philosophical

---

62. E.g., K. J. Popma, J. P. A. Mekkes, S. U. Zuidema, H. van Riessen, A. Troost, J. D. Dengerink, J. Stellingwerff, B. Goudzwaard, H. Geertsema, E. Schuurman, A. W. Begeman, J. Klapwijk, A. Bos, S. Griffioen, G. Glas.

63. E.g., South Africa: H. G. Stoker, T. van der Merwe, D. Strauss, B. J. Van der Walt, E. Botha, Ponti Venter, and others; USA and Canada: H. Evan Runner, C. S. Seerveld, B. Zylstra, J. H. Olthuis, G. J. Spykman, P. G. Schrotenboer, R. Knudsen , J. H. Kok, P. Steen, John Witte, Jr., J. W. Skillen, H. Hart, A. M. Wolters, R. Clouser, H. Van Dyke, R. Sweetman, L. Zuidervaart; Japan: Hizakazu, Inagaki.

and educational compromises. An accommodated view of "faith life" and "theology" impeded not only integrally Christian thinking about reality but also a Christian understanding of scholarship and education. Is it necessary for theology teachers in any institution of Christian education to be ordained by an affiliated faith community? Is "theology" a requisite for all who teach "religion" and who become preachers in organized faith centers? Are Christian ideas taught in non-theological institutions and courses "theological"?[64] Are references to God, Scripture, revelation, depravity, covenant, repentance, sin, obedience, grace, kingdom, etc., necessarily "theological"?[65]

2. As a discipline, philosophy plays a crucial role in theological education, especially with respect matters of "method" and "content" in theology. In this regard, Protestant scholastic thinking complicated, if not obstructed, renewal in philosophy and theology. This problem resulted, perhaps, from a semi-scholastic view of "common grace," advocated in certain Reformed circles, which minimized the depth of human rebellion against God's will for life, including faith life. In that case, integral renewal of it is not matched by a similar renewal in academic knowing and in the teaching of faith life.

A well-intended, but misguided, idea of "common grace" actually obstructs a covenant-centered knowing and educating. To establish an institution of Christian higher education and scholarship is one thing—in fact, it is relatively easy, compared to developing and maintaining it. Only when Christian scholarship, curriculum and pedagogy are interdependent is it possible to talk about "integral Christian" education and scholarship. Only then can colleges, seminaries and universities—building on what is taught in

---

64. In Christian faith traditions, theologians, pastors and students usually receive financial support from often affluent church communities. Most Christian educators and students, especially in poor countries, often cannot huddle together in their struggle against iniquity and their attempt to survive and experience a modicum of shalom. For details, see the problems and needs of the International Association for the Promotion of Christian Higher Education (IAPCHE) since 1975 (cf. www.iapche.org.)

65. My colleague and I in the Philosophy Department at Dordt College were gently but firmly reminded in 1971 by our department chair "to teach philosophy, not theology." After a long discussion with him, he realized that (i) my colleague and I did not confuse philosophy and theology, (ii) we were teaching in a Christian, not theological, way, and (iii) we did not think in terms of philosophers and theology, or as thinkers and believers being separate! Ever since that discussion, our chairman not only supported, but even encouraged, us to teach philosophy Christianly, not theologically. On his deathbed, several years later, he expressed his gratitude for our helping him—and the students, including his two daughters—to be integrally Christian also in philosophy.

Christian homes, elementary and secondary schools— move in the direction of making Christian insights culturally relevant and historically prophetic.[66]

3. From its very start, Reformed higher education created its own nemesis. In a philosophical and educational way, it shot itself, with the best of intentions, "in the foot." The "philosophical" and "theological" ideas of, for example, Arminius cannot be fully and properly understood apart from Beza's philosophy at Calvin's Academy of Geneva and from Gomarus's theological use of Aristotle's logic at the University of Leyden.

The two main scholastic mentors of Arminius were (as indicated above) Beza at the Academy of Geneva and Gomarus at the University of Leyden.[67] These scholars combined elements of Aristotle's logic with their notion of "supra-lapsarian election." Tragically, and ironically, the logical seeds sown in philosophical thinking by two religiously compromising theologians threatened a major dogma in Reformed faith and theology at its very beginning. This irony was continued for several centuries in all required "introductory philosophy" courses in most theological seminaries and divinity schools in the tradition of Reformed higher education.

Much time has been spent, and squandered, on resolving unsolvable problems resulting from misleading anthropological assumptions and their theological implications. Endlessly, numerous theologians debated problems about (i) God's sovereignty and human responsibility, (ii) supra- and infra-lapsarian theories, (iii) divine and human knowledge and their relation to God's will, (iv) impasses in anthropology and epistemology about "objective" and "subjective" knowledge, (v) nature of reason and experience, (vi) relations between theology and anthropology, and (vii) divine revelation in relation to human projection.[68]

4. Certain philosophical problems in the thinking of Luther and Melanchthon in Germany, Calvin and Beza in Switzerland, and Arminius and Voetius in the Netherlands are understandable in light of their historical context and cultural circumstances. To the extent it perpetuated ontological, anthropological and epistemological issues really at odds with God's

66. E.g., Academy of Geneva, University of Leyden, Harvard University and Yale University.

67. The international Synod of Dort met almost a decade after Arminius died in 1609. The chief reason for this Synod was to deal with a confessional conflict between Arminians (or Remonstrants) and Calvinists about philosophically different, even conflicting, ways to understand Scripture.

68. The purpose of all these distinctions is not to indicate they are all Arminian, but to stress that they are problematic.

faithfulness to his covenant promises, an ongoing reformation is called for. Such a renewal is stymied when one quickly appeals to "common grace." Instead, it calls for developing an integrally Christian philosophy. Christians are not free to simply use some existing philosophy. Especially in "philosophy" and "theology," Reformed thinkers have for several centuries been enfeebled, if not handicapped, sometimes even crippled, by questionable thought-patterns about, for example, "reality," "method," "truth," "logic," "being human" and "knowledge" in Western culture.[69]

5. It is common for Reformed theologians to think of the relation between philosophy and theology in terms of "form" and "content," how one thinks and what is thought, how doctrines are formulated and what is believed. This assumption in Reformed thinking reflects, it seems to me, a scholastic view of the relation between nature and grace, what is human and divine, general and special revelation, science and religion, reason and faith, emancipation and authority, subjective and objective knowledge, and projection and obedience. Perhaps in all these instances something is misleading and calls for reforming our view of human "faith life" and "theology."

A goal of this study is to explore the nature, and implications, of distinguishing between function (structure) and direction (religion) in human life, including faith life (to be explained in chapters 9–11 below). Such an approach (a) enhances awareness of Christians and non-Christians about the role of its scholars and teachers about their daily faith life, and (b) deepens the understanding of the scholars and teachers in Christian and non-Christian faith traditions of the nature and ramifications of an unavoidable religious difference, conflict, even clash, in and study of it.[70]

6. The tradition of Reformed higher education, particularly in "theology," was impacted by Greek thinking about such topics as "logic," "method," "truth," "essence," "metaphysics" and "certainty." When Christian faith is thought of as a clear "set of beliefs" to be subscribed to and guarded, then a dynamic biblically directed heart-centered, or religious, renewal is something to be prayed about. When the God of grace, through the Holy Spirit, unleashes a continuing reformation in how Christians think, educate and serve, then there is hope, love and joy in our confused and confusing world.

To avoid the kind of Reformed scholasticism Beza taught at Calvin's

---

69. The effect of Greek *theoria* on theology, faith and religion has been a tendency of Western Christians to accede to intellectualism, cultivate a logos-theory about Christ and not distinguish clearly between intellectual and other forms of knowing.

70. For details, see especially 12 and 20 below.

Academy of Geneva, causing Arminius to become restless and respond in another anthropological way to Beza's dogmatics, it is necessary to sense the debilitating impact of scholastic anthropology and philosophy on theology. Religious synthesis philosophy, especially scholastic theology, has stymied ongoing reformation.

In summary, what is (*de facto*) is not what ought to be (*de jure*). At least four issues in Reformed faith and theology need to be addressed: (a) the relation between faith and theology, theology and philosophy, theology and other disciplines, seminaries and universities; (b) "religion" as part of life or all of life; (c) the difference between Christian and non-Christian faith and their effect on society and culture; and (d) a biblical view of created reality, God's faithfulness, Christian witness, nature of knowledge, structure of society, role of history.

To begin such revisiting of central issues, the next chapters will explore how four Reformed thinkers—Bavinck, Kuyper, Dooyeweerd and Vollenhoven—tried to understand and reform faith life and theology in terms of all of life, a common worldview and clear philosophies.

CHAPTER FOUR

Herman Bavinck (1854–1921)

Salient features of Bavinck's view of faith life, theology and anthropology will be briefly described and commented on in this chapter. Compared to Kuyper's views on faith life and theology (to be described in chapter 5 below), Bavinck was theologically more traditional than Kuyper and culturally less visionary. After a few comments about Bavinck's personal and historical background and understanding of being (ontology) and "thinking" (epistemology), this chapter will focus primarily on Bavinck's view of certainty, faith and will, and conclude with a summary of Harry J. Fernhout's in-depth study of Bavinck's anthropology and its particular impact on his view of religion, faith and theology.

Personal and Historical Context

After studying theology for one year at the Secessionist Seminary in Kampen,[1] Bavinck enrolled in 1874 at the University of Leiden, where in 1880 he received his doctoral degree.[2] That same year, he turned down Kuyper's first

1. Bavinck's father, Jan Bavinck (1826–1909) was a prominent leader in the Secession of 1834, when several thousand members left the Modernist-leaning national Hervormde Kerk. While Jan Bavinck was a pastor in Kampen, the Secessionists established their own theological seminary in 1873. For a brief and helpful introduction to Herman Bavinck as a person, an author and a visitor to North America, see H. Zylstra (1956): 5–11.

2. His dissertation on The Ethics of Ulrich Zwingli deals with practical societal issues resulting from the faith life which Zwingli (1484–1531) had introduced in Switzerland.

request to join him as professor of theology at the Free University Kuyper had established that year in Amsterdam. After being a pastor for one year in a Secessionist Reformed Church in Franeker, Bavinck became professor of theology in 1882 at his alma mater in Kampen. In 1889, he declined Kuyper's second request to join him as professor of theology at the Free University. Three years later, when Kuyper became Prime Minister of the Netherlands, Bavinck accepted his colleague's third (and urgent) request to move from the relatively small city of Kampen to the large and central city of Amsterdam.

Already as professor of dogmatics at a fledgling Secessionist Seminary in Kampen, Bavinck contributed in a significant way to what later was sometimes called "neo-Kuyperian spirituality." In his first inaugural address, in 1882, at the Seminary in Kampen, he focused on "The Science of Sacred Theology," and in his second inaugural address, in 1902, at the Free University, he reflected on "Religion and Theology."[3] In both inaugurals, he discussed two issues which were both crucial and closely interconnected at that time.

After writing his four-volume magnum opus, *Gereformeerde Dogmatiek*,[4] his primary interest shifted from theology (notably dogmatics) to issues related to pedagogy, psychology, natural science, philosophy, ecumenism, culture, and women's suffrage. He traveled to North America first in 1892 and again sixteen years later in 1908 for his Princeton Stone Lectures on "Philosophy and Revelation."

Noteworthy in his thinking was his evaluation of traditional Reformed faith in terms of what is, historically speaking, "Christian" and what is universally considered to be "human". He looked, one could say, at the inside (or Christian) from the outside (or human), not just at what is human in terms of what is Christian. This kind of thinking enabled him to transcend certain limitations in his own Secessionist tradition. Like Kuyper, Bavinck also stressed the need for Christian renewal in what is eminently practical, fully human, not in something "spiritual," "religious," or more important.

---

3. "De Wetenschap van de Heilige Godgeleerdheid" and "Godsdienst en Godgeleerdheid." His main reason for joining Kuyper at the Free University was his desire to develop a biblical worldview, to urge radical obedience to God, and to counteract a mentality of flight from the world in most Secessionists.

4. "Dogmatics" was in his day and age thought of as the epitome of theology. The first volume appeared in 1895, one year after Kuyper published the three-volume *Encyclopaedie der Heilige Godgeleerdheid*. Except for Bavinck's classic dogmatics, no other dogmatics was printed five times within a century. For details about the English translation of his four-volume *Dogmatics*, and about the International Herman Bavinck Conference in Grand Rapids in 2008, see http://www.refdag.nl/website/artprint.php?id=121386.

Bavinck's significance for national, and international, renewal lies more in what he did after 1902, as a co-reformer along with Kuyper, for all of life than in what he had done before 1902, through his major dogmatics, for human faith life.[5] Along with Kuyper, he pressed for a distinctly Reformed way of living in and thinking about the world.

Bavinck's insight into faith life and study of theology, as well as into other areas in life and their related studies, was religiously deep and culturally broad. Two of his many students[6] were Dooyeweerd and Vollenhoven, who five years after Bavinck's death in 1921, were appointed as professors at the Free University in jurisprudence and philosophy respectively.

Ontology and Epistemology

Bavinck's worldview and philosophy affected his understanding of theology as a discipline. This is evident in at least seven different but closely inter-related ways. First, in the spirit of Augustine and Calvin, Bavinck rejected any Anabaptist pietistic acosmism. Any flight from the world does injustice to the biblical meaning of, for example, sin and grace, guilt and forgiveness, regeneration and renewal. Second, in an irenic but non-compromising way, he reached out to talented and influential persons in Christian, and non-Christian, faith traditions, to interact with them about shared human problems and to look for possible practical solutions. Third, in developing his own views about revelation, cosmos, knowledge, society and culture, he rejected the Roman Catholic way in which Aquinas, as a philosophical theologian or theological philosopher, combined Scripture and Aristotle. Fourth, a minor though important disagreement with Kuyper about the nature of revelation and reality, as well as about the relation between theology and philosophy, resembles a subsequent philosophical difference between D.H.Th. Vollenhoven in Amsterdam and H.G. Stoker in Potchefstroom. Fifth, according to Bavinck, practical experience precedes theoretical knowledge, including philosophy and theology. Certainty is not something added, but

---

5. The prominence of dogmatics in theology is not unrelated to the semi-scholastic belief that the content of one's faith can be summarized in a clear and systematic way, made possible by using a right method.

6. Other persons influenced by Bavinck's views are, for example, K. Schilder and G. C. Berkouwer, as theologians; P. S. Gerbrandy, Dutch Prime Minister from 1940 to 1945; H. G. Stoker, a philosopher in South Africa; and J. Waterink, the Dutch psychologist who for years served as personal advisor to the Dutch Royal House of Orange.

rather something integral, to one's daily practical life. Philosophy does not establish certainty, but deepens and broadens it. Sixth, general revelation is presupposed in special revelation; the former precedes the latter. Not in a restricted sense of being a "natural substance," but in an encompassing sense of being "creational," the latter is assumed in both God's grace and human redemption. Seventh, although his creedal stance and general worldview were, in spirit, Reformed, his philosophy of being human (anthropology) and human knowing (epistemology) were influenced by medieval and Protestant scholastic elements. He perpetuated the classic theory of trichotomy, according to which humans consist of "matter, mind and spirit." Furthermore, Bavinck accepted Kuyper's dualistic notion that humans consist of mind and body, i.e., two independent substances arranged hierarchically from higher to lower. As to practical knowledge of Christians, however, he stressed the religious unity of humans as God's image-bearers.

In his anthropology, Bavinck assumed an ontology and epistemology that were in some ways reminiscent of Aquinas's philosophical "critical realism." He rejected modern conflicts between, for example, nominalism and conceptualism, empiricism and idealism, and materialism and rationalism.[7] Central to these conflicts are the complex issues about the epistemic nature of subject and object. In empiricism, truth is essentially objective and discoverable by unbiased (passive) observers, but in idealism truth is subjective and projected by biased (active) thinkers.

To avoid the errors of nominalism and conceptualism, Bavinck advocated a form of critical realism.[8] Science (*wetenschap*) is interested in logical relationships between subject and object, grounded in a scholastic idea of an all-pervasive Logos and its archetype-ectype distinction. The object of science is logical and universal, not individual and particular. True knowledge

7. Bavinck perpetuated the Western mistake of contrasting rationalism with its conceptualism and idealism with empiricism or nominalism. For details, see Vollenhoven and Bril, Boonstra.

8. Because of its pervasiveness in Bavinck's way of thinking, two clarifying comments: (a) "Critical Realism" disagrees with Plato's idea of an objective world independent of one's conception or perception of it, and agrees with Aristotle's notion of forms which have being, or reality, only in things (in rebus),—a view Thomas Aquinas (1225–1274) stressed in his critique of Augustine's Platonism and which the Roman Catholic Church officially sanctioned three times within the last one hundred thirty five years (cf. chapter 14 below); (b) "Critical Realism" refers to Scottish "Common Sense" philosophy, especially that of Thomas Reid (1710–1796) (cf. N. Wolterstorff: 2002) and Scottish theology (cf. J. C. Vander Stelt: 1978, "Scottish Background" 9–35; "North American Context," 36–64, and "Philosophy and Scripture at Princeton College," 65–89).

assumes that reality resides in thought and that it is intellectually accessible in the acts and processes of thinking and understanding.[9]

Critical realism presupposes the existence of eternal truths (*veritas aeternae*), which as a-priori concepts precede argumentation and demonstration. These principles become known through human acts of thinking. Inherent in the structure of reality is a logos, an order, a unity of thought that corresponds to the logos operative in the human spirit.[10] Humans purify and expand the knowledge they gain about this logos in their daily life by means of their involvement in various sciences. Basic to Bavinck's notion of critical realism is his logos-based belief that the difference between practical and theoretical knowledge is not one of kind but of degree.[11]

The epistemology implied in classic critical realism reflects an all-embracing view of God-man-nature. According to this view, God is the principle of essence (*principium essendi*), humans possess the internal principle of knowledge (*principium cognoscendi internum*) and nature provides the external principle of knowledge (*principium cognoscendi externum*).[12] The correspondence between humanity as subject and nature as object is rooted in and determined by the divine Logos. This God-man-nature triad is fundamental in Bavinck's understanding of thinking, being, revelation, man, knowledge, theology, and his view of the relations between theology and philosophy, as well as between theology and all other sciences. He rejected any dualism between Christian faith and human culture.

Concerning the nature of theology and its relation to philosophy and other disciplines, he advocated a theology that differed somewhat from that of Kuyper, his friend and colleague at the Free University. Initially this disagreement was small, but eventually it became sufficiently large for two traditions to develop in circles of Reformed higher education with respect

9. This Thomistic view involves a logos-theory that combines Christian revelation with Aristotelian philosophy. "Science is not about the individual" (*scientia non est singularium*), "the intellect is about the universal" (*intellectus est universalium*) and "the universals are not prior to the thing, but in the thing" (*universalia non anterem, sed in re*). Cf. Bremmer (1961): 155–161.

10. These general concepts are not, in a Platonic way, *ante rem* but, in an Aristotelian way, *in re* and *in mente hominis post rem*. To think of general revelation in terms of critical realism implies the idea that humans possess a subjective ability to discover God and that this urge is the basis for understanding special revelation.

11. For the effects of critical realism on faith life, theology and their interrelationships, see Chapters 14, 15, 18 below.

12. Concerning internal and external principles of knowledge about God, see Bremmer(1961): 163–181.

to the need for ongoing reformational thinking in the Netherlands, South Africa, Indonesia, the USA, Canada, Australia, South Korea, England and New Zealand. In a broad or encyclopedic sense, it is Kuyper, not Bavinck, who introduced at least in principle two new notions: (a) the science (*wetenschap*) of theology is part of the organism of all academic disciplines (*wetenschappen*) and (b) theology presupposes Christian philosophy.

Unlike Kuyper, Bavinck placed "theology," a study of God's revelation, "between" human beliefs about the Creator and philosophy about created reality.[13] He perpetuated the scholastic custom of assigning to theology— in distinction from all other studies—a prominent and leading role within the academic enterprise. Concerning the nature of faith life and the unique role of theology, Bavinck's disagreement with Kuyper was minor compared to that of Rev. Foppe M. ten Hoor, a rigidly Bavinckian but fiercely anti-Kuyperian, theologian in dogmatics at Calvin Theological Seminary from 1900 to 1934.[14]

Despite his laudable and growing ecumenical interests at the Free University, Bavinck continued to advocate a semi-scholastic anthropology, philosophy and theology. In "Thinking and Being," a brief article published in his *Christelijke wereldbeschouwing* (Christian worldview), Bavinck described his view of "the origin, the essence, and the boundary of human knowledge."[15] In it he associated thinking with subject (psychic perception), being with object (physical reality) and truth, the purpose of all science (*wetenschap*), with conformity between intellect and thing (*conformitas intellectus et rei*). This kind of association enables a thinker to avoid the twin dangers of both empiricism and rationalism, or nominalism and idealism. "Being" is known through thinking the way an object is known through a subject. Reliable knowledge of objective reality is known through sensation and representation.

Knowledge involves a "relation between subject and object."[16] Between thinking and being, subject and object, there is a harmony.[17] In terms of Kant's classic formulation, "without representations concepts are empty"

---

13. This difference between Kuyper and Bavinck is evident in the difference between, on the one hand, Vollenhoven and Dooyeweerd, and, on the other hand, H. J. Stoker, W. J. Jonker and J. Heyns in South Africa.

14. For details about his impact on Calvin Theological Seminary in the USA, and the Christian Reformed Church, see Chapter 15 below.

15. For details, see Bavinck (1913): 15–36.

16. Bavinck (1913): 18–19.

17. Bavinck (1913): 21.

and "without concepts representations are blind."[18] Human sensations have a transcendent value. Science assumes "something that remains permanent in the flux of appearances"; that something is "a being, an idea of things."[19] At the center of the human ability to understand is a capacity to acknowledge that nature, or world-out-there, arose out of, and now exists, in ideas.

The scholastic nature of Bavinck's ontology and epistemology is clear from : (i) his acceptance of Christian theism, (ii) his reference to Augustine associating God's Word with *rationes*, (iii) his comments on *prognoosis* and *phaneroosis* and on *universalia* in God and the world, (iv) his comments on the nature of subject and object and (v) his remarks on Wisdom (or Word) and science:

> No matter how we turn it, with the concept truth and science, if we are unbiased and consistent in our thinking, we arrive at Christian theism. Because this teaches us that all things have been brought forth through the wisdom of God's Word and therefore exist, according to Augustine's saying in rationes, in measure, number, and weight.[20]

If the world can be the content of our knowledge, it must itself be clearly and distinctly thought beforehand. Only because in God is the *prognoosis* of all things are these all together the *phaneroosis* of his thought. The *universalia* are *in re*, because they existed *ante rem* in the divine consciousness. The world would not be known to us if it did not exist; but it would not exist if it were not thought beforehand by God.[21] The doctrine of the creation of all things through the Word of God is the explanation of all knowing and knowledge, the supposition of the correspondence between subject and object. Just as the senses are consonant with the elements of things, so does understanding correspond to the thought which combines these elements of things into things, bodies, nature and world:

> The *universalia in re* enter into our consciousness by means of sensory perception through the thinking activity of the νους. The world becomes

---

18. Bavinck (1913): 22; also his statement "neither blind facts, nor empty ideas" (25).
19. Bavinck (1913): 26.
20. "Hoe wij het wenden of keeren, wij komen met het begrip waarheid en wetenschap, indien wij onbevooroordeeld en consequent doordenken, bij het Christelijk theisme uit. Want dit leert ons, dat alle dingen door de wijsheid, door het Woord Gods zijn voortgebracht en daarom naar Augustinus' zeggen in rationes, in maat, getal en gewicht bestaan." Bavinck 1913: 27.
21. Bavinck refers in a footnote to Augustine, Conf. XIII 38 and De Cive XI 10.

and can only become our spiritual possession because, being itself spiritual, it exists logically and rests in thought . . . What is knowable precedes our science, just as the *fides quae* does the *fides qua creditur*. Thinking about this more deeply, all truth is included in the Wisdom, in the Word which was with God and was God. Whoever denies this Wisdom, undermines the foundation of all science, because *qui negat* ideas, *negat Filium* [he who denies ideas, denies the Son].[22]

Humans must acknowledge that Truth exists in the conformity of human consciousness with what is objectively there, i.e., what is perceived, studied, believed and subjected to.

Though they are closely related, wisdom and science (*wetenschap*) are not identical. While science is related to human knowledge of reality through proximate cause (*per causam proximam*), wisdom is related to the knowledge of reality through primary cause (*per causam primam*).[23] Wisdom builds on science; it strives to go beyond it by attempting to penetrate to the primary principles (*prima principia*). It is the object or aim of philosophy. It takes for granted sensory perception and the reliable knowledge of science "that the world rests in thoughts and that ideas control all things."[24] A Christian view of the world assumes a harmony between subject and object, and it calls for a philosophy that is anchored in God's testimony in Scripture.

It is the same Divine wisdom, which gives existence to things and objective validity to our thoughts, grants to things knowableness and to our understanding power of thought, [and] causes things to be real and our ideas to be true. The intelligible in things is the content of our intellect. Both being and knowing have their ratio in the Word, through which God created all things.[25]

Philosophy is not restricted to what is finite, but touches on God as the "last cause of all things." It is in this context that Bavinck stresses the role of religion as something that brings humans "in the first place in contact with God" and determines their "attitude to all creatures," including their sensory affections, concrete representations and total worldview.[26] According

22. Bavinck (1913): 28–29.
23. Bavinck (1913): 30.
24. Bavinck (1913): 32.
25. Bavinck (1913): 33.
26. Bavinck (1913): 34.

to Scripture, the human heart longs not just for a "pure concept of God," but for the "living God himself." Even for the profoundest thinker, there is no justification through a "concept, but only through faith." Such a worldview has to be the same for religion and philosophy, people and scholars, life and school. He concludes his article "Thinking and Being" with a pithy, almost euphoric and somewhat Greek-tinted statement:

> It is the same God whom the pious and the philosopher need and who makes known his works to both. It is the same Word, which has made all things and in the fullness of time became flesh. It is the same Spirit, who renews the face of the earth and changes the heart of the sinner. And, therefore: *verus philosophus amator Dei*, and: *Christianus verus philosophus*.[27]

The Certainty of Faith[28]

Bavinck's philosophical background and stance influenced his anthropology and ideas about religion and faith. His *De zekerheid des geloofs* (*The Certainty of Faith*), 1901, is a clear example of his way of thinking. It provides three things: (a) a penetrating critique of a main feature of his culture; (b) a spirited attack on pietism's flight from the world and secularism's conformity to it; (c) and a biblical perspective on how to live Christianly in modern society. To do these three things, he focused on the pervasiveness of doubt in his day and age and on the great need for certainty in all of life.

By making critical reason the cornerstone of certainty, humans become the ultimate source of truth. Such an intellect-centered idea of truth raises many questions and provides numerous options, surmises and opinions, especially for doubting theologians. If Comte's evolution-centered positivism[29] becomes dominant, then agreement about who humans are, where they have

---

27. Bavinck (1913): 36. The phrases "the true philosopher is a lover of God" and "a Christian is a true philosopher" are taken from Lactantius's discussion of *vera sapientia et religione* in *Divinae Institutiones*, Book IV.

28. Translated from the third revised edition of 1918 into English by Harry der Nederlanden and published in 1980 by Paideia Press, St. Catherines, ON, Canada.

29. Comte (1798–1857) claimed to have discovered in 1822 the evolutionary law of three stages in history: theological (anthropomorphic), metaphysical (depersonalized forces), and positive (simple descriptions of facts).

come from and where they are going will disappear from the horizon of human existence.[30]

More than any other study (*wetenschap*), it is theology's task to reflect on the mysteries of life and to provide "comforting truths." Its "practical" role is "akin" to prescribing "medicine for the ailments of the soul." Theology nurtures the "certainty of faith"(18, 19). As will be seen in a later chapter, implicit in this certainty and truth is the classic Greek idea of faculty psychology. For Bavinck, each of the three human faculties of the soul—in distinction from the human body—i.e., "mind, will, feeling—"finds rest in what it by nature strives towards." While the human mind rests in what is true, or "more profoundly conceived," what is in God, who is "the truth," the human will rests in what is the good and the human sensibility rests on the beautiful (20).[31]

Truth and certainty, though closely interrelated, are not alike. While truth points to a relationship in the scholastic idea of a correspondence between thought and reality,[32] certainty refers to "a capacity, a quality, a state of the knowing subject." Statements or propositions which humans make about the state of their knowing can be one of three different kinds, namely, indifference, doubt, and certainty. The human mind has certainty when it finds "complete rest in its object of knowledge." The "normal and natural condition of the [human] spirit" functions the way health does for the [human] body.[33] In distinction from truth understood in the sense of God's Son, who liberates humans, certainty as such does not liberate anyone. It is possible for humans to find "false rest in an error presumed to be the truth" (33).

The three forms of certainty are scientific, i.e., those "recognized by all

30. Bavinck (1980): 8–13. References to the page numbers of this publication will be placed in parentheses in the text.

31. Bavinck uses this faculty-psychology to describe the Reformation: "Their emotions did not rule their reason, while reason and will did not deny the rights of their emotions. Their hands were never idle. Head, heart and hands worked together in exceptional harmony. They were not pietists with only an eye and heart for the religious life. They were not mystics who retreated into isolation and left the world to its fate. They were not intellectualists and moralists who failed to do justice to the riches of emotional life." Similarly, he described the conflict between orthodox believers (who "no longer confessed their beliefs, but . . . only believed their confessions") and pietists (who "sought the essence of salvation in experience"), between Moravians and Methodists, and between rationalists and mystics (41–48). His semi-scholastic view of faith is evident when he states that "faith is not only trust," but "also knowledge and assent" (50); see also 64–65, 78, and 92.

32. It assumes an ontology based on a speculative view of God's Word as Logos in the spirit of Greek metaphysics.

33. Cf. "Certainty is rest, peace, blessedness. . . ." See (Bavinck) 1980: 20.

but the most hardened sceptic." They are based on (i) senses and observations; (ii) reason or thoughts known immediately through self-evident first principles; and (iii) reason arrived at inferentially through demonstration and proof.

In distinction from these three forms of certainty, there is a fourth form of certainty in the area of religion and morals and based on revelation. It is deeper than "after-the-fact reasoning;"[34] it has to do with faith (21, 22). Being located "in the depths of the soul, in the heart" (22, 23), this certainty cannot be "undermined by scientific argument," nor can it be "convincingly established by it." It is unique in that it rests on "revelation, authority, a divine word, whether true or presumed." Faith's certainty transcends all human doubt. In a sense, faith and religion are synonyms. Religion is "in the first place, faith, i.e., "humility, trust, dependence, obedience, simplicity and childlikeness" (25). Its certainty does not depend on "fallible human insight but on unshakable divine authority." If its basis is the "certainty in the testimony of others . . . and of our own consciousness," then it is comparable to "assumptions and principles of science as a whole" or some "particular sciences."

That our sense perception is reliable, that the outside world has an objective existence, that the laws of thought correspond with those of being and that the so-called axioms are the firm foundation for all knowledge—these and many other postulates cannot be proven but are established by the immediate testimony of our consciousness prior to all proof. Anyone who refuses to proceed on this basis blocks his own way to the truth and falls victim to doubt (24–25).

The full meaning of this fourth meaning of "certainty" is not easy for Bavinck to delineate and hard for the reader of his book to grasp. Though the certainty of faith is comparable to that of "assumptions and principles of science as a whole," scientific certainty may not be imposed on religion, because that would nurture pride, intellectualism, self-elevation, puffed-up knowledge. Bavinck affirms faith's unique certainty when he stresses both "personal trust" and having "faith in the testimony of others." Only when these two forms of certainty are "trustworthy and dependable" is it possible to say that both religion and "theology" depend not "on personal observa-

---

34. For Bavinck, proofs "don't lead the way but trail behind" and apologetics "is the fruit, never the root, of faith." Like A. Kuyper, he rejected the kind of apologetics advocated in Anglo-American Presbyterian theology at Princeton Theological Seminary and, after 1934, in a lingering way, at Westminster Theological Seminary in, respectively, Philadelphia and Escondido.

tion, but on divine testimony and can only be established for us by faith . . ."
(26–27).

> Since in religion not a fallible human being but God himself steps forward
> as a witness, then from this point of view there is no science more certain
> of its subject matter than theology. Its basis and strength consists in *Deus*
> *dixit*, so says the Lord. What human authority can be compared to that of
> the Almighty? . . . .

> There is a certainty that pertains to objective truth and a certainty that
> pertains to the subject's share in the benefits promised by that truth. The
> two kinds of certainty are doubtlessly very closely interconnected, but they
> should, nevertheless, be distinguished and not confused. The act of faith
> by which I recognize the truth differs from the one by which I am assured
> of my own salvation.[35]

Unlike fallible scientific inquiry, imagined ideals and rational propositions, religion presupposes, and appeals to, divine "revelation." A "theology"
which "no longer dares to trace its dogma to a *Deus dixit* (so says the Lord)
has undermined its foundation, lost its stability, and will soon stumble into
ruin. Revelation, divine authority, is the only pillar on which religion can
rest" (52). The fact that there are many forms of religion, even divisions
within a particular religion about "the nature and authority, the content and
scope of revelation" does not result in doubting whether truth can be found.
To doubt anyway would "do violence to our rational and moral nature, which
can never escape the impact of God's majesty" (28).

The power of scientific certainty "rests on rational and therefore more
universal ground" (28), but the certainty of faith transcends the "subjective power" of scientific certainty. Faith's certainty is "the deepest, the most
intimate, the dearest and . . . most tenacious of all . . . Who will put his
possessions, his name, and his life on the line for a purely theoretical truth?
Scientific certainty can't stand up to the torch and the stake" (29). Unlike
"science and art, religion demands a divine certainty" (53).

For Bavinck, human experiences, important as they are, are not the basis
for faith. The objective content of faith, e.g., Christ's resurrection, is presup-

---

35. Bavinck 1980: 27–28. Given Bavinck's acceptance of "critical realism," to "recognize"
something does not imply that the latter is necessarily certain (objective), nor that it is less
certain, even uncertain (subjective).

posed in human experience. The content of faith does not depend on human experience, for "Christianity is not science or philosophy but religion" (73). It does not depend "on our will but on a decree of God" (74) and the Spirit's irresistible call to repentance.

In contrast to confessional theology in seminaries, studies in comparative religion in Religion Departments in modern universities remove this prior commitment to God's revelation, and, as a result, ignore "the superiority of the Christian religion over all other religions" (56). True self-knowledge and knowledge of the world "continually verify the knowledge of God revealed in Holy Scripture"(57).[36] Only such knowledge manifests the true nature and role of faith.

Thinking in terms of a Greek "faculty psychology," Bavinck states that "[f]aith is a function of understanding that has been moved to acknowledge the truth of the gospel by the will. The whole man is therefore involved in believing—with his reason, with his will, with his heart, in the core of his being, in the deepest part of his existence" (78).[37] Biblical faith is the correlate of God's promises: these two realities "address themselves to one another." Consistent with the philosophy of critical realism, Bavinck writes:

> faith is not the ground that carries the truth, nor is it the source from which knowledge flows to him, but it is the soul's organ; it recognizes the objective, self-subsistent truth. Faith is the pail with which the believer draws the water of life from the wellspring of God's Word. In all perception and thought, agreement between subject and object is required" (83).[38]

In addition to the certainty of truth, Christians need the certainty of salvation. These two forms of certainty are, for Bavinck, interrelated. To know something to be certain implies knowing it "spontaneously and immediately."

Genuine, true knowledge excludes all doubt regarding itself. It reaches this certainty not by rational argument, and not by self-reflection or by logical inference; the light that knowledge sheds on the known object immediately reflects back on itself and expels all darkness. This is also true of faith. Faith that really deserves the name brings its own certainty (84–85).

---

36. Bavinck adds: "This is the light on the path that leads through creation, and which is itself clarified and confirmed by all of nature and the whole history of mankind."

37. Bavinck adds: "For faith is not only trust, it is also knowledge and assent" (59). For details about "faculty psychology," see chapter 6 below.

38. Bavinck also uses organ, ground, rock, source, rule, light and lamp as metaphors of faith. For a comparable philosophical thought-pattern in Alvin Plantinga, see chapter 17 below.

Faith is not "an assemblage," nor a "gift . . . imposed from the top upon our own nature, always remaining inwardly alien to it"; rather, it is "a restoration of the right relationship between God and man, the return of the trust a normal child places in his father" (85). Faith is a certainty that "excludes all doubt." Certainty "flows to us immediately and directly out of faith itself." As an "essential characteristic of faith," certainty is "inseparable" from faith (86). Believers become sure of their salvation when they expect it "not from their faith but through faith from God's grace" (87). Doubt and faith do not belong together, for doubt is caused by the old believer, not by the new one.

Bavinck's detailed description of certainty, faith and the interrelation between them presupposes his distinction between what is objective and subjective as rooted in the scholastic notion of reality and knowledge commonly called critical realism.[39] This idea influenced his distinction between truth and salvation, knowing and experience, being and well-being, promises given and promises shared. In all these cases, the former is objective and the latter is subjective.[40]

This is true not only in Christian faith, but also in "historical, temporal and miraculous kinds of faith" (90). Each form of faith "bears fruit according to its object and nature" (91). The difference between Christian and non-Christian faith depends on whether the object is good or bad, rooted in spiritual renewal of the heart or in something that is imagined and projected.

To understand more clearly Bavinck's view of certainty, faith and religion, especially with respect to certain difficulties he encountered in expressing his laudable intentions, calls for a closer look at what he means by being human, i.e., the nature or structure of anthropology.

Philosophical Anthropology

According to Bavinck, humans consist of matter and spirit, or body and soul, as two distinct substances. In a dualistic way, he emphasized the relation or unity between these two independent substances. He associated this unity with something that is inherent in the image of God in humans. In displaying the "oneness of the material and spiritual world," humans mirror the

---

39. For details, see footnote 8 above.
40. Bavinck 1980: 84–87. Certainty differs from any calculation of chances or any experiment.

universe and reflect, microcosmically, God's image and likeness. In humans, "the whole world receives its unity, its goal, its crown."[41]

In a detailed study "Man, Faith, and Religion in Bavinck, Kuyper, and Dooyeweerd," Harry Fernhout[42] indicates that Bavinck introduced in the "spiritual substance" of humans an important, but generally overlooked, distinction between "soul" and "spirit." In his book *Bijbelsche en religieuze psychologie*, Bavinck indicated that "soul" and "spirit" refer to the "same inner man" but they do so in different ways" or as "different sides."[43] While the soul relates to the lower, or "sensory," part of the world, the spirit relates to the higher, or "invisible," part of the world. About the soul, which unites a person's spirit with the body,[44] Fernhout perceptively observed:

> In distinguishing *ziel* [soul] from *geest* [spirit] Bavinck is attempting to give a quasi-structural account of the factor which unifies *geest* and *lichaam* [body] by introducing a 'third' element in man while yet 'avoiding' the pit of trichotomy. *Ziel* becomes the ontologically distinguishable (though not distinct) part of man which serves as the buffer and link between *geest* and *lichaam*. . . . The more Bavinck defines *ziel* as a structural component of man's being . . . the more nebulous and less substantial becomes his understanding of *geest*. Although the latter is something that man has as part of his being, it is not defined as a structural, substantial dimension, but gets the character of a (ruling, monarchial) directional principle. The *geest* is called . . . the principle and the power . . . of life, which is breathed from above. This tendency leads Bavinck to assert that man has a *geest* but is a *ziel*.[45]

For Bavinck, the cosmos is an all-encompassing organism with a built-in hierarchy, in terms of which certain creatures are closer to God as the highest Good. As God's image-bearers, some creatures manifest his divine qualities more clearly than others do. Whatever is higher unifies, organizes, or rules what is lower, and whatever is lower expresses what is higher.[46] Ultimately, God is the Monarch, the Archetype, the Unifying Principle. "All creatures

---

41. Bavinck (1928): GD, II: 604. See Fernhout (1975): 6, notes 7 and 8.

42. H. Fernhout (pp. 10–11)

43. Bavinck (1920): 58.

44. Although Bavinck ascribes a certain measure of independence of the soul from the body. See Fernhout (1975): 7, n12.

45. Fernhout (1975): 7–8; in notes 14 and 15, Fernhout refers to Bavinck, GD, II: 597 and Bavinck (1920): 58.

46. Vollenhoven traced this monarchian conception back to Aristotle's philosophy—for

are the embodiment of Divine Thoughts and display *vestigia Dei* [Divine features]."[47] This is clear from the constitution of humans, in their becoming conformed to God. Being structurally closely related to God and "resembling"[48] him, humans reflect God. In imaging Him, they are the unifying creatures who rule the rest of creation.[49]

In this meticulous study of Bavinck's anthropology, Fernhout indicates a hierarchy in both the world at large (macrocosm) and in each human being (microcosm). God's relation, through human image-bearers, to creation is an archetype for the intra-human relation between a (higher) spirit in the soul to something (lower) in the body. The diversity in the world at large (i.e., the macrocosm) is directed by, and revelatory of, God, and the diversity of the human body (organ of the soul) is unified by the spirit in humans (i.e., microcosm).

As "spirit"—which unites soul and body—the soul acts as the "center" of being human, as the "core" of humanity, or as the "seat and subject of life." The soul is "the form, the motivating power, the principle of the body," while the body is "the matter, the material, the possibility of the soul"[50] There is in Bavinck's anthropology, Fernhout suggests, an "intra-human hierarchical relationship" within the soul, with its three capacities, of which the heart is most important:

> While the spirit (*geest*) is the principle and the soul (*ziel*) is the subject of life in man, the heart is, according to the Holy Scriptures, the organ for his life. It is in the first place the center of his bodily life, but further, in a metaphorical sense, it is the basis and source of all soul life, of emotions and passions, of desire and will, even of thinking and knowing . . ..[51]

Human life expresses itself in different ways: there is life that "encompasses all impressions, senses, perceptions, observations, deliberations, thoughts, knowledge and wisdom." In its higher form, it has "*nous* [mind] as organ

---

details, see Vollenhoven, *Schematische kaarten : filosofische concepties in probleemhistorische verband*, ed., K.A. Bril, P.J. Boonstra, (Amstelveen: De Zaak Haes, 2000)

47. Bavinck, as quoted by Fernhout (1975): 9.

48. Bavinck's term is "verwant aan." See Fernhout (1975): 9–10.

49. Cf. the tendency in traditional and some neo-Calvinist circles to interpret imago Dei in the monarchian manner having dominion, ruling over, being vicegerents or administrative deputies.

50. Fernhout (1975): 11; see also 10.

51. Fernhout (1975): 12.

and expresses itself in words or language." There is also the life of "emotions, passions, inclinations, affections, desires and volitions" that have their origin in the heart. All of these must be led by the *nous* and expressed in deeds.[52] In short, humans have three hierarchically structured organs, namely heart, will and mind. Of these organs, the highest organ is the heart, which directs the organs of the mind and the will.[53]

Faith and Religion

In the tradition of a scholastic anthropology, Bavinck, a very talented Reformed thinker, reflected much about the nature of faith and religion in particular.[54] Basic to the latter is having "a sense of the existence of God" and the human "duty to worship" him.[55] Though devastated by sin, this "natural, universal and necessary"[56] sense has not been lost. He states the following:

> [R]eligion is universal and has great power in life and history. Whether one wants to or not, one always comes up against a certain religious aptitude in man. One can give it various names: *semen religionis, sensus divinitatis* (Calvin), religious feeling (Schleiermacher, Opzoomer), faith (Hartmann), feeling for infinity (Tiele), etc., but it always comes down to a certain aptitude of human nature for awareness of the divine. . . .[57]

> [Even sinful man] remains tied to the heavens. In the depth of his soul he lies firmly anchored to an invisible, supernatural world. In his heart he is a supernatural being; his reason and conscience, his thinking and willing, his wants and inclinations, are grounded in the eternal. And religion is the irrefutable evidence of this.[58]

---

52. Fernhout (1975): 12–13. The "ruling" role of the heart in the monarchian sense and the "directive" role of the heart in the biblical sense.

53. Fernhout correctly indicates in note 35 that Bavinck's use of faculty psychology in his view of the Trinity would have drawn him, had he been consistent, into the monarchian problems that plagued the church during the third and fourth centuries.

54. For Bavinck's view of religion and faith, see Fernhout's analysis in (1975): 15–35.

55. Bavinck (1908): 120 ("besef van het bestaan Gods en van zijn plicht tot vereering"); for English edition, (1909): 142.

56. Bavinck (1955) [GD, II]: 44.

57. Bavinck (1955) [GD, II]: 288–289, as cited by Fernhout (1975): 15.

58. Bavinck (1908): 120, 135–6. Fernhout comments that "Bavinck's words have a ring that

As indicated earlier in this chapter, the three fundamental principles in Bavinck's view of religion are: God as the principle of essence of all religion, revelation as the external principle of knowing, and *imago Dei* as the internal principle of knowing. Integral to (the structure of) being human is having been created in God's image. Religion is a "certain faculty or aptitude of becoming aware of the divine which corresponds to God's objective revelation." God created "not only the light, but also the eye to behold the light."[59] The correlate of "objective religion," or revelation, is "subjective religion," or religion as a habit in human nature. Inherent to the human soul is a capacity, aptitude, power, ability, and the inclination, tendency and disposition to obtain some definite, certain, and indubitable knowledge of God; a knowledge gained in the normal course of development . . . and arrived at in a natural way, i.e., without scholarly argumentation and reasoning.[60]

Revelation is the source of subjective religion and faith, as expression of religion, is "the organ of the soul" that enables humans to acknowledge "objective, self-sufficient truth." Though it is darkened by sin, this capacity for religion has not been eliminated, but it has become impure and given rise to the difference between Christian and non-Christian religion.

Bavinck blurred this sense of a universal religion and its role in the human constitution, with his claim that only Christians have a genuine subjective religion and that non-Christians have something less than a subjective religion.[61] The Spirit can renew the capacity of religion, however, by enabling persons to surrender to God's revelation, so that subjective religion (*religio subjectiva*) is properly correlated with objective religion (*religio objectiva*).

The secret, or "internal principle," of correlating objective religion and subjective religion is God's Spirit,[62] and central to this correlation is faith. Faith has two distinctive features: first, it correlates objective religion and subjective religion, and faith provides "sure and certain knowledge"; and, second, inasmuch as a person is "wholly receptive and totally dependent on

recurs in Dooyeweerd's assertion that all man's functions are rooted in his supra-temporal heart, through which they have reference to the Origin."

59. Bavinck (1955) [GD, II]: 287–290. For details, see Fernhout (1975): 15–25, especially notes 39–41. Bavinck's correlation between objective and subjective religion, between revelation and religion, resembles somewhat Dooyeweerd's distinction between the law-side and the subject-side of reality, including the structure of faith.

60. Bavinck (1955) [GD II]: 58.

61. Fernhout (1975): 19–25.

62. As a result, he "ends up with God in man believing in God." See Fernhout (1975): 21.

God," it indicates "wholehearted trust and total surrender" to God's promises. In such a case, faith is inescapably Christian.

As an innate aptitude, human beings possess such universal faith, even
when it is ignored or not sufficiently recognized. Concerning the content
of faith, revelation determines the aptitude, capacity or role of faith. The
distinction between aptitude and content disappears, however, when the
former is not recognized as a human ability to obtain content, but merely
as something determined by the latter.[63] Using the pail metaphor, if faith is
compared to a pail and Spirit-filled regeneration is compared to water in
the pail, then faith, in the sense of regeneration, is a gift of God's grace, not
a built-in human aptitude to believe in God, in a substitute for God, or in
some pseudo-god.

This way of thinking presupposes Bavinck's scholastic kind of anthropology, which thinks of human faculties as inherent capacities in all humans (whether Christians or non-Christians), which become normative only
when they are activated by the content of revelation.[64] As subjective religion,
faith is a human capacity (*facultas*) that expresses itself through the mind,
or intellect (*nous*), as one of the soul's three capacities. Mind (*nous*) is not
only a capacity for observation, thought, knowledge and wisdom, but also
for religion, because faith—as a restricted part or aptitude of humans—is
distinct from the core of a person's whole or total being.

When faith as a part of human life is equated with faith as religion, as
the heart or center of all human life, then faith functions in a hierarchical
way. As the top or highest capacity of *nous*, which controls and directs human embodied life, the faculty (*facultas*) of faith becomes the highest, most
dominant and directive part in human life. As a result, faith becomes two-
sided: it is related both to God's revelation and to (the rest of) human life.

For a clearer sense of Bavinck's anthropology and its implications for the
meaning of faith and religion and for a better grasp of central issues explored
in neo-Calvinist and neo-Kuyperian circles in both philosophy and theology,
Fernhout's summary of Bavinck's anthropology and view of religion and faith

63. An example of this approach is Barth's docetic view of faith, and, surprisingly, also
Van Til's view of faith and revelation in his apologetics, especially criticism of Dooyeweerd's
idea of faith as a human function and an aspect of created reality.

64. Fernhout comments: "The Cosmonomic Philosophy has gone a step beyond these
problematics by asserting that man has various functions (modes of expression) which are in
their 'make-up' and 'activity,' structurally and directionally, normed by God's Law, and are thus
totally involved in obedience or disobedience to the Creator." Fernhout (1975): 24. For details
on Dooyeweerd, see Chapter 7 below.

deserves close scrutiny. In fact, given its importance and compactness, this summary may require more than one reading. Fernhout writes:

> On the one hand, *geloof* [faith] (and with it, religion) is limited to one part (i.e., *vermogen* [facultas] and organ) of man. In this sense, man's religious or faith *vermogen* stands on equal footing with all his other *vermogens*. On the other hand, however, the monarchian pattern allows Bavinck to give expression to the genuinely reformed emphasis on the all-encompassing, full-life scope of faith (and religion). Because of its place as the highest of man's *vermogens*, coming to expression through the dominating *nous*, religious faith becomes the hierarchical integrating and directive principle, the manifestation of the life-directing rule or power of man's *geest* [spirit]. Thus Bavinck can assert: 'In belief the whole man is involved, with his intellect, with his will, with his heart; (indeed), man in the kernel of his being.' When Bavinck focuses on *geloof* from this point of view, its scope seems to lie far beyond the other *vermogens*; although terms characteristic of the *vermogens* (such as 'knowing' or 'trusting') can be used to try to describe *geloof*, its essence defies delineation. Indeed, when it really comes down to it, *geloof* seems to be much more than a simple *vermogen*. This is evidenced by the fact that Bavinck at times drops the designation '*vermogen*' and calls *religio subjectiva* an organ, seemingly parallel to intellect and heart. But, more importantly, *geloof* is also characterized as the key directive principle in man. It is called a "wonderful and mysterious power" which roots much deeper in human nature than any other power. The character of *geloof* begins to approach that of *geest*, the central, dominating power that expresses itself first through the heart. Thus man's *religio subjectiva* or *geloof* is seen as a structural part of his make-up, but at the same time described as a structure-dominating power, giving expression to what lies at the core of man.[65]

Summary and Assessment

Bavinck's view of faith and religion is not clear. Does faith direct all human capacities or does it refer to only (one of the) three abilities? This ambiguity was evident also in his comments about the certainty of faith when he talked about faith giving rise to certainty, as distinct from scientific certainty based on reason, and about believing in general and five analogies of religious

65. Fernhout (1975): 23.

beliefs like: (i) "immediate knowledge of *principia*"; (ii) "trust in ourselves, in our human perception and thinking"; (iii) "acknowledging the objective existence of the external world"; (iv) "mutual trust on which the whole of human society is built"; and (v) all that which is "done through intuition."[66] All such universal certainties have in common with religious belief the fact that the knowledge associated with them is "obtained immediately, not through reflection" and that "certainty is not secondary to that which rests in consciousness."[67] This ambiguity about "faith" in the sense of subjective religion (*religio subjectiva*) is also reflected in his ambiguity about the nature of "religion." Two dominant and dangerous trends he opposed were: (i), reducing theology to comparative religion studies and a philosophy of religion, based on the assumption that religion is in essence a historical and psychic phenomenon; and, (ii), thinking that science and art are the results of an evolutionary development from primitive religions. To avoid these two prominent dangers, he stressed the real origin and nature of religion not as an additional and superfluous matter, but as one of the essential and basic features of being human.[68]

This emphasis on the central role of religion was hampered, however, by his tendency to stress the diversity of human experience and restrict religion to one of these experiences, namely, as a part of human behavior.[69] He perpetuated the idea that religion is an activity which in a way parallels activities associated with sense perception, science and art.[70] The activities of science and religion parallel each other[71] in that both are interested in knowledge—science in knowledge through the *logos* (*principium internum*) of intelligible things (*principium externum*) and religion in knowledge of God and assurance of salvation.

For Bavinck, science and religion are, however, in a way dissimilar. Unlike science, with its focus on reproducing and multiplying knowledge, religion centers on communing with God and obtaining eternal salvation.

66. Bavinck (1955) *GD*, II

67. Bavinck (1928) *GD*, I: 607–608.

68. This foreshadows what the reformational thinking of Vollenhoven and Dooyeweerd calls "modal irreducibility."

69. In terms of Dooyeweerd's prism metaphor, Fernhout writes: "This limitation is connected with Bavinck's failure to distinguish 'religion' in the limited sense of one of the colors of the spectrum of human functioning from the central religious heart of man which lies at the root of all the colors" (Fernhout 1975: 25).

70. Bavinck (1908): 176.

71. Bavinck (1928) *GD*, I: 238.

Religion has "a different source than science and art" in that it "assumes a revelation."[72] Although they parallel each other as activities, science and religion have different sources and goals: they are "almost independent phenomena."[73] In addition, a scientist is not only a religious being but also a moral one.[74] Despite the fact that his scholastic view of religion hindered and restricted him, Bavinck sensed the need for a better, more central and radical view of religion. He fervently opposed fierce humanistic forces in his day and age. Unfortunately, his Christian thinking was not sufficiently radical or reformational to reject scholastic anthropology based on the three classic Greek faculties of speculation (mind), ethics (will) and emotion (feelings). Religion is something different and something higher than all of that; it must not be something but everything in our life . . . If we want to do full justice to religion, then we have to return to the central unity in man, which lies at the foundation of the differentiation of the faculties and which in Holy Scripture many times is designated as the heart.[75]

Religion is "more deeply rooted in human nature than any other power."[76] It is "not confined to one of the human capacities." It "encompasses the whole man," is "total and central," and uses all the organs of the soul, i.e., *nous*, heart and will.[77] Bavinck writes,

> [It] encompasses the entire man, in his thinking, feeling, and acting, in his whole life, everywhere and at all times. Nothing falls outside of religion. It extends its power over all of man and humanity, over family and society and

72. Bavinck (1928) GD, I: 287–88.

73. This distinction between faith and deed corresponds, in scholastic thinking, to the difference between belief and action, dogmatics and ethics, theology and philosophical ethics. Bavinck (1908): 122 (English edition 1909: 144).

74. Fernhout (1975): 31. Science is one of those "other powers of culture."

75. Bavinck (1921): 14 (iets anders en iets hoogers dan dat alles; hij moet niet iets, maar alles in ons leven zijn . . . Indien wij dus aan de religie ten volle recht willen laten wedervaren, dan moeten wij in den mensch tot die centrale eenheid teruggaan, die aan de differentiatie zijner faculteiten ten grondslag ligt en die in de H. Schrift meermalen als het hart wordt aangeduid, daaruit toch zijn alle uitgangen des levens in verstand, gevoel en wil.). In this context, Bavinck mentions Christ's summary of God's law, and comments that we cannot allow a split in our thinking and living between God and the world, religion and culture, and that "no one can serve two masters." For details about religion, faith and regeneration, see Chapters 9–11 below.

76. Bavinck (1928) [GD, I]: 531.

77. Fernhout (1975): 33: "the nous with its capacity for rational knowledge, 'normally' involved in science, but now directed at knowledge of God, the heart (now directed in fear and hope, sadness and joy, a sense of guilt and forgiveness before God), and the will (showing itself in acts of love and good works)."

state. It is the foundation of the true, the good, and the beautiful. It brings unity, coherence and life into the world and history. Religion is the source for science, morality, and art, and these return to religion to find rest . . . What God is for the world, religion is for men.[78]

This reforming vision is "short-circuited by Bavinck's traditional anthropological framework," however, when he states in a semi-scholastic way that "science, morality and art are rooted in the various capacities of reason, will, and heart," which are essentially independent of religion, but now somehow used for religion. As a result, "religion" is something vertical, not horizontal, focused on and celebrated at special times and places."[79] Given this ambiguity and tension in his anthropology and theology, religion is in Fernhout's view central in "all human life" and, "at the same time very particular and independent, explicitly related to one particular human *vermogen* from which man's other *vermogens* are (up to a point) quite separate."[80] Bavinck's contribution as a Reformed thinker, in the tradition of Calvin and Kuyper on human faith, especially in Christian higher education, is in our world both helpful and problematic.[81]

In Bavinck's work there are at least five important features which are helpful: (i) God's revelation to humans; (ii) religion as a heart-centered response to God's revelation; (iii) a relation between God's revelation and human religion; (iv) the idea that a human must return to God (contra secularism) and back to the world (contra pietism); and (v) the unity and totality of humans living in God's holy presence (*coram Deo*). The cumulative effect of these positive features in Bavinck's thinking underscore the importance of his move in 1902 from the Seminary in Kampen,—where he wrote his magnum opus (the four volumes of *De Gereformeerde Dogmatiek*)—to the Free University in Amsterdam, where he taught theology and wrote *Philosophy of Revelation*, about which he lectured in his Stone Lectures at Princeton Seminary in 1908. His move from the Seminary in Kampen to the Free University in Amsterdam enabled him to do what he had previously taught others to

78. Bavinck (1928) [GD, I]: 278.

79. Fernhout (1975): 33. For details about the general philosophical context of Bavinck's anthropology, see S. P. van der Walt (1953): 11–190, especially 39–47 and 174–190.

80. In note 86, Fernhout comments, "This last point is evidenced by the fact that the nature of science, etc., and their related human faculties are already determined before religion is even discussed."

81. For details about Bavinck's views and influence on Christian Reformed education in Grand Rapids, Michigan, see Chapters 15, 16 and 17 below.

do, i.e., to fight two major dangers: secularism in society/culture and the pietism which was found in Reformed (*Gereformeerde*) traditions which advocated flight from the world. It compelled him to counteract questionable spirits in society and culture and to rethink crucial issues related to such things as revelation, philosophy, religion, experience, history, ecumenicity and Christianity.

Bavinck's philosophical and theological thinking had three problematic issues: (i) an uncritical acceptance of critical realism, whose ontology and epistemology had a Thomistic and Anselmian focus in the way they considered truth, certainty, subjective-objective, correspondence and experience; (ii) a Platonizing/Aristotelian faculty psychology (i.e., anthropology) [concerning] "thinking-willing-feeling" and their inherent problems; (iii) ambiguities about subjective and objective religion, the content of action and faith, the nature of faith and theology, and the relation between religion and theology.

In Reformed circles, Bavinck became the most important Dutch professor of dogmatics since Calvin in Geneva. He taught dogmatics in the tradition of Beza with respect to issues related to philosophy and anthropology at Calvin's Academy in Geneva. In 1902, when Bavinck accepted Kuyper's third request to teach at the Free University, he did not alter his philosophy of reality but continued to teach a scholastically tinted anthropology and epistemology in his understanding of faith life and the study of theology (as will be indicated in Chapter 15 below). For four decades, he was an important, though limited, reformer along with Kuyper, whose views about theology and philosophy will be dealt with in our next chapter.

CHAPTER FIVE

Abraham Kuyper (1837–1920)

Introduction

Central to Kuyper's view was his belief that true freedom is impossible without God's powerful Word for all of life. This Word is the *sine qua non* of
private and public freedom. He applied this insight to his understanding of
faith life, his study of theology and major areas of society that pietist Christians had ignored or minimized, especially in higher education, political life,
socioeconomic issues, medical care and journalism.

His importance is not limited to what he did as a preacher, a pastor
and a professor of theology. It extended to what he did as a reformer, writer,
orator, journalist, strategist, political servant and prime minister. For half
a century, he inspired fellow Christians in the Netherlands, as well as those
he influenced more indirectly in certain regions of Indonesia and South Africa, and in some Reformed/Presbyterian circles in North America. He did
this with his sharp focus on truth, love and justice in daily life. He did not
succumb to a tendency, common among traditional Roman Catholics and
among Protestants in general, to associate Christian living with organized or
institutionalized church life in the midst of a culture shaped by a deepening
secularization and consequences of the Western Industrial Revolution.

He focused on the urgent and complex issue of how Christians should
live in a culture shaped by leaders who were deaf to God's Word revealed in
Christ Jesus. His work, and role, was in a sense comparable to that of John
Calvin more than three and a half centuries earlier. In terms of insights Calvin described in volumes 1 and 4 of his *Institutes of the Christian Religion,*

Kuyper dealt not only with church issues,[1] but also with other pressing issues in his day and age.[2]

After receiving his doctorate in theology at the University of Leyden, he experienced, as a young pastor in Beesd, a tiny hamlet, a major shift in his faith life from a liberalism that shaped his thinking as a student to a radically different, simpler and more relevant (non-biblicistic) scripturally directed way of thinking in the daily life of Christians.[3] Soon after his heart-centered turnaround, he became restless about two things: a culture shaped by rationalism and revolution and a Christian faith limited by creedal navel-gazing and perpetuating misguided ideas and customs in society and culture.

Christians were either too liberal or too pietistic to respond properly to beguiling Liberalism, the Industrial Revolution, speculations particularly in the natural sciences, and effects of Higher Criticism on faith life. For several centuries, Protestant Christians tended to limit their faith life to what was personal and internal, and did not really address a growing deepening and broadening crisis in Western culture.[4]

The Roman Catholic Church reacted to the views of René Descartes (1596–1650) and philosophers and educators he influenced, in a way that vastly underestimated the nature and power of Enlightenment thinking.[5] Not until some three centuries had passed, after rationalism had become a

1. Despite the fact that he was the leader of the "Doleantie," a schism in the national Reformed Church in 1886.

2. For details, see James D. Bratt (1998), Peter S. Heslam (1998), and James E. McGoldrick (2000).

3. See Puchinger (1998): 18–20, 24–27 on Kuyper's "ethical conversion" triggered by (a) his reading, in 1863, of Charlotte M. Yonge's *The Heir of Redclyffe* and (b) the impact on him, while a young pastor, of Pietje Baltus, a simple but scripturally knowledgeable parishioner, who urged him to see and proclaim the full, powerful gospel, rather than a moralistic, superficial liberalism. For details, see Roger Henderson (1992) and McKendree Langley (1988).

4. After the Synod of Dort in 1618–1619, the national Reformed Church did not meet again until 1816, to deal with "state-church" issues within the national Reformed Church. This eventually resulted in the Secession in 1834 and, under the influence of Kuyper, the "Doleantie" in 1886. These two groups united in 1891 and, supported by Kuyper and Bavinck, established the Gereformeerde Kerk. Unlike the Dutch Reformed Church, the Presbyterian Church in English-speaking countries never met after the Westminster Assembly in 1643–1645.

5. An example par excellence of such a compromise is Descartes. When the Synod of Dort met, he met in the city of Dordrecht with elementary and secondary school teachers to talk about the need for a new kind of curriculum and pedagogy. Subsequently, he lived for some time in Amsterdam to develop his philosophy of rationalism. The Synod of Dort influenced Reformed faith life for more than three hundred years, while Descartes's Rationalism shaped Western culture.

major threat, did the Roman Catholic Church—for the first time after the eighteen-year-long Counter–Reformation Council of Trent (1545–1563)— meet to declare at the First Vatican Council (1869–1870) its belief that when the Pope speaks officially (*ex cathedra*), he does so in an infallible way."[6]

Two years later, Cardinal Pecci (elected Pope Leo XIII in 1878) established in Rome the St. Thomas Aquinas Academy, for the purpose of encouraging all Roman Catholic scholars and educators to employ in their philosophy, theology, teaching, preaching and care, the method of thinking of Aquinas (1225–1274). His mind-set or view of reality is crucial to understand the nature, role and interrelation of faith and reason, and of theology and philosophy. In 1879, one year after becoming Pope, Leo XIII published his famous encyclical *Aeterni Patris*. In this encyclical, the Roman Catholic Church elevated the philosophy or method of Aquinas as the model for thinking, reflecting, teaching and writing about philosophical and theological issues. By adopting this philosophical method, all Roman Catholic leaders had to respond to growing crises in that day and age about educational, social, political, economic, medical and faith issues.[7]

In 1880, Kuyper opened the Free University in Amsterdam, in response to serious crises in society and culture. His reason for the bold move to establish this university was to educate a new cadre of leaders, notably in four crucial areas of life: education, law/politics, faith life and health care. For a biblically Reformed influence on society, culture and history, future leaders in vital areas of life must learn how to indicate the depth and scope of God's love and truth, revealed in the incarnate Word and out-poured Spirit, not only in their personal and institutional faith life, but also in what they do in all areas of life.

As indicated in the previous chapter, already in 1880 Kuyper had asked Bavinck[8] to join him in this bold endeavor. From the outset, he sensed the religious depth and scope of God's life-sustaining Word, and the need to avoid both conformity to the world and flight from it. In Christ, through the Spirit, God's Word must be the cornerstone for all personal and public

---

6. Positivism stressed scientific infallibility, whereas the Roman Catholic Church appealed to papal infallibility, and many Protestants relied on Scripture being infallible or inerrant (for details, see J. C. Vander Stelt, 1978).

7. For details, see Chapter 14 below.

8. Earlier that year, Bavinck had obtained his doctorate from the University of Leyden, established in 1575 by William of Orange, a Dutch Calvinist political leader. The first Th.D. recipient at this university was Arminius, a former student of Beza in Calvin's Academy of Geneva. Kuyper also received his Th.D. at this University. For details, see Heslam (1998): 27–56.

life. As a reformer, Kuyper deepened and broadened the meaning of Christian discipleship and did so by stressing its life-encompassing scope and universal implications. The gospel affects every nook and cranny of society and culture. Christian thinking is not an option but a necessity, especially for those not freed from the fang of autonomy-claiming rationalism, or any other "ism" that promises freedom but results in oppression.

Positive Features of His Worldview

Appreciation of Kuyper's understanding of "faith" and "theology" assumes awareness of major problems he sensed in his faith tradition, culture and world. Paramount issues to be addressed were related to the following: (i) the lure of pietism; (ii) endless debates related to impasses between faith and reason; (iii) speculation about the "Creator-creature" distinction; (iv) distinction between the science of Christians and non-Christians; (v) the relation between practical and scientific knowledge; (vi) the importance of philosophy for every science (*wetenschap*); and (vii) the interrelated topics of common grace, creation-fall-redemption and the authority of Scripture.

Time and space do not permit a detailed discussion of the first six of the topics listed above. However, the three sub-themes mentioned in the last item deserve special attention. They provide a helpful context for a clearer understanding of Kuyper's ideas about those first six issues. They also underscore the need for an ongoing renewal or reformation, especially in philosophy and theology.

Common Grace

A unique, though often ignored, feature of Kuyper's view of common grace is that it does not deny, denigrate or mitigate the life-encompassing religious conflict in human responses to God's revelation. On the contrary, Kuyper's articulation of common grace is presupposed in his understanding of a radical conflict.[9] Without his restraining grace, the disastrous effects of human rebellion against God's Word for life would be limitless. Unless the Lord curbs the power of evil in a world filled with defiance against God's Word for life, humans would lose their humanity as responsible creatures.

---

9. For details, see Zuidema (1972): 52–105.

According to Kuyper, without common grace, the powers of darkness would prevent humans from responding in any positive way to the God of life. It reveals God's faithfulness to his Word for reality, including human life, and enables humans to exist, especially amidst any ultimately religious clash within and among humans. The antithetical conflict between, for example, love and defiance, truth and falsehood, obedience and disobedience, redemption and destruction, joy and grief, and life and death is impossible without God's undeserved bridling of ultimate iniquity and opposition. His restraining grace prevents Christians from becoming comfortable with either conformity to the world or flight from it. In principle, common grace provides Christians with the room or space they need to develop a lifestyle that fosters life rather than ruining it. It provides a witness to the Risen One, in whom ultimate authority rests,[10] for the benefit of all humans in society, culture and history.[11]

What prevents this world from falling into a complete ruin are, to use terms unique to Reformed thinking, two kinds of grace: one is biblical, special and particular, while the other is natural, general and common. The secret of the second is the secret of the first kind. Common grace is not unrelated to or outside of the Word incarnate, but is actually rooted in Him (John 1:1–5, 14 and Col. 1:15–20). Christians do not originate the antithesis. Rather, Satan does, together with all who follow the Adversary in rejecting God's holy will for life. Despite humanity's refusal to live by His law of love, God is faithful to his Word. He remains their Creator, maintains the world he made, including His law(s) for human freedom and joy. He continues to manifest his presence as their Maker, even if that demands that His Love be incarnated, killed and raised from the dead. This common grace shown to a religiously lost and wandering humanity causes humans to bow before Him in a spirit of forced and/or spontaneous doxology.[12] Not in the positive sense of approving, but in the negative sense of restraining, common grace bridles Satan's rage by curtailing the evil of human self-centeredness.

Kuyper's emphasis on common grace did not undermine his passion to establish non-ecclesiastical Christian organizations and traditions in addi-

---

10. See Matthew 28:18; John 1:1–5; Col. 1:15–23; and Rev. 1:17–18.

11. The mandate of Matt. 28:20: "Teach them to observe everything I have commanded you. And surely I will be with you always, to the very end of the age" assumes the continued existence of created reality, including rebellious humans.

12. The sequence "common" and "special" reflects an ontic order, and one thinks in a chronological way; when the sequence is reversed, one thinks in a redemptive, or soteriological, manner, in which case "special" precedes "common."

tion to the ecclesiastical ones. By means of Spirit-guided communal insight and prayer, Christians respond to God's Word also in their non-ecclesiastical endeavors in society. To live in a Christian way requires being historically alert and culturally sensitive Light-bearers beyond one's organized faith life. The long series of articles he wrote for a weekly (Christian) newspaper on a wide-ranging set of societal and cultural issues, he published in the three volumes of *De Gemeene Gratie* (1902–1905).[13] Rejecting a pietistic mentality of flight from the world, he urged his weekly readers to see the importance of their living as Christ-followers in every area of life.

A few years later, he wrote a second long series of articles for the same weekly newspaper[14] and published them in *Pro Rege*, vols. 1–3 (1911–1912).[15] His intent with these practical articles was twofold: to oppose both non-Christian and anti-Christian movements in modern society and culture, and to encourage Christians to center their lives in Christ as Lord and Savior, not only at home and church, but also in society, state, science and art. In the preface of this major publication, he stated that his overall intent was "to abolish the demarcation, which has been drawn in our consciousness in a much sharper way than was proper, between our ecclesiastical life and our life outside the church."[16] On the need for Christians to express their faith in terms of a broader view of what life in society really entails for Christ's followers, Kuyper writes,

> . . . whoever speaks of a social problem means primarily that serious doubts have arisen as to the appropriateness of the social edifice in which we live; and that consequently a battle is being waged in the forum of public opinion concerning the principles on which a more appropriate and more inhabitable social edifice may be built. For a social problem to exist only one thing is necessary: that you see that this untenability does not come from incidental causes but from a fault in the foundation of our social association. . . . A social problem does not exist until you exercise an architectonic cri-

13. First published in *De Heraut*, a weekly Christian newspaper (September 1, 1895, to July 14, 1901).

14. *De Heraut* (January 1907–January 1911).

15. Out of deference to Kuyper's vision and work, Dordt College, Sioux Center, Iowa, started to publish *Pro Rege* as an academic quarterly in 1972. For details, see https://www.dordt.edu/about-dordt/publications/pro-rege.

16. See Kuyper (1911), vol. 1: "Pro Rege bedoelt de scheiding op te heffen, die zich in ons bewustzijn, veel scherper dan goed was, tusschen ons Kerkelijk leven en ons leven buiten de Kerk heeft afgeteekend."

tique of human society itself and hence desire and think possible a different structuration of the social edifice.[17]

His view of common grace is important and complex. He stressed it not in order to mitigate the need for special or redemptive grace. On the contrary, the latter is basic, not tangential, to common grace. God maintains his Word for nature, or the world, things Christians and non-Christians experience together. To live in this world is impossible without God's faithfulness to the structure of created reality. What upholds the latter is God's common grace, as will be indicated when we reflect on the next three interrelated issues.

Creation, Fall, Redemption

Kuyper's stress on common grace and its relevance for the structure of society are inseparable from his ideas about the central themes in Scripture of "creation, fall and redemption." To avoid flight from the world and conformity to it, he emphasized what Scripture reveals about created reality, the audacity of humans rejecting God's Word for life and the life-restoring significance of God's grace. According to Kuyper, the world God made, including humanity, was good. Just because humans rejected the Creator's command to love him, this world may not be neglected as being beyond redemption. The human fall removed what God wanted humans to be and to do.

For Kuyper, God's faithfulness to his Word is revealed in a grace to which no recalcitrant sinner has a right. Central to God's grace is the Word incarnate in the life, death, resurrection and return of the "Son of God and Son of Man,"[18] who was made known through the life-restoring Spirit. In this Christ Jesus, as the Light of the world, human disobedience against the Creator and its terrible implications for all human creatures has in principle been overcome.[19] In Christ and through the Spirit, God reveals his mercy-filled claim over "every square inch of life."

Human life is heart-directed, radix-centered, that is to say, profoundly religious. Although Kuyper did not formulate it this way, his still squinting but prophetic perspective can be summarized as follows: humans do not

17. This statement of Kuyper is the secret of H. Evan Runner's classic *The Relation of the Bible to Learning.* (1962), pp. 58–159.

18. See Matthew 28:62 and Acts 7:56; also Daniel 7:13–14.

19. Cf. Kuyper "'Woord God' in drieerlei zin" in *Uit het woord*, vol. 1, 81–85, translated by H. der Nederlanden, "On the Three Senses of 'Word of God,'" (1974).

have religion, they are religious.[20] This simple but radical Scriptural insight compelled Kuyper to raise critical questions about many historically powerful though misleading worldviews and questionable lifestyles.

He wondered whether the Roman Catholic worldview of "nature-grace" was correct. He rejected the liberal Protestant compromise with Enlightenment thinkers. He disagreed with Adam Smith (1723–1790) as an architect of capitalism in his work *The Wealth of Nations*. He spurned the "nature-freedom" dialectics of such culturally powerful thinkers as Kant, Hegel, Marx and Nietzsche.[21]

Pervasive in Kuyper's critical and creative probing is the biblical motif of creation-fall-redemption. It enabled him to start rethinking some questionable features in faith life, the structure of society, the role of education, the effects of the Industrial Revolution, and the meaning of citizenship, art, etc.

Authority of Scripture

The themes of common grace and creation, fall and redemption are, in Kuyper as a driven reformer, inseparable from the authority of Scripture. Combining these three themes enabled him to avoid the fundamentalist-biblicist view of the authority of Scripture. God's revelation is not limited to Scripture as a book, but it is as broad as created reality, including human and non-human history, and it is as palpable and profound as Jesus Christ, the incarnate Word of God.

This life-encompassing revelation,[22] the inscripturated Word, although it is necessary, is not the only source by which humans may learn about God's will. His will becomes known in the world he made and of which humans are the designated caretakers. Scripture is authoritative in the sense that it reminds humans of his life-sustaining covenant with "day and night" and the "descendants of Jacob and David."[23]

---

20. As neo-Kuyperian thinkers like Dooyeweerd, Vollenhoven, Runner and others have emphasized as reformational thinkers (see Chapters 7, 8 and 19 below).

21. See, in this connection, Kuyper's role, with that of his mentor, G. Groen van Prinsterer, in establishing the Anti-Revolutionary Party for the purpose of (re)shaping society in terms of such biblical themes as justice and fairness. For details, see McGoldrick (2000) and Naugle (2002).

22. Cf. H. Bavinck's Stone Lectures in Philadelphia on The Philosophy of Revelation, 1909.

23. Jeremiah 33:25–26: "This is what the Lord says: 'If I have not established my covenant with day and night and the fixed laws of heaven and earth, then I will reject the descendants of

In a public lecture for ardent but mostly non-academic supporters of the Free University in 1899, Kuyper talked about this question: How is a university bound by the word of God? Apart from what precisely he meant by "reformed principles"—a much-used and debated issue in his thinking[24]—his listeners believed he answered that pertinent question in a satisfactory way. In distinction from Lutheran, Pentecostal and Methodist faith traditions, he put his listeners at ease by placing the issue to be addressed within the context of a deeper and broader meaning of God's revelation, i.e., not merely, or primarily, in Scripture, but in creation and Jesus Christ as well as Scripture.[25] To discover the religious unity of being human and the nature of Christian witness, God's written Word has its own unique authority.

One cannot understand God's written Word apart from the world one lives in. It is impossible to know Scripture apart from one's culture. This does not imply that one must subject Scripture's revelation to the norm of one's age or culture. A person's understanding of Scripture is never ahistorical, i.e., isolated from one's experience at a particular time and place. Neither is it restricted to one's personal faith life and/or ecclesiastical tradition. Somehow, it always involves something concerning agriculture, political life, medicine, business, scholarship or anything else one is familiar with.

God's Word is not restricted to Scripture as book, to Jesus Christ as person or to the world as created, if such restriction implies that in each of these three instances the other two are not included. Neither can God's revelation be limited, in any of these three distinct yet inseparable ways, to one's personal inspiration or faith. Such a spiritualized view connotes that the rest of a person's life would, in dualistic fashion, be merely a means to an end, a temporary scaffold to be left behind.

This is Kuyper's most valuable rearticulation, at a time of great spiritual upheaval in Western culture and widespread uneasiness in Christian circles, of John Calvin's perpetual stress on the interdependence of self-knowledge and knowledge of God, and on the need for Christians to live, already here and now, in God's awesome presence (*coram Deo*). This unsophisticated, simple stance is Kuyper's prophetic contribution to the Christian community

---

Jacob and David my servant and will not choose one of his sons to rule over the descendants of Abraham, Isaac and Jacob. For I will restore their fortunes and have compassion on them.'"

24. About this controversy, see Rullmann 1940: III, 152–162.

25. See Kuyper (1899). I'm grateful to Rev. C. Veenstra, a retired pastor in Sioux Center, Iowa, who in 1969 gave me his translation of Kuyper's speech "Band aan het Woord. Antwoord op de vraag: Hoe is een Universiteit aan het woord van God te binden?" for me to use in responding to a few strident biblicist professors at Dordt College at that time.

in his day and age, nationally and internationally, as well as today, locally and globally.[26]

Questionable Features in His Worldview

As with any reformer, Kuyper had his limitations. He was most innovative when he ventured into new areas of reflection and renewal called for by major social, political, economic and other challenges in his country and culture. As to certain traditionally firmly established ways of living and thinking, he was less innovative and reformative, especially in the areas of deeply rooted ecclesiastical customs and scholastically tainted theological thinking.

The conservative tradition he inherited, the threats of modern culture, the fierce opposition of most pastors and theologians to his call to return to God's Word, his limited resources in terms of staff, funding and time, and certain weaknesses in his character—all these require a detailed study of his thinking-pattern(s) regarding at least five issues: (i) the remnants of a dualistic anthropology; (ii) a semi-scholastic and idealistic epistemology; (iii) a dualism in his encyclopedia of the sciences; (iv) a hierarchy in the God-world relation; and (v) a philology unable to acknowledge the full impact of sin and renewal in logic, philosophy and pedagogy.[27]

All these limitations were evident in Kuyper's thinking. Instead of radical change in these five areas, he perpetuated these traditional thought- and act-patterns. They reflect a lingering synthesis mentality in his academic and practical endeavors. Uncritically, he accepted the views of Voetius (1589–1676), a prominent Reformed pietist who advocated semi-scholastic theology, and he was sympathetic to some ideas in nineteenth-century Romantic and Idealist philosophers.[28] Given their relevance for various issues touched on below, only two of them in Kuyper's thinking will be discussed in the rest of this chapter, i.e., his anthropology and his notion of formal faith.

26. For details, see Schrotenboer (1988): 1–2; Skillen (1988): 15–19; Van Dyke (1988): 34–40; Heslam (1983): 1–7; Mouw (1998): 86–87 and McGoldrick (2000). http://www.cpjustice.org.

27. For details, see Dooyeweerd (1939): 193–232, especially 228–232, about human faith as function and about anthropology in general (cf. Chapters 6 and 19 below).

28. Like Calvin earlier, Kuyper had no time for detailed theoretical analyses. For details, see Vander Stelt, "Kuyper's semi-mystical conception," (1973): 178–190.

Philosophical Anthropology

In his detailed study of Kuyper's anthropology, especially with respect to faith and religion,[29] Harry Fernhout highlighted not only reformational but also questionable features in Kuyper's dogmatics as something God revealed to humans through an anthropology based on human "experience, perception or observation."[30] It assumes an anthropology which Kuyper believes is "in" Scripture, but which, in Fernhout's opinion, is actually unconsciously first read into Scripture. Although reality is created by God, it has in Kuyper's way of thinking "a certain independence and lack of direct connection with God."[31] The world of granite, plants and animals stands "over against God, because it is essentially not-God."[32] Contact between God and what is "not-God" is established by humans, who, as God's image-bearers, stand between Him and the world.

> Where God brings his image into the world there comes an end to absolute separation; where God, through his image, enters the world, the latter again comes under God's dominion. Man thus functions as God's vice-gerent, the link bringing the world into contact with God.[33]

This anthropology resembles that of Bavinck, his colleague, who placed anthropology between the Creator and creation. For Kuyper, the non-human world relates to God, the Creator, through the faith of humans in God, and God relates to the non-human world through His human image-bearers: God's vice-gerents manifest his rule over creation.[34]

Like Bavinck, Kuyper rejected the monistic anthropologies of mate-

29. Fernhout, "Man, faith, and religion in Bavinck, Kuyper, and Dooyeweerd," (1975; parts 2 and 3 published in *Tydskrif vir Christelijke Wetenskap*, Potchefstroom, South Africa). For details, see Fernhout (1979): II, 54–71.

30. As cited by Fernhout (1979): 54 and based on Kuyper (1910): II, *Locus de homine*, 4.

31. Fernhout (1979): 55.

32. Idem. For Kuyper, according to Fernhout, created reality "is not all of one kind, but is either closer to God or further removed from Him. A piece of cold, hard granite is furthest removed from God. One could almost say that it is without God; it consists of nothing but matter and in this matter all animation and movement is absent. God is the centre, and if one conceives of the world as a periphery around Him, then the granite stone lies on the outermost circumference. Moving toward the centre, one would find the plant and animal realms consecutively closer to God." Cf. Kuyper (1910): II, *Locus de homine*, 5–6.

33. Kuyper (1910): II, *Locus de homine*, 6.

34. Fernhout (1979): 56.

rialism and idealism, as well as the Platonic trichotomous anthropology of "body, soul and spirit." Instead, he advocated a dualistic anthropology according to which humans consist of body (*soma*) and soul (*psyche*) as two separate substances, one visible, the other invisible.

To stress the unity of man, Kuyper introduced a (non-substantial) qualitative distinction within the (substance of) soul between "psyche" and "pneuma." Unlike psyche, pneuma is not a "substance," nor is it "a third element," but "simply the consciousness" of the two substances of body and soul.[35] This "consciousness" is unique in each person; it points to the ego, or I. According to Fernhout, Kuyper's anthropology can be described as follows:

> As Kuyper spells out his position further it becomes clear that the *ik* (ego) functions as the dominating organizational principle which welds man's two substances together. In this welding process the *ik* functions as the outward manifestation of *pneuma*. *Ik* and *pneuma* are one, but can be distinguished as "outer" and "inner." The *pneuma* is the "driving power" which comes to expression in the "*zelfbewustzijn*" (self-consciousness) of the *ik*; it is the steam that motivates the *ik*. Thus, as with Bavinck, the all-important "third" in man takes on the character of the directive principle setting in motion the hierarchical relation of soul and body. This notion leaves Kuyper (and Bavinck) with a conception that is neither truly trichotomist nor starkly dichotomist. It is not trichotomist since it does not find in man three (structurally conceived) substances; yet it is not starkly dichotomist since it introduces a third "dimension" which certainly acts as if it is substantially different, capable of uniting the other two. As a result, this level becomes cloaked in vagueness, a characteristic which makes it all the more suitable for its key role as dominating, integrating factor.
>
> In Kuyper's terms, the *ik-pneuma* is thus the highest dimension of man's soul. At the same time . . . , the *ik-pneuma* is the centre or core of man's being and works its effects outward. . . . The other dimensions of man would . . . be at once lower and (concentrically) more peripheral.[36]

About a hierarchical difference between what is lower and higher in humans, Fernhout comments that "the dominance or disharmonious functioning of the soma," points to what is "sarx, i.e., the sinful," and that "what is sinful

---

35. Kuyper (1910): II, 32.
36. Fernhout (1979): 58–59.

with respect to the soma is holy in relation to the psyche, and where the psyche has dominion, one speaks of the pneuma."[37]

The (higher) active soul dominates the (lower) passive body and does this by bringing it, via the nerves, into action. As the seat of human consciousness (ik-pneuma), the "I," is the finest dimension and highest expression of the soul. It is intimately connected with human rationality, the brain. Again, Kuyper rejects the trichotomous notion of "three substances" in humans.

We are dichotomists. Even if the distinction between soul and spirit (ψυχή and πνευμα) were able to maintain itself to a certain extent, body, soul, and spirit could never be coordinated. But the antithesis should be between body and soul, and within that soul the distinction between the psychical and the pneumatical should be sought.[38]

This internal principle of domination within man, i.e., psyche over soma, presupposes an external principle of domination upon man: "Just as the soul penetrates and pushes into the body, so God's Spirit penetrates and pushes into our pneumatical consciousness." There is an "indwelling of God in man, just as the soul dwells in the body."[39]

Bavinck divided man's spiritual substance (psyche) into a higher *pneuma* and a lower *ziel* (soul), with its three capacities of "thinking, willing and feeling," Kuyper called the whole spiritual substance in humans "soul" and divided it into (i) *pneuma*, or "I," inherent in the spiritual substance, and (ii) *psyche*, as a lower spiritual substance. Whereas for Bavinck the dominant and unifying principle in man expresses itself in the three faculties of the *ziel* (the lower part of man's spiritual substance), for Kuyper these three faculties are integral to the higher ego-*pneuma* level in man's spiritual substance. About these three classic faculties Kuyper states,

> Man has three increased capacities: the perception capacity, the knowledge capacity and the will capacity. . . . The *facultas percipiendi* is the capacity of our ego to receive in our consciousness (*bewustzijn*) the impressions which correspond to the reality of that which exists and occurs in us and outside us. The *facultas intelligendi* is the capacity to investigate as basis, being and operation, all that which enters via the *facultas percipiendi*, and

---

37. Kuyper (1910): II, *Locus de homine*, 28–29 (as cited by Fernhout (1979): 59).

38. Kuyper (1954): 214.

39. Kuyper (1910): II, *Locus de homine*, 42. This idea of domination affected Kuyper's view of the place of faith—for details, see below.

to form a judgment concerning that which is thus known or investigated. This judgment is either a *judicium abstractum* . . . or a *judicium practicum*. . . . To this faculty belongs the conscience. Finally, the *facultas volendi* is the capacity to posit, in so far as it depends on us, a conclusion of the *facultas intelligendi* as *secunda causa*.[40]

These three interdependent[41] faculties are organized and controlled by a person's ego. The faculty of the intellect, located in the brain, is the closest to the ego and human consciousness. "First a judgment by the *facultas intelligendi* takes place, then the ego comes to know about this, and only when supplied with this knowledge does the ego give an order to the *facultas volendi*."[42] By means of these three faculties, the ego unifies the two basic independent substances in humans, and it does so by giving bodily expression to what humans perceive, know and will.

Despite a relatively small difference in their view of a higher substance in humans, Kuyper and Bavinck agree on the significance of a Greek concept of "faculty psychology" in their anthropology. Both Reformed leaders advocate that the higher substance in humans consists of the Platonic and Aristotelian theory of three basic faculties of "thinking, willing and emotions," symbolized respectively by the head, the hand and the heart. The problematic effects of such an accommodated anthropology on one's understanding of religion and faith life become unavoidable, as will be explained in Chapters 9 and 10 below.

Like Bavinck, Kuyper stressed in his dualistic anthropology, the importance of unity, balance and harmony. Furthermore, in his scholastic thinking two anthropological principles are crucial: (a) a dualistic theory that each human consists of both a lower and a higher substance; and (b) the higher substance expresses itself in the three mental faculties of thinking, willing and feeling. Of these three capacities, the intellect, or mind, is most important. As a consequence of stressing the human mind, or intellect, truth tends to be thought of in terms of reliable scholastic propositional statements.[43]

In terms of such a (philosophical) dualistic anthropology, Kuyper

40. Kuyper (1910): II, *Locus de homine*, 68 (translated and cited by Fernhout 1979: 60–61).

41. Kuyper rejects (Scholten's) empiricism, according to which the faculty of perception determines the faculties of intellect and will.

42. Kuyper (1910): II, 62 (cited by Fernhout 1979).

43. For details, see chapter 6 below about the origin, nature and effects of "faculty psychology."

sensed the nature and impact of three major dangers in Reformed circles that affected the faith life of Christians. In 1900, he published in *De Heraut*, a weekly reformational newspaper, three articles on the dangers of Intellectualism, Mysticism and Practicalism—which, adroitly, he called "little foxes" (*kleine vossen*).[44] These articles focus on the three faculties of "intellect, emotions and will," respectively. On the threat of intellectualism, he writes,

> A sin to which Reformed [Gereformeerde] church life is vulnerable is Intellectualism, the exaggeration of intellectual orientation, a one-sided focus on the power hidden in the world of concepts. Three activities in us must work in balance, three actions, which can be represented by means of the head, the heart, and the hand. The head is the symbol of the intellectual labor, the heart of the emotional movement of the mystical, and the hand of the Christian's activities. If there is to be a balance in our ecclesiastical life, if there is to be a balance in our personal and official (*ambtelijk*) life, then head, heart and hand must cooperate in proper proportion for the total expression of life. But this balance constantly gets lost, the right proportion is repeatedly broken, the harmony that must prevail turns, because of one-sidedness, into discord, and so you see in all sorts of circles and in all kinds of ways the rise of one-sided trends.[45]

Despite the importance of Kuyper's vision and labor as a major reformer, a traditional scholastic element remained in his faculty psychology, structured his anthropology and affected his Greek-tainted view of faith life and discipline of theology.[46] This lingering scholastic feature curtailed his renewed sense of God's Word and of the need of humans to respond in a more wholesome manner. Despite his contribution as an inspired, and inspiring, reformer, a scholastic feature in his thinking prevented him, and others around and after him, from removing certain compromising habits in anthropology in Reformed circles and traditions, especially in Europe and North America,[47]

44. These articles were published in 1901 as *Drie kleine vossen* and based on the Shulamite's complaints about "little foxes, which spoiled the vineyard" (Song of Songs 2:15). Kuyper altered the sequence of these three foxes.

45. Kuyper (1901): 1. For a brief summary of this book, see Rullmann (1940): 227–240. Kuyper associated heart with the human faculty of emotion, and distinguished between mystical and mysticism, affirming the former and rejecting the latter.

46. For details, see Vander Stelt (1973): 178–190, especially 180.

47. Note: Author attended Calvin College from 1954 to 1958 and Calvin Theological Seminary for the spring semester in 1965.

including Calvin Theological Seminary and Calvin College in Grand Rapids, Michigan, as will be indicated in Chapters 15–18 below.

Formal Faith

For Kuyper, faith is neither an option nor an addition, but something integral to being human. In his three-volume work *Encyclopaedie der Heilige Godge-leerdheid* (1893–1894), he discussed, in an historical and systematic way, the place and task of the study (*wetenschap*) of theology in its relation to all the other disciplines (*wetenschappen*) in a curriculum. In response to a rising tide of skepticism at that time, he focused on the presence in all scientific or scholarly enterprises of a faith which reflects an immediate general belief in what humans consider to be certain. It is this sense of certainty, basic to human self-consciousness, which is Kuyper's focus in his thinking about formal faith.

Formal faith is a certain power that enables human consciousness to surrender to what it considers to be true, or ultimate, for the sole purpose of obeying it. He writes,

> Even more effectively than by "wisdom" skepticism is counteracted by faith (πιστις). Faith in this connection is taken formally, and hence considered quite apart from all content. By "faith" here, then, we do not mean the "faith in Jesus Christ" in its saving efficacy for the sinner, nor yet the "faith in God" which is fundamental to all religion, but the formal function of the life of our soul which is fundamental to every act of our human consciousness (*bewustzijn*). . . . To take a position with reference also to . . . "faith and knowledge," it is necessary that we go back to the formal function of faith and investigate whether this function does or does not exhibit a universal character.[48]

Certainty is anchored in formal faith, not in some scientific proof and demonstration. This faith provides humans with a certainty about the reality they perceive, the first principles of what self-consciousness assumes, and the validity of their formulations of general laws provided by the first principles. For Kuyper, faith refers to "that function of the soul (ψυχη) by which it obtains certainty directly without the aid of discursive demonstration."[49]

48. Kuyper (1954): 125.
49. Kuyper (1954): 128–129.

This "faith," as "formal function of the life of our soul," he describes for non-academic readers in his opening remarks on Q&A 59 of Lord's Day 23 of the Heidelberg Catechism, a well-known Reformed creed: "What good does it do you, however, to believe all of this?"[50] He discusses first the need to understand the meaning of faith before he talks about what must be believed (e.g., Apostles' Creed). To do this properly, Kuyper states, one must return, according to Scripture, beyond (*achter*) sin to paradise, and ask the question,

> "Did Adam in paradise, when he still was the way God created him, believe already or not?" If your answer to this is "No," in that case "faith" does not belong to human nature in its completeness; then "faith" is only a temporal expediency, which like a bandage on a wound is applied from the outside; and then Rome must win out, by virtue of her confession that human nature as such is neutral and that all grace, even original righteousness in paradise has been added from the outside as something foreign to our nature.[51]

True self-consciousness does not permit such a view, Kuyper believes. According to official Roman Catholic thinking, faith loses its "human base" (*menschelijken bodem*) and the "work of salvation is dislodged from human nature." According to Kuyper, one cannot be a "child of the Lord" without knowing oneself to be human. Original righteousness belonged to human nature; the loss of this did not result in a loss of human faith, but in a distortion, perversion and corruption of faith.

As "an indispensable component" of human nature, human faith cannot be temporarily lost and then, from the outside, simply added again to human life. Only then can one talk about "the sin of unbelief." Sin is not the loss of faith, but a perversion of it. Because of their importance, some lengthy citations—which, as far as I know, have not been translated into English—from

---

50. Adopted in 1563, one year before Calvin's death. The other two official Reformed Confessions are The Belgic Confession (1566) and The Canons of Dort (1618–1619). For details, see Kuyper (1893) II: 293–354, especially 293–299. The "all of this" at the end of the question refers to everything confessed in the Apostles' Creed.

51. Kuyper 1893: II, 294. "'Heeft Adam in het paradijs, toen het nog was, zoals God hem schiep, geloofd al dan niet?' Antwoord ge hierop: "Neen", welnu, dan behoort het 'geloof' ook niet tot de menschelijke natuur in haar volkomenheid; dan is geloof slechts een tijdelijk hulpmiddel, dat evenals de pleister op de wonde van buiten wordt aangebracht; en dan moet Rome het winnen, krachtens haar belijdenis, dat de menschelijke natuur ons van buiten af was toegevoegd." For information about the reliance of the Roman Catholic Church on the views of Thomas Aquinas, see Etienne Gilson, *The Christian Philosophy of St. Thomas Aquinas* (1956, republished by University of Notre Dame, 1994).

Kuyper's perceptive comments indicate why, in his opinion, it is necessary to think of faith as a formal function.

Only thus do you sense then also the sin of unbelief. As long as faith remains something external, that is added to your nature, it appears to depend on your discretion whether you want to believe or not. If yes, you believe, but the other does not believe, and nevertheless he is just as much human as you are. In contrast, if faith belongs to your human nature in its purity (*gaafheid*), then not to believe is a transgression of your human nature and unbelief becomes a violation of that nature. You are then created in order to believe, destined to live out of faith. Not doing this you are, as a result, deficient as a human being, renounce your nature, and violate your human nature, as that was supposed to be according to God's order and reckoning.

... "[N]ot to believe" is not just a deficiency in your normal function of life, but a turning of that function of life in its opposite. Unbelief is something considerably different and something much worse than not to believe. You cannot simply not believe. You must either have faith, or in you storms and dominates unbelief. ... Of the two one must work in you, either faith according to God's order, or unbelief according to the law of sin. Inasmuch as sin still controls your life, you are a victim of unbelief, and only insofar as sin has been broken in you, faith regained in you the power.

It is due to this then also that Holy Scripture almost never speaks about not believing, but nearly always punishes unbelief as an explicit evil in the sinner.

... The issue then is this, that God the Lord has ordained faith as the higher function of life, which belongs to our human nature. In the first human in paradise, He created the function of life and through faith Adam drank from life from his God. Not to believe anymore was his fall, to which Satan aroused him. What God had said, Adam must not believe anymore. But Satan did not leave it at this. He knew very well that faith remains with the non-sinful [*onzondige*] as long as unbelief has not been substituted for it, and therefore he stimulated Adam still much more not only not to believe God, but to believe him, Satan. "Your eyes shall be opened, and you shall be as God." And with this the turn came in Adam. Faith in God he let go, and at the same moment he turned around in positive unbelief, i.e., in faith in himself and Satan.[52]

52. Kuyper (1893): II, 296–297.

Kuyper's notion of formal faith, is, according to Fernhout, "a universal function of the human ego" that brings humans "face to face" with their Creator, and provides them with a certainty needed in their "many kinds of activities."[53]

According to Kuyper, "all religion assumes communion with something that transcends the cosmos," and in this communion the formal function of faith "obtains its absolute significance."[54] In distinction from the "redemptive" (*zaligmakende*) meaning of faith, on this "most general foundational meaning" (*de meest algemeene grondbetekenis*), Kuyper writes,

> To believe is to know and to acknowledge: I exist not from and through myself, but am of someone, and belong to someone, and exist only through his deed and work. God himself can not believe, because He is self-sufficient to himself, exists from and unto and through himself, and possesses and brings forth out of himself all perfect goodness in himself. If man were like God, then there could also with man be no talk about faith. But now that man is a creature, and not Creator, dependent and not his own master, internally devoid of anything and not self-sufficient—now there must be faith in him, i.e., now he must see and acknowledge that he does not exist for his own sake, nor through himself, but only for the sake and through God, and in like manner that all good gifts do not well up out of him as out of a fountain, but flow to him from God as a Fountain of all good things.[55]

Both the "godless" and the "God-fearing" are as creatures, equally de-

---

53. Kuyper (1954): 65. According to Fernhout, the notion of "formal function of faith" moves in the direction of Dooyeweerd's views about "the anticipation of faith in other functions of human consciousness" and in "the leading character of man's faith in the whole of his life." Bavinck talked about "belief-in-general," arising from man's religious aptitude, not about formal faith as a faculty of man. See Fernhout (1978): 64–65, especially note 54, about problems in Kuyper's view of faith's "formal function" in his distinction between so-called "spiritual" and "physical" sciences.

54. Kuyper (1954): 146 and 149 (translation mine).

55. Kuyper (1893) II: 298. "*Te gelooven* is weten en te erkennen: ik besta niet uit en door mijzelf, maar ben van iemand, en hoor bij iemand, en besta alleen door diens daad en werk. God zelf kan niet belooven, omdat Hij zich zelf genoegzaam is, uit en om en door zich zelven bestaat en alle volmaakt goed in zich zelf bezit en uit zich zelven voortbrengt. Ware dus de mensch als God, dan zou er ook bij den mensch van geen geloof sprake kunnen zijn. Maar nu de mensch schepsel en geen Schepper, afhankelijk en niet zijn eigen meester, innerlijk van alles ontbloot en niet zelfgenoegzaam is, nu moet er geloof in hem zijn, d.w.z., nu moet hij inzien en erkennen dat hij niet om zich zelven, maar alleen om en door God bestaat, en evenzoo dat alle goede gave niet uit hem zelf als uit een fontein opwelt, maar uit God als een Fontein aller goeden hem toevloeit."

pendent on God, whose powers they receive from the "Fountain of all good." Precisely in this respect, they are each other's opposites. The one who believes God "knows all this, acknowledges, sees, wants, and directs himself to it," but the one who is godless "fights, opposes, does not want it, and places a lie against it." An unbeliever does not not believe, but believes falsely, disputes, denies, imagines "reason," "self" or "Satan" to be substitutes for God, claims independence, and believes humans to be their own masters. "The truth that he exists only from, through and for God, he rejects, and the lie that he exists from, through and for something else he accepts. This is his unbelief, and in that unbelief is his sin."[56]

Related to this contrast is Kuyper's view that religion is the correlate of revelation. The one is not possible without the other. Revelation is a "central power" that transcends the world, including humans, and makes religion possible. Both believers and unbelievers sense that perception and knowledge are made possible by a central power, which reveals itself to us, affects us, and touches us inwardly in the core of our psyche. Without it, "religion is inconceivable." Formal faith enables human to appropriate, as it were, "gold from the mine."[57]

God's revelation is important not only for humans, but also for non-human creatures. All creation manifests God's power and glory and is, therein, revelatory. Revelation is not just God's reaction to the human fall into disobedience and restricted to redemption from sin. Revelation is not only soteriological. Human salvation is, in a sense, something accidental in that it "bears an intervening character and remains dependent on the fundamental conception of revelation which is given in creation itself." Redemptive revelation opens the way for fallen humans to be renewed, in a holy covenant-centered, loving way as His image-bearers in a fallen world.

Being human entails, according to Kuyper, having formal faith, which is made possible by God's all-encompassing foundational or fundamental revelation. Through primordial formal faith, each discipline, or science, is linked to the human "I," to religion guided by the central power of God's Word. In this original sense, faith is the way humans meet God in a way not isolated from observation, nor dependent on demonstration and self-consciousness.[58] Faith is inseparable from the human "I," i.e., the human

---

56. Kuyper (1893): II, 299.
57. Kuyper (1954): 148–149.
58. Kuyper (1954): 149. Fernhout indicates that Dooyeweerd states at this point that "the

logos and human pneuma. The human logos has a dual role in revelation: it is the way for humans to receive and to be revelation. This logos

> reflectively [*abbildlich*] reveals something of the eternal logos. . . . And if without lapsing into trichotomy, we may call this finest element in our human being the pneumatical, we define it as being both the choicest jewel in the diadem of revelation and the instrument by which man transmutes all revelation into knowledge of God. Both are expressed in the creation of man after the image of God.[59]

This formal "faith" is the highest capacity humans have to know God. In close relation with the "I-pneuma," formal faith establishes the self-consciousness of humans. This faith points to an extension of human consciousness, an innate knowledge of God, what Calvin called *semen religionis*.[60] Humans bear God's image in that their "I" has the capacity for self-awareness. Such a person, "resting from moment to moment on the omnipresent power of God which is immanent in him, will as soon as the self-consciousness at work in him penetrates to the depth of his being, necessarily come to *cognitio Dei insita* (innate knowledge of God)."[61]

The distinction at the time of Kuyper, and later by persons he influenced, between innate and acquired knowledge of God caused considerable discussion about the meaning of "formal faith." Does it refer to an inherent ability of humans for true self- and God-knowledge? Does human God-knowledge presuppose His revelation and become foundational for human self-knowledge? Is the human ability to know God perhaps an (Augustinian) extension of true human self-knowledge? Is God-knowledge innate, or does it arise from the need to know oneself?

Kuyper distinguished between faith as "capacity" and faith as something innate or "immediately given." He does not separate these two. Whereas faith as capacity (*habitus*) refers to the "instrument side" of faith, faith as innate knowledge points to its "immediate content."[62] While he tended to

---

formal function of faith is totally governed by the material (i.e., content-full) sense of faith in which (Christian) *geloof* and (the content of) revelation are correlates." Cf. Fernhout 1979: 67, and Dooyeweerd (1939): 229.

59. Kuyper (1954): 264.

60. Kuyper (1954): 265.

61. Kuyper (1910): II, 41, 42 (cited by Fernhout (1979): 68).

62. Fernhout (1979): 69. Implied in this stress on "instrument side," not the "content," is that non-Christians do not lack faith, but experience a "positive privation of the faith in-

emphasize the "content" of faith, he maintained both "form," or "instrument side," and "content" of faith when in his *Principles of Sacred Theology* he states

> Faith is indeed in our human consciousness the deepest fundamental law that governs every form of distinction, by which alone all higher "Differentiation" becomes established in our consciousness. It is the daring break of our unity into duality; placing of another ego over against our own ego, and the courage to face that distinction only because our own ego finds its point of support and of rest only in that other ego. This general better knowledge of faith renders it possible to speak of faith in every domain; and also shows that faith originates primordially from the fact that our ego places God over against itself as the eternal and infinite Being, and that it dares to do this, because in this only it finds its eternal point of support. Since we did not manufacture this faith ourselves, but God created it in our human nature, this faith is but the opening of our spiritual eye and the consequent perception of another Being, excelling us in everything, that manifests itself in our own being. Thus it does not originate after the Cartesian style of an imprinted idea of God, but from the manifestation of God in our being to that spiritual eye which has been formed in order, as soon as it opens, to perceive Him and in ecstasy of admiration to be bound to Him. By faith we perceive that an eternal Being manifests Himself in us, in order to place Himself over against our ego, in the same way in which we discover the presence of light by our eye; but what this eternal Being is and what it demands of us, is not told us by faith, but by the innate knowledge of God, presently enriched by the acquired.[63]

Fernhout concludes his scrutiny of Kuyper's view of "formal faith" with two pertinent observations. First, Kuyper viewed faith (and religion) in terms of a Greek (Aristotelian) oriented anthropology. Faith is not just a "limited dimension of man, parallel to many others," but "the pinnacle of *pneuma*, taken up into the dominating, motivating rule" of all human life. In doing this, he ascribed to "faith (and religion) . . . important directive implications for all human life."[64] This inborn capacity to know truth plays a significant, life-encompassing and -directing role.

strument," which is comparable, according to Fernhout, to having the organ of an eye but not using it (70).

63. Kuyper (1954): 266–267; also Fernhout (1979): 69.

64. Fernhout (1979): 70. For the impact of this way of thinking on the role of Christians in society and culture, see Chapter 13 below.

Second, as to a "very peculiar tone" in Kuyper's view of faith, Fernhout called attention to a significant epistemological issue:

> Kuyper uses terms that seem to properly belong to the realm of "analysis," "distinction," "differentiation," "breaking our unity into duality," etc. Thus while Kuyper saw the legitimate place of faith in the doing of science, his own understanding of faith has overtones characteristic of (scientific) analysis. This is not surprising in light of the fact that faith is rooted in man's *ik-pneuma*, which is also designated as *logos*. We have already noted the fact that Kuyper defines the *ik* in terms that are very characteristic of the *facultas intelligendi*. Thus it is to be expected that Kuyper would be predisposed to a rational-logical understanding of faith. This predisposition is further shown in Kuyper's insistence that faith's innate knowledge (i.e., immediately obtained, not logically thought out) must always be complemented by the logical action which can "reduce" or "transmute" it into real knowledge, thus giving rise to innate theology. This rational-logical tendency, however, should not cause us to be blind to the acuteness and biblical soundness of Kuyper's insight that faith has to do with that side of man's creational nature which calls him to come face to face with his Creator.[65]

Four Problems

Regarding Kuyper's attempt to develop a more biblically directed view of higher education, a few brief comments about four more issues in his work as a reforming thinker will be helpful, namely, "faith and theology," "encyclopedia and curriculum," "organic and logical" and "Creator-creation relation."

Faith and Theology

Kuyper did not equate "faith" with "theology," nor did he separate them, although in different ways, they have a religious root and depend on God's revelation. As one of the many disciplines in a curriculum, "theology" is not unique in having a special claim to God's revelation and a privileged or dominant role in the academy. It does not have a monopoly on "truth," what

---

65. Fernhout (1979): 70.

is "supernatural" and "redemptive," and must somehow be related to what is "natural" to human life and learning.

He rejected the traditional scholastic notion that "theology" guides all disciplines in a curriculum. However, since the study (*wetenschap*) of theology is organically related to all human studies, it cannot act as the "queen" of all learning and sciences. As with all other disciplines, theology needs something that only philosophy can provide. For Kuyper, theology is no longer "above" all other academic disciplines in the way, for example, that Beza, Arminius, Voetius and other scholastic theologians had advocated, since theology is part of the whole body of academic disciplines in all colleges and universities.

Kuyper distinguished between "Christian" and "theological." Whereas the former, to use neo-Kuyperian terms, points to a religious, heart-centered, clash between "Truth" and "Lie," the latter is "structural," analytically "correct or incorrect."[66] Just as there is a Christian and a non-Christian scholarship/science, there is a Christian and a non-Christian theology.[67]

Encyclopedia and Curriculum

Kuyper pressed for a holistic curriculum consisting of five distinct kinds of disciplines, viz., (a) physics, (b) medicine, (c) philology, with its four subdisciplines of literature, history, logic and philosophy, (d) jurisprudence, with its two auxiliary disciplines of sociology and economics, and (e) theology, with ethics as its sub-discipline. The disciplines of (b)–(e) are important for doctors, teachers, lawyers and clergy, focus on what is somatic, psychic, human and divine, and zero in on, respectively, body, logic, society and soul.

Two features in Kuyper's more holistic encyclopedia and curriculum are noteworthy. First, a religious conflict in medicine (b), jurisprudence (d) and theology (e) with regard to, respectively, disease, evil and sin. Physics (a) and philology (c) with its two sub-disciplines, "logic" and "philosophy," do

66. About the difference between these two kinds of differences, see chapter 8 below.

67. For details, see unpublished lecture (available in the Archives at Westminster Theological Seminary, Philadelphia, PA) of Robert D. Knudsen on "What evangelicals can learn from Abraham Kuyper and Herman Bavinck as to theological methodology," given at the 19th annual meeting of the Evangelical Theological Society, at the Toronto Bible College, in Canada, on December 27–29, 1967.

not involve a religious contrast, since in Kuyper's scholastic thinking, both "nature" and "reason" are based on God's "common grace."[68]

Second, in the first four curricular categories (a–d), the investigator is, as subject, active, and what is studied is, as object, passive. The opposite is true in "theology" (e) because the relation between "active subject" and "passive object" is reversed in that here not the theologian, but God, is the active "subject" and the investigator, or theologian, the passive "object."[69] Kuyper confused the epistemic "subject-object" relation with the religious "Creator-creature" relation. In thinking about what is "ontic" (ontology) in terms of scholastic knowing (epistemology), Kuyper revealed his Reformed scholastic bias because he thought about theology in an intellective way.

To understand his view of "organic" and "encyclopedic" is not easy. It is inseparably related to a feature in his thinking in terms of what D. Vollenhoven, as historian of Western philosophy, called "intellectual semimysticism." In critique of radical empiricism, especially A. Comte's positivism, Kuyper writes,

> There lies a majesty in the human mind by virtue of which it cannot rest until it has acquired full dominion in the world of thought. It cannot bear the suggestion that there should still be something in the world of thought that has withdrawn itself from the power of its scepter. This impels it to scan not merely the whole horizon of phenomena with its knowledge, but the field of knowledge itself with its thought. An atomistical science offends the unity-sense of its own mind, or, by the pulverizing of the cosmos, robs the mind of confidence of step in its walk. And therefore it is bound to presume a relation between the parts of its knowledge also, nor can it rest until it has seen through that relation organically, because in this way only can science harmonize with the organic unity of its own thinking, as well as with the organic unity of the Kosmos.[70]

"Science" focuses on what is higher, universal and intellectual. Kuyper moved from multiple givens toward relationships, unity and harmony. He thinks in terms of elements and relations, body and soul, lower and higher,

---

68. As will be indicated in Chapters 17 and 18 below, this contestable feature in Kuyper's thinking has been perpetuated at the Free University in Amsterdam and at Calvin Theological Seminary and Calvin College in Grand Rapids, Michigan.

69. See Kuyper (1954): 183–210. For details about "active" and "passive," see Vander Stelt 1974: 184–185.

70. Kuyper (1954): 15; see Vander Stelt (1973): 182.

temporal and eternal, material and spiritual, sensory and logical, experience and thought, subject and object, passive and active, mediate and immediate, atomistic and organic, knowable and knowing.[71] This train of thought is clear when he states,

> The subject of science cannot be this man or that, but must be mankind at large, or, if you please, the human consciousness. . . . Consequently you cannot attain unto a conception of "science" in the higher sense, until you take humanity as an organic whole. . . . If impersonation were in order, this higher factor, this animating and illuminating power, itself might be called "science". . . . Moreover, it is only with this interpretation that science obtains its divine consecration, because that higher factor, which was seen to be the active agent in science, cannot be conceived otherwise than self-conscious; for there can be no science for the human consciousness as such without God to impel men to pursue science, to give it, and to maintain its organic relation. . . . This higher factor, who is to lead our human consciousness up to science, must himself know what he will have us know.[72]
>
> . . . science presents itself to us as a necessary and ever-continued impulse in the human mind to reflect within itself the cosmos, plastically as to its elements, and to think it through logically as to its relations, always with the understanding that the human mind is capable of this by means of its organic affinity to its object.[73]

Organic and Logical

Central to Kuyper's view of "encyclopedic" and "organic" is his understanding of "logical." In a sense, "organic" and "logical" are similar. Both focus on what is universally valid, real, essential and objective. Humans do not impose, but discover, order. At the center of order lies a "logical compulsion." Terms like "order," "organic," "encyclopedic" and "logic" share a common feature:

71. This is also the case when he writes about such paired terms as universal and individual, necessary and accidental, observation and representation, concepts and impressions, one and many, indivisible and visible, logic and moments, biblical revelation and natural revelation, psychical and physical.

72. Kuyper (1958): 63–65.

73. Kuyper (1958): 83.

... the human mind brings about a certain distinction and order in the chaos of our human knowledge, which is not done arbitrarily, but agreeably to a fixed order assumed to be present here. ... Since now that world of our knowledge and that world of phenomena are not chaotic, but organic, our thinking cannot rest till in the treasure of our knowledge it has exhibited such an Encyclopedic order as will harmonize with the organic relation of both of that world of our knowledge and of the world of phenomena. Thus our human spirit is not to invent a certain order for our knowledge, but to seek out and to indicate the order which is already there.[74]

What is "organic," or "logical," is not something observed as being out there in some objective way, but it is something lodged in human consciousness. Rejecting modern epistemological subjectivism, he stressed that humans do not create order, but discover it. At the same time, he thinks, in a semi-mystical way, that within the higher world of human consciousness resides a universal and objective intellect.

The term "scientific" implies that "human consciousness" is essentially intellectual and that the "order" of the world is ultimately logical. This enabled Kuyper to state: "The further science advances, the easier it will be to reproduce the cosmos logically, and to make all its parts to be clearly seen, together with the several relations," and "in proportion as the logical reproduction becomes more accurate, it will image in a more organic way whatever exists organically."[75]

Unlike "general" knowledge, "scientific" knowledge is "systematic, i.e., knowledge orderly arranged."[76] Although humans do not create "order," it does not exist apart from the mental activity of humans. What is in the mind "corresponds" to what is in the world. Everything exists with "relations," which are always "organic," or "logical." In their "logical existence," they are "susceptible to being taken up into our world of thought."[77]

The relations lie hidden in the cosmos, and they cannot be known in their deeper connection, unless we approach this logically existing cosmos as logical thinkers. The science of the cosmos is only possible for us upon the supposition that in our thinking the logical germ of a world of thought is

74. Kuyper (1958): 27, 28.
75. Kuyper (1958): 39.
76. Kuyper (1958): 29.
77. Kuyper (1958): 78.

lodged, which, if properly developed, will cover entirely the logical world of thought lodged in the cosmos. And this provides the possibility of our thinking showing itself actively. As soon as we have learned to know the universal relations that govern the special, or have discovered in those several relations the germ of self-developing thought, the identity between our subjective and objective world of thought enables us to perform our active part, both by calling the desired relations into being, and by anticipating the relations which must reveal themselves, or shall afterward develop themselves.[78]

Creator-Creation Relation

The central impulse of human self-consciousness is not the same as the activity of God, although they exist in a close relationship to each other. The world of "relations" has no existence except for an original Subject, who has thought them out, and is able to let this product of his thoughts govern the whole cosmos. Just because these relations have no substance of their own, they cannot work organically unless they are organically thought, i.e., from a first principle. When we study these relations, we merely think the thought over again, by which the Subject defined these relations when he called them into being.[79]

> And since the object does not produce the subject, nor the subject the object, the power that binds the two organically together must of necessity be sought outside of each. And however much we may speculate and ponder, no explanation can ever suggest itself to our sense, of the all-sufficient ground for this admirable correspondence and affinity between object and subject, on which the possibility and development of science wholly rests, until at the hand of Holy Scripture we confess that the Author of the cosmos created man in the cosmos as microcosmos "after his image and likeness."[80]

78. Kuyper (1958): 79.

79. Kuyper (1958): 77–78.

80. Kuyper (1958): 83. Kuyper wrote about "immediate sight" that takes place "without the bodily eye"—"God's Word opens the outlook before us in which the immediate seeing of the heart of things, this seeing of face to face, shall be the characteristic of our knowledge in another sphere of reality. The accepted use of the word which holds on to the conception of sight in knowledge agrees with Revelation, which points to a science that shall consist in sight." (62)

God as Subject, or Author, of everything creaturely is, philosophically speaking, "a first principle," something basic to all "relations" within, and between, "subjects" and "objects." The relation between "Creator" and "creation" is one of "Archetype" and "ectype," a relation that is derivative, intra-cosmic and studied in the "science" of theology.

In *Principles of Sacred Theology*, Kuyper was still traditional in his (philosophical, anthropological and epistemological) thinking. Although centuries-old scholastic thought-patterns influenced his general way of probing basic issues related to "faith" and "theology," Kuyper was perceptive with his idea of "formal faith" and its implications for the nature of theology. He opened the door, albeit only slightly, for Dooyeweerd, Vollenhoven and other students to think of faith life as something human and as religiously directed in a Christian or non-Christian way.

CHAPTER SIX

Faculty Psychology[1]

Greek faculty psychology had an enormous impact on Western anthro-pology. It created major problems in the study of human behavior, in-cluding faith life and the traditional discipline of theology. It influenced countless theologians in their own training, in their teaching of preachers, pastors, evangelists and missionaries, and in encouraging fellow believers in all their daily tasks to respond to God's love as his grateful people.

The problem concerning a faculty psychology thinking I experienced in a catechism class when my talented and passionate (Christian Reformed) pastor taught us that humans are not only "thinking, willing and feeling," but "also spiritual" beings. As a student at a reputable state high school, I found my pastor's comment that humans are "thinking, willing, and feeling" beings quite helpful, because it dovetailed with what I was learning at the state high school.[2]

Since I was planning to become a preacher, I appreciated my pastor's statement that as humans we are "also spiritual" beings. In an official discussion with four church elders about why I wanted to make public profession of my Christian faith, I shared with them that I agreed with my pastor's teaching that as humans we are "also spiritual." The elders complimented me on my insightful comment that reflected proper biblical self-knowledge.

1. This chapter is an edited and expanded version of a paper given at a Quadrilateral Conference (Free University, Institute for Christian Studies, Calvin College, and Dordt College), held at Dordt College, Sioux Center, IA, 1998—published as "'Faculty Psychology' and Theology" in *Ways of Knowing in Concert*, John H. Kok, ed., Dordt College Press, 2006, 46–59.
2. Brantford Collegiate Institute in Brantford, ON, Canada.

Three years later, it dawned on me that what my church elders told me was actually not astute and that my "self-knowledge" was not really correct. One of my philosophy professors at Calvin College—a classic liberal arts school, influenced by Bavinck's semi-scholastic anthropology and reflected in the teaching of two professors of "Reformed dogmatics" at CTS[3]—encouraged me to explore the nature and implications of what my pastor had taught me in catechism. What did it really mean to be human? What were its implications for my self-knowledge, and for my knowledge of the world, of my fellow humans, and even of God's revelation?

Reflecting on the relation between "thinking, willing, feeling" and "also spiritual," I began to wonder about such a way of thinking in teachers, preachers, theologians and philosophers and about its influence on my dear pastor. His well-meant and well-intentioned comment was interesting, but actually not really helpful in my thought life or in my faith life. Perhaps my pastor's comments were actually not simple, or helpful, but complex, if not problematic.

About the nature of "being human," I was taught in my Christian elementary school for seven years in the Netherlands, in my state high school for two years in Canada, at Calvin College for four years in Grand Rapids, at the Free University for six years in Amsterdam, and at Calvin Theological Seminary for a semester in Grand Rapids. I taught theology and philosophy for more than thirty years at Dordt College, and served on committees that dealt with encyclopedic, curricular and pedagogical issues.[4]

This way of thinking in my own education and as an advocate of integrally Christian living compelled me to avoid any "tripartite" anthropology. As a pastor since 1965, an advocate of ICS in 1967, a teacher of both theology and philosophy after 1968, the author of a dissertation on Philosophy and Scripture: A Study in Old Princeton and Westminster Theology, 1978, and an advocate since 1975 of what in 1989 became known as IAPCHE—in these four ways, I attempted to avoid any Platonic/Aristotelian concept of faculty psychology. This scholastic anthropology affects one's view of such issues as self-knowledge, curriculum and pedagogy, truth and customs, and how humans behave and shape culture and history.

Pervasive in Western thinking is something that is actually complex and even problematic. This chapter centers on what was inchoate in the last four

---

3. About the views of F. M. ten Hoor and L. Berkhof, see chapter 15 below.

4. E.g., tensions between "mental," "volitional" and "effectual" courses in a curriculum and their relation to the study of theology.

chapters (2–5) and what will be dealt with in the remaining fourteen chapters (7–20). It focuses on mainly five anthropological problems in faculty
psychology: (a) Greek background, (b) Reformed scholasticism, (c) Western
anthropology, (d) six examples, and (e) knowledge of God and self and its
effect on human faith life and discipline of it.

Greek Background

The idea of faculty psychology originated in the anthropology of both Plato
(427–347 BC) and his pupil Aristotle (384–322 BC). These two philosophers
stated that the human soul (ψυχη), in distinction from the human body
(σωμα), consists of three fundamental faculties, capacities, or powers. According to Plato, "soul" is an immaterial substance consisting of intellect,
or mind (νους); spirit, will, noble emotion (θυμος); and appetite, passion,
or lower emotion (επιθυμια). The intellect rules the will, which, in turn,
controls the passions.[5]

These three faculties of the soul correlate with three sections of the human body: the head, the chest cavity and the abdomen with its organs of
generation.[6] He describes the role of these three forces, or powers, in terms
of the myth of a charioteer (the intellect) and two winged horses, one of
which is good and cooperative (the will) and the other one initially bad and
uncooperative (passions). The human faculties of intellect, will and emotions
he associates with wisdom, courage and prudence, respectively.[7]

Unlike Plato, Aristotle, his famous student, developed a hylomorphis-
tic view of soul and body not as two separate entities or substances, but as
interdependent features which relate to each other in the way form does to
matter. He disagreed with his mentor's view on the way in which the soul
relates to the body, but he nevertheless perpetuated Plato's idea of "faculty
psychology." The capacities, or powers, of the soul are: (i) the intellect, or
the active/passive mind; (ii) the appetite, or the will; and (iii) the vegetative
soul, or the passions.[8]

5. Plato's *Republic*, 434d–441c. Plato relates these three elements of the soul to (a) the
three functions of the state: deliberative/governing, executive and productive, and (b) the three
motives of wisdom, honor and gain.

6. Plato, *Timaeus*, 69–72.

7. Plato, *Phaedrus*, 246.

8. *De Anima*, 411a24–411b31; 414a30–415a15; 427a16–427b25. For details on the active and
passive mind, see 429b23–430a25. Cf. McKeon (1973): 179–181, 187–189, and 223–4. For the

Both Plato and Aristotle thought that the intellect was eternal, inde-structible and imperishable. The integrity of this most significant human faculty enables humans to focus on truth in a proper way. To determine the essence of being human, the capacity of the intellect guides the capacity of the will, which, in turn, directs the capacity of the emotions.

According to Aristotle, mankind has nothing worthy of consideration as being divine or blessed, except what there is in us of reason and wisdom; this alone of our possessions seems to be immortal, this alone to be divine. By virtue of being able to share in this faculty, life, however, wretched and difficult by nature, is yet so cleverly arranged that man seems a god in com-parison with all other creatures. For "reason is the god in us" . . . and "mortal life contains a portion of some god." We ought, therefore, either to pursue philosophy or say farewell to life and depart hence, since all other things seem to be great nonsense and folly.[9]

Only when the error-free human faculty of the intellect rules the facul-ties of the will and the emotions can the last two abilities become the source for virtue and what is good. When they resist this control, however, they become the origin of vice and what is bad.

The impact of this Greek faculty psychology anthropology on Western philosophy and theology has been enormous. St. Augustine (AD 354–430) used it when he sensed an analogy of the Holy Trinity in the three faculties of the human soul and associated God the Son with intellect (*intelligentia*), God the Spirit with will (*voluntas*) and God the Father with memory (*memoria*).[11]

Thomas Aquinas (1225–1275) believed that the human soul consisted of three faculties, or capacities, namely, intellect, will and passion. As the soul's highest faculty, the human intellect moves the human will and affects the human passions. The negative consequence of human disobedience can be undone only through the "added gift" (*donum superadditum*) of redemp-tive or salvific faith. Only when human will and emotion are subject to the truth(s) of the human intellect is it possible for the virtues and passions of humans to be enhanced and restored. Evil consists of humans rejecting the truth(s) of the intellect and diverting the will from doing what is moral, or good. In associating truth with reason, good with will and evil primarily

---

meaning of psychology in the sense of anthropology in Aristotle's philosophy, see 146–152, especially the last three pages.

9. Cf. Hoekema (1956b): 15. For details, see David Austin Napier, *En Route to the Confes-sions: The Roots and Development of Augustine's Philosophical Anthropology*, (2013,) 348 pgs.

with emotion or passion, Aquinas commented on Galatians 5:17: "The flesh lusts against the spirit by the rebellion of the passions against the reason."[10]

Reformed Scholasticism

To illustrate the influence of scholastic thinking on Reformed theology, it is helpful to look at the views of Andreas Hyperius (1511–1564) and highlight certain features in the anthropology of Bavinck (1854–1921).

Andreas Hyperius

As a theologian and philosopher at the University of Marburg, Germany, Hyperius was the first Reformed theologian who, in a homiletics course, stressed the importance of a common medieval distinction between a popular and a scholastic reading of Scripture in, respectively, church and school.[11] In 1553 he wrote as follows:

> No one is unaware that two ways of interpreting the Scriptures are used in the churches "by those skilled in divine matters,"[12] the one scholastic (*scholasticum*), the other popular (*popularem*). The former is appropriate in the assemblies of learned men and young students who have advanced to some extent in scholarship; the latter is provided entirely to instruct the common people, most of whom are ignorant, uneducated, and illiterate. The former is exercised within the narrow walls of the school; the latter takes place in spacious sanctuaries. The former is concise and compact, smelling of philosophical solitude and rigour; the latter is expanded, free in expression, and diffuse, and indeed delights in the light and forum, as it were, of oratory. In the former most things are examined by the standard

10. *Summa Theologica*, I,95,2. Galatians 5:17: "For the sinful nature desires what is contrary to the Spirit, and the Spirit desires what is contrary to the sinful nature. They are in conflict with each other, so that you do not do what you want." Cf. Hoekema (1956b): 15–16.

11. Cf. *De formandis*. For details, see Sinnema (1999): 128–129, especially note 2; also note 3 about Willem van't Spijker's *Principe, Methode en Functie van de Theologie bij Andreas Hyperius* (Kampen: Kok, 1990). Hyperius focused on the popular reading in *De formandis concionibus sacris seu de interpretatione scripturarum populari libri II* (1553; 1562-edition) and on the scholastic reading in *De recte formando theologiae studio* (1556).

12. See Sinnema (1999): 129n9.

of dialectical brevity and simplicity; in the latter rhetorical abundance and copiousness garner the most favour.[13]

In 1562 he combined this "scholastic-popular" distinction with an anthropology shaped by traditional faculty psychology thinking. The mind, or intellect, plays a more prominent role in determining what is understood than do the two human capacities of will and emotions.

He who teaches in a school knowingly and willingly disregards whatever seeks to arouse good-will and moves the emotions, also [disregards] digressions, extended descriptions, examples, amplifications, elaborate elegance of speaking style, numerous figures of speech; in short all embellishments and adornments of oratory. And indeed he does not try to be devoted to brilliance in speaking, but he is content with a simple, yet plain and clear manner of speaking.[14]

Basic to his view of knowledge is what he had stated six years earlier in *De recte formando theologiae studio* (1556). He developed a scholastic method of interpretation that had "the power to persuade and impress the mind." This method was "suited" for students in "numerous schools and colleges, and savours of something philosophical since it is bound more to dialectical brevity and simplicity (*ad dialecticam brevitatem simplicitatem-que*)."[15] This "scholastic approach" was, according to Hyperius, not a firm "set of doctrines," but "only a method, or way, of explaining the content of theology." According to D. Sinnema, in an attempt to discover a method unique to theology that can help God's people in their daily life, Hyperius opened the door, albeit only slightly, in the direction of allowing a salient feature of scholastic thinking to play an important role in the popular explanation of one's simple faith. He helped prepare the way for what Antoine de Chandieu—another Reformed theologian—later advocated when he

13. As cited by Sinnema (1999): 129.

14. Cf. *Deformandis*. See Sinnema (1990): 130; also 136, where he states that for this method it is "not necessary to move their emotions. The main virtue of a good teacher is clarity and fluency in expression. Prolixity only leads to boredom."

15. See Sinnema (1990): 132; see also note 19 about the second edition of *De recte formando theologiae studio* (1556) published as *De theologo, seu de rationae studii theologici* (1559). Abraham Kuyper summarized its contents in *Encyclopedie der Heilige Godgeleerdheid* (Kampen: Kok, 1908), I:155–165, as did Robert Preus in *The Theology of Post-Reformation Lutheranism* (St.Louis: Concordia, 1970), 82–88.

used "the scholastic method" as "an analytical treatment of theology using Aristotelian logic."[16]

Herman Bavinck

As the leading Reformed theologian in dogmatics at the end of the nineteenth century, Bavinck incorporated faculty psychology in his anthropology in his four-volume work *Gereformeerde Dogmatiek* (cf. Chapter 4 above). In *The Certainty of Faith* (first published in Dutch in 1901 and translated into English in 1980),[17] Bavinck describes his understanding of faith. He correlates human reason, will and emotions with head, hand and heart, respectively, and, when they are viewed wrongly, with intellectualism, moralism and pietism.[18]

He thinks in terms of scholastic faculty psychology when he writes about the nature and role of Christian faith. Faith is "not only trust, it is also knowledge and assent."[19] The truth of revelation can "be recognized only by the conscience, by the heart, by the will"[20]; the "gospel comforts the conscience, brings peace to the heart, strengthens the will; it strengthens the whole person with the power to live a new life."[21] To "believe, freely, willingly and with one's whole mind, one needs a new heart and a changed will."[22] He rejects the experience-centered subjectivism of Rousseau and Schleiermacher when he writes as follows:

The emotions follow understanding, and the will is led by both. Faith is the source of emotional life and the power animating the works of our hands.

16. See Sinnema (1999): 142; also 143. For details about Antoine de Chandieu, see Sinnema 1994.

17. The basic premises of this book presuppose Bavinck's elaborate *Beginselen der Psychologie*, (1897).

18. Bavinck (1980): 40. To highlight the one-sidedness of Moravian and Methodist Christians, Bavinck comments, in a "faculty psychology" way, that "Consciousness was often suppressed for the sake of emotion and will, and there was no harmony between man's capacities and powers" (ibid, 48).

19. Bavinck (1980): 59.

20. Bavinck (1980): 64.

21. Bavinck (1980): 65.

22. Bavinck (1980): 79. It is noteworthy that Bavinck does *not* mention the need for a "new mind." Regarding his tendency to associate "feeling" with "heart," see Bremmer 1961: 223–4.

If faith, however, does not come first, no genuine experience and no true good works can follow.[23]

Clearly, a Greek view of being human that reflected a scholastic faculty psychology had a profound effect not only on Roman Catholic, but also on Protestant, and especially on Reformed (and Presbyterian), ideas about human faith life and the related study of theology. It provided a significant philosophical framework for theological thinking about such issues as the triune God, divine revelation, human existence, the nature of truth, the role of apologetics, the nature of good and evil, and the structure and role of faith.[24]

Western Anthropology

To correlate thinking, willing and feeling as powers of the soul, with what is true, good and beautiful is a main feature in Western thinking. It profoundly affected dominant Western views and theories about what it means to be human, the structure of society, the encyclopedia of knowledge, and the place of scholarship and education with respect to the intellect (Descartes), the will (Schopenhauer) and the feelings (Schleiermacher).

Numerous Western thinkers[25] have used, and continue to use, this classic tripartite anthropology in their worldview and philosophy. This typically Western sense of self-knowledge hugely impacted countless Western thinkers, including such giant philosophers as Kant, Comte and Feuerbach.

Immanuel Kant (1724–1804) structured his famous trilogy on the three basic categories of faculty psychology. In *Critique of Pure Reason* (1781), he focused on the intellect and what is true, in *Critique of Practical Reason*

23. A similar emphasis is present in the anthropological views of Calvin, Hodge and Kuyper.

24. It would be helpful to explore how faculty psychology impacted anthropology and changed from the Greek period through the scholastic period and into modernity.

25. E.g., (i) the dialectical idealist, Francis Herbert Bradley (1846–1924), who associated logic, ethics and psychology with truth, will and the sentient; (ii) the founder of phenomenology, Franz Brentano (1838–1907), who correlated the three modes of intentionality, i.e., judging, loving/hating and representing, with what is true, good and beautiful; (iii) the Marburg philosopher, Hermann Cohen (1842–1918), who related logic, ethics and aesthetics to reason, religion and senses; (iv) Wilhelm Dilthey (1833–1911), an advocate of *Lebensphilosophie,* who viewed society and culture in terms of intuition, creativity and achievement, or knowing, positing and appreciating.

(1788) on the will and what is good, and in *Critique of Judgement* (1793) on the senses and what is beautiful. This detailed and in-depth study impacted a wide range of central issues in philosophy, the encyclopedia of knowledge, the meaning of science (*Wissenschaft*) and numerous disagreements and debates about faith and theology.

Its impact on phenomenology has been pervasive in neo-Kantian circles, with its stress on describing (but not on explaining!) the complexity of human experiences by means of three basic "intentions of human consciousness," i.e., judgment (*Urteil*), love/hate (*Lieben/Hassen*) and representation (*Vorstellung*).[26]

Auguste Comte (1789–1857) focused on the nature of humanity, society and history, and did so in terms of the three traditional faculties of "thinking, willing and feeling." In diverse and detailed ways, he correlated these three human capacities with "thought, action and affection," "source, goal and spontaneity," "intellect, deeds and heart" and "philosophers, workers and women."

In *The Essence of Christianity* (1840), Ludwig A. Feuerbach (1804–1872) discussed the nature of the intellect, the will and the affections in connection with the three human urges of knowledge, choice and love. The ultimate objects of these three human urges are the Father, Son and Holy Spirit. God did not create humans in his image, but humans create God in their image. Feuerbach's anthropology, centered on a faculty psychology, reflected the classic modalistic heresy about God.[27] It also determined the structure and thrust of his major and (in)famous trilogy: *The Essence of Faith according to Luther* (1844), *The Essence of Religion* (1845) and *Philosophy and Christendom* (1859).[28]

The views of Kant, Comte and Feuerbach, as three master thinkers in the last century and a half in Western culture, underscore the enormous impact

26. Other *tripartite* divisions are reflected in pragmatism and other major Western philosophies. For a detailed study, see Tol (1997). For his discussion of C. S. Peirce, one of the three major founders of pragmatism, see Tol (1997): 69–72, especially his comment that feeling, willing and thinking are "three radically different elements of consciousness" and illustrate the three categories of the human spirit (*ibid.*, 72). For details about "faculty psychology" in Comte, Dilthey, Nietzsche, Husserl, Russell and others, see Tol (1997): 139 n11.

27. A heretical doctrine of the second and third centuries AD, about the unity of substance and personality in God, according to which the Son and the Holy Spirit are only "modes" of God the Father.

28. Karl Marx combined the views of Comte and Feuerbach and interpreted humanity, society, culture and history with respect to socio-economic and political issues in an atheistic and human-centered way.

of Platonic/Aristotelian faculty psychology on anthropology, especially in an attempt to understand the nature of human faith life and the study of theology.

Six Examples

The philosophical and theological preference for a tripartite anthropology can be seen in Christian thinking since St. Augustine (354–430), who was influenced by Plato's philosophy, and after St. Thomas Aquinas (1225–1274), who, mesmerized by Aristotle, became the famous synthesis thinker in the Roman Catholic education system. After the sixteenth-century Protestant Reformation, it affected even Reformed higher education regarding the role of reason and theology, especially in higher education. The impact of Plato's and Aristotle's kind of anthropology on theological traditions is clear in six randomly selected instances—four of which are Christian Reformed, while the fifth one is Roman Catholic and the last one is typical of liberation theology.

First Example

Faculty psychology is evident in the anthropology of A. C. Van Raalte (1811–1879). This Dutch preacher emigrated in 1846 to Holland, Michigan, where he became a chief founder of the CRC in the USA. As a Secessionist Reformed thinker, he stressed the importance of both pietism and scholasticism. In his perceptive *Pioneer Preacher: Albertus Christiaan Van Raalte; A Study of His Sermon Notes* (1976), Gordon J. Spykman (1926–1993) highlighted the pietism and scholasticism in Van Raalte's formal theological education in the Netherlands, in his way of thinking, reading Scripture and preaching. About Van Raalte's "Doctrinal Orthodoxy," Spykman wrote the following:

> . . . Van Raalte views the body as the lower part of man's nature. Often he minimizes its importance. At the same time he extols the soul and spirit—which embraces the intellect, emotions and will. These spiritual qualities are the real clue to man's identity. Rather than presenting the Biblical idea of the heart as the all-controlling center of man's whole life, Van Raalte reduces the heart to man's emotions, which together with the intellect and will, form

the structure for his tri-partite view of man's spiritual nature, which stands over against the physical part of his being.

Van Raalte all too readily accepts the problematic as set forth by so many of his contemporaries, defining man as a "rational-moral being." The body does not even enter essentially into such a definition of man. Thus defined, being moral means that man is religious, so that Van Raalte can say that "man is a religious as well as a rational being."[29]

Second Example

In a lecture at a conference in 1997 for Christian Reformed pastors, preachers and evangelists on the subject of "Developing a 'Visual-Based' Oratory," the main speaker, a gifted Christian Reformed pastor and theologian, H. David Schuringa, structured his presentation, and lively discussion, around such scholastic sub-themes as affectionate uses, volitional uses and noetic uses.[30]

Third Example

In addressing practical problems and challenges in modern culture, Carl E. Zylstra talked in his annual presidential Convocation Address at Dordt College in 1998 about "The Moral Academy" in terms of "the Magician, the Intern and the Professor." These three types of people reflect, respectively, sensory experience, morality and truth. These three topics represent what he considered to be the three North American postmodern dangers of deception, relativism and skepticism. To counteract these three threats, he emphasized the importance of their opposites, i.e., transparency, virtue and universal standards.

The laudable intent of Zylstra's Convocational Address assumed the validity of a kind of anthropology which actually reflected what he opposed. His tripartite depiction of the problem and the solution reflects the mindset of a Greek anthropology. It assumes that for Dordt College to be truly human, it must presuppose what it rejects. To explain this conundrum or

29. Spykman (1976): 56.
30. H. D. Schuringa's lecture on "Hearing the Word in a Visual Age" at Dordt College, Sioux Center, Iowa, January 7–8, 1997.

enigma is to indicate that Zylstra—as numerous other Reformed thinkers have done—did this unwittingly, in terms of a Greek notion of "liberal arts" which he was taught as a student at Calvin College and Calvin Theological Seminary, i.e., intellect determines truth and its standards, character focuses on virtue and morality, and perception stresses sensual pleasure and the magic of "smooth talking con men."

Though it was not his intent to do so, the format of his Convocation Address indicates the persistence of a centuries-old scholastic philosophy, theology and education, when he stated that the "inevitable result of intellectual skepticism is finally moral skepticism" and that the "truthful academy needs to be the moral academy as well."[31]

Fourth Example

In *FOCUS*, a publication of the Reformed Ecumenical Council (REC), Robert DeVries, a professor at Calvin Theological Seminary, published several articles on "Catechism, Education and Professionalism: Fresh Looks." The first article he titled "Having Faith—Being Faithful: A Challenge for Educating Youth." He structured his comments in terms of three needs, i.e., orthodoxy (right thinking), orthopraxis (right behavior) and orthopathos (right feeling).[32] Although his interest in the catechetical instruction of young people is commendable, the way he wrote about this crucial issue was essentially the same as what my Reformed pastor taught me in catechism back in 1954.

DeVries perpetuated a scholastic anthropology he had learned as a student during seven years spent at Calvin College and Calvin Theological Seminary. Although he used "aspect" (a term unique to reformational thinking) rather than "faculty" (a term typical of scholastic thinking), he used it in the scholastic sense of "faculty." If faith is thought of as a six-sided cube, three of its axes are orthodoxy, orthopathos and orthopraxis.

The first axis is "Faith as Orthodoxy: The Cognitive Aspect." The axis of right thinking points to "a rational faith, possessing certainty of logical thought." Humans "not only know God" but also "know about God with

---

31. For a copy of Zylstra's address contact Dordt College (www.dordt.edu).

32. See *FOCUS*, 1:3 (Sept. 2001): 2–15. This issue of *FOCUS* was supervised by the Commission for Youth and Christian Nurture of REC. The editor, Jim Lont, referred to these three "rights" as a "hearty three course meal." DeVries based his view on Robert W. Pazmino, *Principles and Practices of Christian Education: An Evangelical Perspective* (Grand Rapids: Baker Book House, 1992), esp. 117–144; cf. *FOCUS* 1 (2001): 3n1.

certainty. God's revelation is clear, certain, and reliable." This cognitive aspect "seeks to understand, or think properly about God and his activities in the world." Humans can "know faith-concepts" and accept "truth-statements at face value." Orthodoxy deals with "doctrines, concepts, and truth-statements." Faith "necessarily includes conceptual knowledge."[33]

Faith involves both "knowledge" and "mystery." Human knowledge of God is "limited," not "complete or exhaustive." Due to the mystery of faith, we talk "about God and the things of God" in terms of "analogy, metaphor, or story." "Ultimately, truth is not fully enclosed in, or identified with, a rational concept, statement or proposition." Being created in God's image, as humans we "find within ourselves an analogy of God." There are "likenesses and parallels" which are both "truthful and reliable" as well as "limited and incomplete." To human analytical reasoning must be added "God's Story"; only then can humans "balance certainty with mystery, knowledge with the incomprehensible."

The second axis of the cube of faith is "Faith as Orthopraxis: The Behavioral Aspect." It focuses on the human "will," "right acting," "right behavior," deeds (cf. James on the subject of "works") in addition to words (cf. Paul on the subject of "faith"). The "actions" of faith are of two kinds: faith as "word" (a form of prayer or petition, expressed in a confession and celebration) and faith as "deed" (a form of developing character, virtues, social justice, sharing in "the mission of God to establish his Kingdom in its fullness.")[34]

The third axis of the cube of faith is "Faith as Orthopathy: The Affective Aspect." It involves the "heart" with its "relationships of values, affections, feelings, and emotions," and expresses itself in faith as "trust" and "community."[35] Because "knowledge is never complete, trust is a necessary component of knowledge. . . . Truth and trust are handmaids of each other." The head, with its truth and rational statements, and the heart, with its relationships and values are necessary: "There is no knowledge without trust," and "no trust without knowledge."[36]

Trust "diffuses itself through, and wraps itself around, cognitive truth and gives truth its stability and reliability." For Christians, this trust enabling them to accept Scripture as God's word rests on what Calvin calls the "inner

---

33. DeVries (2001): 3–5.

34. DeVries (2001): 11–14.

35. See DeVries (2001):7–8. DeVries distinguishes between "heart" and "head": the former does "far more than rationally consider the truthfulness of a particular statement or assertion," since it refers also to "passion" and "intuitions" (8).

36. DeVries (2001): 8.

testimony of the Holy Spirit." Faith involves not just "trust," which is "individual," but also "community," which refers to the church as God's chosen body of believers and to the whole cosmos.[37]

DeVries summarizes his seemingly simple but structurally scholastic[38] and complicated article:

> Each of these six aspects of faith are part of an integrated whole. While each may, at times, serve as the primary focus of catechetical ministry of the church, they may never be treated in isolation from each other. . . . In each age, the church has both succeeded and failed in keeping faith balanced among these six aspects within its catechetical ministry. . . . We need to see catechesis as involving the entire person—mind, heart and will. If Christ is going to find faith on earth when he returns, we must be very deliberate in nurturing that faith in our youth—a faith that involves knowledge and mystery, trust and community, word and deed.[39]

Fifth Example

In *Head and Heart: Affection, Cognition, Volition as Triune Consciousness* (1997), Andrew Tallon, a Roman Catholic theologian, uses faculty psychology in the neo-Kantian phenomenological tradition of Bernard Lonergan.[40] In his writing about "triune consciousness," he assumes an equal partnership of reason, will and affection. In stressing the "partnership" of these three dynamic faculties, he ascribes priority to the faculty of affection, not "intellect," as long as this is done in the "spirit of connaturality," or consciousness of affective intentionality.

"Connaturality brings the whole of triune consciousness to a higher perfection than either "discursive reason" or "deliberative volition" represent, either alone or in combination. Connatural knowledge is more perfect than conceptual knowledge, since it includes all three human intentionalities in a "higher operational synthesis."[41] To ignore, suppress, or elevate "any mode

37. DeVries (2001): 9, 10, 11.

38. This issue will be dealt with in some detail in Chapters 9, 10 and 13 below.

39. DeVries (2001): 14–15. For an example of a more biblically attuned view of catechetical education, see A. De Graaf, *The Educational Ministry of the Church*, 1968.

40. A globally prominent Roman Catholic philosopher/theologian, sometimes called the "twentieth-century Aquinas."

41. Tallon (1997): 259.

of the triad" results in a functional imbalance "in the interpersonal worlds of truth, goodness and beauty, i.e., values that take us beyond our roots as human animals toward the flower of the human spirit. . . ."[42] Scholastic thinking is not restricted to stressing the importance of intellect and truth, but includes acknowledging a kind of anthropology that focuses on the three distinct "capacities" or "faculties" of being human.

Sixth Example

In *Orthopathos: Interlocutor between Orthodoxy and Praxis* (1990), Samuel Solivan focuses on *orthopathos*, a term also used by R. DeVries, albeit differently, as indicated above. As a liberation theologian at Andover Newton Theological School, in Massachusetts, Solivan uses "pathos as a constructive epistemological resource" to emphasize the importance of "pathos as the point of departure for all theological discourse." He views "pain and suffering as an important place from which to do theology." Orthodoxy and praxis have become "polarized" and "sterile" signposts of "vested interests of a class," called "the marketplace of critical cognitive reflection in American theological institutions."[43]

Orthopathos is a "bridge between affirmations made by orthodoxy and the engagement sought by praxis." Pathos is deeper than "passion in a sexual and moral sense" or an "emotional lack of control." It points to "the ontological reality" of "suffering," a "pathetic condition," the "alienation" and "non-personhood" of those who are "poor and marginalized."[44] Such consciousness calls for an appropriating of suffering that leads to "empowerment" and "transforms 'pathos,' in its negative Greek sense of self-alienation and fatalism, into hope." It seeks "to uncover the empowering presence of God in the midst of estrangement" and attempts "to overcome the distance between faith claims that speak of peace at the expense of justice and those that speak of wholeness at the expense of love."[45]

In early Greek thought, pathos referred, pejoratively, to "the indignity of passivity," "something mysterious and frightening." To show passion was

42. Tallon (1997): 290.

43. Solivan (1990): 19; see also p. 66: "The place and nature of most North American liberation praxis has been reduced to scholarly theological forums and other arenas removed if not distant from the cultural matrix of daily suffering."

44. Solivan (1990): 20.

45. Solivan (1990): 21.

equated with being "demon-possessed," rather than with something "closely linked to the Greek concept of divine perfection in the works of Plato and Aristotle." Solivan comments as follows:

For these formative philosophers passivity was incongruent with divine dignity. The Aristotelian concept of First Cause and its accompanying dignity served as the basic assumption about divinity that led to the rejection of pathos as a constructive experience. . ... From very early times the Greeks believed that God, the Supreme Cause, could not be subject to suffering or be affected by anything other than itself. Pathos as an extension of matter was regarded by Aristotle as the passive principle of *pathetikon*. "It is the characteristic of matter to suffer, to be moved: but to move, to act, belongs to a different power."[46]

> The Platonic concept of the human soul, later developed by the Stoics, is that the soul is divided into two compartments: in the upper resides reason, in the lower compartment, emotions; the two tenants have separate ways and manners. Reason was disassociated from the passionate life and sharply contrasted with it. Emotions belonged to the animal nature in humanity and reason to the divine present in humanity. The fleshly and unruly nature of pathos was seen as a source of disaster and evil. On the other hand, reason was understood as an extension of order, light and power that served to raise humanity above the level of the animal. It was this psychological and ontological understanding of humanity that led the Greeks to exclude all emotions from the nature of the Deity.[47]

Reason, not pathos, is the norm. A wise person strives for *apatheia*, freedom from emotions. With this "Stoic ideal of Apatheia" Jewish and Christian morality has tended to "coalesce." Descartes (d. 1650) thought of "emotions and passions as disturbances of the mind," Spinoza (d. 1677) regarded emotions as "confused ideas," and Kant (d. 1804) considered passions as being "without exception evil."[48] In response to this classical Western way of thinking, Solivan writes,

---

46. Solivan (1990): 21; Solivan refers to Aristotle, especially *Nichomachean Ethics*, 1106a7, and *De Generatione*, 324b1, 335b; he quotes Philo's statement that "to act is the property of God, and this we may not ascribe to any created being; the property of the created is to suffer action." Furthermore, he observes that the "idea of God as First Cause" implied that "God was an impassive deity which, having the capacity of moving all things, was itself unmoved. Aristotle's Deity has no pathos, no needs."

47. Solivan (1990): 21.

48. Solivan (1990): 22.

The Hellenistic dichotomy of soul and body, the separation of reason from emotion, is a view foreign to the biblical writers. The Old Testament Scriptures do not share the view that passions are disturbances or weaknesses of the soul, much less the premise that passion itself is evil. For the Hebrew mind the heart was the place of both reason and feeling. The source of evil is not passion or emotion, but rather hardness of heart, callousness and insensitivity. For the biblical writers there is no disparagement of emotion, no celebration of apathy, as with the Stoics. The biblical writers are keenly aware of the importance of pathos in religious experience. A good example of this is the pathetic characteristics of "rua[c]h."[49]

Solivan ends his study of faith by stressing, in a Western way, the importance of human "experience" in addition to humans being rational in their thinking and moral in their actions. Conservative and liberal Christians concentrated more on orthodoxy and orthopraxis than on orthopathos. By ignoring or minimizing the "pathetic circumstances and experiences of the community," orthodoxy and orthopraxis lost the "balance between that which we claim and that which we do as a community." This gave rise to a false conflict between thinking and doing.

As Hispanic Americans we have learned to be binocular in a monocular world and learned to hear in stereo in a monophonic world, the monolingual U.S. . . .. To do theology as an Hispanic American is to think with your heart and feel with your mind. Even as we are the interlocutors between the cultures of affluence and poverty, so we too seek to stand on the boundaries between orthodoxy, calling them both to mutual critique for the benefit of all suffering peoples and as a sign of God's reign among us.[50]

The impact of the Platonic-Aristotelian notion of faculty psychology on Western ideas about being human, about the structure of society, and about the role of faith and nature of theology has been enormous. Today, there is a growing conflict between a prosperous and dominating Northern region in the world and a poor and dominated Southern region. Solivan seeks to address this major problem by using the thought-pattern of faculty psychol-

---

49. Solivan (1990): 22. "*Rua[c]h*" can mean "air in motion," "breath," "wind," "vain things," "spirit," "mind," and "pathos, passion, or emotion" (cf. Hosea 9:7). See Solivan (1990): 22–23.

50. Solivan (1990): 24. For details about what is laudable and questionable about this way of thinking, see Chapter 13 below.

ogy, particularly the importance of feeling and passion. His awareness of the important role of (Christian) higher education in our society and culture, his analysis of reactionary movements throughout history, and his stress on the role of theologians and preachers are significant. The limitations of his fundamentally still scholastic anthropology prevent him from providing a more radical and wholesome way of responding to our troubled world.

Difficulties

Western philosophy and theology are typically tied to an anthropology based on a Greek tripartite faculty psychology. To question the validity of this anthropology is not strange or inappropriate. In fact, not to do this is being short-sighted, even odd. To perpetuate a Platonic and a slightly altered Aristotelian mind-set of a higher soul with three inbuilt capacities, in distinction from a lower body, in our thinking about human faith life and in our study of theology is to limit—and, worse, to undermine—true self-knowledge and genuine insight.

Fundamental questions need to be raised about this kind of (philosophical) anthropology in Western history and culture. Why is the triangular principle of "intellect, volition and sense," or "thinking, willing and feeling," inviolable?[51] Is it unique to Western thinking, or is it universal? Must we think in terms of, for example, "philosophy, ethics and aesthetics," "theory, action and purpose," "what is cognitive, moral and hermeneutic"? Why are these distinctions correlated with the human body parts of "head, hand and heart"? Does a three-pronged anthropology provide true self-knowledge?

The idea of a tripartite soul (psyche) has also resulted in numerous philosophical and anthropological problems for human faith life and the study of theology. Concerning the nature and encyclopedic role of theology in any educational and academic curriculum, faculty psychology has given rise to

---

51. It is hard to establish the exact meaning of these three terms. In general, it can be said that each term is defined in relation to the other two terms. For example, (i) unlike will and feelings, *intellect* refers to the ability to reason, understand and perceive relations and differences, form judgments and draw conclusions; (ii) unlike intellect and feelings, *will* refers to the power of deliberate action, choice, self-direction and control. Being other than having insight, wish, desire, longing, disposition, or inclination, will follows the dictates of the intellect by making a firm resolve and acting on that resolve; and (iii) unlike intellect and will, *feeling* has to do with perception through some physical sensation, resulting in emotion, sentiment, impression, passion, discriminating taste, having a conviction, or heart, for something.

questions about six issues: (i) the meaning of the terms used; (ii) the nature of good and evil and the role of philosophy and logic; (iii) natural theology and apologetics; (iv) the relation between philosophy and faith;(v) the danger of synthesis-thinking; and (vi) the limitations of the concept of the tripartite soul.

First, my pastor's comment in a catechism class several decades ago that Christians are not only "thinking, willing and feeling" creatures," but also "spiritual," raises questions about what is meant by "three capacities," "soul" and the relationship between them. Given the three "psychic" faculties, is there room in the soul for something "spiritual"? Are the three faculties and the "spiritual" complementary? Is the spiritual an addition, something supra-natural? What is the meaning of "soul" and "faculty" in Greek and Western thinking?[52]

Second, implied in any faculty psychology is a questionable, and even unbiblical, view of good and evil. It assumes that the human intellect can know truth and guide the other two human abilities of the soul. Only when both will and feelings obey the truth(s) of the intellect can humans live a good, or virtuous, life. Evil arises when the human will and passions refuse to be guided by the truth(s) of the intellect. The distinction between "good and evil" is disassociated from the religious direction of the soul[53] and equated with something structural within the human psyche.The "good-evil" distinction applies to the faculties of willing and feeling. Focused on truth and error, the intellect is able to correct the good-evil problem in willing and feeling through clearer and better thinking. The good-evil distinction does not apply to philosophy, logic and epistemology—at least not the way they do to will (ethics) and emotions or passions (religion, aesthetics). The Greek idea of truth and evil differs radically from what Scripture reveals about them. The biblical conflict between covenant-keeping and covenant-breaking is not

---

52. *Facultas* is an ability, power, or means of mind, or body, to perform, or do, anything. It applies primarily to mental processes. This Aristotelian use of "power" (*dynamis*) must be distinguished from: (i) "power" in the medieval sense of a branch of learning, or knowledge, particularly in a university setting, and a certain group of teachers of a special art or body of sciences taught; and (ii) powers in the more modern use of "liberal arts," or academic subjects, in distinction from professional, or technical, skills and topics.

53. "Directional" is used here in the sense of life-permeating and -encompassing religious response, in the core of our being, to God's total revelation. Unlike structural distinctions, inherent in the fabric of human existence, the good-evil distinction is not original, but the effect of humans rejecting God's revelation. The good creation is both structurally and directionally good since it points to the Creator.

synonymous with any (non-Christian) Greek faculty psychology concerned with morality (will) and religion (passion), good and bad values, or virtue and vice.

Traditional philosophy, especially the two sub-disciplines of "epistemology" and "logic," tried to avoid, or transcend, what Scripture reveals about the religious difference between obedience and disobedience. A philosophy based on intellect or reason tries to isolate itself from any uncertain opinions. Philosophy does not need religious renewal[54]—after all, philosophy is philosophy, logic is logic and truth is truth.

Third, given its interest in, and access to, truth, in scholastic circles, philosophy, when properly engaged in, is universal in its validity, objective in its foundation, and certain in its conclusions. Until the rise of diverse postmodern forms of knowledge, philosophy provided a reliable basis for other disciplines and derived forms of knowledge.

Not surprisingly, Western traditions in theology and in Christian academic institutions demonstrated a strong predilection for two fundamental beliefs: (i) in addition to their primary interest in revealed theology, a growing passion for (so-called) natural theology, with its Aristotelian/Thomistic emphasis on the first principles of philosophy,[55] and (ii) a need for an apologetics made possible by a common grace that provides a base for different faith traditions and belief systems.[56]

Fourth, given the religious difference and conflict between Greek faculty psychology and Scripture's view of what it means to be human, it is not surprising that the relation between traditional philosophy and Christian thinking has generally been one of suspicion, neglect, or some combination of both. The encyclopedic relation between philosophy and theology has mostly been one of total neglect, subtle compromise or even open conflict.

This ambivalent situation has resulted in many problems, usually with

54. In a public lecture in 1932, which he delivered as the Rector of the Free University, Vollenhoven talked about the need to develop a distinctly "Christian logic." This suggestion was truly radical and offensive, even to Christian professors and preachers. Cf. Vollenhoven (1932).

55. See *Metaphysics*, 1026a10–30. Because it deals with "being *qua* being," or "immovable substance," theology (also known as "first philosophy") is, in terms of its role and scope, a universal science that precedes all other disciplines. According to Aristotle, the essence of all true knowledge is intellectual.

56. In an interview, more than three decades ago, for a position (for which I had not applied) in apologetics at a reputable theological seminary, the **first** question centered on defining "logic" and "truth." I described four forms of logic: Inductive, Deductive, Hegelian and Abductive. The first two forms they liked, but not the last two forms, ostensibly because they were too historical and uncertain.

various significant professional, institutional, curricular, pedagogical and personal implications. Non-Christian philosophy emphasized that natural philosophy must be engaged, if not against biblical faith and theology, then at least apart from it. Christian theology stressed that, unlike natural theology, revealed theology calls for a way of thinking that is independent of both traditional philosophy and anthropology.[57]

Fifth, the harmful effects of a faculty-psychology-based anthropology on the way one thinks about human faith life are evident in many practical and theoretical ways. Theological thinking influenced by Thomist philosophy tends to talk about three features of Christian faith: knowledge (*cognitio*), assent (*assensus*) and trust (*fiducia*). In scholastic Reformed/Presbyterian circles, it is not uncommon to think about God's will and providence in terms of an Aristotelian idea of causality and without doing justice to human responsibility.

Western Protestants often experienced the enfeebling effects of conflicts about which faculty of the soul is primary and determines behavior, including that of faith life. Disagreement about this resulted in much confusion about a faith life centered on the intellect, morality or emotions—and even conflicts between objective doctrines, free will decisions and subjective or pietistic faith experiences, respectively.[58]

Sixth, an anthropology that is based on faculty psychology generally ascribes primacy to the intellect at the center of the soul. Such a self-reliant center actually has no need for a spirituality which permeates and guides all things. Sensing that something was missing in such an intellect-guided faculty psychology, Christians generally rejected such a compromising rational and liberal anthropology, unless, of course, it left some room for a compromise or, better, opted for a truly radical alternative.

In his essay "The Primacy of the Intellect: Greek or Christian?" and "The Primacy of the Intellect: A Tenable Concept?", Anthony A. Hoekema[59]

---

57. See in this connection the relation between philosophy and theology in North American culture, which assumes that, unlike public philosophy, theology is private, equated with "faith" and "religion" and without a right to public funding. For details, see Chapter 2 above.

58. In *Drie kleine vossen* [Three little foxes, 1901], Abraham Kuyper used Song of Songs 2:15 ("Catch for us the foxes, the little foxes that ruin the vineyards, our vineyards that are in bloom") to write about the three dangers of intellectualism, mysticism and activism. In 1961, Henry J. Stob published several articles about three dangers that he called "Minds," for *The Banner*, the denominational journal of the CRC in North America (for details, see Chapter 16 below).

59. Anthony Hoekema (1913–1988) was professor of theology at Calvin College and, for many years, professor of Systematic Theology at Calvin Theological Seminary.

opposed isolating any of the soul's three faculties, and focused on their unity. He warned against the dangers of deifying the intellect, minimizing sin, and allowing any rivalry among the soul's three distinct faculties.[60] He sensed that faculty psychology fostered unsettling problems in faith life of Christians, but was unable to get at the cause of the problem, i.e., Platonic-Aristotelian anthropology with its three-pronged faculty psychology (of thinking, willing and feeling). Hoekema was correct in what he opposed, as is clear from his refusal to locate the secret of being human in the intellect, or some other capacity, of the human soul (psyche). Instead, human life is directed by what Scripture calls "heart."[61] Regretfully, he did not (or perhaps could not) at that time explain what this entails.

In 1954, my pastor was correct in warning me, a catechumen at the time, about the danger of a philosophy that ignores what is "spiritual." He was wrong, however, in allowing a foreign element to influence his own anthropology and theology with his scholastic understanding of two things: (1) the difference between what is human and what is Christian and (2) the distinction between faith life and theology. We need so urgently to have a view of faith life and theology that avoids an anthropology with a faculty psychology. This calls for an anthropology that acknowledges the mystery of knowing God and oneself, daily walking with Him in one's heart in all one's human behavior, also in one's faith life and study of it.[62] Helpful in this respect are the insights of Dooyeweerd and Vollenhoven about four basic structures of created reality. So we turn now to chapters 7 and 8.

---

60. For example, Antonio Damasio's critique of Descartes's one-sided stress on intellect, to the detriment of senses and feelings. For details, see Damasio (1994).

61. See Hoekema (1956b).

62. Regarding the correlation of self-knowledge and God-knowledge, see Calvin, *Institutes*, I.1.i-iii. For details about the need for redefinition and reorientation, see chapters 10–17 below.

PART II

REFORM(UL)ATION

CHAPTER SEVEN

Herman Dooyeweerd
(1894–1977)

To write about H. Dooyeweerd, a student at the Free University in jurisprudence, not theology, who, beginning six years after A. Kuyper's death,
taught jurisprudence at his *alma mater* for thirty-nine years, may come as a
surprise to anyone interested in "faith" and "theology."

After becoming familiar with the depth and scope of what Dooyeweerd
proposed and opposed, I realized that not only "philosophy" but also "theology" can do much harm to one's faith life, also in the tradition of "Reformed"
faith. Having audited his introductory class lectures, discussed basic issues
with him in class and at home, I sensed that where J. Calvin left off as a major
ecclesiastical reformer, four centuries later Dooyeweerd (and Vollenhoven)
picked up the baton as a major integrally Christian philosopher in modern
culture.

The intent of his biblically directed anthropology and its importance
for the structure of society and direction of culture, and the scope of his
philosophical rethinking of created reality and all its disciplines, especially
"theology," will be the main focus of this chapter. To sense what is involved
without losing our way in all kinds of philosophical issues, we will focus
on these issues: (1) background, (2) conflict, (3) meaning, time and law, (4)
anthropology, (5) faith life, and (6) "revelation," "human" and "faith."

Background

Nurtured in the tradition of J. Calvin, J. Althusius, G. Groen van Prinsterer, A. Kuyper, H. Bavinck and others,[1] Dooyeweerd sensed early in his life that being Christian calls for constant renewal in one's life. He saw the need for, and importance of, covenant-living with fellow humans in a troubled society and culture. Badly needed was self-effacing love that enabled persons to live with, and for, others, in a spirit of genuine freedom and justice. He was convinced of the liberating power of God's Word for humans entangled in *structurally* complex socio-economic and political difficulties in a changing industrial culture.

From 1926 to 1965, Dooyeweerd taught jurisprudence at the Free University in Amsterdam. Contrary to a misconception, especially in North American evangelical circles, Dooyeweerd was neither a preacher nor a theologian. On this score, he differed from Kuyper, Bavinck and Vollenhoven. Influenced by his parents and friends, he was fascinated by Kuyper's deep and broad vision and passion for *religious* and *structural* renewal of society and culture.

His initial interest as a student at the Free University in art and music soon made way for a passion to probe *philosophical* issues related to historical and systematic problems in justice and legal theory. In his doctoral dissertation on issues related to Dutch cabinet and state law, he learned how Christians should, and should not, behave as citizens and legislators.[2]

As a civil servant in the Dutch Labor Department in 1916, Dooyeweerd prepared legal briefs and proposals on pressing problems triggered by the Industrial Revolution, particularly its *direct* impact on labor, industry and economic issues and its *indirect* influence on people's health, role of family and place of organized faith, or church, life. Two years later, he published a major study on the nature of, and relations between, municipal monopolies, national hygiene and industrial freedom.

1. For example, J. Woltjer (1849–1917), G. Geesink (1854–1929) and P. Fabius (1851–1931). About views of Woltjer and Geesink, see Klapwijk (1980a): 542–546.

2. When Kuyper was Prime Minister of the Netherlands (1901–1905), Dooyeweerd was 7–11 years old. It is noteworthy that John Calvin also studied jurisprudence, not theology, and that in his doctoral dissertation he focused on the complicated issue of a supreme ruler's relation to law when showing mercy to someone who is guilty, a problem he dealt with later as a refugee, pastor/preacher of fellow refugees, and author of the *Institutes of the Christian Religion*. Near the end of the *Institutes*, he wrote something that caught Dooyeweerd's close attention: *"Civil authority is a calling, not only holy and lawful before God, but also the most sacred and by far the most honorable of all callings in the whole life of mortal men"* (IV, xx, 4.).

At a national annual meeting of legal theorists in 1922, he debated with G. Scholten, a nationally and internationally renowned neo-Kantian legal philosopher, on the extremely sensitive topic of "State Interference and Individual Freedom."[3] Their debate catapulted Dooyeweerd, the youngest participant at that conference, onto the national stage. In disagreeing with Scholten's idealistic neo-Kantian philosophy (cf. Marburg School), Dooyeweerd said that, if compelled to choose between the conflicting norms of the two legal systems Scholten had presented, he would decide in terms of a norm that transcends justice and ethics, viz., divine revelation which says "You shall obey God more than man."

Not unrelated to his clear and, for that day and age, courageous public stance against (neo-Kantian) Humanism at a major international conference of legal theorists and political philosophers discussing how to structure society,[4] was Dooyeweerd's appointment, later that year, as Director of the Abraham Kuyper Institute, the political think tank of the Anti-Revolutionary Party. On the condition he would be allowed to support his *practical* political work with carefully prepared *theoretical* insights into the structure of public life, he accepted his new, and daunting, appointment. Only two years after Kuyper's death in 1920, he played a strategically important role to implement Kuyper's long-standing call for Spirit-filled citizens to acknowledge Christ as the One to whom God has given all authority.[5]

In 1923, in a long article on "The Calvinistic Principle of Sphere Sovereignty," he wrote about the (Calvinist) notion of *law* as something that structures society in terms of God's Spirit-directed love in Christ as "Lord of Lords," and did so without resorting to theocratic thinking. In 1924, he published in *Anti-Revolutionaire Staatkunde*, the Journal of the Anti-Revolutionary Party, his detailed study about an integrally Christian view

---

3. A problem central to the conflict in the USA in 2013 between ultra right-wing, individualistic-libertarian "Tea Party" Republicans *and* other Republicans, Democrats and Independents.

4. An issue that continued to play a pivotal role, especially in Western countries, and that has been responded to in generally conflicting ways resulting in subtle, at times overt, forms of injustice in education, race, gender, taxation, forms of democracy, and such theories as capitalism, socialism and communism.

5. For a summary of the *redemptive* thrust of the *cultural mandate*, see Matthew 28:20. It starts with, but is not exhausted by, Christian *mission* endeavors. North American examples, after the 1980s, of a similar approach to *citizenship* are the Center for Public Justice, Washington, DC, USA, and Citizens for Public Justice, Ottawa, Canada. For details, see www.cpjustice.org/.

of jurisprudence and the need for a Calvinist worldview in terms of a "cos-monomic philosophy" of created reality.

In this pioneering work, he benefited, positively and negatively, from the contributions of his predecessors, including professors. He both deepened their correct views and criticized their misguided views. His passion for *ongoing* reformation of public life compelled him to rethink centuries-old assumptions and beliefs in Western culture, including many basic ideas in his own tradition.

As a practical and probing political pioneer, Dooyeweerd reflected on a wide range of basic terms and realities. These centered not only, or primarily, on such customary topics as faith, religion, kingdom of God, church, love, grace and redemption. They included also, and especially, such terms as "truth," "subject," "object," "meaning," "law," "human," "creature," "relation," "society," "history," "culture," "time" and "analogy." Unlike, usually in con-flict with, the central thrust of Western thinking, he thought about God's revelation, revealed in his law(s), and tried to do so in a covenant-centered, non-speculative, manner about the nature of created reality and the unique role of humans in it.

In his attempt to affirm what is good and avoid what is bad, he tried to stand on the shoulders of his reforming predecessors. His desire was to challenge present and future leaders to lay claim to God's promises for them as citizens in public life and for their theorizing about such life. This pas-sion motivated him as professor of jurisprudence for thirty-nine years at the Free University.[6] Especially in two courses, namely, "Encyclopedia" and "Philosophy of Jurisprudence,"[7] he developed his covenant-centered holistic thinking about "created reality" and concretely applied it in both *legal* and *political* reflection.[8]

6. During 1958–1960, I audited one of his philosophical classes, and until 1964, usually with other foreign students, met with him at his home to talk about issues related to ongoing reformation in Europe and the world.

7. A third area of his expertise was Ancient Dutch Law. His inaugural lecture (75 pages, half of which are endnotes) was about "The Meaning of the Law-Idea for Jurisprudence and Ancient Dutch Law."

8. Recipients of doctoral degrees under his supervision: (i) F. Hommes, his successor; (ii) J. P. A. Mekkes (1898–1987),a high-ranking military officer, confidant of Queen Wilhelmina, mentor of H. Rookmaker, who after World War II mentored F. A. Shaeffer in aesthetics; (iii) Sjoerd Gerbrandy, son of P. S. Gerbrandy, Dutch prime minister exiled to England during World War II; (iv) B. J. Zylstra (1934–1986), professor of jurisprudence and president of Insti-tute for Christian Studies (ICS), Toronto; (v) J. P. Balkenende, Dutch prime minister (2002–2010), whose cabinet was sometimes called "the Dooyeweerd Cabinet." For Dooyeweerd's

Conflict

In 1926, the year in which he was inaugurated at the Free University, Dooyeweerd published in a national philosophical journal a provocative article titled "Calvinisme contra neo-Kantianisme." In this article, he elaborated on issues he had raised four years earlier in his public disagreement with G. Scholten and his supporters. For this biblically directed article, Dooyeweerd incurred the anger of many scholastic *theologians* in his own ecclesiastical Reformed tradition. They disliked his criticism of their uncritical support of neo-Kantian ideas and of their perpetuating scholastic "methods," or ways, of thinking in theology.

They appreciated his generally positive response to Kuyper's meditations and popular lectures, notably his famous Princeton Stone Lectures on Calvinism in 1898. What really irritated them was Dooyeweerd's endorsement of Kuyper's attempt to *dethrone* "theology" by questioning its traditional role in the faith life of Christians and its prominent, or queenly, role in Christian higher education. This opposition, at times even anger, if not outrage, of theologians against the views of Dooyeweerd (and Vollenhoven) climaxed, a decade later, in 1936.

In 1935, Dooyeweerd had published *Wijsbegeerte der Wetsidee*, I-III (*Philosophy of the Law-Idea*) and, one year later, he started *Philosophia Reformata*, an academic quarterly of "Calvinistic philosophy."[9] That same year, Valentine Hepp (1879–1950), successor of H. Bavinck after the latter's death in 1921, who was a rigid and adamant scholastic professor of theology, published a series of pamphlets, called "Threatening Deformation" (*Dreigende Deformatie*), in which he fiercely attacked the "reformational" views of both Dooyeweerd and Vollenhoven.[10]

That same year, the Synod of the Gereformeerde Kerken dealt with the

views, see Dooyeweerd (1953–1958, 1960, 1979, 1986); H. Evan Runner: Chapter 19 below; Bernard Zylstra (1968); James W. Skillen (1974); John Witte, Jr. (2006). For details, see Free University, Amsterdam, and "Dooyeweerd Center" at Redeemer University College, Ancaster, Ontario, Canada.

9. After World War II, the term "Calvinistic" was replaced with "Christian."

10. Hepp's anti-Kuyperian and anti-reformational thinking affected various Christian Reformed theologians, pastors and educators in the USA. In 1937, a Dutch pastor published *Philosophia Deformata* to oppose D. Vollenhoven's anthropology and Christology. Its English translation was endorsed by Rev. Steen and Dr. William Masselink in Grand Rapids. See Chapter 15 below for the criticism of Foppe ten Hoor at Calvin Theological Seminary and for the eleven editorials of Lester De Koster, editor of *The Banner* (official journal of the Christian Reformed Church in North America) in 1973–1974.

public accusation of several pastors and theologians about Dooyeweerd's and Vollenhoven's rejection of scholastic, particularly dualistic, understanding of "soul" and "body."[11] In his response to this open attack of some theologians and their many supporters, Dooyeweerd described in some detail his agreement and disagreement with Kuyper's ideas in two articles, viz., "What cosmonomic philosophy owes Dr. A. Kuyper" (*Wat cosmonomische wijsbegeerte te danken heeft aan Dr. A. Kuyper*)[12] and "Kuyper's theory of science" (*Kuyper's wetenschapsleer*).[13]

At stake in these two articles is something that compelled Dooyeweerd to study a feature in traditional Reformed thinking, teaching and scholarship that reflected a *religious* compromise with unbiblical thinking and a way of living that undermined *Christian* thinking in especially philosophy, anthropology and theology.

The negative, often mean-spirited, response of obstinate theologians deepened Dooyeweerd's belief that the discipline and role of "theology," as understood in Reformed circles, must be rethought with respect to such issues as theology's field of study, its relation to philosophy and all other academic disciplines, the nature of knowledge and science (*wetenschap*), the distinction between "religion" and "faith life," and, last but not least, the meaning of God's revelation.

The reorientation Dooyeweerd (and Vollenhoven) proposed involves a view of "faith" and "theology" that presupposes an integrally Christian view of "reality" and "being human." Such a view calls for a reform(ul)ation of central issues in at least the three major disciplines of ontology, anthropology and epistemology. A biblically directed worldview provides a better, more holistic, awareness of at least three things: (a) the *structure* of faith life and the contours of the discipline associated with it, (b) the *religious* conflict within faith life and between various faith traditions, and (c) the role of a distinct faith-related hermeneutics related to manifestations of God's kingdom in society, culture and history.

One of the crucial insights of Kuyper and Bavinck, which Dooyeweerd (and Vollenhoven) endorsed, was that human life precedes human theory and that, by implication, faith life precedes theology. The distinction between "concrete" and "abstract" knowing is not one of degree, but of kind. While faith life is essentially "confessional," i.e., practical, theology is essentially

---

11. The Synod dismissed all the accusations and exonerated the accused.
12. In *De Reformatie*, 1937.
13. In *Philosophia Reformata* (1931) 4:4, 193–232.

"analytical," i.e., abstract. To distinguish between these two kinds of activities does not suggest they are unrelated, but it highlights their distinctive character.[14]

Ambiguity about this epistemic problem in Roman Catholic and Protestant scholastic thinking Dooyeweerd rejected already as a graduate student in jurisprudence and as a civil servant in the political Kuyper Institute. To misconstrue the distinction between "practical" and "academic" life stymies a holistic view of created reality and the place of humans in it. Instead of fully acknowledging the complexity, even mystery, of God's revelation, theologians have tended to incorporate questionable ways of thinking, with good intentions, but disrupting consequences, and have actually restricted their witness as Christians in a world searching for meaning.[15]

Meaning, Time and Law

Dooyeweerd's *Wijsbegeerte der Wetsidee* (*WdW*), I-III (1935) was published in English, and somewhat expanded form, as *A New Critique of Theoretical Thought* (*NC*), I-IV (1953, 1955, 1957, 1958.)[16] With increasing clarity after his publication of *WdW* in 1935, he focused on five elemental philosophical themes and their interrelationships: (i) transcendental critique, (ii) cosmic time and modalities, (iii) entities and individuality structures, (iv) "enkaptic" interlacements, and (v) distinction between naive and theoretical experience. Of these five themes, especially the second, third and forth themes will be focused on in our inquiry about "faith life" and "theology."

The central and basic theme of Dooyeweerd's philosophy is succinctly expressed in the first subheading of his "Introduction" to *NC*: "Meaning is

14. Not to acknowledge the distinction between these two ways of knowing is typical of Scottish Common Sense Philosophy. For details, see J. Vander Stelt (1978) Chapter 17 below, and especially N. Wolterstorff (2002).

15. For example, common Western distinctions between private and public, faith and reason, church and state, theology and philosophy, sacred and secular, Scripture and science.

16. I (1953): "The Necessary Presuppositions of Philosophy" (566 pp.); II (1955): "The General Theory of the Model Spheres" (598 pp.); III (1957): "The Structures of Individuality of Temporal Reality" (784 pp.); IV (1958): "Index of Subjects and Authors" (257 pp). Other writings of Dooyeweerd: *In the Twilight of Western Thought* (1960), *Roots of Western Culture, Pagan, Secular and Christian* (1979), and *A Christian Theory of Social Institutions* (1986). For studies about Dooyeweerd's ideas, see J. W. Skillen (1974): 274–447; L. Kalsbeek (1975), especially "Introduction" by B. Zylstra, 14–33; J. Van der Hoeven (1978); J. Kraay (1979, 1980); P. Steen (1983); A. Wolters (1983); H. Hart (1984); C. T. McIntire (1985); and R. D. Henderson (1994).

the mode of being of all that is created." He clarified this novel insight as follows:

This universal character of *referring* and *expressing*, which is proper to our entire created cosmos, stamps created reality as meaning, in accordance with its dependent non-self-sufficient nature. *Meaning* is the *being* of all that has been *created* and the nature even of our selfhood. It has a *religious root* and *divine origin.*[17]

For Dooyeweerd's view of "religion," "faith," "truth," "revelation" and "theology" in relation to the "meaning" of created reality, the topics J. van der Hoeven[18] focused on in his lecture at the Dooyeweerd Memorial Colloquium, at Calvin College,[19] are helpful. He focused on "reality," a central theme in Dooyeweerd's thinking. The term "created" that Dooyeweerd used in the terse statement cited above, indicates that

"meaning" is, primarily, no more than a philosophical expression of the all-preceding confession of *faith*, and of *knowledge belonging to* that faith (cf. Heb. 11:3: "It is by faith that we know that the universe was created by the Word of God, so that what can be seen was made by what cannot be seen"): . . . the term "meaning" represents a serious attempt to let the "enlightening" faith in creation have full bearing on the philosophical enterprise, in *its* inevitable and basic orientation to "totality," to reality as a whole. . . . [T]he concomitant and somewhat explanatory terms "reference" and "expression". . . point to the radical and complete *dependence* of *all* there is, in its very being. . . . Generally speaking, precluded is the idea that anything could *exist* in itself and/or could be *known* [by] itself. More specifically, notions like "substance," "essence" and . . . "subject" (or "selfhood") are abandoned, in so far as they reveal philosophical attempts to disconnect . . . something of what is constitutive of its very nature, namely, its dependence, its being-referential and expressive.[20]

17. NC, I, p.4

18. Philosophy professor at the Free University. He studied under Johannes Mekkes, who, Dooyeweerd claimed, understood, better than others, the *dynamis* of his philosophy.

19. A main reason why this Colloquium was held at Calvin College was due to H. Evan Runner (1916–2002) who had taught the views of Dooyeweerd (and Vollenhoven) at this college for thirty years (1951–1981).

20. Van der Hoeven (1978): 133.

Dooyeweerd uses "meaning" in an *ontic* sense: meaning *is* being and being *is* meaning. This equating of "meaning" and "being" leaves no room for the common Western, especially Anglo-Saxon, philosophy that "meaning" is primarily semantic, something humans *ascribe* to things and events, i.e., statements about things which *in* and *of* themselves are not meaning. According to Dooyeweerd, "All that has been created" is "referential-to and expressive-of the Creator-God."[21] Like Luther and Calvin, he rejected the claim of medieval philosophy and theology that "being," or "existence," can be "predicated both of God and of created reality," on the condition this is done "analogically."[22]

While for J. van der Hoeven "meaning" can be considered the **first** "door" to Dooyeweerd's radical philosophy, "time" may be viewed as the **second** "door" to his way of thinking. Both "meaning" and "temporality" are fundamental characteristics of "created reality." According to van der Hoeven (a Dooyeweerd scholar and professor of philosophy at the Free University) "meaning" refers to "the uniqueness and sameness of God's creative power" and "time" to "the track or course" of God's power in unfolding the "coherence-and-diversity" of reality. Just as a "prism" refracts sunlight into different colors, "meaning" differentiates "time" into a rich array of modes of "meaning," ways of "being," i.e., a modal diversity of temporal reality.

In terms of the "prism" metaphor, just as no one color owes its origin to any of the other colors, no one temporal aspect of meaning owes its origin to any of the other temporal aspects of meaning. All aspects of reality are irreducible and rooted in "the fullness of meaning." The various modes of meaning (being) are arranged in an order of "succession," not of "subordination" (cf. Roman Catholic hierarchy) or of "reduction" (cf. totalitarianism).[23] In addition, all modes of meaning are "forward directed" in the sense that earlier, or lower, modes are disclosed by later, or higher, ones. This disclosure reveals the dynamic nature of history, the "unfolding" of creation's "meaning," in response to God, as Creator of everything.[24]

The **third** main door to enter Dooyeweerd's philosophy (of created re-

---

21. Ibid: 135.

22. Ibid: 135–137 for details about *"analogia entis"* thinking.

23. In other words, each aspect of "created reality" is unique, necessary, indispensable and must be recognized and acknowledged, if one wants to do justice to the unity and diversity of created reality. Whereas Kuyper used the principle of "sphere sovereignty" in his view of the structure of society, Dooyeweerd (and Vollenhoven) broadened this view in two ways: (a) they talked about "aspects," not "spheres," and (b) focused on "created reality," not just "society."

24. Van der Hoeven (1978?): 140–141.

ality) is "law." While "meaning" points to "the most basic and most comprehensive characteristic" of creation and "time" indicates the "course" of
meaning disclosure, God's "law" indicates the "structuration," or structure,
of this "disclosure" and the "signs" humans follow to keep this disclosure
moving in the right "direction." This "law" for created reality is unique and
incomparable. It is God-given, not human-made. Humans cannot establish
it in any empiricist or some (neo)Kantian way. Instead, this all-encompassing
"law" is God's Word which is the condition for reality.

Of this unique "law" humans do not have any "concept," but only some
"idea." For this reason, Dooyeweerd indicated that his thinking is essentially a "philosophy of the cosmonomic *idea*." God's "law" is incomparable
to any human law, but points to a "boundary" between God's "Being" and
the "being of the created reality as 'meaning.'" To ignore this "boundary"
and try to form some human "concept" of it is to succumb to some form of
"*speculative metaphysics*."[25]

"Created reality" has two correlated sides: a "law-side" and a "subject-
side." While the "law-side" refers to "*structure*," i.e., "universality and stability," the "subject-side" points to the "*individuality* and *uniqueness*" of everything.[26] Not to see, and properly acknowledge, the correlation between the
"law-side" and "subject-side" of created reality is to succumb to a basically
autonomous, or negative, idea of "law," namely, as some rigid, restrictive or
limiting "entity" between God and created reality. Because of the correlation
between these two sides, when the "subject-side" responds improperly to the
"law-side," the latter is not removed, but asserts itself by judging the human
and, indirectly, the non-human subject-side.[27]

---

25. The distinction between "concept" and "idea" reflects Dooyeweerd's neo-Kantian
background, despite his opposition to it when he disagreed in 1922 with G. Scholten's neo-
Kantian stance, and despite the English translation in 1953 of *Wijsbegeerte der Wetsidee* being
changed to *A New Critique of Theoretical Thought*.

26. J. van der Hoeven (1978): 142–143. Dooyeweerd talks about (i) a "cosmonomic side," or
"order," with its features of "succession and simultaneity," and (ii) a "factual side," or "duration,"
which is always subjected to "order." Cf. *NC* I: 24.

27. *Ibid*: 143–144. The "ultimate judgment of the creatures has been given not to the Law,
but to Him [Jesus Christ] who fulfilled it."

Anthropology

Created reality is dependent on God as the "absolute and self-sufficient" Creator of everything. As a result, philosophy is restlessly "directed towards the totality of meaning," to God as Origin of everything. "Meaning" depends on the "central law" of this Origin, a law that "limits and determines also the center and root" of human existence.[28] Humans exist in a "status of being-universally-bound-to-time," they are all creatures in the "same temporal order." This "temporal coherence" they are able to *transcend*, however, in their "selfhood," i.e., "ego."[29]

> ... within the horizon of *cosmic* time we have no single experience of something "pre-functional," i.e., of anything that would transcend the modal diversity of the aspects. We gain this experience only in the *religious* concentration for the radix of our existence upon the absolute Origin. In this concentration we transcend cosmic time. How could man direct himself toward eternal things, if eternity were not "set in his heart"? Even the idolatrous *absolutizing* of the temporal cannot be explained in terms of the temporal horizon of human existence. For the latter nowhere provides a point of contact for an idea of the absolute, unless it be related a priori to the supra-temporal. This act of concentration presupposes a supra-temporal starting-point in our consciousness.[30]

This "religious center of human existence" is not some Greek metaphysical idea of a "rigid and static immobility," or of a humanistic concept of something "supra-temporal." Rather, the "religious center," or "central sphere of human existence," is "in the full sense of the word a *dynamic* one." The "dramatic conflict between *civitas Dei* (city of God) and *civitas terrena* (earthly city)" takes place in this "central sphere of *occurrence*. . . ."

This "religious center" is related to the "eschatological aspect of cosmic time in faith." In faith, "cosmic time has its limiting aspect." In this mode of human experience, temporal "order" (cf. law-side) and "duration" (cf. subject-side) have a "special meaning." Because the "modal meaning of faith

28. *NC* I: 10–12.

29. *NC* I: 24.

30. *NC* I: 31 The term "pre-functional," used by Vollenhoven and others, Dooyeweerd rejects, since it places "the concentration-point of human existence *in* time" and supposes that the religious centre cannot be "supra-temporal." (*NC I*: 31). For details, see Steen (1983), and chapter 8 below.

... is by its nature related to divine revelation," one can sense only in faith something of what "is or happens beyond the limits of cosmic time."

About the implications of *faith as aspect* for *theology as discipline*, Dooyeweerd believed that theology will "always need this limiting aspect of time in which the cosmic temporal order is indissolubly connected with the revealed supra-temporal realm."[31] These implications presuppose his belief that "religion" must be distinguished from "a faith community." Although they are interrelated, they are not similar. "Religion" refers to the human "ego," to the "radical religious unity," the Origin-directed "totality of meaning of the temporal cosmos." Human *self*-knowledge depends on human *God*-knowledge. This interdependency has its "ground in the essence of religion as the central sphere of our created nature."[32] The selfhood of "reborn" Christians find its "Archimedean point," or "look-out tower," in Christ as the "new root" of humanity. Such a (re)new(ed) center enables humans to testify, in their hearts, to the "Being" of God, to the "meaning" of creation, and to "law" as boundary, in the sense of relation, between them.

Such a radical approach implies acknowledging three fundamental tenets: God's will, revealed in Christ, as the Ἀρχή of the world, the *totality* of all meaning aspects of created reality, and the supra-temporal *unity* of everything. These three tenets, in their unity, provide a religiously integrated perspective on reality. Of paramount importance in such a holistic view of reality is the ontological [not just societal] principle of "sphere sovereignty."[33] This principle does not permit equating any one modality of reality, and its distinct relationships, with any other modality of reality.[34]

Such a view of the human role in society and culture does not permit any specific organized faith community to become *religious* in the sense of all-pervasive and -determining, shaping everything in society and history. God's kingdom is reflected in the *religious* direction (*richting*) in which humans live in everything they do. Religion points to "the connection between

31. NC I: 33. Dooyeweerd comments: "In this special sense must be understood the 'days of creation,' the initial words of Genesis, the order in which regeneration *precedes* conversion etc." For details about this view of "faith" and "time" and their relation to something "supra-temporal" in the human heart, see Troost (2012): 113–118, 222–225 and 438–439.

32. NC I: 54–55.

33. Dooyeweerd accepted Kuyper's notion of "sphere sovereignty," but he deepened and broadened it. He altered it from an idea about the structure of society to a philosophy of all reality, from a *societal* to an *ontological* principle. Evangelical Christians tend to overlook this significant change.

34. NC I: 101–102; about making absolute what is creaturely relative, see 103.

the *meaning* of creation and the *Being* of the Ἀρχή." It is deeper and broader than an established faith community or tradition. The "*temporal meaning of the faith-aspect*" is, although distinct from, not the same as "*the fullness of meaning of religion.*" The latter "transcends the boundary of cosmic time and cannot possibly be enclosed in a modality of meaning."[35]

To equate "religion" with some human "faith" community eventually results in oppressing those who believe differently. Constitutionally, humans are *spiritual*. To be *religious* is not an option, choice or effect of some free will. Not to depend on, and be accountable to, the Creator is an illusion. To be "spiritual" is not an option, but a necessity for them as responsible creatures.

To be human is not restricted to, or centered in, intentional faith activities (e.g., praying, worshiping, meditating, confessing, repenting), nor to a combination of different activities (e.g., a "faculty psychology" with its focus on thinking, willing and feeling, what is true, virtuous and beautiful, or philosophy, ethics and aesthetics). Unlike this traditional (scholastic) way of thinking, Dooyeweerd distinguished between "religion" and "faith life," and associated the former with anything humans do and the latter with a distinct and specific kind of behavior.

Since all human life is essentially *religious*, there is a spiritual struggle also with the "faith life" of humans. While "religion" is total and life-encompassing, faith life is partial and restricted to a specific kind of acting or behaving. Although *organized* faith life cannot avoid the *religious* conflict, it may not be simply, even tragically, equated with the *religious* nature of all human life.

As the absolutely central sphere of human existence, religion transcends all modal aspects of temporal reality, *the aspect of faith included*. It is not at all a temporal phenomenon which manifests itself within the temporal structure of human act-life. It can be approximated only in the concentric direction of our consciousness, not in the divergent one, not as a "Gegenstand."[36]

The "inner essence" of religion is not reducible to some "human experience," as F. Schleiermacher proposed, to some "tremendum" experience of what is "Holy," as R. Otto suggested, nor to some phenomenological "emotional feeling-perception," as E. Husserl advocated. Instead, according to Dooyeweerd, it is "the *ex-sistent* condition in which the ego is bound to its true or pretended

---

35. *NC* I: 104.

36. *NC* I: 57/8. Dooyeweerd states in a note that "the direction and contents of faith are *not* to be understood *apart* from the religious ground-motive by which it is directed and from a divine Revelation, no matter whether the latter is understood in its true meaning, or misinterpreted in an apostatic sense" (emphasis added).

firm ground. Hence, the mode of being of the ego itself is of a religious character and it is nothing *in itself*. Veritable religion is absolute *self-surrender.*"[37]

While the "ego" is the religious "concentration-point" of each individual existence, the entire temporal cosmos is a religious *community*, in which every ego is inescapably bound to other egos. The unity of our existence is both individual and supra-individual. Our I-ness "*points beyond* the individual ego toward that which makes the whole of mankind spiritually *one in root* in its creation, fall and redemption." In Jesus Christ, the second Adam, our "I-ness" is "rooted in the spiritual community of mankind. It is no self-sufficient 'substance,' no 'windowless monad,' but it lives in the spiritual community of the *we*, which is directed to a Divine *Thou*, according to the original meaning of creation."[38]

After the human fall and promise of the Savior, two conflicting spirits vie for control in human life: the "dynamis" of the Holy Spirit and the "spirit of apostasy from the true God." The "first spirit," i.e, Holy Spirit, works through the "power of God's Word" incarnated in Jesus Christ. This power redirects "to its Creator the creation that had apostatized in the fall from its true Origin." It does this through what is basic to our understanding of Scripture, namely, the religious ground-motive of "*creation, fall, and redemption by Jesus Christ in the communion of the Holy Ghost.*"[39]

In contrast to the "first spirit," the second spirit is evident in Western culture and history in two religiously unbiblical ways: (i) Greek "form-matter" and humanistic "freedom-nature" ground-motives, and (ii) the ground-motive of "nature-grace," a pervasive "religious" compromise in all Roman Catholic and Protestant scholastic thinking and behaving.[40]

Despite Dooyeweerd's major reformation of central philosophical issues, H. Fernhout has indicated that Dooyeweerd's view of faith life basically resembles that of Bavinck and Kuyper.[41] This is clear from his emphasis on

37. *NC* I: 58. Dooyeweerd comments that apostate persons, who suppose this "selfhood" to be "something in itself," lose themselves in their "surrender to idols, in the absolutizing of the relative."

38. *NC* I: 60.

39. *NC* I: 61.To ignore, as is often done in Dooyeweerdian circles, "by Jesus Christ in the communion of the Holy Ghost" does injustice to Dooyeweerd's intent and contribution as a Christian philosopher.

40. For details, see *NC* I: 366–413 and II: 104–153.

41. Fernhout (1979): 119. Fernhout taught education at the Institute for Christian Studies, Toronto and was president of ICS (1989–1998) and president (1999–2012) of The King's University College in Edmonton.

a "twoness" in humans, a functioning on two levels: a "temporal" level of a *structurally* diversified functioning of the human body and a "supra-temporal" level of the *religious* depth and unity of humans.[42] In distinction from non-human creatures, the depth-unity of *humans* is not modal, structural or bodily. The quintessence of being human is not some immanence notion of totality, combination of different functions (cf. "faculty psychology"), or even faith life.[43] According to Dooyeweerd, the human "I," or religious-spiritual "center," transcends "the modal diversity of meaning."[44] In stressing the "concentric insight into the root-unity of human existence,"[45] Dooyeweerd perpetuates a questionable feature in the anthropology of H. Bavinck and A. Kuyper.[46]

This center, or "full self," of human existence is *"dynamic"* in the sense that it takes a *religious* stance which, while transcending modal diversity, determines the main *direction* of human life.[47] The source for the conflict in human history between *civitas Dei* and *civitas terrena* lies in the *religious* stance of the *self* before God, as the Origin of meaning, or before an idol or pseudo-god. God is the "religious root" of the "whole temporal cosmos." He wants to relate to this world through the human "I."

Christians respond to God, their Creator, as his image-bearing servants. Through them the real meaning of created reality must become manifest. This "higher principle in humans becomes the directive force which sets the whole of creation going." At the same time, it "serves to introduce unity in the diversity of reality, and it provides the link through which the ultimate Principle . . . steers the world."[48] Since the "I" is not structural, it is not subject to human analysis: it eludes the grip of any concept or definition.[49]

This *supra*-temporal reality is itself "subjected to a central law," with a fullness of meaning derived from the Origin of all things, which *"limits and determines the centre and root of our existence."*[50] Because of this law of God,

42. The terms "level" and "twoness," are Fernhout's, not Dooyeweerd's.

43. Fernhout (1979): 120; see Dooyeweerd 1961: 26, 39; and 1969: III, 89.

44. H. Hart suggests a "threatening dualism" in Dooyeweerd (Fernhout 1979: 121).

45. Dooyeweerd (196)1: 26, 41, to which Fernhout refers.

46. For details, see chapters 4 and 5 above. For a slightly different view of Dooyeweerd on this issue, see A. Troost (2004): 323–325.

47. Dooyeweerd *NC* I: (1961), 20; see also 32.

48. Fernhout (1979): 123. Fernhout comments that, according to J. A. L. Taljaard in *Polished Lenses* (Potchefstroom, 1976), "Dooyeweerd's view of man combines the doctrine of *analogia entis* with the monarchianistic system, so that, analogous to God, man is in effect the origin of the temporal world."

49. Dooyeweerd (1965): 181 about "nothingness."

50. Dooyeweerd (1961): 1, 1; see also 26, 44 about the power of Word revelation.

the "I," about which we have no "concept" or theoretical knowledge, has three basic relations: (a) the whole temporal world and our experience of it, (b) communication with the egos of fellow humans, and (c) the divine Origin in whose image man was created.[51] These three relations can be examined in terms of their "unbreakable mutual coherence" and dependence of the first two relations on the third one. The "religious" law for the "I" is to love God and the neighbor as oneself.

For the "I" to respond properly to this "religious" law of love, it must be gripped "by the power of God's Word revelation." Through God's Word and Spirit, humans obtain a God- and self-knowledge in a non-"scholastic" way. Although he moved in principle beyond the anthropology of Bavinck and Kuyper, Dooyeweerd still struggled to distance himself from the traditional idea that the content of what Christians believe directs the diversity of their "temporal human corporeality."

Unlike the human "I," the human "body" has four "individuality structures," three of which are "modal" (cf. "physico-chemical," "biotic" and "psychical") and one is an "act-structure." Unlike the three modal structures, which are "external," the fourth structure is "internal" in that it points to what is "intentional," to acts of the *total* person. These four individuality structures are arranged in a way that the lower ones are structurally bound to the higher ones.

Being intentional, this fourth structure acts as a "conscious superstratum," which hierarchically subordinates the "unconscious substratum" of humans. The human "act-structure" is "the immediate temporal expression of the human I-ness, which transcends the cosmic temporal order."[52] The "human act-structure" has no modality, or qualifying function, and the human "temporal body" (*lichamelijkheid*) finds its unity not in temporality but in the "I" (*ik*)."[53]

Dooyeweerd described the "human act-structure" in three basic directions,[54] terminologically reminiscent of "faculty psychology," namely, knowing, willing and imagining.[55] The human act-structure, through which the "I" relates to human bodiliness, is the means by which the whole person, consisting of "body" and "soul," becomes a unity. As to the *religious* thrust of

51. Dooyeweerd (1965): 181; also 182.

52. *NC* III: 157, 88.

53. Fernhout (1979): 125.

54. Dutch, "grondrichtingen." The three "directions" of the act-structure correspond closely to the terms "organs" and "faculties" Bavinck and Kuyper used, although Dooyeweerd distinguished these from the traditional idea of "faculties."

55. Dooyeweerd, "Theory of Man," Proposition XXI.

his thinking and its *structural* expression, Dooyeweerd seems to be clearer about the former than he is about the latter. This problem, or ambiguity, Fernhout describes as follows:

> The act-structure is thus the means by which *"dynamis"* enters man's *structural* make-up. "Through the activity of man's soul, the human body . . . received its spiritual character." Through the act-structure, the "human body is the free plastic instrument of the I-ness." The human body is thus the "field of free expression for the human spirit, i.e., for the centre of human existence." Through the act-structure the *ik* comes to express itself bodily." Man's *lichamelijkheid* [corporality] is the stage dominated, shaped and governed by his higher (central) *ik*; once again Dooyeweerd's pattern is directly parallel to that of Bavinck and Kuyper.[56]

Faith Life

Faith life, or experience, is integral to the embodied existence of humans. It indicates one way in which humans experience "creation" in their awareness of God as the Creator of the world. In Dooyeweerd's thinking, creation is "objectively" differently structured, while "subjectively" it is colored by a rich diversity of human experiences.[57] What is novel in this view is that it opposes traditional "faculty psychology" that is focused on "intellect" (scholasticism), "volition" (voluntarism) and "feeling" (subjectivism) as three "capacities" of the "soul" as a "substance."[58]

All human functions are interrelated and interdependent. Humans experience created reality in different ways: e.g., numerical, spatial, kinematic, irritative, biotic, psychic, analytic, historical, lingual, social, aesthetic, economic, jural, 'ethical' and pistic (πιστευω, have faith in, trust, rely on).[59] Comparable to other human experiences, to have faith in reflects a *religious* awareness of, and ultimate reliance on, one's heart-centered response to God's Word for creation.

Faith life, like any other kind of human life, reflects that humans are "spiritual" in their response to God's Word.[60] The secret of such "spirituality"

56. Fernhout (1979): 126, especially Dooyeweerd, Prop. XII, and 1957: III, 88.
57. For details about "objectively" and "subjectively," see chapters 8–10 below.
58. Dooyeweerd (1942): 139, Proposition 17.
59. The number and sequence of these aspects, or modes, continue to be debated.
60. Cf. Dutch "Woord en antwoord" or German "Wort und Antwort."

is not some extraordinary event or some special (supra-natural) sacramental experience. To be human is by its very nature *religious*. Everything humans do, including in their faith life, is a response to God's Word.

As a discipline, "theology" needs a different ontology and different anthropology than what Greek philosophers like Parmenides (sixth to fifth century BC), Plato (428–348/7 BC) and Aristotle (384–322 BC) advocated. It needs an understanding of created reality, including being human, that acknowledges the structural unity and diversity of humans, and does justice to faith life and role of non-human creatures. Comparable to the interest of, for example, logic in what is analytic, sociology in what is social, jurisprudence in what is jural, and biology in what is organic, the interest of "theology" is, or should be, faith life.

Such a study of "faith life" rejects the Greek idea that, unlike other disciplines, "theology" focuses on what is "meta-physical," beyond this world, something Absolute or Ultimate. At least in principle, it is liberated from the unbiblical belief that "theology" is a human study of God through impressive and endless logical probing. Instead, it centers on God's self-revelation to humans how to "walk with Him" in everything they do, also in philosophy, research and teaching future servant-leaders in all of society and culture, not just, or primarily, preachers, priests and pastors. Such an approach frees one from a unbent scholastic "theology" that thinks in terms of God's supranatural "revelation" and human's supra-natural "faith."

Dooyeweerd thought about the faith aspect of both human and non-human creatures. He distinguished between two kinds of "faith aspect" of created reality by calling the human one "subjective" and the non-human one "objective." Humans express their "faith" *actively*, or *subjectively*, in the way they live, and non-human things and events "express" their "faith" *passively*, or *objectively*, in how they influence humans in how they formulate, celebrate, share, develop, etc., what they put their trust in and believe.[61]

Like any aspect of reality, the faith aspect also is not a "thing" or ontic building block. An *aspect* is not a *what*, but a *mode*, a *how*, which in a *temporal* way expresses the *religious* stance of the human "I." Any human act, qualified by one or more human aspects, indicates something of the *totality* of one's whole life, not something of one's *soul* apart from one's *body*, as Bavinck and Kuyper, in dualistic fashion, tended to think.[62]

---

61. Sometimes Dooyeweerd tends to think of "aspects" in terms of *"substances,"* as when he talks about *fields* of expression in which concrete phenomena function. Cf. Fernhout (1979): 127.

62. And as continues to be believed by most (at least Western) Christians, also in faith

Through faith as function "the dynamic directive power of the heart" influences all "other human functions."[63] It affects the meaning disclosure of all human, and non-human, aspects of reality[64] in two directions: a "foundational" and a "transcendental" one.[65] Whereas the "foundational" direction is reflected in the "coherence of an aspect with the lower aspects on which it is founded," the "transcendental" direction is evident in those moments of an aspect which reflect higher aspects in "the cosmic order."[66] An aspect is fully opened-up when it reaches a fullness of meaning that transcends temporal diversity.[67]

This opening-up process of all aspects of created reality finds its rest in human faith as "terminal" aspect or function. Unlike all other human functions, being the last or highest temporal function, faith life cannot appeal to any higher aspect of reality to guide the opening-up process. Instead, as function or aspect, faith is guided "directly by impulses from the religious root of human existence."[68]

Like other human functions, faith life is centered in the human heart which *religiously* directs what and how one believes. In our world of sin (refusing to love and listen to God) this results in the *religious* conflict within and among humans and what influences St. Augustine to write his *civitas Dei* (city of God) and *civitas terrena* (city of the world).[69] In Dooyeweerd's thinking, faith as function "mediates" the *directive* and dynamic impulse of the human heart, and it "effectuates" the *structural* opening process of temporal reality.

The "heart" expresses itself *indirectly* in all human behavior. To do this it needs the link of *faith as function* to direct all other (temporal) human aspects or functions.[70] God's revelation directs the human heart, the impulses of the heart direct faith as a function, and this faith directs the opening

---

traditions influenced by H. Bavinck's and A. Kuyper's anthropology, as reflected in their obituaries in daily newspapers.

63. Fernhout (1979): 127–128. Fernhout indicates that it is more "than simply being that function which comes as close as possible to (explicitly) expressing the fullness of man's unity, the fullness of the root-meaning of his being, which is also operative in all his other functions."

64. *NC* II: 297.

65. This sub-section is very compact. One not familiar with Dooyeweerd's ontology may want to skip this section and return to it after chapters 8 to 10 below.

66. For Dooyeweerd, "retrocipatory" and "anticipatory moments" of that aspect.

67. *NC* II: 52.

68. *NC* II: 293.

69. *NC* II: 299; see also 294.

70. In distinction from Dooyeweerd, Vollenhoven says that "the heart is the functions

up of all other human functions. Faith as function "mediates" the *religious* heart-direction of being human and does so as the "ruling factor" in one's temporal existing before the always-present God as the Origin. As a leading function, faith is "*an original transcendental certainty, within the limits of time, related to a revelation of the Archè (Origin) which captured the heart of human existence.*"[71]

Brief Comments

In the tradition of H. Bavinck and A. Kuyper, Dooyeweerd reflected on "the nature of man and the place of faith and religion in human life." His idea of faith as a structural feature of being human is, however, more fine-tuned than Kuyper's notion of "formal faith" in human consciousness. Regarding "the integral role of faith in leading, and integrating, the diversity of life," he developed a more refined view of life-encompassing Christian faith. However, he still retained a scholastic remnant about "faith" and "religion."[72] This is evident in his understanding of "revelation," "human" and "faith" in the human opening up of created reality.

Revelation

Dooyeweerd associated the anthropological distinction between "I" and "human functions" with "two kinds of revelation," one of which is "pre-redemptive," a "directive Word" which turns "a static structural (law-ordered) creation into action." A more integral anthropology assumes a unified view of revelation—"special" revelation is not more important than "general" revelation, nor is general revelation less important than special revelation.

The *wholeness* of God's Word revelation must be recognized. The diversity of creation exists because of the "many-sided Word of God"; through "Word" God called creation into being, i.e., structured the "responsive existence" of all creatures. Central to God's Word is His love-command, as the expression of the "depth-unity" of God's will. His revelation is "*Word*

---

in unity and the functions are the heart in diversity"—in other words, human heart and functions are one.

71. Fernhout (1979): 129.

72. *Idem*.

revelation" that addresses the "whole" life of humans. In appreciation, and critique, of Dooyeweerd's idea of "revelation," Fernhout correctly says this:

> We are called to confess or believe that the Word [of God] in its centrality calls man in his heart to surrender his whole person to God so that the new life in Christ may encompass his being. In our scientific analysis, we can try to give a limited functional account of these matters. Then we see that functionally the Word of God addresses the whole man by appealing to his faith function, since the latter by nature comes functionally the closest to expressing the wholeness of man's being. On this functional level, the Word calls for man's surrender, no questions asked, and it immediately calls faith to integrate this surrender into all of functionality. But this is only a limited, one-sided analysis of the *whole* picture; man in his heart unity is immediately caught up in this process. *There is no sequential order as in Dooyeweerd's position, in which (only) the heart and the faith function are oriented to directive Word-Revelation and faith stands closer to the heart than the other functions, as if the heart has a supra-temporal spiritual reality apart from the functions.*[73]

Human

Any suggestion of a distinction between temporal and supra-temporal detracts from the wholeness, oneness or integral nature of being human. Though they are distinguishable, the "heart" and "functions" of humans are not in any way separable. In the spirit of D. Vollenhoven's anthropology, Fernhout states that "The heart is the functions in their unity, and the functions are the heart in their diversity."[74] As "depth-unity" of a person, the human "heart" is not "the sum of one's functions," nor a "phantom which cannot be integrally known."

Faith as function is "not the whole of man." Rather, it is "referential,"

---

73. Fernhout (1979): 137 (emphasis added). About Dooyeweerd's use of "faith" in the sense of pistical function, Fernhout comments: "actually this usage contributes to the problems surrounding the nature and role of this aspect. 'Faith' properly has reference to the depth-unity of man or his heart relationship with God. In this sense, all man's functions are dimensions of faith. The aspect as such could perhaps better be designated the *certitudinal aspect*, i.e., that dimension in life which calls man to surrender his being with unquestioning certainty and which calls him to make explicit the ultimate foundations of his life" Fernhout (1997): 138, note 98.

74. For details about this *biblical* anthropology, see Chapters 8–10 below.

points to "an openness in man to what is beyond his creatureliness." This "openness" does not establish a relation with something that gives *religious* "direction" to a static, structural reality. Rather, it *functionally* reveals that humans are rooted either in the true God or in some idol as ultimate validator of life. This openness "belongs to the natural constitution of man." Only when it is "received in Jesus Christ" is it "full and complete."[75]

Faith

In Dooyeweerd's view, the function of "human faith" anticipates, in the greatest degree functionally possible, "the fullness of meaning of reality." Fernhout indicates that Dooyeweerd's "referential mode" of faith makes

> functionally explicit the depth-heart dimension of man's being and its whole dependence on God, through the Word. Thus from this viewpoint, faith can serve to integrate and lead the unfolding of the fullness of meaning in other functions. Religious direction is not mediated to the other functions *via* faith: all the functions are integrally religiously directed. However, within the total context of man's directively-structured functioning, faith plays a leading and integrating role, since its task as a function is to bring out as explicitly as functionally possible Who or What man is at heart living for.[76]

Dooyeweerd's view of faith life was made possible by his anti-secular and anti-scholastic "ontological" and "anthropological" thinking, during the 1920s and 1930s, about the diversity of faith life in a restless world groping for something Ultimate. In a more radical and clearer way, Dooyeweerd's co-founder of *reformational* philosophy, D. Vollenhoven[77] stressed the need for ongoing *reformation* in all life, including "faith life." Already in 1926, he considered replacing "theology" with "pisteology," i.e., study of God *(theos)* with study of faith *(pistis).*[78]

---

75. Fernhout (1979): 138.

76. *Idem.*

77. As well as James H. Olthuis at the Institute for Christian Studies, in Toronto. As a student in ethics at the Free University in Amsterdam, he attended several philosophy classes of Vollenhoven. He supervised Fernhout's M.A. thesis on the views of Bavinck, Kuyper and Dooyeweerd about "faith" and "anthropology."

78. Dooyeweerd did not use the term "pisteology."

CHAPTER EIGHT

Dirk H. Th. Vollenhoven
(1892–1978)

D. H. Th. Vollenhoven deepened A. Kuyper's insight into the importance of "formal faith." He did so by thinking about it within the context of an integral worldview and a distinct approach to basic issues in ontology, anthropology and epistemology. He agreed with Dooyeweerd that the "object" of theology is faith as an aspect of *created reality*, but disagreed with him in certain respects in his ontology, anthropology and view of faith as an aspect of human and non-human reality.

This difference between him and Dooyeweerd will be highlighted below in terms of seven issues: his background, role as pastor and professor, interaction with A. Janse, letter to G. C. Berkouwer, some central themes in ontology and anthropology, a *religious* conflict in faith life and theology, and using "theology" in the sense of "pisteology," i.e., study (*logos*) of human faith (*pistis*).

Background

As a young man, Vollenhoven often talked with his father about various renewal movements and their implications for society and culture. Especially the sixteenth-century Reformation in Europe and the nineteenth-century Reveil (1834)[1] and Doleantie (1886)[2] in the Netherlands fascinated him. Un-

---

1. Also known as Secession (*Afscheiding*), a schism in the national Reformed Church. Partly because of opposition from the national Church, some secessionists moved to the USA and established the Christian Reformed Church in the Holland and Grand Rapids areas in Michigan.

2. The leader of this (second) renewal within the national Reformed Church was

der the influence of J. Woltjer (1849–1917), a classicist and the headmaster of a Reformed Gymnasium in Amsterdam, he developed a deep interest in Greek classical culture.[3]

As a theology student at the Free University from 1911 to 1914, Vollenhoven was, despite his aristocratic background, drawn to a form of Christian socialism and saw the need for genuine evangelism. He studied *classical culture* under J. Woltjer, *philosophy* under G. H. J. W. J. Geesink (1854–1929), and *theology* under H. Bavinck and H. H. Kuyper (1864–1945), son of A. Kuyper. He became entangled in some complex scholastic discussions, and disagreements, about the nature of Christ's "humanity" and "divinity."

As a doctoral student from 1914 to 1918, he tried to understand something of the immense complexity and confusion in modern culture, especially with respect to philosophy. To discover a modicum of clarity lacking in his instructors, he asked for, and received, permission to write his doctoral dissertation *before* completing his studies and taking his final doctoral examination.[4]

In his dissertation, titled *The Philosophy of Mathematics from a Theistic Point of View* (*De wijsbegeerte der wiskunde van theistisch standpunt*), he dealt with the views of Aristotle, Augustine, Brouwer, Descartes, Kant, Leibniz, Lotze, Meinong, Plato, Poincaré and Russell about their ideas in mathematics and speculations about God. His twenty-five rather scholastic "Theses" (Stellingen), attached to his dissertation and open for public academic debate, dealt primarily with ideas of T. Aquinas, A. Einstein, F. Schleiermacher and Lord Herbert of Shaftesbury.

In 1918, after marrying Mien Dooyeweerd, a sister of H. Dooyeweerd, Vollenhoven became a pastor in the Gereformeerde Kerk of Oostkappelle, in the southern province of Zeeland. A consequence of his moving to this small town was its proximity to Biggekerke, a hamlet where A. Janse was a teacher, and the headmaster, of a small Christian elementary school. Shortly after his move to Oostkapelle, Janse, only two years older than Vollenhoven, sent him a letter to compliment him on his dissertation. Unlike academics at the Free University, Janse had—according to Vollenhoven's comment to me in 1964, during an afternoon walk—not only carefully

A. Kuyper. Six years later, in 1892, this movement joined the Secession Church of 1834 and formed the Gereformeerde Kerk (1892–2005).

3. His fluency in Greek and Latin helped him in his later study of the roots of Western philosophy and theology.

4. He passed his comprehensive doctoral exam on July 13, defended his doctoral dissertation two months later, and received his PhD only a few days later, on September 27.

studied his dissertation, but also grasped his detailed analysis of a pressing and complex issue.

Janse's critical comments encouraged Vollenhoven to continue to focus on central philosophical, theological and related issues. He combined this with his deep interest in various practical issues in Christian circles and society at large, which he believed called for reformation. Janse asked Vollenhoven to help him as an elementary school teacher, and headmaster, with various modern pedagogical ideas and practices. In his response, as a rookie pastor, only twenty-six years old, Vollenhoven gave a series of seminars on both Christian systematic philosophy and the anthropological and cultural ideas of H. Poincaré, H. Bergson, A. Einstein and the renowned Marburg School of neo-Kantian philosophy.

In order to study philosophical anthropology, Vollenhoven left Oostkapelle in 1920—the year A. Kuyper died and one year before H. Bavinck died—to study under Felix Krüger, in Leipzig, the evolutionistic ideas of Henri Bergson, Max Wundt and William James.

Pastor and Professor

After his post-doctoral studies in Germany, he served as preacher and pastor for five years in the Gereformeerde Kerk in The Hague. During this period, he had close contacts with his brother-in-law, H. Dooyeweerd, who had become Director of the Abraham Kuyper Institute in The Hague, about mainly the general relation between philosophy and science and about certain special disciplines. With increasing clarity, these two thinkers sensed the "philosophical" importance of the notion of irreducible life-zones and of Kuyper's interest in the unique authority of each life-zone and institution in society. Combining with this a notion already hinted at in his dissertation, Vollenhoven applied Kuyper's principle of *societal* "sphere sovereignty" with his own idea of an *ontic* diversity in the six sub-historical dimensions of the world, viz., the numerical, spatial, physical, biotic, psychic and analytical aspects.[5]

During his five years in The Hague, he lectured on Saturday evenings for a group of Christian high school teachers on general, and some specific, anthropological and pedagogical ideas in N. Hartmann, E. Husserl, K. Barth

---

5. Dooyeweerd focused on such *supra-analytical* disciplines as linguistics, history, sociology, economics, aesthetics, jurisprudence, ethics, and theology.

and A. Janse. During that time, the Gereformeerde Kerk was troubled about the views of Rev. J. B. Netelenbos (1879–1934) regarding three issues: (a) Scripture's "formal," but not "material," fallibility, (b) his nontraditional view of "garden," "trees" and "snake" (Genesis 2 and 3), and (c) a schism in the Gereformeerde Kerk in 1926. Although Vollenhoven agreed with Netelenbos's rejection of how "empiricist-positivist" scholastic theologians read Genesis 2 and 3, he opposed the alternative view of Netelenbos.[6]

This sad ecclesiastical and theological episode deepened Vollenhoven's resolve, as pastor and restless thinker, to understand more clearly two pressing issues: first, what triggered this theological and ecclesiastical conflict about "science," "truth" and "Scripture," and, second, how can the dire need for a better understanding of "reality," including "Scripture," be addressed? What dawned on him was the great need for a Scripturally directed view of "created reality," combined with an ongoing reformation in our traditional thinking, in order to at least lessen, perhaps even avoid, misleading theological conflicts and disruptive ecclesiastical schisms.

To address the first issue became one of Vollenhoven's most important goals for the rest of his life, namely, as a systematic thinker and an historian of philosophy. To respond to the second challenge, he published in 1925 a detailed study of the history of the Gereformeerde Kerk in The Hague, the capital city of Holland, from 1572 to 1816.[7]

Appointed in 1926 as professor of philosophy at the Free University, Vollenhoven dealt in his inaugural lecture with the epistemological issue of the relation between "logos" and "ratio" in Western thinking. From the very beginning of his long career at the Free University, his thinking differed significantly from traditional scholastic philosophy and from typical Western understanding of the history of philosophy. Like Dooyeweerd, he also became increasingly aware of lingering scholastic features in Kuyper's and Bavinck's philosophy and theology and in the views, and practices, of many of their national and international followers.

In the tradition of Reformed higher education since the sixteenth century, also at the Free University all *theology* students were required to take an introductory course in philosophy, including especially logic. Since he was the only philosophy professor at the Free University, he soon experienced,

---

6. Believing the church had treated Netelenbos in an unfair way, Vollenhoven defended him on *legal* grounds.

7. Vollenhoven (1925). De Gereformeerde Kerk vans-Gravenhage (1572–1833). Hague: Bootsma.

as professor of this compulsory course, opposition from traditional pastors and theologians. They disagreed with his strange, if not dangerous, *reformational* ideas. To appease disagreeing pastors and many angry theologians, he clarified his views about "logic" as a discipline (*wetenschap*) in two closely interrelated books: *De Noodzakelijkheid eener Christelijke Logica,* 1932,[8] and *Het Calvinisme en de Reformatie der Wijsbegeerte,* 1933.[9]

His severest critic was Valentine Hepp (1879–1950), who in 1922 succeeded H. Bavinck as professor of Dogmatics and Apologetics at the Free University. In 1935, he ranted against not only Vollenhoven and Dooyeweerd as philosophers, but also against K. Schilder (1890–1952), S. G. de Graaf (1889–1955)[10] and other preachers and theologians. That same year, Vollenhoven, with Dooyeweerd, founded the Association for Calvinistic Philosophy (ACP), which he served as president for twenty-eight years until his retirement as professor in 1963. In 1936, he assisted Dooyeweerd in starting *Philosophia Reformata* as the official quarterly of ACP.

His passion to reach out to students at public state universities in the Netherlands is clear from his establishing a Foundation (*Stichting*), supported by prayers and gifts of academic and non-academic Christians, to enable reformational professors to teach courses in distinct Christian philosophy at all public and reputable Dutch universities.[11]

His initial plan to write several volumes about the history of philosophy did not materialize. Only the first volume, focused on Greek philosophy, was published in 1950. In this publication, he developed his unique "problem-historical method," with its many remarkable and insightful, sometimes almost exasperating, ways of tracing the history of basic Western thought-patterns.[12] He outlined his simplified *history* of Western philosophy in his

8. *The Necessity of a Christian Logic.* H. J. Fernhout, a philosophy student at Dordt College in 1969—later President of ICS in Toronto and The Kings University College in Edmonton—told our class that his father had taken this required philosophy course at the Free University. To complement this study, Vollenhoven published *Hoofdlijnen der Logica* (*Outlines of Logic*) in 1948. For an extensive MA dissertation (538 pp.) about the logic of Vollenhoven, see Theo van der Merwe (1958).

9. *Calvinism and the Reformation of Philosophy.*

10. De Graaf wrote *Verbondsgeschiedenis,* I-II, translated by H. Evan Runner and E. Wichers Runner, 1977–1981, as *Promise and Deliverance,* I-IV. For details, see chapter 19 below.

11. Chairs in Christian Philosophy were established at the universities of Utrecht, Leyden, Groningen and Delft, and, since the 1990s, Rotterdam, Eindhoven and Wageningen. Unlike the first four general universities, the last three specialized in, respectively, business-economics, technology and agriculture.

12. Two students who used the "problem-historical method" in their doctoral disserta-

regularly updated class syllabi,[13] and he developed his *systematic* philosophy, in his tightly formulated lectures, syllabi, articles and public speeches.[14]

Interaction with Antheunis Janse (1890–1960)

Vollenhoven's insights and demeanor as person, pastor and professor were influenced of A. Janse since 1918. Though professionally he was neither a preacher nor a scholar, Janse played a significant role in the initial development of reformational thinking.[15]

Janse, of Huguenot descent,[16] was born in Oostkapelle, not far from Middelburg, where A. Kuyper lived in 1849. After his father died in 1897, Janse, only seven years old, worked, with his younger brother, on their grandfather's farm each summer, to support their poverty-stricken mother. In 1938, at age forty-eight, he described what he had learned during these early difficult, but formative, years. From a simple gardener, who led a Reformed boys club, he learned about "the Calvinistic principle of serving God in all areas of life, not just on Sundays and only in church." He saw the difference between integral Christian living and a popular "ethical, mystical, pietistic form of religion, exemplified by his Reformed pastor."[17] Unlike the simple gardener, his pastor turned his back to the "world" and proclaimed a "religion" as a way to be saved from a deeply troubled world.

His awareness of a conflict in the Christian faith community deepened

---

tions under his supervision were Runner in 1951 and Seerveld in 1958. In his tribute to Vollenhoven, Seerveld stated: "You have taught us to philosophize with the sword of the Spirit. If we have not been very successful in this, it is surely not your fault." See Bril (2005), Bril/Hart/Klapwijk (1973), Wolters (1979), Kok (1998), Bril/Boonstra (2000), Kok/Tol (2005), and Sweetman (2005).

13. For details, see Bril/Boonstra (2000).

14. For details, see Tol (1978), Kok (1988), Bril/Hart/Klapwijk (1973), Kok (1992).

15. See Bennie J. van der Walt's paper "Antheunis Janse of Biggekerke (1890–1960): Morningstar of a 20th century reformation." Koers (2004) 69:2, 221–257. This paper is based on his intermittent research for thirty-five years at Potchefstroom University in South Africa and the Free University in the Netherlands. Van der Walt called for a definitive biography of Janse as an innovative Christian thinker, in order to highlight (i) the need for a general reformation at that time, (ii) his contribution to reformational thinking, (iii) specifics about his anthropology, (iv) the secret of his pioneering work, and (v) the complete list of his writings.

16. Huguenots migrated north after the cancellation in 1685 of the Edict of Nantes in France.

17. Van der Walt (2004): 3.

as he grew older. Dividing life into a "religious" and a "profane" part, and associating the former with God and the latter with humans, violates God's sovereignty. According to Scripture, "The covenant with God has to do with butting oxen and sacrifice, bird's nests and priests, clean linen of the Israelites and their worship, the workers' pay and their tithes, educating children about history and their circumcision."[18]

With only an elementary education, he enrolled in 1907 in a normal school and graduated from it in 1910 as an elementary school teacher. In 1914, he joined the military—the home guard protecting the Netherlands' neutrality during World War I—learned German and acquired many German books. In 1917, he moved to the small town of Biggekerke, in the southern province of Zeeland, where he taught and served as headmaster in a small elementary Christian school until 1942.

Janse wrote many textbooks, illustrated with his numerous drawings. He taught his young pupils that history did not begin with the Egyptians, nor with the Greeks or the Romans, but with God creating the whole world. He wrote extensively about nurture and the process of education. He taught Sunday school, led a Reformed boys club, and served as secretary of a local political committee of the Anti-Revolutionary Party, founded by G. Groen van Prinsterer and A. Kuyper.

He gained the confidence of tradition-oriented, often stubborn, farmers. His secret was his gentle demeanor, clear insight into Scripture, love for God's creation and simple but probing writings. During his weekly walks, he taught his children about distinct features of birds and plants. At the same time, he was aloof, often in his study until two o'clock in the morning, at times even until dawn. He disliked speaking evil of others, but was easily angered by those who perpetrate evil.

In 1929 he indicated in a letter that for "several reasons" he had been "praying to God for a reformation." Two years later he wrote in his diary: "Oh, Lord, remember your covenant. Dry my tears. The mourners of Zion will rejoice when your reformation comes." Seven years later, after experiencing opposition from fellow Christians, he remarked that "Not one single reformation has escaped the cross of Christ." His yearning for a reformation was prompted by his opposition to two major threats in his Christian community: "pietistic theology" and "Reformed scholasticism"—two dangers also Vollenhoven opposed in his preaching, lecturing, researching and writing.

---

18. Van der Walt (2004): 3. Politically, Janse's family supported the Anti-Revolutionary Party (ARP), established by G. Groen van Prinsterer, A. Kuyper and others.

Janse described the danger of pietistic theology in a small booklet, in 1926,[19] about Christians, symbolized by "Ingelse," a person who stresses "mystical inner enlightenment" as the way to obtain "religious certainty." Looking for peace and stability within themselves, not in Christ (Rom. 5:1), they rely on their own "religious experience" of groaning and moaning, or inner "soul-searching," for signs of the Spirit's work in them.[20] Without such signs, they stumble into doubt and uncertainty. Not throwing the anchor of their faith in God, they cast it in themselves and, as a result, "the certainty of faith eludes them."[21] Genuine self-testing requires standing before God, not oneself. Only in that way can one become aware of unbelief and sin, and lay claim to God's infallible and reliable gracious covenant promises. Christians rely on the sovereign God who both demands, and provides, the certainty of faith.

Inseparable from Janse's opposition to pietistic faith was his rejection of scholasticism in faith and theology which focuses on the certainty of sterile concepts. Despite lingering scholastic features in A. Kuyper and H. Bavinck as reformers, these men, and others like them, had urged Christians to think in a more biblically appropriate way. He disagreed with uncritical followers of Kuyper and Bavinck such as H. H. Kuyper and V. Hepp, who canonized, respectively, Kuyper and Bavinck as their predecessors, and perpetuated seventeenth-century stuffy Reformed thinking and acting.

Inherent to scholastic thinking is an uncritical acceptance of a fundamental distinction between sacred and profane, supernatural and natural, holy and secular, or grace and nature. It divides human life into a *God*-related area (e.g., religion, faith, church, theology) and a *self*-related world (e.g., reason, science, politics, philosophy). It fails to distinguish properly between human fallible theology and God's infallible Word(s) for created reality. Scholastic theology lacks both true *self*-knowledge and proper understanding of non-ecclesiastical life and non-theological studies.

In opposing scholastic thinking in theology, especially dogmatics, Janse proposed in his *Dogmatiek als wetenschap* (1939) a more limited role of theology. He rejected the possibility of reasoning one's way up to God, drawing rational conclusions from God as a concept, or developing some logical theses about God. In agreement with preachers like S. G. de Graaf and

---

19. Cf. *Lourens Ingelse: een episode uit het geestelijk leven op Walcheren omstreeks 1788* (*Lourens Ingelse: an episode in the spiritual life of Walcheren district, 1788*).

20. E.g., How is my faith? Am I truly sincere? Am I really aware of my sins?

21. Van der Walt (2004): 6.

K. Sietsma, theologians like S. Greijdanus and K. Schilder, and philosophers like Vollenhoven and Dooyeweerd, he focused on God's living Word, not abstract statements about God.

Already at the age of thirteen, Janse had read *Het echt menselijke: hoe het is gezocht en waar het is te vinden*, written by P. Biesterveld, professor of both philosophy at the Theological Seminary in Kampen and practical theology at the Free University in Amsterdam.[22] In 1919, he responded to Vollenhoven's dissertation with a twenty-one page letter filled with perceptive observations and a number of pertinent questions about fundamental issues.[23] Before most Dutch ministers and theologians publicly discussed the views of K. Barth,[24] Janse published in 1929 "Karl Barth en de waarheid" and, six years later, in *Vox Theologia*, "De Nominalistische Tendens in de Kirchliche Dogmatik."[25]

He worked with Vollenhoven to establish the Association for Calvinistic Philosophy, with Dooyeweerd by publishing an article in *Philosophia Reformata*, and by offering throughout the Netherlands popular courses in "reformational philosophy," sometimes with as many as eighty persons in a course. In 1937/8, he published several semi-popular articles on "Calvinistic Philosophy" in *De School met de Bijbel*, a journal for Christian elementary schools.[26]

His impact on elemental assumptions in reformational thinking and its initial public exposure was remarkable. He addressed the need for a biblically directed view of being human, i.e., anthropology, at the same time Vollenhoven and Dooyeweerd did. Before Janse became familiar with the views of these two reforming thinkers, K. J. Popma—who sometimes has been called a co-founder of reformational philosophy—had close contacts

---

22. *The truly human: how it is sought and where it is found*. He read it six times and underlined it heavily—cf. van der Walt (2004): 9. Because a large part of Janse's huge library was sold and the rest was divided among his children, it is difficult to trace in detail his thought development.

23. In 1918, Janse and Vollenhoven wrote "The Activity of the Soul in the Teaching of Mathematics" (De activiteit der ziel in het rekenonderwijs) for *Paedagogisch tijdschrift voor het Christelijk Onderwijs*. See van der Walt (2004): 10. For details about the relationship between Vollenhoven and Janse, see the extensive Vollenhoven and Janse archives at the Free University in Amsterdam.

24. In 1923, he read Barth's *Römerbrief* (3rd print, 1924) and in 1928, *Kirchliche Dogmatik*, I, 1927. Cf. van der Walt (2004): 9.

25. For further details, see A. Janse on Karl Barth (1987).

26. These articles were published as *Inleiding in the Calvinistische filosofie* (1992) by Buijten & Schipperheijn in Amsterdam.

with Janse, especially with respect to Popma's unusual gift for avoiding the lure of scholastic anthropology.

In appreciation of Janse's significant role during the 1920s and 1930s, Vollenhoven wrote after Janse's death in 1960: "No one could let the old treasures of the Word, freed from all scholastic dust, sparkle in the way Janse could for those who still, or again, wanted to live by the Scriptures as he did."[27] As a prophetic reformer, he made God's Word come alive for his day and age. He used his remarkable gift to discern the spirits of the age that influenced not only pedagogy but also, for example, theology, politics and philosophy.

Regular contact between Janse and Vollenhoven stopped after Germany invaded the Netherlands in 1940.[28] The last time they met was around 1950 chiefly for social reasons to talk about Janse's worsening Parkinson's disease. Before his own death in 1978, and while he was very ill, Vollenhoven read again some of Janse's writings about what it means to be human, and commented that Janse's anthropology was correct.[29]

Assessing Janse's role in the origin of "reformational" thinking, Bennie J. van der Walt, a philosopher in South Africa, suggested that it might be more appropriate to think of a "joint leadership of three persons," not two persons, viz., Dooyeweerd and Vollenhoven, at the beginning of reformational thinking. Janse's unique contribution was his emphasis on "the *basic religious principles* of the Amsterdam Philosophy" which Vollenhoven and Dooyeweerd developed "further in a scholarly fashion."[30]

27. Van der Walt (2004): 8.

28. During World War II: (i) for political reasons, they could not correspond openly, (ii) since 1940, they disagreed about how to react to the German regime in the Netherlands, (iii) because of the effects of Parkinson's disease on him since 1939, Janse had difficulty writing and, eventually, could not speak and move anymore, and (iv) Janse joined K. Schilder in splitting the Gereformeerde Kerk in 1944, while Vollenhoven pleaded with Schilder *not* to split the church. Janse did not really collaborate with Germany. Already in 1932, he rejected the ideology of Fascism and Hitler's National Socialism in Germany and that of Mussolini's in Italy. Despite this critical stance, he refused to participate in the Dutch Resistance Movement against the German invaders, but complied with the pro-German National Social Movement in the Netherlands. For this ambivalent stance, Vollenhoven and Dooyeweerd objected in 1943 to Janse's re-election to the Board of the Society for Calvinistic Philosophy and the Dutch people imprisoned Janse from October 31, 1944, until January 23, 1945. For details about this tragic episode in Janse's life, see Stellingwerff (1992): 155–156 and van der Walt (2004): 24.

29. Cf. van der Walt (2004): 12, who obtained this information from K. A. Bril, a Vollenhoven expert (Bril 1982: 113).

30. Van der Walt (2004): 12. I agree that Janse played a crucial role in establishing "reformational philosophy" but do not believe this warrants thinking of him as a "co-founder"

According to B. J. van der Walt, the significance of Janse's work lies chiefly in its "prophetic character" and emphasis on a "Biblically oriented, pre-scientific worldview." As the movement became "more systematic and schematic," this "prophetic character slipped somewhat into the background." Perhaps, Janse may not have been completely at ease with (what he may have perceived to be) a shift from a prophetic to a more systematic approach. At least, his Parkinson's disease made it impossible for him to continue any participation in the movement after the war.[31]

Janse's bibliography as a reforming teacher and educator for two decades includes ten books, numerous brochures, five hundred articles, a large number of unpublished lectures and speeches, hundreds of letters and his personal diaries. The range of issues he addressed varied all the way from education, pedagogy and psychology, to catechism, history of Reformed faith, Bible studies, dogmatics, theology, and anthropology in light of Scripture, and to a few special issues in politics and philosophy.[32]

For his passion "to live his faith intensely in all areas of life," he was "honored and insulted, knighted and kicked, loved and hated."[33] What im-

---

of this movement. He was a remarkable encourager of this new endeavor of reformational philosophy, but did so in a primarily practical and non-theoretical way. Not just Vollenhoven and Dooyeweerd but also J. P. A. Mekkes, K. J. Popma, H. Van Riessen, H. Rookmaaker, and others resisted the German invasion of the Netherlands.

31. Van der Walt (2004): 12. In North America, H. Evan Runner combined this *prophetic* spirit of Janse with a scholarly interest in the philosophies of Vollenhoven and Dooyeweerd (see chapter 18 below about Runner). At the International Conference of Reformational Philosophy, at the Free University, on August 16–19, 2011, on "The Future of Creation Order" Chris Gousmett, from New Zealand, led a seminar on "Researching all that is 'under the sun.' Creation order, the limits of science and the error of speculation in the thought of Antheunis Janse." I acknowledge my deep appreciation to Frans van Deursen, a Dutch Bible commentator in the tradition of C. Vonk, whose successor he became when the latter died and whose views are reflected in *The True Story of the Whole World, finding your place in the biblical drama*, by Craig G. Bartholomew and Michael W. Goheen (2004, Baker Academic) and available at Faith Alive Christian Resources of the Christian Reformed Church in North America. F. van Deursen gave me in 2003, in Barneveld, the Netherlands, several of Janse's books for my perusal and study.

32. See van der Walt (2004): 13–14. Most important for his anthropology are *De mens als "levende ziel"* (Man as "Living Soul"), (1934), and *Van idolen en schepselen* (Of Idols and Creatures), (1938). For his view of "theology," see his *Dogmatiek als wetenschap en hare wijsgerige motieven* (Dogmatics as science and its philosophical motives), (1939).

33. Van der Walt (2004): 19. Queen Wilhelmina of the Netherlands knighted Janse as a Companion of the Order of Orange-Nassau, he was nominated for a professorship in pedagogy, and he influenced such (Dutch) preachers as B. Holwerda, J. J. Jager, C. Veenhof, G. Visee and C. Vonk.

pressed Vollenhoven about Janse (before 1940) was his insight into the unity and diversity of life, notably the basic thrust of Scripture with respect to, for example, God being sovereign over all of life, His covenant-relation with all human creatures, and the need for Christians to discern the spirits of the age.

Letter to G. C. Berkouwer[34]

In 1928, two years after becoming a pastor, Vollenhoven thought of the study of theology in a way that resembled the way of Dooyeweerd and Janse. This is evident in what he wrote in a letter to G. C. Berkouwer (1903–1994), a young pastor who, eighteen years later, in 1945 was appointed as professor of Dogmatics at the Free University.

In a letter dated October 14, 1927, Berkouwer wrote Vollenhoven—only one year after he became professor of philosophy at the Free University—about six pressing issues: (a) Creator-creature relationship, (b) theology of Karl Barth, (c) Word-incarnate, (d) image of God, (e) meaning of "analogy" and (f) Scripture. In his reply, Vollenhoven raised an issue he considered to be basic and about which Berkouwer had *not* asked him, namely, "What is theology?"

In raising this all-important question, he indicated that fundamental to Berkouwer's six issues was not a problem about "faith" but about the "discipline" (*wetenschap*) of "faith." Vollenhoven commented as follows:

> But the central issue lies much deeper . . . I will gladly share with you my *tentative* opinion, although that should remain between us. Starting with the boundary between God and cosmos: it lies in the law. I see things presently as follows. Science is limited to the cosmos. There is only one truth and, hence, also only one science. Without the fall [science] would have been practiced in an undistorted manner, but now [it] is practiced in a distorted [way]. The difference among people of science is whether or not they recognize this distortion.

Against this background and in terms of his view of the "Creator-creature relationship" and the implied idea of "science," Vollenhoven wrote the following about this "discipline":

34. From 1962 to 1964, as an administrative assistant of Vollenhoven and as a doctoral student in dogmatics under Berkouwer, I discussed several times with both mentors their view of "faith" and "theology."

188

Now, especially, "theology," i.e., pisteology. Indeed, it is impossible that it deals only with Scripture. It has to investigate the phenomena within that sphere; therefore, certainly also "experience," albeit exclusively as normed and norm-acknowledging or *norm-rejecting experience*.[35]

The implications of these compressed observations will be explained later in this chapter and the following three chapters. Vollenhoven's response to Berkouwer's inquiry may seem to be abstract, somewhat strange, if not esoteric. Does replacing "theology," or "study of God," with "pisteology," or study of human faith, not undermine, perhaps eliminate, what for centuries was thought to be unique about the "sacred discipline" of "theology"? Does this not indicate an unbiblical humanistic shift from God to man, revelation to projection, absolute to relative, what is "objective" to what is "subjective"? Does it not open the floodgate to epistemic skepticism, historicism or subjectivism?

One discovers, however, that Vollenhoven's suggestion, already in 1927, to Berkouwer to think of "theology" in terms of "pisteology," is not really subversive, but actually indicative of a (potentially) significant liberating reform(ul)ation of two things: human "faith life" and the classic "discipline," "study" or "science" of it. It does not undermine our knowledge of God, but deepens our awareness of the depth and scope of God's powerful and many-faceted forms of revelation. By implication, it *broadens* the different ways in which humans can hear, and respond to, God's Word not only in their faith life but also in all their ways of living in God's presence (*coram Deo*). It enhances the ability of humans to "walk with God" in whatever they do as His Spirit-filled children, who follow Christ Jesus, the "Son of God and Son of man."

A benefit of thinking about "theology" in terms of "pisteology" is that it enables one to see that *structurally* humans cannot, even if they try, live without faith, and that *religiously* they express their faith in radically different, even conflicting, directions (as will be indicated in Chapter 11 below). It provides a clearer understanding of a similarity and a dissimilarity in Christian and non-Christian faith life. It clarifies our understanding of such common terms as, for example, "religion," "belief," "Christian," "non-Christian,"

---

35. Emphasis added. I am indebted to A. M. Wolters, retired professor at Redeemer University College in Ancaster, Ontario, Canada, for giving me a copy of Vollenhoven's letter to Berkouwer. He had found it in a book of Berkouwer in a second-hand bookshop in the center of Amsterdam. I thank Anthony Tol, a Vollenhoven scholar, familiar with his handwriting, for deciphering his letter to Berkouwer.

"theology," "spirituality" and "worship." Furthermore, it refuses to restrict "religion" to only a part of life, and it distinguishes between "faith" probed analytically and "faith" actually lived and not subject to logical scrutiny.

Finally, and most importantly, "faith" and "theology" will, in principle, be freed from miseries resulting from speculative "theology" influenced by a Greek-tainted, intellect-based, and science-centered view of "truth." Such freedom opens the door to a new way of reflecting on the structure of faith life and the related discipline of (theology as) "pisteology."

Ontology

Vollenhoven's understanding of human "faith life" and the discipline of "pisteology" is closely related to his ontology, or theory of created reality, and its three kinds of laws: (a) God's diverse "structural" laws, (b) His one central *religious* law of love, and (c) "positive" laws of humans in their response to both (a) and (b). As to God's central *religious* law of love, Vollenhoven and Dooyeweerd were in complete agreement. As to the other two meanings of "law," he disagreed with Dooyeweerd in a significant way and developed his own view.

Vollenhoven's path as philosopher and historian of Western philosophy differed from Dooyeweerd's path—as professor in jurisprudence, not philosophy—about chiefly three things: (i) "meaning," "time" and "law," (ii) critique of I. Kant's theoretical thought, and (iii) notion of *four* "religious ground-motives" in Western philosophy. As gifted encyclopedic thinkers, both Vollenhoven and Dooyeweerd were united in their passion to develop a distinct Christian philosophy not about God but about created reality, especially the place of humans in it.

For almost fifty years, they deepened and broadened the tradition of reformers like J. Calvin, A. Kuyper, H. Bavinck and others. In practical and academic ways, they stressed the importance of, for example, love, structure of reality, justice and peace. To oppose deceit and destruction, Christians must reject idolatries, i.e., violations of God's creation resulting from misguided ideologies and human perversions in society.[36] Life-distorting world-

36. "Ongoing reformation" (*doorgaande reformatie*) motivated the Association for Calvinistic Philosophy and its quarterly *Philosophia Reformata*. Their aim was not to encourage integral Christian living only in academic endeavors, especially philosophy, but also in Christian living in, for example, being farmers, laborers, gardeners, school teachers, doctors, veterinarians, business people, politicians, parents and artists.

views signal the presence of a "pseudo-god," an "ism" (an exaggeration of the term to which it is attached), e.g., socialism, communism, individualism, capitalism, intellectualism, fideism, emotionalism, scholasticism.

For a clearer view of the *religious* difference between what is ultimately positive or negative, salutary or damaging, good or evil, Vollenhoven's ontology is insightful and practical. Central to his scripturally guided worldview and philosophy of reality is his notion of three kinds of "law": God's many *structural* laws, His one *religious* law, and numerous human *positive* laws.

Structural Laws

Being subject to, and dependent on, God the Creator, humans have no choice about living as humans in His presence. The intent of God's creative Words and one basic love-command is for humans to acknowledge Him as their Maker and respond to His central love-commandment. His *originating* Words provide the *structural* conditions for humans to be, to function, to respond. Such responses call for humans to acknowledge they are God's vice-regents in His creation.

God's creating Words do not have an ontological status, but are the conditions for, or source of, all creatures, including humans. In their daily life, humans sense there is a diversity in God's Words not just for faith life in isolation from the rest of life (e.g., business, academy, government, recreation, industry, banking, communication). In all of these areas, humans sense something of who God is, and do so in terms of the boundaries of what God did as Creator and expects humans to do as his image-bearers.

Against the backdrop of His *structural* laws for humans, God calls humans to honor Him in everything they do without abstractly speculating about Him. His creative Words are the conditions for the ways in which He reveals himself and for humans to experience His presence. The latter is possible only because His revelation to humans is unique: it is *religious*, i.e., directed at the core, or *heart*, of all human behavior, not just some isolated faith-facet of life. Humans are accountable to their Creator[37] for their responsibilities to fellow humans and other creatures as true care-takers and care-givers.

---

37. This "awareness" can vary greatly, even be denied, but it cannot be replaced, despite the claims of some radical atheists, whose "conscience" is seared because they "suppress the truth in unrighteousness" (Romans 1:18).

God reveals himself in *structurally* different ways to persons, communities, traditions, cultures and generations. In response to the "mystery" of human rebellion against their Maker, God responded in a *positive* way through his mercy-filled love for those who take hold of His promises, and a *negative* way by resisting those who reject His grace-filled love demonstrated in the crucified and risen One.

This life-granting and -assuring Word is the secret of God's covenant faithfulness to His care-takers of the world. In essence, this relation does not, at least not in principle, leave room for intentional compromises in one's walk with God, also, perhaps especially, in speculative thinking. Through his creative Word, God established contact with all His creatures, particularly his human "image-bearers," by virtue of who He is and who they are as his creatures.

Religious Law

God's different *structural* laws for creation are presupposed in His single *religious* law for humans to love Him above all and to love their neighbors as they love themselves. This indicates *how* they respond to Him in all their tasks. Their *humanness* is evident in how they manifest their love for God, fellow humans and even non-humans.

To respond to God's law of love is not an option, but a necessity, i.e., a command. Humans cannot not respond; they have to respond to God's life-giving and -sustaining laws.[38] The issue is whether they do so gratefully or reluctantly, in compliance or defiance. Unlike the *structural* laws, the *religious* law centers on loving him wholeheartedly, i.e., with one's total being. It focuses on one's *spirituality*, or *direction* of the human *heart* in everything we do privately and publicly. It is not focused on only a part of human life. It does not permit a dualism in "how" they live, i.e., the *religious* thrust of everything they do, including, for example, their legislating, farming, banking, eating, relaxing, educating and policing.

Humans are constitutionally *spiritual*. God wants them to be his covenant-people, who know He is faithful to his Word for creation and that they live under the rainbow of His promises. Such knowledge is not some "supernatural" addition to what is natural. Biblically directed thinking rejects

---

38. Cf. "Wort" and "Antwort" (*Woord* and *Antwoord*). For details, see Chapter 5 above, A. Kuyper (1893): II, 294–299.

the worldviews, and implied ways of living and thinking, of both a "pietistic" world-*flight* and a "scholastic" world-*compromise*.

To equate any *structural* law with the *religious* law would be a major mistake. No *structural* law has the depth and scope of the *religious* law. To equate *religious* law with any *structural* law gives rise—as indicated above in this chapter—to an "idol," another "ism." The *structural* laws and the one *religious* law are universal and unchanging.[39] They are the necessary conditions for humans to live in different places, times and cultures. Despite the immense diversity in habits, customs and traditions, the basic human condition is in each instance the same. Humans are responding and responsible creatures, always dependent on God's Word, incarnated in the Christ and revealed through the Spirit. Their fame is to honor and obey that Word; their infamy is to resist and oppose it.

Human responses to God's diverse *structural* laws and His one *religious* law are not sequential, nor separated, but simultaneous and interrelated. Humans cannot observe the former without the latter, or separate, for example, worship and work, Sunday and other days, faith and reason, or vertical and horizontal. Being human cannot be equated with, for example, only acts of feeling, imagining, socializing, interacting or thinking. It always involves revealing somehow one's ultimate trust in what one believes to be most important in life and death. To place one's trust in something ultimate is not a luxury but a necessity, not tangential but essential; ultimately, it is either God or some idol.[40]

Positive Laws

As already mentioned, for humans to respond to God's central law to love Him, their fellow humans and themselves is not an option, but a necessity. Humans are not things, but persons. Unique about them is that their *freedom* is grounded in God's covenant with them and in their living always, and everywhere, in His holy presence. Their secret is living according to God's law of love.

In responding to God's diverse *structural* laws and one *religious* law,

---

39. This does not entail a deistic worldview, but indicates God's faithfulness to his Word for the world he created.

40. Cf. Psalm 115:3–8 and Isaiah 2:8 and 40:18–20 about tempting and deadly idols served and imposed on fellow humans.

humans develop many rules and regulations, or so-called "positive laws," for themselves and others. These human laws are either positive or negative, prescriptive or prohibitive. They indicate what humans perceive God's impinging revelation to be or call for. When these perceptions become routine, they acquire a certain authority, develop into diverse faith traditions, each articulating its own faith content, and establishing its laws that may shape an entire community, culture and civilization.

Cumulatively, *positive laws* indicate assumptions about their (in)sensitivity to God's laws for them and the world. They are human "responses" within, and to, God's created reality. They are *structurally* either correct or incorrect, i.e., appropriate or inappropriate, and *religiously* either obedient or disobedient, compliant or defiant, or some combination of both.[41] They express what a community, tradition or culture believes to be good or bad.

The distinction between human *positive* laws and God's *structural* laws is important and must be upheld. It rejects both "ultra-liberalism," which denies the unchanging character of God's laws for created reality, and "hyper-conservatism," which ignores the changing character of human responses to God's revelation by claiming that earlier human responses to God's revelation are unchangeable.

Walking with God in a covenantal way is a privilege and a challenge, both wonderful and unsettling. It involves being loved by God also in one's innovative ways to explore His dynamic revelation. It does not permit one's faith to fossilize and *religiously* lose its power and vibrancy. Such a daily walk with God—also in philosophy and theology—is not possible without sensing a *religious* tension within the *positive laws* of humans and discovering what needs to be maintained and improved in a loving and wise way.

Religious Conflict

The conflict between "good" and "evil" is evident in the *positive* laws of humans, not in God's *structural* laws and *religious* law of love.[42] Its origin is inscrutable and its nature radical. There is no ordinary solution for it. It is not

---

41. This includes angels, including *fallen* angels, led by Satan and his cohorts, for whom there is no redemption. Knowledge about them is possible only through concrete faith life, not abstract speculations.

42. See Genesis 3:14–24, especially 15 and 20. According to Calvin, our present situation is neither "white" nor "black" but "gray"; the real issue is which one of these two is dominant: "light" or "darkness"? (Romans 7:14–25).

explainable in terms of some social struggle, Hegelian dialectic, economic clash or political conflict.[43] There is no *structural* law for it. God's Word is against it. Its result is a fierce battle between shalom-directed order and chaos-fostering disorder in the hearts of humans in their societies, cultures and civilizations.[44]

Due to the *negative* responses of humans to God's Word for created reality, the *religious* struggle has affected all the *positive* laws of humans in two ways. First, as a result of human trespass of God's *structural* laws and one *religious* law (of love), the *positive laws* humans make for themselves and others in every zone of life and era in history are skewed, no longer fully consonant with God's law(s). Insofar as the latter are ignored or distorted, these positive laws are no longer a blessing for human and, indirectly, non-human creatures.

Second, *positive laws* are also affected by constantly changing personal, cultural and historical situations. Since they are inherently subject to change, it is wrong to simply equate human laws with God's laws. Such equating is misleading, detrimental, potentially disastrous, and, unless terminated, even fatal. What humans have done in the past or are doing presently may not, and cannot, simply be equated with God's will. When this distinction is ignored, humans start to walk in their *own* light, i.e., with their own concocted idols or pseudo-gods. Such *religious* foolishness is an invitation for demonic forces to cause indescribable misery for human and, indirectly, non-human creatures.[45]

The depth and scope of the *religious* conflict between good and evil is not confined to what is spiritual, in distinction from what is secular. It is radical in a life-encompassing way. Since it is centered in the human *heart*, it affects everything humans do in terms of commission and omission. It shapes society, directs a culture and determines the course of a civilization. It is evident in the pain caused by subtle and overt subjugation, audible in those who mourn the loss of life caused by hunger and war, and palpable in those who cry for justice.

---

43. Although his background was aristocratic, already as a student Vollenhoven was deeply troubled about the plight of the poor; during the mid-1930s, he opposed German National Socialism and, after the 1950s, rejected the ideology of apartheid in South Africa.

44. For details, see Chapter 11 below.

45. E.g., the evils of medieval Roman Catholic crusades; millions of Germans, Italians and other Christians shouting, while saluting, "Heil Hitler!" communists in Russia and Eastern Europe; terrorists in Islamic countries; nations and cultures practicing civil-religion; capitalists genuflecting at the altar of mammon.

Because positive laws are made under the influence of deceptive spirits, humans continue to experience the *religious* conflict about what it means to be human. By their very nature, *positive* laws need constant updating. The famous phrase "to be reformed is to be always reforming (*reformata semper reformanda est*)" is applicable to *all* of life, not just one's *faith life*. The *religious* struggle between genuine gratitude and arrogant ingratitude for God's life-giving and -sustaining laws is not original in the sense that God willed it. Rather, as J. Calvin said, this clash is "fortuitous," an unavoidable result of humans rejecting God's will, i.e., law of love.

This all-pervasive *religious* conflict may not be equated with an *encyclopedic* relation between, for example, theology and philosophy, theology and anthropology, or theology and psychology. Nor may it be understood in terms of an *epistemic* distinction between what is objective and subjective, factual and fictional, conceptual and mythical, or literal and metaphorical.

The radical collision between humans rejoicing in God's life-sustaining laws and humans desiring to be a law to themselves by creating their own gods, or "isms," is enigmatic or incomparable. Since it is *religious*, it is profoundly *spiritual* and eminently *practical*. It manifests a radical turnaround to something that is (supposedly) Ultimate and does not require any *intellect*-based theological apologetics. This clash is not explainable in terms of some Platonic or Aristotelian anthropology with its focus on speculative "thinking, willing, feeling" as key to understand both faith life and the discipline of (sacred) theology. The *religious* antithesis[46] is the ultimate conflict in the fundamental direction of human behavior, also in their faith life (*pistis*) and study of it (*pisteology*).

Speculative Theology?

Numerous problems have arisen in traditional encyclopedic reflection about anthropology, theology and their interrelationships. According to Vollenhoven (and Dooyeweerd), there has been a tendency indigenous to Western thinking to conflate the *religious* difference between what is *God*-centered and *human*-centered with the *structural* distinction between the two disciplines of "theology" and "anthropology."[47]

46. Used here in the sense of disobedience to God's will for humans, not in the sense of some Aristotelian logic, Hegelian history, Marxist socio-economics and Smith's employer-worker rivalry.

47. Used here in the sense of *philosophical* anthropology, not in the sense of scholastic "psychology" or "cultural" anthropology.

Such a distorted view of *faith* life and being *human* is incompatible with the biblical view of always living in God's presence (*coram Deo*). It fails to acknowledge that, like all other human studies, "theology" also is a human attempt to understand something that is *structurally* within, not above or beyond, created reality. Like all other academics, theologians act *analytically*, i.e., within the boundaries of being human.

All theology presupposes knowing something about what it means to be human. It involves the discipline of (philosophical) anthropology.[48] It does not have a privilege over other disciplines, including philosophy, to speak about God to humans. On the contrary, all disciplines, including theology, speak in specific ways about human creatures to God. To the extent theology ignores, or minimizes, the importance of anthropology, it will inevitably continue to be shortsighted, introverted, for a while impressive but culturally irrelevant.

If, however, "theology" is understood in sense of "pisteology," then it is no longer irrelevant for anthropology, tangential to a curriculum, something sacred or foreign, an appendix to a "liberal arts" curriculum, a prerequisite for especially (elementary, secondary and tertiary) education and for Christian scholarship.[49] To stress the importance of anthropology for theology does not undermine, or threaten, theology. On the contrary, to ignore it creates problems for theology. Anthropology does not secularize theology, nor does theology make anthropology Christian. What threatens theology is a wrong ontology, a misleading anthropology and a skewed epistemology. The idea that the "object" of theology is unique, i.e., distinct from all other disciplines, inasmuch as it studies "God," "revelation" or "religion" is, in Vollenhoven's thinking, not helpful, but misguided and misleading.

First, in a *structural* sense, the Creator is not a created reality. In every discipline, not only in theology, God is honored, not studied, listened to, not projected; obeyed, not analyzed; worshiped, not dissected; honored, not a concept (of "Being"). He is the Origin of reality, including faith life and analytic life. Through the mystery of the Anointed One and the power of the Spirit, to know this God in one's heart is an amazing privilege.

48. For details, see Chapter 6 above about "Faculty Psychology."

49. From pre-school to elementary, secondary and tertiary education. Historically, the role of theology was associated with the role of organized churches in these three levels of Christian education, and sometimes even graduate education. For details about the Roman Catholic view, see James Tunstead Burtchaell, C.S.C., *The Dying of the Light: The Disengagement of Colleges and Universities from their Christian Churches*, 1998, especially pages ix–xvi and 819–851.

God is not some epistemic cornerstone, an hypothesis for intellectual inquiry, an axiom for linguistic clarification. He is not subject to created reality. As the Ultimate *source for,* and *of,* everything, God is faithful to his Word(s), and wants to be acknowledged in all human activities.

Second, the belief that biblical revelation is the "object" of what theology studies assumes that "reality" is essentially "natural" and studied in non-theological disciplines. The view that the "object" of theology is *Scripture* and one's personal *faith* life, reflects the scholastic notion that "theology" is indispensable for all human behavior and claims for itself the task of directing all non-theological scholarship.

Third, the notion that "religion" constitutes the "object" of theology is not really helpful. Religion is not just a name (nominalism), a "phase" in history (positivism), or a higher part of human life (scholasticism), but points to the heart-centered direction of humans. It does not point to only one "aspect" of being human or behaving. Nor is it restricted to an organized faith community and institution with full-time skilled leaders, programs and budgets. "Religion" is not optional, some addition to one's life, something personal and private. On the contrary, it refers to what is "spiritual," i.e., to the heart-centered direction of what humans do in their life in society and culture.

Vollenhoven rejected the scholastic thought that "God," "revelation," "religion," "faith," "salvation," "church," etc., constitute the "object" of the study of theology. He believed that *formally* "theology" is comparable to any other human discipline. It is impossible to be human without some faith life (*pistical*) that enables humans to do what they do as humans.

Structurally, or formally, "theology" resembles other disciplines such as mathematics, physics, biology, psychology, logic, linguistics, history, sociology, aesthetics, economics, jurisprudence and ethics. All disciplines, and their sub- and cross-disciplines, develop their methods and objectives on what is *structurally* available and analytically accessible.

No study or discipline can escape God's diverse *structural* laws and one *religious* law of love. With *faith life* as its "object," theology, in the sense of pisteology, will not be equated or confused with any other discipline or some combination of disciplines.[50] To ignore this violates the integrity of both theology and the non-theological discipline(s) affected by it.

---

50. For example, "normative," or soft, disciplines, in contrast to anormative, or hard, sciences, as well as disciplines in history and ethics, in distinction from studies in mathematics and technology.

Theology as "Pisteology"

Vollenhoven's suggestion in his letter to G. C. Berkouwer in 1928 to replace the term "theology" with "pisteology" was truly insightful, if not brilliant. As a *doctoral* student in philosophy with Vollenhoven and in theology with Berkouwer in 1963 and 1964, I discussed with them the nature and role of theology and the importance of philosophy for theology, especially dogmatics. These issues influenced me in teaching, for three decades, several middle- and upper-level courses in the Theology and Philosophy Departments, particularly with respect to an increasing ambiguity about the nature of "theology" in our rapidly shrinking "glocal" world.

Christians and non-Christians alike cannot avoid dealing with all kinds of human faith issues the moment they reflect on the personal and necessary, or individual and universal, conditions for, and expressions of, their faith life. Specific features of faith life vary from one faith tradition to another. *Christian* faith communities and traditions reflect in their *acts, contents* and *symbols,* or *metaphors,* that they acknowledge, through Christ Jesus and the Spirit, God as the Creator of the world.[51] This, in turn, shapes their praying, worshiping, catechizing, celebrating the sacraments, interpreting the Scripture, counseling as pastors, reaching out as evangelists, interacting with fellow believers and dialoguing with non-Christian faith traditions. It affects their budgets, judicial arrangements, secretarial and custodial help, pedagogical principles, and social interactions appropriate to a specific faith community.

The wide range of issues to be dealt with in Christian, as well as non-Christian, study of faith life (pisteology) is immense, intricate and volatile. In financially poor and politically precarious situations, faith life tends to deepen and flourish. In financially affluent and educationally well-developed settings, it tends to become outwardly impressive and formal. In times of sudden changes, complex race relations, crises in personal communication, socio-economic struggles, subtle and brutal persecutions, the essence and scope of issues to be dealt with in faith life and "theological" beliefs and education has grown at a breathtaking, if not bewildering, way.

In an encyclopedic, curricular and pedagogical way, to think of "theol-

---

51. In distinction from *covenant living*, kingdom service, practicing justice, making peace, being environmentally sensitive, etc., as life-encompassing expressions of practical Christian living, the *faith life* of humans studied and taught in (Christian) "pisteology" is intentionally aimed at enhancing such responses and avoiding irrelevant speculations.

ogy" in terms of "pisteology" opens the way for a more, not less, scriptural awareness of what *faith life,* and study of it, actually involves. Traditionally, "theology" differed from other disciplines in that it centered on the relation between human life and God's revelation in Scripture and Jesus Christ, as celebrated in certain rituals of organized religion. Such dualism in living and thinking does injustice to the power and scope of God's News for a fascinating, but deeply troubling, world.

To replace *scholastic* "theology" with "pisteology" is one way to react to a growing Western secularism and a stubborn fossilized scholastic thinking. It provides new vistas on our rapidly changing and shrinking world, filled with Christian and non-Christian faiths,[52] to understand each other better and to experience the power of God's Word and Spirit in the crucified and risen One.

Sidebar: Rise and Nature of "Rationalism"

The waning of the *religious* ardor of the sixteenth-century Reformation and the rise of Humanism, Renaissance and Secularism during the Age of Adventure resulted in new forms of *religious* synthesis. Protestants like P. Melanchthon, T. Beza and G. Voetius used certain Platonic and Aristotelian ideas in their theological reflections about Christian faith. That faith lost some of its credibility as a result of many ecclesiastical conflicts, theological squabbles and much creedal confusion. The focus at that restless time in European history shifted to the need to know reality, master nature and develop more certainty by means of new tools of knowing.

From 1600 to 1900, Western culture, especially in its way of thinking, stressed the nature and role of reason. Philosophers directed their attention to epistemic matters related to knowledge, especially the method and scope of reasoning and theorizing. Western thought shifted toward issues in ontology, anthropology and epistemology. Influenced by Greek-Roman thinking, Hellenistic culture stressed the importance of *logos, ratio,* mind, intellect, debating, laws and the nature of human experience. Universal notions, logical concepts, intellectual principles, and *a priori* knowledge in the minds of humans constitute the conditions for human experience and the ground for epistemic certainty.

---

52. The issues and terms mentioned in this chapter focus more on Christian than on non-Christian faith traditions. For Buddhism, Hinduism, Mormonism, Judaism, Islamism, Confucianism, Animism, etc. other topics and terms are more appropriate.

T. Reid's philosophy was shaped by the *religious* spirit of Rationalism. Although ultimate certainty lies in God's revelation, not in human reasoning as such, in a neo-Platonic way Christians placed *a priori ideas* and *numbers* not only in the background in some subservient way, but in the foreground in some God-centered theological way. The collapse of Medieval Scholasticism, the rise of both Humanism and Renaissance, and the limited effect of the Protestant Reformation compelled culturally forceful thinkers to develop a more reliable view of reality with respect to the human ability to know.

In response to a proliferating and debilitating skepticism, and encouraged by the rise of Humanism and Renaissance, a way of thinking arose that opted for a Hellenistic Platonizing focus on universal ideas. Rationalist anthropology curbs uncertainty by stressing certainty and order. Reason, or intellect, provides reliable knowledge about reality and human experience, for example, in *a priori* ideas about Hellenistic virtue and mathematics, medieval *concepts of logic,* and modern *laws of sensation* in the human intellect. Viewing ontology in terms of anthropology is prominent in *modern* thinking, and to think of anthropology in terms of epistemology. In adding *a priori* laws to the mind of humans, Rationalism overestimated human mental capacities.

Rationalism equates the difference between what is *analytical* and *physical* with what is logical and natural. It enables a person to describe what is measurable and knowable, free and necessary, and human subjective and natural objective qualities. The physical world has only *primary*, no secondary, or psychic, qualities. As an idol, Rationalism is a *religion*, which is, in principle, unable to acknowledge God as the Creator of different realms of created reality, each with its intricate *internal* and *external* set of relations. Creation's *regnal* diversity cannot be explained modally by some knowing *subject* as some reified "analytic" unit, or by some physical and measurable *object*.

This Rationalism is subdivided into **early** rationalism (1600–1830) and **late** rationalism (1830–1900). Being more static, **early** rationalism focused on the *content*, or concepts, of self-evident intellectual judgments that precede, and determine, human experience, including one's faith life.[53] It stressed the

53. Cf. D. H. T. Vollenhoven, *Schematische Kaarten: Filosofische concepties in probleemhistorisch verband,* bewerkt door K. A. Bril en Drs. P. A. Boonstra. Amsterdam: Reprohouse, 2000. As an expert in the history of philosophy, Vollenhoven avoided the common mistake of most Anglo-American philosophers—including W. Harry Jellema, N. Wolterstorff and A. Plantinga—who contrast "rationalism" with "empiricism" and cannot explain why both J. Locke and D. Hume were rationalists and empiricists, albeit in a different ways.

importance of clear thinking, proper arguing, debating and drawing conclusions. Being more dynamic, **late** rationalism stressed the *activity* and method of reasoning. It fostered three sub-movements: **Scientialism**[54] with its interest in *theoretical* reason, **Practicalism** with its emphasis on *practical* reason, and **Old Idealism** with its focus on combining these two sub-movements.

Unlike Scientialism (Descartes, Spinoza, Leibnitz, Locke, Berkeley), Practicalism, or Enlightenment (*Aufklärung*), did not think of philosophy primarily in terms of scholarship or natural science, but focused on *a priori* knowledge of all humans in their everyday life (e.g., business, technology, industry, citizenship, art, worship). Reason is not theoretical or abstract, but concrete and cultural. All humans have insight, clarity, certainty, "distinct ideas."[55] Human life flourishes when autonomous *practical* reason guides life, liberates society and shapes culture.[56]

According to Rationalism, the difference between "analytical" and "physical" is comparable to what is "logical" and "natural." It indicates what is measurable, and distinguishes between free and necessary, human and natural, subjective and objective, secondary qualities and primary qualities. The natural world does not have sensory, i.e., secondary, qualities. The philosophy of Rationalism is a religion incapable of (fully) acknowledging God as the Creator of distinct realms, each with its unique internal and external relationships. Creation's regnal diversity cannot be explained by any subject as a reified thinker, or by some measurable object.

As A. Smith's successor in 1764, T. Reid, professor of Moral Philosophy at the University of Glasgow, (i) agreed with G. Berkeley's rejection of materialism and atheism, but disagreed with his equating "being" (*esse*) with "perception" (*percipere, percipi*), and also with his idea that the world is based on spiritual ideas in the Divine Mind; (ii) rejected D. Hume's beliefs

54. Scientific elites deal with complex systems of thought based on *a priori* concepts of physical science (primary qualities), different forms of sensory experience (secondary qualities), and various kinds of logic, ethics, and aesthetics (Newton, Descartes, Hobbes, Spinoza, Leibniz, Locke, Berkeley). Although they focused mainly on (divine) *Logos* and (human) reason, see also such Cambridge Platonists as B. Wichcote, J. Smith, H. More and R. Cudworth.

55. According to I. Kant, "Have the courage to serve your own understanding" is the shibboleth of the Enlightenment.

56. Cf. Vollenhoven's comment in class: "While *scientialism* has slain thousands of Christians, *practicalism* has slain hundreds of thousands of Christians" (cf. Toland's *Christianity not Mysterious* and its negative impact on Christian faith and theology). Included in *anti*-Christian *practicalism* are C. Wolff, D. Hume, R. Voltaire, J.J. Rousseau, d'Holbach and G. Lessing; *semi*-Christian *practicalists* include B. Pascal, J. G. Hamann, G. Carmichael, F. Hutcheson, T. Reid, A. Smith and D. Steward.

that humans have no reliable knowledge about the world, themselves and God, and that matter is reducible to sensation, mind to ideas and causality to customs. His skepticism robs philosophy of its source, knowledge of its foundation, history of credibility, faith of a rational basis, and miracles of trustworthiness. Reid disagreed with Descartes's equating truth with "clear and distinct ideas" and with Locke's idea that "simple and complex ideas" are based on isolated sensory impressions.

CHAPTER NINE

Theology as "Pisteology"

Given H. Dooyeweerd's and D. Vollenhoven's basic view of created reality, I want to reflect in this chapter, and the following three chapters, on the structural diversity in how all humans, both Christian and non-Christian, express their faith life. Minimally, it involves awareness of the distinction between concrete human "faith life" and a study of it in what in Western academies was called "theology."

In this regard, I consider that Vollenhoven's distinction between "primary norms," inherent in God's creative Word *for* humans, and "secondary norms," reflected in the way humans respond *to* God's Word, is crucial. This distinction is not comparable to the difference between what ordained clergy-men and -women do in their part/full-time, so-called "religious" activities[1] and what roofers, judges, doctors, parents, farmers, citizens, bankers, entertainers and garbage collectors do in their daily non-ecclesial jobs.

When humans do not realize God's presence through his life-sustaining laws in their everyday life, they no longer hear his voice, place his Word on hold, elevate their own laws as being basic and central for themselves and their fellow humans. To do this in the best, at least minimally destructive, way, they rely (in Western culture) on what is rational and objective. For advocates of such a response, "God" is an abstraction, a concept, a reality—something non-Christian thinkers tend to speculate about in their thinking and believing.

To resist such speculative thinking and teaching, I struggled—already

---

1. In, for example, their preaching, administering the sacraments, catechizing, shepherding, counseling, and praying.

as a student at Calvin College and a graduate at the Free University, as an ordained pastor in the CRC, as professor in both theology and philosophy at Dordt College, and an advocate for twenty-five years in developing and promoting IAPCHE[2]—with the necessity of replacing scholastic "theology" (study of *God*) with "pisteology" (study of *faith*). To think of "theology" in terms of "pisteology" is being *reformational*; to think of "pisteology" in terms of "theology" is being *scholastic*. The former is helpful in being more radically biblical, while the latter is problematic in being intentionally accommodational.

Many Activities, One "Spirituality"

Vollenhoven's ontological distinction between God's diverse *structural* laws for created reality, including that of humans, and his one basic *religious* law of "love" for humans to be guided by in everything they do in response to His *structural* laws affected his understanding of (philosophical) anthropology. The results of human responses to God's distinct *structural* laws, he called "positive laws." These laws indicate how they react to, i.e., stand under and understand, God's *structural* laws for humans to be acknowledged in a proper *religious* way in their behavior as his caring creatures.

As indicated in the previous chapter, already in 1928 Vollenhoven did not equate, and confuse, "religion" with "faith life," nor did he separate them from each other. Instead—in response to a question of G. C. Berkouwer, a colleague at the Free University—about the nature of "theology," he distinguished between (i) what is *religious* in the sense of radical *heart*-centered and -directed, human response in all of life, and (ii) something humans do in special, intentional, deliberate ways to foster, and share, what they as Christians and non-Christians believe in diverse, often conflicting, ways.

Such a marooned and insulated faith life is, in principle, irrelevant for rest of life in society and culture. It exists for its own sake, is introverted, focuses on endless "theological" introspection, is practically irrelevant, majors in minor issues, elevated above a society and culture "put there" and filled with, for example, educational, political, economic, recreational and sexual idolatry and their anguished perpetrators and victims.[3] Desperately needed

---

2. International Association for the Promotion of Christian Higher Education

3. For example, the misguided view of Christians who advocate a form of Christendom, Theocracy, or National Church or Religion.

is not any (well-meant, but) misguided "private" faith or "public" theocracy, but a simpler, radical, "down-to-earth" scripturally guided (non-biblicist) view of what it means to be human and bear God's image.

What we badly need is a biblical, not a Greek or a scholastic, anthropology which acknowledges that being "human" involves distinguishing between "structure" and "direction," i.e., human "activity" and human "spirituality." To equate "faith life" with "religion," to treat them as equals, is to confuse, and distort, both terms. "Religion" is broader and deeper than what is expressed in actual human "faith life." It does not refer to some higher, supernatural—in *distinction from a lower or natural*—part of human life, as T. Aquinas assumed in his compromised anthropology. Nor is it what, six centuries later, A. Comte, a secularized French philosopher, explained as a lingering remnant of an earlier period of superstition in human history, something no longer needed in a *"positive"* and peaceful era of human history.

Against this kind of scholastic and accommodated form of secularized reason-centered thinking (in Western culture) about "truth," the question of how to educate future leaders—their life-style, society and culture, that according to "reformational" thinking includes shaping, expressing and sharing one's personal and public "faith life" or their *"religion"*—is not restricted to something institutional humans can join, leave, ignore, or abolish.[4] On the contrary, human life is broader than one's "faith life" or "organized religion." Not only in their "faith" (cf. "pistis")—e.g., private and public praying, confessing, repenting, catechizing, celebrating, sharing—do humans display their "heart-directed" *religious* stance as, e.g., composers and performers, buyers and sellers, parents and children, legislators and citizens, teachers and students, inventors and constructors.

In terms of a metaphor, all human activities are spokes in the wheel of life. No one spoke, or combination of spokes, is isolated from the other spokes. Each spoke is crucial for the wheel of life to turn smoothly. The function of each spoke presupposes that of all the other ones. In a sense one could say that, comparable to spokes attached to the hub of a wheel, human acts are related to what is dominant in the human heart.

---

4. As provost of the Free University, Vollenhoven *dis*invited Otto Weber—a gifted German Reformed theologian in dogmatics whom he had met earlier—immediately after he was informed that Weber had joined Hitler's "socialist" movement. Vollenhoven was the *first* Dutch academic leader to do so, according to Dr. G. Hearinck's discovery in 2012. Soon after 1936, Weber ended his membership and opposed Hitler. Cf. my study for G. C. Berkouwer of Weber's *Grundlagen der Dogmatik,* I-II, circa 1700 pages.

Inasmuch as the human heart is centered on the "Beginning and End" (Alpha and Omega) of the "Creator of heaven and earth" (Psalm 121:2), humans can experience in all their activities a serenity surpassing all human understanding. The *structural* diversity in humans is grounded in God's originating Word for created reality; the *religious*, or "spiritual," direction of this behavior displays the direction, or spirit, of a community and thrust of a culture.[5]

All this is true with respect to the covenant God and, *negatively*, to the multiple "idols" humans have fabricated with their own hands and in their own image, and which they genuflect to as the "gods" of strength, riches, power and fame, and which they celebrate at regional and international events as ideals to be remembered and honored. Instead of honoring the God of life, love-defying *self*-centered humans do not bear His image in honor but turn themselves and fellow creatures into "idols" that do not, and cannot, love and provide what humans need most.

When humans for no reason whatsoever oppose God's Word, they do not cease to be religious. Instead, they exhibit their religious nature by making, and turning to, idols, i.e., fake gods, ultimates that do not, because they cannot, deliver what they promise. Self-centered humans who bow at the altars of materialism, political power and outward beauty; philosophers and theologians who thrive on speculating about God and his revelations; mesmerizing orators who manipulate gullible audiences; prophets who profit from imagined revelations—in all these and other misguided cases, the perpetrators and their admirers denigrate in a Spirit-grieving way God's multifaceted and overwhelming revelation.

Such responses distort both human and non-human life. They dampen life's luster and can, indirectly, result in much misery, even death. To the extent humans do not walk with God in all of their responsibilities in life, also in society and culture, they create a vacuum in the house of their personal and institutional faith life.[6] Into that vacuum, i.e., "empty room," it is easy, according to Christ's warning, for evil powers to move in, with their idols,

---

5. E.g., *religious* commitment to a *Pax Romana, Pax Britannica*, or *Pax Germanica*. Bernard J. Zylstra (1934–1986), professor of jurisprudence and first president of ICS in Toronto, Canada, told me, shortly before he died, that he had planned to write a major book on *Pax Americana*. His writings and extensive correspondence—since 2011 located in the Archives of Calvin College in Grand Rapids, Michigan—influenced James W. Skillen, founder and director (1978–2008) of Center for Public Justice (CPJ) in Washington, DC, and Gerald Vandezande, president of Citizens for Public Justice (CPJ) in Ottawa, Canada, and recipient of a national Medal of Honor.

6. Luke 11:24–26.

and do immense damage and cause much misery.[7] Since they are false "gods," idols do not *give* life, but *take* it.

Word-Incarnate[8]

According to Scripture, God affirmed all his promises in the Anointed Savior. As the Word of God, the "Alpha and Omega," Christ Jesus is the "Tree of Life,"[9] the cornerstone of created reality, the ultimate guide for God's image-bearing humans.[10] That this Word of God became human, was incarnated,[11] reveals God's indescribable faithfulness, revealed in his covenant love for a world he created and crowned with humans charged to be his image-bearers. For God's Word to be incarnated in his only Son was not intended to provide merely an interesting, attention-getting, moralistic and superficial *model* to be *imitated*, without requiring a change in one's heart, i.e., in the *religious* direction in which one lives in whatever one does, for example, as spouse, gardener, carpenter, doctor, philosopher, commentator, or ruler.

The reason God's Word—through whom he created the world—had to be "incarnated" was in response to the "mystery" of humans refusing to obey their Maker. As the "Word-made-flesh," God's *own* "Son" would reveal the depth of the Creator's faithfulness to his own promises to them. God did not create his "Word" but, through the latter, created the "world." He promised his disobedient *self*-centered caretakers that only someone who obeys His law of love and bears the burdens of humans who defy the central law of love of their Creator can truly bear his image. Humans had no reason to violate God's simple, yet radical, command to love Him and fellow humans. To walk *with* God, humans need to turn the direction of their heart around, so that *religion* is no longer an option, a part of life, something one has, but a way of living in everything one does, also in one's faith, or pistic, life.

As the second Adam,[12] the "Immanuel" (God-with-us) revealed the

---

7. See Isaiah 1:21–23, Romans 1:18–23, Revelation 18:7–8.

8. The nature of this section is neither philosophical nor theological, but an attempt to summarize compactly what is minimally involved in being "Christian" and to do so in a creedal way.

9. Cf. Revelation 1:8 and 21:6.

10. "Son of Man" is used ten times in Matthew 23–26; see also Daniel 7:13–14 and Acts 7:53–54.

11. This is not only a metaphor, but refers to the mystery of an incomparable reality.

12. "Adam" stands for "humanity" (German, *Menschlichkeit*; Dutch, *mensheid*).

depth of God's covenant faithfulness manifested in the death of the anointed, raised and ascended Word of God, now seated at God's right hand, interceding on behalf of his followers in a world of growing conflicts. His life was fully human: as "the Son of man" he was baptized, tempted, prayed, read the (Old Testament) Scrolls, fasted, broke the bread and drank from the cup, prophesied, returned to heaven, sent the Spirit, (re)directed human hearts, and guided human behavior within his kingdom.

This Word-incarnate experienced, and avenged, God's anger at the rebellion of *self*-centered humans. This self-effacing love of the anointed Savior, through the Spirit, reflected what God's people are called to reflect in everything they do in all their responsibilities or tasks.[13] What this means for our view of the distinct *structure* and *role* of faith life will be addressed in the remainder of this chapter and in the following four chapters.

"Pistical Life"

For humans to place their faith, or trust, in some Ultimate is not strange, unusual, supernatural, or mystical. Nor does it refer, as stated above in this chapter, to what *positivistic* thinkers claim to be a lingering effect of an earlier outdated immature period in history when humans were still superstitious. On the contrary, to have faith in what one believes to be Ultimate is inherent to being human and evident in all phases of human history. Not only is being *religious* not an option; it is a necessity for humans, as is having, developing and expressing their faith not a choice but a requirement for humans in all societies and cultures. Somehow that faith reflects the innate impulse of humans to anchor their life, center their certitudes, establish their priorities and express their doxologies.[14]

The faith life is not an addendum, a supplement, to being human. It is assumed and somehow revealed in intentional, and unintentional, human activities. It is not a luxury, but a requisite to being human. Not to have it cripples human life; it is comparable to attempting to live, for example, without the capacity to sense, imagine, distinguish, communicate, or develop friendship.[15]

For humans to "walk with God," to intentionally live in His presence,

13. About the person and role of Christ Jesus, see John 1, Ephesians 1, Colossians 1 and Revelation 1.

14. Cf. James H. Olthuis, "Towards a Certitudinal Hermeneutic," 1979.

15. Think of a wheel's dependence on all its spokes, or a windmill needing all its vanes, to function properly.

is more encompassing and complicated than limiting it to certain personal and public "faith," or "pistical," customs and events. To equate "religion"[16] with strict and detailed celebrations, at certain times and places, is to restrict God's central law of love in all of life, i.e., to embrace God's covenant with humans as his "image-bearers." When human "faith life" is truly redirected to God's covenant-centered grace, humans can display, through the Holy Spirit, a faith that resists any idols, or pseudo-god. This is, in principle, the child-like agenda of those who walk with the "Lord of life." Followers of the "Way and Life" cannot be "fundamentalists," who focus on a creedal zeal-otry, practice an introverted "faith life" (for their soul), and have little or no interest in the welfare of society and culture.

To equate *religion* with "faith life" may result in one of the following four problems: (i) limiting being Christian to personal devotions, formal worship, knowing Scripture, playing or listening to "sacred" music, writing or reading "Christian" books, producing or watching "Christian" films, or attending "spiritual" retreats; (ii) secularizing the rest of one's life by failing to recognize the *religious* thrust of all human life; (iii) equating the relation between God's Word and human responses to it with the *structural* relation between belief and business, church and state, faith and science, worship and work, evangelism and citizenship; and (iv) thinking of institutionalized "re-ligion" as an add-on, an injection of something sacred into what is (falsely) considered to be independent of God's Word.

To equate "faith" with "religion" is typical of traditional Roman Cath-olic, Orthodox Christian, and Protestant, notably pietist and charismatic, forms of Christianity. In well-established faith traditions, "religion" tends to be associated with well-organized local churches and regional denomina-tions, especially their paid staff, diverse committees, special programs and required budgets. Their focus is primarily, at times exclusively, on "spiritual" discipleship and usually only secondarily, if at all, or at times of crisis, on vocational and cultural issues, in the overall *religious* direction of their daily life in some office, factory, fire- and police-station, bank, court, hospital, army, sport, etc. To think "religion" is something humans can "have" or "not have," be engaged in or ignore, is a temptation that allows the prover-bial Trojan Horse to oppose any Christian wholehearted life of love with its deceitful and deadly powers of wealth and greed, moral perversity, and

---

16. Quotation marks indicate what is "isolated" or "partial," not what is *religious*, i.e., "directional" and "total."

insufferable arrogance to claim the areas of any society and culture vacated by "organized" religion.[17]

Whereas "churchism" equates human "faith life" with "organized religion," creedal traditions or traditional theology, "liberalism" tends to reduce, if not remove, "institutionalized" faith and to focus on what is "good," or beneficial, for human society and culture without having to change the fundamental direction of the latter. "Churchism" senses the need for a biblically directed faith life for society and culture, but it does so in a "scholastic" way by stressing both the vertical, or supernatural, relation of humans to God's revelation and the horizontal, or natural, relation of humans to fellow humans and other natural creatures.

Fundamentally, the shift in so-called "liberal" theology is—unlike that of conservative and pietistic faith life—from God's revelation to human projection, from His Word *for* culture to his presence *in* culture, from a biblically directed faith to some social improvement, or from prophetic pronouncements about the world to "human-centered" views of the world. The pendulum moves from ecclesiastical events, controlled by clergy and theologians, to responses of laity, from orthodoxy to orthopraxis, from believing one's confessions on Sunday to confessing one's faith during the week.

When *religion* is institutionalized, the established, or organized, "church" becomes a prerequisite, the focus of Christian living, how to walk with God in everything one does. To be engrafted, through the Spirit, in Christ Jesus, compels *religiously* turned-around believers to reflect God's powerful love in all human behavior in marriage, family life, civic duties, health care, business enterprises, art events, philanthropies, studying created reality, stewardship, communication, etc.—and, of course, in these, and other, ways to live as His image-bearing caretakers who cannot avoid, but want to be involved in, such indispensable faith-activities as praying, Scripture reading, weeping, sharing, reflecting and celebrating.

To equate the *religious* direction of human life with *structurally* distinct ways of living, e.g., human "faith life," reflects a form of "churchism." Ironically, such a distortion fosters a *religious* secularizing of "faith life" and a spiritualizing of society and culture. *Religion* and "faith life" are, though interrelated, distinct features. To see this enables one to be aware of, and avoid, the dangers of both liberalism and churchism.

---

17. See Christ's comments in Luke 11:24–26—in the context of verses 14–28 about *Jesus and Beelzebub*—about a house with clean swept rooms into which demons moved, controlled the whole house, and ruined it.

The next two sections about "primary" and "secondary" norms, or laws, are consonant with Dooyeweerd's and Vollenhoven's novel thinking about created reality, the *religious* core of being human, God's faithfulness to his covenant with creation and his human caretakers of it, and the nature of such basic terms as truth, unity, diversity, society, culture and history. Given their *religiously* radical, yet anti-revolutionary, philosophy, anthropology and epistemology, I believe it is possible and, for the sake of clarity, necessary that the inherently scholastic term "theology," study of God, be used in the sense of "pisteology," study of faith life.[18]

According to *Webster's New Twentieth Century Dictionary*, 1979, a "theologian" (i) is a student of, an authority on, theology, especially Christian theology, focused on "faith, hope, and charity," (ii) is related to *theologium*, a place for speaking "in the ancient theater, a small upper stage, where the impersonators of the gods in a play appeared," (iii) is one who speculates theologically, reasons upon or discusses God, especially the relation between God and the universe, someone who studies religious doctrines and matters of divinity as expounded by a specific religion or denomination, and (iv) focuses on what is ascetic, biblical, moral, polemic, natural, revealed, systematic and speculative.[19]

Primary Norms

A way to sense what is distinct about faith life is to be aware of what it actually entails. It presupposes a biblically attuned anthropology aware of two things: (i) God's *structural* laws *for* human life, including faith life, and (ii) the *religious* response *of* humans to what God manifests in these laws. While God's laws *for* reality are *primary*, the "positive laws" *of* humans are *secondary*. As indicated in the previous chapter, the secondary laws of humans are shaped by both changing cultural and historical circumstances and by a *religious* heart-centered conflict.

The difference between "primary" and "secondary" laws—consonant with the distinction between "God's revelation for" and "human response to"—is crucial to understand (also) faith life. It is impossible to oppose God's

---

18. Faith (πίστις, "pistis") points to trust, firm belief, certainty, truth, confidence, assurance, reliability, proof, what is fiducial, warrant, etc.

19. Cf. *Webster's New Twentieth Century Dictionary*, Second Edition, William Collins Publishers, Inc., (1979), pages 1892, 1168, 1197.

laws *for* humans without any impunity. Human responses to all God's imperatives *for* life, including faith life, need constant updating to reflect his sovereign will. Such updating requires constant revisiting the meaning of God's "structural laws for" and "human responses to." When the latter move in a *religiously* evil direction, a heart-centered repentance is necessary and God's grace, in Christ through the Spirit, will be celebrated.[20]

Being faithful to his Word for created reality, God calls humans to honor him in the core of their being in everything they do and are interested in. In an all-embracing and -penetrating *coram Deo* way, humans are called to reflect their Maker by representing him in how they love themselves, their fellow humans, and such creatures as animals, birds, fish, water, mountains, flowers, etc. They do so in two distinct, but interdependent, ways: (i) *religiously* in their "heart" in all their tasks and duties, and (ii) *structurally* in specific organized events which are faith-fostering and celebrate the "faith life" of humans at certain times of the day or week and in specific places.

God's full revelation to humans compels us to respond in a general *heart*-centered way and in a specific faith-fostering way. Humans do not determine divine revelation. It is not the "secondary" laws of humans, but God's "primary" laws which provide the basis for created reality, including what humans do explicitly in their intentional "faith life."

Word Revelation

God reveals himself in three distinct, yet closely interrelated, ways. He does this in an *ontic* way through His creative Word, a *salvific* (redemptive) way through the incarnate-Word, and an *instructive* way through the inscripturated Word. The first is foundational for creatures to be, the second for fallen humans to be rescued, and the third for all humans to learn about both of them.

The scope of God's revelation is broader and deeper than Scripture. To think of Scripture as the basic, and most important, form of revelation is not only simplistic but also misleading. Such a reductionist view of God's revelation fosters a way of reading Scripture as though it were a recipe book for faith life, a divine almanac full of practical hints how a person should

---

20. About the mystery, and importance, of the relation between Lord and Spirit, see 1 Cor. 1:7–9, 12:3; 2 Cor. 3:16–18.

live, a model of Christian literature,[21] an example of Christian thinking,[22] a textbook for (natural) science, a source for speculative and sensational prophecies about human history and end-times.[23]

To restrict revelation to an (infallible) inspired Scripture does injustice to the nature and intent of God's written revelation, encourages literalism, fosters biblicism, detracts from the person and work of Jesus Christ, and does not do justice to the importance of God's creational revelation.[24] This way of reading, interpreting, preaching and using Scripture has resulted in considerable confusion in, and between, different Christian faith traditions. Unlike especially various "evangelical Baptist" approaches, a scripturally directed view of reality, including *religion*, calls for acknowledging the full scope of God's revelation about the unity and diversity of reality.

To indicate the precise meaning of God's "Word" with respect to its content for Christians is far from easy. Minimally, at this point in human history, it refers to Scripture's inspired humanly written revelation in various parts of the world and different periods of history. The incarnated Word, as the Anointed (*Christos*), differs from the inscripturated word (*biblos*) in that He is a Person, not a book, in distinction from the Creator's Word (*viva vox*), according to Genesis 1:1–27 and John 1:1–2 as the basis for created reality. Christ Jesus *embodies* God's revelation, reveals who God really is, and did what God wanted humans to do. In originating, and maintaining, His powerful and love-filled Word, God revealed, through his Son, the origin of all meaning, the true nature of human certainty, and the ultimate reason for humans to act as His image-bearing children.

In a lingual way, Scripture points to God's revelation in the world he made, his Son he sent, and his Spirit he poured on a world in great need, even despair. It is God's inspired "love-letter" that conveys what disoriented humans need as an indispensable guide regarding what to believe and how to live in their daily life. It is the main source for humans to learn about, reflect on, and share with fellow humans the intent of God's full, life-encompassing revelation for all creation and humans in it.

---

21. E.g., a professor of English who, in a biblicist way, used Isaiah and Psalms as examples of good literature, without realizing he could hardly claim the same about the book of Revelation, the last book of Scripture.

22. See *Christian Scholars Review,* (2001),4, 381–433.

23. E.g., various pre-millenarian (pre-, mid- and post-tribulation) forms of dispensationalism and their effects on higher education in Baptist churches, mass media and Middle East policy in especially North American circles.

24. For details, see Vander Stelt (1978), especially chapters III, IV and VIII.

Creational Revelation

It is inherent in traditional Roman Catholic, as well as in much Reformed scholastic philosophy and theology to think about God's revelation in terms of "natural" and "supernatural" revelation, correlated with what is "general" and "special," and of humans endowed with the gifts of "reason" and "faith."[25] This way of thinking does injustice, however, to Scripture's content.

Creational revelation is grounded in the Word the Creator spoke. He delighted in what resulted, and promised to be faithful to his Word for creation and its human caretakers. He reassured Adam and Eve of his covenant (of loving sovereignty and sovereign love), provided covenant-clutching servant-leaders to remind them to hear and smell God's Voice in specific rituals and develop a truly distinct lifestyle. Creational revelation is basic for Scripture to be, humans to read it, God's Word to become flesh, the Spirit to be poured out, and the Risen One to return.

God's creational, or *structural,* laws are not static, but dynamic. They reveal His will for creation through its impinging nature. They provide the conditions for diverse human experiences, including their sense of creational revelation and self-awareness. It is impossible to honor God without knowing something about Him as Creator, i.e., without acknowledging that somehow humans reflect His intent and concern.[26] In this regard, though in different ways, both *creational* and *biblical* revelation are authoritative, clear and powerful.

Even non-Christians sense something of God's revelation in their overwhelming experiences of, for example, lightning and thunder, sunrise and sunset, galaxies and stars, mountains and valleys, birds and flowers, human ingenuity and cultural events. To ignore or suppress the simplicity of God's revelation has its origin in their refusal to obey His central love-command, not in his revealing handiwork. Ultimately, humanity's misery arises not from God's revelation, but from refusal to acknowledge the reality of His unavoidable revelation or presence. The problem does not lie in what God has revealed, and continues reveal, to humans. Rather, it lies in humans not hearing, or refusing to hear, his "loving call" to surrender their *heart* to his "calling love" and experience the privilege and challenge of living as his covenant-partners.

---

25. Other related distinctions are everyday life and weekly worship, world and church, culture and Christ, common grace and special grace.

26. Cf. Genesis 2:19 and Isaiah 28:24–26.

Being in their *heart* incurably *religious*, refusing to "walk with God" results, sooner or later, in distortions, or forms of *structural* misery—which alienate humans from each other, perhaps themselves, and even from non-human creatures. Such practical distortions in one's everyday life, in turn, affect what humans do in their actual "faith" (*pistis*) life and in their analytic (pisteological, not theological) study of it.

Given the dynamic character of created reality,[27] unlike *scriptural* and *incarnational* revelation, *creational* revelation may increase, in the sense of become more apparent, as a consequence of human inventions.[28] Human faith experiences, also of creational revelation, are shaped especially in specific events in history and circumstances in society. The society and culture in which humans live leaves distinct marks on all Christian, as well as non-Christian, "faith" acts, events, institutions, habits, customs and traditions.

Christian faith life emanates from a positive *heart*-response of humans to God's call in Christ Jesus, the "only Son of God and Son of Man" and who paid the ultimate gift of Love for his covenant-breakers. In yielding to the Spirit's nudging, a *religiously* turned around faith life seeks to live in the presence, not absence, of their Creator by acknowledging Him as the secret of their life. In their *heart*, in all their spiritual bones, Christians know that *scriptural* revelation is not something merely added to God's *natural* revelation, but assumes and underscore God's all-conditioning and -encompassing *creational* revelation.

The "Good News" is that God's Word is central to Scripture. Not to acknowledge this is not to recognize that *creational* revelation is functionally present in God's will and, consequently, relevant for all one's activities, also with respect to the *structure* of one's faith life. Faith life is not some supernatural, sacred addition to one's natural, "secular," horizontal, mundane or lower life. All humans, Christian and non-Christian, are structured in such a way that they believe, or put their trust in, something or someone. It is impossible to be human without somehow expressing one's faith life. Because of the inexplicable fall, humans place their *ultimate*, or *final*, trust either in the Creator and Redeemer of heaven and earth[29] or in a substitute of their own making that they live, and die, for.[30]

---

27. For an idea about the meaning of "historical" in terms of Vollenhoven's and Dooyeweerd's philosophy, see J. Klapwijk (2007).

28. The power, effect and understanding of these revelations may increase or decrease over time, however.

29. For example, Genesis 1–2, Job 38–39, Psalm 121 and Revelation 21:1.

30. Pre-eminently in the priorities displayed in one's general lifestyle, not necessarily in

Given its dynamic nature, *creational* revelation[31] increases in an exciting and alarming way. The nature and significance of faith life and the awareness of God's creational revelation are impacted by local and global events in cultures, civilizations and historical disclosure. A rapidly shrinking world with dazzlingly speedy ways to communicate and interact impacts the two central *religious* directions and conflicts and the countless *structural* differences within Christian and non-Christian faith (*pistical*) acts, customs, traditions and clashes.

The incarnated Word is central to the Good News of Scripture. Not to acknowledge this undermines the importance of creational revelation and isolates it from God's full revelation in everyday life (cf. homes, work, health, business, education, communication, safety, justice, travel, worship). Faith life is not something supernatural, holy, sacred, "religious" for poor, uneducated, and insecure persons. On the contrary. Religion is not a luxury, an option, but eminently human and necessary anywhere and at all times—from the womb to the tomb. All humans have an irrepressible urge to believe, trust in, rely on someone or something. To be human is to trust in the "God of heaven and earth" or in some speechless idol that victimizes. Creational revelation is foundational for human life. To be human is to respond to God's life-giving and -sustaining *structural* laws, and to do so in terms of the God-given *religious* law of love. To respond in that way is possible only by obediently listening to God's three forms of Word revelation. Christian "faith life" implies two things: a *heart*-directed faith focused on honoring the Creator of everything, and a *structural* expression of such a *religious* stance, that is *structurally* comparable to a non-Christian's *religious* stance and faith life.

Secondary Norms

The difference between *primary* and *secondary* norms corresponds to the difference between structural laws *for* and positive laws *of* humans. The former are God-given and unchanging, the latter human and subject to change. Whereas *structural* laws point to what must be, or what is fundamental,

---

any particular professional activity or special statement of faith. With the exception, perhaps, of a seared conscience of someone who is completely indifferent. However, even then, one's total life reveals what is considered to be of ultimate importance: e.g., hubris, self-infatuation, raw power, fame, wealth, beauty, pleasure, and revenge.

positive laws indicate how humans respond to God's laws, in other words, to laws with the trademark "human-made."

Not to distinguish between these two kinds of norms, or laws, results in a two-fold distortion. To equate God's "laws for" faith life with the "positive laws" of faith life fosters a spirit of "subjectivism" with its inherent threat of relativism. To do the opposite, to equate "laws of" humans with God's "laws for" faith life results in "objectivism" with its inherent danger of conservatism.

No *response* to the norm *for* faith may be treated as a primary norm. Subtle forms of such subjectivism, present also in Roman Catholic, Reformed/Presbyterian, Evangelical and other Christian faith traditions, must be avoided. The danger of such (faith-distorting) subjectivism is evident in the custom, especially in ecclesiastical and educational circles, to think in terms of, for example, faith *and* science, faith *and* politics, faith *and* psychology, faith *and* economics, faith *and* technology.[32] Such a well-intended but misguided approach assumes that "human faith" can function as the norm for the disciplines mentioned.

Western intellectualism has become so subtle, and pervasive, that it has blinded especially theologians to two things: the distinction between "faith life" and "theology" as academic disciplines, and the difference between God's "law-*for*" and human "law-*of*" the structure of human faith. The structure of "theology" as academic discipline differs from the structure of actual faith life or activity—the first is inherently "analytical" and the second "pistical."

Not acknowledging the *structural* difference between acts of faith and acts of theology is comparable to not seeing the difference between certitude and hypothesis, practice and theory, being involved in and stepping back from, actually believing *in* something or someone and thinking *about* such believing. To ignore this distinction is to reject the difference between creeds and symbolics, dogmas and dogmatics, liturgy and liturgics, Scripture reading and hermeneutics, preaching and homiletics, understanding what one reads and hermeneutics.

A proper understanding of "secondary" norms is impossible without acknowledging the cultural differentiation and historical developments in God's creational revelation. The latter is not something "natural," some Greek

---

32. Not human faith but God's Word, with its diverse "structural" laws and one "religious" law, is normative for the "natural sciences" and disciplines in politics, psychology, economics, technology, theology, etc.

metaphysical theory about some ultimate "substance." God's revelation is not anchored in any philosophical or theological theory. On the contrary, it has its origin in the Word of God "through whom, in whom and to whom" all things exist.[33] This powerful Word reveals itself in the response of created reality, especially in what humans do in their faith life. As in all their activities, also human faith is *religiously* grounded, or anchored, either in God's Word or in some "ism" or pseudo-god.

Refusal to bow before this powerful Word has fostered an all-of-life *religious* clash between light and darkness. This conflict affected all the secondary norms of faith life in that they no longer reflect God's central love command. Being a human tradition, faith life is fallible and needs constant updating. Such refinement of faith life calls for an awareness of the nature and intention of secondary norms. The task to maintain, update, deepen, broaden, and, if necessary, correct, these "secondary" norms rests on the shoulders of especially preachers, evangelists, pastors, authors of creeds and testimonies, perceptive liturgists, and wise administrators.

Inasmuch as they comport with God's revelation,[34] secondary norms resemble primary norms in that they guide faith life. As responses to faith's *primary* norms, *secondary* norms may not become *primary* norms for every believer in one faith tradition living in different cultures and times.[35] To underscore the importance of distinguishing between "primary" and "secondary" faith norms, a few comments about creeds, sacraments and preaching will be helpful.[36]

33. Romans 11:36, 1 Corinthians 8:6, Hebrews 2:10. For details, see Troost (2004): 79–80.

34. For problems associated with seemingly endless "because" *(quia)* and "insofar as" *(quatenus)* debates in Reformed faith traditions, see the nineteenth- and twentieth-century discussions in the Netherlands, Republic of South Africa and North America, as well as in Presbyterian circles in Scotland, England, USA and Canada.

35. For example, must Christians in non-Western regions of the world subscribe to, and teach, creeds adopted centuries earlier in very different cultural settings? In the 1950s, a debated issue at Calvin College and Calvin Theological Seminary centered on the role of the *Canons of Dort* (1618/9) in Christian Reformed Church foreign mission in Nigeria.

36. These topics were selected mainly because they touch on central and sensitive issues, and reveal the importance of a distinct Christian philosophy, anthropology and epistemology in notably symbolics, dogmatics, homiletics and hermeneutics.

Creeds

As confessional statements, creeds are carefully worded expressions of what a faith tradition believes. A formidable difficulty in all faith traditions has been the diversity of different, often conflicting, expressions of precisely what is believed and subscribed to. In both Christian and non-Christian faith traditions, creedal statements not only unite but can also trigger more division.

Complicating matters is the fact that "creeds" can be used not only in the sense of verbalizing one's *faith life*, but also in what is firmly stated in, for example, the proclamations of the *Humanist Manifesto I* (1933) and *II* (1973).[37] Comparable faith-like statements are made, and subscribed to, in policies, events, institutions and movements not immediately associated with one's faith life. Rather, they express the fundamental guiding principles of political, medical, educational, social, financial, aesthetic, recreational and other areas of one's life. They reveal more implicitly than explicitly, i.e., more indirectly than directly, a creedal facet of fundamental principles in public law, health care, education of leaders,[38] human interaction, trade and commerce.[39]

What is unique to the *pistical* aspect of created (not imagined) reality is its focus on ultimate principles to which humans commit themselves *explic*itly in their faith life and *im*plicitly in their other kinds of human activities. This "faith" feature of all human life must be acknowledged to begin to sense how different Christian faith traditions—e.g., Christian, Roman Catholic, Greek Orthodox, Russian Orthodox, Lutheran, Anglican, Calvinist, Anabaptist, Pentecostal—influenced what is (non-)negotiable in a society and culture in which a specific (Christian) faith impacts such basic issues as marriage, education, politics, entertainment, warfare and burials.[40]

As to the relation between organized faith life (wrongly called "religion") and the rest of life, creeds are expressions of what humans consider to be most basic, or fundamental, for themselves and fellow humans. They

37. Cf. *The New Humanist* (VI: 3) 1933 and *The Humanist* (XXXIII: 5) 1973, Prometheus Books. Buffalo, New York.

38. E.g., J. Dewey's classic "Educational Creed" regarding foundational principles about truth, learning, curriculum, pedagogy and research.

39. E.g., Adam Smith's capitalism in *The Wealth of Nations* (1776), Pierre J. Proudhon's socialism, K. Marx's *The Communist Manifesto*, and Chairman Mao's *Little Red Book*.

40. Important in this connection, especially in our shrinking world, are the major differences between Christian and Islam, Islam and Buddhist, Shamanist and Taoist, and other faith traditions and cultures.

reveal in them their allegiance to someone, or something, ultimate within the context of their situation in society and culture. As responses to God's *structural* laws *for* created reality, creeds are *secondary* norms, human pistical responses to God's revelation. Their nature and role are determined in two ways: *religiously* by the trust of humans in the triune God or in some idol, and *structurally* by various (Christian and non-Christian) faith traditions.

The plethora of faith traditions reveal subtle differences, even disagreements, among truth-claiming factions also within Christian circles. Serious, even deadly, clashes have occurred within and among such non-Christian faith traditions as Orthodox Judaism and Reform Judaism, Shiite and Sunni Islam, Mormon Church of Latter-day Saints and Reorganized Church of Latter-day Saints, Hinduism and Buddhism, Confucianism and Shamanism, and various sub-conflicts within these traditions.

Sacraments

Unlike the Roman Catholic Church, with its seven sacraments, and many sects which reject most, if not all, sacraments, all Protestant traditions observe only two sacraments: Baptism and the Lord's Supper. In Reformed or Presbyterian denominations these two sacraments are considered to be "seals" and "signs" of Yahweh's covenant-centered love for humans who turned a deaf-ear to his Voice in the garden.

These two "seals" visualize God's promises. They confirm his covenant with His "image-bearing" creatures by validating the reality of what they symbolize. These sacraments symbolize how God delivered his people from forces that oppose Him and seek to destroy them. The symbols of water, bread and wine palpably reflect his love-soaked mercy for humans who want to walk in His way in everything they do as His people.

These two sacraments are not absolute, or essential, for the salvation of humans, nor are they irrelevant, or optional, for humans who as Christians love the Lord God. As "primary" norms, these two sacraments are normative. How Christians respond to these two norms is affected by special circumstances of humans, who administer, and receive, these sacraments. Although they are important, they are not, contrary to Roman Catholic thinking, necessary conditions for salvation. The basis for salvation is God's grace in the Anointed Savior and the Spirit's power.

Through the pistical *subject*-function of the administrators and the recipients of the sacraments[41] and the pistical *object*-function of water in baptism, and bread and wine in the Lord's Supper, God symbolizes and seals his promises to strengthen humans in their trust in him. Through the Spirit, these rituals affirm, and confirm, Christians in their understanding of God's Word and how they respond in a positive and liberating way.

The sacraments as such are not redemptive, do not transmit God's grace (*ex opere operato*).[42] They are not rituals with mysterious powers and immediate effects. The two biblical sacraments indicate that the Spirit provides the "gift" of redemptive faith.[43] They *seal* God's grace in the lives of those who surrender to him and take hold of His promises for themselves and their children.[44] Baptism and the Lord's Supper are *secondary* norms to induce humans to be grateful for *all* God's *primary* norms in all human life, not only in their faith-focused, i.e., pistical, life.

A problem related to how to administer the two main sacraments has to do with the formulas spoken, ways water is used (sprinkling, scooping, immersing, use of fingers),[45] time of administration (children, adults, before or after conversion), shape of bread (whole loaf, small pieces, wafers), cup of wine (individual cups, common cup, grape-juice, water in prison or battle), administering and receiving the sacraments (role of clergy, open or closed communion, gender and age issues), and place of administering and receiving sacraments (sanctuary, home, hospital, chapel, prison, river, swimming pool, fountain).

Disagreements about the nature and role of the Lord's Supper, or Eucharist, resulted in much misery, even deadly conflicts, in different faith traditions of sixteenth-century Europe. Scholastic priests, preachers and pastors discussed, disagreed, and at times resorted to violent clashes. Central in these theological conflicts was the (Aristotelian) Roman Catholic notion of "*tran*substantiation," the Lutheran idea of "*con*substantiation," as well as the Calvinian stress on "realism" and Zwinglian emphasis on "symbolism." Other

---

41. In child baptism, children receive the sacrament *passively* through the *active* faith of their parents, at least under normal circumstances.

42. As a pastor, I was once asked by a stranger at a gas station to baptize his three children, so that they would have "some eternal insurance."

43. See Chapter 10 below about the "gift" of "saving" faith.

44. As they mature, these children are urged to claim the promises symbolized in their baptism, profess God's Name in how they live every day, and to claim these promises someday for their own children.

45. For centuries, Russian Orthodoxy struggled with the issue of which, and how many, fingers must be used in administering this sacrament.

contentious issues centered on the distinction between "clergy" and "laity," especially in connection with serving both bread and wine to the former, but only bread to the latter.[46]

Preaching

Not only creeds and sacraments, but also sermons, homilies, pastoral letters and encyclicals are *secondary* norms. The "Good News" is not an abstract theological product, but an eminently practical and powerful story to be heard and told. It involves close reading, accurate formulation, proper communication. Its message is more than some gripping expression *of* faith life. According to the command of the Risen Lord, just before he returned to the Father, the gospel is intended *for* humans (Matthew 28:19–20, Acts 1:8).

It is not merely a testimony of fallible humans to other fallible humans. It is the Spirit's way of compelling humans to share something that is truly *primary* and, therefore, has to be made known and responded to—also by the preacher involved. Even preaching itself is not a *primary*, but *secondary*, norm. Because it can be done wrongly, it needs to be supervised by the Christian community.[47]

Preaching is a distinct *pistical* act. Not to recognize this may result in confusing, and eventually equating, Word proclamation with interesting moralistic stories, formal *aesthetic* expressions (liturgies, special music, dramas, dances), a variety of *social* events (fellowships, celebrations, clubs), *analytic* activities (discussions, debates, theological probing, doctrines),[48] *psychological* sessions (pep-talks, therapy sessions, counseling, retreats), *economic* issues (offerings, budgets, salaries, tithing, poverty), *political* debates (civil religion, individualism, socialism, fascism, communism, or democratism).

---

46. Other sensitive issues in Protestant, especially Reformed, circles center on such minor issues as replacing wine with grape juice, children participating in the Lord's Supper, relation between sacrament and discipline, replacing bread with coconuts, rice, or fish, and replacing wine with water in times of war and imprisonment. For details, see various ecumenical movements that seek to minimize, or resolve, such legalistic issues.

47. According to 1 Peter 5:2, the proclaimed Word must be truthful and genuine.

48. While preaching and philosophy benefit each other, preaching is not dependent on any philosophy or theology. Both disciplines depend on the proclamation of God's Word. Proper preaching involves claiming the whole world for God, and philosophy and theology study, respectively, God's cosmos and the human and non-human *pistical* aspect of it.

Proper Word proclamation either enhances, quickens or kills positive faith-responses of humans.[49] As was the case with "creeds" and "sacraments," the difference between positive and negative responses is determined by how humans react in the center, or core, of their being to God's Word. Being essentially *religious*, humans cannot escape placing their trust in something they assume to be ultimate. The latter may manifest itself in, for example, a radical indifference, seared conscience, a fatal addiction. If God's Word *of,* and *for,* humans is not central, then soon human idols will play a *religiously* "anti-thetical" role in society and culture.

Biblical preaching does not consist of first reading certain human experiences *into* Scripture and then, illustrated by Christ's life and work, reading them *out of* Scripture, and thereby impressing mesmerized listeners. On the contrary, it calls for penitent and faithful bowing of the speaker and the listener to the "Alpha and Omega," i.e., the Creator and covenant-keeping Father, who calls his image-bearing creators to return to Him (Revelation 2–3). Such genuine proclamation avoids the snare of "moralistic" stories profound on the surface but only veneer-deep, attractive but not substantive.

Non-Christians are not *non*-believers, but believers whose "faith life" moves, because of ignorance, compromise, or opposition, in the wrong *religious* direction. Christian living reflects a lifestyle of being aware of God's awesome Presence in everything one does. By thinking in a biblically directed and covenant-oriented way, Christians can, and should, develop an anthropology without the two Platonic-Aristotelian speculative ideas of (i) a "substance" called "soul" and (ii) a "faculty psychology" made up of three distinct, and interdependent, faculties of "reason," "morality" and "passion" (for details, see Chapter 6 above). The *intellectual* capacity to know "truth" is considered to basic to the capacity to be *moral,* or *virtuous,* and these two capacities enable humans to be *emotional,* or *passionate,* even *religious,* in their response to God's gracious love. It is impossible to break the crust of such scholastic anthropology without a *religious* renewal and *structural* reform(ul)ation of "faith life" and traditional "theology" in Christian colleges, seminaries and universities.

Without such a change, preachers may, despite their good intentions, actually give listeners, if not stones for bread, actually stale, if not spoiled, bread. Such preachers, and parishioners, may become unbiblical, lose their restorative power, experts in proper formality. Proper preaching is not focused on only the "faith life" of humans to the exclusion of other ways in

---

49. Cf. Colossians 2:8.

which humans live and which are thought to be secondary, mundane, secular, not "spiritual," or "religious," merely a means to an end, a way to "make money" in order to support a church budget, a mission, or faith cause. As an eminently practical, radical and liberating activity, preaching reminds humans to hear the Creator's call to bear his image by feeding the hungry, helping the dependent, seeking justice for the oppressed, providing water for the thirsty, inviting strangers, healing the sick, remembering the imprisoned (Matthew 25:31–46).

Human deliberate *faith* life is, in distinction from all other forms of human life, unique in that it reminds all other human ways of living not to act in isolation from, or in conflict with, what humans do as farmers, bankers, governors, educators, entertainers, doctors, newscasters, internet surfers. In tangible ways, Christians reflect God's grace in a world filled with subtle and damaging forces of darkness. Not only in their intentional "faith life" but in all of life humans must reflect God's life-restoring grace and redemption.[50]

A much debated issue in *scholastic* and *experiential* faith traditions is the problem of a Platonic-Aristotelian philosophy with an inbuilt "anthropological" and "theological" debate about whether preaching is something "objective," "subjective," or both of these combined. Scholastic preaching (homiletics), stressing the importance of reason, resulted in an intellect-based disagreement about the essence of sermonizing. Advocates of "objective" preaching stressed that the truths proclaimed reflect an intellect-based view of created reality. As a result, preaching consists of communicating clear "doctrines" as carefully articulated concepts.

In distinction from an objective, or rational, view of truth, reality and faith, other preachers emphasized what is "subjective," more experiential and practical. The focus is not so much on the human intellect, but on what is more "volitional" and especially "affective." Faith life stresses the features of feelings, warmth, experience, spirit, vitality, passion and enthusiasm.

This conflict in especially traditional Reformed and Presbyterian faith traditions about so-called "objective" and "subjective" preaching reflects a tension in traditional Western thinking about human "faith life" and study of "theology." This is the reason for the widespread homiletical distinction between what is doctrinal and personal, universal and individual, absolute and relative, general and particular, or impersonal and existential. These

---

50. Cf. (in a general, not biblicist, way) about marriage (Colossians 3, Ephesians 3–6), justice (Psalm 72, Romans 13), wealth (Isaiah 3, James 5:4), emotions (Hebrews 12:5–7, 1 Peter 4:12–14).

problems, in turn, centered on the differences between, for example, exposition and application, explanation and revival, being abstract and practical, thinking and feeling, knowing and experiencing, ideas and tears, revelation and projection.[51]

That this unceasing pendulum between "objective" and "subjective" resulted in unnecessary problems for faith life, is, though understandable, foreign to what is really simple and powerful kingdom proclamation. Since it is living and active, God's Word has no room for human-made enfeebling dilemmas. His Word is a power unto salvation (1 Corinthians 1:18–19) that separates joint and marrow (Hebrews 4:12) and leaves no room for dilemmas resulting from some dualistic anthropology in which the (higher) soul—apart from the (lower) body—possesses three distinct "faculties" called intellect, will, and feelings.

Kingdom preaching avoids the speculative problem of something being either *objective* or *subjective*. To avoid such *scholastic* impasse-thinking calls for a genuine heart-centered awareness of God's Word for, and in, created reality and the dependence of humans on it. When preaching consists of a sharing of intellectually *objective* truths, the content of human faith tends to become a set of doctrines or some theological beliefs. To reject such an intellect-based objective truth, K. Barth (1886–1968), an existentialist theologian, believed that *in* the event (*Ereigniss*) of "preaching" Scripture *becomes* the Word of God.

When preaching focuses on what is *subjective*, Scripture tends to be viewed, and used, primarily as a book of human experiences and projections, and their implied fears and hopes. Such a subjectivist approach does injustice to the God-breathed nature of Scripture as a compass *for* whatever humans do in nurturing their faith life. In proclaiming his three-fold (creational, incarnated and inscripturated) Word, God challenges human image-bearers to acknowledge him as covenant God, the source of the "structurally" diverse laws for reality, and the single *religious* law to love Him in everything they do in all their tasks. Mesmerized by the love of His liberating Word, Christians know that God addresses them through the Spirit and the Risen One, who is the key to reality (Colossians 1:15–20). God calls humans, who lost their way in paradise, to return and live under the umbrella of his love (Romans 15:4, Revelation 2 and 3).

---

51. Dutch Reformed theology struggled for several centuries with a closely related debate about "objective" (*voorwerpelijk*) and "subjective" (*onderwerpelijk*) preaching. For details, see J. W. Maris, *Geloof en ervaring: van wesley tot de pinksterbeweging*, 1992, especially the English summary, 267–274.

Range of Issues

A study of "faith life" in terms of "pisteology"—not "theology," a scholastic study of God's revelation in terms of endless "faith-reason" issues—is integral to reforming thinking about the *structure* of all faith life. Its wide range includes such factors as geography, structure of society, kind of culture, period in history, commitment to God or a phantom. The following categories and related lists are illustrative, not exhaustive. They highlight a wide range of significant issues in faith life. Each general category includes, or involves, several specific terms and issues related to that category.

The aim of listing these categories is to convey what is, at least potentially, involved in a biblically simpler, encyclopedically more appropriate, and locally and globally more relevant sense of how humans cultivate and express their faith. It provides a clearer sense of why, how and where Christians and non-Christians agree or disagree in their daily faith life, in our rapidly shrinking world, filled with hope and fear, happiness and misery.

Place of Worship

House, catacomb, mountain, tent, chapel [hospital, funeral, rest home, campus, military], cathedral [design, architecture, liturgical center, acoustics], monastery [Eastern, Roman Catholic, Protestant], synagogue [Judaism], stake house [Mormons], reading room [Christian Science], mosque [Islam], meditation room [Buddhism], reflection center [Unitarian].

Music

Choir [a capella, quartet, soloist, chant], hymn, [lament, requiem, praise, Geneva tunes], instruments [drum, strings, trumpet, flute, organ, piano, ensemble, even a saw], accompaniment [pianist, organist].

Communication

Preaching, publishing [pamphlets, tracts], technology [mass media, radio, television, video, film, overhead, internet], translating [sacred texts, commentaries], evangelizing.

Academy

Theology [seminary, curriculum, divinity school, mission school], department [Bible, theology, religion], content of faith [dogmatics], preaching [homiletics], interpretation [hermeneutics], pastoral care [poimenics], faith instruction [catechism].

Emotions

Feelings, excitement, solemnity, comfort, sorrow, mourning, grief, sickness, healing, guilt, loneliness, anger, boredom, joy, hope, doubt, repentance, addiction.

Interpretation

Sacred documents [Torah, Scripture, Qu'ran, Book of Mormon], synod [council, pastoral letters, encyclicals], worldview [being human, structure of society and culture, view of history], listening, hearing, discernment, wisdom.

Instruction

Catechism, faith lessons, Bible studies, devotions, faith exercises, memorization, *lectio divina*, indoctrination, imagination [plays, paintings, pictures, liturgical dramas, dances, statues], age levels, challenged members.

Finances

Faith budget, vow of poverty, tithing, sacrifice, deacons, tent-ministry, salary, soup kitchens, state support, insurance, legal fees.

Government

Political issues [oath, court, church and state], idols and ideology [communism, socialism, capitalism, militarism, racism, democratism], civil religion, tax-exemption, freedom and toleration, persecution [Jewish, Christian, Islam, Mormon, Humanism], conscientious objection [military exemption], chaplains.

Rituals

Private devotion, public worship, role of tradition, altar calls, burial rites, funerary art, hand- and foot-washing, rosary, call-to-prayer, sacraments, wedding ceremony.

Prayer

Form [long, short, private, public, posture, spoken, silent, sung], effect [power, healing, guidance], expression [formal, spontaneous], context [celebration, war, health, disaster].

Anthropology

Soul-body dualism [meaning of heaven, death and resurrection], conflict between biblical meaning of "heart" and Greek "faculty psychology," anthropology [humanism, evolutionism, pragmatism], ontology and epistemology [mysticism, scholasticism, existentialism, pragmatism, postmodernism].

Idolatry

Private and public idols, cultural expressions, "law-of-sin-unto-death," judgments, martyrdom, pseudo-revelation and pseudo-religion, conflict between and among idols, subtle and seductive powers.

Monasticism

Vows, reaction to fossilized faith and decadent culture, monastic orders and liturgies, problem of human-God and human-world relations, role of celibacy.

Male/Female

Gender issues [different male-female relations], phases in life [babies, children, teenagers, adults, seniors], faith traditions [lifestyle, devotional life, education, celebrations], ceremonies [private and public, role of sacraments, nature of funeral], sexuality [purity, perversity, divorce and therapy].

Missions

Evangelizing [strategies, proselytizing, deprogramming], use of apologetics [identity, adaptation, debating], faith of converts [exciting, tender, unsettling], differences in Christian and non-Christian traditions, local and/or global.

For a bird's-eye view of the ontology, anthropology and epistemology implied in the faith life described above, we turn to our next chapter. To counteract the traditional discipline of "theology," with all its inherent problems, I believe, after five decades of probing, that to think of "theology" (study of God) in terms of "pisteology" (study of faith life) is not less, but more, biblical, not compromising, but more radical, not avoiding God's impinging revelation, but stressing it with respect to at least two fundamental issues: (a) *religious* divergence, even clash, between Christian and non-Christian living, and (b) "structural similarities" in all human faith traditions. The faith life of non-Christians is "structurally" human, but *religiously* non- and, potentially, even anti-Christian.

CHAPTER TEN

Structure of "Pisteology"

L ike all other studies, theology presupposes basic philosophical, anthro-pological and epistemic assumptions. This is evident in what during the last century a growing number of *religiously* perceptive Christian, though not theological, thinkers have indicated.[1] Their scripturally directed studies of different intricate structures of created reality enabled them as God's image-bearing creatures, especially in their faith life, not to speculate or major in minors.

Whatever God created depends on both his imperatives, commands, or laws, and on being faithful to his handiwork. This amazing reality, in which humans bear his image in their daily tasks, consists of four distinct interrelated and interdependent realms, viz., "things,"[2] "plants," "animals" and "humans." Structurally, God's commands are diverse. He commanded the non-human world (of things, plants and animals) simply to be, and the human world (fourth realm) to live in his love-filled delight in the world of his image-bearers. The nature of human responses to their Creator's Word is succinctly summarized in the Dutch and German phrases "Woord en antwoord" and "Wort und Antwort."

To catch a glimpse of the wonderful and intricate nature of created re-

---

1. For details, see Chapters 4–5 and 7–8 about the views of A. Kuyper, H. Bavinck, H. Dooyeweerd, D. Vollenhoven and many others influenced by them. Cf. Kuyper (1908), Dooyeweerd (1953–1958), Vollenhoven (2006), Heslam (1998), Van der Kooi and de Bruyn (1999).

2. "Things" are inanimate—in distinction from biotic (plants), psychic (animals), or religious (humans)—physical (energy, causality, force), or kinematic (motion, trajectory, travel).

ality, one must think about normal human experiences in terms of their distinct qualities. Each "facet" of human experience presupposes, points to, or reflects the other facets of life. Stated philosophically, each feature is an "aspect" (not a "thing" or "concept" of something), a feature, mode, way, dimension, facet or quality of a specific human experience of created reality. Each category listed below indicates a specific "way," or "manner," in which humans function, or behave. The ontic condition, i.e., reality, of each "mode," is highlighted by a verb, and the command character of that "dimension" by an exclamation mark.

Divine commands for:	Irreducible functional responses to:
Trust!	*Pistical*—certitude, assurance, commitment
Be reliable!	*Ethical*—troth, pledge, being faithful, loyalty
Be just!	*Jural*—fairness, recompense, equity, compensation
Stylize!	*Aesthetic*—suggestion, style, allusiveness, fashion
Optimize!	*Economic*—being frugal, stewardship, scarcity, thrift
Commune!	*Social*—sharing, fellowship, interrelation, club
Signify!	*Lingual*—depiction, signification, denotation, sign
Form!	*Technical*—making, training, shape, production
Discern!	*Analytical*—distinguishing, discernment, distinction
Be sensitive!	*Psychical*—sensing, feeling, emotion, passion
Grow!	*Organic*—growing, genesis, vitality, animation
Be energetic!	*Physical*—exerting, force, vigor, causality
Move!	*Kinematic*—moving, trajectory, travel, journey
Be extended!	*Spatial*—extending, expand, place, space, distance
Be unity!	*Numerical*—quantify, wholeness, measure, totality

An "aspect" of created reality is not an entity, thing, activity or event. In pointing to a universal mode, or dimension, of reality, it assumes, or presupposes, their existence. To catch a helpful glimpse of the structure of created reality, we must be aware of the rich modal diversity in how humans respond to God's diverse modal laws for daily life, including faith life.

A proper experience-based insight into created reality (cf. ontology) provides a glimpse of the structure of (Christian and non-Christian) faith life. Assuming this to be the case, we do well to replace "theology" (study of God) with "pisteology" (study of human faith life).[3] Based on God's three-

---

3. K. J. Popma (1903–1986), a prominent *reformational* philosopher, philologist, commentator and novelist, suggested that the difference between "religion" and "faith" is that the

pronged, i.e., creational, biblical and incarnated revelation, the study of faith life provides a clearer understanding of consensus and conflict between and within different faith traditions. It also counteracts a tendency of well-meaning theologians who perpetuate irrelevant and speculative ideas.[4]

To think of "theology" in terms of "pisteology" helped me in my (i) graduate studies at the Free University, (ii) work as preacher/pastor in the Bethel CRC in Newmarket, (iii) brief stint as promoter in Eastern Canada and USA of the ICS in Toronto, (iv) three decades of teaching philosophy and theology at Dordt College in Iowa, (v) writing and publishing my doctoral dissertation, *Philosophy and Scripture: A Study in Old Princeton and Westminster Theology*, 1978,[5] and (vi) international and global challenges for three decades (1975–2005), as secretary, speaker, boardmember and president of IAPCHE.[6] All these, at times unsettling, experiences convinced me of two things: first, structural resemblances in conflicting human faith traditions, and, second, a *religious* conflict between Christian and non-Christian faith traditions.

Living in a global village filled with human faith traditions that shape communities and cultures and compete for dominance, it is not a luxury, but a necessity, to have another look at a fossilized tradition of glib talking about such terms as "faith," "theology," "religion," "truth," "love," "church" and "Christian." However, faith life and its discipline of "pisteology" affirms what is good in traditional "theology" and rejects what is bad in, for example, any intentional *scholastic* theology. It seeks to avoid unfounded suspicions, endless theological debates and alienating conflicts. It opposes dogmatism and relativism, and avoids majoring in minor issues in our restless and troubled world.[7]

---

former centers on the *relation* between God and humans, and the latter on the human *response* to God in the *act of trusting.*

4. K. Barth, K. Schilder and G. Berkouwer, to mention only some theologians. I discussed with Berkouwer his ideas about (i) various creedal issues during the 1920s in the Gereformeerde Kerk, (ii) central issues in Barthian theology, and (iii) his experiences as one of the two Dutch Reformed guests the RCC had invited to "observe" the Second Vatican Council in 1962.

5. Published by Mack Publishing Company, Marlton, New Jersey, USA (354 pages); for his invaluable assistance, I am profoundly indebted to Dr. Lefferts Laecher for his interest, immense assistance and gracious demeanor.

6. International Association for The Promotion of Christian Higher Education.

7. More is needed at this time in history than merely rearranging some theological deck chairs on the titanic boat of unending "faith-reason" debates about scholastic thought- and act-patterns and their detrimental effects on (not biblicism, but) biblical faith.

Four Meanings of "Faith"

Humans experience the world, including themselves in it, in many different ways. Given the basic features of biblically directed reforming philosophical thinking (cf. Chapters 7–9 above), the fifteen[8] aspects of created reality, listed above in this chapter, point to a great diversity of ways in which human interact with it. They indicate how every aspect of created reality affects, and is affected by, all the other aspects. In other words, the study of "pisteology" is "special," not general, "particular," not foundational, "reforming," not scholastic.

In terms of God's all-embracing revelation through His Word and Spirit, a distinction must be made between (i) the structure of faith life (cf. "act," "content" and "aspect") and (ii) the religious direction in which humans move in their faith life. Given its non-structural nature, the latter is not accessible to "theology," nor even to "pisteology."

Faith as "Act"

Faith as a human "act" (verb) precedes faith as "content" (noun) and is qualified by a specific "aspect" (dimension) of created reality. These structural features of faith life differ from *religious* faith in that the latter reveals either wholehearted relying on, or trusting in, the Creator. It is a heart-directed restless groping for, and depending on, a human-made substitute or pseudo-god, unable to walk, see, hear, respond, rescue, deliver or redeem. *Religion* and "faith life" are not quite the same. While the former focuses on the "heart-centered" direction of **all** human life, the latter focuses on human faith as it is expressed, namely, as only **part** of human life.[9]

Cultivating one's faith life is misguided when it is *isolated* from one's heart-centered allegiance to God, the Creator. The different ways in which humans express their faith with others humans reflect what they believe to be most important in life. As in all structurally diverse human actions, human "faith" life is *religiously* guided by the human heart.

---

8. The number, and sequence, of the various aspects are still debated: e.g., is "irritability" an aspect located between the "biotic" and "psychic" aspects, and is the "imaginative" aspect, assuming it exists, pre- or post-analytical?

9. This distinction differs from such traditional distinctions between what is private and public, vertical and horizontal, primary and secondary, or organized religion and secular society or culture.

234

Integral to faith life is faith instruction, i.e., what and how to believe, proper worship, pastoral care, stressing God's promises, leaning on the Creator as the source of truth, comfort, justice, joy, peace, etc. The norm for all human life (*religion*) and "pistical" life ("faith" life), together with all other forms of human life, is God's full, or three-pronged, revelation. Ultimately, the norm for human life is neither "religion," nor "faith" since both of these are human responses to God's impinging revelation as the Creator, Redeemer and Comforter.

To say that the Christian faith is the norm for all human beliefs, attitudes, ways of thinking, etc., assumes that Christians are the standard for the behavior of humans. This well-intended but subjectivist tendency tends to be advocated in "evangelical" traditions.[10] The relation between internal attitudes and external actions is "reciprocal"[11]—"action and faith, like action and attitude, feed one another."[12] Though the primacy of God's "revelation" is not ignored for Christian living, including thinking and scholarship, "faith life" tends to play a subjectivist normative role.

In the New Testament, the apostle John used "faith" as a verb some eighty-eight times in the sense of placing one's "trust in a person." This use of faith shifted later from a personal trusting "in" a person to a general formulation "about" a person, and, eventually, to "assenting" to unambiguous propositional statements with inherent proofs and certainties.[13] This scholastic (Platonic) view of faith resulted in numerous complicated debates in Christian academic centers about, for example, the difference between "saving" and "non-saving" faith.

Faith as "Content"

The "content" of proper human faith depends on how they as humans respond to God's life-giving and -sustaining Word. That Word is the ultimate norm for all human faith. It is not the result of humans' *pistical* projection,

---

10. See David G. Meyers, "Faith and Action a Seamless Tapestry" in *Christianity Today* (XXIV:20) 1980, 16–19. About assumptions in teaching, preaching, counseling and child rearing, Meyers states ". . . we are as likely to act ourselves into a way of thinking as to think ourselves into a line of action"(16). Faith can be a *source* of action, but also a *consequence* of action.

11. Meyers (1980): 17.

12. Meyers (1980): 18.

13. Cf. James 2:19: "You believe that there is one God. Good! Even the demons believe that—and shudder."

but of God's sovereign revelation as the Creator. For humans to respond to His life-giving and -upholding laws is not an option, but an obligation.

The "content" of faith is not the result of wishful thinking, something faddish, a changing personal or communal myth. To the extent it is the latter, faith is superficial, flimsy, outwardly strong, but inwardly only veneer-deep. Such humans behave as weathervanes, easily thrown off course by numerous *pistical* crosscurrents and aberrations. Because such faith life is *religiously* not really rooted in the tree of life, it is easily exploited by charismatic gurus and egocentric shysters.

Non-Christians, including nominal Christians, lack staying power, solidity, "substance." They do not really know the life-changing and -encompassing joy at the core of their being. Constantly, they adjust to personal, communal and cultural changes. Instead of focusing on "what" is really important in daily life, they focus only on what they like, look for public affirmation, build ever-larger businesses, gain political power, become prophets by profiting from cultural renown.

The distinction between the "act" and "content" of faith is evident in all (oral or written) faith traditions. Whereas the "content" of faith is generally thought to be foundational and universal, the "acts" of faith tend to be more practical and dealt with in pastoral care and advice.

These two main parts of human faith relate to each other as "center" (content) and "circumference" (act). The depth of the former is evident in the relevance of the latter. When they are disconnected, the "center" faces a crisis, loses its integrating power and becomes irrelevant. If the opposite happens, the practical part must either be updated or removed. For various historical reasons and with many practical consequences, every major faith tradition experiences sooner or later locally, or globally, a crisis in its relevance and identity.

In this respect, medieval philosophical and theological inquiries about God as a rational and impersonal "It" (*Id*), even when combined with a biblical "God" (*Deus*), caused considerable crises in Western Christianity. It resulted in a sacerdotal church, shaped by Scripture *and* neo-Platonic and Aristotelian thinking in both philosophy and theology. This, in turn, gave rise to a complex scholastic system of beliefs about God, humans and the relations between them. As a result, as an organized "religion," the Roman Catholic Church adopted and conveyed—through seven salvation-conveying and -assuring sacraments—and shaped an accommodated faith life of millions of Christians in Europe and various regions of the world.

The crisis resulting from this spreading accommodating Christian faith

236

life triggered the sixteenth-century Protestant *religious* renewal. What made the Reformation so important was its opposition to two central issues: (a) the scholastic assumption that humans are "reasoning" and "believing" beings, and (b) the notion of hierarchy in the structure of human faith life and the related distinction between a higher (sacred) faith life and lower (human) life, i.e., church and society and culture. Given its (Hellenistic) stress on the "intellect," faith as "verb" turned into faith an act of "assent." That change undermined the certainty of biblical faith.

In returning to a more scriptural view of faith ("act" and "content"), M. Luther, J. Calvin and others sensed a need to turn away from a scholastic view of an abstract God wrapped in multiple sacramental blankets. These reformers focused on the biblical story of God's creation, the fall of humans, salvation in Christ Jesus and the work of the Holy Spirit, as the only way for restless humans to experience God as the only resting place for humans here and now.[14]

To sense such features of redemptive faith as its depth, wings, power, comfort, assurance and change in times of health and sickness, prosperity and poverty, peace and war, it is helpful to distinguish between faith as "act" and faith as "content," Living in a world of immense *religious* confusion and restless search for hope, we do well to focus not just on faith as "act" and "content," but also on "faith" as an "aspect" of created reality, and its relevance for human faith life.

Faith as "Aspect"

When I taught a course on "structure of faith," the students were surprised by the importance of faith as an "aspect" of created reality, not just of humans. Every aspect of created reality reflects, and affects, different ways, or modes, of all human living, including their faith life. The structure of any human act, movement or institution is influenced by an aspect of reality that qualifies such behavior. In this respect the structure of human "faith life" resembles the structure of, for example, family life, healthcare, justice, industry, recreation, communication, and art. Since they are analytical, "aspects" are not entities or concrete things, but abstract features of entities and activities.

---

14. See *Institutes*, II, ii, 1–7, 542–543. Cf. P. G. Schrotenboer's "Academic Freedom" about the role of theology in this context. For the corrosive effect of "doubt" and need for the certainty of faith, see Heb. 11:1, Rom. 14, and Jude 22.

Structurally speaking, humans are not qualified by only one aspect of their life e.g., "pistical." They are also qualified by their juridical, social, artistic, analytic, psychic, physical and other facets of being human. All human activities, or events, are qualified by a specific organizing principle, which unifies them all. A particular or leading aspect may qualify what humans do when they interact with the world around them. Humans experience created reality not just in physical, social, financial, aesthetic and recreational ways, as well as in a distinctly "pistical" way in their faith life (cf. symbols of sun, moon, rainbow, flowers, water, wine, music, cross, flame, fire, posture).

Implied in such a non-speculative, yet helpful and practical view of faith life is the importance of thinking about "faith life" in terms of the "pistical aspect" of what humans express in their faith life. This can be indicated in terms of five aspects of created reality, which play a subordinate, but important, role in human "pistical" life—the "ethical," "formative," "aesthetic," "psychic" and "physical" aspects.

The ethical aspect of created reality plays a significant role in faith life. Without it, faith malfunctions and loses its credibility. In a secondary, not primary, *pistical* sense, the features of loyalty, troth, fidelity, vows, marriage, and wedding are important in the faith life of (both Christian[15] and non-Christian) persons, small groups, communities, traditions and cultures.

The formative aspect of created reality is evident in the features of faith life related to nurturing faith, training followers, developing faith strategies, impacting the shape of society, form of culture and course of history. As to the range of options "whom" and "what" to influence with one's faith life is pistical in a "formative" sense. Though these two are interrelated, and affect other human acts, to "change" and to "trust" are structurally different. To elicit a change in a person's faith reflects a *formative* feature in one's "faith life." Any "formative" human act depends on the reason for the change. It may be personal, political, social, economic, cultural, etc. In short, the "formative" aspect of human living affects, and is affected by, one's "pistical" life.[16]

The aesthetic aspect of created reality has often been misused, or insuf-

15. The precise nature of these "ethical" features in the faith life of Christians differs from that of non-Christians. Sometimes these features are more obvious in the latter than they are in the former; in that case, Christians can learn from non-Christians about such virtues as friendliness, fellowship and loyalty.

16. Changes in faith life are difficult to implement, as is clear from "hot-button" issues associated with some creedal statements, institutional habits, gender issues, worship styles, kinds of church order, etc.

ficiently recognized, in "scholastic" faith and theology. This aspect centers on human imagination, which C. Seerveld at ICS has called "allusivity."[17] This feature of faith compels humans to explore going beyond what is intellectually accessible. Faith life exceeds what can be expressed systematically, formulated propositionally, or summarized in clear and detailed creeds.

Human faith is more complex and powerful than analytically knowable statements about faith life. Allusiveness leaves room for all kinds of images, allusions, metaphors, stories, plays, kinds of music, dances and mime in something that is engaging and even overwhelming. Imaginative creative reaching for, or alluding to, does not permit truth to be entombed in logically clear definitions and intellectual certainty.

Instead of avoiding faith metaphors, the aesthetic aspect of faith life welcomes them. It uses allusive faith metaphors as God's "tent," "eternal life," "heavenly banquet," God as "father," God as "mother," etc.[18] Structurally, the aesthetic feature of "faith life" is the condition for poetic jubilation and lamentation, and for music to those "filled with faith" to soar on wings of praise and to bow in grief and repentance. It is the fountain for stories and parables that allude to what is mysterious, yet real.[19]

The psychic aspect of faith is evident in the very structure of human faith life. As to its distinct nature, "faculty psychology" has caused considerable confusion. It assumed the Platonic and Aristotelian notion that "feeling" is one of the three "faculties," or "capacities," of the "soul"[20] a substance, in distinction from the "body" as substance. According to scholastic anthropology, what is "psychic" is not an "aspect" of created reality, but an inherent "capacity" of the human "soul."

This kind of (Western) synthesis thinking caused major problems not just in the three classic disciplines of philosophy, anthropology and epistemology, but also in the two disciplines of "psychology" and "theology" and their interrelationships. For example, is neurosis an emotional disturbance

17. See Calvin G. Seerveld, *How to Read the Bible to Hear God Speak: A Study in Numbers 22–24*, Dordt College Press and Toronto Toppence Press (2003), and *In the Fields of the Lord; A Seerveld Reader*, edited by Craig Bartholomew (2000).

18. See C. F. Henry, *God, Revelation and Authority*, especially Seerveld's (i) critique of Henry's rationalistic view of truth and his inability to do justice to such faith metaphors as "core," "root," "rock" and "bottom," and (ii) stress on the need for symbols that highlight the magnitude and inscrutability of truth.

19. See "Imagination: That Other Avenue to Truth." (note: could not confirm source) And rejection of empiricism's idea of truth and aversion to the role of imagination.

20. "Thinking" and "willing" are the other capacities. Cf. chapter 6. above.

that affects faith life, or is it pistical malfunction that influences one's feeling life, or, is it both, or neither, of these?[21] Or are emotions and impulses subconscious, i.e., independent of one's firm faith, or are they pathological indications of a distorted faith life? Is the act-structure of one's "pistical" life affected by an unusual "physical" and "psychic" aberration that will prevent the human "I" from behaving holistically? Or does the neurosis indicate an inability of the human "I," or "self," to be fully committed?

To equate *faith* life with *emotional* life makes it impossible for traditional theology to distinguish clearly between "mystical" or "experiential" faith and "psychology." Usually, the latter wins out over the former, because it tends to interpret human faith "acts" and "contents" as human projections of psychic needs and wants.

The physical aspect of faith life is evident in all faith life. Without going into details, but merely to illustrate, it is common to describe faith life by using "physical" terms like "road," "path," "movement," "way," "walk," "force," "cause and effect," "weight," "fall" and "rise." These faith characteristics apply also to such physical features of buildings, budgets, location, offices, events and instruments of faith life.[22]

Faith as "Direction"

The effect of humans defying God's central command to love him and their fellow humans was the *religious*, i.e., *heart*-centered, conflict between being either grateful for, or defiant of, his life-sustaining Word. "Faith" refers not just to the structural issues all humans share ("act, content, aspect"), nor to a Thomistic "supernatural addition" to what exists naturally. Instead it points to the important distinction between *religion* and *structure*. Unlike *structural* faith that is observable, analyzable and can be conceptualized, *religious*, or *directional*, faith has to do with the mystery of human radical obedience and disobedience.

The secret of this "faith" does not reside within wayward humans. It has

21. Perhaps, a sixteenth modality called "irritability," located between the "vital," or biotic, and "emotional," or psychic? Cf. footnote 8 above. To introduce a new modality needs more substantive argument. Also, irritability is very negative as opposed to the other modalities which express a positive function. Irritability seems just one kind of psychic response.

22. For other aspects of created reality determining the structure of faith life, including the jural, economic, social, lingual, analytical, biotic, kinematic, spatial and numerical dimensions, see Vollenhoven 2006 and Dooyeweerd (1953–58).

to do with the reliability of God's Word and Spirit. Desiring to be their own law-givers, humans rejected being God's loving image-bearers. In his letter to Christians in the prominent city of Ephesus, Paul wrote,

> As for you, you were dead in your transgressions and sins, in which you used to live when you followed the ways of this world and of the ruler of the kingdom of the air, the spirit who is now at work in those who are disobedient. All of us also lived among them at one time, gratifying the cravings of our sinful nature and following its desires and thoughts. Like the rest we were by nature objects of wrath. But because of his great love for us, God, who is rich in mercy, made us alive with Christ even when we were dead in transgressions—it is by grace you have been saved. And God raised us up with Christ and seated us with him in the heavenly realms in Christ Jesus, in order that in the coming ages he might show the incomparable riches of his grace, expressed in his kindness to us in Christ Jesus. *For it is by grace you have been saved, through faith—and this not from yourselves, it is the gift of God—not by works, so that no one can boast.* For we are God's workmanship, created in Christ Jesus to do good works, which God prepared in advance for us to do.[23]

When humans rejected God's Word, his central love command, they became restless, explored other ways to live, created their own gods and worshiped them as idols. Only two heart-centered responses to God are possible to his life-giving and -saving Word and Spirit, namely, a positive and a negative one.[24] Plato and Aristotle did not have this central law of God's love for humans in mind when they developed their dualistic anthropology of a (lower) "body" and a (higher) "soul" with the three "capacities" of "thinking, willing and feeling."

---

23. Ephesians 2:1–10, emphasis added (NIV).

24. D. Morey is clearly *scholastic* in his view of faith as "gift" when he says that faith is an "elusive and ambiguous word" used in two senses: (a) a *secular* sense of "knowledge" and what is "reasonable" based on "accumulated data" and "sufficiency of the evidence," and (b) a strict *religious* sense of something "supranatural" beyond "feeling" and "natural reason." Such a *pistis* is not merely a "mental exercise," but involves, according to Heb. 11:1, "trust and confidence" and "commitment" as "irrevocable acceptance." It refers to God's gift to humans, that activates their "spirits to enable them to interact with His Spirit," to a "new birth," something beyond what is "mental" and "feeling" and yet includes both of these capacities. For details, see "Theology Forum: The Essential Meaning of Faith," O. Gruenwald, ed., International Christian Studies Association, pp. 4 and 11.

A Spirit-filled heart-centered response to God's Word provides humans with a certainty "passing all understanding."[25] It nurtures an openness to his revelation and irresistible passion to be directed as a child of God in everything one does. Without such love, no renewal in human behavior is possible in any community, society and culture.

This "gift" of faith cannot be acknowledged without confessing it is undeserved and it calls for a Hallelujah response. The depth of God's love is centered in the life, death and resurrection of "the Son of God and the Son of Man," in whom to live is a privilege. The Spirit prompts humans to thank God for such love and wonder of genuine freedom. Such a simple, but powerful, walk with God calls for renewal in one's *heart*-directed functioning in all one does, including one's *faith* life and the study of it.

Failure to distinguish between the three *structural* features of faith (act, content, aspect) and its religious role caused many problems in Roman Catholic, Orthodox and Protestant faith traditions. In his intransigent critique of Roman Catholic and Protestant liberal thinking about "reason" and "nature," K. Barth (1886–1968) stressed that, unlike "faith" and "revelation" which are given to humans, "religion" is essentially projected by humans.

Barth contrasted God's dynamic self-revelation with a God who is projected by humans and never judges, but only advises. He stressed God's judgment that culminated in the paradox of Love-personified and Love-crucified, i.e., in God's "No" (*Nein*) to any "boomeranging" human faith. Christian faith responses to God's existential, or moment-to-moment, events (*Erreichnisse*) are impossible. Such responses undermine, even jeopardize, the ultimate "triumph" of God's sovereign grace. In terms of Barth's "existentialist" thinking, God "creates" the human capacity to believe.

In other words, biblical *faith* was seen to point to God's "gift" of grace, not to human faith in the sense of "act," "content" and "aspect" of created reality.[26] "Faith" is authentic when it is existential, i.e., "actuated," only a "gift" of God's "trumping" grace. To think about "faith" in terms of *structure* is human-centered anthropology, not God-centered theology, humanistic, not biblical.[27]

---

25. For Paul about faith-in-Christ in connection with "love" and "knowledge," see Romans 12:2, Ephesians 3:19, 4:17–32 and 5:1–2.

26. For this reason, neo-orthodox, or Barthian, theologians criticized, often rejected, the movement of *reformational* thinking in all the disciplines, especially theology.

27. S. U. Zuidema, philosophy professor at the Free University, perceptively stated in a lecture on "*dialectical*" thinking that K. Barth did not see the relevance of God's "creational" revelation for humans to enter, and live in, God's kingdom in Jesus Christ. G. C. Berkouwer

Despite significant differences in their dogmatics,[28] K. Barth at first in Germany and then in Switzerland, and Klaas Schilder (1909–1952) in the Netherlands (and some followers in North America) agreed on three issues: (a) the nature of "faith," (b) the role of "theology," and (c) their view of "anthropology" and "philosophy." Schilder also stressed "faith" as God's "gift" of grace and failed to account for the *structure* ("act," "content" and "aspect") of human faith, since it distracts from God's sovereignty, centers too much on the role of philosophy and anthropology,[29] and gives rise to a false faith. God always provides both salvation and faith, the latter in a "constantly new way."[30]

The impact of Schilder's view of "faith" on the discipline of "theology" was such that during the 1930s, D. Vollenhoven and H. Dooyeweerd agreed with his anti-scholastic stance and the need for renewal in the (Dutch) Gereformeerde Kerk. However, they parted ways with him, especially after 1944— shortly before the end of World War II—when he caused a major split in the Gereformeerde Kerk. The main reason for their disagreement with Schilder centered on four crucial, and interrelated, issues: (a) the meaning and role of creational and scriptural revelation, (b) the role and task of philosophy and theology, (c) the nature and scope of "common" and "special" grace, and (d) the stubborn and endless scholastic debates centered on "faith and reason."[31]

These discussions during the 1940s—when bombs dropped and freedom-fighters were imprisoned and killed—centered on the meaning of "human," "heart," "religion," "revelation," "covenant," "faith," "kingdom," "church," "Scripture," "Christian" and "theology." At such a critical time of

---

emphasized the "correlation" between human "saving faith" and "God's grace." In discussing with him the structural meaning of human faith, he did not reject my probing, knew about Barth's "existentialist" leaning, and stated that his own main concern was Scripture's idea of "salvific faith" and in that respect, like K. Barth, he sought to challenge Roman Catholic and both liberal and scholastic Protestants to rediscover the gospel and live by faith.

28. For example, their views on God's eternal decrees, the person and work of Christ, the nature of history, character of church, role of proclamation, and Scripture as God's Word.

29. For details, see his discussion in "The Heidelberg Catechism" of Q & A 21, Lord's Day 7, about true faith and all its benefits.

30. Cf. five kinds of faith (historical, temporal, blind, small, salvific), role of the Spirit, meaning of "Amen," and importance of God's promises.

31. Cf. three conflicts: (a) Gereformeerde Kerken: in 1944, Vollenhoven pleaded with Schilder, even one hour before he split the church, not to proceed with the schism; (b) Association of Calvinistic Philosophy about the need for creedal subscription as condition for membership in the Association; (c) Christian community, church and kingdom, Kuyper's idea of societal sphere-sovereignty.

major societal and cultural crises, Vollenhoven, Dooyeweerd and many others[32] reflected on a wide range of issues in different disciplines. They did this in a *reformational* way in especially philosophy, anthropology and epistemology. Hints of what rethinking involved with respect to the nature of faith life and study of theology will be indicated below.

Inherent Features of Faith Life

Every thing, person, event, organization, or institution functions in all the "modes" of created reality as indicated above in this chapter. Assumed in the modal diversity of the world is an underlying unity. Whatever can be said about the distinct features of any modality, they all belong together in that they reflect a certain mode of reality. Since each aspect of reality is unique in relation to all the other ones, each aspect has its own distinct nature.

This principle of "unity-in-diversity" is evident in two ways: *inter*-modally "between" different modalities, and *intra*-modally "within" each modality. For this reason, non-pistical aspects play a role "within" each mode of human experience, including the pistical one. They are present not in their original way, but in a pistical way.[33] Each feature in a modality reflects the features of all other modalities, but does so in a way determined by that modality.

These few (rather abstract) philosophical statements become clear, and show their practical relevance in every particular discipline, including "theology" in the sense of "pisteology." This indicates that any study of faith life is structurally not simple but intricate. Faith life also reflects the modal diversity of created reality. As a result, *non*-pistical modes of reality play an indispensable "structural" role in each study of human faith (pistical) behavior. They do so not in their *original* sense, but as analogical, or extended, moments in faith life.

A modal "difference" does not imply modal independence but, due to modal "diversity," a modal "universality." This is the ontological basis for the immense variety of *analogical* moments in all modes of human life, including "faith life." Structurally, all *analogical* moments in faith life resemble, reflect

---

32. For example, J. P. A. Mekkes, K. J. Popma, S. U. Zuidema, J. Van Riessen, M. C. Smit, G. C. Berkouwer, H. Ridderbos.

33. In the former case, the principle of "sphere sovereignty" applies, in the latter case the principle of "sphere universality."

or echo all non-pistical dimensions of created reality. The structure of human "faith life" is related to the structure of *all* human life. As a consequence, all non-pistical aspects of created reality play an indispensable role in all (Christian and non-Christian) faith life.

Because the pistical aspect is the "last" modality in the order of an increasingly *analytical* complexity,[34] analogical moments in pistical behavior are "analogies," which in a "retrocipatory" way point to earlier, analytically less complicated, modes of reality.[35] Unlike any other aspect of created reality, the pistical modality has (structurally) no "anticipatory" moments.

The two columns below of "Modality" and "Character" point to the structure of created reality, and the third column of "Examples" calls attention to the analogies, or "retrocipations" integral to the faith life of all (Christian and non-Christian) humans. These analogies provide a helpful glimpse of the intricacy and richness of faith life.

Modality	Character	Examples
Pistical	Certitude	Since it is the *core*, certitude is not an analogy, but the nucleus of all analogical moments, or retrocipations, of pistical life.
Ethical	Troth	*Fiducia*, faithfulness, loyalty, trustworthiness, dependability: e.g., *pistical* meaning of bridegroom and bride, husband and wife, marriage and adultery, wedding and divorce.
Juridical	Retribution	Justice, justification, righteousness, discipline, penalty, recompense, courtroom, guilt, lawyer, crucifixion, persecution, punishment.
Aesthetic	Allusiveness	Suggestiveness, imagination, solemnity, style, drama, liturgy, decorum, icons, sculptures, choirs, chants, symbols.
Economic	Frugality	Sacrifice, free grace, price, payment, ransom, tithing, cost of discipleship, reward, faith budget, diaconal care, riches of faith, treasures, poverty of unbelief.

34. Vollenhoven does not talk about faith as "terminal" function in the way Dooyeweerd does because of his ideas about the restlessness of meaning and the transcendental direction of reality and human thinking. They do agree, however, that the analogical moments in faith are only "retrocipatory," not "anticipatory."

35. Unlike the monistic "monad theory" of Spinoza and Leibniz.

Social	Fellowship	Fellowship of believers, congregation, denomination, organized church, brothers and sisters in the faith, spiritual retreat, sect, excommunication.
Lingual	Symbol	Banners, creeds, pictures, speaking in tongues, sermons or homilies, water, bread, wine, cross, gestures, rooster, colors, prayer shawl, rosary.
Historical	Formation	Influence, impact, tradition, change, progress, regress, deformation, reformation, adaptation, revolution, renewing, culture, civilization.
Analytical	Distinction	Understanding, insight, knowledge, *cognition*, studying faith traditions and texts, distinguishing, discernment, learning, pisteology, catechesis.
Sensitive	Feeling	Joy, enthusiasm, sensitivity, fear, stability, anxiety, depressed faith, insecure faith, needs of faith, release from guilt, effects of forgiveness.
Biotic	Vitality	Rebirth, regeneration, fruits of faith, growth of faith, living or dead faith, bud and flower of faith, tree of life, faith as mustard seed, growth of love.
Physical	Energy	Power, intensity, force of faith, foundation of faith, faith as a rock, cornerstone, fortress and bulwark, effect of faith,
Kinematic	Motion	Pilgrimage, journey, movement, path, way, direction of faith, running the race, exercise of faith, flight of faith, bowing down, reaching out and up.
Spatial	Extension	Ups and downs of faith, inner and outer, room for hope, prayer closet, transcendent and immanent faith, problem of extra *calvinisticum*.
Numerical	Number	Unity, quantity, diversity, triune God, cabalism, one day as thousand years, role of 3, 4, 6, 7, 12, 40, 1000, 144,000, finite and infinite.

To think in terms of radical (covenant-directed) "pisteology," not accommodating or compromising (scholastic) "theology," the importance and implications of studying and teaching faith life in a simpler, clearer and more relevant way are substantial. It opens a clearer awareness of the nature and importance of, for example, **inter**-modal relationships in created reality and **intra**-modal relations within each aspect of reality. It enhances our ability to address major problems and many misleading dilemmas in faith life related to important glocal practical, academic, cultural and historical issues.

The **first** benefit is that the pistical mode of human experience will no longer be thought of in terms of the Roman Catholic "grace-nature" distinction. Central to the latter is a "whole-part" view, in which faith life is equated, and confused, with faith as a "supernatural gift," an add-on, to natural and rational human life. It thinks of faith life in terms of organized religion, i.e., church as an institution, headed by the Pope, which directs human life as something natural and rational and subordinate to the guidance of the Church.[36]

The **second** benefit is that it discloses that ignoring, or misinterpreting, any analogical pistical moment may reflect some form of mysticism, asceticism or spiritualism. Paul's statement that "all that which is without faith is sin"[37] does not mean that any non-pistical activities—for example, doing business, playing games, political involvement, sexual intercourse, building a house—are essentially unrelated to faith life and, worse, even unspiritual and non-religious.

Not to distinguish between one *religious* and many *modal* differences reflects a neo-Platonic worldview and lifestyle. It thinks of "evil" as something that is spiritually *higher* having contact with what is naturally lower, and of "good" as when the *lower* sensory world reaches for the higher world of truth. Such a vertical "ascent theory" violates the nature of created reality. Mistakenly, it views the "anticipatory" moments in every modality to be (more) spiritual and the "retrocipatory" moments in every modality to be (more) carnal.[38]

Any attempt to explain the difference between "good" and "evil" in terms of some created diversity distorts the integrity and meaning of life. To ignore the rich diversity built into created reality is to yield to the lure of reductionism and to open the door to distortions and "isms." Any distorted ontology violates the integrity of human life, results in skewed philosophies, misguided anthropologies, speculative theories about faith life, even possibly some form of persecution.

The nucleus of the pistical modality is not restricted to any one, or any combination, of all its analogical moments. To violate this rule in Christian faith traditions results in the faith-related problems and aberrations of, for

36. This view of faith life contributed to the rise of medieval Christendom, diverse forms of Theocracy, and subtle forms of Ecclesiasticism.

37. Romans 14:23: "everything that does not come from faith is sin."

38. Similarly, Paul's statement "not all things are lawful" (1 Cor. 6:12) does not imply asceticism. Paul rejected the idea of being subjected to certain cultural customs. In terms of the context of the letter, he considered *certain customs* to be *lawful*, not evil.

example, work righteousness, scholasticism, doctrinalism, emotionalism, simony, cabala theories, moralism, unitarianism, asceticism or mysticism.

The **third** benefit is that it acknowledges that the *religious* conflict is fully creaturely, i.e., has its origin in human defiance of God's will. The source of this conflict within, and among, humans is not God, but the human rejection of His Word for created reality. Humans wanted something other than what is "thetical," positive, or good. Contrary to the dominant belief in our world, the source of the human predicament lies in the human refusal to "hear" the Good News and to bow before the Word of life and for life.

The *religious* conflict between rejecting God's revelation and affirming it may not be equated with the *structural* difference between what is "pistical" and "non-pistical." The fundamental conflict in human life is not between faith and feelings, theology and psychology, sacred and secular, higher and lower, church and state, calling and job, or what is God-centered and human-centered. It is different and deeper than that. It is all-pervasive, present not only, or primarily, in pistically qualified events, institutions and traditions, but also, at times perhaps more clearly, in family, academic, political, industrial, economic and recreational life.

Subject-*Subject* Relationships

Any human community consists of multiple *subject-subject* relationships, or ways in which its constituents interact with one another. This is true also of a *faith* community with its intricate network of "I-you," "I-we," "we-they," "they-us" and "they-they" relations. Relationships within the same realm differ from relationships between different realms. The former are "intra-regnal" (human-human), the latter "**inter**-regnal" (human-animal, human-plant and human-thing). While the former are heart-centered, the latter are involved in faith life only indirectly, as objects.[39]

The human subject-subject (**intra**) relationships affect, and are affected by, all kinds of subject-object (**inter**) relationships. Although animals, plants

---

39. The Creator-creature relationship is unique, not comparable to any human subject-subject relationship. To equate these two relationships distorts the Creator and creation. Humans who "covenant" with one another do so as creatures, never in a way God covenants with creatures. God is the origin, or condition, for the structure of reality, something no human is, or can be, for fellow humans. In all their acts and relationships, humans must acknowledge the uniqueness of God's relation to created reality and, vice versa, humans must acknowledge this in their relation to God.

and physical things cannot believe, they can, and do, play an important role in faith life. In numerous ways, they enrich human life, including faith (pistical) life. In wonderful, often surprising ways they are the creational conditions for humans to express, and enrich, their faith life.

All human "subject-subject" relations presuppose an all-encompassing and -permeating covenant of God with humanity's two covenant heads, viz., Adam and Christ. For fallen humanity, the Anointed Savior, i.e., Christ Jesus, revealed God's law of love and, through the Spirit, the "fountain" "and "tree" of life.[40] Rooted in "the way and the truth and the life" (John 14:6), humans hear again God's call to kingdom living, already here and now.

To behave according to God's three-pronged (creational, incarnated, inscripturated) revelation affects all human activities and relationships. To state it succinctly, though a bit abstractly, human *religious* response to God's central love command affects all (**intra**) "subject-subject" relationships and (**inter**) "subject-object" relations. Christian faith life is not isolated from one's everyday jobs and professions (cf. pietism or fundamentalism), nor is it added to one's natural or cultural life (cf. Roman Catholic accommodation), but it is, at least in principle, the most significant reason for hope in a deeply troubled world.

The distinction between "Church" as new humanity in Christ[41] and "church" as an organized faith community[42] is important—the former is not reducible to the latter, nor is the latter the same as the former. As to the *religious* direction of all human life, there is a certain correspondence between "pistical" and other organized (but non-pistical) traditions. A small cell of just a few Christians may become an embryo that not only gives birth to a new "faith" community, but also provides a glimpse of the structure, or contours, of a Christian society and culture. Key to such an eminently practical witness is the call to fellow humans to return in their heart to God. One's whole personal and public life needs to reflect the redeeming claims of God's imperial and kenotic law of love. To pass on to others God's "holy kiss," or to think of slaves as "brothers and sisters," reveals the nature, and consequence, of God's life-restoring kingdom of love.[43]

---

40. See Psalm 1, John 1, Colossians 1, Ephesians 1 and Revelation 1.

41. Also "body of Christ" and "royal priesthood," etc. For details, see chapter 13 below.

42. Also in non-Christian faith traditions such as synagogue (Jewish), kingdom hall (Jehovah's Witness), stake house (Mormon), mosque (Islam) and temple (Buddhism).

43. About "holy kiss," see Romans 16:16 and 1 Thessalonians 5:26, and about treating a slave as a brother, see Philemon 16–17. Unlike the kiss of a slave on the master's *feet* and of a pupil on the *teacher's hand*, a Christian's "holy kiss" is given, without bowing down, on the

Church as Human Faith Community

Structurally, a human *faith* community has its own distinct office-bearers. Their task is to equip men and women, young and old, poor and rich, sick and healthy, weak and strong, to rely on God's love-filled promises revealed in the birth, life, death and resurrection of God's only Son. They may not misuse their role and authority. Those who violate God's law of love are not shepherds but hirelings.[44] True servants are self-effacing in their tasks of proclaiming, pastoring, instructing, counseling, and enabling fellow-believers to live as renewed, and renewing, creatures.

In diverse societal, cultural and historical circumstances, Christians experience a wide range of joys and griefs, and develop new customs in their faith life about meaningful membership, many responsibilities, role of men and women, liturgical habits, catechetical instruction, visiting those who are sick and poor, who mourn, and who share the Good News with non-Christians.

With respect to being "organized" or "free," Western Christianity has at least six kinds of Church Order: Early Christian, Roman Catholic, Anglican/Episcopalian, Reformed/Presbyterian, Methodist/Congregational and Independent/Charismatic. Each has its own peculiar view of clergy, laity, ordination, gender issues, financing, leadership[45] and a concomitant view of the *structure* and *religious* direction of the culture in which we live.

Relationships within, and between, different *faith* communities, commonly called "church traditions" are influenced by a variety of *faith* factors that determine the purpose and agenda of each community. As indicated earlier in this chapter, features that influence the structure of faith life may be some or all of the following:

Numerical	Small, large, many, few, dozens, hundreds.
Spatial	Urban, rural, coastal, prairie, desert, valley, mountain, inner city, harbor, prison.
Kinematic	Mobile, nomadic, stagnant, changing.

---

cheek of humans. Paul neither approves the *status quo* of slavery, nor acts in a revolutionary manner, but places the dynamite of God's love under the foundation of slavery, in order to foster proper inter-human relationships.

44. See the graphic description in Ezekiel 34 of the self-centeredness of shepherds who instead of caring for others, misuse them for their own benefit.

45. For example, minister, superintendent, elder, deacon, charismatic person, pope, archbishop/bishop/priest, etc.

Physical	Strength, energy, resources, environment.
Biotic	Growth, stage, development, unfolding, maturity, health, vitality.
Psychic	Openness, reservation, anxiety, joy, mood.
Analytical	Discernment, education, instruction, catechism, knowledge, understanding.
Formative	Traditions, conventions, habits, customs, experiments.
Social	Tribe, race, community, relationship, cell group, fellowship, retreat.
Lingual	Symbol, liturgy, communication, gesture.
Economic	Riches, poverty, jobs, blue-white collar worker, lower middle and upper class.
Aesthetic	Art, music, song, harmony, style, sculptures, statue, choirs.
Juridical	Nation, law and order, party, court, discipline, guilt, judgment, censure.
Ethical	Single, couple, family, widow-widower, friend, loyalty.
Pistical	Christian faith community, non-Christian faith community.[46]

Church as Body of Christ

Humans express their faith life not only functionally in a *structural* way, as indicated above, but also in a *religious* way through the central spirit reflected in the main direction of the human heart. In the same way, for example, academic centers, cultural associations, political parties, business enterprises, labor movements, medical centers, and human faith institutions are *religiously* guided, or directed, by human heart-centered response to God's full revelation.

As to relationships in *non*-pistical life between what is private and public, individual and institutional, there are three distinct, but closely interrelated, temptations: first, to **correlate** "private" with religion or church life, and "public" with being a citizen in a state or a member of a society; second, to **equate** "private" with personal life and "public" with impersonal life; third, to **associate** "organized church" with what is vertical, and "God's kingdom" with what is (more) horizontal in some post- or pre-millennial way.

The contours of faith life are influenced by personal, cultural and histor-

46. The Society for the Scientific Study of Religion (SSSR) focuses on empirical studies, especially the six natural, quantitative, or scientific features of faith life. In distinction from the SSSR, the American Academy of Religion (AAR) stresses more the nature of historical, cultural, and social features of faith traditions.

ical circumstances in different parts of the world. The *faith* life of students may reflect, positively or negatively, the influence of their parents and/or teachers. The particular *faith* life of an office-worker, doctor, soldier, lawyer, corporate executive, commentator and entertainer may skew one's allegiance to certain cultural forces and assumptions.

In their daily life, humans experience things that are normal and abnormal, meaningful and senseless, redemptive and destructive. They do this in the way they know themselves, think of their calling, perform their tasks, interact with fellow humans and relate to non-human creatures. Such biblically *directed* (not biblicistic) self-knowledge enables Christians to be Spirit-led in shaping the *structure* of their faith life and to indicate thereby the *religious direction* of their whole life.

Subject-*Object* Relationships

In addition to **intra**-regnal subject-*subject* (or human-human) relationships, there are three kinds of **inter**-regnal subject-*object* (or human-nature) relationships, viz., human-*animal*, human-*plant* and human-*thing*. Scholastic thinking does not acknowledge this structural feature of faith life. This deficiency is perhaps an ascetical feature of a dualistic anthropology according to which faith life is "spiritual" or above the bodily part of human life.

Animals, plants and physical things have an important role in faith life.[47] They do this in two ways: as created entities for humans to care for and use and as **objects** with a symbolic role in the *structure* of human faith. There are numerous studies in human faith traditions about the role of animals, plants and physical things to express, and enrich, faith life.[48]

It was especially this section of an upper-level special topic course on "Structure of Faith," attended by mostly non-theological students, which surprised me with their positive response. They were struck by its practical relevance for faith life, its intricate nature, its importance for their careers, and significance for dialoguing with fellow Christians and especially with non-Christians. It deepened their environmental interests and desire to learn more about how faith life relates to the rest of human life and to the mar-

---

47. As they do in other forms of human life, e.g., farming, mining, business, fishing, space exploration.

48. For the *pistical* meaning of faith symbols, shields and other insignia, see Rudolph F. Norden, *Symbols and Their Meaning* (1988), St. Louis: Concordia Publ. House.

vel of the non-human world. Studying "theology" in terms of "pisteology" enhances studying Christian and non-Christian faith more meaningfully.[49]

To acknowledge the importance of God's *creational* revelation for the *structure* of faith life does not undermine faith life, but enhances it. The intent of the resume below about the three primary pistical categories of "subject-**object**" relationships is to call attention to their existence and to deepen of our understanding of faith life and the need for thinking about theology in terms of pisteology.

Human-*Animal*

A brief survey of animals used as symbols in the (OT and NT) Scriptures, and experienced in the structural features of faith life, indicates the importance of the "**subject**-*object*" distinction:

Dove	Peace, gentleness, purity—associated with God's Spirit and its fruits.
Lamb	Innocence, gentleness, weakness, sacrifice.
Goat, ram, pigeon	Atonement, sacrifice, covenant treaty (Gen. 15:13).
Eagle	Protection, providing care, soaring eagle as symbol of love.
Horse	Strength, conflict, war, might.
Mule	Stubbornness, humility.
Peacock, phoenix	Resurrection, immortality of Christ and of Christians.
Butterfly	Process of a crawling larva from cocoon to mature butterfly; symbolizes movement from life to death to resurrection to immortality.
Ant	Work, cooperation, strength in unity.
Fox	Deception, slyness, threat, subtlety.
Quail	Food, manna, care, daily sustenance.
Locust	Punishment, plague, judgment, curse.
Raven, vulture	Destruction, death, decay.
Snake	Deception, idolatry, healing.

49. Their positive response is one of the chief reasons for me to write this book. It is my fervent wish that nationally and internationally especially non-theological students will benefit from my probing and encourage theology students and teachers to become more aware of these issues.

Fish (*ichthus*)	"Jesus Christ, Son of God, Savior"
Pelican	Mother bird plucking open her breast and self-sacrificially feeding the young with her own blood, typifying the self-giving Savior (Rev. 5:9).
Rooster	Temptation to deny the Lord, alertness to faithfulness, being watchful to confess the Lord (on top of many Protestant church steeples in Europe).
Lion	Courage, strength, danger, winged lion in "Mark's Gospel" depicting Christ's deeds.
Ox	Sacrifice in Old Testament, winged ox in Luke's Gospel, pointing to Christ's sacrifice.
Cattle, sheep	Blessing, being cared for, wealth, being lost and found (Isaiah 53).

These animal symbols indicate that familiarity with God's *creational* revelation is not a speculative luxury, but a necessary condition to understand the structural nature of faith life. The "objective"[50] faith features of animals highlight various qualities of human faith. It avoids the error of an ascetic allegorizing of faith life and the danger of spiritualizing the world of animals. It deepens human experience, including understanding faith life with respect to faith as "act" and "content."[51]

This down-to-earth view of human faith underscores the need to acknowledge the structural nature of human faith. The latter does not depend on a profound, or so-called spiritual, insight of reputable theologians, or on some speculative theory of famous philosophers. According to Vollenhoven (and Dooyeweerd), practical life, including faith life, precedes any theory about life. Familiarity with non-human creatures is a necessity, not an option or luxury, to sense the intricate structure of faith life. In recognizing the "objective," or symbolic, importance of animals in their faith life, Christians know that animals also are God's creatures and are His handiwork. Knowing distinct features of animals can help Christians in their daily faith life.

Because they are creatures, animals are not gods to be worshiped. There

---

50. Not "subjective" for the simple reason that these creatures are not human, do not have a "heart," are not God's image-bearing responsible caretakers, who can break covenant with Him and, after repentance, "walk" with Him again in love.

51. It avoids reducing truth to logical concepts, scholastic propositions, or abstract doctrines for dogmatic or systematic theologians to debate endlessly and result in conflicting schools of theology and almost endless ecclesiastical schisms.

are no "holy" cows, monkeys, birds, lambs or snakes. To deny this is to misuse them.[52] Humans can use certain features of animals, or some other (non-human) creature, as "symbols" that point to the calling of daily walking with God, who (being faithful to his covenant promises) sent his only Son to become "the sacrificial lamb." Through the Holy Spirit, Christians, whose life is rooted in the Living Word, reject all idols, or gods, their own hands have made.[53]

Human-*Plant*

Also in the world of plants, a great diversity deepens, and expands, human sensory and analytical awareness about the structure of faith life. In Scripture and Christian faith traditions, there are numerous examples of the "objective" role of plants in the (subjective) faith life of humans. This is especially evident in Christ's references to plants in his parables about God's kingdom. For example:

Cedars	Strength, reliability, durability.
Lilies	Beauty, tenderness, new life, eternal life, annunciation, Easter.
Vine	Salvation, unity, or bond, with Christ.
Thorn, thistle	Anger, curse, sweat, toil, pain, difficulty.
Tree	Positively as shade, protection, life and fruit; negatively as idolatry.
Mustard seed	Power, vitality, growth.
Wheat, weeds	Harvest of believers, punishment of unbelievers.
Fig tree	Blessing, curse.
Sprout, shoot	Covenant promise, branch of Jesse's house (Zech. 3:8; Isaiah 11:1).
Fruit, harvest	Result, produce, maturity, growth, ingathering, celebration, rest.[54]
Olive tree	Anointing, peace, remedy against pain, Spirit, peace (Zechariah 4).
Palm branches	Victory, triumph, reception, confirmation, welcome.

52. According to Deut. 5, animals also rest on the seventh day of the week and benefit from the liberation of God's people from bondage to slavery.

53. Cf.(a) **Inter**-regnal subject-*object* (human-*nature*) and **intra**-regnal subject-*subject* relationship; (b) distinct realms (things, plants, animals, humans); (c) speculations—"sacred numbers" (cabalism), ultimate "space," divine "energy," infinite "force," "Ultimates" based on "human projections."

54. Cf. Psalm 1, John 15, Romans 12:2, Colossians 2, Ephesians 4:12–20, Galatians 5:22–23.

Human-T*hing*

Examples of how *physical* things play an "objective" role in faith life, according to Scripture and Christian worship:[55]

Bread, water, wine	Sacraments, cleansing, assurance, seal, sign.
Yeast, leaven	Penetrate, influence, perversion, spoil.
Chalice	Forgiveness, joy, blessing, suffering, death.
Cornerstone, capstone	Rock, firmness, solidity, security, source, fountain.[56]
Furniture	Pulpit, font, table, altar, prayer chamber, lamp (Psalm 119:105).
Scroll, book	Bible, hymn, register, church bulletin.
Harp	Joy-filled worship, foretaste of sinless life in new world.
Anchor	Ship held in place, believers in Christ (Heb. 6:19–20).
Ark, boat	Ship saved from flood as sign of Church, or new humanity, saved in Christ.
Stone, wood, metals	Tabernacle, temple, synagogue, images, church building, cathedrals, statues.
Light	Penetration, victory, festivity, life.
Stars, rainbow, cloud	Assurance, promise, threat, theophany, Morning Star (Rev. 22:16).
Shell	Baptism, cleansing water.
Armor, breastplate, sword	Spiritual warfare, protection, strength, safety (Eph: 6, Heb. 4:12).
Cross	Shame, honor, boasting (Gal. 6:14).
Incense	God's people as a fragrant offering and sacrifice (Eph. 5:2).
Keys	Absolve, excommunicate, incorporate, bind (Matt. 16:19, 18:18; John 20:23; Rev. 22:22).

55. As in the case of human-animal and human-plant, the human-thing relationship is highlighted in terms of Scripture, not in terms of non-Christian faith traditions.
56. Cf. 1 Corinthians 10:4, Psalm 18:2 and Matthew 7:25, 16:6.

Summary

The idea suggested in the last three chapters and proposed in this chapter is about the possibility and benefit of thinking about "theology" in the sense of "pisteology." This proposal does not dishonor God's revelation or replace God-centered thinking with a human-centered approach, or exchange firm "objective" truth with some shaky "subjective" truth. On the contrary! It seeks to supplant scholastic philosophy, anthropology, epistemology and theology by stressing the depth and scope of God's Word in a religiously radical and covenant-centered way.

The anthropological distinction between the *structure* of faith life (cf. act, aspect, content) and the *religious* direction (cf. positive-negative, repentance-defiance) implies that human life in terms of its *religious* thrust and concrete faith expression are distinct, yet related, i.e., they are neither identical, nor are they separated. The distinction between *structure* and *religious* direction of faith life may be present also in non-Christian traditions. In both instances, there is an inconsistency between the *structure* of faith and its *religious* direction. Depending on the final outcome, it may turn out to be both positive or negative: the faith life of Christians may be religiously wrong and that of non-Christians may be *structurally* correct.[57]

As to the *structure* of faith life, Christians and non-Christians have much in common. When *religious* conflict between them does appear, a life-encompassing clash may result and, in extreme cases, call for a parting of the ways, and perhaps give rise to life-or-death situations. To reflect on the nature of such a radical conflict in faith life, and the rest of human life, we turn to our next chapter.

---

57. Cf. James 2:14–26 about having "deeds," but not "faith." Only the power of God's Spirit can resolve the puzzle of human resistance.

CHAPTER ELEVEN

Religious Conflict

Introduction

The *religious* conflict, mentioned in especially Chapters 7–10, is reflected in the "spirit," "way" or "direction" in which humans have responded to God's all-encompassing (created, incarnated, written) revelation. What induces this spiritual, heart-centered struggle within, and between, humans, and what indicates how humans relate to non-human creatures?

In violating God's central love-command, humans who were originally not *self-centered* wanted to be self-sufficient, their own lawgivers. As a result, original, and all subsequent, human cultures battled relentlessly to provide proper priorities. After the Risen One returned as "Prince of Peace" to the Father, the Holy Spirit, at Pentecost, moved thousands to respond to the power-filled preaching of Peter, who only a few weeks earlier had denied knowing Jesus. Subsequently, countless humans locally, regionally and eventually even globally believed the Good News. The result was communities and traditions in which followers of the Lord Jesus sensed the power and mystery of God's grace-filled covenant faithfulness to humans.

In a *religiously* radical way, Christians experience God's liberating love in who they have become, the source of their hope in a world filled with pain and suffering, confusion and frustration. This occurred also in Europe. To deal effectively with the enormous challenges and problems of medieval society and culture, various prominent Renaissance, Humanist and Rationalist thinkers sensed a need for a new view of how humans should live and explore a new way to structure society. Needed is a culture without conflicts resulting from institutionalized faith life. The response was to ground free-dom and tolerance, which it is claimed are inherent in universal reason, and which supposedly enable humans to avoid rigidity and conflicts resulting from different forms of organized "religion." After all, it is asserted that faith life is private and personal, not public and central to society and culture.

Essentially, human responses to God's threefold (created, incarnated and inscripturated) revelation are always *religious* in the sense of being ul-timately obedient or disobedient, proper or improper, positive or negative.[1] Humans cannot not respond. Respond they must. They are "responsible" creatures.[2] This responsibility involves minimally two prominent issues: (a) a *self*-awareness that enables humans to catch a sense, or glimpse, of their role in society, culture and history, and (b) the importance for humans to look back, around, up and ahead, always reflecting His Love, as his caretakers, in everything they do in their educational endeavors, teaching and exploring in all the disciplines, also in such major disciplines as philosophy, anthro-pology, epistemology and so-called "theology."

The heart-centered *religious* clash in the immediate and ultimate di-rection of human history is too prominent to be ignored, too pervasive to be regarded as irrelevant, irrational or a residue of superstition. Being not *structural*, but *religious*, this spiritual difference between Christian and non-Christian is not analyzable, measurable nor enforceable, but only referred to, or hinted at, in terms of what directs humans in how they respond to God's all-embracing Word and Holy Spirit. To ignore this is to be shortsighted, sanction major land grabs, allow sex-trafficking, condone persecutions be-tween, even within, Christian and non-Christian faith circles.

The *religious* conflict manifests also in the way *self*-centered humans pollute rivers and lakes, ruin forests and pollute the air, and misuse fellow humans and other creatures. To damage the *structure* of created reality harms not just, for example, physical, psychic, social, jural and political, but also human faith (*pistical*) life. For Christians, the latter involves more than, for example, praying, meditating, reading Scripture, receiving or administering the sacraments, spreading the Good News, and celebrating God's call to love Him and those around us.[3]

1. For using these terms in a non-structural sense, see Chapters 1, 7–10.

2. Cf. H. Hart, *Understanding Our World: An Integral Ontology* (1984)(especially ix-xxii and 437–458.

3. What this means in other areas of human life (e.g., business, industry, politics, sports, emotions, education, art) should be spelled out in those areas and their studies, not in theo-logical seminaries.

Unavoidable Conflict[4]

The goal of God's one central command to love Him and fellow humans was not to create, but to prevent, a problem. In that sense, evil is not *structural*, but *directional*. God did not create it. There is no reason for it. After He had created everything, including humans, He saw that it was good. The conflict between good and evil is not inherent in, but integral to, being human. This enigmatic, puzzling conflict has affected all humans and cannot be "explained."

To "explain" it anyway is the epitome of evil. Why humans failed to do what their Creator told them to do as His image-bearers, and did what He warned them not to do as His gardeners in paradise—all this is a mystery. There is no reason, or explanation, for it. The result of this human hubris would have been catastrophic were it not for God's faithfulness to his Word for creation and covenant promises to humanity. The consequence of human rebellion against the Creator and of God's faithfulness to promises is such that there is an unavoidable conflict in the *religious* response of humans to His law of grace-filled love.

This conflict is *religious*, i.e., *directional*, not just *structural* in terms of conservatism and modernism, Jerusalem and Athens, Hegel's triadic society, culture and history, and Marx's communism in the East and Smith's capitalism in the West. It refers to an invisible, yet real, tension in private and public faith life. It indicates the way of life in which humans behave in everything they do consciously or habitually, intentionally or unintentionally, in every zone of society and facet of culture. Contrary to what is traditionally assumed in all, especially higher, education, this fundamental, or *religious*, conflict is present in three interlocking ways: "what" is studied, the "act" of studying, and the "relation" between these two.

Western culture experienced the consequences of local, regional, often incidental, "religious" conflicts between institutionalized human faith traditions without really redirecting the *religious* direction of society and culture. When Western Christians compromised the central thrust of God's redeeming Word through the accommodating activity of theologians and preachers, the nature of the gospel became a complex problem that depended on personal preferences.[5]

4. At first, I used "antithesis." Given the use of "*religious*" throughout this study, I returned to the term "conflict," since it indicates more clearly the radical nature of the renewal needed in all human behavior, not merely in faith life.

5. Cf. ecclesiastical hierarchy, "health and wealth" preachers, fame-seeking orators, charismatic mis-leaders.

This was evident already in early Christianity, Eastern Orthodoxy, Roman Catholicism and Protestant—Lutheran, Anglican, Reformed/Presbyterian and Baptist—conflicts, each claiming to be necessary and calling for changes in personal and institutional faith life, at times resulting in one or more schisms.[6] Conflicting faith traditions challenged Christians to determine whether the conflict was *religious*, i.e., directional, truly radical, or only peripheral and tolerable.

According to Scripture, the *religious* struggle within, and among, humans, became evident when they rejected God's command to love Him and each other. Taking the place of rebelling humans, Christ Jesus, the Word-incarnate, answered God's call by giving his life for them and, after returning to the Father, sent the Spirit, and his disciples spread the good news to Jews, Greeks, Romans and others. His followers soon experienced radical opposition to those who, gripped by the Gospel's power, had indicated the new *direction* in which humans can experience the joy of living in God's kingdom already now and here through the Spirit and in Christ Jesus.

In the fourth century, Augustine, and Luther and Calvin in the sixteenth century, responded in similar ways. During the closing decades of the nineteenth century, two (of the numerous) ambassadors of God's Word in Western Europe were G. Groen van Prinsterer and A. Kuyper who stressed the need for a radical, or *religious*, response to a growing Humanism, Liberalism and Pietism in churches, society and culture. In the twentieth century, challenged by Kuyper's simple but radical worldview, H. Dooyeweerd and D. Vollenhoven developed an integrally Christian way of thinking and teaching.

For these two persons, and others who joined them, including many preachers, *religion* is not an option or something partial, but essential to being human; it is not an addition, but radical and total, reflected in everything humans are and do. It affects everything humans do, not just their faith life (*pistis*) as a (religious) addition to their social, educational, political, agricultural, artistic, medical and industrial life. In fact, it influences the structure of a society, the nature of a culture, and the unfolding of human history.

It rejects humanism, fosters humility and assumes that God is faithful to His promises, maintaining his love-command, even if it requires sacrificing his Son for human violators of it, raising Him from the tomb, seat-

---

6. To equate secondary with primary issues in faith results in a form of denominationalism. A senior college student evaluated my teaching as follow: "I've been trying to get through this class *without learning anything*. . . . I do not want to remember anything of this course, because it differs from my *religion*."

ing him at His right side, and unleashing the Spirit to turn human hearts around to experience the marvel of God's grace in his kingdom. Already here and now, Christians can live, work, think and teach by keeping their eye on the Risen One, especially in times of opposition and persecution. Genuine heart-centered faith leaves no room for hubris and provides a certainty in life and death. In everything they do in their daily life, humans are called to move in the right *religious* direction in their constant "walk with God" everywhere.

It is distinctive of Christian living, also in philosophy and "pisteology," to endorse what is positive, or good ("thesis") and reject what is negative, or evil ("anti"). To resist what is good ("thesis") is, I believe, *religious*, not merely *structural* (e.g., physical, psychic, analytic, social, political, ethical). It refers to an unexplainable rejection of God's life-sustaining and redeeming love, moving in a misleading, even deadly, *religious* direction in human behavior. It involves a conflict that is radical, not peripheral, total, not partial, life-encompassing, not merely an addition. *Heart*-centered (Christian) faith is *religious, spiritual, directional* in all human behavior, not only in organized faith life, commonly called "churches."

Truth and Falsehood

The *religious* conflict presupposes a tension between what is right or wrong, life-enhancing or life-threatening. It is total, radical and all-embracing. It involves abandoning the path of life and joy and walking on a pseudo path of arrogance and grief. This change in the basic direction of one's whole, not only one's private and personal, life includes socio-political issues, cultural challenges and historical changes.

Advocating a faith based on intellectual brilliance, an infallible natural science, or dream of an absolute tolerance reveals the depth and implications of humanistic intolerance. This kind of intolerance is, ironically and paradoxically, detrimental to what is necessary to sense, and experience, a modicum of a stable society and culture.[7]

What the *religious* conflict ("antithesis") between life and death, "truth"

7. This Western reason-based enlightened notion of being free *from* any Divine revelation—and from any human, especially political, role of faith—is related to an uneasiness in non-Western cultures about Western liberal democrat*ism* and humanistic individualism, which minimizes, ignores, even opposes, the role of "faith" in everyday life, especially political life.

and "falsehood," is really about is reflected in the Old Testament account of the clash between David and Goliath. That battle was not merely bodily, physical, ethnic, political, or "pistical." It was total, radical, spiritual, directional, an "either-or" situation between the God of life and the pseudo-god of raw power. It indicated the childlike faith of a young God-fearing shepherd with a sling as he faced the huge defiant and mocking giant carrying a large sword. In this clash, neither Goliath's arrogance, nor David's trust in, and reliance on, God's covenant faithfulness is explainable.[8]

To live Christianly in all of life is not impossible. Its possibility is based on God's covenant faithfulness, his grace based on the sacrifice, and victory, of Jesus, his only Son. It is not human thinking and knowledge which is the key to knowing what it means to be human. Only in their childlike "walking with God," also in their probing into the meaning of created reality, can humans experience something of what it means to be "at home" with God here and now.[9]

In walking with God, or "living in His presence" (*coram Deo*), Christians indicate something of God's truthfulness in created reality, despite opposition from fellow humans and their own lingering resistance to rely on all His promises. Truth is not something that probing thinkers and searching mystics alone are privileged to discover. God's living Word is concrete and practical, evident in the love His image-bearers reflect, in a Spirit-filled and -guided way, as, for example, parents, farmers, rulers, judges, soldiers, teachers, merchants, doctors, artists and even entertainers.

To know "Truth," humans need to walk with God, be aware of His impinging revelations and guidance in their daily life. Such a walk with God is not the same as being a member of an "organized church," becoming "religious," joining a "religion." "Truth" has to do with proper spirituality, or direction, in everything one does. It does not depend on a philosophical or theological scholastic study of topics like "God," "created reality" or "being human" (trilogy of logic, ethics, passion). Truth is not first of all theoretical and abstract, but practical and concrete. It indicates how humans are directed in their daily behavior by the grace-filled "gift of faith," through

8. Cf. an editorial of Harry der Nederlanden, a former mine worker: "But where's the Goliath rising up over against me hurtling insults at the God of my people? Maybe I am part of Goliath now. Just as I adapted quite easily to the ethos of the mines, so I have also adapted to North American society." Cf. "David, a few smooth stones, and life in the mines," *Christian Courier* (February 16, 2005), 3–4.

9. Christians need not die to be with God. They are with God already here and now, and will continue to be in their state of death, in the Risen One.

which sinners are engrafted onto the "Tree of Life,"[10] i.e., Christ Jesus, "the way, the truth, and the life" in whom all things cohere (John 1:3, 4, 14 and Colossians 1:15–50).

Not to respond *positively* to God's three-pronged (created, incarnated, inscripturated) revelation is to respond *negatively*. In that case, one moves in a *religiously* wrong direction, acts "antithetically," lives "the Lie," opposes the living Word. In his response to conniving Pharisees, Jesus said: "You are from below; I am from above. You are of this world; I am not of this world. I told you that you would die in your sins; if you do not believe that I am the one I claim to be, you will indeed die in your sins" (John 8:23–24). To those who opposed him, he said,

> If God were your Father, you would love me, for I came from God and now I am here. I have not come on my own, but he sent me. Why is my language not clear to you? Because you are unable to hear what I say. *You belong to your father, the devil, and you want to carry out your father's desire. He was a murderer from the beginning, not holding to the truth, for there is no truth in him. When he lies, he speaks his native language, for he is a liar and the father of lies.* Yet because I tell the truth, you do not believe me! Can any of you prove me guilty of sin? If I am telling the truth, why do you not believe me? He who belongs to God hears what God says. The reason you do not hear is that you do not belong to God.[11]

To those who believed him, however, Jesus said: "If you hold to my teaching, you are really my disciples, then you will know the truth, and the truth will set you free" (John 8:31–32). The difference between those who understood Christ and those who did not is *directional*, not *structural*, *religious*, not *analyzable*. It is good news to be responded to in deep joy, not something to be unhappy about because they are focused on a god of their own making, namely, "father Abraham." In centering their faith life on their forefather "Abraham," the Pharisees were "antithetical."

This fourth *"directional"* use of "faith" differs from three *structural* usages of "faith" (for details, see Chapter 10 above), viz., (i) faith as verb, or "act," (ii) faith as noun, or "content" of what is believed, and (iii) faith as an

---

10. See Genesis 2:9, Proverbs 3:18 and 11:30, Psalm 1:1–3, Romans 11:11–24, especially verses 22–24, and Revelation 22: 2, 14.

11. (Emphasis added) John 8:42–47; see 51–55: "I tell you the truth, if a man keeps my words, he will never see death. . . . Though you do not know him [God], I know him. If I said I did not, I would be a liar, but I did know him and keep his word."

"aspect" of created reality. The fourth usage centers on what is unexplainable and overwhelming, namely, "faith" as God's "gift" of grace to self-centered, stubborn, "antithetical" humans to turn around and surrender to their Creator and call Him, in the name of His Son and through the Spirit "Abba (Father)." This "gift" of faith is the secret to *religious* renewal in the way humans can, and are called, to live anywhere in this world.[12]

What is at stake in this *religious*, i.e., directional or spiritual, struggle in the world since the beginning of human history is aptly described in the book of Proverbs in terms of a woman named "wisdom" and another woman called "foolishness." They represent, respectively, obedient and disobedient responses to God's life-affirming commandment to love.[13] This central law is not antithetical or destructive. To think it is the cause for the *religious* conflict within, and among, humans is to believe two colossal myths: first, that humans, who thank God for His grace and who love fellow humans, even when they are their enemies, are "abnormal," and second, that humans who reject God's law of love and the only Savior of the world are "normal." To believe this epitomizes the deception of unbelief, subtlety of evil and depth of Satan's fury.

A common mistaken view of this all-pervasive *religious* conflict is the idea in academic, political and other public circles, that Christian faith is personal and private and that a "non-religious" stance is imperative for a peaceful society and culture, especially in academic, economic, political, technological and recreational life.[14]

Exiled by hostile (chiefly Roman Catholic) powers in France, J. Calvin had become a refugee already at age twenty-seven. Writing on behalf of fellow French refugees, who, like him, were accused of being dangerous, he described what the conflict was really about. In the "Preface" to the first draft of the *Institutes*, in 1536, he wrote to Francis I, King of France, about

12. Regarding "faith" as *gift* of God's grace, see Paul in Ephesians 2:4–10. Faith as 'gift' results in conversion, i.e., turning back to God (cf. Dooyeweerd (1953) I:59 and 61). The *gift* of faith is not a human act, but evidence of God's "mercy," namely, sinners becoming "new creatures" and the promise of a new heaven and earth (cf. Psalm 57:1, 1 John 5:4–5 and 11–12, Isaiah 65:17–25). Ephesians 2:4–10 is central to G. C. Berkouwer's extensive dogmatics and H. Ridderbos, notably in his *The Coming of the Kingdom* (1962) and *Paul: An Outline of His Theology* (1975).

13. Cf. Proverbs 1–9 and 31 about lady "wisdom," *and* chapters 10–30 about a wise and a foolish woman.

14. For a skewed view of the *religious* "anti-thesis" of, for example, (i) dualistic Christians in the Middle Ages, (ii) theocratic-leaning Christians, since the sixteenth century, in Europe, Latin America and North America, and (iii) especially Evangelical faith traditions, with respect to their understanding of such terms as "religion," "church," "kingdom of God," "discipleship."

those who "blame us for all the disturbances, tumults and contentions that boil up against us" and described that blame by citing of Elijah's comment to Ahab, king of Israel: "[I]t is not we who either spread errors abroad or incite tumults; but they who contend against God's power."[15]

Lie as Parasite

The diabolical "Lie" has no substance, basis or validity. It is the epitome of deception, an unparalleled temptation that unleashes indescribable anxiety and misery. It is not original, but parasitical, a satanic deception that acknowledges the truth of the Creator by opposing Him. It feeds off God's revelation by questioning its reality while opposing it. The umbilical cord of the Lie is its truth-dependency—it appears under the guise of truth. Though not original, the *religious* antithesis is a formidable subtle force with, unless halted, devastating consequences.

No human tradition, social institution and form of culture is as such, or inherently, antithetical to what God created. What *is* unique to evil and human sin is that they are *abnormal*. They feed off life, in order to destroy it. They do not foster fellowship and wholeness, but incite animosity and discord. For stubborn, unloving humans to be positive ("thetical") is possible only when, through God's incarnated Word and Holy Spirit, they return "home" and live as His love-filled image-bearers. Ignoring God's law(s) for life is being negative, rejecting what is good, living in an "antithetical" way.[16] The *religious* clash is 'existential,' not original or something God created. The *religious* conflict is not between what is higher, and sacred, in distinction from what is lower, and natural, in human life.

15. Responding to Ahab, king of Israel, who had said to Elijah: "Is that you, you troubler of Israel?," Elijah replied: "I have not made trouble for Israel. . . . But you and your father's family have. You have abandoned the Lord's commands and have followed the Baals." [In his translation of Calvin's *Institutes* (1960), F. L. Battles indicated that Calvin more often quoted Scripture *ad sensum* than *ad littteram*. . . ." See "Translator's Note," 1960: xxiv.]

16. Cf.1 John 2:1–19. A. Kuyper called Christians "abnormalists," who know they are sinners, and referred to non -Christians as "normalists," who are not aware of being sinners. He thinks of humans in their present situation as sinners, not, as John did, in terms of God's original and final intent. Cf Psalm 139:21–22: "Do I not hate those who hate you, O Lord, and abhor those who rise up against you? I have nothing but hatred for them; I count them my enemies." In the next two verses, the psalmist does not retract this unusual prayer, but asks God to see if he is in any way "offensive" and to lead him "in the way everlasting." Only Jesus Christ fulfilled this prayer in a loving, or thetical, way.

Any *religious* bifurcating in the way humans live violates the unity and intent of God's all-embracing revelation. Such a *religious* inconsistency lures humans to become victims of wealth at any cost, the raw power of self-centered bankers, the chest-thumping fame of athletes, the role of self-centered philanthropists, and the fame of popular preachers and pop-theologians who specialize in "religious" issues often at the expense of their so-called "faithful" followers.[17]

According to Scripture, "evil" and "devil," sin and suffering, always reflect an "idol," an "ism," an exaggeration of the word to which it is attached—e.g., Humanism, Rationalism, Individualism, Capitalism, Democratism, Communism, Socialism, Materialism, Pragmatism, Racism, Atheism, Hedonism, Sexism, Nihilism. None of these are original, or will be ultimate. They are parasitic, presuppose what they reject, i.e., the Creator and His creation.[18] As surrogate gods, they reflect *religious* rebellion, Satan's wish to *be*, not to *have*, the law-giver. Compared to God Almighty, idols[19] are "human-made," fakes, surrogates, "no-things," "figments of one's imagination." For the prophet Jeremiah, an idol is "a scarecrow in a melon patch"; it seems real, but is not. Idols are unable to "speak" and must be "carried," since they cannot walk."[20]

God determines the laws for justice, truth, integrity, gentleness, joy, order, service and peace. Antithetical to His will for human life are the evils of, for example, injustice, greed, falsehood, duplicity, brutality, misery, anarchy, exploitation and war. In order to rescue recalcitrant humans and save a sin-riddled world, God sent his only Son (John 3:16) and poured out His Spirit.[21]

In summary, to prepare for the rest of this chapter and the two chapters

17. For details, see VanderStelt (1978) about beliefs of Presbyterian theologians who advocated libertarian ideas about society, government, economics and education based on the rationalistic philosophy of Thomas Reid, John Locke and Adam Smith.

18. Cf .Genesis 1:31: "God saw all he had made, and it was very good."

19. Idols can be associated with natural forces, a person's body, family life, race or color, and with such human idols as fame, greed, individualism, do-goodism, denominationalism, Calvinism, fideism. For details, see Bob Goudzwaard (1984), and, although less clearly, a North American evangelical like Herbert Schlossberg (1990).

20. Jeremiah 10:5. He tells victims of ruthless powers that their oppressors are only "scarecrows." "Do not fear them; they can do no harm, nor can they do any good." For his comments about idols and their origin, see especially Jer. 10:8–9.

21. The depth and scope of John 3:16 assumes awareness about four things: revolting angels in heaven, human fall on earth, relation between heaven and earth, and the diverse ways in which the "anti-thesis" affects humans, society, culture and history. See A. Kuyper (1923): 5–19 and 200–292; K. Schilder (1929): 3–86.

thereafter,[22] at least five comments about the *"religious* conflict" will be helpful: **(1)** the *religious* conflict, i.e., "anti-thesis," is not limited to a disagreement within, and between, organized Christian and non-Christian faith traditions. It refers to a heart-centered, basic refusal to live within the liberating boundaries of God's covenant with fallen humanity and the privilege of responding as His image-bearers; **(2)** the conflict between humans and God was, though not "caused" by Satan, not unrelated to his "antithetical" defiance of the Creator;[23] **(3)** the *religious* conflict is not merely a simple "either-or," "positive-negative," or "us versus them" issue. Both are reflected in human life, including faith life, as Paul aptly indicated in Romans 7:14–25, especially "For what I do is not the good I want to do; no, the evil I do not want to do—this I keep on doing"; **(4)** the depth and scope of the *religious* antithesis presupposes God's covenant relation with humankind and the way of hearing God's voice accordingly. It calls for incessant "dying and rising" with Christ, trusting in God's abiding love, and gratefully loving Him in everything we are, do, and have; **(5)** because the *religious* conflict is radical and inscrutable, no rational probing, philosophical reasoning, logical searching, epistemic debating and theological probing can explain it.[24]

Thetical and Antithetical

The result of humans not doing what God told them to do was the directional, or *religious*, conflict in human behavior. The goal of His three-pronged (creational/incarnated/written) revelation is positive, not negative, i.e., thetical, not antithetical. The intent of fallen humans, however, is to be antithetical. But God's continued revelation protected defiant humans from being victimized by their predicament outside the God-intended paradise. His overpowering grace embodied in the incarnate One and poured out Spirit is the "secret" or "key" to the continued existence of the world as created reality.

22. For details about "idols," see A. Janse and D. Vollenhoven about "heaven and earth" and "angels and humans" in chapter 9 above, and "truth and lie."

23. The relation between sinful humans and fallen angels is not a reason for humans to blame fallen angels for their own rebellion and misery on earth, nor to absolve themselves of their calling to be God's image-bearers.

24. See Paul's remarkable description in 1 Corinthians 1:18–31 about Christ as God's wisdom and power in connection with (a) the weakness of philosophers and scholars, (b) a "stumbling block to Jews and foolishness to Gentiles" and (c) the paradox of the "weakness of God" and "strength of man."

The conflict between "thetical" and "antithetical" indicates that God is the source of what is "good" and that humans are called to reflect His image by rejecting what is "evil." Humans move in the wrong *religious* direction when they do not rely in their diverse tasks on God's covenant faithfulness, revealed in the Savior who, on their behalf, or for their sake, endured God's wrath on self-centered humans. Without God's faithfulness to his Word for created reality, affirmed in His mercy, and promised to undeserving caretakers, humans would be unable to live and call upon Him. Being faithful to his Word, God calls humans to honor Him by discovering his structural laws for daily life and doing so in a wholehearted, amen-like, way to His one single call to love in whatever they do here and now.[25]

The key to such a response is determined by the human "heart," or "place" (A. Kuyper called it "plek"). This is where the "spiritual conflict" arises between listening and defying, serving and exploiting, carefully tiptoeing through creation and lovelessly trampling upon God's creatures. This "spiritual," or *religious*, conflict permeates everything humans do in whatever they do in their life in community and society.[26]

To "describe" this conflict is easier than to respond to it. The latter is demanding, time-consuming, even dangerous, if not life-threatening. This basic strife affects all of human life, not just institutional, or organized, faith life traditionally, often glibly, called "religions." Such conflict is potentially dangerous, even deadly, when it is perpetrated by a tradition that is "turned-in-upon-itself" (*incurvatus in se*) and violates the law to love human, and non-human, creatures.

Which "spirit" prevails in one's "heart" determines all human "functions," not merely one's faith (pistical) life. It affects everything humans do, privately and publicly, in compliance with, or defiance of, the God of life. Does it reflect the love and grace-filled God of "heaven and earth," or does it reflect a private or public handmade idol? Just as a wheel's hub and rim, center and circumference, are inseparable, the human *heart* and the diverse functions of humans cannot be separated. Human "heart," or *religion*, and human—Christian and non-Christian—"faith life" are distinguishable but not separable.

---

25. Cf. Micah 6:8: "He has showed you, O man, what is good. And what does the Lord require of you? To act justly and to love mercy and to walk humbly with your God."

26. Cf. Genesis 3:15 and Romans 1–3. According to K. Barth, sin can only be confessed, not explained; to explain sin is sin.

Antithesis and Solidarity

The *religious* conflict cannot be eliminated by anything humans are able to do *structurally*. The humans' refusal to do what God told them to do resulted in their attempt to hide from His face. To recover from their fall, humans could not rely on a certainty inherent in Platonic and Aristotelian faculties of "thinking, willing and feeling." God assured his covenant-violating image-bearers of His covenant faithfulness for a world with human caretakers, who rejected their Maker's intent for humans to be *religiously* redirected on the road of life and away from misery and grief.[27]

The nature of the *religious* conflict is such that it does not eliminate what Christians and non-Christians share: they live in the same world as humans. Their solidarity as humans is assumed in whatever they do in all their cultural, also academic, endeavors[28] in God's garden, also in the study of "theology." About the relation between "antithesis" and "solidarity" K. J. Popma wrote:

> God himself proclaimed the antithesis, in order to remove the historical vacuum after the fall into sin. That does not mean that we can always precisely indicate how the antithetical situation exists; but it does mean that the antithesis cannot be abolished through a solidarity found in its background. . . . But just as we cannot always tell exactly how the antithetical situation has been structured, so also we cannot tell precisely what the configuration of humanity's solidarity is. It does seem prudent to expect much from the solidarity; and it is a given about which we begin to understand something when we observe that solidarity delineates itself against the antithesis as its permanent background.
>
> We cannot trace with precision the paths of antithesis and solidarity. We can develop a principled knowledge of both, but we cannot map that knowledge with exactness. Therefore, we must be aware of the possible presence of unresolvable tensions as such.[29]

---

27. Though the difference between "those who shrink back and are destroyed" and "those who believe and are saved" (Heb. 10:39) is ultimate, both responses are human. See also those mentioned in Matthew 7:21: "Not everyone who says to me, 'Lord, Lord' will enter the kingdom of heaven, but only he who does the will of my Father who is in heaven." Brutal dictators, serial killers, moral perverts, etc., remain human.

28. All academic schools reveal this tension, including theological seminaries.

29. Popma (1969): 52. .

The simultaneity of *"religious* conflict" and "human solidarity" is noticeable in all human activities, including those related to their specific faith life and study of it. The *religious* clash in humans was not mitigated by God's general revelation and common grace. His faithfulness to his Word for creation and his central law of love to all humans is presupposed in the sense that it makes this conflict in how humans live even possible.[30]

In rejecting Positivism's emphasis on scientific objectivity and the supposed irrelevance of God's revelation for humans to know truth, A. Kuyper stressed not only the personal and cultural importance of Scripture's witness to truth, but also the *religious* antithesis, i.e., spiritual conflict it evokes. In all society and culture, including the academy, the contrast between Christian and non-Christian commitment and living cannot be avoided.[31] It is deep and broad, not optional or peripheral. It is internal, invisible, *religiously* real. It reveals a human struggle between two opposite directions of human behavior.

Vaguely, humans sense this conflict in their repressed inklings of God's impinging revelation. However, they suppressed its relevance. In an "abnormal" way, disobedient humans do not sense, if at all, God's impinging power, or celebrate His faithfulness to his own Word for the world cared for by His image-bearers. Breaking covenant with Him, humans turned their backs to their life-giving and -sustaining Creator, and wanted to determine for themselves how to live in His world.[32]

In the "spirit" of A. Kuyper, H. Dooyeweerd distinguished in his "transcendental critique of theoretical thought" between two polarities: (i) a limited polarity *within* the non-Christian ground-motives of Greek "form/matter" and Modern "freedom/nature" thinking, and (ii) a large polarity *between* Christian and non-Christian thinking.[33] While he stressed the second

30. Cf. Kuyper's semi-scholastic and -mystical view of the encyclopedia of knowledge about "natural" and "cultural" sciences (*wetenschappen*). For details, see Vander Stelt (1973): 178–190.

31. Cf. A. de Bondt's (undated) book about the depths of Satan, in the areas of family, church, state, society, nations, science, art, technology and cults.

32. See A. Kuyper, *Pro Rege*, I-III and *Lectures on Calvinism* (1908), and Peter S. Heslam, *Creating a Non-Christian Worldview: Abraham Kuyper's Lectures on Calvinism* (1998). In "De Antithese," an unpublished lecture at the annual meeting of ARP (Association for Reformational Philosophy) January 1, 2000, J. Hoogland talked about some key issues regarding the meaning of "antithesis" in a polarized society. He suggested an alternative approach to (a) a coherent "worldview" with an implicit ontology and (b) a different idea of the context of giving meaning ("zingevingskader") in connection with "truth" and "faith."

33. This *third* approach, described as a form of "synthesis" thinking, tries to resolve con-

conflict, he did not forget the importance of Christians being engaged in heart-to-heart discussions with non-Christians about their basic differences.

Such a dialogue across the great *religious* divide is necessary since all humans, living in the same world, are exposed to God's creational revelation, and therein experience a commonness, or solidarity, with fellow humans. Given this *structural* solidarity, a *religiously* serious thinker welcomes self-critique, explores what may be wrong in one's own view, and correct in the views of someone else. Christian thinkers also must learn to be explicit about what is implicit.[34]

C. Seerveld clarified the distinction, and relation, between *religious* conflict and *structural* solidarity when he wrote about three horizons and ways of human knowing, viz., "truth," "correctness" and "accuracy."[35] He stated,

> It is very important to distinguish the different horizons to knowledge, the varying structural aprioris which limit and require obedience of human knowledge. Beside the root law of Truth are what I shall call the test of cosmic correctness and the criterion of accuracy.
>
> 1. Achieved knowledge is *true* if the product develops Christ's lordship of the world (rather than the devil's) and pleases Him.
>
> 2. Knowledge gained is *correct* if the relative states of affairs known are kept relative, limited, related to the rest of the world in its (proper) place.
>
> 3. Knowledge obtained is *accurate* if the subject's knowing agrees with the structural laws (needing to be more-or-less correctly posited by man in the light of Truth) concerning a particular feature or function of a knowable object.[36]

First horizon. "Truth" refers to "the way God does things," his "staying-power," his "deeds" which "hold" and are "trustworthy, certain of fruit, ef-

---

flicts between non-Christian and Christian thinking by combining both through compromising both.

34. W. Harry Jellema and Henry Stob, precursors of Reformed Epistemology at Calvin College, interpreted "antithesis" more in terms of "spiritual" conflicts among humans and institutions. In his "transformational" approach, J. Klapwijk believes Dooyeweerd's transcendental critique of theoretical thought is not sufficiently clear. Instead of polemic thinking about starting points, presuppositions and principles, a thinking in terms of consequences, implications and conclusions of views is required.

35. See Seerveld (1971): 161–175, especially 161–169, and notes of J. H. Kok, Dordt College, in his response to Richard Mouw and a Protestant Reformed pastor on "Common Grace and the 9/11 World Trade Center Attack," Dordt College, Iowa, 2002.

36. Seerveld (1971): 164–165.

fecting what will last." Whenever "Truth" appears, there is "a God-revealing, a faithful healing dynamic that enriches those who are responding to its development." It gets persons "actively caught up in the fabric of protecting, strengthening, sense-opening communion with the almighty holy One."[37]

To recognize the human "heart-depth" is the secret of the "Truth-depth" of human experience. Truth is "the matrix within which God's creatures are to live and move and have their meaning. Truth is accepted, lived, acted out, or disobeyed."[38] It is "the most fundamental, the largest, final horizon within which human knowing necessarily takes place."[39] Directionally, or *religiously*, the opposite of Truth is the Lie (John 8:44).

Second and **Third** horizons. "Correct" and "accurate" knowledge are not so much *directional* as they are *structural*. "Correct" knowledge concerns the "rightful place" of things and events, their proper "context" within the "cosmic order." When they are viewed incorrectly, some form of distortion and idolatry results. "Accurate" knowledge has to do with specific features and behavior of particular things. The effect of an inaccurate understanding may be a malfunction with serious, although initially limited, negative consequences.

What complicates matters is that those who live the Truth can have *in*correct and *in*accurate knowledge, and that those who *religiously* live the Lie can have "correct" and "accurate" knowledge of the world. As to "accurate" and "correct" knowledge, Christians and non-Christians can experience, despite their *directional* conflict, a significant *structural* solidarity.

Non-Christians underestimate, or attempt to ignore, this complex state of affairs to the extent they think about "religion" as referring to only a part of human life and limited to what is personal in connection with faith life and related disagreements and conflicts.

---

37. Seerveld (1971): 161–162. Seerveld contrasts this covenantal nature of truth with the scholastic and linguistic meaning of truth.

38. Seerveld (1971): 163. Regarding "Truth" in relation to Christ, see John 5:33; 8:31–32, 34; 14:6. Truth has a "jealous and exclusive character." To keep silent and remain ignorant about God is "still nose-thumbing at God."

39. Seerveld (1971): 164. With various false dilemmas in everyday life for all humans (for details, see chapter 12 below).

Conflict and Pistical Life

Given the deeper and broader meaning of "antithesis," the *religious* conflict is not restricted to organized *faith* life and traditions. Nor does it refer to what is popularly, although improperly, called a "church-world" issue. A conflict is *religious* when it is *heart*-centered, i.e., broader and deeper than organized *faith* communities and traditions. A *religious* conflict manifests also in political, economic, social, artistic, educational and other forms of human behavior.[40] It is radical in the sense that it directly affects all human life and indirectly even non-human life (e.g., animals, plants, water, soil, air), the structure of society, thrust of a culture, and role of regional and global pseudo-gods.

Such "antithetical" forces, and unavoidable crises, may appear to be not of primary, but secondary, importance in many Christian and non-Christian faith traditions, while they actually cause much misery through the "sin" of omission. When *structural* problems in faith life—caused by well-intended, but misguided, theologies—play a *religious* role, they give rise to anger and hostility, even clashes. Such struggles within Christian organized faith traditions result in much grief, loss of credibility, endless squabbling and splintering, fueled, consciously or unconsciously, by accommodated ways of (theological) thinking and claiming to be biblical.[41]

Non-Christian faith traditions also experience the grief of faith ("pistical") conflicts, as is evident in, for example, (a) the African Gold Coast, between black art of "private deity" cults and "public tribal" cults, (b) clashes in China between Confucianism and Taoism, and between these two traditions and heterodox Buddhism, and (c) deadly clashes in Iran and Iraq between Shiite and Sunni Muslims.[42]

Unlike *religious* conflicts in Christian faith traditions, cultural, especially educational, differences in denominational traditions are hard to deal with

---

40. During World War II, I saw "Gott mit uns" (God with us) inscribed on the belt buckles of German officers. Fifteen years later, while in Amsterdam, I heard Richard Nixon's response, over the radio, to a reporter's question in Germany why in his public speeches in the USA he talked about God in some, but not in other, parts of his country. In a Machiavellian way, he responded, "It pays politically to put some of that God-stuff in there once and a while."

41. I experienced this in three different countries (the Netherlands, Canada and USA) in the areas of education, family life, industry, and organized faith community.

42. Cf. the conflict in India between Brahminism and Buddhism, disagreement in Jewish communities between Orthodox Jews and Reform Jews, the Muslim clash between Mutazilites and Sufites in Syria and Iraq.

in a proper way. A major reason these conflicts vary so widely is that they call for major reflections about the meaning, or nature, of "reality." This problem involves at least three crucial philosophical assumptions: (a) an "ontology" related to conflicting ideas about "monism" and "dualism," (b) an "anthropology" anchored in the classic Platonic and Aristotelian tripod of "truth, virtue, emotion," and (c) an "epistemology" grounded in basically pagan assumptions about "faith," "reason" and their "interrelations."

Concerning the *structure* of faith life, terms like heresy, schism and deviance are prominent.[43] They refer to practices, beliefs, customs and institutional formulations of firmly held beliefs about, for example, the "truth of love" and "love of truth," which, when they become suspect, foster alienation and result in a parting of ways. What is considered to be misleading is then abandoned, and what is believed to be essential is assumed to be truth. Such a struggle may somehow result in a further disclosure of the riches of God's Word which, through the Spirit, may enable humans to hear God's Word in a new way and to reflect His image in a clearer way.

"Faith life" is one of the many ways in which humans respond to God's command to love Him in everything they do. The *structure* of such faith life, though not isolated from it, does not completely reflect one's heart-centered *religious* (re)direction of life. The *religious* conflict is present in all human "pistical," and "non-pistical," life in society and culture. The actual conflict between "Truth and Lie" is not recognized when it is somehow equated, and confused, with what is personal and public, church and state, having religion and rejecting it, faith and reason, sacred and secular, or Scripture and science.[44]

The conflict is expressed in human questioning and doubting, ignoring and rejecting God's love, breaking relations with vital God-centered causes and movements. It thrives in traditions and cultures in which the depth of God's covenant love is not known. When humans refuse to respond in an affirmative way to God's love command, faith life is no longer orthodox, but heterodox, not merely functionally defective, but *religiously* antithetical.

It differs from what Noah did when he "walked with God" as he built the ark, and what Abraham did as an itinerant sheep-farmer. It differs from what critics and comforters such as Jeremiah and Isaiah did at a time of major

43. From a non-Christian humanist perspective, especially in secularized Western culture, "sect" refers to something "non-Christian," "religious," or "denominational."

44. What is "structurally" wrong may be "religiously" right, and what appears to be right, may actually be false. This conundrum is indicated in the bloody Thirty-Year Religious Wars in Europe (1618–1648).

national and international crises. Centuries later, (i) Stephen, a deacon (Acts 6–7), became a martyr; (ii) Saul, an expert in Jewish and Roman culture, experienced his radical *religious* turnabout while he was on his "heretic-hunting" trip to Damascus (Acts 9:1–39) and was renamed Paul; and (iii) John, "apostle of love," as an aged pastor was imprisoned on the isolated island of Patmos.

Followers of Christ do not live in a religious and in a secular world, a supernatural and a natural realm, or in a prayer-closet and on the stock-market. Faith life is structurally embodied. It involves human urges, calls for discernment, is known by its symbols, practices fellowship, influences all vocation, affects true citizenship, establishes friendships, develops proper discernment. They oppose "antithetical" living and move in the right *religious* direction. To reduce what is *religious* (cf. total) to what is *structural* (cf. partial) is wrong, and to do the opposite, turn what is structurally partial into something ultimate, is idolatry, a pseudo-*religion*.

Compared to the one *religious* conflict, organized, or ecclesiastical, disagreements are less, if at all, consequential for society and culture.[45] Being *structural*, they are institutionally identifiable and manifest only indirectly the *spiritual* direction of the human heart.[46] In a differentiated society, faith (pistical) differences tend to be (i) more private than public, (ii) more controlled than diffused, (iii) more interested in settling theological disputes than in highlighting the power and scope of the gospel, (iv) more focused on debating theories about "salvation" and Christ's "return" than about matters of hunger, injustice, greed, violence, fame, reputation, power and success.

The distinction between *religious* (cf. heart) and *structural* (cf. pistical) enables one to gain a better understanding of diverse faith traditions in, for example, (a) early Jewish and Greek traditions, Eastern and Western communities, Roman Catholic circles, relations between Roman Catholics and Protestants, and (b) in the latter, such divisions as (i) Lutherans, Anabaptist and Calvinists, (ii) Anglican/Episcopalian and Puritans, and (iii) Reformed and Presbyterian traditions and their various sub-branches.[47] The existence

---

45. Except, notably, when a faith community attains a position of authority in a society or culture, e.g., Medieval Christendom, Protestant Theocracies, etc.

46. E.g., the disconnect between personal faith and church life in North America and the basic dynamic of a society and with millions of *born-again* Christians dominated by the evils of individualism, pragmatism, greed and violence.

47. **Reformed** traditions in the Netherlands and North America: National Reformed, Secessionist Reformed, Christian Reformed, Netherlands Reformed, Protestant Reformed, Canadian Reformed, and United Reformed. **Presbyterian** traditions, for example, Presbyterian

of so many, often competitive, Christian faith traditions in Western culture is perplexing and confusing. For Christians to divide, harass, at times even sue, fellow Christians about ostensibly creedal, unbiblical, even antithetical issues, indicates the subtlety of evil even within Christian circles.

This schismatic (mainly Western) mentality was directly, and indirectly, based on a Greek-scholastic notion that the essence of "Truth" is not only "Scripture-directed" but also "theology-oriented and based." Intentionally and unintentionally, followers of Jesus Christ, who is "the way, the truth, and the life," need not rely *only* on God's powerful three-pronged revelation (creation, Scripture, incarnated Word), His covenant-centered "Good News." Failure to rely on God's covenant faithfulness expressed in His one law of love, and instead turning to utilize Platonic and Aristotelian ideas about "Truth" and "Reality" has impacted the meaning and role of "theology" as discipline.

Persecution and Martyrdom

The presence of sin and evil is evident in all humans. Given its *religious* nature, it consists of an uneasiness and tension, a private and public struggle, subtle and overt forms of persecution, perhaps even martyrdom. Opponents of Christian faith have often been charismatic persons, who used their cultural power, backed up by military might and financial resources, in order to impose their ideology on fellow humans by treating them as "objects" to be used, abused and removed.

Idols are inherently imperialistic, demand total allegiance, want complete control and involve some form of oppression. They seek to dethrone their rivals; jealousy motivates and may consume them. Their striving is *religious*, all-consuming, something demonic, even if it means devastation, or "hell on earth." Given their "to be or not to be" mentality, idols lack longevity; they survive only for a time. This frantic rivalry of idols will continue until the Risen One returns to his Father's world. Human history is filled with *religious* clashes between demonic forces.[48] These battles between pseudo-gods will culminate in the final clash between "truth" and "falsehood."

Church in USA (PCUSA), Orthodox Presbyterian Church (OPC), Presbyterian Church of America (PCA), Bible Presbyterian Church (BPC). Baptist tradition is, given its independentist nature, the most diversified faith tradition in North America and the world.

48. See Santayana's pessimistic comment that human history is a long series of little victories on the road of ultimate defeat.

Human history is filled with conflicts between freedom and slavery, hope and fear, joy and despair. This conflict is unavoidable for humans who experience both the grace of God's reliable faithfulness and the subtle deceptions of humans who create their own pseudo-gods. Disciples of the Anointed Savior, who is "Truth-personified," cannot avoid in this life some form of oppression or persecution, triggered by humans who create, and serve, fake-saviors. For descriptions in the New Testament about Christian martyrs, see especially Hebrews 11 and Revelation 1 and 21.

This *religious* conflict in (especially Western) culture tends to be more *structural* than *religious*. Dissensions within, and among, organized churches, or faith communities, often involved issues related to church-state issues, the nature of conversion, compulsory conversion, vested interests of clergy, socio-economic support, crusades, "religion-culture" and "faith-reason" issues.[49] Also included is the intermittent ecclesiastical suppression of vulnerable women, humans with abnormal bodies, strange behavior and a strange faith life somehow linked to witchcraft.[50]

In general, persecution tended to embolden the faith life of Christians (and non-Christians).[51] It was not always overt, political or fatal. In urbane cultures, it tended to be subtle in social, psychic, academic, aesthetic and financial ways. Tragically, the effect was often a broken spirit, a form of death, a relief from personal and public harassment.

The grace-filled "gift" of *religious* conversion resulted in a joy and peace that passed all human understanding. It made possible a true *religious* com-

49. For details, see Paul Marshall with Lila Gilbert, *Their Blood Cries Out: The Worldwide Tragedy of Modern Christians Who Are Dying for Their Faith*, 1997. Marshall was born in England, graduated from, and taught political theory at, the Institute for Christian Studies (ICS) in Toronto, and joined the Freedom House in Washington, DC, USA. Others who share his views about justice and freedom are John Witte, Jr. and Johan van der Vyver, at Emory University, Atlanta, and James W. Skillen, founder and first director (1978–2008) of the Center for Public Justice (CPJ) in Washington, DC, and author of several justice-related books and numerous articles.

50. Witchcraft is complex and varies greatly: (a) "white magic" involves charms and spells used for benevolent purposes; (b) "black magic" appealed to the devil to perform evil, and to "pacts" to help the devil. In Europe, witches were burned as *heretics*, and in New England they were hanged as *felons*. Between 1580 and 1680, about 3,500 humans were executed. In 1691, in one day 23 adults and 15 children were killed in Mohra, Sweden. In the seventeenth century, 28 persons were killed in New England in 1692. For details, see Brian P. Levack, ed., *Witchcraft, Magic & Demonology*, 12-volume anthology of scholarly articles (Hamden: Garland Publishing). See also Melton (1983): 22–25; Bratt (1992): 8–10.

51. Evident in the faith commitment of twentieth-century Japanese Shinto-inspired kamakazi pilots, as well as in modern Islamic Jihadist terrorists.

mitment in one's whole life, including "faith life," concerning what is truly central and primary. This gift enabled martyrs to relativize their present predicaments by considering them not to be primary, but secondary. The difference between the "Truth" of God and the "Lie" of Satan is radical and definitive—while the former is victorious, the latter is conquered and condemned. The secret of all Christians, in both "life and death" is the definitive, child-like, life-saving "slingshot" of the great David, "Son of God and Son of Man," in his love-filled response to the God-mocking taunts of the sword-swinging "Goliath," who for his defying mockery, was fatally slain.

Summary and Transition

The issues dealt with in this chapter center on the *religious* conflict in humans between "Truth" and "Lie." In a parasitic way, the latter depends on the former. Despite its ultimate perversity, Satan's "antithetical" response to God's full revelation does not remove human solidarity. In a twisted way, it makes the *religious* struggle within, and among, humans possible, also in their faith life.

This *religious* heart-centered conflict results in not just personal but also public problems and an all-pervasive struggle. In a Spirit-directed love-filled way Christians seek to reduce, not remove, the *religious* conflict within, and among, themselves—even in non-Christian circles. Such a heart-centered way of living always involves a *religious* struggle in everything they do in this life.

In thinking about teaching the Good News, and sharing it with others, Christians need God's grace to avoid debilitating "scholastic theology." To walk with God in a childlike yet radical way is an immense privilege for those who thank God for His covenant faithfulness, uniquely revealed in the Anointed One who, through the Spirit, calls humans to come home, bow at the cradle of the "Word-made-flesh," and indicate what "walking with God" really means and can subtly be lost from sight (Chapters 7–10 above).

The focus of the next two chapters will be on the diversity and complexity in Christian organized faith traditions (Chapter 12), and on certain basic, but crucial, hermeneutic issues related to our hearing God's Word as his image-bearing readers of Scripture (Chapter 13).

CHAPTER TWELVE

Diverse Faith Traditions

In light of the ideas about faith life and related studies of traditional theology and proposed pisteology, as described in the last five chapters, the nineteenth-century Western notion of "comparative religions," also called "religious pluralism," is, though in some ways helpful, flawed in that it assumes the validity of a typically Western rationalist understanding of both "faith" and "religion." Given its subtle mind-set, "religious pluralism" has been so powerful that to press for renewal in this area presupposes knowing what it thinks it actually is. To do the latter, we turn next.

Basically, it assumes that genuine tolerance between conflicting faith traditions is possible not with, but without, a *religious* change. Is the notion of a world without conflicts not an illusion of an outdated Humanism? Do *religious* differences in faith life not foster strife and result in conflict, sometimes even persecution and martyrdom? Is it, in principle, even possible for different faith traditions to tolerate a form of ultimate toleration? Is unlimited toleration tolerable—does it not foster chaos?

In order to sense the central issue(s) in different human faith traditions and implied *religious* conflicts, the studies in "comparative religion" by Ernst Troeltsch, in nineteenth-century Germany, and Wilfred C. Smith, in twentieth-century North America, are hugely important. In their influential ecumenical endeavors, they popularized certain philosophical principles. The focus of this chapter will be to summarize and briefly evaluate their main tenets, concluding with some suggestions for a different understanding of such terms as "pluralism," "truth," "dialogue," "tolerance" and "conflict."

Origin of "Comparative Religion"

Disagreements in Germany about the possibility, and nature, of "comparative religion" centered on the meaning of the two basic terms: "comparative" and "religion." In *Nathan the Wise*, a drama written by Gotthold E. Lessing (1729–1781), three main European faith traditions are described, namely, Christianity, Judaism and Islam. In Jerusalem, Nathan, a Jewish business-man, Saladin, a Muslim sultan, and a Christian temple administrator are engaged in a conversation.

Having lost his wife and seven sons during a pogrom night, Nathan wrestled with the issue of God's control in the world. As a result of his quest, he gained considerable wisdom about life in general and his own life in par-ticular. Saladin asked Nathan what he thought about the truth of the three main monotheistic European faith traditions. In his response, Nathan told the sultan a fable about three rings.[1]

A long time ago, a man in the East owned an expensive ring with a gor-geous opal stone. This ring possessed the secret power to make its faithful bearer become greatly admired by God and humans. One time, this ring came into the possession of a father who loved his three sons equally much. He promised to give each one of his sons this ring, without telling that son he made a similar promise to the other two sons. To avoid a predicament at his death as to whom he would give the ring, he had a goldsmith make two identical rings.

These two copied rings looked so much like the original ring that even the father could not tell the difference between the original ring and its two copies. Secretly, he gave each one of his sons a ring. After his own death, none of his sons knew who had the right to claim to have the original ring. In the same way, Nathan claimed, it is impossible to determine which one of the three faiths—Jewish, Christian or Islam—is the true one.

When Saladin expressed his surprise about the similarity of the three rings and said that the three faiths were distinct *only* in terms of what each faith wore, ate and drank, Nathan interrupted by saying "but not in essence, not in the grounds to which each one appeals." They are all based either on recorded his-tory or on mere tradition. We all trust what our parents told us, or what others have modeled for us with their deeds of love and faithfulness. Saladin agreed.

---

1. About this fable, see Verkuyl (1989): 26–28, former Reformed missiologist in Indonesia and professor of missions at the Free University in Amsterdam. The story of the three rings is often told in circles of Free Masons, of which G. E. Lessing was an active member.

Continuing the fable, Nathan narrates how the three sons went to a judge to obtain a decision in the matter. Each son swore that the ring he received was from his father, and doubted the veracity of the two brothers who claimed the same thing. The judge indicated that only the father could indicate who has the authentic ring, unless, of course, the opal stone on the ring has the miraculous power to indicate that whoever wears the ring shall be loved by God and people. The ring that cannot accomplish this is not the true or original one.

Because the true ring possesses this power, the final verdict of the judge will be as follows: if you have personally received the ring from your father, you must regard it as genuine and do your utmost to show its authentic nature through your good deeds of love to everyone, tolerance for others and inner surrender to God.

When your descendants reveal this miraculous power of the ring, they will, after a thousand years, appear again before a judge, wiser than I, who will come with a final verdict. In response to Nathan's challenge to Saladin to be the man the judge called "wise," Saladin retorted: "I, Nathan, I who am dust? I, a nothing?. . . Oh Nathan! Nathan! No, the thousand years of your judge have not yet passed. His judgment seat is not mine. Go, oh go! But be my friend!"

In response to the intolerance of medieval Roman Catholic Christianity and seventeenth-century bloody Religious Wars, eighteenth-century Europe stressed *reason* and *tolerance,* not faith, superstition, witchcraft and heresy hunting. Lessing welcomed the emancipation of Jewish communities, established close friendship with Moses Mendelssohn, a Jewish philosopher, and advocated enlightened dialogues with Islamic believers. Humanity can redeem itself by living a virtuous life and, in the end, obtain immortality. Christianity, Judaism and Islam share a common interest in God, virtue and immortality.

What these three faiths have in common must be accented and what is unique about each must be relativized. It is impossible to determine now which faith is true—*that* will become clear after thousands of years! No faith is wholly right, nor is it wholly wrong. Lessing was passionate in his firm belief that in human history "education" and "revelation" are correlates, which pass through three important, and distinct, phases. In *The Education of the Human Race,* Lessing claimed that whereas *earlier* "revelation" guided the "reason" of humans as children, *now,* all at once, "reason" provides clarity for mature humans about the nature or meaning of "revelation."[2]

2. Cited by Beck (1966): 231.

Through the reciprocal role and influence of "revelation" and "education," the latter matures and becomes increasingly more, and the former becomes increasingly less important. The basic movement in human history is from childhood to youth to adulthood, Old Testament to New Testament to Enlightenment, or enjoyment to honor to duty, the lower to the higher to the highest part of life, individual to communal to ultimate progress, in short, from rational maturity to moral development.[3]

Not just the three Western (monotheistic) religions, but all religions are variations of the same religion. All faiths are alike; they all seek truth. No one faith, or religion, has the truth.[4] To make one faith absolute is to equate one wave with a vast ocean, or with a tsunami with all its devastating consequences. Fundamental to this approach are three beliefs: (a) tolerance is an absolute principle anchored in reason, (b) immortality is the final reward for being and doing good here and now, and (c) revelation presupposes human self-realization and projection of what is transcendent and divine.

The *scientific* method used in studying the history, philosophy and sociology of religion brackets all issues related to absolute truth. The notion that all religions are equal removes the need for any *religious* conversion. To insist on conversion indicates arrogance and intolerance. Diversity in faiths is inevitable, but disagreements, especially conflicts, between them must, and will, ultimately be resolved in a *rational* way.

According to Immanuel Kant (1724–1804), true knowledge never transcends human experience. It is limited to space, time and causality as basic categories of the human mind. This is evident in the rigor of mathematics and all natural sciences built on it. However, in "moral" and "religious" studies not "pure" science, but "practical" reason, dominates, since in them not facts but such values as God, freedom and immortality are central.

In the spirit of Kant's radical enlightenment philosophy, G. W. F. Hegel (1770–1831) claimed reason to be the key to reality, history and religion. Through the dialectical "thesis, antithesis, synthesis" process,[5] history culminates in the Absolute. Cosmic reality is grounded in, and accessible to, reason. Such a restless rational reality is historical in a paradoxical, yet unifying, way. Only as an ingredient, i.e., as a relatively minor component, does it include Christianity.

3. Beck (1966): 226–239.

4. Verkuyl (1981): 26ff.

5. Three terms *other* thinkers used to describe Hegel's way of thinking or method of philosophy.

Historicist Baden School: Germany

In their critique of Kant's and, especially, Hegel's thinking, Wilhelm Dilthey (1833–1911) and Wilhelm Windelband (1848–1915) developed their own view of history and scientific method. Their views of "truth" and "method" differed significantly from that of Kant and Hegel, their two giant predecessors. With their own understanding of " truth," "history" and "scientific method," they started the Baden (also called Heidelberg or South-West German) School, with its own distinct view of "reality," particularly "faith" and "religion."

Wanting to combine neo-idealism and *Lebensphilosophie*, **Dilthey** focused on the dynamic nature of history. This stress affected his idea of "cultural," in distinction from "natural," studies in such disciplines as philosophy, theology, sociology, jurisprudence, psychology and economics. Central to culture and history is the inherent teleology of human consciousness in the triplex acts of intuition, creativity and achievement.[6] Since they are historical, human knowledge and truth are always changing. Being human, ideals are essentially "subjective norms" and "objective goals."

Proper cultural understanding (*Verstehung*) involves a method that does not (abstractly) explain lived-through human experience (*Erlebung*), but only "describes" it. The movement of history has its own "subjective" and "objective method," i.e., a method that is particular and general, individual and universal. Life (*das Leben*) exists in and for itself. Being self-contained, it defines itself. "Past," "present" and "future" are related to each other as "significance" (*Bedeutung*), "value" (*Wert*) and "goal" (*Zweck*). "Development" (*Entwicklung*) from the past, via the present, to the future determines "totality" (*Sinn*).

Windelband tried to go beyond Kant concerning the distinction between "history" and "nature," and their related studies. He did not rely on the exact sciences of nature, but on a "scientific" method of studying history. In *History and Natural Science* (*Geschichte und Naturwissenschaft*), 1894, he focused on the "normal consciousness" (*Normalbewustsein*) of humans, i.e., on what is universally True, Good and Beautiful.

He distinguished between "nomothetic" and "ideographic" methods. The former is common, natural, necessary, objective and universal, typical of the method used in mathematics and natural science. The latter, however, is interested in history and culture, focuses on values, norms, ideals and oughts, and zeros in on what is unique, spiritual, subjective, particular,

6. For details, see Chapter 6 above on "Faculty Psychology."

transcendental—in short, anything that is *free*.[7] In ethics, aesthetics, religion, law and politics, humans create their own objective, universal and transcendental norms.

Ernst Troeltsch

As an historian and social scientist, E. Troeltsch (1865–1923) taught "theology" for twenty years (1894–1915) at the University of Heidelberg[8] and "philosophy of history" for several years at the University of Berlin. His agreement with the Baden School of thinking is clearly evident in his three major publications: *Protestantism and Progress: A Historical Study of the Relation of Protestantism to the Modern World* (1906), *The Social Teachings of the Church* (1912) and *Christian Thought: Its Origin and Application* (1923).

His influence on (i) history, faith, religion, theology and church in general, (ii) ecumenical reflection and behavior in Christian circles, especially the World Council of Churches, and (iii) Wilfred Cantwell Smith in North America has been phenomenal. A brief, sometimes a bit abstract, summary of his "method" and basic ideas in studying different faith traditions, or "religions," is necessary to sense the dire need to rethink the meaning of "theology."

He was passionate about discovering the proper way, or *method*, to understand historical change. Unlike "scientific" methods used in the study of universal and timeless regularities in natural science, the *method* required in any historical study concentrates on what is human, particular, individual, personal, meaningful and transcendental in society and culture.

Partly due to the influence on his thinking of Max Weber (1864–1920), his colleague at the University of Heidelberg,[9] In Troeltsch's view, what is

---

7. Also H. Rickert (1863–1936), Windelband's successor at the University of Heidelberg and a leader in the South-West German School of philosophy, stressed the limitations of natural science and need for a "scientific method" in studying what is unique (*einmalig*), particular, historical. Nature's laws can be *explained*,, but cultural values must be *understood* and the meaning (*Sinn*) of life must be *interpreted*. For details, see his *Sciences of Culture and Nature* (1899) and *Philosophy of Life* (1920).

8. Where also W. Dilthey and W. Windelband had taught.

9. Max Weber (1864–1920), a scholar, historian, and politician in Heidelberg and München, used Troeltsch's method to study the relation between socio-economic and religious thought patterns. His rationalist, value-free view of the social sciences influenced modern

unique about human truth is that it is religious, points to something universal, is a deflection, or refraction, in time of truth beyond historical change. Sensing the dynamic of human history and the danger of historicism, he tried to avoid stumbling into the abyss of relativism. Throughout his life, he tried to acknowledge the relativity of culture and the constant changes in history and, at the same time, to leave room for what is transcendent, or universal, and to prevent human life from meaninglessness and history from collapsing.

In a penetrating study of Troeltsch's thinking, Jaap Klapwijk indicated how Troeltsch lived between historicism and relativism, reflected on its paralyzing consequences, and pressed for a form of cultural-social and religious renewal.[10] Troeltsch stressed that what is changeable in culture and history is *not* accidental, or adventitious, but constitutive of the reality of "society," "culture" and "religion."

Although his historicist view was initially welcomed as an expression of human ingenuity and freedom, it resulted in considerable anxiety and insecurity. Historicist thinking started to question its own answers and achievements. When abiding principles for "reason" and "faith" disappear, truth disappears in the fog of change and doubt. After becoming aware of the danger of radical relativism in social philosophy and cultural ethics, Troeltsch backed away from the edge of despair and did not plunge into the abyss of absolute doubt.

His interest in Western awareness of different world religions and unsettling questions about whether Christianity is absolute or relative did not capture the imagination of Western thinkers until four decades later in the 1960s. An important reason for this delayed reaction was the response of many theologians and certain philosophers, who became interested in two new developments: (a) "the sudden rise of Barthianism, especially its fierce opposition to the ultra-liberal views of Ernst Troeltsch" and (b) "the deluge

---

sociology and studies in comparative religion. This historicist method is pervasive in his *The Protestant Ethic and the Spirit of Capitalism* (1904/5), *The Religion of China: Confucianism and Taoism* (1915), *The Religion of India: The Society of Hinduism and Buddhism* (1916/7), *The City* (1921) and *Wirtschaft und Gesellschaft: Grundrisse der Verstehenden Soziologie*, Vols. I-II (1922). He stressed the changing nature of social action more than the abiding structure of society.

10. For details, see Klapwijk (1970): 1–468, who traces Troeltsch's change from A. Ritschl's anti-historicist ethical position to (a) the historicism of metaphysical idealism in J. G. Fichte and G. W. F. Hegel, (b) the neo-Kantianism of W. Windelband and H. Rickert, (c) the *Lebensphilosophie* of H. Bergson and (d) the radical individualism of M. Weber. See Klapwijk (1970: 19–33) for a summary of these four different philosophical positions of Troeltsch.

of existentialistic philosophy, which with its retreat from culture, society and history . . . retreated into the stronghold of an internal and supposedly absolutely free existence."[11]

A major challenge for Troeltsch was to understand how Christianity's absoluteness is related to its historical and sociological reality. In addition to the worlds of "nature" and "human spirit," there is the world of "variable forms of culture." Conditioned by their time and environment, human "forms" and "norms" are subject to change. Historical consciousness does not restrict human understanding. World history implies a development in which humans move from being determined by primitive "natural" impulses to a form of ethical, or spiritual, freedom and to determining their own future. For years, Troeltsch grappled with this difficult issue. While history freely creates its course, it is at the same time restricted in its path inasmuch as faith life is determined by historical, especially societal and cultural, changing conditions.[12]

Humans need an ultimate norm in order to have some stability and certainty. At the same time, those familiar with history know that what was once believed to be absolute is later thought not to be true. Dogmatic beliefs of medieval Christianity and of modern Enlightenment may later not be believed in the same way. Troeltsch wondered whether Christian faith in Western culture is the best expression of absolute truth.[13]

If it is true that all faith, or religion, including that of Christians, is particular, not universal, or local, not global, then a genuine comparing of different faith traditions is not only superfluous but also impossible. Is Christian faith so intermingled with Greek-Roman, European, and/or Euro-American culture that it is no longer truly global? Perhaps it is "absolute" only in a local sense?

In "Absoluteness and Historicity: Questions about the so-called Absoluteness of Christianity," Klapwijk distinguishes between two kinds of absoluteness, namely, "ecclesial orthodoxy" and "liberal theology." According to

11. Klapwijk (1970): 19–20 *Theologians* are interested in Troeltsch's view about the history of religion, *philosophers of religion* in his idea of "religious apriori," *historians* of religion in his cultural analyses, *sociologists and ethicists* in his studies of the social teachings of the church and various groups, and *general philosophers* in the meaning and problems of historicism.

12. In this respect, the impact of Weber's views on Troeltsch are clear. Cf. Klapwijk (1970): 25–30 and 245–288.

13. About the last two paragraphs, see Klapwijk (1970): 21–26, 27–29 about Weber's influence on Troeltsch from 1907–1915 regarding the impact of the structure of society on the shape of Christianity (cf. "church," "sect" and "mysticism").

the former, God's revelation in Jesus Christ and Scripture is *supra*-natural, i.e., unchanging, outside and surpassing history, not subject to the vicissitudes of temporal life. According to the latter, humans' moral improvement—an unfolding from a primitive faith to a world religion—reaches its absolute end in modern Christianity. For an improvement to occur, history is essential and unsurpassable.[14]

Klapwijk rejects "ecclesial orthodoxy" and "liberal theology," because they assume a misleading "absolute-false" distinction. They presuppose the *scholastic* principle of a dualistic reality and the Hegelian notion of an *absolute* history. Neither position can do justice to, for example, Christian and non-Christian faith, how God acts in the history of nations, and why human God-knowledge has been darkened and suppressed.[15] It is too simplistic to equate the difference, and struggle, between Christian and non-Christian faith with simply the "God-human" distinction. The light of God's revelation is too bright for this, despite human distortion of it through accommodated religiosity and apostate idolatry. Klapwijk writes further:

> Against scholastic supernaturalism it must, in my opinion, be objected that no single religion can simply be called a human or natural invention. All religions, even the deepest apostate idolatry and the most audacious ideology are still divine in the sense of being related to God and his unceasing revelation. Idolatry is precisely for that reason so bad because man in this case does not act apart from God, but in aversion from the living God. Consequently, idolatry does not presuppose the absence but the presence of God, the God to whom also Christian faith is related.[16]

The uniqueness of Christianity does not lie in the scholastic notion of something *supra*-historical (Aquinas), or *end*-historical (Pannenberg), but in its *historicity*. With the exception of Jewish and Christian faith traditions, including their secularized expressions such as Western Idealism, Positivism and Marxism, a remarkable feature in most world faith traditions is the **absence** of *historical* awareness. They tend to center on "the fixed fate, the endless repetition, the periodic return, the eternal struggle between good and evil, the arbitrariness of the gods." They focus on the "spell of a mythical

---

14. Klapwijk (1995): 33–35. This article was published earlier in 1978 and 1993.

15. Klapwijk (1995): 35–37, notably his references to Acts 14:7, Romans 1:18–19, 21–22, Acts 17:23, 27, and John 4:22.

16. Klapwijk (1995): 37.

primeval event." They are curtailed by a form of "eschatological unraveling."[17] The course of history is basically meaningless and inevitably subject to decay.

Troeltsch reacted negatively to any mythical scholastic, and neoscholastic, inability to do justice to what is "historical," i.e., to the societal and cultural characteristics of all human beings.[18] Instead, he looked at all these significant features of everyday human life in terms of his own *historicist* view of "faith," "religion," "theology" and "christianity." In this regard, his impact has been enormous on subsequent thinking about the diversity of faith traditions and the growing need for new ways to acknowledge, and understand, countless human faith traditions.

Wilfred Cantwell Smith: North America

What E. Troeltsch did in Germany with his historicist explanations of different faith, or religion, traditions, W. Cantwell Smith (1916–2000) did in North America. He was Director of the Institute of Islamic Studies at McGill University in Montreal, Founder of the Religion Department at Dalhousie University in Nova Scotia, and Professor of Comparative History of Religion at Harvard University. His most important books are *The Meaning and End of Religion* (1978), *Faith and Belief* (1979), and *Towards a World Theology: Faith and the Comparative History of Religion* (1981).[19]

Fundamental to his view of human life, in general, and faith life and theology, in particular, was a mind-set that resembled that of W. Dilthey and W. Windelband in "philosophy" and E. Troeltsch in "religion" and "theology." He claimed that everything in human life and culture is "in flux." The only

17. Klapwijk (1995): 38. See especially pages 39–41 for Klapwijk's comments about the (a) uniqueness of God's revelation in Jesus Christ, (b) its importance for the origin, existence, and final destiny of created reality, (c) the task of Christians to celebrate, make known and tentatively give concrete expression to new life in Christ as lion and lamb, (d) avoiding thinking that redemptive history is *above, outside, beyond* profane rather than at the *core* of history, and (e) doing so not only in faith life but also in the fullness of one's economic, social, ethical and political life.

18. In a *formal* sense, these features resemble the approach Marxism advocated in an anti-Christian way.

19. Reading these books for the first time in 1984/5, I realized their significance for my interest in "faith life," "religion" and "theology." His spiraling and probing analyses are both intriguing and questionable. His earlier *Questions of Religious Truth* (1967) and *Belief and History* (1977) are preparatory for his classical trilogy that I use in this chapter.

exception to this claim, however, is his firm belief that reality is essentially "in flux." This historicist "method," or way of thinking, was pervasive in all his probing studies. That "truth" is constantly in flux affected his view of "faith" and "religion" in an, irony of ironies, a systematic and predictable way. This influenced his view of reality (ontology), humanity (anthropology), knowledge (epistemology), way of thinking (methodology) and understanding of faith (theology). All these disciplines guided him in his meticulous, principled inquiries as an historian of faith and theology. Except for an element of postmodern thinking,[20] his method resembled that of such Baden School thinkers as especially W. Dilthey and E. Troeltsch about what is transient and what is unchanging in human (faith) life.

To enter into Smith's way of thinking, a brief summary of its two issues will be helpful: *first*, his "historical" method with respect to the content of knowledge and the distinctions, and difference, between a "mundane" and a "transcendent" world, and, *second*, his view of eight terms, especially with respect to such topics as "faith," "religion," "belief" and "intelligibility."

"How" one studies determines, and is determined by, "what" is studied. The "method" and "content" of knowledge are interdependent. They both express the presence, not disappearance, of "religion" as something that is "active, momentous, with its own initiative" and that lies "below us . . . around us and within us and above us."[21] The interdependence of "how" and "what" indicates two things: (a) the "transcendent reference" of all religious phenomena in all faith traditions and (b) the diversity within each of them, and the vitality of faith as activity and its ever-changing nature in each (organized) religion.

While on the "personal level," *method* focuses on discovering some "meaning in modern life," on the "group level" it tries to turn our "emerging world society into a world community."[22] Unless humans understand each another across religious frontiers and learn to live together, in spite of their faith differences, the "prospects for our planet's future" are not bright. Due to

20. In his Foreword to Smith's *The Meaning and End of Religion*, John Hick, an advocate of Smith's views, indicates that according to modern linguistic sociology of knowledge "our ways of perceiving the world are profoundly affected by concepts with which we select, group, and organize the multiplicity of events" and that these concepts enable us to talk about "coherent meaning" in our view of human life, including religion, i.e., faith life (cf. Smith 1978: ix). Smith, however, refers to this way of philosophizing as "meaningless patter of language gone awry" (Smith (1978): 155).

21. Smith (1978): 5, also 1–4.

22. Smith (1978): 8.

the "sheer fact of change"—the whole world is in constant "flux"—"religion" is basically "historical, i.e., evolving, in process." As result, the enormous variety of religious phenomena has become "bewildering," their interpretation "a cacophony" and their total effect "inebriating."[23]

Any talk about the universal nature of religion, the abiding essence of Christianity, or the claim that only one religion is true and all others are false, must be avoided. In Western culture and history, Christianity thought of itself as possessing, along with Scripture, a true "system of beliefs." In viewing itself as being superior to all non-Christian faith traditions, it prevented itself from properly understanding, and relating to, non-Western faith traditions.

To remove this Western arrogance, Smith looked for a way for Christian and non-Christian faiths to understand the role of faith in a way that enables them to tolerate differences in faith. He distinguished between what is personal and impersonal, knowing religiously and knowing conceptually, approximating truth and reifying it, being an engaged participant and an abstract thinker, loyalty and rationality, what is particular and generic, individual and universal, or existential and intellectual.[24]

These distinctions reflect the unique features of human life and the traits of scientific knowledge. In this context, Smith distinguished between "faith" and "religion," two terms central to his passion as an ecumenical historian, to his rejecting any restricting view and misguided practice, and to discover proper human understanding and corporate living.

He spurns any "conceptually identifiable," or "systematic religious entity," viewed as "a distinct community."[25] Such faith is the result of a standard and gradual "reification," which stresses "preaching," focuses on "the emergence of followers," shapes "an intellectual community" and defines the "actual pattern of its institution."[26] Such an "institutionalization" is a reification, in which terms and attention "shift from personal orientation to an ideal, then to an abstraction, finally to an institution."[27] The moment "religion" claims

---

23. Smith (1978): 9 and 114. Traditional trite answers are not acceptable, such as "all religions other than one's own may be ignored," "all religions are essentially the same," or "all religions other than one's own are wrong" (10).

24. See, for example, Smith (1978), especially 19–22, 67, 76, 125–141, 144–147. To "reify" means to make a thing of "faith" and everything related to it. Any "thingified" religion must be avoided.

25. Smith (1978): 119.

26. Smith (1978): 67.

27. Smith (1978):76.

it has the definitive, true and exclusive "system of doctrines," faith becomes "congealed," "reified," "definable" and "substantial."[28]

These distinctions culminate in the misleading distinction between "faith" and "religion" that is rooted in, and expressive of, the most encompassing distinction between "mundane" and "transcendent." In terms of this ultimate distinction, Smith rejects any reified, or "thingified," religion, and is passionate about studying the astonishing diversity of faith traditions in our shrinking world. About the ontological distinction in his anthropology, epistemology and faith studies, as an *historicist ecumenist*, Smith writes,

> We speak of the life of religious man seeming to be somehow in two worlds, the mundane realm of limiting and observable and changing actuality and a realm transcending this. What is the nature of that transcendent sphere, and what is the nature of its relation to this mundane one, are questions on which, to put it mildly, there is no general agreement. Whether the transcendence is the human imagination at work or the fantasy of subconscious neurosis, or the meaningless patter of language gone awry, or the ideological superstructure of a particular economic situation; or whether it is a real world, or more real than this immediate one, or is this immediate one perceived more truly; and whether, if it is real, it is personal, Jesus-like, rational, formless, moral, punitive, unknowable—all these are questions on which intelligent men have taken varying stands.... *In fact, the divergence of answers is one part of the very matter that one is trying to understand. Room for this multiplicity must therefore be provided in the conceptual framework with which one approaches the task.*[29]

Rather than solve the problem of the relation between these two worlds, scholars should "postpone" taking a stand on this metaphysical issue. Instead, they should "outflank" this difficulty and get on with their task, as historians, to think about the "religious life" of humans in terms of the "link" between these two realms. While the "mundane" realm is observable and knowable, the "transcendent" one remains elusive and unknowable.

The history of religion "in general" and each religion "in particular" consists of human "participation in an evolving context of observable actu-

28. Smith (1978): xiv, xii-xiii. Religions are not "contraposed socio-theological entities" (xvii). Smith is not alone in questioning the adequacy of the term "religion." In a different context and for different reasons, others also have been critical of this term—e.g., Karl Barth, Emil Brunner, Paul Tillich, C. S. Lewis and Dietrich Bonhöffer. See Smith 1978: 125ff.

29. Smith (1978): 154–155 (emphasis added).

alities," something "not directly observable by historical scholarship." Neither of these two "realms" (aspects, parts, elements or concepts) in human history may be neglected. The historian must "separate them in intellectual analysis, retaining both."[30] The "mundane" realm points to the "cumulative tradition," the "transcendent" realm to human "faith," and the "living person" to the link between these two.

Both "cumulative tradition" and "faith" are requisite "to conceptualize and to describe anything that has ever happened in the religious life of mankind." They can be used "equally by sceptic or believer, Muslim or Buddhist, Episcopalian or Quaker, Freudian or Marxist or Sufi." This approach provides a "method that will humbly yet deliberately" enable humans to investigate the diversity of faith problems, and to do so without adopting any "prior solution."[31]

The cumulative tradition refers to "the entire mass of overt objective data that constitute the historical deposit, as it were, of the past religious life of the community in question"—e.g., temples, scriptures, theological systems, dance patterns, legal and social institutions, conventions, moral codes, myths—"anything that can be transmitted from one person, generation, to the other, and that an historian can observe."[32]

Contrary to what *positivist* historians claim, this tradition is not a "closed system." At its center is a human agent with a "spirit in some degree open to the transcendent." This tradition is "observable" as well as "dynamic" and "diverse."[33] In this context, Smith talks about seven interrelated issues: Faith, Belief, Understanding, Intellect, Religiousness, Intercommunication, Self-consciousness and *Humane* knowledge.

30. Smith (1978): 156. The relation between "mundane" and "transcendent" is viewed in terms of early Christian thinking about Christ's "human" and "divine" natures.

31. Smith (1978): 157.

32. Smith (1978): 156–157. Observable data are "overt manifestations across the centuries in their resplendent or grotesque variety" (155).

33. Smith (1978): 161 and 168. Openness to transcendence expresses freedom from anything static, rigid and objective.

Faith

Faith indicates that humans are *"homo religiosus."*[34] This "global human quality" is a "normal," "uniform" and "central category."[35] "To have faith is to be human, in the highest, truest, sense."

> The various religious systems of the world are not fancy elaborations tacked on to human history as curiosities over and above the standard human. They are, rather, the principal attempts at being human. . . . A person is not a human being and then also a Jew, or also a Christian, or a Muslim.[36]

It points to "inner religious experience," an "impingement" on a person of what is "transcendent, putative or real."[37] It reveals a human "involvement (*engagement*) with what is transcendent." It constitutes the "meaning (*raison d'être*)" of life, shows that humans can be "at home in the universe," expresses "the final truth of mankind" and reflects a serenity associated with what is profound, ultimate and ineffable. Faith undergirds, informs, precedes, transcends and eludes all human formulations about the transcendent.[38]

It is not "automatic." Humans are naturally prone to abnormality. Christians talk about the Fall as a difference between "pristine and actual condition," and Western philosophers talk about the difference between "rational and irrational."[39] Nor is faith "supernatural" in a Roman Catholic sense. It is

---

34. Smith (1979): 129.

35. Smith (1979): 130, 133, 135, 136.

36. Smith (1979): 138. Smith rejects the secularist notion that faith is "something extra" to being human and its impact on epistemology, political science, structure of school systems, and programs of foreign aid (139–140). He rejects any "negative secularism," which claims that "faith in whatever form" does not "really matter" and should be ignored. Such a view is "resented in Asia and will not survive Western dominance. It is developing into a tragedy internally in Western life, engendering a pitiably dehumanized society." Secularism does not challenge humans to acknowledge that "unlike crocodiles," to be human is something "transcendent," not merely an "empirical concept."

37. Smith (1979): 156; also 140.

38. Smith (1979): 12, 16. Christians and Buddhists (20–31), Muslims (33–52) and Hindus (53–68) have this kind of faith.

39. Smith fulminates against positivism and rejects "unfaith" and "nihilism." Cf. Smith (1979): 132–135.

something "ubiquitously astonishing," a "strange dynamic towards becoming our true selves, or becoming divine."[40]

The ability to devote oneself to transcendence is not definable.[41] It is loving what is transcendent by participating in it.[42] It is deeper than religion, not open for inspection by an observer. It involves the human ability "to symbolize," or "live loyally," in terms of something "transcendent" in one's life.[43] Faith itself cannot be seen. It is "more than human,"[44] calls for taking a "flanking" step, inquiring into its "role," not "nature," in one's life. In distinction from Western "religion," it focuses on "something, or Someone, behind or beyond Christianity, or Buddhism." It can be expressed in words, rituals, morality, art, institutions, law, community and character. It is broader and deeper than "religion." It requires being an "engaged participant" (*engagé participant*) in what is investigated.[45]

Faith is "ever changing, ever accumulating." Each religious person is "the locus of an interaction between the transcendent, which is presumably the *same* for every man . . . and the cumulative tradition, which is *different* for every man."[46] It is not "a generic entity, but a living quality," not "a fixed something, but the throbbing actuality of a myriad of someones." It is not "a static, complete, definable, metaphysically given." It has "continuity," although it is not an abstract "identity." It differs "any morning" from what it was the "preceding afternoon."[47]

There is no "generic"—Christian, Buddhist, Hindu or Jewish—faith. In God's eyes, each human is a person, not a type. Nothing can be called "*the* Christian faith."[48] Faith is indicative of a person's "present awareness of eternity." What humans "have in common" lies in their response to "the transcendent itself."[49]

Smith is not interested in "cleaning," "rearranging," "enlarging" or "replacing" the window of any inherited view. He rejects any "amalgam of inner

40. Smith (1979): 142. He distinguishes between reaching and being reached, time and eternity, historical particularity and transcendence.

41. Smith (1979): 103–104.

42. Smith (1979): 117.

43. Smith (1979): 141.

44. Smith (1979): viii. Unlike relatively constant beliefs, faith always varies.

45. Smith (1978): 19. To equate "faith" with "religion" is doing "too much, and at the same time too little."

46. Smith (1978): 186 (emphasis added). Such "faith is new every morning." (187)

47. Smith (1978): 189, 190.

48. Smith (1978): 191.

49. Smith (1978): 192. In short, "The traditions evolve. Men's faith varies. God endures."

piety and outer institution that at a certain stage in their dynamic development was intellectually reified under the terms 'religion' and 'religions.'"[50]
He presses for a different "conceptual apparatus," one which consists of the
dynamic factors of "historical cumulative tradition" and "personal faith of
men and women."[51]

Belief

As a system of dogmas, belief is not faith, but may lead to it.[52] Whereas
"faith" centers on the human *relation* to transcendence or God, "beliefs"
focus on *statements* about faith, formulations, systems, concepts, propositional truths, what is observable, time-bound, standard practice.[53] They are
empirical, culture specific, intellectual ways to secularize being human or
mundane-minded.[54]

Equating "doctrine" with faith as "primary religious category" reveals
a Western fixation on apologetics, which shows some beliefs to be correct
and true and judges other beliefs to be wrong and false. A person can "have"
belief, not faith. Faith is a verb, something one does. Belief can be an "avenue
for" faith, but also an "obstacle to" it; one can affirm belief, but reject faith.
Since the rise of Enlightenment in Western culture,

> Christian discussion centered on transcendent realities, and not on faith, man's
> relation to them, but on the conceptualizations of both, on man's relation to
> those conceptualizations: on believing. The difference was subtle but profound.
> . . . A new situation arose where, to some significant extent, those who believed
> the doctrines have faith, and those who did not believe, did not.[55]

50. Smith (1978): 193, 194.

51. Smith (1978): 194. He wonders whether using "religiousness," or "piety"—and drop-
ping "religion(s)" and "the religion" from "serious writing and careful speech within twenty-
five years"—might not produce a "truer faith in God and a truer love for their neighbour" and
for scholars in "a clearer understanding of the religious phenomena" studied. (195)

52. Smith (1979): 104. He predicts that "No future age will ever again translate *credo* as
'I believe.'"

53. For a detailed discussion of issues, see Smith (1979): 105–127, especially 121–127.

54. Smith (1979): 143–144. Belief emphasizes knowing without understanding (146), views
doctrines as beliefs (147), depersonalizes and detranscendentalizes reason, denatures truth, is
technocratic and scientific (148), reflects Western narrowness and arrogance, truncates human
knowing (150) and is "objectivistic, thing-oriented." (152)

55. Smith (1978): 123.

To ascribe primacy to beliefs is to grant them "veto" power "over entry into the kingdom."[56] To reject this practice does not imply dispensing with "intellectuality," nor does it endorse the Roman Catholic idea that faith "includes belief but goes beyond it."[57]

Understanding

Rejecting positivist "knowing" and Western "believing," Smith stresses the "Baden" view of "understanding." Not intellectual truth, but "recognizing" or "seeing the point" is crucial.[58] It is "humane" in that it shows concern for the neighbor, implies change of mind and heart and enables humans to be "potentially persons of faith." It is "comparativist" in that it provides a "compelling vision of diversity" and enables humans to live in an "interpenetratingly complex" world.[59] To live in a Christian, Jewish, Islamic, Buddhist, Hindu, or any other culture calls for rethinking the meaning of such terms as "faith," "context," "cohesion" and "planetary."

Understanding rejects oversimplified Greek, ecclesiastical, Western and natural scientific "binary classification of true/false."[60] It is wrong to absolutize one's own position and relativize that of others. To be a "relativist without being a nihilist" is possible when one acknowledges that "understanding the position of others is a function of one's own position."[61]

> No one (group) of us deserves the genuine respect of the rest of us. Perceiving, conceiving, articulating our apprehensions, thinking, believing, are something that we human beings do in diverse ways. We therein constitute (potentially) a corporate global community of a now self-conscious intellectual pluralism . . . through our several disparate loyalties to truth and our mutual respect for each other, to move severally and jointly closer to that truth, and hence away from the grosser cacophonies of that relativism.
>
> . . . [F]or a comparativist, the truth may be conceptualized as something

56. Smith (1979): 125. Also, "Faith is not to be subordinated to belief, nor to anything else mundane." All religious forms are at best strictly secondary, derivative from and answerable to "transcendent reality and truth." (125)

57. Smith (1978): 124.

58. Smith (1978): 127; see also (1979): 148–149.

59. Smith (1979): 150–1.

60. Smith (1979): 152, 153.

61. Smith (1979): 155.

that both is immanent within, and transcends, any given formulation of it in any given system. . . . [The] truth of what one believes—even of what one sees; even of what one experimentally verifies—is never the whole truth.[62]

Transcendent truth is possible only "insofar" as one apprehends it and "is apprehended by it."[63]

Intellect

Unlike "faith" as a human *quality* that enables one to reach out towards Truth, "intellect" is a human *characteristic* with a role in "faith" that is comparable to its role in "human life."[64] The two main features of faith are "insight" (belief, knowing that) and "response" (sensing transcendence, going beyond belief). To isolate these two from each other is to confuse "faith" with "beliefs," or not to acknowledge one's limitation and become judgmental of others.

"Insight" points to what goes beyond this world, or transcends one's apprehension of others. "Response" has to do with saying "Yes!" to recognized truth, knowing that truth is greater than one's vision of it. Faith must be "continuous" with faith in earlier ages. The similarity of "faith" to "insight" implies that the intellectual dimension of faith is necessary to "reach out beyond" what one's mind can manage. Faith may not "wallow innovatingly in sentimental a-rationality." It encourages human involvement with ideas, moving upwards and seeking to comprehend more. As "an attitude to truth," faith reaches for "the closest approximation to the truth of which one's mind is capable."[65]

> In its intellectual dimension, faith is first of all *recognition* of truth, *insight* into reality; and its *conceptualizations* (the "belief" that goes with it) must on the one hand be sincere, *subjectively*, a close approximation to what one personally apprehends (is apprehended by), and on the other hand be valid, not only in the *objective* sense of being a significantly close approximation

62. Smith (1979): 156.
63. Smith (1979): 157. "Such a relativism is far from nihilism," says Smith. (157) It would be "unintelligent as well as discourteous not to give heed to those few that have been cherished by scores of millions of persons, for many long centuries, and on the basis of which civilizations have been built and sustained. . . . These are not merely mundanely significant facts but are also significant to transcendent truth." (158)
64. Smith (1979): 158.
65. For details, see Smith (1979): 166–168.

to Reality, the final Truth, but also in the dynamic and demanding sense (thus *linking the subjective and the objective*) of the closest approximation possible.[66]

Unlike "ordinary knowledge," the intellectual dimension of faith recognizes what transcends one's interests, situation and ascertained knowledge. It centers on the "will" of the knower to want to "apprehend" truth. Being neighbor-directed and inclusive of human mutuality, truth permits pluralistic relativism; "acceptance of diversity enriches rather than undermines one's own apprehension of truth."[67] Faith is "intellectually vacuous" unless it strives for the "highest approximation" of truth, moves from "a self-regarding to a self-transcending living." Smith's commitment to the *universality of reason* is clear when he states "that reason is in principle universal, and that in the intellectual realm human kind converges. Truth is ultimately one, although the human forms of faith decorate or bespatter our world diversely."[68]

Religiousness

The traditional meaning of "religion" is a dialectical process between a mundane "overt tangible tradition" and a transcendence-directed "vital personal faith." Personal faith is fully observable and not restricted by any intelligible limits. Its effect is manifest in the constantly expanding deposit the historian scrutinizes.[69]

Terms like "religion," "religions" or "the religion" are no longer tenable. More appropriate are terms like "religiousness" or "piety" without the plural or a definite article. Religion is not a noun or "entity," i.e., something one *has*, but adjectival in the sense of *being* religious or *participating* in transcendence. Phrases like "historical tradition" and "personal faith" are more appropriate.[70]

66. Smith (1979): 169 (emphasis added).

67. Smith (1979): 170.

68. Smith (1979): 172. "[U]ltimate truth-and-reality transcend(s) every human relation with it" and at no ontological level is Christian faith timeless and distinct (1979: 329, fn. 1). It is possible to talk about the "faith of an intellectual" and "the intellectualization of faith" (1979): 334, fn. 15.

69. Smith (1978): 187.

70. Smith (1978): 195. These concepts are not intellectual requirements, nor metaphysical realities, but "historical actualities."

Two themes in "global history" of the human "quest" for God and of God's "seeking" humans, converge in the human faith "response to God's initiative" or " self-revelation." This "ongoing and multi-faceted" converging process is evident in all sectors and phases of humanity and in all faith traditions. Basic to history is the human quality of faith to "transcend" oneself and become "informed by the universe's transcendence." "Human history is the history of religion, and the latter is the history of salvation by faith. Faith is man's participation in *Heilsgeschichte*."[71]

Intercommunication

This "method" (of thinking historically) fosters intercommunication among all faith traditions. "Dialogue" replaces polemic apologetics, theological debates, and monologues of preachers and missionaries. This is easier in Hindu and Chinese than in Christian and Muslim traditions, which need a more intelligible and satisfying expression of faith for their members and theologians.[72] Due to rapid changes and increasing faith diversity, particularly in Christian circles,

> faith itself continues to be precious and of transcending significance. It is no secret that the Church is consciously in need of a new theology that will empower Christians to be at once more modern and more devout, that will nourish a faith more closely attuned both to contemporary history and to the fullness and majesty of God. The two important movements of Christian thought in the twentieth century so far, liberalism and neo-orthodoxy, have been oriented to one or other of these, not to both.[73]

71. (*History of Salvation*) Smith (1979): 140. Cf. "Faith bespeaks involvement in transcendence. Any anthropocentrism, then, betrays our human cause if it is not also theocentric or, to shift to the Buddhist or Greek mode, metaphysical." The human capacity for faith is "a divine gift." (1979): 139–140.

72. Smith (1978): 197. He comments, "If the Islamic community can reformulate its position in the modern world in a way that takes fully seriously not only the faith of other men but also the historicity and dynamic of its own tradition past and present, the profoundly personal quality of faith and the profoundly transcendent quality of its immediate reference, then it would seem if the opinion of an outsider may be tolerated that its contemporary religious crisis will be solved."

73. Smith (1978): 198. He adds, "To such a Church the present analysis is offered, in the bold hope that conceivably it might be able not to answer the questions that press hard but to

The challenge for Christian, Islam and other faith traditions is not to perpetuate traditional theological thought-patterns, but to capitalize on "new knowledge, new opportunities, new responsibilities."[74]

An "observer" interprets what he "sees," but an "engaged participant" interprets what he "knows or feels." We must construct "a single theory" that will serve a "merging" of observer and participant. "People of faith" are "incipiently or potentially members of the total corporate religious complex of mankind, composed of different but no longer separated communities."[75]

Knowing one's *own* faith and that of *others* requires an interpenetration of different faith traditions. Humans are becoming more "self-conscious" and "more unified, for good or ill." They need to shape a world which "different religious communities can jointly approve" and participate in.[76] The two levels of "empirical evidence" and "theological truth," or what is mundane and transcendent, must be "unbifurcated" and display an "interrelated intelligibility" which only a historian, not a philosopher, can ascertain.[77]

Such a world is directed by the "faith" factor, in contrast to, and in conjunction with, the "mundane" factor. This determines the *two* meanings of "the end of religion," namely, "God" it points to and may lead to, *and* abandoning the traditional concept of "religion" and all its "paraphernalia." A person's faith is legitimate only when it contributes to the modern task of "together constructing a brotherhood on earth deserving the loyalty of all our groups."[78]

In *Towards a World Theology* (1981), Smith describes what is actual, unique and reflective of human dignity in an ever-changing and dynamic world. He writes,[79]

For the moment, I am arguing only that on earth what the communities have had in common is that their several histories, individually already

---

provide a prolegomena of thought within which those questions could be tentatively answered by men of sufficient faith and intelligence."

74. Smith (1978): 199.

75. Smith (1978): 200.

76. Smith (1978): 200–2001. These initiators of the next phase of the world's history can do so "more intelligently if they can be more flexible and more embracing, more penetrating and truer, than in the past has been either available or necessary."

77. Smith (1978): 5–6, 15–17.

78. Smith (1978): 2001–2002. Smith is writing "from within the Christian Church . . . university . . . [and] mankind."

79. See Smith: (1981) :3, 5–6, 15–17, 20 about his passion to stress the ever-changing character of this world.

complex, can be understood, and indeed can be understood better, and in the end can be understood only, in terms of each other, as strands in a still more complex whole.[80]

The "rich religious history of humankind" as a global community (with its hagiography, prayer beads, flowers, greetings cards, rites, notions about God, Scripture, devil) has fostered "a new empirical awareness of historical interrelation" that "approximates more closely to the truth" than did "the less well informed notion of disparate entities . . . in sharply boundaried compartments."[81]

Religious life is not a stable system. "Spiritual truth is not . . . permanent amidst historical flux, impermeable and uniquely our own so as to cut ourselves off from other groups and their allegiances."[82] Religious diversity is a problem *within* and *among* all faith communities, although less in Buddhist and Hindu than in Muslim and Christian traditions.[83] Because religion is "a response to a divine initiative," the historian can only approximate the ideal by describing "different things in different centuries, in different countries, among different strata." To view "historical process as the context of religious life" and "participation as the mode of religious life" enables one not to impose "ideational patterns" on life and to avoid misguided "dichotomies."[84]

In the historical "divine-human" process, humans "find God" and "God finds" humans. As "historical" beings, humans interact with what is "mundane" and as "spiritual" beings they are open to what is "transcendent." To be "religious" in a Christian, Muslim, Buddhist or Secular way is a "creative

80. Smith (1981): 6. He comments, "An ambition of mine has for some time been to try my hand, before I die, at writing a world history of religion in the singular: century by century, rather than in the more customary fashion of system by system." Smith taught a course at Harvard University on "Historical Interrelations among Religious Traditions" and refers to the innovative studies of R. N. Bellah and E. A. Burt (195, 199, endnotes 2 and 21–23).

81. Smith (1981): 18. Smith also says, "We have all along been participants in the world history of religion, although we did not know it . . . until recently we knew it only imaginatively, mythically, in the form of legends and of tales. The breakthrough is that now we do know it, accurately. I, for one, rejoice." (20)

82. Smith (1981): 22.

83. Smith (1981): 23, 24. Buddhist faith emphasizes the process of "interiorising" through adding on, subtracting from, modifying, inheriting, passing on, perpetuating a continuing movement, and the notion of a flowing river. It does not think in terms of comparative religion, with its focus on a common thread, denominator, or essence, but concentrates on what is more fluid, dynamic, dialectical, personalist, and "faith-like;" for details, see 25–29.

84. Smith (1981): 33.

act," a "participation in a community in motion."[85] In this becoming self-conscious, the "process of each is becoming conscious of the process of all."[86] As the human community moves from "its inherited past" into "an uncertain future,"

> the present members constitute that present phase as each plays his or her part in the company of fellow members and in the constant presence, dimly or deeply perceived, of that transcendent power *in whom we all live and move and have our being.* It is the quality of their participation that each finds his or her life opened to the divine; that each is, if one likes the term 'saved'. . . . through participation in a religious tradition each of us participates in the life of God.[87]

New today is the emergence of an awareness of "the unitary religious history of humankind." To be rigid about one's own faith and hostile about the faith of others is no longer possible.

> Given the hostility among communities, ranging from open warfare on the battlefield to intellectual and emotional boundaries of stupendous rigidity, I am not unaware of the boldness of this concept. . . . What is beginning to happen around the earth today is the incredibly exciting development that will eventually mean that each person, certainly each group, participates in the religious history of humankind—as self-consciously the context for faith.
> . . . I am a Presbyterian; yet the community in which I participate is not the Presbyterian, but . . . the Christian. I participate as a deliberate though modified Calvinist in the Christian community, . . . In much the same way, I choose to participate as a Christian in the world process of religious convergence. For, ultimately, the only community there is, the one to which I know that I truly belong, is the community, world-wide and history-long, of humankind.[88]

---

85. Smith (1981): 34–36. His shortest paragraph in all his writings is perhaps: "That context is always in process." (36)

86. Smith (1981): 37. Interested "in more intimate appropriations" and "interpenetration," Smith stressed "mutual interaction" not externalistic "influence" centered on origins and causality—for details, see 38–42.

87. Smith (1981): 42 (emphasis added).

88. Smith (1981): 44.

What is most transcendent, intimate and personal cannot be compre-hended, only apprehended. An expanded consciousness that enhances self-consciousness opens new vistas on what it means to be human. It calls for a "revolutionary rethinking of theology" in the area of comparative reli-gion. Though "*continuous with classical rationalist and humanist traditions*" (emphasis added), it rejects the idea that knowledge consists only of what is natural or objective, and the scholastic belief that religion is something added to being human. It abandons the Western Enlightenment dichotomy between "secular" and "religious"[89] and the distinction between "natural" and "supernatural." We are not "human and, *in addition*, Buddhist, Hindu, Muslim, rationalist-humanist, or whatever."[90]

This bifurcation advocated by Western secular intellectuals and tra-ditional Church thinkers has "tended to distort Western interpretation of religious matters" and truncated its ability "to see human spirituality as a day-to-day dimension throughout the world."[91] History is "foundational" for theology. The transcendent feature of human affairs is beginning to dawn. Understanding "human history" involves understanding the "human spir-it"[92] and its multiple religious forms.

Self-Consciousness and Humane Knowledge

The difference between "human" and "humane" sciences is that the former focuses on what is objective, external, out there, and the latter on what is subjective, internal and manifest in society and history. *Self*-consciousness is the mode of humane knowledge.[93] It contains subjective and objective knowledge, and moves, through approximation, beyond them to an "unre-lentingly rigorous, critical, rational"[94] objectivity. It moves from conscious-

89. Smith (1981): 47–52. Western faith in reason is one form of human faith: "the reason-*versus*-faith debate has actually been a polarity between faith in reason and faith in God." (52)

90. Smith (1981): 53. The Greek-metaphysical, or new secular, way "is certainly not the only way; certainly not the foundational way; and not self-evidently the best—truest—way." (53)

91. Smith (1981): 54.

92. Smith (1981): 55. "The time has come . . . to move rationally beyond it, in what I will call the humane sciences."

93. This view is in line with W. Dilthey's nineteenth-century idea of truth and history and M. Polanyi's twentieth-century theory of truth and science.

94. Smith (1981): 57, 59. To treat a person as subjective or objective is irrational, destruc-tive and fallacious (58, 60).

ness to *self*-consciousness (man), to *critical* self-consciousness (science) and, finally, to *critical-self* consciousness (corporate).[95]

To be human is to be self-conscious, self-transcendent, have a sense of justice, imagination, freedom, truth, compassion, wickedness and deception, being remorseful and forgiving.[96] One's perception of, for example, space, temple and symbol is "incontrovertibly part of its truth." But truth is broader than what is given or apart from humans.

> The truth of the temple manifestly lay not in the building itself as an object but in the significance for, and interaction with, these men and women. . . . The notion of temple, and that of symbol in general, are humane concepts, not objective. No building is objectively a temple. No space is objectively sacred. No object is objectively a symbol, in and of itself: an object becomes a symbol in the consciousness of certain persons.[97]

In terms of W. Dilthey's historicist philosophy, the "meaning" of things lies in their relation to "persons," not in things as "objects."[98] Though aspirations, imagination and fears are not objects, they are "real" and "knowable" through a "conceptual apprehension" of "corporate critical self-consciousness."[99] Any inter- and intra-cultural apprehension of truth (about oneself, neighbor or God) involves interpretation, a standing in someone else's shoes, an understanding (*Verstehung*), a sympathetic living into (*Einfühlung*). Subject and object, knower and known, are interdependent.[100]

A critical consciousness avoids an objectivist mind-set, which controls, manipulates and alienates other humans by robbing them of their freedom. "Objective" knowledge in a humane world is "immoral." The "we-they" fallacy disrupts the community. Inasmuch as "socially friendly" persons are "objectivists," they are sectarian, idiosyncratic, esoteric, void of humility.[101]

95. Smith (1981): 59. Moving from the world of nature to the world of man is complete "when human self-consciousness becomes fully critical and concrete, ideally embracing us all both in our diversity and in our personalism" (59).

96. Smith (1981): 61. Such critical self-consciousness is "trans-cultural" (62).

97. Smith (1981): 63. For a *non-historicist* view of "objective" and "subjective," see chapters 9 and 10 above.

98. Smith (1981): 64. Behavioral sciences cannot "fully" or "accurately" do justice to the truth of things. According to Dilthey, human behavior must "be seen and interpreted as within a context of the consciousness that gives meaning to their lives and to their behaviour" (65).

99. Smith (1981): 66.

100. Smith (1981): 67–69.

101. For details, see Smith (1981): 70–76.

Secular sceptics and Christian believers fought each other in Western culture. They joined hands and felt superior when they traveled abroad. They did not realize that across the centuries and the world humans know each other in mutuality, trust and equality. This hubris in "Western academic scholarship" has caused much resentment on the part of Asians.[102]

Western culture needs to stress "humane knowledge" or "corporate self-consciousness." Merely knowing is not enough for someone to become a "new kind of person." Only by becoming one community, can persons, who are "lesser," in part overcome their "lessness" and become "more fully human." The "truth of all of us is part of the truth of each of us."

"Comparative religion" assumes that *humane* knowing is "a 'we' or 'us' kind of knowing, generative of partnership, of mutual understanding."[103] Faith life involves not only "will, emotion and intellect,"[104] but also "practice, community, participation, and much else."[105] The diversity of religious groups is determined "more by ideas than by piety," more by "the ideational aspect" than by faith. Apart from humans, an object is not a symbol, nor is any Platonic ideational pattern, or proposition, a symbol, as phenomenologist thinkers claim. "Symbols" are significant in their "total coherence," which provides a framework for interpreting "the factual data and concrete events and spiritual propensities of the person's or society's life."[106]

Western culture is known for its dichotomy between "religious" and "secular." Religion is only an item, a sector in life, alongside other sectors. Unlike Westerners, Asians do not think in terms of "objects of nature," but, more humanely or holistically, in terms of what is "religious" or objects as symbols of what is transcendent. Symbols "teach" and "express" what is "other and greater" than themselves.[107] In this context, the issue of "truth" arises. Smith wondered whether it is possible to be a "relativist without being a nihilist."[108] As an historicist thinker, he commented on four issues: "religious pattern," "symbol," "verification" and "group self-consciousness."

---

102. Smith (1981): 78, also 77, 79. Smith thinks of the growing alienation, resentment, drugs, malaise of personal and social life, and revolts of many Western university students.

103. For this paragraph, see Smith (1981): 79–80.

104. For details, see chapter 6 above.

105. Smith (1981): 81.

106. Smith (1981): 82–83. Symbol is a humane, not an objectivist, concept. Only for persons who participate in transcendence does an object become a symbol (85, 87, 88).

107. Smith (1981): 90.

108. Smith (1981): 89. How can one acknowledge the immense diversity of religious patterns without despairing?

Religious pattern. Truth depends on "faith-transcendence," on what is universal, unchanging and unitary. Knowing objects as symbols of transcendence enables one to make knowledge *humane* and enlarge one's religious horizons.

Symbol. It is not the same as "accepting" a religious position. Being person-centered, symbols are particular and, with respect to their conceptual frameworks, multiple. They do not indicate that one has "joined the community of those for whom the symbol is cogent." They weaken the "boundaries segregating off religious communities radically and finally from each other." "[B]eing a Hindu and being a Buddhist, or being a Christian and not being a Christian," cease to be stark alternatives.[109]

Verification. This principle is important for "understanding." A "statement about a group of persons is valid" only when it can "be appropriated by those persons.[110] To look at the world through an ever-growing and -widening humane consciousness is key to a collaborative and comparative approach to truth.[111] Such verification is *rationalist,* when it refers to a knowledge "all intelligent men and women, participants and observers, can share and jointly verify by observation and participation," and *practical,* when observers understand it as wise participants in the form of "mutual intelligibility—which eventuates in the community."[112]

Group self-consciousness. In a global state of "group self-consciousness," we know what it means to be religious and rationally understand, and to approve each other's faith. A modern Christian and a modern Muslim converge intellectually.

The study of comparative religion is the process, now begun, where we human beings learn, through critical analysis, empirical inquiry, and collaborative discourse, to conceptualise a world in which some of us are Christians, some of us are Muslims, some of us are Hindus, some of us are Jews,

109. Smith (1981): 90–91. See 91–94 about moving from externally knowing facts to humane understanding, from reification to interpretation, passive belief to active faith, empirical religion to religion in the context of transcendence, thinking about truth in a logically bifurcated (true/false) way to seeing it in a critically self-conscious, historical and corporate way.

110. Smith (1981): 97.

111. This principle K. Barth rejected when he advocated *die Aufhebung der Religion* [the abolition of religion] and claimed Christian faith to be exclusively about salvation Smith (1981): 100.

112. Smith (1981): 102.

some of us are sceptics and where all of us are, and recognise each other as being, rational men and women.[113]

To resolve faith conflicts, humans must learn to live in global solidarity. Believing that any statement "about personal faith" is potentially "intellectually persuasive" for someone of another faith, Smith writes,

> Some traditionalists would maybe shudder to think of going along with me, a Christian, in perhaps speculating . . . that *no statement about Christian faith is valid to which in principle a non-Christian could not agree.* Theologians have not usually adopted such a principle, I guess . . . we shall not fully sound the depths of this suggestion; but it may be borne in mind. I deem it more promising than one might at first suppose. At least intelligibility, if not acceptability, is a possible and fruitful criterion.[114]

In explaining a statement about his faith to "an intelligent, modern, devout, informed, Muslim or Hindu friend," Smith hopes that such a person would "understand, and yes, in the end, would accept" his statement. Such a person need not believe anything he does not find "intelligible and intelligent."[115] Humans are "diverse," not "incongruous"; human "solidarity" precedes human "particularity" and is part of "self-transcendence." True knowledge is self-knowledge on a "global scale"; it calls for "disciplined self-consciousness."[116]

Theology of Comparative Religion?

A theology of religion that looks "from within one tradition or community" out upon the faith life of other groups or traditions is untrue. It fails

---

113. Smith (1981): 101. This quotation is preceded by the disclosing sentence: "Several years ago I had occasion to characterise the study of comparative religion as moving from talk of an 'it' to talk of a 'they'; which became a 'we' talking of a 'they'; and presently a 'we' talking of 'you'; then 'we' talking 'with' you; and finally . . . a "we all' talking together about 'us.'"

114. Smith (1981): 101 (emphasis added).

115. Smith (1981): 101–102. "If this dream seems inept to anyone," it may be so "because that person is disdainful of all religion, or of all religion other than his own . . . ; or because he or she is disdainful of reason; or is unaware of modern developments in the religious history of the world, with its interactions among diverse communities. . . ."

116. Smith (1981): 102,

to assume that all humans think of themselves and their fellow humans "as fellow participants" in one global human community. The secret of Smith's approach is to "recognise the faith of other men" and that "there are no *other* men."[117]

In this secret, Smith both denounces and advocates. He rejects the traditional theological *comparativist* account of religious diversity. It is not helpful to someone eager to know, it is "relativistic" to think all options are "equally open and cogent," and it serves a "dogmatic" apologist to debate as a Christian.[118]

To understand religious faith from the outside is to subject it to alien categories. Theology is the *"intellectual expression"* of human *"faith"* as something *"central, total, supreme,"* which enables a person to be *"open to the infinite"* and *"see all that is finite in relation to that infinite."* Only from the inside can one theologize.[119] All human knowledge is self-knowledge, and all theology is *self*-theology. It is irrational to talk about a "theology of religion, the religion, or the religions." Theology is not less than Christian, Islamic, Hindu, etc.[120] A static view of faith and theology is wrong. Humans are not restricted to any limited involvement and logical paradoxes. In their thinking, humans must transcend "the adjectival truth of any particular group."[121]

The terms used in the Schleiermacher-Troeltsch and Barth-Kraemer traditions must be transcended, because they perpetuate the formulations of classical Christian theology, as well as Islamic, Hindu, Buddhist, Jewish and academic-humanistic thinking. The new terms must avoid "universality and absolutism" and stress the role of transcendent involvement. Traditional teaching, defending, attacking, debunking or explaining must be replaced with new ways of inquiring and understanding religions. In this lies "the

---

117. Smith (1981): 101.

118. Smith (1981): 108,109.

119. Smith (1981): 110–111 (emphasis added).

120. Smith (1981): 112.

121. Smith (1981): 113, also 112. As a *universal* "quality of human life," faith is "an orientation of the personality, to oneself, to one's neighbour, to the universe;. . . a way of seeing the world and of handling it; a capacity to live at a more than mundane level, to feel, to act in terms of, a transcendent dimension" (113–114). As a *particular* "concept," faith refers to (a) early Christian community, (b) modern need for meaningful life, (c) Luther's idea of how we are saved, (d) Schleiermacher's simple or pious faith, (e) gradual reifying of Calvin's doctrinal formulations and institutional practices and deist-humanist ideas of natural religion, (f) Barthian idea that faith is Christian and "religion" is non-Christian, and the Roman Catholic belief that faith is necessarily Christian, and the opposite of faith is non-faith or infidelity (117–121).

incipient endeavour to understand faith as a universal human quality."[122] As an "intellectual" (theologian) and a "Christian" (member in Church), Smith pressed for a theology informed "by hope and by love."[123]

Critical of traditional *objective-genitive* "theology" focused on "comparative religions," Smith developed a *subjective-genitive* view of "religion" based on "a global and verified self-consciousness of religious diversity." Since "all theology is self-theology" and may not "exclude" religion,[124] the method of "comparative religion" must include "oneself" and embrace "pluralism." If it does this, "theology" can still be used in that *new* sense. "It can be qualified by such adjectival terms as Christian, Jewish or Hindu, as long as it does not dilute, but actually transcends, that particular faith. It cannot be "a theology of faith from the outside," nor "simply the personal statement of a single individual."

> The theology of comparative religion, accordingly, must be the product of thinkers who see, who feel and, indeed, who know men and women of all religious groups and all centuries, as members of one community, one in which they themselves also participate. And this situation is just beginning—but *very* incipiently—to emerge.[125]

Ideally, a theology of comparative religion must be "acceptable to, even cogent for, all humankind." Its data must be "the history of religion."[126] The idea that theology explicates "revelation rather than history" perpetuates a false dichotomy. All revelation "has taken place in history."[127] The task of theology is *"to make rationally intelligible the meaning of human life in*

122. Smith (1981): 122. "The last hundred years have seen the universities doing an impressive task of uncovering, reporting, analysing, the data of the variegated religious traditions of the world. If during the next hundred years we can make a comparable effective study of faith in its many forms, the results will be momentous" (122).

123. Smith (1981): 123. In scholastic fashion, Smith talks about "secular intellectuals" and "religious" intellectuals: the former focus on what is "true," the latter on what is "good."

124. Smith (1981): 124.

125. Smith (1981): 125.

126. Smith (1981): 126. Smith criticizes two major misconceptions: (a) that theological colleges, theological seminaries and religion departments, associate history of religion with "religious communities other than their own," and (b) that history "excludes any transcendence reference" and is "closed system." (127)

127. Smith (1981): 127. He does not reject using the conceptual category "revelation," as long as it is done in an "intellectually appropriate" way, i.e., within an "awareness of what in fact has been going on." (128)

faith, and of the world in which that faith is lived."[128] Such a "global" and "collaborative" theology reflects Smith's dream of a world community, to "participate Christianly in the total life of mankind—the intellectual life, and the religious, as well as . . . the economic, and political."[129]

Noteworthy is Smith's account of an *imaginary panel presentation* between someone from six (other than Christian) faith communities, the last one being a "secular rationalist." On behalf of "fellow sceptics," this person indicates at the outset that they have had "to live in a world lacerated by religious strife," but now welcomes the invitation to talk about "a theology of comparative religion." He indicated that *secular rationalists* believe the notion of God to be wrong, religious symbols to be merely symbolic, welcome sophisticated analyses in psychology and social structures of religion, and are open to talking about faith as a constitutive component of being human.[130]

In the context of such panel discussion, they need to show humility and admit that "rationality" and "goodwill" are not premises to start from, but problems to be dealt with. Secular society is not necessarily a good society, because it, too, is confronted by lethargy and boredom. Its universities, or temples, struggle with "a loss of faith," especially with respect to "wholeness, integrity, loyalty, freedom, rapport." Like comparative religion thinkers, they also are interested in "a general theory of human attempts to find or to give meaning in, or to, human life."[131] They want Christians to respond to them not with rejection, but with reconciliation.[132]

According to Smith—as the imaginary panel chairman—all participants want to approximate truth, be content with partial truth, press for a dynamic vision, develop a historical way of apprehending truth, and serve fellow humans in this endeavor.[133]

---

128. Smith (1981): 128 (emphasis added). "Christians think Smith is not Christian enough, while many Muslims, Jews, Buddhists, and others think he is too Christian in his orientation, innuendo, and preconceptions." (128)

129. Smith (1981): 129. Smith adds, "And I invite others to do so Jewishly, Islamically, Buddhistically, or whatever—including humanistically."

130. Smith (1981): 130–146, particularly 146, " Man is *homo symbolicus;* and may well be *homo religiosus.*"

131. Smith (1981): 146, 147.

132. Smith (1981): 148, 149, especially the secular rationalist's question: "Your 'we', enlarged to include Buddhists and Jews and all, ought somehow also to include us too, ought it not?"

133. Smith (1981): 150

The discussion thus far will have prepared us also for the use of the word 'theology' in an altogether informal sense. By it I mean, quite literally, talk about God; or more generically, about the transcendent dimension of human life and of the universe, to which the history of religion (the history of man's spirit) bears witness and which it elucidates, and to which Christians have historically given the name 'God.' I do not primarily mean . . . a formal systematic theology in the sense of an established discipline. . . . My aim is to make a small contribution to talking about comparative religion in relation to God, or to talking about God in relation to comparative religion.[134]

Smith provides a full and final view of comparative religion in "A Theology of Comparative Religion for those among us who are Christians," the penultimate chapter of his *Towards a World Theology*. He rejects all "boundaried," i.e., "self-sufficient," theology which treats the faith of other communities as "objects" one makes pronouncements about. Instead, he advocates a comprehensive kind of human faith by focusing on *corporate, critical self-consciousness* with its stress on "universalisability" and "intellectuality" of such terms as "God," "religion," "history," "faith," "church" and "revelation."

God indicates a consciousness that "He transcends" whatever humans "personally have the wit or even the grace to mean by the term. . . . Let the word 'God' mean to each of my readers whatever it does mean personally to him or her, as atheist; or if not one, then what he or she thinks that it has meant to theists."[135]

Religion refers to continuous creation, not some 'big-bang' theory of origins. The notion of "reformation" in the sense of going back to the origin, what is pristine, a "once-for-all" attitude reveals a backward-looking mentality.[136] It assumes that "history" is injected into, added from the outside, to what was originally true, genuine, without accretion.[137]

History does not point to the past, to be studied, but to the present, to

134. Smith (1981): 151. The omitted part in this citation is a parenthetical comment which hints at Smith's view of dogmatics, namely: "That establishment, those inside it know, is currently groping for direction; new light must come to it from outside the 'discipline.'" He observes: "Usually, those who talk about God (those who speak theologically) talk about only one religious complex. Usually, those who talk about comparative religion do so without talking about God." (151)

135. Smith (1981): 152–153.

136. Smith (1981): 154. This disposition reflects enlightenment, deist and nineteenth-century linear thinking.

137. Smith (1981): 154–155.

be observed, and to the future as something new. It is an ongoing, dynamic movement of persons who, through faith, move forwards, not backwards (to "founders"), because they are in touch with, and touched by, transcendence. In this movement, even myths play a factual role. By tracing "what truly happened" (*was wahrlich geschehen ist*), one separates fact from legend.[138]

Faith is something by which also a Muslim is saved "—a sinner, yes, but *simul justus et peccator*."[139] One is saved "by faith," but faith need not be Christian: it can differ "in form, not in kind." Stated in a theologically and historically correct way, "just as Christians have been saved by faith of a Christian form, so have Muslims by faith of an Islamic, Andaman Islanders of an Andaman faith."[140] Some Christian and Muslim theologians believe such faith is "a sheer gift from God, and cannot be induced by anything that men and women do."[141]

Church is, as in any other religious community, "a divine-human complex" in motion. It involves one's "relationship to God" through participation of that person in one of the religious communities. Cosmic salvation is "the same for an African tribesman and for a Taoist and for a Muslim as it is for me, or for any Christian."[142] The idea that "only Christians" can be saved is wrong, even "blasphemous." When St. Paul proclaimed that "faith in Christ, or faith in God through Christ, saves, he had never heard of faith in the Buddha, or of faith in God through Islamic patterns." Smith comments,

> Those of us who have heard of these and know something of them must affirm with joy and triumph, and a sense of *Christian* delight, that the fact that God saves through those forms of faith too corroborates our Christian vision of God as active in history, redemptive, reaching out to all men to love and to embrace them. . . .
>
> Faith is a global human quality. And the religious history of the world is

138. Smith (1981): 155, 156–163.

139. Smith (1981): 165. For details, see 166–167. The phrase is from Martin Luther—"At the same time righteous and sinner." Smith's distinction between "historian" and "theologian" is riddled with epistemic and methodological problems.

140. Smith (1981): 167, 168. "Salvation" in this context means being "saved from nihilism, from alienation, anomie, despair, from the bleak despondency of meaninglessness. Saved from unfreedom, from being a victim of one's own whims within, or of pressures without; saved from being merely an organism reacting to its environment." (168)

141. Smith (1981): 169. Such faith saved Muslims from "ego-diffusion" and their societies from chaos, although Islamic patterns also permitted stupidities and brutalities to occur, just as also Christians were imperfect and guilty of the horrors of Crusades and Inquisition. (169)

142. Smith (1981): 170.

the record of God's loving, creative, inspiring dealings with recalcitrant and sinful but not unresponsive men and women. Christians He saved through Christ's death and resurrection, through membership in the Church, . . . Buddhists He saved through the teachings of the Buddha; through the imaginative memory of His person.

God is more imaginative than we Christians used to think. And man more responsive. God has participated more richly in human affairs, man has participated more diversely in God, than we once knew. All human history is *Heilsgeschichte.* . . .This has always been true; although we are the first generation of Christians to see this seriously and corporately, and to be able to respond to the vision.[143]

Revelation is "inductive, universal and Christian," and it is "continuous" in "history, humane intellectuality, theology, and especially faith." Smith emphasized revelation's "continuing contemporaneity." Just as a *symbol* does not carry "meaning" in itself, but mediates between particular persons and a transcendent reality, so also *revelation* consists of particular persons and what is transcendent, i.e., Himself.[144] In "doing justice," humans participate in the life of God, and God communes with humans.

The Qur'an as a book and Jesus Christ back then and there are as such objective revelations of God. It is improper to say that God revealed Himself in them in an absolute and impersonal way or to state that God revealed Himself *to me* as a Christian through Christ.[145] A Christian may never say that God has done so "fully" and "only" in a special way. Revelation points not to "fullness" but to "transcendence."

> I would accordingly suggest that theology abandon the use of concepts that give rise to statements such as 'God is fully revealed', or 'God was revealed in Christ.' The good news is not that God did something centuries ago in Palestine, however big that was; but that He can and may do something . . . salvific, however small our capacity, for you and for me today. The locus of revelation is always the present, and always the person. The channel of revelation in the Christian case, Christ, is a figure in history. But history, I have insisted, moves forward, and is the process by which He comes to us;

143. Smith (1981): 171, 172, 173. He rejects "one strand of Christian thought since 1800 and certain specific but minor formulations from earlier times," e.g., the belief that *only* Christians are saved.

144. Smith (1981): 173.

145. Smith (1981): 174.

is not something to be studied backwards, as the process by which we try to recapture Him.[146]

It is not the *first* century which is most important, but the present, or "contemporary experience." Today He is born (*hodie natus est*), today He is risen. Transcendence, i.e., God in the shape of Christ, which entered life anew in the past, continues to do so "every year, even every day" in the lives of Christians.[147] This form of Christian theology calls for a "rational interpretation of the known data" and to do so in an "unabashedly theocentric" way." Smith calls all who "insist that Christ is the centre of their lives" to rediscover that "God is the center of the universe."[148]

Vocabulary, Truth, History

Smith's interim conclusion is that what is new in Christendom's view of human religious history with respect to ultimate reality and truth is the manifestation, at this stage in history, of "pluralism." Given its "inherent aspiration to universally valid truth," it is not just the *intellect* which must move "through and beyond" this phase, but also *faith* must do this. Because it is "personal, particular, historical" and since the finite apprehends the infinite only finitely, "faith" also is historical, moving and only partly communal. Today the faith community is rapidly enlarging and intellectuals are forced to rethink the "relation of the specific to the generic." To move through and beyond "the several theologies of comparative religion . . . towards something still more universal" is today not an option but a necessity. To move towards "universal truth," Smith stresses three important issues, namely, "vocabulary," "truth" and "history."[149]

146. Smith (1981): 175.
147. Smith (1981): 176. "To over-simplify: a transforming power was continually received, an ability to love, to forgive and to know forgiveness, to discern and to live in loyalty to the intangibles, to recognise justice and mercy and compassion as ultimate, suffering as potentially redemptive and a proximate price of righteousness, oneself as cosmically significant and one's neighbour equally. . . . These things actually happened, generation after generation, in the lives of millions of people." (176)
148. Smith (1981): 177.
149. Smith (1981): 181–186.

Vocabulary

More adequate categories are needed for four traditional terms: faith, salvation, theology and God. The universal term **faith** refers—in the tradition of the Baden School of philosophy and anthropology—to what is "religious" or "transcendental" in life, and the term **salvation** has lost its traditional meaning, especially in Western culture, and has been replaced with terms like "liberation," "shalom" and "identity."

The concept **theology**—disliked by Buddhists and Western humanists—should perhaps be substituted with "philosophy," advocates of "philosophy of religion" claim. Such a change involves exchanging classical love of a transcendent yet humane wisdom for a positivist practicing of philosophy as a mundane craft, something Christian, Muslim and Jewish theologians would not welcome. Because of a pusillanimity of spirit, i.e., timidity or lack of courage, Smith does not want to replace "theology" with (the Baden term) "transcendentology."

The concept **God** has engendered much debate. As symbol, it points to something transcending all human conceptualization. Not all humans find the term "transcendence" "congenial and rich." Does it refer to, for example, a "He," a "She," or both? To an "He/She," or an "It"? To "Truth, Beauty, the Good and Justice"? For Christians "God" means "Him whom Jesus Christ has revealed," but for Muslims it refers to "Him who speaks to us through the Qur'an." Is "God" a reality humans respond to, search for, perhaps both, i.e., "a reality that they responded to by searching for it"? Smith does not define the concept "God" but tries to make our self-consciousness "more corporate and more historical" and thus "bridge the gap between specific and generic."

> I have urged, then, that our conceptualising, and our understanding of each other's concepts, be anchored in history, even for history-transcending and self-transcending concepts such as 'God.' . . . 'Transcendence,' 'theology,' 'God,' or some counterparts to them, are important to keep or to develop, lest sight or feel be lost of what some would call the objective pole in religious experience.[150]

150. Smith (1981): 186. He adds, "My emphasis on corporate self-consciousness might seem to lend itself to a charge of collective subjectivism, despite my disclaimers, were there not dramatically included within it that historically persistent consciousness of a surpassingly great Other."

Truth

"Truth" in religion has to do with intellectual interpretation of the world as understood in faith. Religion *is* not in all instances true, but *becomes* true in particular persons, nor are religious statements always true.[151] The West can learn three things from the Orient: (a) "arriving at more accurate discriminations between more true and less," (b) the truth of myths, and (c) a pluralism involving agreeing to disagree conceptually. In return, the Orient can learn from the West's long and profound thinking about the (a) significance of history and its (b) influence on religion.

In opposition to current Western epistemology "oriented more to science than to history, more to things than to persons, and more to individualism than will probably endure," Smith proposes a historically self-critical and universalist epistemology that fosters a "corporate critical self-consciousness in the religious realm." In this respect, "the comparative study of religion" might contribute "more to the development of Western epistemology" than, *vice versa*, the latter to the former. Understanding religion is integral to "man's general aspiration to truth."[152]

Rather than defend the "truth of transcendence itself, the reality of God," or "the divine," before the bar of modern sceptics' logic and worldview, Smith calls the latter before the bar of world history to "defend their curious insensitivity to this dimension of human life."

> Seen in global perspective, current anti-transcendent thinking is an aberration. . . . After all, the overwhelming majority of intelligent persons at most times and places, and all cultures other than in the recent West, have recognised the transcendent quality of man and the world. To be a secularist in the negative sense is to be oddly parochial in both space and time, and to opt for what may alas be a dying culture.[153]

---

151. Smith (1981): 187; also his parenthetical comment: "(Besides, one must note that the period is now coming to an end when one imagined that a religion consisted primarily in a set of propositional tenets, each either true or false. Though that period was short-lived, the position was strong enough to have done much damage)."

152. Smith (1981): 189.

153. Smith (1981): 189. He thinks that the "larger frame" of his historical method provides a way to avoid another parochialism, the false dilemma of nihilistic positivism versus Christian, or Greek, metaphysical speculations.

Truth is not found objectively in history, but apprehended through history. Insofar as truth "is true, it transcends history" and is, for that reason, "inherently a transcendent as well as a humane concept." This fact allows a historian "to combine a basic respect for, basic acceptance of, others . . . not an arrogant sitting in judgement on them. . . ." Looking beyond propositions and symbols to the persons they served, and past even these persons to the truth to which they responded in their particular manner and setting, we find ourselves in a "vastly improved position critically, yet charitably, responsibly, non-idiosyncratically, to formulate the truth for us. May a theologian reasonably do less?"[154]

History

The historical dimension is apparent in that humans live in two dimensions: the historical and the transcendent. These two dimensions "interpenetrate in our lives," are formalized in religion, indicate what the "religious systems of the world have in common," and are dynamic, i.e., focused more on becoming than on being.

All world religions are now for the first time "faced with a joint challenge: to collaborate in building a common world," in which we can "all live together." Not conflict between religions, but juxtaposition is required, made possible by mutually agreed awareness of differences. Authentically perceiving each other as religious persons, rather than conceptualizing one another's positions, increases a common worldwide consciousness. From "monologue of proselytising missions," we moved to "dialogue," and now we must move to "colloquy," to "a side-by-side confronting of the world's problems," not to a "face-to-face confronting of each other."[155] Smith ends his *Towards a World Theology* as follows:

> It is through His participation in the religious history of the world (and in the Western case, also the history of the Graeco-Roman tradition) that He has chiefly entered human lives to act in human history. Right now, He is calling us to let Him act through new forms, continuous with the old, as we human beings across the globe enter our strange new age.[156]

154. Smith (1981): 190. While truth remains transcendent, our formulations of it are only approximations, since they are always particular, historical and contingent. (191)
155. Smith (1981): 193.
156. Smith (1981): 194.

Assessment

Positive features

First, the scope and depth of Smith's study is phenomenal. He senses the need to think holistically and globally, rejects non-historical ideas about truth, and stresses the importance of rethinking the meaning of "reality," the role of "transcendence," the dynamics of "history," the importance of "philosophy," "anthropology" and "epistemology"—especially the distinctions between *humane* and *natural* and *subjective* and *objective* knowledge.

Second, he acknowledges the *religious* nature of Western "secularism," rejects classic positivism, warns against nihilism, is troubled about crises in modern faith life, probes local-global religious conflicts, develops a mind-set and vocabulary that influenced the World Council of Churches, and avoids secondary disagreements in Roman Catholic and Protestant thinking.

Third, he is aware of the complexity of faith life, the role of philosophy in theology, the need to replace monologue with colloquy, the danger of conceptual rigidity in the Western faith of Christians, and the importance of global rethinking of issues related to "religion" and "faith."

Negative Features

First, his monumental scholarship reveals an *uncritical* acceptance of the Baden (Heidelberg or South-West German) School of Philosophy. His train of thought moves along on the rails laid down by the three classic *historicist* thinkers: W. Dilthey, W. Windelband and E. Troeltsch. Their thought-pattern shaped his ontology, anthropology and epistemology about, for example, *self*-consciousness, self-*consciousness*, the role of faith in determining human experience, equating an idea of "transcendence" with God, and the dynamic of human history.

Second, his commitment to a Greek idea of "intellect," his idea that critical rationality provides the cure-all to conflicts related to faith and religion problems, and his belief that humans have the capacity to discover what is transcendent in different faith traditions and, thereby, to prevent humans from approving nihilism and succumbing to chaos.

Third, his belief that the universal power of "transcendence" influenced his view of "God," "love," "grace," "faith," "religion," "truth," "unity" and "meaning." As a result, the *fourth,* i.e., mysterious, meaning of faith as "gift"—which involves repentance and results in heart-centered renewal—is compromised. The *religious* conflict between Christian and non-Christian living is not radical, but only one of "degree." The power of God's three-pronged revelation for humans to respond to God is not acknowledged.

Smith's engaging insights turn out not to be biblically directed, but to be basically *Western* in his reliance on human reason, use of a rigid "method," or way of thinking, about truth advocated in the Baden, or Heidelberg, School of thinking. Although *structurally,* his approach provides some helpful insights, the central *religious* thrust of his philosophy and his theology of "comparative religion" is Western in reflecting fundamental assumptions of Western philosophers and theologians whose thinking moved along the two rails of the Greek idea of "truth" and "reality."[157]

---

157. Two comments: (a) missing in Smith's thinking is the role of God's created, incarnated and inscripturated revelation. God's Word does not guide his thinking about religion; (b) the traditional scholastic view of "religious diversity"—not mentioned in this chapter—will be touched on (briefly) in chapter 18 below.

CHAPTER THIRTEEN

Hermeneutic Issues

To think about faith life in terms of "pisteology," not "theology," as suggested in the last four chapters, assumes a holistic way of living in, and thinking about, created reality. The method and content of such a study attempts to avoid two questionable features in Western culture: Platonic and Aristotelian scholasticism and modern Kantian and Schleiermacherian projection theories about especially "truth," "faith," "religion," "revelation" and "God," in various Christian faith traditions.

The focus of this chapter will be on exploring an appropriate way to read, interpret or understand the acts and contents of faith life. As a subsidiary discipline of "pisteology," *pistical* hermeneutics affects at least eight issues: revelation and religion, Christ as "key," written Word, terminology, then/there-now/here, proclaiming and interpreting, revelation and norms, and selective hearing. The intent is to be explorative, not exhaustive, about the main features of "hearing" God's Word for one's general *self*-awareness and specific *faith* life.

Revelation and Religion

The mystery of God's love-filled mercy is the answer for self-centered humans to hear the voice of the Creator, to be free to develop a practical perspective on human life and history.[1] A heart-centered *religious* turnaround of

---

1. For example, Paul and Lydia, as described in Acts 16:14.

men and women, of all ages and races and places, enables humans to "hear" God's liberating Word and permits it to redirect their whole life. Such a turnabout is, in principle, life-encompassing in whatever humans do as His image-bearers. Any *half*-heartedness results, sooner or later, in inconsistencies, personal and interpersonal violations of God's law of love. Humans are essentially *religious*: to be human is to be *religious* and to be religious is to be human.[2] For all (Christian and non-Christian) humans, "religion" is deeper and more encompassing than any carefully structured fellowship and worship at specific times, places and projects, in special buildings, with specific budgets, and their distinct theological seminaries.

"*Religion*" and "*religious*" refer, in this book or study, to what (un)consciously humans do in their response to what is Absolute or Ultimate. It reflects the "spirituality" of one's way of living. It is not restricted to a specific facet of life, block of time or activity in one's life. It is not merely some vertical dimension added to one's horizontal, autonomous, self-sufficient living.

God's one, but three-pronged, revelation is inconceivable without some human response to it. At the same time, without His created, incarnated and inscripturated revelation, any human *religious* response to it is impossible. Even a negative human response to God's revelation is possible by virtue of His all-of-life embracing presence. Due to His awesome presence God's people work out their salvation with "fear and trembling."[3] His revelation is essentially perspicuous, reliable and authoritative, unlike human responses in the *religious* direction of their *faith* life.

The relation within humans between their "inner" and "outer" selves, i.e., their "heart" and "functions," is such that, although distinguishable, they are not be separated from each other. The human "self," or "I," responds in an ultimately obedient or disobedient way to God's impinging revelation guaranteed in His covenant faithfulness.

Christ as "Key"

God's revelation began when He created the world. Without this *creational* revelation, which includes humans as His image-bearing caretakers, it is impossible to fathom what it means to be human, i.e., a self-conscious creature, who acknowledges the Creator by obeying His central love command. This

2. For details, see chapter 19 below.
3. Cf. Philippians 2:12.

322

revelation is assumed in God's *incarnated* revelation in His Son—through whom the world was created—as the Anointed Savior, i.e., Christ Jesus, to redeem desperate humanity. God's *inscripturated* revelation reminds humans about His covenant faithfulness and the power of God's yearning for a wayward and reclaimed world.[4]

The "Alpha" and "Omega," beginning and end, of created reality are centered in God's Word "through, in and for whom" everything was made that has been made.[5] In the fullness of time (*kairos*), that Word became human, or "flesh," in the one Word in, and for, the world.[6] Through their dying in His death on the cross and their rising in his resurrection from the tomb,[7] those who follow the Word-made-flesh are, already now and here, at peace with the God of life. Engrafted into the Tree of life, Christians are rooted, have a global Light in the Lord of lords. In the Spirit, they have a lookout tower, can scan the horizons of culture and history, have reason to hope in everything they do, also in their *faith* life.

Through God's redirecting *gift* of faith, Christians are gripped by His incredible, astounding grace. Sensing something of the depth and scope of God's love command, they are eager to read His *written* revelation about His loving power and powerful love. Not to acknowledge this new reality is to ignore countless women and men throughout the world, whose renewing experience did not depend on complicated hermeneutic theories, but on the power (*dynamis*) of God's story that they read, believed and shared.

The power of such a heart-centered revelation and *religious* response was not eclipsed by things they did not understand in Scripture.[8] The Savior (Jesus), who in the New Testament is called "the way and the truth and the life,"[9] is the embodiment of the Anointed ("Christ") in the Old Testament. The sheep of this Shepherd know that the Father sent Him to take their place, pay their ransom, bear His fury for breaking His love, and bond them to Him in the Spirit.

In response to this wonder of God's revelation, humans are called to express their joy in the second Adam, their only hope and security in both life and death. No theory of hermeneutics can explain this mystery of love. It is the basis for knowing the Word-personified, who, through the Spirit,

4. Cf. John 1:18.
5. Cf. John 1:3.
6. Cf. Galatians 4;4–5.
7. Cf. Romans 6:4.
8. See, for example, Roy Clouser (2001): 273–293, esp. 289–292.
9. John 14:6.

provides the key to unlock God's self-sacrificing love (*agape*) for humans who turn a deaf ear to the full revelation of God, their Maker and Provider.

The response of most Pharisees, scribes, Sadducees and Zealots to the personified Word in centered on their refusal to acknowledge the "heart" of God's revelation, i.e., the Lord Jesus Christ. The Anointed One is the *key* to Scripture, the knob that opens the door to *religious* renewal. As God's written love-letter, Scripture zeroes in on the *religious* thrust of human life. It is the *spiritual* compass for true piety in everything humans do privately and publicly.

Written Word

Being focused on the heart, i.e., on the *religious* direction, Scripture is not some almanac, or recipe book, with all kinds of prescriptions for what to do, or not do, in specific circumstances. Nor is it a book filled with *proof*-texts for such things as psychology, political problems, ethical issues, economic policies, genres of literature, natural science, educational theories, scholastic debates or theological speculation.

Neither the Old Testament nor the New Testament[10] is textbook. Both Testaments are *faith-focused* libraries of sixty-six[11] books of various lengths that cover at least two thousand years. They provide positive and negative guidelines for humans in often complex personal and societal situations. They indicate to God's people and, through them, to other humans that He is faithful to his covenant with creation, no matter what humans do in it.

The Bible is not a book of concepts, intellectual truths or propositional statements. Neither is it a collection of moral stories with ethical principles for theologians to speculate about and preachers to impress listeners with. It is not some manual that teaches how to combine walking with God with accommodational thinking. It does not sanction the use by medieval theologians of Greek ideas about, for example, "being," "substance," "thinking/willing/feeling," "four causes," "truth" in order to develop, and explain, faith life for learned clergy who then explain the gospel to clergy-dependent listeners.[12]

---

10. As well as many other ancient, including apocryphal, writings during the Old and New Testament eras.

11. The Roman Catholic Church includes seven more books.

12. Nor does it justify what Theodore Beza did in his inaugural lecture in 1559 at the

Its clarity is centered in Christ Jesus, who embodies God's covenant promises to a partially self-oriented humanity. Its perspicuity does not consist of what is "logical," "literary," "historical" or any combination of such features, nor does it lie in any economic, political or social quality.[13] The focus of Scripture is the Creator of everything, who is faithful to his covenant with created reality, especially human image-bearers in their creation, fall, redemption and return to their love-commanding/demanding Maker.

Scripture is unique in that it centers on the heartbeat of God's Word. This is what makes Scripture *normative* for all human life, particularly faith life. In this respect, Scripture is its own interpreter. Although apart from human faith in the Savior, Scripture cannot be properly understood, its normative character is not based on *our* faith in the Lord, but in *God's mercy* in Christ Jesus.[14]

As book (*biblos*), Scripture is creaturely, not something divine. Unlike any other book, Christians believe it is God's inspired "love-letter" to a world in need. It is the means for the Spirit to open human hearts for its amazing story of salvation and redirection of human life to the Creator-Redeemer.[15] Through the Spirit, the written Word directs searching readers to His love and to rejoice in the Father's forgiveness, having a new lease on life, and experiencing a peace passing all understanding.

The Good News of the written Word[16] enables humans to yield to its liberating power and take hold of God's life-granting promises. Openhearted Scripture readers need not lean on philosophical, theological or hermeneutic theories to understand Scripture's central message. They sense the need to stop doing what they have been doing and turn around in the core, or the "I," of their being and to redirect their whole life.

Such a response to God's Word removes, at least in principle, divisive differences between, for example, conservatives and progressives, and compels them to follow the Spirit's leading. It does not permit false dilemmas, resulting from misguided theological conflicts, to rob from them the joy and certainty of true faith.

---

opening of J. Calvin's Academy in Geneva when he encouraged the Reformed community to use Aristotle's views about reality and truth (for details, see chapter 3 above).

13. E.g., respectively, capitalism in North America, Puritanism in New England colonies, and liberation theology in Latin America.

14. See Luke 24:13–35 about the Risen Lord conversing with travelers to Emmaus.

15. For example Lydia (Acts 16:14).

16. For details, see chapter 19 about John Kraay and Anthony Tol, eds., *Hearing and Doing: Philosophical Essays Dedicated to H. Evan Runner* (1979).

Instead of nurturing a dynamic, not simplistic, or childlike, not child-ish, Christian faith, philosophical theologians or theological philosophers developed complex theories about God's revelation and faith life with their distinct ways of interpreting Scripture. They developed rigid "methods" and "doctrines" and imposed them on their fellow Christians. These, in turn, tended to result in misleading contrasts, futile debates, unnecessary conflicts, painful schisms, even political and military struggles.

These conflicts usually centered on issues related to the nature of reality (ontology), the meaning of being human (anthropology), the role of knowl-edge (epistemology), the place of faith life, the structure of society (culture), the discipline of theology (encyclopedia), or any combination of these disci-plines. Prominent in this respect are the differences, even conflicts, between, for example, (a) transcendence and immanence, (b) objective and subjective revelation, (c) theology and anthropology, (d) Word *as* Scripture and Word *in* Scripture, and (e) Scripture with infallible facts and interpretation-free concepts *of* revelation and K. Barth's neo-orthodox stress on Spirit-directed witness *to* revelation revealed *in* Scripture.

Christians cannot avoid thinking of God's (threefold) revelation through the lenses of their personal experiences and common faith traditions. To admit this does not undermine Scripture's authority, nor prevent Christians from knowing truth. On the contrary, it is the only way humans understand God's written Word. What is crucial is whether their discerning of God's revelation is heart-centered and indicative of covenantal allegiance and joy. The issue is whether the discernment is a *genuine act of faith* or merely an analytic affirmation of theological statements.[17]

Scripture requires its interpreters to rely on God's infallible promises, guaranteed by the Spirit's overwhelming power. Scripture is the Spirit-guided means for young and old, rich and poor, uneducated and educated, male and female, healthy and sick, to read about and do what delights the Creator of heaven and earth.[18] A *heart*-centered, Spirit-directed *religious,* response to God's written Word does not need *scholastic* dualism, nor any "gnostic" mysticism. Prompted by the outpoured Spirit, humans respond in faith to God's love narrated in Scripture and centered in the Incarnate Word.

---

17. Regarding the distinction between confessional (*pistical*) and "*theological*," see chap-ters 9 and 10 above.

18. Of course, this involves translators (from Hebrew, Aramaic and Greek) and presenters and explainers of the content of both Testaments.

Terminology

It not easy to indicate the exact meaning of "hermeneutic." Minimally, it involves interpretation. "What" is interpreted, and "how" this is done, in relation to an assumed worldview are unclear. Does it refer to a creedal, or confessional, way of reading Scripture?[19] Or does it imply some (post) modern view of reality, being human, way of knowing (epistemology)?[20] Is interpreting Scripture not theocentric, or "objective," not anthropocentric, or "subjective"? Is it more important for modern pastors and theologians to be exposed to multiple postmodern theories of faith and belief? Can one avoid the multiple hermeneutic debates today and their often conflicting theological probing? Why not simply focus on an infallible Bible as norm and develop a personal and practical way to read and interpret Scripture?

We need both a general hermeneutic to interpret created reality and a specific one to interpret the nature of faith life. Such an interpretation is not primarily pistical, but a step removed from one's daily faith. It is a specific interpretation *in*, and *of*, faith life. Such an act is not *pistical* but *analytical*. Just as theology, in the sense of pisteology, is abstract, i.e., analytic, so does a hermeneutic faith life involve a form of theoretic knowledge.

Given the contours of the ontology indicated in chapters 7 through 10 above, the distinction between the *leading*, or qualifying, and *founding*, or supporting, functions of faith life is crucial. All faith life has various *foundational* aspects that play a significant supportive role in faith life. Included in the foundational aspects are the psychic, analytic, lingual, technical/cultural, social, economic, aesthetic, juridical and ethical aspects of created reality.[21]

Given its qualifying, or leading, role in faith life, the *pistical* aspect is not reducible to any *foundational*, or supporting, aspect. Any reduction in this context results in a distortion in which a *secondary* aspect of faith life assumes a *primary*, usually moralistic, role. Structurally speaking, Western faith traditions focused for centuries on such *secondary* features as what is "grammatical," "factual" and "intellectual," or "lingual," "historical" and "analytical," features of "pistical" life. Stressing these three sub-aspects was helpful. It was also a hindrance, however, in that it impeded a richer and

19. A Roman Catholic, Eastern Orthodox, Russian Orthodox and Protestant (Lutheran, Calvinist, Anabaptist) way of knowing or interpreting reality.

20. Cf. rationalist, existentialist, language/analytical and other forms of postmodern philosophy.

21. And the earlier, or foundational, numerical, spatial, kinematic, physical and biotic aspects of created reality.

fuller sense of God's "inscripturated" revelation and the need for a *pistical* hermeneutic of Scripture reading and understanding.

First. Scripture is not a book of different *languages*, genres of literature, kinds of grammar and series of exemplary lessons. Its main purpose is to evoke a wholehearted response from its readers and listeners in their private and public *faith activities* related to their Scripture reading, prayers, devotions, laments and songs. The intent of all their faith-related activities is to grow in the awareness of the nature and scope of the uniqueness of the relation between one's self-knowledge and knowledge of God, i.e., human religion and divine revelation. It expresses a freedom-in-submission, *religious* sense of being rescued, of the Creator-Redeemer.

Second. Scripture is not a summary of surprising, if not unsettling, events. Careful Scripture reading and sharing the Good News in historically meaningful and culturally relevant ways, and in all (early, elementary, secondary, tertiary and undergraduate) education about created reality in light of God's power-filled Word—this is the Holy Spirit's way of influencing the *religious* direction of a community, culture and civilization. On this score, Scripture resembles any other *pistically* qualified document, even non-Christian and anti-Christian ones.[22] Unlike any other human document, Scripture's role is distinct in that it is the Spirit's way of convicting, and convincing, humans of all ages and places, privileged and neglected, healthy and sick, etc., to live in a love-filled, self-sacrificing and life-redeeming way.

Third. Scripture is not a compilation of helpful truths, statements, aphorisms or examples of *practical* wisdom. It reveals God's faithfulness to his reliable promises and how recalcitrant humans can, through Christ's Spirit, respond to powerful forces of iniquity, brutality and even death. Central to Scripture is God's promise of life, command to love, depth of grace and redemption, and his kingdom of peace passing all understanding.

Central to His holiness is his opposition to any power of grief and destruction. His holiness is evident in two ways: (a) His fierce warnings against man-made idols that cannot deliver what they promise, and (b) His holy wrath on the epitome of human folly, audible in the piercing "Why" of His *only* Son for the sake of a lost humanity.[23]

No hermeneutic theory can circumvent the basic problem the Bible

---

22. E.g., *Qu'ran, Communist Manifesto, Humanist Manifesto, Little Red Book* in China, and *Book of Mormon*.

23. Matthew 27:46: "About the ninth hour Jesus cried out in a loud voice, *"Eloi, Eloi, lama sabachthani?"* (My God, my God, why have you forsaken me?).

addresses. Scripture's message is deeper than what Greek thinking focused on with its (in)famous intellectual probing, stress on moral freedom and passion for justice. Scripture addresses the *dis*integration of human life, the need for *re*integration of distorted life, and covenant-centered forgiveness, and childlike prayers and praises.[24]

While for Christians the norms (*regula fidei*) for their whole life, especially faith life, are based on Scripture, pistically *deviant* persons do the same, but they appeal to Scripture to give their deformed faith some credibility.[25] Also *accommodating* scholastic thinkers, including theologians, try to harmonize their ontology, anthropology, epistemology, role of faith by appealing to specific passages in Scripture. This tendency can affect also *reformational* thinking.

What complicated matters in biblically orthodox faith traditions is the hermeneutics of certain church leaders and theologians. They interpreted Scripture in ways that tacitly, or openly, for personal or complex historical reasons, approved such evils as slavery, civil religion, militarism, capitalism, communism, apartheid, abuse of women, secularism and dictatorship.[26] Stressing *sola Scriptura* is no guarantee against questionable ways of reading Scripture and developing a wrong hermeneutic.

Protestant reformers did not always agree among themselves how to interpret Scripture.[27] This is clear from the way they dealt with scholastically complex issues related to the Lord's Supper, child baptism, the general notion that what Scripture does not forbid is permitted, and the Puritan view that what Scripture does not explicitly command is forbidden.[28] Perhaps ascribing a "normative" role to a particular faith tradition within institutionalized churches weakens the principle of *sola Scriptura*?

Then/There-Now/Here

How can the message of such an ancient document as Scripture (*then*), written and compiled in a different cultural setting and in another part of the

24. For details, see chapters 7–11 above.

25. Cf. the apt Dutch phrase *"Elke ketter heeft zijn letter"* ("Each heretic has his verse").

26. For example, Locke in England, Kant in Germany, Kautsky in Western Europe and Russia, health/wealth gospel in the USA, and apartheid advocates in South Africa.

27. For example, the medieval four ways, or levels, of reading Scripture: literal (facts), allegorical (what to believe), moral (what to do) and anagogical (what to hope for).

28. With its tendency to downplay God's *non-written* revelation.

world (*there*), be correctly understood and communicated today (*now*) in an historically different setting (*here*)? What is the relation between *then* and *now,* and how can the distance between *there* and *here* be bridged?

Do these two forms of relationship presuppose certain concepts about supra-natural, or non-historical, truth (T. Aquinas, T. Reid, B. B. Warfield), based on "psychological" similarity and universality (S. Freud, C. G. Jung), the result of existential decisions (M. Heidegger, P. Tillich, W. Pannenberg), or the residue of ancient and modern myths and symbols (M. Eliade and J. Campbell)?[29]

The "truth" of the words, sentences, episodes, stories and books of Scripture is centered in God's faithfulness promised, and embodied, in the Lord Jesus Christ. Its life-redeeming power is evident in the Spirit-directed followers of the Redeemer, who move in the wake of His victory. Comparable to differently shaped and colored feathers of a hunter's arrow are the words of God's love-commands and promises revealed back "then" and "there" and which continue to guide His people "now" and "here."

The Bible is not a collage of stories, filled with moral lessons, for humans to consider and emulate. This Book is God's way to encourage humans to read, hear, reflect and share with others the essence of true love in daily life. It reveals the origin, nature and purpose of created reality, and it does this through the response He expects from humans as His covenant-partners. He prompts them to behave responsibly on their short, but important, journey to the *eschaton,* where and when evil, oppression and tears will be no more. Proper reading and understanding of this relatively old Book is not the privilege of, for example, lingual experts, creative theologians, or popular preachers who revel in various hermeneutic *theories* and *methods* focused more on the "how" of Scripture than on its "what" or "content."

To sense, and acknowledge, the central thrust of Scripture without ignoring important details of this millennia-old written revelation of God calls for a heart-centered awareness of Scripture's unique message. It calls for a careful listening to God's voice, an openness to His life-saving mercy, and a readiness to share this with fellow humans. Such redemptive knowledge of God's will for society, culture and history is always deeply personal and communal, never merely private and individual. To interpret and rightly hear His Word is first of all practical, life-changing, and vision-sharpening for the benefit of other humans, both locally and globally.[30]

---

29. This list of positions, and advocates, is illustrative, not exhaustive.
30. For example, the role of Noah, Abraham and, uniquely, Christ Jesus.

Such a hermeneutic of Scripture calls for a simple, and vibrant, childlike reliance on God's Word revealed in "the Son of God and Son of Man." Such walking with God determines human knowledge of God and self, within the context of His covenant with creation and humans in it.[31] This covenant God affirmed when, through the "gift" of faith, and prompting of the Spirit, humans hear His voice when they read Scripture.[32] Such a discernment does not depend on any intimidating hermeneutic theory of interpretation. *Religiously* redirected humans learn gradually, sometimes suddenly or through protracted struggles, what being Spirit-led implies for their liberating journey on the path of truth.[33] The *words* of Scripture point and are subservient to this overpowering *Word* of God.

In this regard, the intent and context of the words of Scripture are essential. Not to recognize this forestalls the reader from sensing rich nuances, or helpful nuggets, in the story of Scripture. Unique geographic, lingual, personal, social, cultural and historical features of the written *words* of God's one *Word* are important. Specific names, aspects, stories and events provide necessary clues about the nature of God's revelation and human response to it. Regarding God's promises, blessings, patience, warnings, anger, nearness, forgiveness and encouragement, Scripture reveals the ups and downs, stability and struggles, and anxieties and joys of faith life.

These nuances are not merely to be noted and quickly ignored, but to be carefully noted and reacted to. They are mini-invitations for readers to respond more wisely in their daily walk with God in whatever they do. Christians reflect a new way of living, through the Spirit and in the Word, by acknowledging God's basic law of love in all their responsibilities and tasks.

To do this always and everywhere is difficult. Christians do not sufficiently see, let alone acknowledge, the close relation between *faith* life— often erroneously equated with organized "religion"—and the *rest* of life, especially business, politics, economics, sexuality, entertainment and race relationships. Three wrong views about the relation of *faith* life to the rest of life are *separating* vertical from horizontal, *equating* spiritual with practical, and *elevating* what is pistical to something cultural.

First, *separating* confessional faith life (pistical) from what is cultural is typical of Pietism's world-flight disposition, and of the Neo-Orthodox

31. See Calvin, *Institutes of the Christian Religion*, I, 1, *1–2*.

32. E.g., Council of Jerusalem (Acts 15:1–21).

33. Cf. Old and New Testament, especially the letters of Paul, writings of John, book of Hebrews and book of James; *Belgic Confession* of Guido de Brès, written in prison, *Barmen Declaration* against Fascism, *Belhar Confession* against Apartheid and slavery.

distinction between "text" and "context" in Scripture (cf. K. Barth, R. Bult-mann). **Second,** *equating* universal statements of Christian faith with Hu-manistic principles (cf. Liberal theologians). Rejecting God as the sovereign Law-giver in his primary laws for created reality, it views Scripture as the result of human projections and myths that reflect the human challenges and struggles in life (cf. M. Eliade, J. Altizer). **Third,** *elevating* a faith tradition, together with its culture, to something national or universal. This danger conservative Christians tend to favor. They stress clear statements about central beliefs, tend to revel in scholastic thinking about salient beliefs, and relativize the effects of historical circumstances and changes (cf. V. Hepp,[34] J. Rushdoony).

Proclaiming and Interpreting

The way one views the three misleading stances mentioned above, and the *reformational* stance suggested in this study, impacts not only our read-ing/interpreting Scripture, but also how the gospel is proclaimed. Sermons, homilies, devotionals, retreats, etc., reflect how the central message of God's written revelation is understood and conveyed.

In distinction from *juridical* proclamation in some courtroom or leg-islative hall, preaching is a human faith activity associated, if it is *Christian*, with Scripture-oriented worship in a public, or private, place, in order to share the Good News with fellow believers and those eager to hear it. If it is *non-Christian*, it is associated with whatever is communicated and done in synagogues, mosques, temples, meditation centers, witness-halls, even with sun-worshipers on warm beaches.

In Christian faith circles, proclaiming the gospel and administering the sacraments of baptism and Lord's supper[35] are usually done by ordained persons in organized faith communities. How they understand, and com-municate, God's Word influences not only the *faith* life of their fellow be-lievers but somehow also other areas of their life—e.g., marriage and family, political life, caring for non-human creatures, educational programs, social interaction, business policies, courtroom practices, military conduct and

34. Valentijn Hepp (1879–1950), successor of Herman Bavinck in 1922 as professor of dogmatics at the Free University. In his method of thinking, he was one of the most scholastic thinkers in the history of Reformed dogmatics.

35. The five additional sacraments in Roman Catholic and Eastern Orthodox faith tradi-tions are confirmation, penance, holy orders, marriage and extreme unction.

medical care. How Christians interpret Scripture—and non-Christians their distinct books and rituals—affects their principles and priorities in their life.

Compared to other human activities, faith activities are not so-called holy or supernatural experiences, but thoroughly human. Preparing and delivering sermons, personal and public gospel sharing, praying and interceding are fully human or ordinary, not special or religious. Genuine faith life assumes that a person is aware of problems to be addressed, issues to be dealt with, power and limitations of faith life, and willingness to review one's (lack of) self-understanding and (in)ability to hear God's Word in His written revelation.[36]

Faith life, with its distinct structure, exhibits a wide range of features, dimensions, aspects and facets. Included in these "structural" facets of faith life are nine aspects of reality—*psychic*: disposition of human faith, excitement, confidence and openness; *analytical*: clarity, discernment, insight and ideas of faith; *lingual*: different languages, translations, metaphors, symbols, body language; *social*: class, community, tribe, race, fellowship, organization; *formative-technical*: skill, technique, training, control, impact; *economic*: proper balance of time, words and space, fast/slow and brief/long, benefit, value, sacrifice, offering; *aesthetic*: style, composition, drama, rhythm, imagination, poetry, music, liturgy; *juridical*: authority, discipline, constitution, regulation, ordination, rights, freedom, excommunication, plagiarism; and *ethical/trothic*: honesty, trustworthiness, reliability, deception, manipulation.

Minimally, these nine empirical sub-aspects of faith life, together with the four "earlier" aspects,[37] of created reality are somehow present in *all Christian **and** non-Christian* faith activities. This includes such *pistical* issues as preaching, sacramental rituals, liturgical programs, spiritual retreats, devotional activities and faith reflections. To be aware of these *structural*—in distinction, not separation, from the central *religious* direction—aspects of faith life leaves no room for the docetic temptation to "spiritualize" the testimony of God's Word by turning it into something mystical for searching humans and away from the only source of comfort for discerning Christians here and now.[38]

36. For details about these issues in relation to ontology and anthropology, see chapters 9 and 10 above.

37. Not included in this list of human faith's features are the *numerical, spatial, kinematic* and *biotic* dimensions, which, in scholastic theology, have resulted in speculative problems about the meaning of "numbers," "infinity," "eternity," "time," "space," "causality," "movement," "organic or growth" in theology and faith.

38. Cf. Lecture of David Lyon on "Surveillance" in Chicago, IL, June, 2007.

To think of *proclamation* in terms of any one, or combination, of the inherent features[39] of pistical experience is misleading. It may confuse preaching with giving *psychic* pep-talks, mesmerize gullible listeners with *logical* arguments and proofs, impress worshipers with masterfully crafted prayers, and deliver stunning *literary* orations. It may reduce Scripture interpretation and proclamation to a veneer-deep "health and wealth" proclamation, liturgies to artistic masterpieces and riveting performances, and the "Bread of Life" to crumbs of moral lessons that are profound only on the surface.

Misleading Scripture interpretation and proclamation stifles true faith life and genuine discipleship. It encourages listeners to yield to a non- or, worse, anti-Christian faith life and usually self-centered lifestyle in society and culture. Such superficial reading of Scripture and interesting, though powerless, preaching may encourage even non-Christians to criticize Christians for their irrelevant faith and inability to address the real needs of humans.

Every faith tradition displays the *structural* features inherent in faith life.[40] Given its stress on the importance of clarity, logic and philosophical issues, scholastic theology cannot do justice to the intricate and complex nature of faith life. Their Greek-tinted anthropology and epistemology forces them to oversimplify the actual nature of human *pistical* experiences. There has been an extensive debate during the last decades about the relation between the human **pistical** act of *proclaiming* and its concrete interpretation, and the **analytical** act of *interpreting* and its hermeneutic method. The distinction and relation between these two closely interrelated human activities is basic to hermeneutics.

For a bird's-eye view of the wide range of issues involved in any scriptural anthropology and faith hermeneutics, a brief list of basic differences between *reformational* and *scholastic* thinking will be helpful. It includes such central hermeneutic issues as the following: meaning and substratum, interpretation and fact, religious and empirical, metaphorical and literal, symbolic and factual, subjective and objective, belief and analysis, redemption (*Geschichte*) and secular history (*Historie*), power and text, kernel and shell, primary and secondary, essential and accidental, substance and form, central and peripheral, or message and myth.

---

39. The philosophical term for such structural features of faith life is "*retrocipatory* moments" (cf. chapters 9 and 10 above).

40. In their commitment to some *pseudo*-Ultimate, also non-Christians (cf. farmers, politicians, doctors, bankers, parents, etc.) remain fully human. Non-Christians do not cease to believe in something that is (for them) "ultimate."

Being engrafted, through the Spirit, into Christ[41] as joint-heirs, Christians live already now in God's presence. They sense the pulsebeat of God's revelation. This joy in God's covenant-love is the reason for their faith to blossom and bloom in the sunlight of God's grace. This is what breaks the proverbial vicious hermeneutic circle, because His life-given Word is heard again. It is interpreted, and proclaimed, in a way that enables them to respond in a life-saving way. Christ Jesus is the "key," and the Spirit the power, to turn humans back to God. This enables Christians to be rejuvenated and able to read God's "booked" revelation in an inspiring way. This covenant-centered, Spirit-directed, heart-gripped experience of God's *agape*-love enables humans to know something that surpasses all human understanding. Thus the familiarity and strangeness of God's incarnated Word (*Christos*) and His inscripturated revelation (*biblos*) will be heard and shared with humans in need of a peace that all "hermeneutics" must begin and end with.

Revelation, Experience, Norms

Revelation[42] refers to some kind of manifestation, authorization, communication or illumination. It points to something that comes to humans, something they experience in an overwhelming, transcendent, or ultimate way. It has a grounding, centering or (re)orienting effect on those who are its recipients.

Experience indicates a great diversity in ways humans respond to God's laws, or words, for creation, share with others in the way they shape life, set goals for themselves and fellow humans, and do things with them for the well-being of God's world. It is not limited to what is physical and sensory, but includes what is social, industrial, economic, aesthetic, juridical, ethical and pistical. All human experiences are *religiously* directed and *heart*-centered.[43]

Norms point to what is *structural*, to primary, or fundamental, laws of

---

41. For details, see Romans 5:12–21, 6 and 8.

42. Not in a Roman Catholic "natural-supernatural," or Protestant "general-special," sense of revelation, but in the holistic sense of three forms of one revelation: created (*Logos*), inscriptured (*Biblos*) and incarnated (*Christos*) revelation. The last form of revelation does not relativize, or replace, the first two forms of God's revelation, but is the secret, or "key," to embodied holy/human love.

43. This leaves no room for a dualistic anthropology in which the "body" is merely a natural/temporal means for a spiritual/eternal "soul."

God, according to which created reality is what it is. They indicate the ways, or parameters, for humans to respond to Him in all their responsibilities and tasks. To ignore, violate or disobey any of these laws disrupts life, fosters abnormal behavior and deepens human misery.

In Western culture, norms are generally understood in terms of the "positive laws" of humans, the dominant mores of a community and main customs of a tradition. Being time- and space-conditioned consequences of human *responses*, they must be distinguished from God's primary and unchanging laws. "Positive laws" are human-made, not God-given. They indicate what is unique about each community and tradition. Being cultural and historical, they are subject to change, a major source of conflicts, irreconcilable disagreements and fatal clashes.

The traditional study of theology, especially the sub-discipline of hermeneutics, will benefit from a clear(er) understanding about the terms "revelation," "experience" and "norms," and their various interrelationships. This presupposes a new, or *reformational*, view of created reality (ontology), being human (anthropology) and human knowledge (epistemology). It calls for a liberating way of thinking, not a traditional one grounded in a Greek thinking about, for example, reality, humanity, knowledge and truth.

A new hermeneutic of Scripture interpretation and gospel proclamation requires thinking about God's Word not just, or primarily, in terms of a "booked" revelation (*sola Scriptura*), but in terms of the Word through whom everything was created and who became incarnate in the Anointed Savior. About that powerful Word, Scripture is God's testimony that must be read, interpreted and shared with all humans. It guides Christians in their thinking about what is *normative* in their *experience* of God's threefold *revelation*.

To recognize this revelation presupposes faith as a "gift" of God's grace. Such faith provides humans with an awareness of something transcendent and, at the same time, revealed in the fullness of time (*kairos*). This awareness arises from an irrepressible human *religious* sense. Though it is not restricted to any specific or identifiable human *act* of faith, it is indicative of God's unavoidable and impinging presence. Humans have no option whether or not to respond to God's revelation. Being incurably *religious*, they cannot avoid God's presence in time and space.[44] Their response is appropriate only when, and to the extent, they acknowledge his *structural* laws for created reality, including humans, and his central, or *religious*, law of love for humans

44. See Psalms 14 and 139 about this human inability.

in whatever they do. Such positive responses must be the *religious* thrust, and aim, of all human life, and intentionally celebrated and enhanced in all specific human faith activities.

A *religiously* disobedient response to God's Word manifests itself in faith life in the form of idol worship. God's three-pronged revelation is what makes any all-pervasive human response possible. The relation between God's revelation and human *religion* is in that sense one of correlation: no revelation without *religion* and no *religion* without revelation.

"Spirituality" is not some added feature of being human, i.e., something gnostic or esoteric which humans can do without. On the contrary, it is essential in that it points to the central and all-encompassing *religious* nature of being human, the secret of one's daily life, the ultimate direction in which humans journey, the core of discipleship. It is not partial but total, not optional but essential. It is evident in all human personal experience and public behavior. It is misleading to equate *faith* life, as one kind of experience, with *religion* and, furthermore, to restrict the latter to any organized religion or faith community.

God's revelation calls for, and involves, human responses to it in an appropriate way. The relation between God's revelation and human *religious* experiences of it cannot be described in terms of any "objective-subjective" paradigm. To equate revelation with *Scripture* as something *objective*, i.e., true and reliable, and human *experiences* with something *subjective*, i.e., uncertain and unreliable, reflects the major impact of *scholastic* thinking about truth and certainty on both hermeneutics and theology.[45]

To ignore the importance of "revelation," "experience" and "norms," especially their intricate interrelationships, results in at least three questionable views of created reality. **First**, stressing *revelation* and *norms*, but downplaying the role of human *experience*, fosters a spiritualistic world-flight disposition. One talks quite readily and openly about the truths of God's revelation, but hesitantly, if at all, about the diverse responsibilities human have to respond to God's revelation. It tends to minimize the significance of human experience and the importance of living in a distinctly Christian way in everything one does.

A **second** distortion occurs when scriptural *revelation* is read, in a humanistic or "liberal" way, in terms of human *experiences* and ever-changing *norms* of shifting circumstances and customs. In this case, *revelation* depends

---

45. For details, see VanderStelt (1978): 271–335. In *Twilight of Western Thought*, 17–18, H. Dooyeweerd associates "objective truth" with the scholastic notion of "naive realism."

on human aspirations and projections. It does not allow God to reveal himself to them by urging them to respond to Him in loving obedience and genuine gratitude. Instead, humans create their own gods and worship them through their idolatrous concepts and imaginations that image them, rather than they image Him.

A **third** distortion involves focusing on *revelation* and *experience*, but minimizing the importance of *norms,* i.e., the "positive laws" of humans. This danger is typical of the tendency of *conservatism* to lean in the direction of legalism. When humans look to the past, i.e., turn their face (of faith) to what is behind them, they back themselves hesitantly and fearfully into the future. They fail to acknowledge the dynamic character of God's revelation, the importance of human history, the forward-look of God's people in their present comfort, the vision and witness reflected in the way they live. It tends to view God's revelation in terms of a strict set of (prescribed) doctrines to be believed, despite changed, and changing, personal, societal and cultural situations. The effect of such a mind-set is the threat of fossilizing one's faith life.[46]

These three distortions of God's *revelation*, human *experience* and creational *norms* have given rise to, respectively, relativism, dogmatism and some combination of these two wrong views.[47] Proper awareness of "revelation," "experience" and "norms" and their interrelations calls for a different ontology, anthropology, epistemology and study of faith life—one that is covenant-centered and focused on walking with God in an all-of-life-encompassing way. Acknowledging God's *creational, incarnational* and *scriptural* revelation deepens human awareness of God's awesome and wonderful presence. It urges humans to live *coram Deo*, experience His kingdom of love and press for covenant-oriented shalom.[48]

46. See the warnings from such Old Testament prophets as Jeremiah, Ezekiel and Amos, from New Testament experiences of John the Baptist, Jesus Christ, Stephen, Paul and John.

47. It is possible to *err* in the way one sequences **REN**, namely, revelation, experience and norms. For example: **ENR**: from "experience" to norms to revelation (evolutionism); **NER**: from "norms" to experience to revelation (humanism); **RNE**: from revelation to norms to experience (cf. intellect-centered scholasticism).

48. Covenant-centered hermeneutic is not (neo-)scholastic, liberal, or neo-orthodox, nor is it pietistic, fundamentalistic or individualistic. Its focus is on down-to-earth Christian discipleship in everything one does, also academically in philosophy and theology.

Selective Hearing

Humans cannot not respond to God's revelation. To respond is not an option, nor a projection. It is inherent, i.e., essential, to being human. The issue is not *whether* humans respond, but *how* they respond. For them to plug their ears, close their eyes, deny His three-pronged revelation is to violate God's loving sovereignty and sovereign love. It does not, and cannot, remove Him and His diverse ways of revelation.

That humans respond in different ways to God's revelation reflects their selective hearing. As responsible and accountable creatures with their inherent, though often suppressed, awareness of their Creator, humans hear something of God's sovereign voice in themselves and in the world around them in numerous overt and subtle ways.

The two most basic ways are, as indicated above, *directional* and *structural*. Although they are distinct, they are inseparable. The first way points to the difference in the *religious* or *spiritual* struggle in human behavior between loving obedience and loveless disobedience, and the difference between God's delight and his displeasure or anger. The second way is *structural*. It reflects the variety of cultural and historical settings in which humans shape, and express, their faith life in their personal, local, regional, cultural, economic, political and other circumstances.

For a *reformational* alternative to traditional theological (Western) hermeneutics centered on "method" and "message," and their interrelationships, and on the "concepts" or, for example, "revelation," "faith," "spiritual(ity)" and "interpretation," the approach suggested in chapters 8–12 above is important. At least seven features are central to hermeneutic issues in all faith life: (i) correlation between revelation-religion, (ii) three forms of God's Word, (iii) one *religious* law of love, (iv) diverse *structural* laws of human faith, (v) positive responses or laws of humans, (vi) heart-centered and -directed human behavior, and (vii) the distinction between *"religious"* and *"pistical."*

Hermeneutics in any discipline presupposes God's three-pronged revelation and is shaped by the distinct structural human response to it, also in the study of human faith *(pistic)* life. Crucial in such a study is the combination of "hearing" and "doing." What humans hear, i.e., are overcome by, in their *heart*, the core of their being, directs everything they do, not only their faith *(pistic)* life, but *religiously* in everything they do in their life. Proper *acts* of faith—e.g., praying, repenting, trusting, worshiping, pleading—indicate, express, make concrete the power of the amazing "gift" of God's grace that shapes the faith life of humans with respect to its "act," "content" and "aspect" and (re)formative witness on society, culture and history. Such *hearing* is not the product of any hermeneutic method, but the effect of a *religious* regeneration, a rebirth made possible by the "gift" of faith or response to God's redemptive revelation.[49] Such a *hearing* of God's voice, through his Word and Spirit, provides a witness for a deeply troubled world.

The structure of faith life is *pistic*. It reflects, and affects, directly or indirectly, the way humans behave in, for example, their social, sexual, agricultural, economic, political, educational, medical and recreational life. In their present fallen situation, humans are called to respond in a positive way to God's *mercy-filled* central love-command by walking personally and communally on the road of life, not death, joy, not grief, as children of the God of Mercy.

The distinction between Christians and non-Christians is that the *hearts* of the former center on God's faithfulness and covenant promises. When the *religious* direction of one's *pistic* life is renewed, faith life expresses an amazing depth, power and scope of God's grace-filled love. This is something non-Christians do not understand; they move in a *religious* direction in which they don't discern His voice or sense the depth of His full revelation, but they create for themselves, and somehow impose on others, an immense diversity of pseudo-gods. They create their own gods, develop their own rituals and paraphernalia that express and foster their faith. Since the Fall, humans have created an immense variety of pistic distortions in, for example, the idols of power, greed, fame, egoism, vanity, perversion, cruelty, even death.

The central "methods" developed , and often (mis)used, to "interpret" God's revelation are often related to the structure of faith life with respect to its "activities," "contents" and "aspects." Secondary, or subsidiary, issues tend to be determined by one's personal and/or institutional faith life, and by such features as local customs, socio-economic conditions, political ideologies, philosophical differences, aesthetic sensitivities, educational customs, natural disasters, personal conflicts and human tragedies. Some, or all, of these influence humans in the way they *hear* and *read* God's written revelation in different faith traditions throughout history.

Given the nature of created reality, the structure of faith life does not change. As it did in the past, so it does now, and will do so in the future—

---

49. *Heart*-centered *hearing* is not *theory*-dependent. For details about genuine *hearing* in one's daily life with respect to the meaning of such terms as "heart-centered," "religious" and "religions," see chapter 20 below.

always, of course, in terms of the customs and needs of society and culture at the time. Whereas the faith responses of Christians to God's revelation remain *religiously* unchanged, the forms of their *structure* do change, culturally and historically, in both positive and negative ways.[50]

Not to distinguish between *religious* and *structural* has resulted in much confusion, wasting of energy and time, even crippling conflicts and tragic deaths, in both Christian and non-Christian faith traditions.[51] What has complicated matters in faith life is that all sorts of changes in personal, socio-economic, political and cultural circumstances have influenced, negatively or positively, the power and vitality of all human faith communities and traditions.

Summary

A proper pistic hermeneutic is not interested in developing a definitive exegetical method and homiletical skill. Its focus is on something *religiously* deeper and empirically simpler, something traditionally ignored as not being theological, philosophical or biblical. Scripture reading aimed at truly "hearing" God's warning love, and loving warning, implies a hermeneutic that addresses minimally three interrelated challenges in especially Western theology: selective hearing and reading of Scripture, church and kingdom, and scholasticism.

First, selective hearing and reading is a major problem. All readers of Scripture read it with their own eyes, hear God's voice with their own ears, walk in the Lord's way with their own feet, experience His presence with their own sensitivities, and reach for God's hand with their own hands. When they do this in a dependent, childlike and heart-centered way, with everything they are and need, their hearing is authentic and will, through the Spirit, (re)direct their faith life and deepen their understanding of the power and comfort of God's written Word.

---

50. The difference between "unchanging and changing" reflects a distinction, not division, separation or "two-realm" theory, between "*religious* and organized faith," or "heart-direction and faith as function," evident also in Jewish synagogues, Christian churches, Islamic mosques, Buddhist temples, Mormon stake-houses, Jehovah's Witness kingdom halls and Baptist assemblies.

51. The *religious* conflict *between* Christian and non-Christian responses to God's (three-pronged) revelation is "anti-thetical," while conflicts *within* any "organized religion" occur in both faith traditions, often for comparable societal and historical reasons.

Second, the life-encompassing, Spirit-guided and history-directing *kingdom of God* compels disciples of the Lord Christ Jesus to behave confidently, in fear and trembling, in His presence in their reading and hearing of His written Word. Interpreting and acknowledging His "inscripturated" revelation is not the privilege of any established church, or *organized* religion, with its distinct rituals, detailed creeds, impressive programs, hierarchic clergy, imposing buildings and large budgets. God's people, or the body of Christ, is not limited to any congregation, denomination, organized faith or *institutionalized* religion. No single Spirit-filled and -directed faith community exhausts the scope and power of God's kingdom. A dynamic, i.e., stirred and stirring, Spirit-prompted Christian faith commitment functions as a diving board for those who mount it to stretch their arms to jump up and forward and dive into the pool of God's love and swim in the pool of His kingdom.[52]

Third, to replace "theology" with "pisteology" is impossible without rejecting the classic "two-realm" dualism inherent in scholastic thinking, mind-set, paradigm or way of living. In principle and practice, scholasticism cannot do justice to minimally three things: God's three-pronged revelation, integral human covenant-living, and acknowledging that faith life is—like any other expression of human life—basically *religious*, not *intellectual*.

In summary, Christian living does not restrict *religion* to a part of human life with respect to, for example, time, place, career, priority or importance. Responding to God's love is radical and total. What is *structurally* not "pistical" in nature is not some "lower," "temporary," "natural," or "rational" neo-Platonic means for some higher and eternal purpose. A *reformational* view of created reality rejects the classic idea that "theological" hermeneutics is essential to faith, the nature of which is truly spiritual. Without pandering to modern and postmodern *religious* relativism, a reformational view does not want to perpetuate *scholastic* thinking and living.[53]

Major implications of questionable thought-patterns in traditional Christian higher education will be highlighted in the next five chapters. The official stance of the Roman Catholic Church about "faith and reason"— based on the medieval philosopher and theologian Thomas Aquinas"—will be highlighted below in terms of three papal encyclicals issued in these

---

52. Matthew 28:20: "and teaching them to obey everything I have commanded you. And surely I will be with you always, to the very end of the age." For details, see H. Ridderbos: *The Coming of the Kingdom* (1962).

53. Traditional theology has problems with the distinction between primary and secondary issues, the nature of religion, the meaning of human, the structure of faith life, the essence of philosophy and theology, and the contours of a Christian mind.

years: 1879, 1950 and 1998. In the following four chapters (15–18), the influence of Roman Catholic *scholastic* thought-patterns on "philosophy" and "theology" in Christian Reformed higher education at, for example, Calvin Theological Seminary and Calvin College, in especially the nineteenth century, will be indicated with respect to the meaning of especially such pivotal terms as "reality," "human," "truth," "revelation," "religion," "theology," "Word of God," "faith and reason" and "liberal arts."

PART III

ACCOMMODATION

CHAPTER FOURTEEN

Three Encyclicals: 1879, 1950, 1998

While the Protestant Reformation rejected many questionable beliefs and practices in the faith life of the Roman Catholic Church (here-after RCC), it generally continued to think about the essence of "reality" in terms of what is "true, good and beautiful," i.e., classical "liberal arts," also with respect to the nature and role of "theology."

Western "faith life" and "theology" were greatly influenced by the thought-pattern of Thomas Aquinas (1225–1274), the renowned medieval philosopher and theologian. *Negatively*, though indirectly,[1] it contributed to Martin Luther's break with the faith life of the RCC, when he, in 1520, surrounded by students who sang "Te Deum Laudamus," publicly threw the Papal Bull of Excommunication in a university bonfire. *Positively*, and directly, however, the Roman Catholic Counter Reformation perpetuated a form of scholastic thinking. Since then, via the backdoor of higher edu-cation, that view of theology impacted most Protestant higher education, including that in Calvinist traditions.

Nearly five centuries after the Protestant Reformation, it is imperative to understand the nature, scope and implications of T. Aquinas about "faith," "reason" and their interrelationships in the RCC. There is no better way to do this than to have a close look at the only three "encyclicals"[2] centered on "faith" and "reason," i.e., *Aeterni Patris* (1879), *Humani Generis* (1950) and *Fides et*

---

1. Nominalism's opposition to scholastic thinking influenced Luther as student, professor of philosophy, and reformer.

2. Combination of the Greek words *en* (in) and *kyklos* (circle). An "encyclical is a letter of

Ratio (1998). After indicating the reasons for, and central thrust of these three encyclicals, they will be briefly evaluated in terms of their role in all Roman Catholic educators and scholars, especially philosophers and theologians.

Background and Context

The Protestant Reformation occurred in critical reaction to the Roman Catholic faith tradition which had developed over more than a thousand years. Inwardly and outwardly, it broke apart Constantinople- and Rome-centered Christianity and gave rise to Lutheran, Calvinist, Anabaptist and Anglican faith traditions. To curb this major disintegration and regain its earlier prominence, the Roman Catholic Church undertook a major Counter Reformation. Central in this seventeen-year-long counter-offensive were the meetings of the Council of Trent (1545–1563).[3]

This extended Council reformulated basic Roman Catholic teachings and introduced many ecclesiastical reforms so comprehensive in their scope that the Roman Catholic Church (RCC) did not officially meet again until three centuries later[4] in Vatican I (1869–1870).

The intent and scope of the Council of Trent was mainly ecclesiastical. It did not address the Church's view of educational matters related to, for example, philosophical and anthropological issues. The views T. Aquinas developed, two centuries earlier, did not really enable the RCC leaders to address what triggered the Protestant Reformation. In fact, they encouraged appreciation for the Classical Humanism of L. Valla (1407–1475), welcomed Renaissance thinking in D. Erasmus (1469–1536), and tolerated the Rationalism in R. Descartes (1596–1650).

Not until three centuries later—when Pope Leo XIII stated in 1879 that in philosophy and theology T. Aquinas is "the angelic doctor in the Church"— did the RCC address the need for and the contours of "Christian philosophy."[5]

---

the bishop of Rome and successor of St. Peter, to . . . all the Christians all over the world." Cf. Anne Freemantle, ed., *The Papal Encyclicals in their Historical Context* (1956): 21.

3. Dates of the sessions: Dec. 13, 1545, to Sept. 17, 1549; May 1, 1551, to April 28, 1552; Jan. 18, 1562, to Dec. 4, 1563.

4. From the time of Calvin's death in Switzerland (1564) to Kuyper's conversion, as pastor, in the Netherlands (1864).

5. From the sixteenth to the nineteenth century, Lutherans, Calvinists and Anglicans were influenced by the views of, respectively, P. Melanchthon, T. Beza and R. Hooker about basic philosophical and anthropological issues. Cf. chap. 3 above.

As in Protestant traditions,[6] Roman Catholic faith focused mostly on what is personal, ecclesiastical and theological. In thinking, general education, scholarship and philosophy, the focus shifted increasingly towards anthropology (not theology), especially with respect to human senses and reason, i.e., epistemology and philosophy.

From the sixteenth to the nineteenth century, Europe experienced philosophically[7] a growing focus on an inflated view of *reason*. In Roman Catholic and Protestant academic circles *reason* and *faith* were thought to be compatible. This compatibility began to be questioned during the seventeenth century and challenged in especially in the eighteenth century in the curricula of state universities and, sometimes, even theology departments. This secularization affected not only theologians but also pastors and educators in their view of faith life and theology in both Roman Catholic and Protestant educational traditions.

During the nineteenth century, major intellectual and cultural revolutions jolted Western society and even the world.[8] For example, Benthamist utilitarianism in England, Comtean positivism in sociology and technology in France, and romantic philosophy and art in Germany undermined traditional Roman Catholic and Protestant ideas about truth, society and culture. The role of *faith* and *reason* changed after the nineteenth-century Industrial Revolution, Marx's *Communist Manifesto* (1848), Darwin's *Origin of Species* (1859), the rise of historicism and higher criticism in Germany, Nietzschean and Kierkegaardian irrationalism,[9] and twentieth-century existentialism.

In reaction to spreading irrationalism and relativism, philosophers stressed the enlightenment tenets of an inherent goodness and unlimited

6. Except Anabaptists who, because of their *gnostic* worldview, showed no, or very little, interest in philosophy.

7. For an analysis of different philosophical systems, see Vollenhoven (1892–1977) as an expert historian of philosophy. Unlike Dooyeweerd, he did *not* describe Western philosophy in terms of four "religious ground-motives," but in terms of specific "philosophical currents and conceptions." For details, see various major books published by Bril, Tol and Kok between 2004 and 2010 by Dordt College Press.

8. The French Revolution shocked Europe and, after Napoleon's campaign in 1812, also Russia. At the Vienna Congress (1815), conservatives revolted against liberals. Belgium gained independence from the Netherlands in 1830. For twenty years, revolutions rocked Greece, Poland, Austria, Hungary and Germany. The Crimean War started in 1854, and in 1870 France and Prussia fought each other. The USA fought against England in 1812, initiated its Monroe doctrine in 1823, and experienced a Civil War in the 1860s.

9. Irrationalism is a focus on something other than reason (e.g. experience, feelings, will) in philosophy. It does not mean that the thinking is rationally incoherent.

progress. Rational education, fused with technical skills, helps humans to control personal and societal evil. Enlightened scholars, teachers and scientists are the high priests of a new culture. The epitome of humanism was eminently expressed in the slogan "no God, no Master" (ni Dieu, ni Maître). Humans can tear down jails through *public* education and *state* universities filled with enlightened citizens.

It is at this critical juncture in Western culture and history that the RCC met at Vatican I (1869–1870),[10] chiefly to address not creedal and ecclesiastical issues, as it did at the Council of Trent (1545–1563),[11] but a rising tide of cultural and societal problems and crises. In this critical context, the RCC declared, for the *first* time, the notion of Papal "infallibility," when the Pope speaks *ex cathedra*, i.e., officially, as Christ's vicar.[12] Only two years later, Cardinal Giuseppe Pecci founded St. Thomas Aquinas Academy in Rome, in order to encourage all Roman Catholic educators, notably philosophers and theologians, in the world to think, and teach, in terms of the philosophy and method of Thomas Aquinas.

Aeterni Patris (1879)

One year after Vincenzo Pecci became Pope Leo XIII (1878), he published on August 4, 1879, *Aeterni Patris* (hereafter *AP*).[13] In it, he told all Roman Catholic thinkers and educators throughout the world to view Thomas Aquinas as their "angelic teacher" and use his "philosophy" and "method" in their response to the modern challenges. Forty-three years later (1922), Pope Pius XI (1922–1939) said that *AP* "so far surpasses all other deeds that, if he had

---

10. During this difficult period, the Dutch Reformed Church experienced the *Reveille* of 1834 and *Doleantie* of 1886. These two renewal movements affected Dutch culture and society in three ways: (i) the writings, and leadership, of Guilluame Groen van Prinsterer (1801–1876), a historian and statesman; (ii) H. Bavinck (1854–1921), a professor in theology at a seminary and the Free University and a senator in the government: and (iii) A. Kuyper (1837–1920), a prolific author and major reformer in higher education, church life, national politics, labor and journalism.

11. A comparable focus was evident in the (continental and international) Reformed traditions at the Synod of Dort (1618/19) in the Netherlands, and in the Presbyterian tradition at Westminster Assembly (1643) in England.

12. In reaction to a spreading uncertainty in Western culture, the RCC promulgated the doctrine of *Papal* infallibility, Protestants stressed *Scripture's* infallibility, and humanist reformers, educators and scientists emphasized *rational* and *scientific* infallibility.

13. One year later, A. Kuyper opened the Free University in Amsterdam.

done nothing else, it alone would have been sufficient to make his name as a major pope immortal."[14]

Throughout his long pontificate (1878–1903), Leo XIII prompted Roman Catholics to develop a distinct culture of thinking and behaving for the benefit of humanity. In his passion to shape a new intellectual elite, he rejected the notion that modern science and traditional (scholastic) thought are incompatible. The philosophy and theology of Thomas Aquinas are normative for all Roman Catholic thinkers and educators. Opposition to his encyclical deepened his resolve to revive Aquinian thought- and act-patterns in Roman Catholic academic and teaching enterprises[15] in Italy, France, Spain, Latin America and elsewhere in the world. In 1889, he rejoiced in the founding of Roman Catholic universities in Washington, *USA*, Ottawa, *Canada*, and Freiburg, *Switzerland*, the Advanced Institute for Thomist Philosophy, and the Leo XIII Seminary at the University of Louvain in *Belgium*.

His successor, Pius XI (1922–1939) endorsed *AP*, and **Pius XII** (1939–1958) talked about *AP* in his lecture to Jesuits and Dominicans in 1946 and

14. H. Bailors, 'Voorwoord' to *"Aeterni Patris,"* published in Series *Ecclesia Docens: Pauselijke documenten voor onze tijd*, Hilversum(1948), 5. This encyclical is, in his opinion, "a historical event of the first order." On pages 7–10, Bailors indicates that V. **Buzzetti** (1777–1824), in the small town of Piacenza in Italy, had *opposed* any attempt to harmonize Cartesian rationalism, Augustinian platonism and Lockean empiricism with Roman Catholic traditionalism, ontologism and with semi-Hegelianism, and *proposed* to return to the views of T. Aquinas. Three of his students were sons of a Sordi: Giuseppe, Serafino and Dominico. **Serafino** influenced P. Luigi Taparelli d'Agzeglio (1793–1862), rector of the Thomistic Collegium Romanum (1824–1829), who encouraged Joachim Pecci (later, Pope Leo XIII) to make a thorough study of the views of Thomas Aquinas. **Dominico** encouraged P. Matteo Liberatore, member of the Dominican *Societas Jesu* and author of *Institutiones Philosophicae* (1840) (eleven editions within few years), with its strong emphasis on Aquinas. Many ethical and juridical issues were published in the Thomistic journal *La Civilta Catolica* in 1850. Between 1852 and 1872, twenty-five Dominicans published twenty-five folio-size volumes on the philosophy of T. Aquinas. As a result, interest in the philosophy of Thomas Aquinas was on the rise also in Spain, France and Germany. For details, see Bailors, 7–10.

15. He encouraged bishops in Spain, Mexico, Brazil and Peru to advance Aquinian scholasticism, and insisted on establishing new bishoprics, in which Thomism would be taught in all new theological seminaries. In a decree on August 4, 1880, exactly one year after his encyclical *Aeterni Patris*, he declared Saint Thomas to be the patron of all forms of Christian higher education. He encouraged gifted Thomist scholars throughout Italy to become professors in Rome and direct various study institutes. His brother, Cardinal Joseph Pecci, established, and directed, an Academy for Aquinas Studies in Rome. The Dominicans published a new edition (*editio leonina*) of all the works of T. Aquinas. He recommended that various journals address general cultural problems in terms of specific Aquinian ideas and methods in philosophy and theology.

summarized it in 1950 in his *Humani Generis*. Forty-eight years later, **John Paul II** (1920–2005) described, in some detail, the views of Aquinas in *Fides et Ratio*. In short, *Aeterni Patris* is basic to *Humani Generis*, and both of them to *Fides et Ratio*.

The primary purpose of this chapter (the longest in this study) is not to debate but to call attention to the nature of (i) the "faith and reason" problem, (ii) indicate the RCC view of reality, religion, revelation, philosophy, theology, scholarship and education, (iii) highlight a mind-set that constricts Christian discipleship, and (iv) may be helpful to sense certain semi-scholastic features in Reformed thinking, scholarship and teaching at, for example, Calvin Theological Seminary and Calvin College in Grand Rapids, Michigan.

Introduction

As the "common and supreme teacher of the peoples," the Church has the "authority to train the minds to faith . . . contend forever against errors" and safeguard "the integrity of the faith." All studies, notably philosophy, must due to "the gravity of the subject and the condition of the time . . . respond most fitly to the excellence of faith, and at the same time be consonant with the dignity of human science."(1)[16]

I: Practicing True Philosophy (2–9)

The "strifes" and "troubles" that threaten the RCC arise from "false conclusions" about "divine and human things" in schools of philosophy. It is in the "nature of man to follow the guide of reason in his actions, if his intellect sins at all his will soon follows . . ." Though a "sound mind" takes a "stand on true and solid principles," philosophy cannot combat and root out "all errors." For this, the "light of faith" is necessary, the "powerful help of Almighty God" to dispel "error."

> But the *natural* helps with which the grace of divine wisdom. . . has supplied the human race are neither to be despised nor neglected, chief among which is evidently the *right use of philosophy*. For not in vain did God set the *light*

16. Parenthetical numbers indicate paragraphs.

of reason in the human mind; and so far is *the super-added light of faith* from extinguishing or lessening the *power of intelligence* that it *completes* it rather, and by *adding* to its strength renders it capable of *greater* things (emphasis added).(2)

True philosophy defends "revealed doctrines." To call people back to "the paths of faith and salvation" implies taking advantage of "human science," reason may not be "belittled, nor undervalued."(3) True philosophy "tends to smooth and fortify the road to true faith," to "prepare the souls . . . for the fit reception of revelation."(4) About "divine things," God manifested truths that "human intelligence could not attain by itself." With "the help of divine authority they may be made known to all" without "any admixture of error."

> Hence it is that certain truths . . . bound by the closest chains to the doctrine of faith, were *discovered by pagan sages with nothing but their natural reason to guide them, were demonstrated and proved by becoming arguments. . . .*[17] [H]uman wisdom and the testimony of our adversaries serve to support the Christian faith—a method . . . adopted by the holy Fathers of the Church. . . . [about] the Hebrews, who, when about to depart from Egypt, were commanded to take with them the gold and silver vessels and precious robes of the Egyptians, that by a change of use the things might be dedicated to the service of God which had formerly been the instruments of ignoble and superstitious use. . . .[18] But if natural reason first sowed this rich field of doctrine before it was rendered fruitful by the power of Christ, it must assuredly become more prolific after the grace of the Savior has renewed and added to the *native faculties of the human mind.* And who does not see that a plain and easy road is opened up by such a *method of philosophic study?* (emphasis added).(4)

This philosophy is important for faith in general and for Christian faith. Reason *demonstrates* that God exists, knows all things, is "truth itself" that neither deceives nor is deceived. By "reasonable consent" those who believe the gospel "subject their intelligence and judgment to divine authority."(5) Reason affirms the credibility of both the Gospel and the Church.

---

17. Cf. Romans 1:20 and 2:14–15.

18. More than a dozen church fathers are mentioned, including Origen, Gregory of Nyssa, Basil the Great, Jerome, Justin, Irenaeus, Cyprian, Lactantius and Augustine.

Philosophy provides "solid foundations" for faith, and does this as "a perpetual and varied service" through "sacred theology," a "most noble of studies," which helps humans to know revealed doctrines and gain precise insight. The "integrity of life and love of faith" needs "a mind rounded and finished by philosophic studies." Knowledge of sacred dogmas must be sought by means of an analogy of the things known from the connection of "mysteries one with another and with the final end of man."(6)

The "glory of philosophy" is that it is "the bulwark of faith and the strong defense of religion." (7) In defending faith against attacks on the truth, Greek philosophy is "the hedge and fence of the vine." Christian faith used "human reason to repel . . . the attacks of adversaries by the hostile arms which human reason itself supplied."[19] Christian teachers need "philosophy" to resist assertions contrary to revealed truth.[20]

This path of "venerable antiquity" must be continued. Supernatural truths "far beyond the reach of the keenest intellect," may not be denied, measured by one's own standard, or interpreted at will, but must be accepted "with a humble and full faith."(8) In the case of doctrines, however, which "human intelligence may perceive . . . philosophy must make use of its own method, principles and arguments"—on the condition that this intelligence does not "withdraw from divine authority." What is against "faith," wars against right "reason." A philosopher knows he violates "faith and laws of reason" when he accepts conclusions opposed to revealed doctrine.(8)

Foolish people "repudiate the most sublime truths, and reject the divine gift of faith, from which the fountains of all good things flow out upon civil society."(9) As "mistress of truth," faith is not enmeshed "in the snares of error," nor tossed back and forth "on the waves of fluctuating opinion." Combining "obedience to the Christian faith" with philosophy the latter can be done "in the best possible way."

> . . . the splendor of the divine truths, received into the mind, helps the understanding, and . . . adds greatly to its nobility, keenness, and stability. For surely that is a worthy and most useful exercise of reason when men give their minds to disproving things which are repugnant to faith and proving the things which conform to faith.(9)

19. For example, Paul, who had learned from "the true David to wrest the sword from the hands of the enemy and to cut off the head of the boastful Goliath with his own weapon." (7)

20. As Augustine testifies, "if reason is turned against the authority of sacred Scripture, no matter how specious it may seem, it errs in the likeness of truth; for true it cannot be." (7)

The "holy" faith confers "great benefits" on reason: "like a friendly star, [it] shines down upon his path and points out to him the gate of truth beyond all danger of wandering."

II: *True Philosophy Serves Revealed Truths* (10–16)

Against espousers of "false and incongruous things" and of "vague and doubtful opinions" about Divinity, the origin of things, the government of the world, knowledge of the future, evil, virtue and vice, and eternal beatitude, Greek and Latin apologists compared and sifted ideas in terms of Christ, as the "restorer of human science . . . in whom are hid all the treasures of wisdom and knowledge." (10) In addition to Justin Martyr, Boethius and Anselm, Leo XIII refers to twenty Western and Eastern Christian apologists, the greatest of them being Augustine. About him, he writes this:

> Of a most powerful genius and thoroughly saturated with sacred and profane learning, with the loftiest faith and with equal knowledge, he combated most vigorously all the errors of his age . . . subtly he reasoned on the angels, the soul, the human mind, the will and free choice, and religion and the life of the blessed, on time and eternity, and even on the very nature of changeable bodies.(13)

Leo XIII comments on the "doctors," or "scholastics," of the Middle Ages, who collected, sifted and stored up "in one place, for the use and convenience of posterity, the rich and fertile harvests of Christian learning scattered abroad in the voluminous works of the holy Fathers." About Pope Sixtus V (1585–1590), he comments,

> There was founded . . . the *scholastic theology*, which two glorious doctors in particular, the angelic St. Thomas and the seraphic St. Bonaventure . . . set in order and beautified, and skillfully arranged and clearly explained in a variety of ways, handed down to posterity. (14)
> . . . the knowledge and use of so salutary a science . . . must always be of greatest assistance to the Church, whether with the view of really and soundly understanding and interpreting the Scriptures, or more safely and to better purpose reading and explaining the Fathers, or for exposing and

refuting the various errors and heresies; and . . . need of confirming the dogmas of the Catholic faith and confuting heresies.[21](15)

While Sixtus V focused mainly on scholastic *theology*, Leo XIII, three centuries later, talked also about scholastic *philosophy*,

Although these words [of Sixtus V] seem to bear reference solely to Scholastic *theology*, nevertheless they may plainly be accepted as *equally true of philosophy* and its praises. For the noble endowments which make the Scholastic theology so formidable to the enemies of truth[22]. . . . are only to be found in a right use of that philosophy which the Scholastic teachers have been accustomed carefully and prudently to make use of even in theological disputations. Moreover, since it is the proper and special office of the Scholastic theologians to bind together by the fastest chain human and divine science, surely the theology in which they excelled would not have gained such honor and commendations among men if they had made use of a lame and imperfect or vain philosophy. (16)

III: Aquinas, Master in Connecting Revealed Truths and Philosophy (17–23)

Of all the Scholastic Doctors, Thomas is the "chief and master of all." He was a "lover of truth for its own sake" and was "richly endowed with human and divine science." He touched on "the laws of reasoning, on God and incorporeal substances, and man and other sensible things, on human actions and their principles."(17) He pressed his "philosophical inquiry into the reasons and principles of things" in a "most comprehensive" way that for posterity contained "the seeds of almost infinite truths." He used "philosophical method" to refute errors in former times and put to rout errors that "might in after-times spring up."

21. The context of the comments of Sixtus V is the Protestant Reformation and the rise of Rationalism.

22. As Sixtus V said, "that ready and close coherence of cause and effect, that order and array as of a disciplined army in battle, those clear definitions and distinctions, that strength of argument, and those keen discussions, by which light is distinguished from darkness, the true from the false, exposed and stripped naked, as it were, the falsehood of heretics wrapped around by a cloud of subterfuges and fallacies." (16)

Again, clearly distinguishing, as is fitting, reason from faith, while happily associating the one with the other, he both preserved the rights and had regards for the dignity of each; so much so, indeed, that reason, borne on the wings[23] of Thomas to its human height, can scarcely rise higher, while faith could scarcely expect more or stronger aids from reason than those which she has already obtained through Thomas.(18)

Most men of the "highest repute in theology and philosophy" mastered "with infinite pains the immortal works of Thomas." Almost all founders and lawgivers of religious orders[24] required their members to study and adhere to the views of Thomas.(19) He "reigned supreme" in ten "celebrated schools and universities" in Italy, France and Belgium. (20) Nine pontificates since the fifteenth century praised his "wisdom." (21) The four Councils of Lyons, Vienna, Florence and Vatican I used his ideas to oppose errors of Greeks, heretics and rationalists.

At the Council of Trent (1545–1563), the Church Fathers made Aquinas "part of the order on conclave"[25] through placing on the altar, along with Scripture and the decrees of the Pontiffs, the classic "Summa" of Aquinas, in order to "seek counsel, reason, and inspiration" from it.(22) A "last triumph" of this "incomparable man" is the "homage, praise, and admiration" he received even from "the very enemies of the Catholic name." Some heretics openly "declared that, if the teaching of Thomas Aquinas were only taken away, they could easily battle with all Catholic teachers, gain the victory, and abolish the Church."(23)

IV: *Restoring the Philosophy of Thomas Aquinas (24–31)*

Only the views of Aquinas can counteract the decay in both philosophy and theology. Sixteenth-century "innovators" philosophized "without respect for faith" and developed often clashing ideas about knowledge and moved "from doubt to error." New philosophies and theologies lacked a "firm and stable" foundation. They must be approached in the way of the "Scholastics," so that "revelation and reason" united in it, may continue be the "invincible bulwark of the faith."(24)

---

23. The metaphor of "wings" is prominent in John Paul II's encyclical *Fides et Ratio* of 1998.
24. E.g., Dominicans, Benedictines, Carmelites, Augustinians and the Jesuit Society.
25. A "conclave" is a private meeting of cardinals, chiefly to elect a new pope.

With his eye on the future as a philosophical and theological thinker, Leo XIII challenges all Roman Catholic scholars and teachers to provide the next generation with "the purest streams of wisdom flowing" from the Angelic Doctor. (26) To counteract the "machinations and craft of a certain false wisdom," educators must stress "sound doctrine," "convince the gain-sayers," and "guard against all who are alienated from the faith, hate Roman Catholic institutions, and claim reason as their only "mistress and guide."(27)

> . . . we think that, apart from the supernatural help of God, nothing is better calculated to heal those minds and to bring them into favor with the Catholic faith than the solid doctrine of the Fathers and the Scholastics, who so clearly and forcibly demonstrate the firm foundations of the faith, its divine origin, its certain truth, the arguments that sustain it, the benefits it has conferred on the human race, and its perfect accord with reason, in a manner to satisfy completely minds open to persuasion, however unwilling and repugnant. (27)

Reviving Thomism is necessary not just for church and society, but also for the "liberal arts" and the "physical sciences." Without Aquinian thinking, philosophy leans to "error" and joins "folly."(29) Both "liberal arts" and "physical science" benefit from the "force and light and aid" of "judiciously taught" philosophy.[26] To defend the Catholic faith, advance the "good of society" and benefit "all the sciences," Leo XIII emphasized the "wisdom of St. Thomas" and cautioned against misleading young minds through "subtle" and "careless" ideas of thinkers who deviate from the views of St. Thomas.(31)

Conclusion (32–34)

AP ends with (i) an appeal to the God of all knowledge and understanding (32), (ii) a statement about Aquinas "that whatever he knew he had acquired not so much by his own study and labor as by the divine gift" (33), (iii) a prayer that the RCC open its "senses for the understanding of wisdom," (iv) an appeal to the "efficacious patronage" of the Virgin Mary, "the seat

---

26. With its (Aristotelian) ideas about facts, corporeal things, laws of nature, role of "natural" law or order in society, principles of unity and mutual attraction amidst diversity, and about the role of human intelligence in moving philosophically from "sensible things" to "searching into the mysteries of nature."(29)

of wisdom," and her advocates, Joseph, Peter and Paul (33), and (v) a papal blessing.(34)

Preliminary questions

My initial response to *AP* about "faith" and "reason" in Western culture is two-fold: an admiration for its intent and clarity, and an uneasiness about its *religious*[27] thrust. Without going into details at this time, various probing questions arise about issues related to "faith and reason" and "theology and philosophy" in the Roman Catholic tradition of classic *scholastic* thinking:

1. Does *AP* assume the validity of Greek "faculty psychology" in its anthropology that focuses on *reason*, which guides the human *will*, and it, in turn, directs human *affections*?
2. Is the truth of "faith" similar to the truth of "theology," i.e., are both essentially "intellectual"?
3. Is *error* associated with intellect and philosophy, *sin* with human will and ethics, and *religion* with passion and experience?
4. Can philosophy, without faith's assistance, "combat and root out all errors," or is it fulfilled by the light that faith provides?
5. Is "faith" associated with what is supernatural, the content, or doctrines, of the RCC, or primarily with God's "gift" of grace in the radical conversion of humans?
6. Does a "nature-grace" synthesis, or mind-set, enable the RCC to incorporate elemental pagan and modern "secular" ideas in its view of God, humans and the world?
7. Is the difference between "theology" and "philosophy" comparable to that between "faith" and "reason"?
8. If the goal of philosophy is to contemplate God, does that imply that theology is the goal, or epitome, of philosophy?
9. Does a Pope's response to dangerous trends in Western (and global) thinking and his emphasis on the human need for God's supernatural revelation not deepen the difficulty when he returns to T. Aquinas, the "Angelic Doctor," and underestimates the human plight?
10. How has *AP*'s view of "mind," "faith" and "truth" impacted the nature

27. As used in the *reformational* sense throughout this entire book.

of apologetics and the possibility of non-Christians to become Roman Catholic in the way they think and live?

11. How has *AP* influenced the relation between faith and theology, truth and philosophy, the nature of the "liberal arts," and the structure of society, notably the state?

Humani Generis (1950)

In *Summa Pontificates* (1939), Pius XII (1939–1958) affirmed the law of solidarity and love and rejected any state absolutism; in *Mystici Corporis* (1943), he opposed rationalism, materialism and mysticism for denying the Creator-creature distinction; in *Mediator Dei* (1947), he warned against mysticism, quietism and humanism. He stressed in many of his speeches the importance of the "angelic St. Thomas" and the threat of philosophical relativism, determinism and existentialism.

In *Humani Generis* (1950)—hereafter *HG*—focused on "Some False Opinions Which Threaten to Undermine the Foundations of Catholic Doctrine," Pius XII dealt with issues in "theology," "philosophy" and "exegesis."[28] He rejected any philosophy that denied unchanging truth, did not like scholasticism, denigrated ecclesiastical authority, belittled natural knowledge about God, and questioned the credibility of external revelation.[29]

He warned against moral agnosticism, war atrocities, pantheism, evolutionism, dialectical materialism, existentialism, historicism, belittling human reason and ignoring the teachings of the RCC.[30] *HG* focused on the future, not the past, on being irenic to those who tone down their ecclesiastical stance. Scholars and educators must look for kernels of truth in all positions and propositions, focus on issues of faith and morality, bring clarity in "theology," "philosophy" and "exegesis" and in "scientific studies" when Roman Catholic thinking is antiquated.

28. In dealing with philosophical errors affecting Christian faith life, this encyclical resembles the encyclicals *Quanta Cura* (1864) of Pius IX (1846–1878) and *Pascendi Dominici* (1907) of Pius X (1903–1914).

29. Mulders, *HG*, 7. Mulders believes that an improper balance between wise conservatism and careful progressivism is traceable to wrong philosophy.

30. According to Cardinal Ratzinger, pope from 2005–2013, as indicated by G. C. Berkouwer (1964) 55.

Introduction (1–13) and Part I (14–28)[31]

Central to three main modern errors in *theology* are skepticism, dogmatic relativism and ignoring the authority of the Church in biblical exegesis. The **first** theological error is to free Roman Catholic dogmas from past formulations. To reformulate expressions used in Scripture and by the Church Fathers is permitted only to renew theology, not to denigrate *speculative* theology and ignore traditional terms and scholastic thinking.[32]

Terms to be avoided are "immanentism or idealism or existentialism, or any other system," if the intent is to indicate that "the mysteries of faith are never expressed by truly adequate concepts, but only by approximate and ever changeable notions."[33] The history of dogmas is not just "a reporting of the various forms in which revealed truth has been clothed."(15) Perfecting and enriching theological terms is permitted, but not a *total* reformation of theology. The Church is not bound to any "system of philosophy." Roman Catholic teachers base their dogmas on "principles and notions deduced from a true knowledge of created things." Such knowledge enlightened the "human mind through the Church."(16) Terms and notions "habitually used by scholastic theologians" cannot be replaced with "conjectural ones," or "unstable tenets of a new philosophy." *Speculative* theology is based on proper "theological reasoning."(17)

The **second** theological error is to ignore the teaching authority of the Church. Scholastic theology does not prevent development, nor does it obstruct science. (18) In light of the Roman Catholic distinction between

31. As in the case of *Aeterni Patris*, these headings are not taken from the encyclical, but are mine.

32. See in this connection the modernist views of Garrison-Lagrange at the beginning of the twentieth century; the excommunication of Alfred Loisy and George Tyrell in 1908; the anti-modernist oath in 1910; H. Bouillard's views in 1941 regarding Aristotelian, Hegelian, and Heideggerian thought forms and their effect on theology and doctrinal utterances; the ideas of Henri de Lubac about dynamic development, relativity and limitations of human knowledge, influence of biblical theology, and expressing treasures of the past in molds of the present. Cf. Berkouwer (1958) 33–43 and (1964) 55–56. See Meuleman about two things: (i) the School of Lyon-Fourvière (Daniélou, de Lubac and von Balthasar, with their stress on heart, faith and missions, rather than on scholastic method) 3–6, and (ii) Daniélou's notion of different incarnations of Christianity and the relativity of scholasticism, Bouillard's suggestion that scholasticism is replaceable, and de Lubac's Platonic understanding of the relation between natural and supernatural realms, 6–12.

33. Theology may not "substitute a new concept in place of the old ones . . ."

"ordinary" and "extraordinary,"[34] an *encyclical* is "ordinary" in that it calls for "intellectual" agreement about any *doctrinal* issue touched on in an encyclical. Not any "faithful" member, or theologian, but the Church's Teaching Authority "determines how a doctrine is contained in the sources of revelation."(21)

The **third** theological error is violating the Church's Teaching Authority in matters related to *exegesis*. This can be done in four ways: (i) believing that only spiritual and moral truths are free from error, (ii) distinguishing in Scripture between what is infallible and divine and what is fallible and human, (iii) ignoring the analogy of faith and the tradition of the Church, and (iv) contrasting what is spiritual, or symbolic, with what is literal in Scripture.(23)

"Theological" errors include rational knowledge humans have about God, His foreknowledge of free human denial, the gratuity of a supra-natural order, and the reasonableness and credibility of Christian faith.[35]

II: (29–34)

Concerning errors in *philosophy*, especially "existentialism," themes to be preserved are trust in human understanding, submission to the Church's authority and respect for Church tradition. Unlike agnosticism and positivism, human understanding, when shaped by a healthy philosophy, can lead to true knowledge of God's natural law in one's inner being, attain changeless truth, and demonstrate, without the help of revelation, the existence of one personal God.

The depth and scope, clarity of formulation, and relevance for both philosophy and theology, of *HG* is similar to *AP* (1879). This is clear from the following quotations:

> It is well known how highly the Church regards human reason, for it falls to reason to demonstrate with certainty the existence of God . . .; to prove

34. Papal infallibility is not a personal quality, but an imparted attribute dependent on the Spirit's assistance. It refers to a pope's *ex cathedra* pronouncements on matters of faith and morals. For details, see Berkouwer (1964) 17–25.

35. Other errors mentioned in this list have to do with denying the existence of angels as personal beings, the origin of the world, the difference between matter and spirit, the distinction between original and actual sin, beliefs concerning Christ's atonement for humans, the meaning of substance in the dogma of transubstantiation, the Church as Christ's mystical body, and eternal salvation through the Church. (25–27)

beyond doubt from divine signs the very foundations of the Christian faith; to express properly the law which the Creator has imprinted in the hearts of men; and finally to attain to some . . . fruitful notion of mysteries. But reason can perform these functions safely and well only when . . . sound philosophy . . . safeguards the genuine validity of human knowledge, the unshakable metaphysical principles of sufficient reason, causality, and finally the mind's ability to attain certain and unchangeable truth.(29)

[T]he Church demands that future priests be instructed in philosophy "according to the method, doctrine, and principles of the Angelic Doctor," since we well know from the experience of centuries, the method of Aquinas is singularly preeminent both of teaching students and for bringing truth to light; his doctrine is in harmony with Divine Revelation, . . .(31)

The method of St. Thomas[36] suits all knowledge, scholarship and education. It purifies, completes and enriches insight only when it is developed within the perspective and boundaries of the RCC.[37]

Given the Church's adoption of (Plato's and Aristotle's) "faculty psychology" about intellect, will and emotion, in philosophy and theology, Pius XII opposed—more explicitly than Leo XIII had done in *AP*—those who criticized the Church for stressing "only the intellect in the process of cognition, while neglecting the function of the will and the emotions." Pius XII stated in this connection,[38]

Never has Christian philosophy denied the usefulness and efficacy of good dispositions of soul for perceiving and embracing moral and religious truths. *In fact it has always taught that the lack of these dispositions of good will can be the reason why the intellect, influenced by the passions and evil inclinations, can be so obscured that it cannot see clearly.* Indeed, St. Thomas holds that the intellect can in some way perceive higher goods of the moral order, whether natural or supernatural, inasmuch as it experiences a certain

36. This method is known for "its clear exposition and solution of questions, its accurate definition of terms, its clear-cut distinctions." (32)

37. The scholastic speculative idea *about* revelation, as communication of the truths of Scripture and tradition, combined with faith as starting-point, cannot be harmonized with the *neo*-Thomist interpretation *of* revelation, which assumes a distinction, in Scripture and tradition, between primary revelation of reality and secondary revelation in human concepts and words. Cf. Meuleman, 6–12.

38. Because of its importance and density, this long citation may require more than one reading. With respect to the meaning of "connaturality," see chapter 6 above.

"connaturality" with these goods, whether this "connaturality" be purely natural, or the result of grace. . . . [I]t is one thing to admit the power of the dispositions of the will in helping reason to gain a more certain and firm knowledge of moral truths; it is quite another thing to say, as these innovators do, indiscriminately mingling cognition and act of will, that the appetitive and affective faculties have a certain power of understanding, and that man, since he cannot by using his reason decide with certainty what is true and is to be accepted, turns to his will, by which he freely chooses among opposite opinions.(33)

III (35–39) and Conclusion (40–44)

About the positive, or natural, sciences (35–39), *HG* does not exclude evolutionism with respect to the human "body," not the "soul" which God creates, rejects what is hypothetical and accepts the authority of the Church.[39] The Church addresses philosophical issues in "faith" and "theology," instructs bishops and supervisors to heed the Church's instructions, warns educators not to stray from the truth, and blesses the RCC.

Initial Evaluation

HG does not so much warn and judge but tries to find a balance between law and freedom. By criticizing in a spirit of renewal, it wants to avoid confusion by stressing the need for intellectual submission to the teaching authority of the Church caught in the vortex of a groping world.

The "form" and "content" of "truth" belong together. The words and ideas of humans may change, but Divine revelation, as articulated in the RCC, does not. Certain concepts are not subject to change. Although T. Aquinas is, unlike Scripture, not canonical, his "method," i.e., way of thinking, does accord with divine revelation and is helpful to defend Christian faith. What is needed is not a subjective *interpreting* theology, but an objective *reasoning*, or speculative, theology. Since "will" and "affections" can hamper "reason," the RCC advocates that humans need supra-natural revelation.[40]

---

39. The Pope rejects the polygenic theory that Adam refers to a group of ancestors, not one ancestor.

40. For details, see Meuleman, 15–27. He points out that the pope wants to maintain the

For though, absolutely speaking, human reason by its own natural force and light can arrive at a true and certain knowledge of the one personal God . . . and also of the natural law, which the Creator has written in our hearts, still there are not a few obstacles to prevent reason from making efficient and fruitful use of its natural ability. The truths that have to do with God and the relations between God and men, completely surpass the sensible order and demand self-surrender and self-abnegation in order to be put into practice and to influence practical life. Now the human intellect, in gaining the knowledge of such truths is hampered by both the activity of the *senses* and the imagination and by evil *passions* arising from original sin (emphasis added).[41]

Both "reason" and "church" are indispensable. What the Pope regrets about erring members of the RCC is that "the more firmly they accept the word of God, so much the more do they diminish the value of human reason, and the more they exalt the authority of God the Revealer, the more severely do they spurn the teaching office of the Church . . . to preserve and interpret divine revelation."[42]

HG rejects irenicism, or "theological pacifism and egalitarianism,"[43] advocated in existentialist philosophy and modern theology, with respect to the *intention* of the Church in formulating dogmas, the inadequacy of all formulations, the inexhaustible nature of truth, and the limits of the traditional teaching authority of the Church. Whereas Leo XIII in *AP* focused chiefly on dangerous developments *outside* the RCC, Pius XII in *HG* concentrated mainly on erring currents *within* the Church. Both encyclicals used the method of the "Angelic Doctor" to express dogmas and their formulations.[44]

1. *HG* does not explain the Thomistic "method" but assumes its validity with regard to controversial issues in philosophy and theology in a

---

dogma of transubstantiation, that the natural is impossible without the supra-natural, and that the Church is the mystical body of Christ.

41. *HG*, 2. It is noteworthy that "reason" is **not** mentioned in this context. See also par. 3: "the natural light of reason alone" can prove with certitude "the divine origin of the Christian religion," but "prejudice or passion or bad faith" can refuse and resist "the evidence of external proofs" and "the impulses of actual grace."

42. *HG*, 8. Advocates of this "new theology," about which this pope warns, ascribed a more important role to Scripture than they did to the views of Aquinas. For a critique of Pius XII's warning against this renewal, see Meuleman, 27–38.

43. *HG*, 11.

44. G. C. Berkouwer (1964) 55.

changing and insecure world. It warns against thought-patterns inconsistent with the way of thinking T. Aquinas developed.[45]

2. In responding to modern neglect of, and opposition to, God's revelation, *HG* reminds Roman Catholic educators, scholars and professors
to acknowledge God's revelation in terms of Scripture's testimony and
the (medieval) belief that humans know truth also intellectually.

3. The nature of "truth" presupposes a Platonic and Aristotelian ontology,
anthropology and epistemology, not in isolation from but fused with
biblical themes in the ontology and methodology of the philosophy and
theology of Aquinas.

4. The distinction between "reason" and "faith" is one of degree, not kind.
Both terms are related to divine revelation, but do so in different ways.
Restless reason finds its ultimate repose in faith. The home of *natural*
reason is *supra-natural* faith: reason and faith are co-dependent. The
response of faith to God's revelation is somehow triggered by innate
human reason.[46]

5. Incorporated in *HG*'s (dualistic) anthropology is classic Greek "faculty
psychology" with respect to "soul" (in distinction from "body") which
influences the meaning of terms like "intellect," "reason," "truth," "belief,"
"dogmas," "logic," "apologetics" and "liberal arts."

Fides et Ratio (1998)[47]

Before he became Pope John Paul II (1978), Karol Wojtyla was already a
reputable thinker. His admiration for Thomas Aquinas, as philosopher and
theologian, surpassed even that of Leo XIII (1878–1903), author of *AP,* and
Pius XII, author of *HG.* He worked for a decade on this detailed encyclical

45. The intent of this chapter is to indicate the nature and scope of scholastic thinking in
philosophy and theology, not to argue the pros and cons of this synthesis thinking.

46. By implication, while the creedal "content" of *faith* and *theology* in Aquinian and
Calvinist, i.e., Roman Catholic and Reformed/Presbyterian, traditions differ, their ontological
and epistemological mind-sets, or ways of thinking, display certain similarities about reason
and faith, philosophy and theology, and their interrelationships.

47. **Note to reader:** the way I dealt with *AP* and *HG* above I will use also in *FR,* i.e., first
describe, in some detail, what the Pope states about "faith," "reason," and their interrelationships, and then raise some basic issues about his views. Readers not familiar with traditional
Roman Catholic thinking may need to read my summary of the views of John Paul II more
than once, and perhaps review the issues raised at the end of *AP* and *HG* and will be raised
at the end of *FR.*

on "human reason and its necessary relationship to faith."[48] In comparison to the two earlier encyclicals on this complex issue, *Fides et Ratio (FR)* elaborates in great detail the meaning of reason and faith, philosophy and theology, and their interrelationships.

Its essence is summarized in the opening statement: "Faith and reason are like two wings on which the human spirit rises to the contemplation of truth. God has placed in the human heart a desire to know the truth—in a word, to know himself—so that, by knowing and loving God, men and women may also come to the fullness of truth about themselves (cf. Ex. 33:18; Ps. 27:8–9; 63:2–3; Jn 14:8; 1 Jn 3:2)." The next 108 paragraphs elaborate on this brief statement.

Introduction (1–6)

Eastern and Western[49] humanity is on a journey "to meet and engage truth more and more deeply." It urges humans to probe the meaning of terms like "reality," "truth," "human," "evil," "death," "life" and "future."[50] Through the "gift of the ultimate truth about human life," the "Paschal Mystery,"[51] the Church serves humanity with the "diakonia of the truth," now understood "in part," later in its "fullness."[52]

Philosophy focuses on reason as an "innate property" interested in "the reason for things and their purpose," how "different human cultures are complementary" and express their "native and seminal wisdom."(3) To discover the "ultimate truth of existence," humans "wonder," i.e., have an innate capacity to "speculate" about, for example,

> . . . principles of *non-contradiction*, finality and causality, . . . concept of the person as a *free* and *intelligent* subject, with the capacity to know God, truth

48. Kenneth L. Woodward in "Uniting Faith and Reason," *Newsweek* (October 26, 1998) 67. Woodward commented that it is "further evidence that his legacy as a Christian Humanist is more important—comprehensive—than his occasional headline making pronouncements on abortion and birth control."

49. North and South are not mentioned but "West" and "East" are.

50. Cf. (1). Such a search is evident also in the quests of Confucius and Lao-Tze, teachings of Buddha, poetry of Homer, tragedies of Euripides and Sophocles, and philosophies of Plato and Aristotle.(1)

51. Cf. Jesus Christ, as "the way and the truth and the life" (John 14:6).

52. Cf. 1 Cor. 13:12. Cf. paragraph (2).

and goodness . . . certain fundamental moral norms which are shared by all. . . . [B]eyond different schools of thought, there exists a body of knowledge which may be judged a kind of spiritual heritage of humanity. . . . Once reason successfully intuits and formulates the first *universal principles of being* and correctly draws from them *conclusions* which are *coherent* both *logically and ethically*, then it may be called *right reason* or, as the ancients called it, *orthos logos, recta ratio* (emphasis added).(4)

Through proper use of reason, philosophy can "know fundamental truths about human life." This knowledge is "indispensable" to understand "faith" and to communicate "the truth of the Gospel."(5) Reason yearns to know "ever more deeply" and seeks a truth that "transcends" all human subjectivity. Philosophy lifts its gaze to "the truth of being," something not "limited and conditioned." It rejects agnosticism and relativism, any "pluralism" based on ever-changing ideas. Distrusting the human "capacity for knowledge" results in "partial and provisional truths" and dodges problems about the meaning and ultimate foundation of human, personal and social existence. Bearing the "Revelation of Jesus Christ," the RCC must "reflect upon the truth." Theologians and philosophers need to restore to our "contemporaries a genuine trust in their capacity to know" and urge "philosophy to recover and develop its own full dignity."(6) *FR* focuses on "truth itself" and its "foundation in relation to faith."

The need for a foundation for personal and communal life becomes all the more pressing at a time when we are faced with the patent inadequacy of perspectives in which the ephemeral is affirmed as a value and the possibility of discovering the real meaning of life is cast into doubt. This is why many people stumble through life to the very edge of the abyss without knowing where they are going. . . . With its enduring appeal to the search for truth, philosophy has the great responsibility of forming thought and culture; and now it must strive resolutely to recover its original vocation.(6)

I: The Revelation of God's Wisdom (7–15)

When "truth" and "philosophy" are disconnected, statements about faith, revelation, Jesus Christ, Father, Spirit and mystery may seem to be problematic.[53]

53. For example, "At the origin of our life of faith there is an encounter, unique in kind,

However, their full meaning is clear and simple, when they are thought of in terms of patristic thinking, the Council of Trent (1548–1563), Vatican I (1869) and Vatican II (1962) about *super*natural revelation and a knowledge of "faith" surpassing the knowledge of "human reason."(8) In terms of Vatican I, the truth of philosophy and revelation is "neither identical nor mutually exclusive."[54] There is a "twofold order of knowledge,"

> . . . not only as regards their source, but also as regards their object . . . one by natural reason . . . the other by divine faith. With regard to the object, because besides those things which natural reason can attain, there are proposed for our belief mysteries hidden in God which, unless they are divinely revealed, cannot be known. *Based upon God's testimony and enjoying supernatural assistance of grace, faith is of an order other than philosophical knowledge which depends upon sense perception and experience and which advances by the light of the intellect alone* [emphasis added]. Philosophy and the sciences function within the order of natural reason; while faith, enlightened and guided by the Spirit, recognizes in the message of salvation the "fullness of grace and truth" (cf. Jn 1:14) which God has willed to reveal in history and definitely through his Son, Jesus Christ (cf. 1 Jn 5:9; 5:31–32).(9)

Supernatural revelation, which calls for faith and is salvific, is "immersed in time and history" and perfected in the Word-made-flesh. (10) God "sent his Son, the eternal Word who enlightens all people, so that he might dwell among them and tell them the innermost realities about God."[55](11) In the Incarnation, God "forged the enduring and definitive synthesis which the human mind of itself could not even have imagined: the Eternal enters time, the whole lies hidden in the part, God takes on a human face."(12) The Church "constantly progresses towards the fullness of divine truth, until the words of God reach their complete fulfillment in her."(11)

A "coherent understanding" of this mystery comes through "faith alone."(13) It acknowledges the "divinity, transcendence and supreme free-

---

which discloses a mystery hidden for long ages (cf. 1 Cor. 2:7; Rom 16:25–26) but which is now revealed: In his goodness and wisdom, God chooses to reveal himself and to make known to us the purpose of his will (cf. Eph 1:9), by which, through Christ, the Word made flesh, man has access to the Father in the Holy Spirit. . . . This initiative is utterly gratuitous, moving from God to men and women in order to bring them to salvation."

54. This formulation is reminiscent of Chalcedon's description of Christ's human and divine natures.

55. Cf. John 1:1–18.

dom" of God's revelation, gives "assent" to the "gift" of the truth of "divine testimony," and "urges reason to be open to it and to embrace its profound meaning." Such "assent," which displays the "spiritual nature" of "the intellect and the will," is the "consummate expression" of human "freedom" and "self-realization." In the "act of faith," freedom reaches "the certainty of truth and chooses to live in that truth."(13) The passions of reason to know

> serve to lead the search for truth to new depths, enabling the mind in its autonomous exploration to penetrate within the mystery by use of reason's own methods. . . . Yet these signs also urge reason to look beyond their status as signs in order to grasp the deeper meaning which they bear. They contain a hidden truth to which the mind is drawn and which it cannot ignore without destroying the very signs which it is given.(13)

From Vatican I (1869) and Vatican II (1962) "emerges a novel consideration for philosophical learning."(14) This "point of reference," anchored in revelation, is essential to know the "mystery of human life," a mystery that refers back to God's mystery, which the human mind cannot "exhaust" but only "receive and embrace in faith." Reason has its own "field of investigation in which it can enquire and understand" in a way "restricted only by its finiteness before the infinite mystery of God." This "universal and ultimate truth" excites the "mind to ceaseless effort" and "impels reason continually to extend the range of its knowledge until it senses that it has done all in its power, leaving no stone unturned."[56]

The lodestar directing humans is the "absolute truth" of God's revelation. (15) It invites humans to be "open to the transcendent," while respecting "their autonomy as creatures and their freedom."[57] This revelation is not a "product" of human reason, but something "gratuitous" that "stirs thought and seeks acceptance as an expression of love."

> The ultimate purpose of personal existence, then, is the theme of philosophy and theology alike. For all their difference of method and content,

---

56. Cf. Anselm's statements that God is "that than which nothing greater can be conceived (*non solum es quo maius cogitari nequit*)" and "greater than all that can be conceived (quiddam maius quam cogitari possit)."

57. Cf. references to John 8:32, "You will know the truth, and the truth will make you free;" Deut. 30:11–14 about "the word" being near you, in you, in your heart, enabling you to do it; and St. Augustine: "Do not wander far and wide, but return unto yourself. Deep within man there dwells the truth (*noli foras, in te ipsum redi. In interiore homine habitat veritas*)." (15)

both disciplines point to that "path of life" (Ps. 16:11) which, as faith tells us, leads in the end to the full and lasting joy of the contemplation of the Triune God.(15)

II: *Credo ut Intelligam (I Believe in Order to Understand) (16–23)*

Reflecting "deep intuition,"[58] wisdom literature thinks about the relation between knowledge of "faith" and "reason." Whoever "loves and seeks the truth" reasons "intelligently,"[59] not "abstractly," the way Greek philosophers and Egyptian sages did and modern thinkers do with their "different kinds of knowing." A wise person focuses on Scripture's "indissoluble unity between the knowledge of reason and the knowledge of faith."(16) It does not deny "reason's autonomy," nor reduce its "scope for action," but points to Israel's God acting in human experience and history. The "inner eye" of "faith" opens "the mind to discover in the flux of events the workings of Providence,"[60] and "reason" helps humans to "know which path to take . . . within the horizon of faith." In order to know themselves, the world and God, humans need "reason" and "faith," each with its "own scope for action."

The distinction between "reason-faith" is inseparable from the "human-God" distinction. The former explores "truth" through reason, the latter searches the "origin of all things," the "fullness of the mystery."(17) A wise person has three rules: keep searching for truth, avoid pride in thinking, and live in the "fear of God."[61](18) To ignore these rules is to risk failure, become fools with a "deficient" knowledge neither wrong nor false, but *incomplete.*

As to "nature," as the "first stage of Revelation," humans can "rise to God."[62] Not to know the Creator is the result not of "reason" but of an "impediment" in the *"free will"* of humans, their "sinfulness." Reason should not be "overvalued," but must be used "within the larger horizon of faith." Only faith-enlightened reason can discover "the deeper meaning of all things," including one's own existence.(20)

In the Old Testament, knowledge is not a matter of "careful observation", but implies a necessary link with faith and revelation.(21) *True* knowledge calls for reason to enter "the realm of the infinite." The search for truth begins

---

58. And expressing "the voices of Egypt and Mesopotamia." (16)
59. Cf. apocryphal sources: Wisdom 9:11 and Sirach (Ecclesiasticus) 14:20–27.
60. "The human mind plans the way, but the Lord directs the steps" (Proverbs 16:9).
61. Proverbs 1:7; Sirach 1:14.
62. Cf. Wisdom 7:17, 19–20; 13:5.

in reason and ends in faith. Reason's search for what is "beautiful, good and true"[63] implies strain, toil, doubt, leaning on God.(21)

Perhaps most important in *FR* are the comments about humans' ability to know God "through the mind" both before and after their primal disobedience. John Paul II states,

> Through the medium of creatures, God stirs in reason an intuition of his "power" and his "divinity" (cf. Rom 1:20). This is to concede to human reason a capacity which seems almost to surpass its natural limitations . . . by discoursing on the data provided by the senses, reason can reach the cause which lies at the origin of all perceptible reality. In philosophical terms, we could say that this important Pauline text affirms *the human capacity for metaphysical enquiry.*
>
> . . . But because of the disobedience by which men and women chose to set themselves in full and complete autonomy in relation to the One who had created them, this ready access to God the Creator was *diminished.* . . . All men and women were caught up in this primal disobedience, which so *wounded reason* that from then on its path to full truth would be strewn with obstacles. From that time onwards the human capacity to know the truth was impaired by an aversion to the One who is the source and origin of truth. It is again the Apostle who reveals just how far human thinking became distorted and inclined to falsehood (cf. Rom 1:21–22). The eyes of the mind were no longer able to see clearly: reason became more and more a prisoner of itself. *The coming of Christ was the saving event which redeemed reason from its weakness,* setting it free from the shackles in which it had imprisoned itself (emphases added).(22)

Reason's autonomy is "limited," not "full and absolute." Disobedience is to ignore the "knowledge" God's revelation provided within the horizon of faith. Reason as such is "wounded," "impaired," "distorted," "empty," turned into a "wisdom of this world," not "wisdom of God revealed in Jesus Christ."[64] In his move from *Credo ut Intelligam* to *Intellego ut Credam,* the Pope indicated the essence of his (scholastic) synthesis thinking:

---

63. About this (Platonic-Aristotelian) triad "beautiful, good and true," see chapter 6 above.

64. Humans are "wounded," not depraved, rebellious, defiant, actively protesting, intentionally spurning. The depth of the human fall is mitigated, partial, relative, due more to wrong faith than to wrong reason. Cf. I Cor. 1:20–28]

Of itself, philosophy is able to recognize the human being's ceaselessly self-transcendent orientation towards the truth; . . . The preaching of Christ crucified and risen is the reef upon which the link between faith and philosophy can break up, but it is also the reef which the two can set forth upon the boundless ocean of truth. Here we see not only the border between reason and faith, but also the space where the two may meet.(23)

III: Intellego ut Credam (I Understand in Order to Believe) (24–35)

In the human heart is "a seed of desire and nostalgia for God."[65] It starts with "reason's capacity to rise beyond what is contingent and move towards the infinite." Philosophy has its own "specific tools and scholarly methods."(24) *Theoretically*, it is reason's interest in truth, and *practically*, it is the will's "free and rightly tuned" decisions to do good, acknowledge values and walk from happiness to perfection.(25)

"Truth" centers on what is universal and ultimate.(26) As the "ground of all things," it provides a "final explanation," "supreme value," and end to "all questioning." The *search* for the "certitude of truth" (philosophy) and "absolute value" (ethics) is basic to human existence.(27) The *levels* of truth are based on "immediate evidence," reason's "speculative powers," "religious truths" grounded in philosophy, and answers of "different religious traditions" to "ultimate questions."(30) In addition, there are "simply believed" truths.

To seek "truth" is also to live by "belief."(31) Being often "richer than mere evidence," beliefs imply an "interpersonal relationship" that is deeper than merely knowing. Humans will "entrust themselves to the truth" that others declare to them, as is evident in the "witness of martyrs," who show a love that needs no long "arguments" to convince others.(32)

The search for truth reaches for an "ulterior truth" which explains the "meaning of life" and ends in "the absolute." Truth is encountered, and recognized, in two ways, namely, "reason" and "trusting dialogue and sincere friendship." This "unstoppable" discovery of truth ends in Christian faith, draws humans into the "order of grace," and offers "true and coherent knowledge of the triune God." It reaches its fulfillment in Jesus Christ as the Truth.(33)

65. Cf. Acts 17:22–27.

The unity of truth is a fundamental premise of human reasoning, as the principle of *non-contradiction* makes clear. Revelation renders the unity certain, showing that the God of creation is also the God of salvation history. It is one and the same God who establishes and guarantees the *intelligibility* and *reasonableness* of the natural order of things upon which the scientists confidently depend, and who reveals himself as the Father of our Lord Jesus Christ. This unity of truth, natural and revealed, is embodied in . . . Christ, as the apostle reminds us: "Truth is in Jesus" (cf. Eph 4:21; Col 1:15–20).[66](34)

IV: Relation between Faith and Reason (36–48)

Early Christians referred to "Moses and the prophets," "natural knowledge of God" and the "voice of conscience" in every person. Rejecting "divinizing" anything in "nature," Paul associated revelation with philosophers who opposed myths and with mystery cults of "divine transcendence." They linked "reason and religion" by appealing to "universal principles" and proposing a *"rational foundation for their belief in the divinity"* (emphasis added). In stressing "universal reason," they replaced "superstition" with "the concept of divinity" and purified "religion, at least in part, . . . by rational analysis."

In this respect, the Fathers entered into *"fruitful dialogue with ancient philosophy, which offered new ways of proclaiming and understanding the God of Jesus Christ"* (emphasis added). (36) Irenaeus and Tertullian rejected gnosticism for its "esoteric speculation,"[67] as well as any subordinating of "Revelation to the interpretation of the philosophers."(37) Although at first philosophy was more "a disturbance than an opportunity,"[68] because of its "search for truth," philosophy became less elitist and gradually something that was universally accessible. Because "access to the truth" implies "access to God," a positive engagement with philosophy provided helpful insight on the condition that it was done with "cautious discernment."

Many paths lead to truth, but only Christian truth has redemptive value, namely, in the revelation of Jesus Christ. According to Clement of Alexandria, the Gospel is a "true philosophy," which like the Mosaic Law, is an "instruction, prepared for Christian faith." In rendering sophistry

---

66. See also John 1:14 and 18; Colossians 1:17; and Acts 17:23 ("What human reason seeks 'without knowing.' ")

67. Cf. Paul's warning against worldly philosophy and vain deceit (Col. 2:8).

68. With respect to "the proclamation of the Risen Christ by way of a personal encounter which would bring the listener to conversion of heart and the request for Baptism." (38)

impotent and disarming those who betray truth, *Greek philosophy is rightly called the hedge and the protective wall around the vineyard*" (emphasis added).[69](38)

In using philosophy, not all Christians were uncritical.[70](39) **Augustine** (354–430) developed, according to the Pope, "the first great synthesis of philosophy and theology," a "unity of knowledge, grounded in the thought of the Bible, confirmed and sustained by a depth of speculative thinking." (40) About the relation between Church and Athens, faith and Greek thinking, theology and philosophy, the Church fathers sensed both "its positive aspects and its limitations." Instead of simply transposing "the truths of faith into philosophical categories," they disclosed "all that remained implicit and preliminary in the thinking of the great philosophers of antiquity."

> ... theirs was the task of showing how reason, freed from external constraints, could find its way out of the blind alley of myth and open itself to the transcendent in a more appropriate way. Purified and rightly tuned, therefore, reason could rise to the higher planes of thought, providing a solid foundation for the perception of being, of the transcendent and the absolute.
>
> They fully welcomed reason which was open to the absolute, and they infused it with the richness drawn from Revelation. This was more than a meeting of cultures, with one culture perhaps succumbing to the fascination of the other. It happened rather in the depths of human souls, and it was a meeting of creature and Creator.(41)

For **Anselm** (1033–1109), the *intellectus fidei* reveals a tension between faith's priority and reason's search. The task of reason is not "to pass judgment on the contents of reason," but "to find meaning, to discover explanations which might allow everyone to come to a certain understanding of the contents of faith." The intellect seeks what it loves, i.e., "truth," and does so by "reasoning." Faith's task is to understand its object with the help of reason. At

69. For example, Origen (185–254) used Greek philosophy, but about the immortality of the soul, human divinization and origin of evil, he changed it profoundly.

70. Also, "The name 'theology' itself, together with the idea of theology as rational discourse about God, had to this point been tied to its Greek origins. In Aristotelian philosophy ... the name signified the noblest part and the true summit of philosophical discourse. But in the light of Christian revelation, what had signified a generic doctrine about the gods assumed a wholly new meaning, signifying now the reflection undertaken by the believer in order to express the true doctrine about God." (39)

the summit of this search, reason "acknowledges that it cannot do without what faith presents."(42)

As in *AP*, *HG* and *FR* also pay special attention to the contribution and originality of **T. Aquinas** (1225–1274) in his contacts with Arabian and Jewish thinkers, who had developed great expertise in Greek philosophy, especially the views of Aristotle. Between faith and reason there is a "harmony," because "both come from God,"(43) Faith does not fear reason, but "seeks it out and has trust in it." Illumined by faith, "reason" is *"free from the fragility and limitations deriving from the disobedience of sin and finds the strength required to rise to the knowledge of the Triune God"* (emphasis added). As a masterful synthesizer of "faith" and "reason," T. Aquinas is *"a model of the right way to do theology"* and *"a pioneer of the new path of philosophy and universal culture"* (emphasis added). The "brilliance of his prophetic intuition" consists of his reconciling "the *secularity* of the world and the *radicality* of the Gospel." In essence: "Just as grace builds on nature and brings it to fulfillment, so faith builds upon and perfects reason."(43)

The "primacy of wisdom," as "gift of the Holy Spirit,"[71] enables a person to make "a judgement according to divine truth." While *faith* "accepts divine truth as it is," *wisdom* is complemented by the intellect's "capacity" to explore "reality" and by a *theological* wisdom, based on "revelation" to explore the contents of "faith" and the "very mystery of God." Having the Spirit as its source, *truth* is universal, objective and transcendent; it produces a philosophy of "what is."(44)

In the **late Middle Ages**, the difference between reason and faith, the two main forms of learning, turned into "a fateful separation." Philosophy became "independent of the contents of faith," tried to replace faith, even mistrusted reason itself.(45) During the **nineteenth century**, liberal theology, positivism and atheism turned this "separation" into an "opposition" between reason and faith. This, in turn, fostered a philosophy of nothingness, in which the search for truth ceased, everything was considered to be "fleeting and provisional" and the search for meaning became an "end in itself."(46)

This limiting of philosophy from "universal wisdom and learning" to merely one area of "human knowing" marginalized philosophy. Reason no longer contemplates "truth" but promotes "utilitarian ends" and serves "enjoyment and power." As a result, humans experienced alienation and are

---

71. Unlike knowledge as an "intellectual" virtue obtained through study, wisdom is "from on high."

threatened by what their intellect achieves and will desires. They live in fear. Not to "know the truth," nor to "seek the absolute" obscures reason's "true dignity." Despite all those who drive a wedge between faith and reason, "precious and seminal insights" are still possible and contribute to the discovery of truth.[72] Not to link "faith" and "reason" impoverishes both.

> Deprived of reason, faith has stressed feeling and experience, and so run the risk of no longer being a universal proposition . . . faith then runs the grave risk of withering into myth or superstition. By the same token, *reason* which is unrelated to an adult faith is not prompted to turn its gaze to the newness and radicality of being.[73]

Faith and philosophy must recover their unity and live in harmony with their nature and not compromise their mutual autonomy. The *parrhesia* (freedom) of faith must be matched by the boldness of reason.(48)

V: The Church's Interventions in Philosophy (49–63)

The "constitutive status" of philosophy is to be autonomous about its "principles and methods." The church does not have her own philosophy, nor does she prefer any special philosophy.[74] Throughout history, however, philosophy has been "deficient," advocated "false and partial theories," opposed Christian teaching, operated with assumptions, and arrived at conclusions incompatible with the "word of God and theological enquiry." Especially with respect to "God, the human being, human freedom and ethical behavior," the church needs to witness to the truth by serving *recta ratio*, i.e., reflect "rightly upon what is true."(50)

Because reason is "wounded and weakened by sin" and as a result of a proliferation of complex "systems, methods, concepts, and philosophical

72. E.g., its penetrating analyses of perception and experience, what is imaginary and unconscious, personhood and intersubjectivity, freedom and values, time and history, even death. (48)

73. "The notion of "radicality of being" is central to the philosophy of Aquinian and Anselmian *realism*.

74. How to harmonize this idea with the endorsements by the Council of Trent, *Aeterni Patris*, *Humani Generis* and *Fides et Ratio* is difficult, if not impossible, to explain, unless Thomism is *not* seen as a particular philosophy, but as a way to combine reason and faith, philosophy and theology, and autonomy and revelation. See (64) below.

themes," the church at times must intervene to encourage philosophy to stay on the path of truth that leads to a "recognition of the mystery." (51)

For this reason, for the first time in history, Vatican I (1870) commented, in its Dogmatic Constitution *Dei Filius*, on the relation between "reason" and "faith." It censured any *fideistic* distrust of reason's natural abilities and any *rationalistic* notion that only "faith" provides knowledge.(52) With respect to "faith" and "reason," the role of revelation and natural knowledge of God's existence, the RCC rejects fideism (radical traditionalism) and rationalism (ontologism). It affirms the "unity of truth," the "contribution of rational knowledge" to knowledge of faith, and the distinction between "the mysteries of faith and the findings of philosophy." *Dei Filius* talks about "two orders of knowledge," states that faith being "superior" to reason does not imply a "divergence between faith and reason." God "reveals the mysteries and bestows the gift of faith" and endows the human spirit with "the light of reason." God does not "deny himself," nor can "the truth ever contradict the truth."(53)

The Pope warns bishops about the dangers of phenomenist, agnostic and immanentist philosophies, "marxist" thinking in certain liberation theologians (54), "deep-seated distrust of reason" and chatter about "the end of metaphysics." Philosophically incompetent theologians "allow themselves to be swayed uncritically." Modern cultural shifts encouraged a resurgence of fideism, a disparaging of "speculative theology," and an abandoning of "traditional terminology."(55)

> In brief, there are signs of a widespread distrust of universal and absolute statements, especially among those who think that truth is born of consensus and not of a *consonance between intellect and objective reality*. . . . It cannot but encourage philosophers—be they Christian or not—to trust in the power of human reason . . . [I]t is necessary not to abandon the passion for ultimate truth, the eagerness to search for it or the audacity to forge new paths in the search. It is faith which stirs reason to move beyond all isolation and willingly to run risks so that it may attain whatever is *beautiful, good and true*. Faith thus becomes the convinced and convincing advocate of reason (emphases added). (56)

The Church is interested in the "basic principles of a genuine renewal of philosophical enquiry." *AP* (1879) took a step of "historic importance for the life of the Church. To this day, it remains the one papal document of such authority devoted entirely to philosophy." In showing how "philosophical thinking contributes in fundamental ways to faith and theological learning," Aquinas has been of "incomparable value" to recover the practice of a "philosophy consonant with the demands of faith." He distinguished "perfectly between faith and reason" and united them in "bonds of mutual friendship, conceding to each its specific rights and to each its specific dignity."(57)

Most eminent twentieth-century Roman Catholic theologians, whose views influenced Vatican II (1962), benefitted from revived Thomistic philosophy,[75] especially in a chapter on anthropology about humans being created in God's image. Their dignity and superiority over the rest of creation affirms "the transcendent capacity of human reason." The ending of this chapter was a "constant reference-point" in John Paul II's teaching, also in *FR*.

> "The truth is that only in the mystery of the Incarnate Word does the mystery of man take on light. For Adam, the first man, was a type of him who was to come, Christ the Lord. Christ, the new Adam, in the very revelation of the mystery of the Father and of his love, fully reveals man to himself and brings to light his most high calling."(60)

With "surprise and displeasure," the Pope reacts to the diminished interest, after Vatican II, in scholastic philosophy and a lack of interest in any philosophy.[76](61) He states that "philosophy is fundamental and indispensable to the structure of theological studies and to the formation of candidates for the priesthood."(62) A proper theological curriculum presupposes "a special study of philosophy." The medieval "constructive harmony of philosophical and theological learning" must replace the modern "indiscriminate acceptance of any kind of philosophy."(62) The "intimate bond" between "theological work" and "philosophical search for truth" must be restored.(63)

75. John Paul II also refers to other philosophies "of great influence and lasting value," e.g., impressive systems of idealism, faith viewed in terms of moral consciousness, an analysis of immanence that opens a window onto the transcendent, and understanding faith in terms of a phenomenological method.

76. The Pope gives three reasons for this disenchantment: (i) distrust in reason, (ii) focus on anthropological issues resulting in marginalizing philosophy, and (iii) an inculturation of faith without doing justice to traditional ways of thinking. (61)

VI: Interaction between Philosophy and Theology (64–79)

Theology is a "reflective and scientific elaboration of the understanding of God's word in the light of faith."(64) The latter involves two methodological principles: hearing of faith (*auditus fidei*) and knowledge of faith (*intellectus fidei*). The former provides theology with the content of revelation, as expressed in tradition, Scripture and "magisterium," and the latter prepares theology for a correct philosophy, i.e., "speculative enquiry," into "knowledge and personal communication, especially the various forms and functions of language."(65)

The *intellectus fidei*, proposed in Scripture and interpreted by the Church, has an "innate intelligibility," or logical consistency. It grasps "the logical and conceptual structure of the propositions," which frames "the Church's teaching" mainly to indicate "the salvific meaning of these propositions for the individual and for humanity."[77](66) In distinction from "moral" theology,[78] "dogmatic" theology concentrates on "the universal meaning of the mystery of the One and triune God and of the economy of salvation," and does this as "a narrative" and "above all, in the form of argument."[79] Dogmatic theology needs a philosophy of three things: being "human," the "world," and "objective truth as its foundation."(66)

"Fundamental" theology justifies and expounds "the relationship between faith and philosophical thought." To accept God's revelation is based on "naturally, or philosophically, knowable" truths. Theology shows that faith knowledge enables reason to obtain truths "from its own independent enquiry" and accept revelation without "compromising the principles and autonomy of the mind itself."(67)

> Faith will thus be able "to show the path to reason in a sincere search for truth. Although faith, a gift of God, is not based on reason, it can certainly

---

77. This ends with a stress on the Eucharist and assent of faith: "From the sum of these propositions, the believer comes to know the history of salvation, which culminates in the person of Jesus Christ and in his Paschal Mystery. Believers then share in this mystery by their assent of faith." (66)

78. With its use of concepts like "moral law, conscience, freedom, personal responsibility and guilt," partly dealt with in "philosophical ethics." For details, see paragraph 68 below.

79. The concepts used must be "critical and universally communicable," and the issues dealt with are, for example, the language used in speaking about God, the relations within the Trinity, God's creativity in the world, the relation between God and humans, and Christ's divine-human identity. (66)

not dispense with it. At the same time, . . . reason needs to be reinforced by faith, in order to discover horizons it cannot reach of its own."⁸⁰(67)

History, science, issues of faith and culture and cultural pluralism are important, but they cannot take the place of "typically philosophical and critical thinking." Going beyond the "particular and concrete," philosophy focuses, as T. Aquinas said, on different worldviews and cultures, not on what people think, but on "objective truth."⁸¹(69) Philosophy and theology have a boundless desire for "truth" in all cultures. This "desire for knowledge" indicates the human interest in what is "universal" and "transcendent" as different paths to "truth" reflects culture's "intrinsic capacity to receive divine Revelation" and expresses the transforming power of Christianity.⁸²(70–71)

The way Christianity faced the task of inculturation when it encountered Greek thinking, so today it faces a similar challenge in its encounter with the cultures of China, Japan, India and Africa. Proper inculturation reflects three things: (a) the universality of the human spirit, (b) what the church learned from Greco-Latin culture through insights gained from modern dialogues with Eastern cultures, and (c) not allowing one cultural tradition to change and oppose other traditions.(72) The relation between theology and philosophy can "best be construed as a circle," as follows:

> Theology's source and starting-point must always be the word of God re-vealed in history, while its final goal will be an understanding of that word which increases with each passing generation. Yet, since God's word is Truth (cf. Jn 17:17), the human search for truth—philosophy pursued in keeping with its own rules—can only help to understand God's word better. . . . It is as if, moving between the twin poles of God's word and a better under-standing of it, reason is offered guidance and is warned against paths which would lead it to stray from revealed Truth and to stray in the end from the truth pure and simple. . . . This circular relationship with the word of God leaves philosophy enriched, because reason discovers new and unsuspected horizons.⁸³(73)

80. Quotation is taken from John Paul II's *Letter to Participants in the International Congress of Fundamental Theology* on the 125th Anniversary of *Dei Filius* (September 30, 1995).

81. "It is not an array of human opinions but truth alone which can be of help to theology."(69)

82. And, implicitly, the message and method of the Roman Catholic Church.

83. The pope refers to "great theologians who also distinguished themselves as great philosophers" and who produced writings of "high speculative value," such as Gregory of

As to the nature of "Christian faith," three are philosophical stances: independence from the gospel, Christian philosophy, and handmaiden of theology (*ancilla theologiae*). The **first** stance refers to a time before Christ, cultures unaffected by the gospel, and philosophy based solely on reason and obeying its own rules. Though disabled by an inherent weakness, it looks for truth within the "natural order" and is only implicitly open to what is "supernatural."[84] Its stress on "rigorous rational criteria" ensures that its results are "universally valid."

> This also confirms the principle that *grace does not destroy nature but perfects it*. The assent of faith, engaging the intellect and will, does not destroy but perfects the free will of each believer who deeply welcomes what has been revealed (emphasis added).(75)

The **second** stance, "Christian philosophy," is useful as long it does not indicate an "official" Church philosophy, but merely "a Christian way of philosophizing, a philosophical speculation conceived in dynamic union with faith."(76) Christian philosophy has a "subjective" and an "objective" aspect. The former indicates that faith "liberates" reason from the philosophical presumption of ignoring "data of Revelation."[85] The latter points to the "content," or "certain truths," of Revelation that might not have been discovered by "reason unaided, although they are not of themselves inaccessible to reason."[86] The truths of faith can broaden "reason's scope for action." Instead of becoming theologians, philosophers work on their "own terrain and with their own purely rational method, yet extending their research to new aspects of truth."(76)

The **third** stance, philosophy as *ancilla theologiae*, points to theology's need for a philosophy of theology to use "concepts" and "arguments" and to confirm "the intelligibility and universal truth of its claims." By adopting

---

Nazianzus and Augustine; Anselm, Bonaventure and Aquinas; Newman and Rosmini; Maritain and Gilson in Western culture; and Soloviev, Florensky, Chaadaev and Lossky in Eastern contexts. (74)

84. This "openness" distinguishes it from those modern thinkers who believe that philosophy is "independent," "self-sufficient" and "separate" from faith and revelation.

85. E.g., evil and suffering, personal nature of God, meaning of life, and the metaphysical question "why is there something rather than nothing." (76)

86. E.g., the rationality of the truths of a free and personal God, the reality of sin, a person as spiritual being, and, more recently, history as event, "the possibility of man's supernatural vocation" and "original sin itself."

philosophy, theologians affirm philosophy's autonomy and require philosophy to undergo certain "profound transformations." The relation of philosophy to theology is not one of "servile submission," but (in Aristotle's sense of experimental science) something ancillary, a help or servant, to "prima philosophia."

> The term can scarcely be used today, given the principle of autonomy to which we have referred, but it has served throughout history to indicate the necessity of the link between the two sciences and the impossibility of their separation . . . The truths of faith make certain demands which philosophy must respect whenever it engages theology.(77)

For T. Aquinas "the guide and model for theological studies" and all "truth" seekers,

> the demands of reason and the power of faith found the most elevated synthesis ever attained by human thought, for he could defend the radical newness introduced by Revelation without ever demeaning the venture proper to reason.(78)

> By virtue of the splendour emanating from subsistent Being itself, revealed truth offers the fullness of light and will therefore illumine the path of philosophical enquiry. In short, Christian Revelation becomes the true point of encounter and engagement between philosophical and theological thinking in their reciprocal relationship.[87](79)

VII: *Current Requirement and Tasks (80–99)*

To understand "human existence, the created world and God himself," the "mystery of the Incarnation" is key. It pushes philosophy to its limits by pressing reason "to make its own a logic which brings down the walls within which it risks being confined." In the Word Incarnate, "human nature and divine nature are safeguarded in all their autonomy, and at the same time

---

87. He concludes by citing Augustine: "To believe is nothing other than to think with assent . . . Believers are also thinkers: in believing they think and in thinking, they believe . . . If faith does not think, it is nothing." Also, "If there is no assent, there is no faith, for without assent one does not really believe."

the unique bond which sets them together in mutuality without confusion of any kind is revealed."(80)

Modern culture is experiencing a deep "crisis of meaning," resulting from proliferating data and facts and from fragmented knowledge evoking radical doubt expressed in scepticism, indifference and nihilism.(81) To counteract this threat, three things are necessary.

First, a philosophy, in consonance[88] with God's word, to reclaim "its sapiential dimension as a search for the ultimate framework of the unity of human knowledge and action."

Second, a philosophy that verifies the human capacity "to . . . reach objective truth by means of that *adaequatio rei et intellectus* (similarity of reality and intellect) to which the Scholastic Doctors referred." Although due to sin certitude about reality is "partially obscured and weakened," it is still possible to "know and grasp the clear and simple truth" of a knowable reality. To understand the "ontological content" of what the apostles John and Paul said about "the very being of Christ," theology needs "a philosophy which does not disavow the possibility of a knowledge which is objectively true even if not perfect."[89](82)

Third, implied is a "sapiential and analytical knowledge"[90] with a "metaphysical range" and an ability to transcend "empirical data in order to attain something absolute and foundational in its search for truth.(83) The "concept of personal dignity" implies an encounter with "being" and with "metaphysical inquiry." The metaphysical dimension of reality opens up in truth, beauty and moral values of humans, in being itself, and in God.

> The word of God refers constantly to things which transcend human experience and even human thought; but this "mystery" could not be revealed, nor could theology render it in some way intelligible, were human knowledge limited strictly to the world of sense experience. Metaphysics thus plays an essential role of mediation in theological research. A theology without a metaphysical horizon could not move beyond an analysis of religious experience, nor would it allow the *intellectus fidei* to give coherent account of the universal and transcendent value of revealed truth.[91]

88. The engagement of philosophy "in the search for the natural foundation" of life's meaning "corresponds to the religious impulse innate in every person."(82)

89. This is equally true of "the judgments of moral conscience."(82)

90. A "requirement for knowing . . . the ultimate foundation in the Supreme Good, God Himself."(83)

91. He adds:"If I insist so strongly on the metaphysical element, it is because I am con-

To stress "metaphysics" is helpful to react positively to modern hermeneutics and language analysis. Faith assumes the human ability to express
"divine and transcendent reality in a universal way."[92] Without it, there would
be "no Revelation of God, but only the expression of human notions about
God and about what God presumably thinks of us."(84) This sapiential task
of philosophers is to develop "a unified and organic vision of knowledge."[93]
The Church must recover "the profound theological tradition of earlier times
and the enduring tradition of that philosophy which . . . can transcend the
boundaries of space and time."(85) This is necessary to avoid eclecticism,
historicism, scientism, pragmatism and nihilism.

FR acknowledges the insights of modern logic, language philosophy,
epistemology, philosophy of nature, anthropology, affective aspects of
knowledge, and existential freedom. It warns against the "principle of immanence" which provokes "radical requestioning of claims once thought in-
disputable." Postmodernity in aesthetic, social and technological disciplines,
even philosophy, is ambiguous. It must be rejected for opposing certainties
and advocating the absence of meaning and "everything is provisional and
ephemeral."(91)

The study of theology centers on understanding revelation within the
context of changing situations and cultural settings. Essentially, theology
focuses on the "ultimate truth . . . of the living God and his plan for salvation
revealed in Jesus Christ." This truth challenges both theology and philosophy. Their methods differ, but in their joint effort, they reach for "universally
valid truth," for "sincere dialogue," curbing conflicts, and journeying toward
full truth.(92)

The chief aim of theology is to understand "revelation" and "content of
faith." Its nucleus is to contemplate the "mystery of the Triune God," especially God's "kenosis" or self-giving love. For the "meaning" of texts, theology focuses on the truth to be "grasped and explained" and does so in
conjunction with the critical and vital role of philosophy. Human language

---

vinced that it is the path to be taken in order to move beyond the crisis pervading large sectors
of philosophy at the moment, and thus to correct mistaken modes of behavior now widespread
in our society."(83)

92. That is, in an "analogical" way.

93. For the following reason: "The segmentation of knowledge, with its splintered approach to truth and consequent fragmentation of meaning, keeps people today from coming to
an interior unity." This basic postulate is "in organic continuity with the great tradition" of the
ancients, the Church Fathers, the masters of Scholasticism, and the basic insights of modern
and contemporary thought regarding "philosophy's demand for autonomy." (85)

"embodies the language of God, who communicates his own truth with that wonderful 'condescension' which mirrors the logic of the Incarnation."(94)

Only by means of a hermeneutic "open to the appeal of metaphysics" can the "absoluteness and the universality" of truth be reconciled with "the historical and cultural conditioning of the formulas which express that truth." One moves from historical and contingent circumstances to a truth that transcends these situations. Although truth is known in history, it is not "confined to time and culture" but "reaches beyond history."[94] (95)

In addition to properly interpreting texts, there is the "more delicate and demanding task" of understanding "revealed truth," i.e., articulating the "*intellectus fidei.*" This calls for a "philosophy of being." Reducing the "truths of faith" to mere "rules of conduct" is "superficial." (97) About the need for, and nature of, "philosophy of being," John Paul II states:

> Set within the *Christian metaphysical* tradition, the *philosophy of being* is a dynamic philosophy which views reality in its *ontological, causal and communicative structures*. It is strong and enduring because it is based upon the *very act of being itself*, which allows a full and comprehensive openness to reality as a whole, surpassing every limit in order to reach the One who brings all things to fulfilment. In theology, which draws its principles from Revelation as a new source of knowledge, this perspective is confirmed by the *intimate relationship which exists between faith and metaphysical reasoning* (emphasis added).(97)

Theology serves primarily proclaiming the faith and catechizing the "mystery of the living God." Philosophy can help elucidate the relation between "truth and life" and "transcendent truth and humanly comprehensible language." This involves "a reciprocity between the theological disciplines and the insights drawn from the various strands of philosophy."(99)

94. About basic concepts retaining their "universal epistemological value," i.e., "the truth of the propositions in which they are expressed," to endure in the Church's tradition, see especially section 96.

Conclusion (100–108)

Basic to *FR* is the relation between faith and philosophy. It impacted the "development of culture," "patterns of personal and social behavior," and "theology and its disciplines." The Pope states,

> I have judged it appropriate and necessary to emphasize the value of philosophy for the understanding of the faith, as well as the limits which philosophy faces when it neglects or rejects the truths of Revelation. The Church remains profoundly convinced that faith and reason "mutually support each other"; each influences the other, as they offer to each other a purifying critique and a stimulus to pursue the search for deeper understanding.(100)

As "science of faith," theology challenges reason to "remain open to the radical newness found in God's revelation" and to glimpse "new vistas of further meanings." This science must recover a correct relationship to philosophy, and the latter in relation to theology.(101) To stress the relevance and range of philosophical thought enhances human dignity and gospel proclamation. Philosophy enables one to discover two "profound needs" that God inscribed in humans: "their capacity to know the truth and their yearning for the ultimate and definitive meaning of life."(102)

With reference to Pope Paul VI's call in 1975 for an "evangelization of culture," John Paul II applied *FR* to thinkers who "explore more comprehensively the dimensions of the true, the good and the beautiful to which the word of God gives access."(103) Because philosophy is "often the only ground for understanding and dialogue with those who do not share our faith," Christian philosophers must be guided by a "deeper understanding given them by the word of God" and provide a "comprehensible and appealing" reflexion for those uninterested in "the renewal of humanity."[95](104)

Theologians pay "special attention to the philosophical implications of the word of God" and must indicate "the speculative and practical breadth of the science of theology." Given the "intimate bond" between theological and philosophical wisdom, they concentrate on the "metaphysical dimension of truth" as a way to "enter into a demanding critical dialogue" with traditional and contemporary philosophy, "whether consonant with the word of God

---

95. "A philosophy in which there shines even a glimmer of the truth of Christ, the one definitive answer to humanity's problems, will provide a potent underpinning for the true and planetary ethics which the world now needs." (104)

or not."(105) **Philosophers** recover "in the flow of an enduringly valid philosophical tradition" the wide range of "wisdom and truth—metaphysical truth included—which is proper to philosophical enquiry," and they do so always striving for truth, "alert to the good which truth contains." **Scientists** concentrate on the "sapiential horizon" knowing that "the search for truth" is "never-ending" and points beyond "to something higher than the immediate object of study, to the questions which give access to Mystery."(106)

Pope John Paul II ends *FR* by appealing to the intercession of Mary, the "Seat of Wisdom" and "a true parable illuminating the reflection contained in these pages" as follows,

> *Just as* the Virgin was called to offer herself entirely as human being and as woman that God's Word might take flesh and come among us, *so too* philosophy is called to offer its rational and critical resources that theology, as the understanding of faith, may be fruitful and creative. And *just as* in giving her assent to Gabriel's Word, Mary lost nothing of her true humanity and freedom, *so too* when philosophy heeds the summons of the Gospel's truth its autonomy is in no way impaired. Indeed, it is then that philosophy sees all its enquiries rise to their highest expression. . . . In her they saw a lucid image of true philosophy and they were convinced of the need to *philosophari* (philosophize) in Mary (emphasis added).(108)

Threefold Assessment

Western culture experienced three major *religious* crises. **First**, when Hellenistic-Roman culture, affected by Platonic/Aristotelian ideas of "truth" and "reality," was threatened by a debilitating scepticism, though somewhat restrained by a certainty inherent in the Good News,[96] but the latter, though radical, struggled with ways of thinking and behaving shaped by a pagan Constantinian culture. About a millennium later, in response to a spreading barbarism and increasing conflicts between Christian, Jewish and Muslim faiths, T. Aquinas developed his masterful *religious synthesis* of God's Word revelation with Greek notions of "truth" and "reality."

Second, a major *religious* crisis within Western Christianity was triggered by various factors: (a) disintegration of imperial Christendom, (b)

---

96. Cf. Rodney Stark, *The Rise of Christianity: A Sociologist Reconsiders History.* Princeton, 1996).

William of Ockham's nominalism and inherent rejection of "method" and "truth" proposed by Aquinas, (c) the rise of Early Humanism, (d) negative effects of the Protestant Reformation, and (e) the rise and effects of scepticism in leading academies. In response to this major *religious* crisis in Europe, the four movements of Humanism, Renaissance, Reformation (Luther, Calvin) and Rationalism (Descartes) arose.[97]

About three centuries later, in response to a crisis due to an inflated "reason" and deflated "faith," the RCC addressed the nature of, and relation between, faith and reason, theology and philosophy, and church and culture. In response, *AP* (1879) was adopted to help Roman Catholic thinkers and teachers to do justice to both faith and reason

Third, a pressing problem in mainly Western culture was triggered by a deepening relativism in *atheistic secularism* and a *postmodernism* that threatened both "reason" and "faith." In response, the RCC published *HG* (1950) and *FR* (1998).[98] Remarkable about *FR* is its detailed elaboration on the way *AP* talked about the scholastic "method" of thinking and way of acting in daily life that Aquinas proposed more than seven centuries earlier.

Pervasive in *AP*, *HG* and *FR* are *terms* like "truth," "revelation," "wisdom," "God," "speculation," "metaphysics," "being," "incarnation," "analogy," "harmony" and "assent," and *topics* like "faith and reason," "theology and philosophy," "intellect and will," "natural and supernatural." Each one of these presupposes, and refers to, all the others. All three encyclicals reflect an accommodational view of both "reason and faith" and "philosophy and theology."

Two Wings and One Body

The two wings of "faith" and "reason," or disciplines of "theology" and "philosophy," mentioned at the beginning of *FR*,[99] are central to what keeps the

---

97. A Membership in the Roman Catholic Church did not affect Descartes in his rationalistic thinking. When the Reformed Synod (1618/9) met in Dordrecht, the Netherlands, Descartes—still a young man—talked with some school teachers in that city about the need for new, i.e., rationalist, ideas and methods in teaching children and young people.

98. This situation is not unrelated to the sudden decline of Christian faith in Western culture and its phenomenal expansion in non-Western regions of the world.

99. George Vandervelde, "Will the Wings of Faith and Reason Support Us?," a review in *Christian Courier* (December 11, 1998) 13. Vandervelde (1940–2007), a *reformational* scholar in theology, taught at the Institute for Christian Studies (ICS) in Toronto. As an expert in

"bird," or body of truth, airborne within the Christian community caught in the vortex of perilous *religious* crisis.

Although it is used in all three encyclicals, especially in *FR*, the precise meaning of "reason" and "faith" is not immediately clear. Although they influence each other, faith is not the same as, but other than, reason, and the latter is not the same as, but other than, the former. While reason refers to what is basic, natural and true, faith points to something ultimate, supernatural and crowning.

In addition to "reason" and "faith," "desire" also is basic to knowing and believing, moving from natural to supernatural, searching for truth and adoring what is divine, starting with autonomy and ending with dependence. Reason and faith are *similar* in that they act as "wings" that uphold the "body" of humanity and truth. They are *dissimilar* in that reason is foundational for faith—not *chronologically* in the sense of earlier-later, but *essentially* in the sense of source and vision, knowledge and *sapientia*, wisdom and judgment.[100]

The relation between them is one of rapport and compatibility. This congruence has its origin in mainly Aristotelian thinking, and it was adopted by Aquinas in his concept of these two terms and their interrelationships. It assumes Plato's and Aristotle's anthropology with its inbuilt "faculty psychology," i.e., a "soul" with three faculties of intellect, will and feeling. Being most important, the *intellect* helps humans avoid error and walk on the road of truth.[101] It guides the human *will* and, by means of its decisions, human *feelings*. In this way, human *will* moves towards the *good* and refrains from *evil*. Furthermore, for Aristotle the human soul is the (higher) *form* that actualizes the human body as (lower) *matter*.

"Reason" focuses on the first principles of philosophy and of "natural theology." Though self-sufficient, the intellect needs the help of faith, divine revelation and Christian theology. The relation between *reason* and *faith* is one of a continuum, and, consequently, their difference is one of degree, not

---

Roman Catholic thinking, he met with John Paul II in Rome and had extensive discussions with Joseph Ratzinger, who as Benedict XVI succeeded John Paul II and retired as Pope in 2013. (Vandervelde's mentor was G. C. Berkouwer, at the Free University in Amsterdam, one of the only two Dutch *Protestant* theologians—the other one was Heiko A. Oberman—invited to attend Vatican Council II, 1962.

100. Wisdom enables one to make three kinds of judgments: spiritual, philosophical, based on intellect, and, based on Revelation, theological. Cf. *FR* (43).

101. In a *scholastic* way, "truth" points to something intellectual, or speculative, and to something other than the Greek intellect (2 Thess. 2:1–12). Cf. *Fides et Ratio* (53).

kind: it is *structural*, not *directional* (or *religious*).[102] As a result, the distinction between "theology" and "faith" is no longer clear—in fact, it becomes quite confusing.

In a scholastic way, the RCC emphasizes the necessity of reason and philosophy to prepare humans for God's supernatural revelation and Christian faith. Inseparable from this approach is the importance of "apologetics" in Roman Catholic faith traditions in order both to establish contact with non-Christians and to defend Christian faith.

The relation between "reason" and "faith" parallels that of "philosophy" and "theology." In both instances, "reason" and "philosophy" refer to what is human, natural and autonomous,[103] and "faith" and "Christian theology" indicate what is revelational, supernatural and heteronomous.

Scholastic "ontology" and "anthropology" affected not only the disciplines of philosophy and theology, but also various pedagogical, curricular and cultural issues in Christian scholarship and all (higher) education. Of the three stances cited in *FR*—two of which are *bad* in that they prevent the *"body* of truth" from flying, and one is *good* in that it enables the *"body* of truth" to soar. The three stances, are: (i) "philosophy" independent of theology, (ii) "theology" as "Christian philosophy" independent of philosophy, and (iii) "philosophy as handmaiden of theology" (*ancilla theologia*).[104] The stance *assumes* that "reason" and "philosophy" indicate that what is "Christian" is *faith* based on *supernatural* revelation. In other words, theology's two wings of "reason" and "faith"[105] keep the *body* of universal truth aloft. This is the RCC's response to a crisis created by the twin dangers of "intellectualism" and "fideism."

More elemental than the "two wings" (reason and faith) is the "body" (bird) to which the wings are attached. The nature of this "body" is such that the two wings are not tangential, but essential, even integral, to the "body of truth." Given the weight of the "body," the two wings must flutter rapidly and in harmony to keep the body of truth towering above the cacophony of a confused, and confusing, world. In this respect, the mind-set of Aquinas is pervasive in the three encyclicals listed above, especially in *FR*.

---

102. For details, see Chapters 9 and 10 above.
103. Cf. *FR* (48).
104. See *FR* (74).
105. Cf. *FR* (76).

Analogy of Being

The backbone of the *body* of truth consists of a *metaphysics*, an "autonomous"[106] intellectual speculation centered on *being-as-such*, on something the Creator and creation have in common. For philosophers and theologians (83), "metaphysics" (going beyond nature) is not a luxury, but a necessity, not an option, but an obligation. Reason, in the service of faith, probes, or pries, into understanding what non-humans, humans, and God share in their essence. Reason in the sense of knowing "being" is the handmaiden of faith.

The notion of "analogy of being" (*analogia entis*) is basic to the ontology of Aquinas.[107] The truth of the relation between Creator and creation and of the Word-Incarnate is assumed and demonstrated in the mystery of the Eucharist (*FR*, 80), in the role of the RCC in the world, including that of the Pope as Christ's vicar and shepherd of God's people, also in Christian scholarship, teaching and education. It is fundamental in the Roman Catholic view of "truth" and "reality." It is basic to such *terms* as "assent," "reason," "faith," "analogy," "truth," "being," "substance"; *topics* such as "faculty psychology" and the notion of "adopting from and adapting to"; *relations* such as "natural and supernatural," "reason and faith," "philosophy and theology," "culture and church"; and *methods* used in introductory philosophy courses, in apologetics and in ways to incorporate non-Christian ideas.[108]

Educational Strategy

A papal messenger, Malespine, reported in 1598 to the RCC that the Calvinist "heresy" within only a few decades had become sufficiently strong in Poland to threaten the RCC there. A bishop from Krakow informed the pope that, as in other West European countries, Poland also was becoming a victim of the Reformation started by John Calvin in Geneva.

In response to the threat of the Protestant Reformation in Poland, the Pope sent hundreds of Jesuit priests and educators, immersed in the ideas and methods of Aquinas, to Poland in order to regain control over all, par-

---

106. In an Aquinian, not modern rationalist and secularist, sense. Cf. Arvin Vos (1985).

107. Although for different reasons, related to the role of creational revelation, this theory is rejected by neo-Calvinist and Barthian thinkers.

108. In distinction from *terms, themes, relationships* and *methods* in rationalism, existentialism, phenomenology, pragmatism, analytical-language philosophy, and postmodernism in Western culture, as well as from thought-patterns indigenous to non-Western cultures.

ticularly higher, education, to prevent the demise of Roman Catholicism there. This tactically wise strategy was so successful that within a generation the Genevan Reformation was halted in Poland and the demise of the RCC there averted.[109]

Inherent in the three encyclicals is an *accommodated* anthropology that complicates the meaning of "faith life" and "theology." It calls for a better view of the disciplines of philosophy and theology and a clearer sense of the difference between Christian and non-Christian thinking, educating and impacting society and culture. All three Popes stressed the human need for (*super*natural) revelation, including the importance of the relation between the first Adam and Christ as second Adam (*FR*, 60) and the work of the Holy Spirit in the life of Christians.[110]

The crises in modern culture compelled the RCC before the twenty-first century to maintain its traditional *religious* dualism and related *scholastic* notion of truth and education.[111] In doing this, it continued to mitigate the depth of human rebellion against God's Word by saying that humans are "wounded" and "weakened" beings, who live in error, not defiance and rebellion. It thinks of faith's "content" primarily in terms of truths, or propositions, which humans assent to, and believes that the mystery of the incarnate Word somehow affects how humans think about the relation between reason and faith.

The discussion about the difference between classic *accommodational* thinking in the tradition of the RCC and simpler, but more 'radical,' *reformational* thinking in some Reformed and Presbyterian circles will continue to receive considerable attention. The focus of that dialogue, or debate, will include the nature of faith and theology, the structure of created reality, and

109. For details, see A. A. van Schelven, "Polen," in his (posthumous) publication in 1965 on the history of Calvinism, pp. 7–62, especially 8, 15–21, 43–44, 61. For an example of a similar strategy Pope John Paul II used in the publication, as late as 1989, by the Vatican's Congregation for the Doctrine of Faith of "an oath of fidelity to all church teachings" to be taken by "all newly appointed professors of theology or philosophical ethics at Catholic colleges and universities." For details, see Debra E. Blum, "Vatican Publishes Oath of Fidelity to Church Teachings to Be Taken by Theology Professors at Catholic Colleges," in *The Chronicle of Higher Education*, A 13–14, March 15, 1989.

110. After Vatican II, much has been written about the need for a more biblical approach in various emphases and customs in the Roman Catholic Church. For details, see G. C. Berkouwer.

111. Although the Roman Catholic Church does not prescribe a particular philosophy, it does require that the method (and philosophy) of T. Aquinas be taught and adhered to. For details, see *FR* (50 n. 35); as well as 76, 78, 79 and 83).

the role of philosophy, principles and practices in all, especially higher, education in all areas of life in an exponentially shrinking world community with diverse societies and cultures.

We turn to the next four chapters for a close look at the subtlety, complexity and importance of specific issues related to believing and thinking, faith and philosophy, preaching and educating in a classic (Christian) Reformed educational community in the USA.

CHAPTER FIFTEEN

Calvin Theological Seminary

The encyclicals *Aeterni Patris* of Leo XIII (1879), *Humani Generis* of Pius XII (1950), and *Fides et Ratio* of John Paul II (1998) indicate the Roman Catholic reliance on the philosophy and method of Thomas Aquinas (1225–1274). His influence on Christian higher education, including Reformed and Presbyterian ideas about philosophy and theology, has been subtle and formidable.

Between *Aeterni Patris* in 1879—one year before A. Kuyper opened the Free University in Amsterdam—and *Fides et Ratio* in 1998, Calvin Theological Seminary (CTS) and Calvin College (CC) incorporated ideas about reason and philosophy, faith and theology, and their interrelationships into their teaching that significantly contributed to the nature of "Reformed Epistemology" (RE).

Two philosophical traditions played a significant role at CTS and CC. The first one was the influence of Herman Bavinck's scholastic views of "reality" and "truth"—resembling the essence of "Scottish Common Sense" philosophy—on theology at CTS (since 1876) and philosophy at CC (since the 1930s) through W. Harry Jellema and Henry J. Stob (who in 1954 moved to CTS to teach moral philosophy). The second influence came via Nicholas Wolterstorff and Alvin Plantinga (students of Jellema), who combined Anglo-American linguistic-analytic philosophy with "liberal arts" thinking at CC and who, in the 1980s, founded[1] Reformed Epistemology with its view of both "knowledge" and "reality."

---

1. With two Anglo-American philosopher co-founders, W. P. Alston at Syracuse University, and G. I. Mavrodes at the University of Michigan.

These two fledgling institutions developed views about reason and faith, philosophy and theology, metaphysics and knowledge, reality and truth, which significantly shaped Christian Reformed higher education, as will be indicated in the next three chapters.

After World War I and II, the Christian Reformed community struggled to determine its place in the USA and, since the 1950s, in Canada. This scramble, affected by worldview and cultural differences, caused considerable debate, disagreement, even some conflict, between a more culture-avoiding and a more culture-engaging approach.[2] This difference was, in subtle and complex ways, directly related to the distinction between, for example, special and general revelation, saving and common grace, and the vertical relation to God and the horizontal relation to the world. It affected the editorial policies, debates and disagreements of the two prominent Christian Reformed journals for many years: *Torch & Trumpet (Reformed Outlook)* and *The Calvin Forum (The Reformed Journal)*.[3]

Foppe M. ten Hoor (1855–1934)

Foppe M. ten Hoor contributed to this debate. In the Netherlands, he was a Secessionist (1834) pastor since 1864 and opposed the notion of a *national* Reformed (State) Church. Emigrating in 1896 to the USA, he served four years as a pastor in a Christian Reformed Church in Grand Rapids. From 1900 to 1924, he taught at CTS a course on Reformed Dogmatics, based on Bavinck's *Gereformeerde Dogmatiek*, I-IV.[4] Already in the Netherlands, he opposed Kuyper's view of Christian higher education, especially his explanation of "theology" as described in his monumental *Encyclopaedie der Heilige Godgeleerdheid*, I-III.

He believed that theologians are preachers and that preachers are theo-

---

2. After World War II, thousands of neo-Kuyperians migrated from the Netherlands to Canada and some to the USA and joined the Christian Reformed community. This influx of neo-Kuyperian Christians resulted in a divergence within the North American Christian Reformed community, especially in education, labor unions, citizenship, agriculture and business.

3. James D. Bratt and Ronald A. Wells, *The Best of The Reformed Journal* 2011: xiii-xvii (Jon Pott's "Publisher's Note") and 1–9 ("Introduction").

4. Bavinck taught Reformed Dogmatics at the Secessionist Seminary in Kampen, which his father had founded, and where ten Hoor had studied theology.

logians.[5] To be a theologian is ecclesiastical, not something academic.[6] To teach theology is the responsibility of the church as an organized "institution," not of some nebulous, or non-ecclesiastical, "organism," like Kuyper's Free University.[7] The "object" of theology is Scripture, i.e., God's written revelation. Theology is not some academic study of faith life and religion. It focuses on God's written Word as understood by the instituted church, not within a state, or some society-controlled, institution. Theology is not some intra-mundane discipline: although *in* the world, it is not *of* the world.

As professor of Reformed Dogmatics at CTS for twenty-four years, ten Hoor rejected Kuyper's distinction between human *ectypal* and divine *archetypal* revelation in Kuyper's anthropology and understanding of knowledge, encyclopedia and academic discipline.[8] Not even in a formal sense is theology a human science. There is no difference between "faith life" and "theology": being a theologian and being a Christian are interchangeable.

His anti-Kuyperian stance was clear also in his disagreement with Bavinck's move in 1902 from the Theological Seminary to the Free University. As a Christian Reformed pastor and theology professor for almost three decades (1896–1924), ten Hoor nudged many Christian Reformed pastors and teachers to reject Kuyper's understanding of "church" as a non-ecclesiastical "organism" and of "theology" as a discipline in a university department.

His pietist slant affected his critical, even negative, attitude to culture and passion so as to regard "theological" and "Christian" as being interchangeable.[9] Scripture is basic for theology, not the academy.[10] Theology

5. For details about ten Hoor's views, see R. H. Bremmer (1961): 46–53 and 393–424.

6. F. ten Hoor appealed to J. Calvin's idea that teaching is the fourth ecclesiastical office, in addition to those of elder, deacon and pastor/preacher.

7. He rejected Kuyper's notion of "sphere sovereignty" as described in his Opening Address of the Free University in 1880.

8. For details, see VanderStelt (1973): 178–190.

9. About the complicated political, ecclesiastical and educational structure of the Dutch "ordo duplex" about the role and place of theology in state universities and denominational seminaries, see Vroom (1997): 210–231. For more on Christian Reformed clergy and theologians who perpetuated ten Hoor's view of theology and resisted Kuyper's ideas about Christian higher education, see Rev. Steen and three Masselink preachers and teachers.

10. Ten Hoor's opposition to Kuyper's and Bavinck's ideas about Christian scholarship and higher education influenced the Christian Reformed Church to view Calvin College as a "denominational" school of Christian higher education, unlike Dordt College in Iowa, Trinity Christian College in Illinois, Kuyper College in Michigan, The King's University in Alberta, Redeemer University College in Ontario, and the Institute for Christian Studies in Ontario— each in its own way bound by God's Word, yet free from *ecclesiastical* control. For details, see R. VanderVennen (2008).

should not be taught, or studied, in some university. It must be offered, and controlled, in a distinct theological seminary.

Ironically, however, as will be indicated below, ten Hoor advocated not only a form of *pietism*, but also a form of *scholasticism* during his long teaching career as professor of Reformed Dogmatics at CTS, and through his many students as preachers and teachers in the CRC in the USA.

Influence of H. Bavinck (1854–1921)

The philosophical and theological impact of Bavinck on the CRC and its distinct educational tradition has been significant, even more important than that of Kuyper.[11] His thinking influenced the theology of L. Berkhof[12] and the thought-patterns of Henry J. Stob at CTS, and, either directly or indirectly, affected crucial ideas in such leading thinkers at CC as, for example, W. Harry Jellema in philosophy, C. Jaarsma in education, and N. Wolterstorff and A. Plantinga in epistemology, as will be indicated in chapters 17–18 below.

Bavinck's inaugural lecture at the Theological Seminary in Kampen, in 1882, centered on "The Science of Sacred Theology," and his inaugural at the Free University in Amsterdam in 1902 focused on "Religion and Theology." In 1908/9, he gave his L. P. Stone Lectures on "Philosophy and Revelation" at Princeton Theological Seminary and lectured on that topic in seven other places in the USA.[13]

---

11. For details about Bavinck and Kuyper, see Chapters 4 and 5. Since the close of the twentieth and start of the twenty-first century—with a decline in the CRC's *reforming* role in society in especially the USA, Kuyper's vision is seemingly starting to replace, at least restrict, ten Hoor's *pietist* and *scholastic* use of Bavinck's approach.

12. Author of *Systematic Theology* (hereafter *ST*), (1938) (5th printing, 1953). A highly condensed version of this 784-page magnum opus was used for many decades as a manual in most Christian (Reformed) high schools in the USA. A condensed version of *ST* was used as a prescribed textbook (*Manual of Reformed Doctrine*) at CC. Since 1938, the uncondensed text of *ST* was a must-study about Reformed doctrine at CTS and a main source for *ecclesiastical* examination for all who wanted to be preachers/pastors in the Christian Reformed Church.

13. Published in 1909 by Longmans, Green, and Co, and reprinted by Baker Book House Company, Grand Rapids, 1979. Chapters I-VII, delivered at Princeton Theological Seminary, focus on philosophy of revelation and revelation's relation to philosophy, nature, history, religion, and Christianity. Chapters VIII-X deal with revelation's relation to religious experience, culture and the future, and were delivered in Grand Rapids and Holland, Michigan, and in Chicago, Louisville, Brunswick and Paterson, NJ, and New York.

For more than a century, his *Gereformeerde Dogmatiek*, I-IV, 1895–1901,[14] played a significant role in Christian Reformed higher education, especially with respect to methodological issues related to the nature of truth, the role of philosophy and the discipline of theology.

He vigorously opposed pietism and, like Kuyper, was deeply interested in societal and cultural matters, philosophical issues in anthropology, particularly knowledge and psychology, and challenges in education and pedagogy. His primary focus from 1880 to 1902 at the Theological Seminary centered mostly on ecclesiastical and theological issues, but that changed after he moved to the Free University. From 1902 until his death in 1921, he deepened and broadened his interest in philosophical issues related to societal, cultural matters. As a member of the Upper Chamber, he dealt with many complex issues in the Dutch government. Kuyper concentrated on detailed political issues, especially as Prime Minister; Bavinck focused less on detailed church issues and more on larger social, political, cultural and general renewal. As an irenic and ecumenical thinker, he emphasized authentic Christian living in a restless world and the importance of testifying in one's everyday life to the world's Savior.

One of his top students from 1911 to 1914 was D. H. T. Vollenhoven,[15] who continued his studies at the Free University until 1918, chiefly in philosophy under the supervision of professor G. Geesink.[16] Vollenhoven's close friend at the Free University was H. Dooyeweerd, a student in jurisprudence and legal theory.[17] The parents of Vollenhoven and Dooyeweerd were strong supporters of Kuyper's distinct confessional stance, cultural vision and academic endeavors. They encouraged their sons to familiarize themselves with the need for an ongoing reformation (*doorgaande reformatie*) in all of life, not only in one's ecclesiastical life.

Although they appreciated the well-intended *religious* basis of the phi-

14. 2nd printing, 1906–1911; 5th printing,1995; English translation, 2008.

15. During these three years (1911–1914), S. Volbeda studied at the Free University. For details, see below.

16. About Vollenhoven's doctoral dissertation on a theistic critique of a modern philosophy of mathematics, see Chapter 8. G .H. J. W. J. Geesink (1854–1929) was an eloquent preacher and gifted professor of theology, logic, epistemology, history of philosophy and psychology and the author of *Van's Heeren Ordinantien* (*About the Lord's Ordinances*) *Vol. I-IV*. Regarding scholastic elements in his philosophy and way of thinking, see A. Tol and John H. Kok 2005.

17. Contrary to a mistaken notion in North American "evangelical" circles, Dooyeweerd never studied theology, nor was he ever a pastor. He wanted a "Christian," not "a theological," philosophy, anthropology, jurisprudence, etc.

losophy taught at the Free University, they began to question certain basic anthropological issues in the views of Bavinck, G. Geesink and other professors. They sensed an incongruence between the laudable *religious* intent and the actual content of what their professors taught. As a result, they started to question certain philosophical assumptions in traditional Reformed thinking. Their growing unease centered mainly on the meaning of being human, image of God, truth, knowledge, faith and reason. In philosophy and theology, they sensed a tendency to fossilize certain thought- and act-patterns. Raised in a traditional Reformed environment, they sensed the prevalence of ideas and customs that are really at odds with the heart, or core, of covenant-living, also in one's thinking. They sensed, and rejected, any dualism in anthropology, and the danger of scholastic thinking in areas of their interest. Hence, in their academic activities, they pressed for a scripturally directed, not biblicistic, way of thinking about created reality and the unique role of humans in it.

Vollenhoven and Dooyeweerd liked Bavinck's focus on the triune God, the uniqueness of creation, God's life-giving laws, his revelation to and covenant with humans, human rejection of his law of love, and his call to love Him as their Maker and live in a *coram Deo* manner. In the 1920s and 1930s, they went public in their attempts to reform(ulate) certain traditional assumptions in ontology, anthropology and epistemology, and to react to a negative response of mainly preachers and theologians in Reformed (Gereformeerde) circles. Their rejection of lingering scholastic ideas in Bavinck (and Kuyper) centered on the meaning of such traditional terms as "truth," "reality," "reason," "causality," "faith" and "soul-body" dualism.[18]

As Rector Magnificus (Provost) of the Free University, Bavinck had given a public lecture on "Christian Worldview" (Christelijke wereldbeschouwing).[19] In three carefully structured and interrelated parts, which reflect his uncritical acceptance of Greek "faculty psychology," he indicated the three ways humans think of the relation between the Creator and created reality: Part I, "Thinking and Being" (Denken en Zijn), Part II "Being and Becoming" (Zijn en Worden) and Part III "Becoming and Acting" (Worden en Handelen). In **Parts I and II,** he focused on the *epistemic* harmony be-

18. One could add "faculty psychology," subjective-objective, and individual-universal. For details about Bavinck, see R. H. Bremmer, *Bavinck als Dogmaticus,* (1961), especially 46–54 about his disagreement with ten Hoor's opposition to Kuyper's idea of "theology;" also, *Herman Bavinck en zijn Tijdgenoten,* (1966), notably 194–198, 249–252, and 263.

19. *Christian Worldview,* 1904, published by Bos in Kampen; 2nd rev. edition, (1913) used here; 3rd ed. (1929).

tween "subject" and "object" and *ontic* harmony between "thinking" and "being" (cf. Apostles Creed, article 1, about God as the foundation of all knowledge and science).[20] In **Part III**, centered on "Becoming and Acting," he focused on "ethos" (ethics), not on "physis" (nature). Humans are not free to do anything they want, but free to act "morally," i.e., to behave according to the norms of "the true, the good, and the beautiful."[21] Truth is "objective" in the sense of "independent" of humans. Near the end of this public lecture, Bavinck stated,

> . . . just as the wisdom of God became flesh in Christ, so truth ought also to become part of us, in the way of freedom it must become our own personal and spiritual possession, through a living and authentic faith it must be turned into an integral part of our own thinking and acting, and then propagated beyond us, until the earth is full of the knowledge of the Lord. That is what the Reformation wanted.[22]

The impact of Bavinck's logically articulated dogmatics on Christian Reformed thinking has been greater than Kuyper's less carefully formulated dogmatics. As to his way of thinking in *De Gereformeerde Dogmatiek* (*GD*), volumes II-IV presuppose the philosophical principles he described in *GD* I. After his detailed description of the "name," "concept," "encyclopedic place," "method," "structure" and "history" of dogmatics, Bavinck wrote 411 pages to explain the basic principles incorporated in theological dogmatics.

20. Bavinck (1913): 21. For details about "thinking" and "being," especially the relation between subject and object, humans and the world, ideas in God and in humans, see 15–36, esp. 27–29, as well as the statement on 33: "The intelligible in things is the content of our intellect. Both, being and knowing, have their ratio in the Word, through which God created all things" ("Het intelligibele in de dingen is de inhoud van ons intellect. Beide, het zijn en het kennen, hebben hun ratio in het Woord, waardoor God alle dingen schiep.") For details about "Thinking and Being," see Chapter 4.

21. Bavinck (1913): 69–106, especially 69–71. According to Bavinck, Kant's mistake was to make what is moral the basis for religion and theology, rather than making religion and theology the basis for morality (cf. 74).

22. Bavinck (1913): 106 ("Maar gelijk de wijsheid Gods in Christus vleesch geworden is, zoo behoort de waarheid ook in ons in te gaan, zij moet in de weg der vrijheid ons eigen persoonlijk en geestelijk eigendom worden; door een levend en waarachtig geloof moet zij in een bestanddeel van ons eigen denken en handelen worden omgezet, en dan buiten ons worden verbreid, totdat de aarde vol is van de kennis des Heeren. Dat heeft de Reformatie gewild.") Rejecting autonomy and anarchy and recommending theonomy, God's truth is not something "purely supernatural and transcendent above us," but in the way of freedom is our personal possession (108).

Three key principles guided Bavinck in his thinking: (a) "general principles" in **science** (cf. rationalism, empiricism, realism) and **religion** (cf. essence, seat, origin); (b) "external principles" (cf. revelation, nature, Scripture); (c) "internal principles" about four issues: (i) meaning, (ii) four methods of "historical-apologetic," "speculative," "religious-empirical," and "ethical-psychological," (iii) faith and its basis, and (iv) faith and theology.[23]

These three principles shaped Bavinck's discussion of "God" in GD II, 1897, in some 369 pages, which W. Hendriksen in 1951 edited, translated and published as *The Doctrine of God*.[24] It has been a passion in Christian Reformed theological and educational circles to understand the philosophical features in Bavinck's theology. Perhaps this may account for the puzzling *reason*-slanted title *Our Reasonable Faith*, given in 1955, to H. Zylstra's translation from Dutch into English of Bavinck's *Magnalia Dei* (God's wonderful, marvelous or praiseworthy deeds), 1909, a *doxological* synopsis of *GD, I-IV*.[25]

Bavinck's chief interests as professor and close colleague of Kuyper at the Free University from 1902 until his death in 1921 were not dogmatics and related issues in theology, but specific issues in, for example, anthropology, philosophy of revelation, education, politics, warfare, culture, young people and amusement, and ecumenical relations—within the context of God's redemptive call to a fallen and struggling humanity and to resist, through the Holy Spirit, further *religious* secularizing of society and civilization.[26]

As to Bavinck's legacy in Christian Reformed circles, two events at CTS and CC in 2008 are noteworthy. A century after Bavinck delivered his L. P. Stone Lectures in Princeton, under the auspices of the Dutch Reformed Translation Society and general editorship of J. Bolt at CTS, Bavinck's *Essays*

23. In a sense where Bavinck **ended** his discussion of basic principles in dogmatics, my study **begins**.

24. William Hendriksen (1900–1965) was born in the Netherlands, migrated to the USA in 1911, graduated from Calvin College in 1924, Calvin Theological Seminary in 1927, and Princeton Theological Seminary in 1948 with a Ph.D. After serving in four large Christian Reformed congregations in Michigan, he taught New Testament at CTS from 1943 to 1952.

25. Henry Zylstra (1956), professor of English at Calvin College, wrote in the Preface of his translation of Bavinck's book: "*Our Reasonable Faith* is less technical, less exclusively professional, more popularly intended than the *Dogmatics*, and is more fully supported by Scriptural reference and annotation, but it is, like the larger work, a book of basic Christian dogma. It presents clearly and in fine perspective the fundamental doctrines of Biblical teaching" (p. 6).

26. One of Bavinck's last reports in 1920/1 to the Synod of the Gereformeerde Kerk focused on young people, entertainment, and culture. His balanced approach on these practical issues was not reflected in a report in 1926 at the Synod of the Christian Reformed Church in the USA about entertainment related to card-playing, dancing and theater attendance.

on Religion, Science, and Society was published in English, together with the first English translation of his *GD*, I-IV.[27]

Later in that same year, a three-day international conference, organized by CTS, met at CC, under the general (laudatory) theme of "A Pearl and a Leaven: Herman Bavinck for the Twenty-First Century." Of the many presentations at this academic commemorative event, four focused either completely, or in part, on philosophical matters: (i) D. Sytsma, "Herman Bavinck's Thomist Epistemology: The Argument and Sources of Bavinck's *Principia* of Science"; (ii) T. G. Van Raalte, "*Unleavened Morality?* Herman Bavinck's Contribution to Natural Law Debate"; (iii) J. S. Hocking, "Herman Bavinck's Doctrine of Revelation: Beyond Dogmatism and Relativism"; and (iv) Nicholas Wolterstorff, "Herman Bavinck and Reformed Epistemology."

Samuel Volbeda (1881–1953)[28]

In 1915, one year after he received his Ph.D. from the Free University in Amsterdam for his dissertation on "De intuitieve philosophie van James McCosh,"[29] S. Volbeda gave his inaugural lecture at CTS on "Het wezen der religie" (The essence of religion). He dealt with a fundamental issue in Bavinck's (and McCosh's) scholastic thinking about a philosophical core issue in Reformed (and Presbyterian) theological thinking at that time, at least in principle, operative at CTS and CC (and Princeton Theological Seminary).

27. Published by Baker Academic, with John Bolt as editor. Harry Boonstra and Gerrit Scheeres translated Bavinck's *Essays*. Parts of *GD*, IV were edited and translated by John Bolt and published by Baker Books as H. Bavinck, *The Last Things: Hope for This World and the Next*, 1996.

28. He graduated in "literature" at the (Christian Reformed) Theological School in Grand Rapids (1901) and in "theology" at this School (1904), served as pastor in two churches (1904–1911), obtained his Th.D. from the Free University (1914), and taught at CTS for *thirty-eight* years: in Church History (1914–1926) and Practical Theology (1926–1952), and served as President of CTS (1944–1952). For details, see Peter De Klerk 1985: 39.1–39.15.

29. James McCosh (1811–1894) studied at the Universities of Glasgow and Edinburgh, was a Presbyterian pastor for sixteen years in Scotland, taught philosophy for sixteen years at Queen's College in Belfast, was president and professor of philosophy at Princeton College, NJ, USA (1866–1888). At the age of eighty-two, he was the *only* USA philosopher to speak at the *first* World Exposition in Chicago in 1893. His Scottish "Common Sense" philosophy (cf. T. Reid's philosophy of Realism, about which N. Wolterstorff published a major study in 2002 (for details, see Chapter 17). In many ways, Bavinck's philosophy resembled that of T. Reid and J. McCosh (cf. Vander Stelt 1978: 83–89).

Instead of talking about "essence" and "religion" as "two metaphysical disparate entities, between which a relation exists"(11–12),[30] Volbeda focused on "religion" not just as a concept but as a reality. To establish a concept of "religion" is prerequisite to "arrive at the logical fixation of its essence. After all, essence and concept are correlates. The essence is the ontological content of the concept, and the concept is the dianoëtic reproduction of the essence."[31] About "religion" as an "objective ontological given," he states that it is

> . . . a reality in a genuinely essential sense, which exists *for us* admittedly only if through logical assimilation it has become our spiritual possession. . . . a reality in a truly essential sense, which in the very modality of the knowledge we have obtained about it, provides us with the guarantee of its independent existence."[32]

Since "religion" is the "gate" for the cosmos to reach for the Eternal, the "ladder" by which God's handiwork climbs to "God's never-dying light," it must be "amenable" for "inversion" in terms of "logicality."[33] The secret of such a "transition" is using the proper "method." As elsewhere, also in "religion" the goal is not "speculation," but "logical reproduction of objective reality." The method used should not be the medieval "deductive" one, however, but the Baconian empirical "inductive" one.[34]

A crucial feature of a "Christian Method" is *rebirth* (*palingenesis*). The difference between "belief and unbelief" consists of the difference between "regeneration" and being "dead in sin." Those who take "rebirth" seriously "tremble before God's Word." They are not satisfied with "religion as such"

---

30. According to R. Harms, archivist at CTS and CC, Volbeda's inaugural lecture has—to his and my surprise—not been translated into English. For the Dutch passages I translated and cited, see the footnotes for page number(s).

31. Volbeda (1915): 12: ". . . de logische fixeering van haar wezen te geraken. Wezen en begrip zijn toch correlata. Het wezen is de ontologische inhoud van het begrip en het begrip is de dianoetische reproductie van het wezen."

32. Volbeda (1915): 12. ". . . het objectief ontologisch gegeven . . . een realiteit in zeer wezenlijken zin, die weliswaar *voor ons* eerst bestaat als zij door logische assimileering ons geestelijk eigendom is geworden, maar die in de modaliteit van de kennis die wij van haar hebben verkregen de garantie van haar zelfstandig bestaan ons aanbiedt."

33. Volbeda (1915): 13.

34. For details, see Volbeda (1915): 13–15. Volbeda rejects I. Kant's idea that "objective reality" (Ding an sich) depends on "knowledge acquiring spirit" (kennis nemendes geest) of humans (Ding fur uns).

in their own soul and in that of others, when they brush aside "the logically designated source of knowledge for the object of their investigation."[35]

Another feature of Volbeda's "Christian Method" is *Scripture* as God's special revelation. It has a "central and controlling place" in the life of Christians, not as a "lexicon" to consult when knowledge is "insufficient," but as a "lamp" for our feet "to clarify what is dark." Religion has to do with the relationships of both humans to God and of God to the life of humans. Because religion is "objectively" lost, out of order (*ongereede*) and "subjectively" distorted (*verstoord*), humans have lost their ability to perceive and judge in a reliable way.[36]

The "religious, or, if you will, theological life- and world-view Scripture provides for us," is "impossible for pseudo-religions to evaluate in their own light, which is darkness." Through faith, Christians learn five things from Scripture:

> *what* religion is according to its idea, as determined in God's counsel according to the good pleasure of his will; *what* it was according to the reality of creation, when its idea in the beginning was changed to fellowship with almighty God and sparkled in the splendor of his glory; *what* it became, when the ethical power of sin, which Satan projected in the world of the human spirit, threw itself on her and corrupted her; *what* remained of it beyond the world of palingenesis on the basis of an indestructible peculiarity of human nature under the basking of God's common grace and to the extent these remnants can make an appeal to the name of religion; and, finally, *what* it becomes through the restorative grace of our Lord Jesus Christ, the Son of God. (emphasis added)[37]

35. " . . . de logisch aangewezen kenbron voor het voorwerp van hun onderzoek voorfbijgaan." (16)

36. All they can do is moralistically rely on statistically analyzed ever-changing situations, without a "normative idea" of religion. What is empirically best and ideally normative are as far apart as "the west is removed from the East." See 17 and 18.

37. "Wat de religie is naar haar idee, zoals als die in Gods Raad is gefixeerd naar het welbehagen van zijn will; wat zij was naar de werkelijkheid der schepping, toen haar idee in den beginne in levensgemeenschap met den almachtigen God was omgezet, en schitterde in den luister naar haar heerlijkheid; wat zij werd toen de ethiche macht der zonder, door Satan in de wereld van den menschen geest geprojecteerd, zich op haar wierp en haar denatureerde; wat van buiten het gebied der palingenesie overbleef op den grondslag van de onvernietigbare eigenheid des menschelijke natuur onder de koestering van Gods germeene gratie, en in hoeverrre deze resten op den naam van religie annspraak kunnen laten gelden; and eindelijk, wat zij wordt door de herstellende genade van onze Heere Jezus Christus, den Zoon van God" (18).

Because of sin, the understanding of the human heart, "the sanctuary of religion," is not the source of (true) religion, but the Word of God is, since it is "eternally certain and teaches wicked people wisdom."[38] It does so in three ways: thetical (essence of religion), historical (course of religion) and therapeutic (new life in Christ Jesus).

Scripture is our source of knowledge about religion because it teaches "the origin and essence" of being human (*den mensch*) and provides the "broad anthropological basis" on which religion rests, and "the pure, clear knowledge of the adorable essence" to which humanity related itself religiously.

Two misconceptions that must be avoided are the idea that Scripture is the only source of knowledge for religion, and thinking that psychological and historical studies of religion are not fruitful. "Just as generally speaking special revelation, however much it has its own roots and is inspired by its own thought, is, nonetheless, built on the broad foundation of general revelation, in the same way also Theology gladly receives the supportive services of the history and philosophy of religion."[39]

Whereas the first *methodological* question centers on the "source of knowledge" (*kenbron*) of religion, the second one focuses on "how the discovered givens serve a constructive unity according to the twofold requirement of reality and science combined."[40] The consciousness of a believer appropriates the substance of scriptural revelation in a splendid independent way.

This "spiritual reality, called religion, is a phenomenon controlled by a unity of thought, which, through logical analysis, can assuredly be explicated in terms of its constitutive elements . . . [without] for a moment losing the internal unity." Believers must "explain the cognitive dispersed elements of religion" and do this in terms of the unity of reality.[41] What compels that

---

38. Volbeda (1915): 19.

39. "Gelijk in het algemeen de bizondere openbaring, hoezeer ook op een eigen wortel stoelend, en van een eigen gedachte bezield, niettemin op den breeden grondslag der algemeene openbaaring is opgetrokken, zoo ook ontvangt de Theologie bij haar studie van de religie gaarne de hulpdiensten van de geschiedenis en de wijsbegeerte der religie." (21) Volbeda adds that this is especially true when the "supportive services are rooted in palingenesis and subjected to the regimen Sacrae Scripturae."

40. ". . . hoe dienen de gevonden gegevens tot een constructieve eenhbeid naar den dubbelen eisch der werkelijkheid en wetenschap ineengezet" (21).

41. "Whoever notices trees has for that reason not yet seen the forest" (Wie bomen opmerkt ziet nog daarom niet het bosch). (22)

constructive work is the impulse of life peculiar to our consciousness and corresponds to the postulates of cosmic reality.[42]

Now the question could arise whether our consciousness, due to the imperfection of religion, lacks all warranty that the givens which Holy Scripture provides for our knowledge of religion are properly perceived and completely gathered, and, moreover, that, if it succeeded in the former, these data are now, according to the demands of reality and logicality, architectonically correctly organized/accounted for ("adstrueert").[43]

For Volbeda, the damaging consequences of sin affected our human consciousness much more in robbing truth of its content than in disturbing the human logical capacities and functioning. Admittedly, the analytical distinction between the "logical" and "ethical" consequences of sin has hardly been undertaken, to the detriment of a Christian theory of knowledge and epistemology.

Although the technical term "religion" is not used in Scripture, it is better than the term "worship of God." Scripture gives humans the task to express its witness in natural ways for modern consciousness. The "fundamental relation between man and God," or "essence of religion" (*religio*) is more important than worship for three reasons: (a) "worship" is merely "liturgical" and, in Methodist fashion, equates "religion" with "church attendance"; (b) it is more an "utterance, revelation, expression" of "religion" than "religion itself;" and (c) worshiping God is only part, not all, of religion.[44] "Religion" refers to the "most fundamental relation" of humans to God. It is used by "the rationalist, the nomist, the mystic" alike. Given its Latin origin, "religio" is used internationally and has a "universal" meaning.[45]

Having focused on the "psychological," or "anthropological," meaning

42. ". . . noopt tot dien constructieven arbeid de impulse van het eigen leven van ons bewustzijn, die Tetullinaus' zeggen: anima naturaliter christiana, bevestigt, en op de postulaten der kosmische realiteir correspondeert." (22)

43. "Nu zou de vraag kunnen rijzen, of ons bewustzijn niet een oorzaak van de onvolkomenheid der religie allen waarborg mist, dat het de gegevens die ons the Heilige Schift voor de kennis van de religie biedt zuiver waarneemt en volledig verzamelt, en vervolgens dat het, zoo het al in het eerstgenoemde slaagt, deze data alsnu naar de eischen der realiteit en der logiciteit architectonisch juist adstrueert." (22)

44. Volbeda (1915): 23.

45. Volbeda (1915): 24. These three types reflect the classic "faculty psychology" of thinking, willing and feeling (for details, see chapter 6 above).

of "essence of religion," Volbeda describes what "Gereformeerde" theologians meant by *religio subjectiva*, in distinction from *religio objectiva*.[46] In *GD* I (238–290), Bavinck—Volbeda's mentor—retained this distinction, but focused on the "Essence, Seat and Origin" (Wezen, Zetel en Oorsprong) of the "religio subjectiva." About this Bavinckian view, Volbeda comments,

> . . . that the habitus religionis (subjectiva) through the influence of the religio objectiva (which according to the author is "identical with God's revelation") turns into activity, does not, in my opinion, provide the right to call that "revelation of God" religion. One could just as well call religio subjectiva revelatio objectiva. . . . If religio objectiva is identical with God's revelation, as Dr. Bavinck remarked, why then not be satisfied with that old tested and excellent name and leave the name religion without further qualification to what presently is called religio subjectiva. One can then forcefully maintain that the religion of humans awakens and develops just as little without the influence of God's revelation as the eye sees without light and the ear hears without airwaves.

The starting point for determining what in a Biblical sense is meant by religion lies in the Locus de creatione ad imaginem Dei hominis (The topic of the creation of humanity in the image of God, the traditional name for this section of theological dogmatics). This doctrine forms the cornerstone of all anthropology with the adjuncta of hamartology and soteriology. On close inspection, precisely this truth offers us the key to the secrets of christian cosmology. Now by this creation, according to the image of God, the broad foundation on which it rests must not be lost sight of and which lies in the intimate relation which connects the Creator and the works of his hands. That fundamental idea of creation Holy Scripture itself interprets for us in the statement that παντα εκ του θεου [everything is from God], and precisely for that reason each moment is δι αυτου [through Him], and through what is constant εις αυτον [in Him] moves in the direction of their

46. Volbeda (1915(: 25. About the speculative and complicated distinction between *religio subjectiva* and *religio objectiva*, see p. 26. How do the qualifying characteristics "*subjectiva*" and "*objectiva*" relate to "religion"? Is it possible for "the *religio subjectiva*, when I make it the object of my investigation, to be called *religio objectiva*, and the *religio objectiva* to become for God *religio subjectiva*"? Or must both forms of religion be viewed in terms of "subjectiva" as being "*in*" and "*objectiva*" as being "*outside*" humans, or does "*subjectiva*" refer to one's "practice" of religion and "*objectiva*" to the influence of someone else's religion? According to Volbeda, both are unacceptable.

purpose. To show ontologically how the elements of reality in everything constantly correspond to this three-fold relation exceeds our capacities by far. God is great, and to discover his work to perfection, the infinity of Him, whose essence is *actus purissimus* [purest action] is not permitted for finite essences such as we are. The *how* escapes our searching look, the *that* stands firm for us on the basis of God's revelation. With this Word of God in our possession, we fight against all *gnostic emanation*, which conflicts with the infinitas Dei; all *pantheism*, which clashes with the testimony of our self-consciousness, and all *deism*, which elevates the creature to a false independence.[47]

For Volbeda, the intimacy of God's relation to the cosmos is not "ethically" rooted in His "will" to be intimate with the works of his hands, but

47. Volbeda (1915): 27–28: ". . . dat de habitus religionis (*subjectiva*) door inwerking van de *religio objectiva* (die naar den auteur 'identisch is met de openbaring Gods) in activiteit overgaat, geeft m.i. geen recht die 'openbaring Gods' religie te noemen. Men zou evengoed de religio subjectiva revelatio objectiva kunnen noemen. Maar men noemt het licht nog niet oculum objectivum omdat het op oculaire absorpsie is aangelegd en daarvoor is bestemd, en het oog door de instraling van het licht tot optische actie overgaat. Indien de religio objectiva met de openbaring Gods identisch is, wat Dr. Bavinck opmerkt, waarom zich dan niet tevreden gesteld met den alouden beproefden, uitnemenden naam, en de naam religie zonder nadere bepaling overgelaten aan wat thans religio subjectiva heet. Men kan dan verder met nadruk handhaven, dat des menschen religie zoomin tot ontwaking en ontwikkeling komt zonder de inwerking van Gods openbaring, als het oog zonder licht ziet, of het oor zonder luchtgolvingen hoort.

Het uitgangspunt voor de bepaling van wat in Bijbelsche zin onder religie te verstaan zij ligt in den Locus de creatione ad imaginem Dei hominus. Deze leer vormt de hoeksteen van heel de anthropologie met haar adjuncia van harmartologie en soteriologie. Op de keper beschouwd, biedt juist deze waarheid ons ook den sleutel tot de geheimen der christelijke kosmologie. Nu moet bij deze schepping naar den beelde Gods de breede grondslag waarop het rust niet uit het oog verloren woirden, en die gelegen is in de intieme relatie die de Schepper en het werk zijner handen verbindt. De gansche kosmos is eene *schepping* Gods. De grondgedachte der Schepping interpreteert de Heilige Schrift selve voor ons in de uitspraak dat *panta ek tou Theou*, en juist hierom elk oogenblik *di autou* zijn, en door het constante *eis auton* zich in de richting van hun bestemming bewegen. Ontologisch aan te toonen hoe de elementen de realiteit op deze driedelige relatie in alles en bestendig corresponderen gaat ons vermogen ver te boven. God is groot en zijn werk tot de volmaaktheid te vinden, laat de oneindigheid van Hem, wiens wezen *actus prurissimus* is, niet toe aan eindige wezens als wij zijn. Ontgaat het *hoe* aan onzen zoekenden blik, het *dat* staat echter voor ons vast op grond van Gods openbaring. Met dit Woord Gods in den hand bestrijden wij alle *gnostiswche emanatie*, die met de infinitas Dei in strijd is; all *pantheisme*, dat tegen het getuigenis van ons zelfbewustzijn vloekt, en alle *deisme*, dat het schepsel tot een valsche zelfstandigheid verheft."

much more grounded "metaphysically," as a consequence of the free "De-cretum Dei," in the "nature of things." God was "free" to create the world, but "how" he wanted to be "intimate" with the world, he had no other way at his disposal than that of creation. For this reason, John 3:16 is the "locus classicus" to highlight God's "intimacy" with the world. It is "the basis for the service which God's creation shows as organ" of his "Self-revelation and Self-glorification."[48]

Given the "intimacy" between God and His creation, it is impossible to understand correctly God's image in man—the "compendium naturae"—apart from "any preformative antecedents" in creation. Volbeda stated: "This humankind (mensch) possesses in its being created according to God's im-age, which determines its characteristic feature (nota characterisca) the com-plementary element, for which his surrounding cosmos calls."

> The cosmic, in distinction from the theological, motive for the creation of humankind according to God's image must for that reason be sought in the disclosure to actuality of the potentiality of fellowship with God, which through creating was placed in the cosmos. By holding on to this cosmic motif, we avoid the false notion as though the comprehensive and representative character of humans remains ethereal, i.e., would have a ratio [reason] in God, *above*, but would not have a ratio [reason] in the cosmos, *below*. At the same time, this interrelation of mankind and cosmos casts a surprising interpretative light on the uniqueness of mankind, which resides in its being created in God's image.[49]

Volbeda makes three comments about God's image in humans. *First,* Scripture does not state that humankind *"is"* the image of God. For Bavinck,[50] "Image" and "likeness" are not in God, but in humans, not "increata or ar-

---

48. Volbeda (1915): 28. This "intimacy" indicates that not only "humans exist in eternity," but also the "cosmos."

49. Volbeda (1915): 29. "Het kosmische in onderscheding van het theologische motief voor de schepping van den mensch naar Gods beeld moet derhalve gezocht in de ontplooiing tot actualitiet van de potentialiteit der gemeenschap Gods, door schepping in den kosmos gelegd. Door dit kosmische motief vast te houden vermijden wij de valsche voorstelling, als zou het comprehensieve en representieve karakter des menschen in de lucht hangen, dat is, wel een ratio in God zou hebben, *boven*, maar niet een ratio zou hebeen in den kosmos, *beneden*. Tevens werpt deze interrelatie van mensch en kosmos een verrassent interpretatief licht op de eigenaardigheid des mesnchen, die in zijn schepping naar Gods beeld gelegen is."

50. *GD*, II, 509.

chetypa" but "creata or ectypa." Only by "analogy" is being human "like," not the same as, or identical with, God.[51]

Second, the "total human being, that is in terms of soul and body" is created in God's image. Scripture "strictly maintains the essential difference between soul and body." It has "cut the root of idealism and materialism" by indicating that "both body and soul are created in God's image." We may "not separate what God has united," or has created as an "organic" whole. Humans are associated with the cosmos, which depends on its Maker, but does not image him. In their body, humans have much in common with animals, but in the "rationality and morality" of their "spirit," they show a "striking parallel" with angels. The "material and spiritual" are integral to the human task of developing dominion in terms of God's image.[52]

Third, the image-of-God for all mankind leaves no room for individualism. It affects the manifestation and our understanding of God's providence, and has implications for our view of such topics as "religion," "being," "consciousness" and "regeneration."[53] For the purpose of this chapter (and the next three chapters) Volbeda's comments near the end of his Inaugural are revealing. What makes it possible for humans to know the triad "God, self and the cosmos" is the ability the Creator gave them to inquire about "the image of God."

> The synthesis of *understanding* and *will* lies in connection with each of the members of the trio in the delicately strung *feeling* of humans. The religious reaction, which arises from the depth of being, and which, under guidance of the Spirit of God, looks for a way to the mirror of consciousness, can, therefore, find no other intermediator than the facultates animae, regardless of whether one thinks about this in a dicho- or trichotomistic way.[54]

It is necessary to hold on to "the total apparatus of the soul" and the idea "that the human spirit has as its first calling, and finds its greatest meaning,

---

51. Volbeda (1915): 30, 31. Christ is called "the image of God" in 2 Cor. 4:4 and Col. 1:15; cf. John 14:9 and Heb. 1:3.

52. Volbeda (1915): 32, 33.

53. For details, see Volbeda (1915): 33–41.

54. Volbeda (1915): 42. "De synthese van verstand en wil ligt met betrekking tot elk der leden van de trias in het zoo fijn besnaarde gemoed des menschen. De religieuse reactie die uit diepte van het zijn opkomt, en zich, onder leiding van den Geest Gods, een weg naar den spiegel van het bewustzijn baant, kan dus geen ander intermediair vinden dan de facultates animae, onverschillig of men deze dicho- of trichotomisch denkt."

in the knowledge, service and enjoyment of God." After all, "each capacity of the soul finds, . . . in the totality of its varying operations, its raison d'être primarily and mostly in the relation of religion. This is what our Calvinistic, theological life-view demands."[55] Giving religion a "preformative basis in a theologically founded cosmos" conquers "all dualism."

The "common capacities of the soul" are also "the organs of religion." This addresses the threefold epistemological question of "how the perception of the divine being must be thought," how "God is the object of our thelematic [willing] activity," and "how the activity of feelings with respect to God must be thought." The basis for a thinking-willing-feeling understanding of "religion" lies in the "theistic doctrine of God's immanence."[56] This "action of God," which "religion awakens in us," is not an "action at a distance," but "a penetration of the essence of God to the root-fibres of our existence."[57]

Being light, not darkness, God "offers warranty that, humanly speaking, the essence of God lends itself for logical assimilation in an absolute way for Himself and a relative way for us to the extent He pleases to reveal Himself to us and according to the mensura humana of our receptivity."[58] Volbeda closed his inaugural lecture by urging his audience to thank God that "the building of God's church and Kingdom has a scientific (*wetenschappelijk*) basis according to Gereformeerde principles. By studying at this institution your spirit receives the theoretic and practical invitation (*plooi*) to unfold in the richest and most forceful way. . . ."[59]

55. Volbeda (1915): 42, 43.

56. Volbeda (1915): 43.

57. Volbeda (1915): 44. He refers to Acts 17:28: "In Him we live, we move and have our being." How this awareness of "the Eternal" comes about has still not been answered.

58. Volbeda (1915): 44. For a striking similarity between this scholastic way of thinking and that described in the next three chapters, see especially A. Plantinga in Chapter 18.

59. Volbeda (1915): 47. In "Samuel Volbeda and the Christian Reformed Pulpit," Rev. Charles Greenfield wrote, after Volbeda's death in 1953, about his "expository," "eloquent" and "thematic preaching," known for its "Itsitis Syndrome," i.e., a "theme divided into three points, each beginning with *its*." According to John H. Kromminga, President of CTS for thirty-eight years, "No other man has so influenced the preaching in Christian Reformed pulpits as he." He taught students "to search for one basic concept of the text" and with "extreme care and exactness . . . the words of the theme and of the outline which developed the theme." Also Catechism preaching is "dogmatical," i.e., it must "speak as the Lord speaks"—even though "the Lord does not speak theology," since the latter "lacks the resoluteness which preaching needs. . . ." For details, see *ORIGINS*, VI: 2, 19–21.

Louis Berkhof (1873–1957)

No one else in the Christian Reformed community and tradition popularized Bavinck's view of faith and theology as much as did L. Berkhof, an ardent advocate of Reformed dogmatics. He graduated from the Christian Reformed Theological School in Grand Rapids in 1900, was pastor in a local CRC until 1906,[60] taught Exegetical Theology at CTS from 1906 until 1914, New Testament until 1926, and dogmatics from 1932 to 1944, and served as CTS's president during his last thirteen years of teaching (1931–1944).

His most important publication—in the tradition of Bavinck's *GD*, I-IV, is his *Reformed Dogmatics*, I-II, 1932, primarily aimed at his students at CTS. Six years later, his *second*, revised and expanded edition appeared under the changed title—without any explanation—of *Systematic Theology* (*ST*).[61] This mysterious change may reflect the desire of Berkhof and/or of William B. Eerdmans, the publisher, to associate it, perhaps for promotional reasons, with Charles Hodge's *Systematic Theology*, I-III, at Princeton Theological Seminary. In the "Preface" of the *fourth* reprint in 1949, Berkhof wrote

> It is not necessary to say much about the nature of the work, since it has been before the public for more than fifteen years and has been used extensively. I have every reason to be grateful for its kind reception, for the favorable testimony of many reviewers, and for the fact that the book is now used as a textbook in many Theological Seminaries and Bible Schools in our country, and that requests were even received from abroad for permission to translate it into other languages.[62]

Shortly after his *Reformed Dogmatics* appeared in print, he was asked to write a "brief manual" of his two large volumes, to be used in Christian (Reformed) high schools, as a required textbook in theology classes at CC,

60. During this time, he received his B.D. degree from Princeton Theological Seminary and completed a correspondence course at the University of Chicago. For details, see Peter De Klerk (1980), pages 2.1 to 2.52.

61. In 1909 William B. Eerdmans, the publisher, visited B. B. Warfield at Princeton Theological Seminary and H. Bavinck at the Free University in Amsterdam. In 1910, he started to publish other books in "Systematic Theology" (not "Reformed Dogmatics") and perhaps he urged Berkhof to change the title of this work. For details about Wm. B. Eerdmans, Sr. see Larry ten Harmsel with Reinder Van Til's helpful book, (2011): 19–20.

62. Berkhof 1953: 7. By 1977, fifteen reprints were published. For details about reprints and translation into Spanish in 1969, see P. De Klerk (1980): 2:14.

and even to assist catechism teachers in Christian Reformed Churches.[63] In response, Berkhof wrote *Manual of Christian Doctrine* in 1933. His *ST* was reprinted thirteen times, translated into Japanese in 1952, Spanish in 1966, and Chinese in 1974.[64] In the "Preface" to his first edition, he wrote,

> Mindful of the great importance of the *proper indoctrination* of the young people of the Church, I did not have the courage to refuse, but undertook to prepare a brief manual. The work seemed particularly important to me in view of the widespread *doctrinal indifference* of the present day, of the resulting superficiality and confusion in the *minds* of many professing Christians in the insidious errors that are zealously propagated even from the pulpits, and of the alarming increase of all kinds of sects. . . . If there ever was a time when the Church ought to *guard her precious heritage, the deposit of the truth* that was entrusted to her care, that time is now. I have tried to give a rather comprehensive and yet concise statement of our *Reformed conception of the truth*, and sincerely hope that its *clarity* may not have suffered through its brevity. . . . (emphases added)[65]

The impact of his *ST* has been enormous in CRC in the USA during most of the twentieth century, and elsewhere in the world in English and through the Spanish, Korean and Japanese translations of it. This impact has been both laudable and detrimental: the former, in terms of its confessional (pistical) intent, the latter with respect to its scholastic anthropology and methodology in describing Christian faith and its understanding of the vague term "theology."

Without denying Bavinck's, ten Hoor's, Volbeda's and Berkhof's laudable intentions—this study is *not* a heresy-hunt—we need to become aware of scholastic views of the meaning of such basic terms as essence, existence, being and attributes, knowableness and names of God, shibboleths of "soul" and "body," nature of "truth," meaning of "imago Dei," avoiding intellectual impasses, the impact of being Reformed by using *philosophically* questionable ideas about faith and science, ontology/ethics/passion, the puzzle and scope of sin, God's central law of love and daily walking with Him, also in philosophy and (what is traditionally called) theology.

---

63. Even in the 1980s, some elders used the *Manual of Christian Doctrine* to teach teenage catechumens.

64. P. De Klerk (1980): 2.14.

65. Berkhof (1953): 5–6.

Berkhof's "doctrine of God" in his *ST* and *Manual of Christian Doctrine* is basically similar to that of Bavinck. He assumed Bavinck's view of this doctrine—which, four centuries earlier, T. Beza taught at J. Calvin's Academy in Geneva—about ultimate being, being human, knowledge and truth, concepts, clarity, doctrine and certainty. Through the back-door of classic Reformed theological thinking, a number of scholastic ideas impacted Reformed teachers in classrooms, preachers on pulpits, instructors of catechumens, elementary and secondary teachers at Christian schools, and the faith life and worldview of numerous Christian Reformed persons.

Unlike such *reformational* thinkers as D. H. T. Vollenhoven and H. Dooyeweerd since 1926 at the Free University, Berkhof already in 1906, especially after 1926 as professor of dogmatics, did not *reform(ulate)* Bavinck's philosophical stance. Instead, he perpetuated at least three fundamental features of Bavinck's thought-pattern, namely, (a) the distinction between God's "incommunicable" and "communicable" attributes, (b) a discussion of "attributes" in terms of an anthropology based on a (higher) "soul" and (lower) "body," and (c) a "faculty psychology" about the human capacities of the soul's "intellect, will and feeling."[66]

As to the *religious*[67] direction of Christian higher education, in "theology" at CTS and of "liberal arts" at CC, during the first decades of the twentieth century, Berkhof played a key role. His passion to be Reformed, desire to be scriptural, and respect for Bavinck's way of thinking were generally appreciated in Christian Reformed circles. In fact, he perpetuated a three-century-old tradition of a kind of Reformed orthodoxy that incorporated into its view of God's threefold (creational, incarnational, and biblical) revelation certain questionable features in the understanding of certain views and methods in "faith" and "theology."

In 1938 Berkhof changed the title of his expanded *Reformed Dogmatics* to *Systematic Theology*. The change from "Reformed" to "Systematic" and "Dogmatics" to "Theology" is significant. As far as I know, Bavinck did not equate "reformed" with "systematic," nor "dogmatics" with "theology." For him, "Reformed" refers to what is creedal, i.e., confessional, not "logical"

---

66. For details, see Bavinck *Gereformeerde Dogmatiek, II* 149–225, and Berkhof (1853): 64–81, especially 65: "In its whole fabric and constitution it reveals the clearest traces of an infinite *intelligence*, of the deepest, highest and tenderest *emotions*, and of the *will* that is all-powerful. Consequently, we are constrained to mount from the world to the world's Maker as a Being of intelligence, sensibility, and will, that is, as a person" (emphases added).

67. Understood in a biblical *reformational*, not scholastic *accommodational*, way.

or "systematic," and "dogmas," though significant, are not equated with the study of "theology."

Living in North America four decades after Bavinck wrote *GD* I-IV, Berkhof was in a sense *more* scholastic than Bavinck. He echoed, in a somewhat amplified way, "doctrines" as conceptual and propositional pieces of the puzzle of an intellect-leaning faith and Scripture as providing *proof*-texts for theology. In shifting from "dogmatics" as the *capstone* for theology to what is *foundational* for all of life, including all academic disciplines, "theology" begins to play a subtle *religious* role. As a consequence, theology (as study of God) becomes something that directs and guides, shapes knowledge, one's worldview, all Christian education and scholarship.[68]

This problematic feature of Berkhof's view as Professor of Dogmatics contributed to a way of thinking and teaching, in mainly Christian Reformed circles, about: (i) being human and knowing, i.e., anthropology and epistemology, (ii) "soul-body" dualism, (iii) Greek "faculty psychology," centered on thinking-willing-feeling, and (iv) the nature and role of "faith" and "reason," "religion and science," "theology and philosophy" and "special and general revelation."

Berkhof, since 1906 a colleague at CTS of ten Hoor, who taught Reformed Dogmatics for a quarter century, succeeded ten Hoor in 1932 for fourteen years of teaching, writing, preaching and speaking about many Reformed principles. At the same time, he was accompanied for decades by Volbeda.[69] He did so as a Reformed scholastic thinker about such topics as truth, dogma, method, general and special revelation, common and special grace, communicable and incommunicable attributes of God, church and state, religion and science, theology and philosophy, soul and body. His influence on Christian Reformed preachers in the USA, foreign missionaries, professors at CTS and CC, most teachers and administrators in elementary and secondary schools, and other leaders in society and culture has been significant.

---

68. For decades after 1933, students at Calvin College were required to take a course in which Berkhof's *Manual of Christian Doctrine* was the textbook. Students often memorized these abstract distinctions without really understanding them.

69. Church historian (1914–1926) and professor of Practical Theology, especially Homiletics (1926–1952), i.e., teaching ministers how to preach (cf. "Itsitis", i.e. stressing "three point" sermons).

CHAPTER SIXTEEN

Calvin Theological Seminary: Henry J. Stob (1908–1996)

Henry J. Stob graduated from CC (1932) and CTS (1935), received his Th.M. from Hartford Theological Seminary (1936) and Ph.D. from the University of Göttingen, Germany (1938). After a brief visit at the Free University[1] in Amsterdam in 1938 or 1939, he taught Philosophy from 1939 to 1954 (except for 1944/5) at CC, and Moral Philosophy and Apologetics at CTS from 1952 until his retirement in 1975.

He co-founded in 1951 *The Reformed Journal* (*RJ*)—an independent journal, funded for four decades by William B. Eerdmans, Sr. and William B. Eerdmans, Jr.[2]—for the purpose of articulating what is distinctive in the thinking of the Christian Reformed intelligentsia at CC and CTS. This journal caused considerable discussion within, and beyond, Christian Reformed circles. Like W. Harry Jellema, his former colleague at CC, Stob was fond of using the term "mind." Jellema had used it to highlight three mind-sets and phases of thinking in the history of Western philosophy, viz., Ancient Greek Mind, Medieval Christian Mind and Modern Secular Mind. Stob used the term, however, not so much in a "philosophical" as in a mainly "ethical," or "moral," way with respect to issues involving "liberal arts" education, Christ

---

1. Vollenhoven and Dooyeweerd told me they appreciated his visit, but because it was brief and mostly social, they did not have a substantive (*inhoudsvolle*) discussion with him about the need for, and nature of, *reformational* philosophy.

2. Concerning Henry J. Stob, see James D. Bratt and Ronald A. Wells, editors, *The Best of The Reformed Journal*, Eerdmans (2011) esp. "Introduction," 1–9; Larry ten Harmsel *with* Reinder Van Til, *An Eerdmans Century 1911–2011*, Eerdmans (2011) especially "Coda" by Jon Pott, 207–212.

& Culture issues, Christian and non-Christian relations, and various mentalities within Christian Reformed circles.[3]

The focus of this chapter will be on three articles he wrote when he taught Philosophy at CC and seven articles he published after he moved (across the campus) to teach at CTS in the areas of Moral Philosophy and Apologetics. His love of the classic expression of St. Augustine (354–430), namely, "faith seeking understanding" (*fides quaerens intellectum*)[4] is clear in his thinking and all his writings.

Articles Written at Calvin College

1. "Philosophy and the Bible" (1943)

In "Philosophy and the Bible," Stob referred to Scripture as a "divine gift," a "word from beyond," a "set of value judgments" directed at human "will, emotions and understanding." The Bible is a "communication of facts, truths, ideas—a body of propositions setting forth the actual and the real," a "medium of an assertion to be affirmed," which "conveys God's Word" and demands "unconditional submission."[5]

Unlike Scripture, "philosophy" is about "theoretical knowledge and systematic interpretation of the cosmos as a whole." Its focus is the "interrelation and interaction of things." As "a set of mutually implicated propositions," it is a "coherent, logically articulated, system of truths." Being something to be "argued and critically appraised," philosophy makes human "life and experience intelligible."[6]

The relation between "Scripture" and "philosophy" can be seen in four ways: (i) non-existent (ancient period), (ii) negative (modern times), (iii)

---

3. Cf. "Note to a College Freshman" (1952), "The Mind of the Church" (1957), "The Mind of Safety" (1957), "The Militant Mind" (1957), "The Positive Mind" (1963). For details, see Stob 1981: 229–239 and 183–217. For its clarity, essence and importance of his lectures at CC and CTS and other publications, I will focus on "Note to a College Freshman" in *The Reformed Journal* (1952).

4. For details, see *Seeking Understanding: The Stob Lectures 1968–1998*, Calvin College and Calvin Theological Seminary, Eerdmans (2001) 550 pages.

5. Stob (1981): 173.

6. Stob (1981): 174. In a way typical of traditional Reformed thinking, the distinction between, on the one hand, Scripture and philosophy, and Revelation and philosophy, on the other hand, is not mentioned.

Thomistic (medieval *subordinated* to and *isolated* from Scripture) and (iv) integrated (philosophy based on religious commitment, or transcendent assumptions about Scripture). As to the fourth way, "religious" must be distinguished from "theology" and "cultus" (prayers, worship). Unlike any *intra*-cosmical relation to **nature** (cf. things, plants, animals) and **values** (cf. intelligence, community, morality), "religion" centers on the *extra-cosmical* relation of humans with **God**.[7]

In 1943—i.e., four years after his social visit in 1938 or 1939 with Dooye-weerd and Vollenhoven in Amsterdam and a brief discourse with them about their way of thinking, Stob used such traditional terms as "religion," "religious" and "heart" not in any *reformational* way[8] but in the traditional *substantive*, i.e., scholastic, way. He assumed the validity of Greek anthropology with its inherent "faculty psychology."

This explains, at least in part, his "philosophical" academic and non-academic disagreement in Christian Reformed circles quite soon after H. Evan Runner joined the philosophy department at CC in 1952. About Runner's *reformational* view that humans are essentially "religious" in that in their "heart" is an "unanalyzable unity" which directs everything humans do, Stob states,

> *Living, feeling, willing, and thinking are merely so many functions of man, so many aspects of his being. His being or essence lies under and beyond. The central thing in man is neither body, nor spirit as such, nor any specific function of either, but that deeper something of which the functions are the functions. It may be called the "core" or the "heart" of man, but the name we give it is relatively unimportant.* The important thing is not to confuse it with any of its expressions or activities. In any case, it is here, in his heart, at the point which sustains and underlies all his intracosmic relations, that God impinges on man. Here, at the deepest, all-determinative level of his existence, man's fundamental nature is constituted by the specific character of the relation he sustains to God. Here, at the core of his being, man is religious. (emphasis added)[9]

---

7. Stob (1981): 174, 175, 176. As "a fundamental divine-human relation," religion has to do with an attitude of humans towards God—either to love or to hate, to acknowledge or to ignore, to be aware or to be unconscious" (177).

8. It rejects the idea that philosophy is "metaphysical" and that theology provides "systematic knowledge" about God.

9. Stob (1981): 177–178.

Mistakenly, Stob associated the scholastic idea of "faculties" (feeling, willing, thinking) with the *reformational* notion of "functions" and facets." In other words, he used the terminology of "reformational" thinking, but continued to think about "religion" as *something* "central" in humans, an "ever-present subject" in all human behavior. Christian thinkers do not move apart from "faith," but have a "transcendent vantage point," are directed by "the world's maker and interpreter," in short, they are enrolled in "the school of God."[10]

Stob does not elaborate how this *extra*-cosmical relation of humans to **God** directs or influences the *intra*-cosmic relation of humans to **nature** (physical, biological) and **values** (rational, moral, social). As a Christian, he admits that "reality" is not "self-interpretive" or "self-explanatory," but is "ontically distinct from its creator" and "unable in itself to account for even its existence, much less for its more specific qualities."[11]

2. "A Note to Young Seminarians" (1952)

Sensing the danger of "scholasticism," in "A Note to Young Seminarians"—published in *The Calvin Forum*—Stob warns against the "dry-rot of barren and abstract scholasticism." However, he still talks about a seminarian's call as a "sacred ministry" and stresses the need for theologians to be "disciplined by logic, history, and philosophy." As "an intellectually articulated account of revealed truth," theology "enjoys primacy among us." It has its own "worth" and "ends," its own "system of truths" that is "valid independent of its functional efficacy." As a "system of meanings," theology has "its own right of being understood." Classical theological literature not only informs, but also forms, liberates and puts us in "contact with the Living Word—i.e., the Scriptures" as witness to God's presence in Christ and the Spirit.[12]

Although "theology" is "abstract," detached, a product of thinking, somewhat removed from concrete reality, it must be sensitive to revelation. "Living theology" implies a "living faith," in which "truth is *'felt'* and experienced" and a "living church," community, or kingdom, of Christians, in which "theological truths" liberate, enrich and direct the moral conduct of

---

10. Stob (1981): 176, 177, 178.
11. Stob (1981): 178.
12. Stob (1981): 131–132.

people. It is the "awful responsibility" of theologians to ensure "that their existential import becomes apparent."[13]

3. *"Note to a College Freshman" (1952)*

In his clearly formulated "Note to a College Freshman," Stob stated that "mind is as different from brain as soul is from body" and "as different from intellect as whole is from part."

> Mind is *intellect, will, and feeling* (emphasis added) fused into one. Mind is what you are on the deeper level of your being. It is the spiritual measure and size of you, the conscious center and core of you. It is you at the point where you most centrally confront the world. Mind sets your perspectives, determines your judgments, dictates your loyalties. It defines you.
>
> The mind that is in you . . . is the product of many historical forces and influences. Not all of these . . . were under your direction and control. Yet many of them operated with your consent and under your active governance. This means that you have been an agent in the making of the mind you have. For its present set and temper you must, in consequence, accept the responsibility. And you must accept the same responsibility for its future form and texture.[14]

This advice, which is based on Stob's *Theological Reflections* and lectures on Ethics, reflects his stance as professor of *philosophy* at CC and of *ethics* at CTS. Through the "liberalizing and formative influences" of college education, students shape their "mind after the best and most enduring pattern that exists." The goal of "a good college, a liberal arts college, a Christian college" is to provide "the ideal mind." This "more acceptable kind of mind" was "delineated and recommended" by Plato, "the arch opponent of the Sophists." Unlike the Sophists, who focused on what is individual, subjective, provincial, idiosyncratic and undisciplined, Plato believed that the central focus of a "liberal—that is a liberalizing—education" is "the human mind," i.e., the "broader mind of man" which concentrates on what is universal, objective,

---

13. Stob (1981): 134; see 133. His comments on p. 135 about theological maturation, critical self-examination and present cultural crisis, especially the interrelationships between these three, compels a careful reader to question his exaggerated estimate of "theology" and to want to know more about scripturally directed *non-theological* disciplines.

14. Stob (1981): 229 (emphasis added).

shared, common and disciplined. Only such education provides a measure of "dignity and freedom."[15]

Only three kinds of mind exist: (i) "your own mind in its sheer particularity," (ii) the ideal mind of higher level education which "shares in the common human mind," and (iii) to transcend even this mind and reach one's "ultimate range and scope," "the mind of Christ." In terms of the famous Platonizing-Augustinian motto of CTS, viz.,"faith seeking understanding" (*fides quaerens intellectum*), Stob comments,

> Just as the movement from the *first* mind to the *second* was not a mere negation of the first, but an enrichment and enlargement of it (a finding of it through losing it), so the movement from the second to the *third* does not involve the abandonment of the second, but the inclusion of it within a larger perspective, a subordination of it to a higher, indeed, the highest, *ultimate rationality.* To be truly educated, to be completely liberated, to be wholly enlightened, is to share *in Christ the thoughts of God* and thus to transcend the relativity not only of the subjective but also of the merely human. To understand ourselves, to understand the world, to truly and fundamentally understand anything at all, we must take up position neither in the individual nor in the race, neither in sophistic intelligence nor in human rationality, but in *the Truth himself,* which is what is meant by taking on the *mind of Christ* (emphases added).[16]

It is difficult to shake off the "confining chains" of one's "discrete individuality." Years of "discipline and training" are required for an educated person to acquire "objectivity and universality." Attaining "the mind of Christ" is more difficult, since it is "in the first instance a miracle and a gift, and only secondarily an achievement and possession." No one is "educated," just as no one is "saved," unless one is shaped by "the Word and Spirit and the whole

15. Stob (1981): 229–231. The Christian student must "get beyond, transcend his private self" and "become a man," living "under an objective and universally binding law of righteousness and truth"—"Even Plato saw this. . . . And he was right. This does not mean that we must have Plato's mind. But we can and must adopt Plato's suggestion that the narrow mind of the Sophists 'be replaced by that broader mind which lifts us out of our privacy and identifies us with mankind'" (1981: 237, 238).

16. Stob (1981): 231. These three "minds" Stob associates with, respectively, "technical schools [which] do not educate," "a secular college of liberal arts [which] does educate" and "a Christian college" which makes an effort to "form in the student a Christian mind."

of God's creation into conformity with the mind of Christ, to be fashioned anew in the image and likeness of God."[17]

The "root" of man is located between the "surface" (body, feelings, manners, overt judgments) and the "mind" (self, entity) of a person. To think of "root" as "the proper object of educational forming" is not something "impious and impossible," and to view the "surface" as the object of education results in a superficial form of education. *Mind* does not lie on the deepest, but on a deeper, level of human existence. The human mind is "subject to the direction of the heart," and the heart "directs our judgments and volitions." Though it is "less basic than the heart," mind is "fuller and more basic than the intellect, since intellect, will, and feeling are included in it." Being two distinct things," "mind" and "heart" are not the same:

> The heart is the religious ground of our being; it lies below the threshold of our consciousness; it functions on a transcendental level of our existence; it cannot be altered by an activity of man, and it undergoes no process of development as such; it cannot be educated; when changed it is changed in an instant through the miracle of regeneration; it determines but is not determined by our choice and decisions. . . .
>
> The mind, unlike the heart, can be altered or improved by taking care. The mind is, as I told the freshman, the actual you, in distinction from what you are in principle and promise. It is you in your concrete existence. It is you in your empirical totality. . . . It is the conscious center of you. . . . It is you as made and still unmade, as being and still becoming.[18]

Stob associates the relation between "mind" and "heart" with the difference between "common grace" in the hearts of unregenerate humans and an "unqualified and absolute antithesis" in the hearts of those who are regenerate. He states,

> The unregenerate heart, because of common grace, does not come to full expression in the unbeliever's mind. The regenerate heart, because of sin, does not come to full expression in the Christian's mind. . . . There is not an absolute antithesis between the Christian and the non-Christian "mind."

17. Stob (1981): 231–232. The quotation about "the mind of Christ" Stob repeats verbatim on p. 237 and adds "it is this kind of forming, this kind of education, that a Christian college, and only a Christian college, undertakes to do."

18. Stob (1981): 235.

He who is in his heart a Christian, is in principle Christ's, may have a mind that embraces egregious error and breathes a reprehensible spirit. He who is in his heart a non-Christian, is in principle Satan's, may have a mind that embraces much truth and breathes a temperate spirit. In the case of both the Christian and non-Christian, the mind, though for different reasons, can be false to the heart.

... One is compelled to say that the Christian both has and has not the *mind* of Christ. In speaking of the *heart* one may not use an expression of this kind. One may never say that a Christian both has and has not a new heart.[19]

Educated persons share a "common property" with respect to the laws of "logic, mathematics, and the like"; the "non-Christian has this knowledge, combined with much that is false, but not by a law of right. It is borrowed or poached, poached from the Christian universe whose Christian character he is concerned to deny but cannot destroy." Due to God's goodness, unbelievers pour "treasures of knowledge into a coffer, accessible to all, but really owned by Christians only." He challenges freshman students to,

> raid that coffer and thus "enlarge the cramped perspective of the cabined self," become "kin to the large minded men who have created our art and science," and attain "in some measure to the dignity and freedom of disciplined man."
>
> But I had more to tell him. He was not to forget that he was a Christian. He was not to spend his time at college becoming *human merely*. He was to become a Christian man. It was not that he should become human first and then Christian. That would be preposterous. ... His appropriation and assimilation of knowledge should be Christian assimilation in which facts are shorn of the spurious interpretation put upon them by the non-Christian, and set in a framework differing at the root from that employed by those who are not in Christ. The knowledge and experience he acquires should go to form a Christian mind, a mind governed in all its range by the new heart born of grace.[20]

Through the "narrow aperture of the isolated self" it is possible to find "a little bit of truth, as the Sophists prove," and through the "broader mind

19. Stob (1981): 236. The problem of a biblical view of "heart" and Greek "faculty psychology," or liberal arts, echo Bavinck's problem.

20. Stob (1981): 238.

of man" one can see "more truth, as Plato proves," but only by looking at the world through the "mind" the Spirit of Christ gives can one "see things as they truly are." Only by taking up position in "the Truth himself," or "the mind of Christ," is it possible to truly understand ourselves, the world, or anything at all.[21]

Given Stob's mind-set about "truth" and the essence of "liberal arts" education, it is not surprising, but only logical, that, several decades later, CC adopted "Minds in the Making" as its official campus-logo. It captures not only Stob's thinking, teaching and view of Christian "liberal arts" education, but also the vision of his slightly older colleague, W. Harry Jellema. It indicates (a) the *direct* impact of both Jellema and Stob as two (scholastically leaning) philosophers and educators on most Christian Reformed preachers, professors, school teachers, artists, scientists, writers and (b) their *indirect* influence on other well-intending and gifted servant-leaders in, for example, medical and psychic care, civic life, business, law, communication, etc.

Basic to the "mind" of CTS and CC is Augustine's phrase "faith seeking understanding" (*fides quaerens intellectum*). Implied in this Augustinian motto are at least five features: (i) three forms of truth, viz., little, more, and full; (ii) three levels of education: individual, liberal arts, and Christian; (iii) a process of "appropriation" and "assimilation"; (iv) a distinction between "objective" and "subjective" knowledge, "redeeming" grace and "common grace," love and truth, and religion and science; (v) Greek "faculty psychology" and a "theological" form of accommodation.[22]

---

21. Stob (1981): 238–239.

22. For details, see the insightful analysis of (i) Daniel A. Napier—a former philosophy student of Dr. Robert Sweetman at the Institute of Christian Studies (ICS) in Toronto—*En Route to the Confessions: The Roots and Development of Augustine's Philosophical Anthropology*, especially Chapter 6: "Augustine's Account of Contemplation: Perverse and Redemptive Ascents in the *Confessions*," 213–293; (ii) Steven D. Boyer and Walter B. Huddell III, "Mathematical Knowledge and Divine Mystery: Augustine and His Contemporary Challengers," *Christian Scholar's Review*, XLIV: 3, 207–235, 2015; and (iii) Jonathan Reimer, review of Garry Wills *Font of Life: Ambrose, Augustine, and the Mystery of Baptism*, Oxford Univ. Press (2012) published in "*Books & Culture*," July/August (2015) p. 16.

Articles Written at Calvin Theological Seminary

4. *"On Taking Too Much Philosophy"* (1953)

In this brief but important article, Stob focused on the need to develop "a Christian mind" that enables one to "judge all things by Christian standards," i.e., to use the "perspective of the Faith" to utilize "the best that has been thought and said by Christians" and obtain "Christian profit from the study of non-Christian thought." About the "religious root of all philosophy," he emphasized that only by carrying "something to pagan books" is it possible to take "something of lasting value from them." In keeping with "God's preserving grace" in Christ, students need to own and claim "truth wherever it is found."[23]

5. *"The Warrant for Theology in a Scientific Age"* (1953)

In the depth and scope of this article, Stob provides a clear glimpse of an affinity between his way of thinking and that of two co-founders at CC, three decades later, of Reformed Epistemology (RE). In putting "religion and Christianity on the defensive," secularism had made theologians "nervous and uneasy" about the "anchorage" of theology "in a transcendent reality."

To "boldly affirm God's existence" and explain "the meaning of his being and acts for the entire world," theology must "reassert its right to be heard" and to do so by "convincing a science-oriented generation" that theology is "a veritable science, relevant to people of any age and capable of illumining the totality of existence." Theology is "worthy of assent—even the assent of the most critically intelligent."[24]

In this regard, seven Christian assertions can be made: (i) as an "infinitely good, wise, and powerful being," God "*exists*," "is *real*," although "lifted above the world in true transcendence," and always "present to it in grace and judgment"; (ii) God "created the world . . . out of nothing," and being "real," this "dual" world consists of the Creator as "necessary being" and creature as "contingent being," neither of which can be "univocally subsumed under one category"; (iii) being created in *"God's image,"* man is "in touch"

---

23. Stob (1981): 70–71.

24. Stob (1981): 75. To believe this problem is unique to "theology" assumes the secularist notion that non-theological disciplines function without a faith in anything ultimate.

with Him and in "free responsibility" a member of *God's* "*Kingdom*," of which the Christian "*church* is the earnest and the symbol"; (iv) falling into "the power of *sin*," the human race became the "heir of *death*"; (v) out of *pity*, God restored man to "self-integration, social cohesion, and transcendent peace"; (vi) God revealed his nature and purpose in the words, person and deeds of *Jesus Christ*; (vii) believers in Jesus Christ are in principle *new creatures*.[25] These seven "Christian affirmations," and their "subordinate statements," provide theology with the necessary credentials of a science.

Six general criteria of any "rationally grounded and intellectually structured" *science* are equally applicable to the science of theology: (a) a determinate *object*, subject matter, facet, or dimension of experience, (b) an object that is *real*, or existent, not imagined or projected, (c) a *relation* between object of knowledge and knowing subject, (d) fidelity to the *canons of rationality* with respect to internal consistency and external coherence, (e) *evidence* to validate the assertions made, and (f) *serving* the human community in deepening and extending its understanding of the universe.[26] These *philosophical* remarks of Stob about the "science of theology" call for some elucidating comments about these six criteria.

(a) *Object of theology.* Unlike formal and natural *sciences* (arithmetic, geometry, physics), human and social sciences (human experiences) and *philosophy* (ontology, metaphysics, structure of cosmos, what is ultimate, absolute and unconditioned), *theology* "posits or recognizes an object, not in, but beyond, above, and outside the world."

> Its object is the *supernatural*, the *transcendent*, the independent and eternal principle of existence, the super-cosmic ground or cause of everything other than itself. Its object, in short, is *God*—the "Holy One." It should be added that, though God (better: God in his disclosures) is the object of theology, theological thought is not restricted to God. Theology has to do with the world, too, especially with man, but with both of these only in relation to God.[27]

(b) *Warrant for the supernatural.* The concept God as "supernatural intelligence and will" refers to "what is real," something that "exists," "Existence

25. Stob (1981): 76.
26. Stob (1981): 77.
27. Stob (1981): 78. For details about the "object" of theology, see chapter 2 and what will be indicated in chapters 17 and 18. Reformed Epistemology assumes such a view of theology.

itself," "the source and ground of all else that has being." *Theology* thinks in three ways about God's existence: *first,* logical inference (Unmoved Mover and Ultimate Designer); *second,* rational thought (concept "God" implies "existence"), and *third,* direct, non-inferential awareness, "seed of religion" (*semen religionis*) or "sense of divinity" (*sensus divinitatis*), or "universal sense of moral obligation," in Augustine's and Calvin's view of God as "Ultimate Obliger" (Romans 1 and 2).[28]

(c) *Object of knowledge and knowing subject.* The correspondence between "God" and "man" implies the doctrine of "image," and the relation between "man" and "world" involves the doctrine of "creation." Man is "intelligent," the world is "intelligible" and God, as precondition of science, is "the link between knower and known." However, between theology and all other sciences is "a very great difference." Whereas "theology" involves a cognitive relation with "God," in "science," including "philosophy," the cognitive relation of humans is with the "world."

In the latter, the "subject" takes the *"initiative"* to know (grasp, discover, comprehend) the "object," and it uses the tools of "observation, experience and reason." In (the science of) *theology,* however, God is not an "object" to be "discovered, ferreted out, analyzed, mastered, reduced to an idea," but He "a subject, agent," a *"Person,"* who takes the "initiative." To "be known" God does the "approaching," makes the "disclosure," or *"reveals* himself." Basic to theology are "revelation and faith," not "discovery and reason."[29]

As in any science, also in theology the *method* used must be "suited to its object." Since God is known because of his initiative, the "very *shape* of theological knowledge" differs from human knowledge about "merely cosmic realities." The "supernatural" and "absolutely transcendent" God, "even when revealed and 'known,' remains the ultimate 'Mystery.'"[30] Theology may not bring "God down to the level of the creature." "[F]itted to the object of knowledge," theological knowledge is neither "univocal," or like, nor is it "equivocal," or unlike, but "analogical."[31]

(d) *Canons of rationality.* Theology is "a concatenated assemblage of

28. Stob (1981): 79.

29. Stob (1981): 80. For a comparable distinction between theology and other sciences, see the epistemology of Bavinck and Kuyper in chapters 4 and 5.

30. Quoting A. C. Bennett, "the Unseen is foreign to the native air of our minds. . . . Though grasped, it is not comprehended." It "reveals" and "conceals" itself, it is "known in a cloud of unknowing."

31. Stob (1981): 81. This is reminiscent of T. Aquinas. For details, see chapters 14 above and 17- 18.

harmonious truths" which permits "paradoxes," but not "contradictions." A mind "fashioned in the school of God" cannot embrace "both A and Non-A, except perhaps *dialectically*." Theological "coherence" involves "a single unified universe of knowledge" that is "compatible" with what has been "*revealed*," not in "conflict" with what has been "discovered." For this reason, theology "gladly utilizes all relevant materials and insights which other sciences contribute."[32]

(e) *Evidence and validation.* To meet the "rational" demand for "evidence," theology must obey "the logical laws of critical thinking." Through its own "proofs," "demonstration" and "heuristic proposals," it must illuminate experience and "*validate*" itself as science. Theology is not a "mere precipitate," or "mere hypothesis," based on inquiry and logical procedures, of ordinary experience. Rather, theology is "a response to, and systematic articulation of, divinely revealed truths." It is testable through its "*explanatory efficacy,*" its ability to "order and interpret the whole range of human experience" and "disclose the hidden structures and meanings of cosmic reality." A willing mind need not "demonstrate," or "prove," theology.[33] Christianity opens a perspective on the world corroborated by bringing all of "reality in support of the choice."[34]

(f) *Service of theology to humanity.* Being focused on the "supernatural" and "extra-cosmic realities" of the living God, as "chief discipline," theology is "religion made articulate."[35]

6–7. *"Three Minds" (1957, 1961)*

Unlike the way W. Harry Jellema used "mind" to depict three different ways of thinking in the history of Western philosophy, Stob wrote about three co-existing mentalities, which he called "minds," within Christian Reformed thinking about being "in" the world without being "of" the world. Two of

32. Stob (1981): 81.

33. Perhaps the somewhat odd expression "willing mind" is related to Stob's view of "will" and "intellect" and thinking about, respectively, "ethics" (freedom, choice) and "metaphysics" (reality, truth, A and Non-A).

34. Stob (1981): 82.

35. Stob (1981): 83. He concludes his article with a quote from Cardinal Newman's comment in "The Idea of a University": ". . . the omission of Christian theology from the list of recognized sciences is not only indefensible in itself but prejudicial to all the rest" and is (Stob adds) "injurious to human society."

these "minds" are *negative*: (a) being *safe*, or withdrawn, and (b) being *militant*, or combative; the third one (c) is *positive*: it reaches out and is redemptive.[36]

The first two "minds" are closely related to different opinions within Christian Reformed circles about the role of "common grace" in both everyday and academic life. In his article "The Militant Mind," Stob writes about what is "true, good and beautiful," warns against forgetting that these virtues can arise from a "totally corrupt" fountain,[37] and indicates that "even unregenerate culture" is a mixture "of grace as well as of sin."[38] Christians do "not view the world only in the perspective of the absolute antithesis." He stated the following:

> There is an absolute antithesis, although I should prefer to call it radical. The antithesis is, deep down, between the regenerate and the unregenerate heart, and it makes its presence felt in culture. But there is more than sin in the culture of the unregenerate; there is the *common grace* of God and his mercy to men in flight from him. Because of this fact, obscured I fear in militancy, is that we may and indeed must take to ourselves many of the fruits of worldly effort. This will leave us with much to oppose, for there is expressed in the worldling's work not only God's grace, but also the sinner's opposition to the person and purpose of God. However, while we should not make ourselves guilty of adopting what we should oppose, we should also not oppose what we are required to appreciate and adopt, for we should be guilty then of opposing God himself (emphasis added).[39]

He rejects any dualism between fideism and rationalism about what is supernatural and natural, the relation between belief and learning, religion and knowledge, and faith and reason. Instead, he accepts A. Kuyper's idea of a faith-conditioned conflict between "two scientific systems," not merely a

36. Stob (1981): "The Mind of the Church" (183–186); see also "The Mind of Safety" (187–194), "The Militant Mind" (195–209), and "The Positive Mind" (211–217). The first three articles were published in 1957 and the fourth in 1961, in *RJ*.

37. Stob (1981): 198, together with what is "right, and holy"; see also 208.

38. Stob (1981): 209.

39. Stob (1981): 209. Stob refers in his article to Calvin's *Institutes*, II.ii.15: "If we regard the Spirit of God as the sole foundation of truth, we shall neither reject the truth itself, not despise it, wherever it shall appear, unless we wish to dishonor the Spirit of God. . . . Let us, accordingly, learn by their example how many gifts the Lord left to human nature even after it was despoiled of its true good."

conflict between "faith and science."[40] The influence of "religion," or "faith," on "natural and formal science" is not direct, but "indirect," and actually only in "philosophy." According to Kuyper, philosophy is "the true and 'proper' locus of the antithesis in the realm of theoretical activity."

Any distinction between "Christian and non-Christian *facts*" Stob rejects. He ends his "Faith and Science" discussion in a semi-scholastic way, as also A. Kuyper had done. It is only when one moves up the scale of the "sciences" and gets into those concerned with humans and their values that what it means to be Christian clearly and unequivocally appears.[41]

8. *"Calvin and Aquinas"* (1974)

In memory of the 700th anniversary of T. Aquinas, Stob stated in "Calvin and Aquinas" that "in the mountain range of sanctified reflection two peaks stand out above the rest," namely, Augustine and Aquinas.

> These two estimable thinkers effected a vaster and more influential synthesis of Christ and culture, theology and philosophy, than have any others in the history of the church; and every thoughtful and well-directed Christian student, interested in these central issues, has had to go to school with them. It would be futile, and perhaps perverse, to inquire which of these two—*the Plato and the Aristotle of the Christian tradition*—should be given primacy. Protestantism has, to be sure, been shaped prominently by St. Augustine, but no responsible Protestant has thought it fitting to ignore St. Thomas, and none has found it possible to evade the thrust of his searching analyses (emphasis added).[42]

Centering his comments on what is basic for "Reformed" Protestants, who do *"not* heed the admonition of Leo XIII to pattern themselves on Thomistic lines," Stob states that key to the "intellectual engagement" of

---

40. Stob (1981): 19–20, where he quotes from Kuyper's *Lectures on Calvinism*, 176.

41. Stob (1981): 22; see also 21. Stob's quotations from two of Dooyeweerd's writings to support his own view of "faith" and "fact" do not sufficiently take into account the "religious" intent and depth of Dooyeweerd's "transcendental critique of theoretical thought." Stob still thinks in terms of Kuyper's traditional (and questionable) idea of "science," "subject and object," "logic," "truth," and "common grace." For details, see "A. Kuyper" and "H. Dooyeweerd" in chapters 5 and 7.

42. Stob (1981): 126. This commemorative article appeared first in *RJ* in May-June, 1974.

Christians with "the wider world of thinking and understanding" is "the relation of the Revelation in Christ, the eternal and incarnate Logos, to that Reason, or immanent Logos, which prevails in universal culture." As to the possibility of "grace-induced faith" to participate in the "rational pursuit of truth, goodness, and beauty," he stressed the importance of "the relation between religion and science, Christ and culture, revelation and reason, theology and philosophy, grace and nature, and the like."[43]

Combining the *origin, form* and *content* of Judeo-Christian and Greco-Roman wisdom brought about a "clash" between divine revelation and human inquiry, prophecies and arguments, a personal God and an impersonal principle. About four centuries later, three other ideas developed concerning "revelation and reason." Instead of theology and philosophy being in *conflict* with one another, "faith" and "reason" can be viewed as being: (a) *compatible,* having the same Logos and being similar, (b) *complex,* or *dialectical,* a Yes and No, the former being "above" the other (Aquinas), and (c) *transformational,* one "uses" the other and "changes" it (Calvin).[44]

Whereas Roman Catholics stressed "nature" and "grace" more than "sin," and Lutherans concentrated on "grace" and associated "nature, reason and culture" with "sin," Calvinists stressed "creation" (nature), "fall" (sin) and "redemption" (grace). For Aquinas "nature" is basic; for Calvin "creation" is fundamental. According to Calvin "nature and natural reason . . . have been despoiled by sin, and they can be retrieved and utilized only after they have been renewed by grace, and only after they have been viewed and exercised in the closest possible association with faith."[45]

9. "Personality, Human and Divine" (1981)

In this article, Stob reflects on God, humans, and their interrelationship. Not in Socrates, Plato or Aristotle, but in the incarnate One did "God become

43. Stob (1981): 127.

44. Stob (1981): 127–129. "The Christ that the church most decisively confessed was neither the Christ *against* culture, nor the Christ *of* culture, but either the Christ *above* culture or the Christ who *transforms* culture. What came to be almost universally advocated in Christendom was some sort of *synthesis*" (129).

45. Stob (1981): 130. Stob criticizes Aquinas for endorsing Aristotle as philosopher, rigidly distinguishing between theology and philosophy, denying the possibility of a Christian philosophy, being too rationalistic in arguing for God's existence, being too empiricistic, and advocating an ethics of natural law.

intelligible as a person." Only in Jesus, who is one with the Father, do we have a concept of "a dignification of man and humanization of God." The "Trinitarian controversies" deepened this conception. As a "category of thought," the idea of "personality" first developed in the course of "speculations," or "intellectual formulations of beliefs" about God.

As a "philosophical principle," this "ontological discussion" was present in the Nicene Creed.[46] It attempted to express "the plurality in distinction from the unity of the Godhead" by using *"persona"* (Latin: mask, actor, role) and *"hypostasis"* (Greek: existence, not appearance) as "synonyms" which modify "one another."[47] In addition to *"life"* and *"consciousness,"* to be a "person" requires: (i) *"rationality,"* or *"thinking consciousness,"* (ii) being an *"individual,"* which involves "uniqueness, incommunicability, and substantiality" and "a multitude of other selves," (iii) possessing *"self-consciousness,"* or "both subject and object at once," (iv) *"volition,"* "will" and ability "to initiate actions, to be a cause, to choose, to override necessity, to create," (v) *"permanence, continuity, self-identity,"* or "memory," and (vi) *"capacity for morality,"* opting for one of two proposed courses, behaving as a "responsible subject."[48]

The *"reality"* of "personality" is a "metaphysical" problem that calls for "epistemological groundwork." According to Augustine, the reality of a person's "selfhood" is "indubitable," an Archimedean "fulcrum," a "self-consciousness" with a "certainty" about "the order of being," especially "logical order," and some "assignable property."

> Our certainty of self as manifested in these [human] activities is therefore a certainty of personality, which is nothing more nor less than a unity of psychical states. Thus Augustine provided himself with a secure beginning and subsequently made all his ideas center about the principle of the immediate certainty of inner experience. He is followed in this primary faith by all reputable theistic thinkers.[49]

"Personality" is "the only thing we know most surely and the principle of all knowing." It is "our best approach to reality." According to H. Bavinck,

---

46. Stob (1981): 54–55.

47. Stob (1981): 55.

48. Stob (1981): 56–57. In short, a person is "a consciousness which thinks; which is unique; which distinguishes itself from things, from other persons, and from its own states; which is self-conscious; which acts; which persists; and which is capable of morality."

49. Stob (1981): 58.

The only way by which we can come to reality is that of self-consciousness. And this approach determines our basic category, so intimately bound up with ontology. It is from the personality of man, the one reliable datum of experience, that, philosophically, we arrive at personality of God. We make the inescapable assumption that *reality must be the most intelligible in terms of the highest we know*, that reality must somehow consist with our best notion of it, that *thought*, in other words, *has ontological validity* (emphasis added).[50]

Since it is philosophy's "ultimate category," a theist ascribes "personality" not just to "finite" reality, but also to "Ultimate Reality." Even though formal proofs for God's existence are inadequate, for theists every "judgment" has a "transcendental reference" that "sustains" it and is "beyond ourselves."

For our thought we need an ultimate validator and for our moral striving we need an ultimate norm. And if these circumstances, independently considered, do not get us God, they constitute an *overwhelming presumption* in favor of his existence, and combined with the deliverance of religious experience carry for many full conviction (emphasis added).[51]

Aware of the "ontological implications of finite selfhood," Augustine used an "ontological argument" to "arrive, philosophically, at the certainty of God." According to Plato, finite human self-consciousness entails an "entity" endowed with "will, intellect, and emotion," that aspires towards "truth, beauty, and goodness" as "something transcendent and universally valid," which humans are "compelled to affirm" by "denying it." For Augustine, Plato's "incorporeal and abstract" universals are not "self-existent," but are "united" in God's "ideas." Because "truth, beauty, and goodness" reside in God, one must "ascribe to him intelligence and will" and "think of him as a person."[52]

This ultimate "person," who is "intelligible" as "law-giver," is not some

50. Stob (1981): 58.

51. Stob (1981): 59.

52. Stob (1981): 60. Bavinck claims something similar in *Philosophy of Revelation*, although he does so not in terms of a "contemplation of the knowledge relation," but through "psychological introspection" as an immediate given in experience—a "self" is not some mere or "bare existence," some general "what," but a "particular existence," a specific "what," a "hampered, finite, dependent self," or, as Bavinck says, something "limited, temporal, creaturely" with a "feeling of dependence." Because finite consciousness is "free and personal," also "Ul-

"absoluteness" (deism), or "the All" (pantheism), but something the concept "one independent ground of all things" points to, viz., "transcendence and immanence." The "superiority" of God's selfhood is "indubitable" to anyone who believes in God as the Creator. Being created in "the likeness of God, humans bear his image." Especially in the "selfhood" is that "affinity" manifest.[53]

The truths of God's *existence, ability* to hear and *willingness* to help are "propositions" that underlie *"all* prayer." Although "theistic proofs" do not satisfy the canons of "strict logic," God's "intelligence and power," moving from "the infinite to the finite" into human "minds *directly,*" lay claim to their "conscience." Possessing a "native and indelible awareness of God" (*sensus divinitatis*), humans "affirm" him or, apart from grace, create a *substitute* for him.[54]

Though "incomparable in his glory," God is in a "real sense like us." Being both "individual" and "social," God is "distinct from, though in relation to mankind," fully aware of its needs. He is "a centered self possessing all the marks of selfhood—life, intelligence, volition and affection." As "a person," God "lives, perceives, understands, wills and feels."

> Of course, his personality is infinitely complex (consider his triune nature) and it transcends the limitations that characterize our own (which is only analogous to his). But this means that he is not less, but more personal than we are—more acute, more aware, more sensitive than we shall ever be. It is this fact that justifies prayer. God is not a mere object, but a subject; not a thing, but a self. And though he has no ears (for he is not corporeal), he is infinite *Spirit,* and this enables him to hear.[55]

This exalted God, with "omniscient intelligence," became *"incarnate"* and in an "immanent" way understands those who pray. Being "love," he is

---

timate Reality (God) must be personal, for the finite cannot exceed the infinite." This kind of argument is not a "philosophic proof," but the effect of "reflective thinking" (60).

53. Stob (1981): 63. Stob rejects the view of R. H. Lotze (1817–1881) in *Microcosmos* (1856–1864) that "divine personality" is based on the "subject-object aspect of selfhood" and that the "personality" of humans is only a "faint image of its glorious and perfect antitype" in God. Stob's *scholastic* view of "image of God" is evident when he asserts that "as with an acorn," "growth" is the law of the "developmental and aspirational qualities of the selfhood," in which the "potential perpetually outruns its *actus,*" and has "a transcendental reference. It never is what it may be. It has infinity to traverse and is always on its way" (63).

54. Stob (1981): "Prayer and Providence," 84–86.

55. Stob (1981): 88.

determined "*not to be alone,* but to *share* his blessedness and felicity with others." In creating man, he enlarged "the intra-trinitarian community" to permit "*others* to be insinuated into the divine life . . . [and] participate in the Kingdom and enjoy the divine fellowship."[56]

As to "the person and work of Christ," Christianity is "final and absolute." It reflects God's way of "dealing with men and of man's graciously initiated response" to this divine activity. The Christian religion is different, unique and absolute, set over against "every ethnic faith." The "antithesis" is not "primarily" between "two histories," "two lives" or "two theologies," but in the conflict between the two "principles of sin and grace."[57] It is "effected by the supernatural and absolute power of grace . . . mediated to the world through Jesus Christ and the Spirit." The result is a "great gulf" between those who, "called out of the mass of men" are in Christ "saved from condemnation" *and* those who, yielding to the devil's temptation, "fell away from God," "came into the power of sin," and, "outside of Christ," live from "the principle of sin."[58]

The key to "religion" and "religious life" is provided in the "revelation set down in the Christian Scriptures, the Bible. . . ." Such "faith" is offensive to those who do not believe it, but a welcome to those who know that not "improvement" but repentance from serving false gods is called for.[59]

The *radical* difference between Christian and non-Christian religion does not imply a "*negative* judgment" on all non-Christian religions. In four ways—(a)*sensus divinitatis/cognitio dei innata,* (b) general revelation, (c) common grace, and (d) special revelation—it calls for appreciating certain features in other religions through borrowing from them, memory or tradition. Christianity is "the *denial* of the ethnic faiths and the fulfillment of them" or "a rejection of them and an answer to their questions." Mission is "*necessary*" and "*possible.*"[60]

56. Stob (1981): 89 and 90. "In short, *communion* was his goal—not for his own sake (for he was always in communion), but for the sake of man" (90). About *redemption, providence,* and *preservation,* see 91–93.

57. Stob (1981): 120.

58. Stob (1981): 122.

59. Stob (1981): 122–123. Stob's use of "faith" (in "judgment of faith") in the sense of "faith" as *gift*—not as human *activity, content* and *aspect* of reality—reflects his traditional (scholastic) view of "religion" and (semi-Lutheran?) idea of an "antithesis" between "grace" and "sin."

60. Stob (1981): 123–124.

10. "Faith and Reason" (1981)

Stob writes about "two distinguishable spiritual functions" that seemingly "trace two divergent paths to truth." These two "avenues to truth," and corresponding "types of knowledge," relate to "natural truths," known "independently of faith," and to "supernatural truths" never known by "reason." These two "independent processes" require acknowledging the "territorial rights" of each and not allowing any invasion of the one into the other. What is personal, individual, private and irrational may *not* determine what is natural, public, demonstrable and scientific. Christ may rule in a person's heart, but not his head. Personal faith and impersonal reason are not the same.[61]

Given life's "inviolable wholeness," Stob rejects this theory of the relation between faith and reason. As "abstractions," such terms as Man, Reason and Faith are only "indirectly" relevant to life, meaningful only as "adjectives" in the sense of "particularity," e.g., "*this* man" and "this man's *use* of faith and reason." Faith and reason are "natural functions, common to all men, and integral to their native constitution. Man is a reasoning and believing animal. . . ." As with "faith," "reason" also is a "function," an "expression of the man," something "specific in reference and personal in character." Therefore,

> If the man be Christian, the expression will be Christian; there will be a Christian exercise of reason. . . . Reason will be exercised not only in conformity with the laws of thought as a form of obeisance to the *Immanent Logos*, but also, and that unflinchingly, in subjection to the *incarnate Logos*, which is the Christ, and the *inscripturated Logos*, which is his Word. Christian reason, like Christian faith, will be childlike, humble, obedient. . . . Christian thinking will be . . . thinking conditioned by the character and nature of the thinker, and by the thinker's basic loyalties. It will not be something separate from faith, but rather something joined to faith in the deeper unity of selfhood. It will not be neutral, in the sense in which that word has become a kind of shibboleth, but will be colored and controlled and "biased" by the immediate apprehension of that truth which, though not perceived apart from thought, is never the deliverance of thought, but always *a miracle and a gift*. It will be thinking in the shadow of Christ and of his cross; or, to put it somewhat differently, a thinking "prejudiced" in favor of *The Truth* (emphases added).[62]

61. See Stob (1981): 39–41.
62. Stob (1981): 41–42 . He indicates that a "Christian science" will differ in degree,

Any "antithesis that separates the student in us from the Christian" destroys our "essential unity" and makes us "lame and ineffectual both in our religion and in our science." This call to bring every thought "into captivity to the obedience of Christ" is biblical, but—as will be indicated in the next two chapters—his view of faith, reason and their interrelationship remains in essence scholastic.

As "instrument of the Spirit," a "new divine organ," or the "result of a miracle," "faith" as "deed and gift of God" is not based on "reason," "experience," "a condition," or a "work" rewarded with salvation. It is "active" in apprehending and "passive" in "accepting" salvation; it is not "superimposed, a kind of superadditum," but a "movement of the whole personality" in "subjection to God."[63]

> Faith . . . whatever else it may be, certainly includes intellectual assent to definite propositions. It is a belief in certain facts and a certain interpretation of those facts. . . . It changes not only one's system of thought but also one's self. . . . It involves the acceptance of a definite witness to a definite redemptive act.[64]

In "Notes on the Philosophy of St. Augustine" (1973), Stob states that the "temper, approach and spirit" of Augustine's philosophy reveals a "religious" and "inward" feature, a certain Platonic "openness," evident also in the thinking of Anselm, Calvin and Pascal.[65] It implies a (Christian) search for salvation that coincides with a (philosophical) search for truth. God is both a "subject" to be loved and an "object" to be known. Piety and reflection, worship and inquiry, love and logic, light and truth, praise and knowledge, and illumination and apprehension belong together in the way *faith* and *reason* do. As the *sine qua non* of wisdom, "faith" centers on *God,* and as what makes humans unique, "reason" enables humans to discern truths, particularly about the cosmos. As subject of knowledge, *man* is a "unity" of "reason" and "will" (moral choice) and "commitment" (religion). Theology is

---

method and conclusions from a science that rejects "the assistance of a supernatural revelation," and that this difference will be "most apparent in the sciences of the spirit, and especially in philosophy." What a "religiously oriented metaphysics" entails depends on the meaning of "science," "fact," "interpretation," "system" and "similar indefinite concepts."

63. Stob (1981): 162, in "The Doctrine of Revelation in St. Paul," in *CTJ,* 1966.

64. Stob (1981): 163.

65. Stob (1981): 43–44. The observation is based on Augustine's *De Civitate Dei, De Trinitate, De Doctrina Christiana,* and *Enchiridion.*

not differentiated from philosophy. To understand Christian belief, thinking needs to be guided by the community of believers.[66]

In distinction from "nature," "sense" and "body," this "inward" character in humans points to their "mind," "reason" and "consciousness." This self-knowledge and openness to divine truth is made possible by God's "descent in grace" and human "ascent in search." The "ontological gap" between Creator and creature is not bridged by divine grace, nor by human virtue. It is impossible to know oneself without knowing God. There is no "final synthesis between the agape motif of Paul and the eros motif of Plato, between the God-centered philosophy of revelation and the man-centered philosophy of the Greeks."[67]

As to the "soul's desire," in Augustine's thinking, the cosmos "lies midway on the scale of reality between the being who created it and the non-being out of which it was created." Since it is "shot through with contingency," the cosmos "neither wholly is nor wholly is not." Of this cosmos, man is the "highest part."

> Above him is God, below him is nature. He is linked with nature through the body . . . with God through the soul. Nature and the body are next to nothing, the soul is next to God. The soul, therefore, lies midway between God to whom it is subject, and nature over which it is lord. Let the soul, then, reflecting upon itself, seek her own place in conformity to her nature, under Him to Whom she is to be subjected, above the things over which she is to be placed; under Him by whom she ought to be ruled, above the things which she ought to rule."[68]

Because it is not "sufficient to itself," the soul is "dynamic," "restless," filled with a yearning for something "outside" itself to "complete" it. The soul desires the "happiness" of "truth, beauty, goodness." This desire for happiness and love is "natural" and "universal." The soul's inner "desire" assumes that "God" is man's "Good" and is found "only in and through the soul lifted up above the world of sense, of matter, and of flesh."[69]

To understand the "revealed truths . . . apprehended and accepted by faith" about God, man and their interrelations, Augustine had to "theol-

---

66. Stob (1981): 45–46.

67. Stob (1981): 46–48. "Theocentrism" does not permit "an egocentrism inherited from the Neoplatonists" (48).

68. Stob (1981): 49 (reference to *De Trinitate*, I, x,5).

69. Stob (1981): 49.

ogize," or "philosophize." For this, he used the "intellectual" tools of neo-Platonic thinking, terms, concepts, categories, principles and frameworks in vogue at that time.

> He adopted its general spirit and direction; used many of its directions; profited from its analyses; and in general identified himself with its temper and outlook. In Augustine's hand, consequently, Christianity took on a Neoplatonic *form*. His philosophy can thus with considerable justice be called a *Christian Platonism*.[70]

To use these available "thought structures," Augustine sometimes had to "rupture" its scheme, "misconstrue" Christian teaching, and "import alien matter" into it. At the same time, he believed, as Calvin did later, that Christians may "appropriate" truth "not foreign to the pagan and the unbeliever."[71]

For two things, Stob criticized Augustine's way of thinking: (a) his "one-sidedly ontological" philosophy involves "a contemplative engagement with eternal ideas" that ends up with "mystic flights to non-sensuous realms." This ignores the importance of "the created cosmos," and fosters a concept of the soul's "immortality" that does injustice to human "naive experience or common sense," and (b) the notion of a "scale of being" (Being, cosmos, and non-being) and the distinction *within* the "cosmos" of "man and nature," "soul and body," leaves no room for "theistic" thinking and opens the doors to "monistic and emanational" theories.[72] For this criticism, he referred to the important assumption in Reformed Epistemology at CC, viz.,

> An entity possessing the powers of intellection and volition may perhaps be said to be closer to God than one which lacks these powers, but then not

---

70. Stob (1981): 50.

71. Stob (1981): 51 and 52. He refers to Calvin's comment about freely using the contributions of "the impious" (*Institutes*, II, xi, 18) and Augustine's statement "Let every good and true Christian understand that truth, wherever he finds it, belongs to his Lord" (*De Doct. Christ.*, I, xi, 18).

72. Stob (1981): 52–53. Instead of a "ladder of existence with its four rungs of God, soul, body, and nothing," Stob states that between "God and the created cosmos" a "most fundamental distinction," or "metaphysical gulf," exists, and that "non-being" is not "something," but "precisely nothing," although in Christian metaphysics the term can designate "the realm of God's possibility."

in any ontological sense, but only in the spiritual and ethical sense of being able to apprehend and respond to God.[73]

11. "Moral Philosophy and Theology" (1976)

In writing about "moral philosophy and theology,"[74] Stob reveals the center and contours of his thinking. Philosophy is a "theoretic and systematic construction interpretive of the various aspects of reality." As a "particular science," theology focuses on "a single aspect of reality," viz., "religion," or "heart," and uses "concepts, categories and assumptions open to philosophical scrutiny and appraisal." This "immediate relationship of the self to God" is *"vital and affective,"* an *"elemental affection of the heart, a fundamental movement of the soul, a basic attitude of the self"* (emphasis added).[75]

The two basic "attitudes" of loving or hating, being reconciled or unreconciled, believing in or disbelieving God are not "determined by reasonings or independent volitions," but they "determine all reasonings and volitions." The "choice" Christians make in this regard is "divinely and miraculously conditioned" and, "constrained by a divine compulsion," compels them to be "committed to obedient thinking."[76]

Salient features of Stob's moral philosophy are seven principles[77]: (i) *God-man-nature* as ontological paradigm, (ii) *God* as "ultimate environment" or "last boundary" of human existence, as basis for "will" and "morality," (iii) *law* as something that is subordinate and calls for obedience, (iv) T. Aquinas as thinker about happiness, universal good and seven virtues (cf. faith, hope, love as *"christian"* virtues, and prudence, courage, temperance and justice as *"common-grace"* virtues), (v) "ethos" as "external" and "ethics" as "internal" doing, (vi) a distinction between "spiritual" and "natural," the

---

73. Stob (1981): 53. Stob ends his article by stating that "Augustine is and remains a most distinguished teacher of the church, a saint of the first magnitude, and a thinker who cannot be circumvented by anyone who aspires to do philosophy or theology in this or any future age." For details, see chapters 17 and 18 below.

74. The foundational and complex issues in Stob's Moral Philosophy can be summarized as follows: (i) relation between Creator and creation, (ii) meaning of human, natural and law, and (iii) nature of truth, knowledge, culture and history.

75. Stob (1976): 31, 32.

76. Stob (1976): 34.

77. Based on his "Ethics: With What Does It Deal?" in *CTJ*, 11:1 (1976) pages 34–60, and his unpublished class lectures, given to me in 1965 when I enrolled at CTS for one semester as a prerequisite to becoming a pastor in the Christian Reformed Church of North America.

former more evident in the "image of God" and the latter evident in God as "causality," and (vii) "will" associated with the "logical power of thought," "thinking" and "aspiring."[78]

The proper object of ethics is *not* God as the "Unchangeable One," "Goodness itself," or "source and guarantor" of everything, but, rather, the "voluntary conduct" of humans as God's "image-bearer" in their "moral struggle between good and evil."[79] As "science of the moral life," ethics centers on "an aspect of human conduct which is neither open to sensible observation nor amenable to causal explanation." God judges humans "supremely" about what his "image-bearers do in imitation of him." He judges them in terms of norms that are absolute and universal, not "relative and contingent." To be moral is to do what is "good," display "virtue," or use the "will" as a "native and inalienable property or organ" to distinguish between "good and bad."[80]

Given the antithesis between sin and grace[81] (Gen. 3:15), moral judgment does not permit "syncretism" in one's behavior. As to the *content* of ethics in relation to God's revelation in the "incarnate and inscripturated Word," the structures of human behavior are "incompatible."[82] The *ground* of ethics is the "Ultimate Reality" of Love, rooted in the "nature and will of God" as "the bedrock on which the cosmos rests." Love "impinges upon and merges with metaphysics and theology." The ideals of ethics are "objectively real," not unstable and changing, nor "outside the domain of knowledge." The basis of "morality, or ought," is the "is" of Love.[83]

78. Stob (1976): 34, 41–42. Stob sometimes uses *reformational* terms in a traditionally *scholastic Reformed* way—e.g., man's behavior "functions through every aspect of the created world"; man exhibits "in himself all the modalities of being distinguishable in creation"—arithmetical, geometrical, physical, biological, psychical, logical, historical and moral sphere; "although each man's aspects and functions are unique, each is tied with every other and is affected by them"; and "moral life, though not the product of physical, biological, social, economic, and other forces, is nevertheless lived in the context of such forces, and cannot escape their influence" (40 and 44).

79. Stob (1976): 37.

80. Stob (1976): 46, 47–51. The struggle is typical of ethical, not intellectual, or emotional, life.

81. The "antithesis" of (human) "sin" is not (God's) "grace," but (human) obedience, and the opposite of (God's) "grace" is not (human) "sin" but (God's) judgment. This statement of Stob reflects his acceptance of (Greek) "faculty psychology."

82. Stob (1976): 54.

83. Stob (1976): 56, 57. He adds that ethicists, who think they are not metaphysicians, have "not thought their position to the end" and are, by focusing on "becoming" instead of "being," pragmatists and "anti-metaphysical" (58).

Metaphysics and ethics are "interdependent": the former focuses on "truth" and the latter on "goodness."[84] Good and evil are not "existences," but "distinctions" that enable humans to move forward on the road of responsibility.[85] Ethics cannot "resist the inner compulsion to advance beyond itself." For that reason, ethics is not separable from the "underlying *system* of truth—called philosophy, theology or metaphysics—which delineates the Ultimately Real and sets forth the basic structure of the cosmos in which the moral life is lived."[86]

Faced with "competing systems of reality," ethics must decide between "rival definitions of what is the ultimate justifier of moral principle, moral judgment, and moral behavior." In an ultimate sense, it depends on "the result or outcome of our metaphysics or theology," our "all-encompassing world and life view." About the latter, he comments,

> The decision in favor of this or that "system" is prior to the construction of the ethic. As Professor Jellema says: "Ethics may clarify the decision; show me something of what is involved in it; contribute to the intelligence of the decision; but it cannot furnish the last ground for the decision." For that is a religious, and not a merely moral act.[87]

According to Stob, the distinction between "religious" and "moral" presupposes a Greek view of "metaphysics," "theology" and "ethics": the first two studies focus on what is (intellectually) "true" or "false," the third on what is (morally) "good" or "evil."

Summary and Comments

Without a radically *religious*[88] renewal, the identity and importance of integrally Christian higher education weakens and runs the risk of subtly and gradually disappearing. The philosophical views of Henry J. Stob at CTS—and, by implication, of W. Harry Jellema at CC—will be helpful before we turn to the last two chapters in this considerably larger than initially in-

84. Stob (1976): 58. "Truth and goodness are inseparable, and our view of the one determines our view of the other."
85. Stob (1976): 58.
86. Stob (1976): 59.
87. Stob (1976): 59.
88. Used in a *reformational*, not an *accommodational/scholastic*, sense.

tended study. Not to be engaged in *religious* renewal in our "heart," the core of being human in whatever we do, is a subtle temptation in all Christian—Orthodox, Roman Catholic, Protestant, Reformed/Presbyterian, Anglican/Episcopalian, and Evangelical—traditions of all, especially higher, education, in the nebulous discipline of "theology."

Within a relatively short span of time, this became evident in Calvin's Academy of Geneva (est. 1559), and, eventually, even the Christian Universities of, for example, Leyden, Princeton, Yale and Harvard. In principle, this can happen also to educational institutions like CC and CTS[89] to the extent they incorporate ideas in their thinking that are *religiously* inhibiting in our understanding what is unique about created reality, especially about humans bearing His image.

At CC both W. Harry Jellema and Henry J. Stob, and at CTS, for almost thirty years, Stob called medieval scholastic thinking "Christian Mind." For Jellema, "truth" and "reality" (ontology) and for Stob, "being human" and "ethics" (anthropology)—both of these echo (i) St. Augustine's (fourth-century) neo-Platonic thinking, T. Aquinas' (twelfth-century) use of Aristotle's philosophy, combined with Augustine's theology, (ii) T. Beza's (sixteenth-century) inaugural lecture at the opening of the Academy in Geneva, and (iii) H. Bavinck's (nineteenth-century) *Reformed Dogmatics*, with its "biblical" intent but "scholastic" use of traditional philosophical assumptions about such basic terms as "reality," "truth" and "certainty."[90]

This affected also his view of "faith," "religion," "doctrine," "revelation," "salvation" and "discipleship" with respect to basic issues in *ontology* (essence, boundary and created reality), *anthropology* (soul-body dualism) and *epistemology* (knowing, truth, logic).

Reformed thinking and teaching at CTS (and CC, as will be indicated in Chapter 17 and 18) reflected "scholastic" ways of thinking about especially "philosophy" and "theology," their interrelationships, and their relation to other disciplines (*wetenschappen*). The philosophical track Bavinck used, in the 1890s, in especially volume I of his *GD*, I-IV, in the Netherlands,

---

89. As well as in other schools such as Dordt College, Trinity Christian College, and Kuyper College in the USA; Institute for Christian Studies, Redeemer University College, and The King's University College in Canada.

90. The Christian Reformed community in North America needs to make a *critical* study of H. Bavinck's philosophy, anthropology and view of education. For details, see R. H. Bremmer, *Herman Bavinck als dogmaticus* (1961) J. H. Kok N.V. Kampen about Platonic, Aristotelian and Aquinian elements in Bavinck's thinking.

L. Berkhof used extensively in his *RD*, 1933 (*ST,* 1938), and Henry J. Stob incorporated in his role as professor of Ethics and Apologetics at CTS.[91]

The cumulative effect of pervasive Reformed scholastic thinking in philosophy, theology and ethics has been a predominantly neo-Platonic Augustinian and Aristotelian Aquinian view of truth and reality and its impact on faith life, theology and (all levels of) Christian education and scholarship.

Distinct features in Stob's thinking, teaching and writing as a Reformed theologian, ethicist, apologist and commentator are the following twelve examples:

1. Emphasis on Scripture (*sola Scriptura*) as God's written word and on Jesus Christ, as God's Son, the Word-incarnate.
2. Use of scholastic methods and concepts in his view of, for example, "reality," "intellect," "mind," "truth," "freedom," "causality" and "virtues."
3. A dualistic view of soul and body, faith and reason, special and general revelation, special and common grace, vertical and horizontal relations, religion and culture, theocentric and anthropocentric.
4. He taught numerous preachers, teachers, colleagues and other servant-leaders to perpetuate his view of "integrating" Scripture with some Greek ways of thinking, and even resisted a biblically directed simpler and more radical view of "integrally" Christian living in society and shaping culture.
5. He focused on "deep thoughts"[92] in: (a) pre-Christian thinkers like Parmenides, Socrates, Plato and Aristotle, (b) scholastic theologians, philosophers and educators, and (c) non-Christian scientists, logicians and other experts who lacked critical discernment.
6. He did not really discuss the real differences between two Christian Reformed traditions in theology, ethics, economics, citizenship, etc., in

91. Reflecting on his advisory role in the "Plato Club" at CC, Stob indicated in his *Memoirs* that four of its eleven members in 1951 were Dewey J. Hoitenga, Jr., C. Seerveld, A. Plantinga, and N. Wolterstorff. Hoitenga taught philosophy at Grand Valley State University in Michigan; Seerveld taught Aesthetics at Trinity Christian College, in Illinois and at the ICS in Toronto (1976–1996); Plantinga and Wolterstorff co-founded, in 1982, at CC, Reformed Epistemology (RE). Cf. Henry Stob, *Summoning Up Remembrance* (Grand Rapids: Wm. B. Eerdmans Publishing Co., 1995) 313; also 218, 284.

92. As a member of the "Plato Club" in 1957/8, sponsored that school year by H. Evan Runner, I (we) read H. Dooyeweerd's *New Critique of Theoretical Thought* and reflected extensively on the pros and cons of Dooyeweerd's *reformational* thinking in philosophy and other disciplines, including theology, and of classic, or traditional, *Reformed* thinking.

terms of God's all-encompassing Word, which in Christ (the Truth, the Way and the Life) calls humans to image Him as his children.[93]

7. His motto was Augustine's neo-Platonic phrase "faith seeking understanding" (*fides quaerens intellectum*), the official motto of CTS.

8. Given his Greek anthropology with its inherent "faculty psychology," the "intellect" focuses on what is "true/false," and "will" on what is "good/evil," i.e., respectively, "truth" and "ethics."

9. Stob thinks in terms of three levels of human existence: what is natural, human decisions and the relation of humans to God.

10. His essay "Too Much Philosophy and Warrant for Theology" (1983) may have influenced A. Plantinga to write his major *Warranted Christian Belief*, 2000—the similarity between Stob's view of "Calvin/Aquinas" (1974) and Plantinga's comments about "The Aquinas/Calvin Model" (2000) is noteworthy.

11. His (in)famous *Banner* articles on the three mind-sets in the Christian Reformed Church reflect an anthropology based on Greek "faculty psychology" about the meaning of being human.

12. As "chief" of all "authentic sciences," the study of theology is about "supernatural realities, with extra-cosmic verities," and centers on such things as "religion," the "eternal and living God," the "influences of religion"—in short, "theology is religion made articulate."[94]

To learn more about issues raised above and living as we do in a *religiously* troubled world filled with major local, regional and global problems and challenges, we turn now to what is praiseworthy and problematic in (Christian) Reformed philosophy, theology and related academic endeavors, in an attempt to explore a simpler and more radically biblical way of local and global thinking and living.

93. As a member of the "Plato Club" in 1957/8, sponsored that school year by H. Evan Runner, I/we read H. Dooyeweerd's *New Critique of Theoretical Thought* and reflected for hours on the difference between his (*reformational*) thinking and that of some prominent (*Greek*) philosophers.

94. Stob (1981): 83, in "The Warrant for Theology in a Scientific Age," (1953) written while he taught at Calvin College.

CHAPTER SEVENTEEN

Calvin College:
Nicholas Wolterstorff (1932–)

Introduction

"Reformed Epistemology" involves a philosophical study of human faith life, including theology, by means of a form of *accommodational* thinking about the meaning of such terms as faith, reason, theology and philosophy, especially the relation between faith and reason, knowledge and metaphysics, the meaning of "liberal arts" and a distinct view of "truth."

It assumes certain philosophical and anthropological ideas in the mind-set of Calvin Theological Seminary (CTS, established 1857) and Calvin College (established 1920),[1] combined with a modern way of thinking influenced by Scottish "Common Sense" philosophy and modern Anglo-American linguistic-analytical method. N. Wolterstorff's and A. Plantinga's way of thinking reveals the major impact on their thinking of their two chief philosophical mentors, viz., W. Harry Jellema (1898–1982) at Calvin College and Henry J. Stob (1908–1996) at both Calvin College and CTS.[2]

---

1. The Theological School of the CRC consisted initially of a three-year *literature* department (which in the 1920s became Calvin College) and a three-year *theology* department. Calvin College has always been the *official* college of the CRC (cf. Richard H. Harms, *Calvin Spark*, Fall 2009, 14). After World War II, thousands of mainly neo-Kuyperian Dutch immigrants came to North America, especially Canada. This influx of immigrants affected the dynamics and divergence within the CRC in the USA and Canada, especially in higher education, labor unions, citizenship, agriculture and business.

2. H. Stob was an ordained minister in the CRC (1952–1975). He taught Philosophy at Calvin College (1939–1943 and 1946–1952), and Philosophical and Moral Theology at CTS

These two scholars in, respectively, "philosophy" and "ethics" advocated a semi-scholastic view of "knowledge" and "reality."

The background of the Society of Christian Philosophy, established in 1978, assumed the validity of traditional "faith and reason" thinking and its encyclopedic implications for theology, philosophy and other academic disciplines.

Ever since the 1920s, the CRC has experienced an uneasiness about its nature and role in North American culture, reflected in the difference, sometimes conflict, between a culture-shunning and a culture-improving disposition, a kind of pietism and cultural relevance, stress on antithesis and common grace, special and general revelation, a religion, or faith life, focused on God and an involvement in society. This ambiguity, at times tension, was evident in the editorial policies of the two leading CRC journals, *The Torch & Trumpet* (later *The Reformed Outlook)* and *The Calvin Forum* (later *The Reformed Journal*).

In their study of especially theology, of being Reformed and of other religions, students at CTS and Calvin College were taught to think in terms of Scripture (*sola Scriptura)*, and in other courses, including philosophy and ethics, in terms of traditional Western ideas about, for example, intellect, logic, essence, truth, relation, and reality in a way that was somehow influenced by the thought of such major Greek thinkers as Parmenides, Socrates, Plato and Aristotle.[3]

Reflecting on his role as the designated advisor of the "Plato Club" at Calvin College, Henry J. Stob stated that in 1952 two of its (eleven) members were A. Plantinga and N. Wolterstorff.[4] Three decades later, these two per-

---

(1952–1975). He was a founder, and longtime editor, of *The Reformed Journal*, an intellectually influential publication (cf. Peter De Klerk (1980): 35:1–14).

3. Especially as philosophy students at Calvin College from 1954 to 1958, many of us participated in sometimes heated discussions on campus, in local restaurants, Plato Club sessions, the office of *Chimes*, the College student publication, about whether Socrates was *a half-*christian, the relevance of a distinct voice in different societal institutions, need for a *christian* philosophy, role of biblical love in "religious" conflicts. We appealed to insights gained from philosophy professors, especially W. Harry Jellema, H. Stob, H. Evan Runner and others, and issues raised in the Plato Club and the G. Groen van Prinsterer Club. For details, see H. Stob, *Summoning Up Remembrance* (1995), 218, 284, 313.

4. As well as Dewey J. Hoitenga, as will be indicated below. Another member of this Club was Calvin Seerveld, who, at the advice of H. Evan Runner, continued his doctoral studies at the Free University in Amsterdam and became interested in the *reformational* worldview and philosophy of D. Vollenhoven and H. Dooyeweerd. He taught philosophy and aesthetics at Trinity Christian College, Palos Heights, Illinois, and at ICS in Toronto.

sons founded Reformed epistemology (RE), known for its scholastic thinking about the relation between such fundamental issues as faith and reason, theology and philosophy, metaphysics and anthropology, knowledge and truth.[5] They tried to combine a biblical faith with a Reformed philosophy Jellema had taught them and with a Reformed epistemology that some students had developed about proper ways of thinking.

In distinction from classical "Reformed" philosophy and knowing, H. Evan Runner introduced in 1951 at Calvin College (and, in some cases, CTS) a more "reformational" thinking about the "structure" of reality, the nature of worldview, the role of philosophy, and ways of knowing. After 1967 Runner had a great impact on the Institute for Christian Studies in Toronto (ICS) through a total of about a dozen professors—of which six had been his students—in a wide range of disciplines.[6]

The difference between these two educational traditions gave rise to two paths in scholarship and teaching, each with its own method, way of thinking and philosophical assumptions. What compels them to dialogue in speaking and writing—also in this study—is their common faith in the triune God and reliance on His covenant promises fully revealed in Christ Jesus and confirmed by the Spirit. The issues dealt with affect philosophy, anthropology, epistemology and each discipline, or science, that seeks to understand the difference between "integral" and "integrated" Christian living, thinking, teaching and witnessing—with respect to the depth, scope and power of God's Spirit-filled and Christ-centered kingdom in teaching, studying and scholarship.

Both traditions are challenged to make a *religious* difference in the disciplines of philosophy, anthropology and epistemology, especially in an increasingly secularized culture and world. In terms of the "horse-saddle" metaphor, both traditions may be riding in similar saddles, and yet move in diverging directions in their thinking about and educating the next generation of humans to act always and everywhere as God's image-bearers. In short, what does it mean to be "spiritual" as members of a "church," or organized "religion," but not in our human behavior as lawyers, bankers, artists, farmers, logicians, philosophers, educators, pastors, priests and, lest we forget, theologians?

5. Semi-scholastic features still lingered in the views of such reformers as J. Calvin, H. Bavinck and A. Kuyper.

6. And, since the 1950/1960s, at Trinity Christian College in Palos Heights, Illinois, the 1970s at Dordt College in Sioux Center, Iowa, and the 1980s at The King's University, Edmonton, Alberta, and at Redeemer University, Ancaster, Ontario.

Almost immediately after Runner joined the Philosophy Department at Calvin College, disagreements arose over his views about the nature of truth and the meaning of "religion," how to live in one's thinking, including theorizing, as God's people, who live as Christians. Not just "how" but also "what" he taught tended to create problems about the meaning of, for instance, creation, being human, revelation, religion, truth, philosophy, theology, worldview, culture, accommodation and being Reformed. Differences of view were evident in some classrooms, the coffee shop and *Chimes*, the campus student paper. The debates centered on issues related to the importance of theory, the nature of theology, the relevance of philosophy, the role of logic, the meaning of facts, implications of "common grace," and the essence of "liberal arts" education.

W. Harry Jellema (1898–1982)

The difference in 1951 between W. Harry Jellema,[7] Chair of the Philosophy Department, and for more than twenty years teacher of a Platonic-leaning philosophy about truth, reality, ethics, etc., and, on the other hand, H. Evan Runner, a non-Dutch and originally Presbyterian "reformational" thinker, was substantial. In Runner's view, religion, revelation, reality, truth, knowledge, and the rejection of certain features in St. Augustine's philosophy and theology had affected a way of believing and thinking at both CTS and Calvin College with respect to the meaning of revelation, reality, religion, knowledge, truth, image-bearing and covenant-living.

Two of Jellema's more prominent students were N. Wolterstorff and A. Plantinga. After his death in 1982 (the year in which RE was founded), they commented on Jellema's major role in advancing classical "liberal arts." According to Wolterstorff, "in many and profound ways, Calvin College is the expression of the work and vision of Dr. Jellema." He ended his tribute by stating "we shall carry on as he taught us."

In a more detailed way, A. Plantinga wrote about Jellema's contribution:

Although he was a man of razor sharp intellect, Jellema wasn't first of all

---

7. W. Harry Jellema obtained his Ph.D. in 1922, for his dissertation on Josiah Royce, from the University of Michigan. He taught at the University of Indiana (1935–1947) and at Grand Valley State College in Michigan (1963–1975). Henry Stob (1908–1996) was Jellema's colleague in philosophy at Calvin College from 1939 to 1943 and 1946 to 1952; from 1953 until he retired in 1975, Stob was Jellema's philosophical companion at CTS.

a close or exact thinker; his metier was the method of broad vistas, not that of the logical microscope. Many of us came deeply under his spell. . . . [He] was perhaps the premier teacher of philosophy of his generation. . . . [W]hat was especially striking about Calvin [College] then—as about Calvin now—was the serious and determined effort to ask and answer the question of the relation between scholarship, academic endeavor, *the life of the mind on the one hand and Christian faith on the other. . . .*

[He saw] four fundamentally religious stances that have dominated Western intellectual and cultural life. There was the Ancient Mind, typified best by Plato; then the Medieval and Christian Mind; then the Modern Mind; and last—and in his judgment certainly least—the contemporary mind, whose contours and lineaments, though not yet wholly clear, are fundamentally naturalistic. . . . Most important, however, he looked to the history of philosophy as a means of coming to see how to be a Christian philosopher—how, more generally, to combine the life of the mind with the Christian faith.[8]

Dewey J. Hoitenga Jr. (1931–2005), another one of his outstanding protégés, arranged on his chief mentor's retirement from Calvin College in 1963, for him to join the Philosophy Department at Grand Valley State University in Allendale, Michigan, until Jellema's final retirement in 1975. Shortly after Jellema's death in 1982, Hoitenga stated the following:

Professor Jellema's favorite philosopher is Plato, and his favorite textbook, *The Republic.* Like Emerson, Professor Jellema sees that Plato, inspired by Socrates, is the quintessential model of "philosophy itself." Plato not only

---

8. "Harry Jellema, 1893–1982," *ibid.*, 37–39 (first published in *The Reformed Journal*, July, 1982). In his "W. Harry Jellema: A Former Student Remembers," John Beversluis writes that Jellema was "an education professor's nightmare," who was always ten minutes late, didn't hand out a syllabus, never took roll, asked few questions, and after distributing the final exam went home with no proctor in class. He also stated that Jellema "had little real interest in what was going on in contemporary American, British, and Continental Philosophy," that he liked Jellema's pithy statement "More important than *what* you think is the mind *with which* you think;" and that he never really understood what Jellema meant by the arresting phrase that we need to be "patterned by the good"—ibid, 41, 42, and 44. C. Stephen Evans, a former member of Calvin's philosophy department, ended his review—titled "Plato Was Right All Along: The Beautiful, the Good, and God"—of Robert Adams's *Finite and Infinite Goods: A Framework for Ethics* (Oxford University Press, 1999) somewhat nostalgically: "Alas, we live in a world where Platonism, particularly theistic Platonism, is unlikely to be taken seriously." Cf. *Books & Culture* (July/August, 2001), 18–19.

asks the right questions, but opens up the entire range of possible answers. Most important is Plato's vision: a vision of *man as a rational, moral being, in touch with a transcendent Good that gives ultimate meaning to all existence.* Plato, foremost among the pagans, *sets the stage for Christianity.* St. Augustine, and Calvin, too, praised—and used Plato when they came to articulate the fullness of the Gospel—the Good made personal in God, and the eternal *Logos* made flesh in Jesus Christ.

Plato also held, Professor Jellema fondly explains, that *philosophy is the pervasive essence of all true education. . . .* This is important because as Professor Jellema points out, *education and religion* lie at the heart of the just society, the true commonwealth. It was Plato, he goes on, who first drew, in philosophy, the distinction between the fallible kingdoms of men and *the true kingdom whose "pattern" is "set up in the heavens." What Plato, however, could only seek in "discourse" has been made manifest, both in word and deed, to Christians in the kingdom of our Lord* (emphasis added).[9]

In *Faith and Reason from Plato to Plantinga: An Introduction to Reformed Epistemology* (1991), Hoitenga provided a detailed account of Jellema's philosophical background and legacy. It was deeply rooted in Platonizing Augustinian thinking preferred in Calvinian academic centers. Philosophically, Calvin College reveals this in its firm allegiance to a "Christian liberal arts" way of thinking and teaching.[10]

This study provides a helpful historical overview of and insight into RE, adopted in 1982 by the Society of Christian Philosophers, established in 1978. It focuses, or centers, on issues related to faith and reason, theology and philosophy, religion and facts, etc. In the first and third paragraphs of

9. He goes on to say, "Of books and articles Professor Jellema published very few. He was rather the scholar-teacher, and the teacher *par excellence*, and he lives on today in the one way a teacher can—not on the shelves of a library, but in the lives of his students." Cf. "W. Harry Jellema Professor of Philosophy Emeritus" in *William Harry Jellema, 1893–1982*, Memorial Booklet (Grand Rapids: Calvin College Library, 1982) 9–10. In similar fashion, Kenneth Konyndyk remarked, "While some regret he was not a writer, I believe he would rather have his legacy be his students than a shelf of books." Cf. "In Memoriam: William Harry Jellema," *ibid*, 47—first published in *Calvin College Spark* (December, 1982). Hoitenga points out that for Jellema the traditions of *Afscheiding* (1834) and *Doleantie* (1886), represented at Calvin College, parallel in a sense the distinction between "faith and learning," "religion and learning," or "pietism" and "political and cultural activism."

10. Hoitenga's study helped me to understand more clearly Jellema's courses at Calvin College when I studied there in the 1950s.

the Epilogue,[11] Hoitenga comments on the background and context of RE as follows:

> I have finished my account of the origin and significance of Reformed epistemology. Its central claim is the immediacy of our knowledge of God. We do not, in the first instance, know God by inference or testimony but by direct acquaintance with him. A closely related claim is that we cannot easily remain indifferent to the God whom we know by such direct acquaintance. Thus our knowledge of God is like our knowledge of every other fundamental kind of reality—physical objects, their properties and relationships, other persons, right and wrong, good and evil, and the elementary objects of logic and mathematics.
>
> If our knowledge of God consists primarily in *a direct acquaintance with his presence in our minds*, in our lives and in the universe, it does not follow, of course, that such knowledge arises apart from the *inferences of reason* or the testimony of other human beings. Indeed, this direct way of knowing God is as dependent on the *inferential workings of reason* and on human testimony as is the direct knowledge of anything else. . . . [A]s with sticks and stones, much of what we know about God we cannot know without making inferences either from what we are told (by other human beings or by God himself) or from what we see directly for ourselves . . . (emphases added).

The rise of what became known as RE[12] at Calvin College is not surprising given the scholastic features in the anthropology taught at CTS and Calvin College in theology and philosophy. The background of Christian Reformed thinking is the classic tradition of fourth-century neo-Platonic Augustinian and thirteenth-century Aristotelian views of T. Aquinas about reality, being human, truth, faith and reason.

The nature of being human (anthropology) and knowing (epistemology) affected theology and philosophy with respect to the nature of faith and reason, knowledge and metaphysics, education and truth, anthropology and "liberal arts" in institutions of higher education, including CTS.

---

11. Hoitenga Jr., (1991): 235–236.

12. Chief Anglo-American *philosophical* founders of Reformed Epistemology are William Alston at Syracuse University, Alvin C. Plantinga at Calvin College and Notre Dame University, George I. Mavrodes at Michigan University, and Nicholas P. Wolterstorff at Calvin College and Yale University.

Awareness of two main academic traditions[13] in Christian Reformed higher education is necessary to sense the difference between *Reformed Epistemology* and the *reformational* philosophy that H. Evan Runner introduced in 1951 at Calvin College and which in 1967 resulted in the opening of the ICS in Toronto, Canada. The difference in these two traditions in North America of Reformed higher education is evident in their methods, or ways of thinking, discussions about the meaning of "biblical" and "scholastic," how to gain clarity about the structure of "reality," the meaning of *religion*, the difference between obedience and disobedience, the clash between "walking with God" and defying His love.

Christian "Liberal Arts"

Before the 1980s, Wolterstorff already talked about five interrelated problems inherent in Jellema's view of Christian "liberal arts" education. In "Beyond 1984,"[14] he wrote that Kuyper's neo-Calvinism took root in North America by way of Jellema's advocating Augustine's notion of two spiritual kingdoms: the City of God (*civitas Dei*) and the City of the World (*civitas mundi*) and their interrelationships. These two kingdoms require a special kind of education. The goal of such education is to transmit "humanity's knowledge" in three distinct ways., viz., shaping a "way of thinking," calling for a "moral character" and a specific "mode of piety."[15] Since it centers on the "totality of life in a kingdom," education is essentially "extraordinarily holistic."[16]

The structure and thrust of these two kingdoms is, according to Jellema, determined by the "mentality, or mind," of its members.[17] Each citizen develops a kingdom "mind" in terms of "the social and cultural expression of that mind." The goal of classic education is to disclose the nature of kingdom citizenship. If it involves identifying oneself with *civitas Dei*, then, as a result of sin, an ultimate struggle between two kingdoms is unavoidable. Education is essentially "formal" in that it focuses on "what is," develops "certain skills"

---

13. The third tradition, pietism, did not result in any philosophical tradition at Calvin College, nor at CTS.

14. Cf. *Philosophy of Christian Education* (1986).

15. Understood as "emotion" in terms of Greek "faculty psychology" about "thinking, willing and feeling."

16. Wolterstorff (1986): 4.

17. Wolterstorff associates "mind" with "world-and-life-view," "world-view" or "vision" (1986): 4, 5, 12.

and fosters a "will to culture." It forms in students a *"Christian mind"* that will *"express* itself in a specific cultural and social situation."

Not just *what* the mind thinks is important, but also *how* it thinks. Christian thinking presupposes a "classical mind."[18] *Formal* education enables one to become familiar with various "minds," including the "Christian" mind.[19] Proper education for citizenship in the *civitas Dei* assumes a clear grasp of medieval "Christian" thought. College-bound high school students must be educated in "Christian liberal arts," not in industrial, commercial and domestic thinking.

Wolterstorff has two reservations about this view of his mentor's thinking, namely, it does not, in his opinion, sufficiently recognize the "struggle for justice" and significance of "delight and worship." Jellema's "religious depth-analysis" centers too much on "products of intellectual and literary culture." More is needed than a Christian mind. In this respect, Wolterstorff is *less* scholastic than his mentor and stresses more the actions of the Christian "mind." To "think about" the world is not the same as "to be in" the world. Christian education implies a way of "being-in-the-world," i.e., an "education for shalom." "Thought" and "action" go together.

According to Wolterstorff, radical thinking results in radical practice.[20] Truths are not so abstract that the "tendency or disposition or inclination" to act accordingly does not result in a change in society and culture.[21] A "praxis-oriented" scholarship and education needs a "new anthropology," one in which "action as a whole" is more than only an expression of "thought and will." Human behavior is affected by an "interaction with reality."[22] The human "self" is not an "imperial entity, defined by just thought and volition, floating unencumbered above the world of body and history."[23]

18. For the citations in this paragraph, see Wolterstorff (1986): 6, 8 and 9. This meaning of "mind" is reflected in the Calvin College slogan "Minds in the Making."

19. Wolterstorff (1986): 13.

20. For details about "shalom," see Wolterstorff, *Until Justice and Peace Embrace: The Kuyper Lectures for 1981,* at the Free University in Amsterdam, 1983. Some thirty years earlier, H. Evan Runner had already stressed "action" in a *reformational* way through the power (*dunamis*) of God's Word and Spirit.

21. See Wolterstorff (1984): 20–23. "They want their emotions stirred, their loyalties enhanced, their minds filled with glittering thoughts; but actions changed? No" (24). The three processes that shape action are discipline, modeling and giving reasons.

22. For Jellema, the aim of "liberal education" is "intellectual and moral," in which "ultimately the intellectual is for the sake of the moral." Cf. *The Curriculum in a Liberal Arts College,* 16, cited by Wolterstorff, 27, note 4.

23. Wolterstorff (1984): 25. His "new anthropology" is still medieval in the sense that it

The scholastic view of "faith" and "reason" in W. Harry Jellema determined certain, not all, features in Wolterstorff's philosophy, anthropology and "theology," especially with respect to worship and hermeneutics.[24] While accepting his mentor's scholastic anthropology, including its "faculty psychology" (thinking-willing-feeling), Wolterstorff has gone beyond his mentor in stressing the need for "justice" and expressing "delight." Jellema's impact on him was major with respect to the scholastic trilogy of what is *true* (scholarship, education), *good* (economic order, justice) and *beautiful* (imagination, music, art, worship). It is also evident in (i) his review of Pope John Paul II's major encyclical *Fides et Ratio*, 1998, (ii) his view of "faith" and "philosophy" and comments about "reason" and "religion," and (iii) his acceptance of Scottish "Common Sense" philosophy.

Review of *Fides et Ratio*

Wolterstorff's view of faith and reason, theology and philosophy, Christian and general knowledge resembles the philosophical and anthropological thought-pattern of the Roman Catholic Church since the Middle Ages. In his review of the encyclical that Pope John Paul II published in 1998 and aptly called *Fides et Ratio (FR)*, Wolterstorff calls for another reflection on the difference, not similarity, between *scholastic* and *reformational* thinking about "faith life" and the discipline of "theology." To do this in a biblically wholesome, yet distinct and drastic, way requires more than another "epistemological" study. It calls for a careful systematic view of scholastic Roman Catholic and Protestant, especially Reformed (and Presbyterian) ways of thinking about faith, reason and their relationships.

The main focus of this chapter is to reflect on Wolterstorff's view of *foundational* issues often ignored in well-intended but misguided Christian educational traditions. Western philosophy and theology are filled with endless "faith-reason" debates about *what* a study of faith life really entails and *how* such a study can be engaged in. What does being "reformed in a reforming way" mean for human learning, teaching and holistic Christian living, not just in "theology" but in all human analytic tiptoeing through creation?

---

presupposes "faculty psychology" with its "thinking" (truth), "willing" (morality), and "feeling" (passion, commitment, experiences).

24. Especially in his position as Noah Professor of Philosophical Theology at Yale University.

Wolterstorff's reaction in 1999, one year after *FR* was published, reflects a way of thinking he learned from Jellema, his mentor at Calvin College. Reading this wide-ranging encyclical, centered on "Faith and Reason," with the "eyes and mind . . . of a philosopher who stands in the Reformed tradition of Christianity," Wolterstorff finds himself "in almost complete agreement with what the pope says about the relation of faith and reason."[25] What *FR* states is "true and needing to be said." There seems to be a "convergence" between Roman Catholic and Reformed traditions.[26] Wolterstorff is in full agreement with its central argument. Its significance for theology and philosophy lies in its "intervention" in recent developments in these two disciplines.

The "hermeneutical key" to unlock the main theme of *FR* lies, Wolterstorff thinks, is the "distinction between *properly functioning* human reason and human reason as it *actually functions* in its fallen state." While the Pope is "confident and optimistic" about the former, he is "eminently realistic and, on occasion, even judgmental" about the latter.[27] Philosophy is "autonomous" in that reason is "by its nature oriented to truth and . . . equipped with the necessary means to arrive at truth." Philosophy's "formulations" are, however, "shaped by history and produced by human reason wounded and weakened by sin." Wolterstorff comments:

> Well! "Reason wounded and weakened by sin"—no Calvinist could ask for more. "Reason oriented by its nature to truth and equipped to arrive"—no Catholic could ask for more than that. Indeed, in one brief extraordinary paragraph of just two sentences, the pope puts both themes together: "it was *part of the original plan of creation that reason* should without difficulty reach beyond the sensory data to the origin of all things: The Creator. But because of the disobedience by which man and woman chose to set them-

---

25. "Faith & Reason," *Books and Culture* (July/August, 1999) 28–30. Wolterstorff reacted with "awe and astonishment" to this papal Letter—its argument is "vigorous and visionary," even "extraordinary." His only reservations concern the Pope's views of a "core consensus" in the history of philosophy, the "authoritative status of tradition," and the "role of Mary." For a somewhat more critical, although still positive, reaction to *Fides et Ratio*, see A. Plantinga in chapter 18 below.

26. Wolterstorff (1999): 29. It is an "extraordinarily rich and dialectically subtle encyclical" (30).

27. Wolterstorff (1999): 29. He adds that Roman Catholics speak "too little of the actuality of fallen reason [and] too much of the ideality of properly functioning reason" and that Calvinists have "majored" in reason's "fallenness" and "minored" in its "proper functioning."

selves in full and absolute autonomy in relation to the One who had created them, *this ready access to God the Creator diminished* (emphasis added)."[28]

Essentially, Wolterstorff agrees with the traditional view of faith, reason and relations between them. *Reason* impels humans to "seek the truth," raise "why" questions and "discover the meaning of life." It compels humans to move "beyond partial and fragmentary truths toward universal and absolute truth." It enables them to reach for "something ultimate," the "ground of all things," a "final explanation," something of "supreme value that refers to nothing beyond itself and which puts an end to all questioning."[29] Although it can "discover the Creator," reason is not able to discover "the nature and deeds of the Creator." To do that, *reason* needs faith.

Faith is necessary to accept divine "revelation," through the Church as message bearer, about the "nature and deeds" of God, the Creator. Revelation does not repudiate, or reject, reason, but perfects it. Truth unites reason and faith. It consists of both the goal, and attainment, of reason *and* the content of revelation. While truth is a human achievement, revelation is a divine gift. Faith does not make "reason" passive in response to the gift of revelation, but enables reason to deepen the search for truth. In agreement with patristic and medieval thinking, "faith seeking understanding" (*fides quaerens intellectum*), faith enables "the mind in its autonomous exploration to penetrate within the mystery by use of reason's own methods. . . ." Through *faith* revelation seeks "acceptance as an expression of love" and through *reason* revelation stirs "thought."

"Weakened and wounded" reason fails to achieve what it was originally able to do. Sin is an impediment: it causes reason to take "wrong turns" and results in possible conflicts with revealed truth. In addition to supplementing, or aiding, reason's attempt to attain to truth, faith and revelation are necessary to correct, and guide, this endeavor of reason. To accomplish this, the Roman Catholic Church needs the assistance of philosophers, theologians, bishops and all other members to provide a "critical discernment" that ensures reason's proper reflection on truth (*recta ratio*).

About *theology*, especially after the rise of phenomenology, linguistic philosophy and deconstructionism, Wolterstorff remarks that too often in

---

28. Cf. Wolterstorff's comment: "Of course, there will continue to be disagreements on the details of reason's powers when properly functioning and on the extent to which the wounds impair proper functioning."

29. See Wolterstorff (1999): 29.

recent years "theology has been in headlong flight from metaphysics—that is, from a willingness to speak about God in particular and reality in general." However, he thinks that theology does not need "metaphysical timidity," but must boldly affirm revealed truth that transcends and surrounds us: "Revelation is not just 'God-talk,' but talk *about* God—*true* talk."[30]

About *philosophy*, he states that an anti-metaphysical disposition has become so prevalent today that "reality has receded ever further away"—so much so that even questioning the need for any talk "about reality at all" has disappeared. What is needed today is what the Pope calls "Christian philosophy," i.e., "philosophical speculation conceived in dynamic union with faith." The Pope's "good word for reason, and for faith as reason's ally" is praiseworthy. Given "the extraordinary dignity of human reason" and "the love displayed by God in revealing to us dimensions of truth that would otherwise have eluded us," Wolterstorff hopes, as "philosopher and Reformed Protestant, that the pope's call for boldness will embolden theologians and philosophers to do exactly what he is calling for."[31]

Wolterstorff's positive, even glowing, appraisal of *FR* is (in his Jellema/Stob thinking) evidence of a common scholastic understanding of faith, reason and interrelationships. Basically, he accepts the Pope's *Aquinian* manner of phrasing the problem and ingeniously employing the metaphor of two wings of "reason" and "faith" which, in tandem-fashion, support the moving "body" of Truth. As a philosopher, Wolterstorff is uncomfortable with the notion that sin is more than being "wounded" and "weakened." As a philosopher, he basically endorses *FR*'s view of the depth and solution of the human predicament.

Wolterstorff's view of (i) reason, faith and their interrelationships, (ii) philosophy, theology and their interrelationships, and (iii) the relation of both to Truth is still "Reformed," in a traditionally semi-scholastic sense. A similarity between Augustinian/Aquinian thinking (and living) in the Roman Catholic Church and Wolterstorff's response to *FR* is not insignificant, and does not indicate a heresy but underscores the need for more *integral reformational* thinking, in especially philosophy, anthropology, epistemology and traditional theology. In short, Wolterstorff's reaction to typically Roman Catholic thinking is not sufficiently critical but still *religiously* accommodational with respect to the nature of, for example, "truth" and "reality."

---

30. Wolterstorff (1999): 29.
31. Wolterstorff (1999): 29.

Faith and Philosophy

Basic assumptions in RE's view of faith and theology, belief and theory, and theology and philosophy are evident in various writings of N. Wolterstorff. In "Faith and Philosophy," the first chapter in *Faith and Philosophy: Philosophical Studies in Religion and Ethics* (1964), published in honor of W. Harry Jellema and edited by A. Plantinga,[32] Wolterstorff describes his understanding of "faith" and "philosophy." In the Preface to this *first* RE publication, Plantinga summarized Wolterstorff's view (and his own, as will be indicated in Chapter 18 below) about this issue in RE:

> Wolterstorff points out that a philosophy is usually (though not always) an elaboration and defense of a very broad perspective or unified set of beliefs. A religious faith likewise involves such a unified set of beliefs. Hence, philosophy and faith stand in complex and many-faceted relation permitting of various degrees and kinds of conflict and accord. For almost any well-developed philosophy there are religious faiths with which it conflicts; and for almost any religious faith there is a philosophy with which it conflicts.[33]

For Wolterstorff, if the goal of philosophy is truth and if truth depends on reason, objectivity, universality and factuality, then the history of philosophy shows that agreement is impossible about what philosophy really is. Common to all traditional philosophical systems has been the belief that "there is or ought to be a barrier between the realm of philosophy and the realm of faith which prevents any crossing, and especially prevents a man's faith from interfering with his pursuit of philosophy and with his attempt to solve the philosophical problems. Objectivity is assured for philosophy and face is saved for faith by allowing no interaction."[34]

This situation calls for a closer, and critical, look at the "relevant features" of philosophy and faith. "Philosophy" consists not just of "insight,

---

32. In his "Foreword," Henry J. Stob writes: "This collection of essays is issued by his students, friends, and colleagues in honor of W. Harry Jellema, whose retirement this summer at the age of 70 closes a period of exceptional service to Calvin College, the Reformed community, and the cause of Christian philosophy" (v). Regarding Jellema's influence, he comments: "Let it merely be said that he "placed an indelible stamp upon Calvin College and upon the many students who, since leaving his classroom, have entered graduate school and from there have gone out to spread his influence on many campuses throughout the land" (vii-viii).
33. Plantinga (1964): ix.
34. Plantinga (1964): 8.

vision, scope, etc.," or an "outpouring of 'this I believe' utterances," but of "argument and counter-argument."[35] A "method" for solving a specific philosophical problem readily becomes the key to solving "all philosophical problems." The interrelationship between "method" and "theme" gives birth to a "philosophical perspective." Instead of being a "super-science," philosophy is "synoptic" in that "growth of a philosophical perspective cannot be stopped." Wolterstorff comments,

> A philosophical perspective is inherently expansive, dynamic, proliferative: the procedure, the method, the court of appeal, the authority which the philosopher regards as competent to solve one philosophical problem he also regards as competent to solve a great many more, and perhaps *all*, philosophical problems.[36]

> A sharp distinction between method and results might be satisfactory if the structure of a philosophical perspective were like that of a mathematical proof—axioms, rules of inference, and theorems. But its structure is more like that of a sonata movement. The musician starts with a theme and then develops it—plays it backwards, upside down, backwards and upside down both faster, slower, broken up. Still, it is always the same theme; and in each new development we see a new facet of an old theme. Someone else might have taken the same theme and written a very different movement. But, on the other hand, an unfinished sonata movement can be completed by someone else. A composer's style is not something separable from his works; yet it is something more than his works. One can accept a philosopher's method and disagree with some of his results; yet a philosopher's method is seen in his results.[37]

Today, philosophy is, though less "systematic" and "speculative," still "synoptic." Although it is not merely a technique to "describe and prove," philosophy continues to be "the elaboration and defense of a *Weltanschau-*

35. Plantinga (1964): 9. Elaborating on the role of arguments, especially the relation between premise and conclusion, Wolterstorff refers mainly to Descartes, Hume, Kant, Plato, Berkeley, Moore, Wittgenstein and Mach (10–20).

36. Wolterstorff (1999):20. For example, for Descartes "the court of appeal" was "clear and distinct ideas," Hume "mental images" and "custom," positivists "science and logic," Moore "common sense and logic," and later Wittgenstein "logical grammar" and "conventionalism" (20–21).

37. Wolterstorff (1999): 21.

ung, an interpretation of our human condition. The philosopher is after the meaning and 'hang' of things; today as always he has a vision of the whole structure of men's thoughts."[38] In concluding his remarks about the "relevant features of philosophy," he discloses a central feature of RE when he states,

> The rise of analytic philosophy, like the rise of any other philosophy, has caused a change in the whole intellectual scene. The fact that there are today a great many things about which the philosopher does not wish to talk, topics which he regards as outside his field of competence, is part of his conception of how things hang together. To see nothing but technical "objective" discussions in present-day philosophy is to come in at the middle of the development section and insist that there is no theme, only notes. In Schoenberg too there are some themes; only, it takes some listening.[39]

Wolterstorff does not talk about "faith" in terms of "necessary and sufficient conditions," nor in terms of those who normally use this word. Instead, in terms of Paul's use of the word, he indicates how "faith" changes, pervades and unifies everything. "Conversion" changed Paul's "religious beliefs," affected his "ultimate concern," shaped his "moral outlook," altered his "attitudes," determined his "worship" and "rituals," and influenced his "religious experience" (cf. mystery, awe, wonder, vision). Faith caused a pervasive change in his life—he became "a new being," it changed his "doing, trusting, and feeling."[40]

It is difficult, if not impossible, to determine what "essential thing" in faith changed Paul's life.[41] In terms of Martin Luther's insight, central to religious faith is "trust in" and "loyalty" to something "ultimate." This being "one of its dominant features," Wolterstorff states that faith bears a "most significant relation to philosophy."[42] If "faith in" is

> the dominant and organizing feature, then we can understand something else which Luther hints at, and which a good many religious people claim— namely, that the opposite to particular faith is not the absence of faith, but rather a different faith. . . . It seems most unlikely that some men have no

38. Wolterstorff (1999): 21.
39. Wolterstorff (1999): 21–22.
40. Wolterstorff (1999): 24–25.
41. For a detailed description of the statement "Faith is different things to different people," see page 28 of Wolterstorff (1999).
42. Wolterstorff (1999): 28.

ultimate faith in anything at all—though "ultimate" has to be understood here in the somewhat odd sense of allowing several competing faiths to be equally ultimate. Whether we put our trust in science, or reason, or humanity, or the nation, or the Party, still it is trust. It is not, then, that some men have a way of life determined by trust and loyalty, and that others do not; but rather that their ways of life are different, determined by different trusts and loyalties.[43]

The **relation** between philosophy and someone else's faith, and, vice versa, between faith and someone else's philosophy, will most likely, since the pre-Socratics, be one of "conflict." One's specific philosophy of the world tends to intersect with one's specific faith, or way of life—not with any "*particular* issues involved," but with respect to "the basic appeal of the philosopher and the basic trust and loyalty of the man of faith."[44] Specific views of a philosopher and general ways of a person of faith do not conflict. However, when the "implications" of a philosopher's appeal and the "trust" of a person of faith are pressed, then a conflict arises.

Such a conflict will be either superficial or strong. In case of a *superficial* conflict, one may surrender certain views of faith without abandoning the philosophical method adopted; and the same is true, *mutatis mutandis*, for philosophy with respect to faith. In the case of a *stronger* conflict, the features of the universe the philosopher appeals to are "those in which he places his faith," and this, ultimately, gives rise to "secular theology."[45] In summary, "a philosophical appeal is typically not neutral with respect to faith,"[46] and, conversely, "an ultimate trust and loyalty is typically not neutral with respect to a philosophical appeal."[47]

The relation between "philosophy" and "faith" is not one of mathematical deductive consistency. It may be possible for a person's "philosophical perspective" to be independent of his "way of life"—his "philosophical appeal" may be independent of his "ultimate trust." A person's dominant

43. Wolterstorff (1999): 29.
44. Wolterstorff (1999): 30.
45. Cf. Descartes, Spinoza, Locke, Kant, some positivists, and certain pragmatists.
46. Plantinga (1964): 31; also "given any philosophical appeal, there are usually certain trusts and loyalties which conflict in one of the ways indicated with that appeal." Wolterstorff comments that "[s]ome faiths are not very pervasive."
47. Plantinga (1964): 31; also "that given any trust and loyalty, there are usually certain philosophical appeals which conflict in the ways indicated with that way of life." Wolterstorff adds "some philosophical methods are not very expansive."

philosophical interest need not be only in problems raised by a person's "particular faith." When a philosopher's attention is not focused on his faith, his "philosophical appeal may not have a positive and direct relation to his ultimate trust.[48] When a conflict does arise between "philosophy" and "faith," however—when "faith exercises a formative influence on his philosophy, or vice versa"—then we are faced with "a contrast between reason on the one side and faith on the other." Such a contrast is not one of "rationality versus bias," but a conflict between "two trusts," or "an ultimate appeal and an ultimate trust."[49]

Wolterstorff ends his "Faith and Philosophy" article by reflecting on Paul's use of "mythical or symbolic language" to describe what he believes. His language differs considerably from the language "customarily used by philosophers."[50] Although to translate "symbolic statements of religion" into the language of philosophers is "fraught with difficulties,"[51] it is not impossible to answer any "questions" about such language. A possible solution may be to think in terms of three analogies: (a) the nature of, and relation between, a poem and a paraphrase of a poem, (b) loving a girl and studying a girl, and (c) a carpenter describing a painting and a critic analyzing a painting's depth.

This view about "reason," "faith" and their "interrelationships" is pervasive in RE's thinking. It is central to how Wolterstorff, Plantinga and others discuss such topics as rationality and theism, reason and religion, being a philosopher and a Christian, rationalism and fideism, and evidentialism and foundationalism.[52]

---

48. Wolterstorff (1999): 32.

49. This calls for a "choice, in the last resort" that goes beyond "rationality and irrationality, or rationality and non-rationality" (32).

50. Wolterstorff (1999): 33.

51. For example, God as First Cause, heart as transcendental ego, predestination and indeterminacy, creation manifesting God's glory, and teleological arguments.

52. He lectured on this topic in "Theory and Practice, or Theory and Commitment: II," in 1978, at the Second Conference of what is now called the International Association for the Promotion of Christian Higher Education (IAPCHE) on the general conference theme "Justice in the International Economic Order." Cf. Wolterstorff (1978): 78–98. For a *reformational* reaction, see H. Hart's "Theory and Practice (A Response)," 99–103.

Reason and Religion

In *Reason within the Bounds of Religion*, 1984,[53] Wolterstorff focused, in a way characteristic of RE, on the "relation" between "reason" and "religion," not on the terms of reason and religion as such. His thinking about this "relation" moved along the path Jellema and Stob had taught him and which he himself had traveled after publishing his "Faith and Philosophy" in 1964 and as described above in this Chapter. Reversing the sequence of "religion" and "reason" in I. Kant's classic *Religion within the Bounds of Reason* (*Religion innerhalb die Grenzen der bloszen Vernunft*), Wolterstorff placed "reason" within the bounds of "religion" and reflected on "religion" within, or in the context, of "control beliefs" in one's thinking and theorizing.

In his "Introduction" to *Faith and Rationality: Reason and Belief in God* (1983), which he co-edited with A. Plantinga,[54] Wolterstorff indicated what distinguishes this publication from many other studies about "faith and reason." It is the result of a one-year project in the Center for Christian Studies at Calvin College on the general theme of "Toward a Reformed View of Faith and Reason."[55] These essays contain "a weaving in and out of four fundamental themes," namely, (i) "the collapse of *classical foundationalism*," (ii) "the evidentialist challenge to religious belief" in European Enlightenment, (iii) the role of "Calvinist" or "Reformed epistemology," which bears "a close affinity to positions long held on the relation of faith to reason by the Continental Reformed (Calvinist) tradition,"[56] and (iv) whereas American Evangelical

53. Grand Rapids: Wm. B. Eerdmans, 1976 (1984, 2nd ed.). In 1975/6, he lectured on this topic at Dordt College in Sioux Center, Iowa. Recommending this book, G. I. Mavrodes wrote: "How can a scholar remain true both to a Christian commitment and to scientific research? . . . [This] is a probing and challenging book that helps integrate academic inquiry with Christian faith." Cf. H. Hart, "Critical Reflections on Wolterstorff's *Reason within the Bounds of Religion*," unpublished paper, Institute for Christian Studies, Toronto, 1980. Dutch translation: *De rede binnen de grenzen van de religie*. Amsterdam: Buijten & Schipperheijn, 1993.

54. Indiana: University of Notre Dame Press, 1983, 1–15. For a review, see Stephen Wykstra, *Faith and Philosophy*, 3:2 (April 1986) 206–213.

55. Senior fellows of the Center for 1979/1980: D. Holwerda (theology), G. Marsden (history), R. Manweiler (physics), A. Plantinga (philosophy), N. Wolterstorff (philosophy)—from Calvin College; G. Mavrodes (philosophy) from the University of Michigan; student fellows R. Veenstra, M. Hakkenberg, P. Pereboom; adjunct fellows W. Alston (philosophy) from Syracuse University; H. Hart (philosophy) from the Institute for Christian Studies in Toronto. Cf. Wolterstorff, "Introduction" 9.

56. No mention is made in the book, not even in a footnote—despite H. Hart's partic-

academics assumed that science and Christianity are ultimately compatible, Continental Reformed thinkers did not exclude the possibility of conflict between *reason* and *faith* and at times rejected science in order to hold on to Christian faith. The essays by A. Plantinga, W. Alston, N. Wolterstorff and G. Mavrodes (the four founders of the Society of Christian Philosophy) address "in depth" in an illustrative, not exhaustive, way the *"rationality of Christian belief,"* and suggest "new ways of approaching" matters related to that issue (emphasis added).[57]

The first part of this publication centers on "the rationality of Christian belief" and the second part on the traditional debate about "reason" and "faith." The "bearing of faith on theorizing" is not dealt with, at least not explicitly. Wolterstorff concludes his "Introduction" with some comments about "the *core* of faith" and the relation of faith to "the believing of propositions."[58] Instead of "exploring the ordinary use of the word 'faith' and then defining the derivative phrase 'Christian faith,'" he summarizes how "faith" is used in Scripture.[59] It refers to *trusting*, relying on, believing in or having confidence in, and it involves *obedience* to God. In the New Testament, it refers also to Jesus himself and the *kerugma*, or proclamation, of what he said and did.

This apostolic "message" includes "belief," i.e., acceptance of something with "propositional content" (*quae creditur*). The *what* of faith does not permit any "attitude of cautious tentativeness" on the part of the believer, nor is it the outcome of any "labored deliverances of theologians."[60] Though "faith as a whole" is more than "belief," it does call for "believing the words of the one trusted" and the "specifications of that message" for one's life. It entails "various beliefs about the working of God in one's experience," as well as the belief "that God exists."[61] What is believed, or accepted, is not *"merely* believed" but also "known." Because the apostle John often talks

---

ipation as adjunct fellow at the Study Center—of the sixty-year tradition of *reformational* philosophy since the 1920s, which H. Evan Runner, since 1952, had introduced as professor of philosophy and, since 1954, as sponsor of the Groen van Prinsterer Club at Calvin College (and CTS) in Grand Rapids, and, since the 1960s, in neo-Kuyperian circles, in Canada, especially as mentor of what today is the graduate Institute for Christian Studies (ICS) in Toronto.

57. G. Marsden and D. Holwerda focused on "some features of the historical setting" of this issue (9).

58. Wolterstorff (1983): 10.

59. For Wolterstorff's reliance on R. Bultmann's "highly tendentious" view of *pistis* in Kittel's *Theological Word Book of the New Testament*, see his endnote 1 on p. 15.

60. Wolterstorff (1983): 13.

61. Wolterstorff (1983): 14.

about "knowing and believing" and "believing and knowing,"[62] Wolterstorff wonders about a

> natural sequence in the relation of belief and knowledge. Does belief find its fulfilment in knowledge, as Augustine so consistently taught, or does knowledge somehow find its fulfilment in confessing belief? Bultmann's comments on this seem correct: the two are indissolubly bound up together. In antithesis to Gnosticism it is apparent that knowledge can never take us beyond faith or leave faith behind. As all knowledge begins with faith, so it abides in faith. Similarly, all faith is to become knowledge. If all knowledge can only be a knowledge of faith, faith comes to itself in knowledge. Knowledge is thus a constitutive element in genuine faith.[63]

Scottish "Common Sense" Philosophy

With respect to the issue of "faith and reason," Wolterstorff respected the views of Thomas Reid (1710–1796), the founder of Scottish "Common Sense" philosophy, or "Realism." Reid became a leading thinker for most Presbyterian theologians, pastors, and college and seminary professors in Scotland and North America, and even in some prominent Evangelical circles.[64]

In a public lecture on "Reid's Contribution," Wolterstorff talked in 1983, one year after co-establishing RE, at the thirtieth Annual Philosophy Conference, at Wheaton College in Illinois, about Scottish "Common Sense" philosophy, especially the significance of Reid's thinking for "reformed epistemology." In a "qualified and clarified" way, he agreed with Reid's "basic insight" about "a general theory of justified belief." In providing a "criterion

---

62. See John 6:69, 17:8, and 1 John 4:16.

63. Wolterstorff (1983): 227. For details about "knowledge of faith," see Chapters 11 and 12 above, especially Augustine's neo-Platonic expression "faith seeking understanding" (*fides quaerens intellectum*), the motto of CTS and stressed especially by Henry J. Stob.

64. E.g., Carl F. Henry (1913–2003), the first editor of *Christianity Today* (1955–1968), whose understanding of reason, rationality, truth, certainty, apologetics, etc., comported completely with T. Reid's philosophy. John Witherspoon (1723–1794) taught Reidian philosophy for two decades at Princeton College; Samuel S. Smith (1750–1819) popularized it; Alexander Green (1762–1848) and James McCosh (1811–1894) advocated it for several decades in their views about reality, society, and theology; B. B. Warfield (1851–1921) advocated it at Princeton Theological Seminary; J. Gresham Machen (1881–1937) incorporated basic features of Reidian philosophy in his teaching at Westminster Theological Seminary in Philadelphia. For details, see John C. Vander Stelt (1978) (republished, 2013): 9–64.

of justified belief," Reid made it possible to "displace the discredited *foundationalist* theory" and to acknowledge that "beliefs are to an extent, and in certain ways, within the control of our *wills*" (emphasis added).

Not only the "belief-disposition structure" of human knowledge is important, but also the "motivational structure" of knowledge. A "full-fledged theory of justified belief" calls for a "belief-formation" which acknowledges that "the corpus of a person's belief emerges from complicated interaction between belief-dispositions and his motivated undertakings."[65]

In *Thomas Reid and the Story of Epistemology* (2001),[66] Wolterstorff stated that this book was perhaps his most significant *philosophical* publication. He worked on it for some twenty years. In the Preface, he stated that in the latter part of the eighteenth and in most of the nineteenth century, T. Reid was "probably the most popular of all philosophers in Great Britain and North America and enjoyed considerable popularity on the continent of Europe as well."[67] After his almost complete disappearance for almost a century from Western academic circles, there is today a remarkable renaissance in Reidian studies and ideas.

> It was about twenty years ago that I first read Reid, for reasons that I now cannot recall. I had the sense of discovering a philosophical soul mate: a metaphysical realist who was also, in his own way, an *antifoundationalist*. I suppose I also had the vague sense of having discovered a religious soul mate, less I think because Reid was a Christian philosopher, though he was, and more because of the fundamental role in his thought of ungrounded trust. I resonated with his *antirationalism* (emphasis added).[68]

---

65. Unpublished lecture, 27. In a paper at this conference on "The Common Sense Tradition and American Evangelical Theology," Mark A. Noll talked about (a) epistemological, (b) ethical and (c) methodological/scientific facets of Common Sense philosophy. About (a) he said that "Epistemological Common Sense seems to have entered most deeply into the evangelical consciousness, and in fact to have become almost indistinguishable from the more general Christian belief that our perceptions of the world may be relied upon, not just because they are part of Common Sense, but *because this is the way God has made the world*" (emphasis added), and about (b) he stated that "Ethical Common Sense has had less effect on Reformed and Lutheran strands of evangelical theology, more on Arminian and Holiness [strands]" (Unpublished lecture, 29).

66. Cf. series *Modern European Philosophy*, Robert B. Pippen, general editor. Cambridge: University Press (2001).

67. Wolterstorff (2001): ix.

68. Wolterstorff (2001): x.

Finding Reid's philosophy "fascinating" and "baffling," Wolterstorff wrote a book about his theory of knowledge in an attempt to produce an *"interpretation"* of Reid's epistemology, not to provide a "full treatment," or "exegetical study," of his philosophy, nor to be fully engaged with the "scholarly literature on Reid." His intent was to provide "a guide to reading Reid, so that his genius can come to light."[69] Not to become distracted by some provocative ideas in Reid's philosophy, he stated: "I restrained myself and simply presented my interpretation of what Reid was trying to say."[70] Ever since the rise of RE at Calvin College,[71] Wolterstorff was drawn to Reid's understanding of knowledge and philosophy of "realism."

His attraction to Reidian philosophy was triggered not merely by central issues in RE, but also by its (a) stress on "realism," (b) congruence with scholastic features in Herman Bavinck's thinking, (c) effect on numerous Presbyterian and many Evangelical theologians, (d) resemblances with Jellema's and Stob's thinking at Calvin College and CTS, and (e) difference between RE in the USA and Reformational Philosophy (RP) since the 1930s in the Netherlands and Runner's arrival in 1951 in Grand Rapids, Michigan, and the opening of the ICS in Toronto in 1967.

According to Reid, knowledge is an *original judgment* about what is permanent in the subject, as the one who knows, and what is inherent in the object, as something known. Features of reality such as "existence," "substance" and "cause and effects" suggested in human sensations are not merely names, or fictions, but "real," and reliable, "conditions" in all human experience and knowledge. Truth presupposes, is based on, a "common sense" in

69. Wolterstorff (2001): xi.

70. Wolterstorff (2001): xii. E.g., "Philosophy in the Middle Atlantic and Southern States—Metaphysics and Morals" in *A History of Philosophy in America,* Vol. I, by Elizabeth Flower and Murray G. Murphey (New York: C. P. Putnam's Sons, (1977) 277–361. Also Michael DeMoor, "Not Ideas About the Thing but the Thing Itself: Thomas Reid's Epistemology in the Light of Aristotle's *De Anima*," partial fulfillment of the degree of Master's of Philosophical Foundations (N. Wolterstorff as outside advisor) at the Institute for Christian Studies, Toronto, (2003).

71. In a public lecture in 2008 at the International Herman Bavinck Conference—organized by CTS and held at Calvin College—to commemorate Bavinck's Stone Lectures on *Philosophy of Revelation* at Princeton Theological Seminary in 1908, Wolterstorff remarked near the end of the Conference that the name "Reformed Epistemology" was possibly not the most appropriate appellation for what he (and Plantinga) had in mind in 1983. The suggestion "Anselmian Epistemology" he found interesting and deserving of some consideration. Given Wolterstorff's and Plantinga's interest in "Common Sense" philosophy, perhaps "Reidian Epistemology" may be a more apt appellation.

the consciousness of human thinking. The human mind is a court of appeal, which provides the knowing subject with practical and theoretical concepts, self-evident propositions requiring no prior reasoning, i.e., insights basic to belief and invulnerable to doubt.

The intuitive propositions of humans, guaranteed by God, possess a revelatory power. Being part of the intellectual constitution of the human mind, this irrepressible and reliable "common sense" awareness accompanies human sensations and memory. Instead of needing verification, the human mind verifies everything. The principles of "common sense" thinking enable humans not only to know *that* something exists but also *what* that something really is.

The truths of "common sense" are either necessary or contingent. The six *necessary* truths are grammatical, aesthetic, logical, mathematical, moral and metaphysical.[72] From these six necessary truths, twelve *contingent* truths can be delivered.[73] Knowledge is externally and internally grounded in *facts*, i.e., based on *senses* used in a broad way,[74] and includes *moral* experiences of humans as independent substances. In terms of Reid's idea of "facticity," one could say that in studying the human mind, Reid extrapolates the science-ideal.[75] Concluding his discussion of Aristotle's logic and need for a better *Organon* than the one of Aristotle and Francis Bacon, Reid states,

> It is of great consequence to accurate reasoning to distinguish first principles, which are to be taken for granted, from presuppositions which require proof. All the real knowledge of mankind may be divided into two parts: the first consisting of self-evident propositions; the second, of those which are deduced by just reasoning from self-evident propositions. The line that divides these two parts is to be marked as distinctly as possible and the principles that are self-evident reduced, as far as can be done in mathematics from the beginning, and has tended greatly to the advancement of science.

72. Examples of "necessary" truths are the self-evident beliefs that perceived qualities belong to bodies, that conscious qualities are inherent to the mind, and that from marks in the effects an intelligent design can be inferred as the cause.

73. E.g., what is perceived through the senses really exists, and the intellect has power over the will.

74. In other words, not in the limited empiricist sense of only psychic perception.

75. On the title page of his *Inquiry into the Human Mind or the Principles of Common Sense*, Reid reproduced Pope's motto, "Account for moral as for natural things" and Newton's statement, "If natural philosophy, in all its parts, by pursuing this method, shall, at length, be perfected, the bounds of moral philosophy will also be enlarged."

It has lately been done in natural philosophy and by this means that science had advanced more in a hundred and fifty years than it had done before in a thousand.[76]

His anthropology is basically still dualistic: "soul" and "body" are two distinct substances. The soul consists minimally of the "faculties" of "intellect" and "will." The former has nine abilities, or powers, viz., external sense, memory, conception, abstraction, judgment, reasoning, taste, morality and consciousness. The power of "judgment," which accompanies the *active* power of the perceiver, enables humans to know intuitively, i.e., immediately, the object of perception.[77]

In using all their intellectual powers, humans discover the *rationally anchored principles of common sense* and the structure of life and culture accordingly. The belief that the objects of these intellectual powers really exist precedes all argumentation, i.e., it does not depend on any act of human reasoning. It comes with a certainty so strong that humans act on it in a way mathematicians do an axiom. One either resists or acknowledges, but cannot avoid, this powerful, overwhelming "common sense" of the Almighty's handiwork. The *facts* of religion and science are real, not fictions. They reveal God's presence, i.e., are His voice. In this way, as a "moderate" clergyman, Reid harmonized faith and reason, religion and science.

For more than a century, this Scottish philosophy of Realism, with its distinct epistemology, was adopted, modified and popularized in especially Scotland and North America. This "rationalistic practicalism"[78] influenced especially Reformed (and Presbyterian) theologians, preachers, educators and philosophers[79] in their use of basic terms like reality, truth, being, human, faith, knowledge, certainty, revelation, reason, theology and philosophy.

76. Reid, *Inquiry*, 1764

77. Unlike *perception*, in which the perceiver is active and knows the essence, or object, in *sensation* the perceiver merely feels, is passive and subjective.

78. This terminology reflects D. Vollenhoven's detailed, distinctive description of the Western history of philosophy.

79. A precursor of Common Sense philosophy was **G. Carmichael** (1672–1729), son of a Presbyterian minister. As professor of Moral Philosophy since 1694 at the University of Glasgow, he focused on the intellectual powers of humans and on natural religion. His successor, **F. Hutcheson** (1694–1746), son of a Presbyterian pastor, continued this stress on human mind and moral dignity, especially the notion of an implanted, intuitive, immediate moral sense in six forms, two of which were "beauty" and "virtue." At the core of the human mental capacity lies "right reason," with its self-evident truths of first principles which infallibly guide, and ultimately validate, reliable knowledge that accompanies human behavior.

Such basic terms in Scottish "Common Sense" realism seeped into thought patterns at CTS and affected philosophy at Calvin College in the (Socratic) teaching of W. Harry Jellema, the captivation of Wolterstorff and Plantinga in "linguistic-analytical" thinking, and was formalized in the founding of RE. The two official Christian Reformed centers of higher education, viz., CTS and Calvin College, developed a way of thinking in which Bavinckian scholastic elements in philosophy and theology resonated with salient features in "common sense" thinking at CTS (F. ten Hoor, S. Volbeda, L. Berkhof),[80] Princeton Theological Seminary (G. Vos , C. Hodge),[81] and especially Calvin College (Wolterstorff, Plantinga) with their interest in the Anglo-American linguistic-analytic way of "doing philosophy" about faith and reason, religion and science, belief and truth, church and culture, being Christian and philosophy.

Preliminary Evaluation

Wolterstorff's writings are lucid, engaging and challenging in the areas highlighted above, especially his passion for justice, call for a wholesome economy, genuine shalom in an aching world, and an aesthetically more gripping and diverse form of worship.

His worldview is more holistic and biblical. It enabled him to reject the kind of "liberal arts" education his main mentor, W. Harry Jellema, taught at Calvin for five decades. Being more "Kuyperian" in his concern about

---

Practical rationality is key to avoid skepticism, protect Christianity, and acknowledge human greatness. One of his gifted students was **Adam Smith** (1723–1790), the founder of free-market Capitalism, which Karl Marx opposed over a century later with his Communism. **Thomas Reid** (1710–1796) succeeded A. Smith in 1764.

80. E.g., John Bolt in systematic theology, John Cooper in apologetics, Richard Muller in the history of Reformed theology, and Neal Plantinga, until 2011, President of Calvin Theological Seminary, a graduate of Calvin College and CTS, whose father taught education at Calvin College and whose brother Alvin co-founded RE .

81. Geerhardus Vos (1862–1949), graduate of Princeton Theological Seminary (1883–1885), after teaching Systematic and Exegetical Theology at CTS (1888–1893), returned to PTS to teach Biblical Theology for twenty-nine years (1893–1932). Samuel Volbeda studied and taught at CTS, received his Th.D. in 1914, from the Free University on *De Intuitieve philosophie van James McCosh*, a prominent advocate of Scottish "Common Sense" realism and keynoter at the First International World Exhibition, held in Chicago in 1893 (for details, see chapter 16 above). For details about Realism, see Elizabeth Flower and Murray G. Murphey (1977): 203–273, esp. 232–241.

culture than his mentor, Jellema, has enabled Wolterstorff to appreciate certain features in reformational thinking by professors at the ICS in Toronto.[82]

Like Jellema at Calvin College and Stob at CTS, Wolterstorff also accepted Plato's and Aristotle's view of classic "faculty psychology," known for its stress on the three human capacities of "thinking, willing and feeling." In the tradition of the Roman Catholic Church and most, if not all, Reformed philosophers and theologians, Wolterstorff assumed that the human "will" (morality, virtue, justice, economy) and "passion" (religion, feeling, art, music) is either *good or bad*—in distinction from human "reasoning" which is essentially either *true or false* (emphasis mine).

His interest in the importance of Scottish "Common Sense" thinking, especially for the relation between "faith" and "reason" is important for at least three reasons: (i) it coincides with H. Bavinck's impact on Foppe ten Hoor's anthropology at CTS with respect to being human and the nature and role of dogmatics, (ii) it is evident in the anthropology of Samuel Volbeda, and (iii) why during the 1970s Wolterstorff lectured several times at Wheaton College, Illinois, on the importance of T. Reid's philosophy, and why he spent some *twenty years* (emphasis mine) studying his views, publishing perhaps his most important philosophical/epistemological book simply called *Thomas Reid and the Story of Epistemology.*[83]

His appreciation of Reid's "epistemology" is essentially still scholastic, or accommodational, in that it focused more on the "how," or "method," of thinking than on its content, leaving the impression that the former is key to the latter. Given the essence and scope of this chapter and to prepare for the transition to our next chapter focused on the epistemology and philosophy of A. Plantinga, I decided to do something unusual, but helpful, viz., add a sidebar on a *reformational* account of Western Rationalism since the fifteenth century.

---

82. Dr. P. Bremer, retired professor at Kuyper College, Grand Rapids, who pre-sorted H. Evan Runner's library to be entered in the archives of Calvin College, told me in/or around 2010 that he had seen a brief positive note that Wolterstorff had sent to Runner about his decision in the early seventies not to move to the ICS in Toronto but remain at Calvin College. Unfortunately, this note was lost.

83. For the nature and impact of Scottish "Common Sense" philosophy on mainly Presbyterian theology in the USA, see my *Philosophy and Scripture: A Study in Old Princeton and Westminster Theology*, doctoral dissertation at the Free University (Mack Publishing Company, Marlton, New Jersey, USA, 1978).

Sidebar: Rise and Nature of "Rationalism"

1. The waning of sixteenth-century Christian thinking and the rise of Humanism, Renaissance and Secularism, during the Age of Adventure, gave rise to new forms of synthesis-thinking in such Protestant theologians as P. Melanchthon, T. Beza and G. Voetius, who incorporated various Platonic and Aristotelian ideas in their views about the nature of Christian faith. The latter lost some of its credibility and renewing power triggered by ecclesiastical conflicts, theological debates and creedal confusion. The focus in Europe shifted to new ways of knowing reality, mastering nature and exploring new ways of knowing.

2. From 1600 to 1900, Western culture changed its ways of thinking by reflecting more on the nature and role of reason. It zeroed in on epistemic matters related to how and what humans know, i.e., on the method and scope of reasoning and theorizing. Increasingly, pressing issues in ontology, anthropology and epistemology, influenced by Greek Hellenistic and Roman culture, emphasized the importance of *logos* and *ratio*, intellect and mind, ways of debating, nature of human experiences and laws. Universal ideas, logical concepts, intellectual principles and *a priori* forms of human knowledge influence the experiences and basic certainties of humans.

3. Thomas Reid's philosophy also displays the *religious* thrust of Rationalism. Ultimately, certainty lies in God's revelation, not human reasoning as such. In a neo-Platonic way, Christians place their *a priori ideas* and *numbers* not in the background in a hidden or subservient way, but in the foreground of a God-centered theological way. The collapse of medieval scholasticism, the rise of Humanism and Renaissance, and the effect of Protestant thinking motivated culturally influential thinkers to develop a trustworthy view of reality with regard to their human ability to know.

4. In response to a proliferating skepticism, and encouraged by the rise of Humanism and Renaissance, a thinking arose that favored a Hellenistic Platonizing stress on universal ideas. Rationalistic thinking helped curb insecurity by focusing on certainty and order. Reason provides reliable knowledge about reality and human experience.[84] *A priori* ideas of earlier Hellenistic virtues and mathematics, fused with "medieval" concepts of logic

84. In "The Word of God and Learning," Wolterstorff rejected H. Evan Runner's notion of a "doctrine of the a priori" when he (NW) stated "there isn't any such thing as *the* doctrine of the a priori, only a number of different doctrines all bearing vague resemblances and going under the same name. . . . There is no such thing as *the* concept of reason (*The Reformed Journal*, December 1960, p. 19).

and "modern" laws of sensation and intellect, became prominent in *modern* thinking in ontology, anthropology and epistemology. By incorporating *a priori* laws in the human mind, "Rationalism" contributed to an overestimating of human mental capacities.

5. Rationalism tended to equate the difference between *analytical* and *physical* with what is logical and natural, measurable and knowable, optional and necessary, subjective and objective. The physical world has only *primary*, no secondary or psychic, qualities. Rationalism is an intellectual idol, functioning as a *religion*, which is, in principle, unable to truly acknowledge God as the Creator of distinct realms, each with its own *internal* and *external* relations. Creation's immense diversity is not explainable by any knowing human *subject* as a reified, or bloated, thinker, nor by any physical/measurable *object*.

6. "Rationalism" can be subdivided into Early Rationalism (1600–1830) and Late Rationalism (1830–1900). **Early** Rationalism is primarily *content*-centered, concept-focused, interested in intellectual judgments that precede, and determine, human experience, including human faith life.[85] It stressed clear thinking, proper arguing and drawing appropriate conclusions. **Late** Rationalism is more dynamic, in that it focuses on the *act* of reasoning and importance of methodology. This difference gave rise to three sub-movements: **Scientialism**, interested in *theoretical* reasoning, **Practicalism**, focused on *practical* thinking, and **Old Idealism**, which attempts to combine these two methods.

7. Unlike "Scientialism" (cf. Descartes, Spinoza, Leibnitz, Locke, Berkeley), "Practicalism," or Enlightenment (*Aufklärung*), did not think about philosophy in terms of scholarship and natural science, but of *a priori* knowledge of humans in their everyday life (business, technology, industry, citizenship, art, worship, cook, barber, legislator, etc.). Reason is not first of all theoretical, or abstract, but concrete, eminently practical, cultural. All humans have a measure of insight, certainty, knowledge and wisdom.[86] *Practical* reason guides life, liberates society, shapes culture and directs history.[87]

---

85. Cf. Vollenhoven, *Schematische Kaarten: Filosofische concepties in probleemhistorisch verband*, bewerkt door K. A. Bril en Drs. P. A. Boonstra. Amsterdam: Reprohouse, 2000. As an expert in the history of philosophy, Vollenhoven avoided the mistake of most Anglo-American philosophers—including W. Harry Jellema, N. Wolterstorff, and A. Plantinga—who contrast "rationalism" with "empiricism" and cannot really explain why J. Locke and D. Hume were both rationalists and empiricists in their philosophy, albeit in different ways.

86. Cf. I. Kant's statement as the shibboleth of Enlightenment: "Have the courage to serve your own understanding."

87. Cf. Vollenhoven's comment in class: "While *scientialism* has slain thousands of Chris-

8. According to Rationalism, the difference between "analytical" and "physical" is, in a way, comparable to what is "logical" and "natural." It indicates what is measurable, i.e., what is free and necessary, subjective and objective, and secondary and primary. The physical world is void of sensory, or secondary, qualities. In a sense, Rationalism is a form of *religion*, unable to truly acknowledge God as the Creator of all unique realms, each with its own *internal* and *external* relations to all the others. This *regnal* diversity of created reality is not explainable in terms of a *subject* and object, i.e., a reified thinker and a measurable *object*.

9. In 1764, Thomas Reid succeeded Adam Smith (1723–1790)—who wrote *The Wealth of Nations*, with its focus on capitalism, and *The Theory of Moral Sentiments*, with its stress on "moral consciousness" and "sympathy"— at the Glasgow University in Scotland. He agreed with G. Berkeley's rejection of materialism and atheism, but disagreed with his equating "being" (*esse*) with "perception" (*percipere, percipi*) and his belief that the world is based on spiritual ideas in the Divine Mind. Furthermore, he rejected David Hume's beliefs that (a) humans do not have reliable knowledge about the world, themselves and God, and that (b) matter is reducible to "sensation," mind to "ideas" and causality to "customs." Hume robs philosophy of its source, history of credibility, knowledge of a foundation, faith of a rational basis, and miracles of trustworthiness. He also disagreed with R. Descartes's equating truth with "clear and distinct ideas" and J. Locke's view that "simple and complex ideas" are based on isolated sensory impressions.

---

tians, *practicalism* has slain hundreds of thousands of Christians" (cf. Toland's *Christianity not Mysterious,* and its negative impact on Christian faith and theology). Included in *anti-Christian practicalists* are C. Wolff, D. Hume, R. Voltaire, J. J. Rousseau, d'Holbach and G. Lessing; semi-Christian *practicalists* include B. Pascal, J. G. Hamann, G. Carmichael, F. Hutcheson, T. Reid, A. Smith and D. Steward.

CHAPTER EIGHTEEN

Reformed Epistemology:
Alvin Plantinga (1932–)

Given his interest in linguistic-analytic philosophy, known for its distinct method of "doing philosophy,"[1] Alvin Plantinga's thinking also reflected the scholastic mind-set of W. Harry Jellema, his main mentor at CC. His understanding of faith-and-reason-related problems in Christian Reformed and other Christian and non-Christian traditions compelled him, as co-founder of Reformed Epistemology, to concentrate on the nature of, for example, "Being," "Substance," "image of God," the "Aquinas/Calvin" model, and the papal encyclical *Fides et Ratio*.

Ontology: "Being" and "Substance"

Plantinga's view of "Being" is clearly expressed in his (I believe, first) philosophical article published for the Christian Reformed community. What he

---

1. A method that focuses on *how* one thinks and uses language as a means to understand the *what* of one's philosophical assertions. *What* one claims or asserts depends on *how* one argues, is aware of lingual usages, sensitive to logical processes, i.e., to the "what if . . . then what?" or "if this . . . then that" way of reasoning. To listen to, or read, such thinkers/debaters, one is soon tempted—unless one has expertise in "doing philosophy"—to close the book or leave the room, something that happened when a rather large audience at a philosophy conference at a Christian college dwindled to only a handful of persons, including W. P. Alston and A. Plantinga. Invited to a discussion at the University of Toronto with W. P. Alston—a co-founder of Reformed Epistemology—I was advised by the person who invited me to focus not so much on "what" Alston would say as on "how" he reasoned, the "method" of his thinking.

assumed in this article has remained central in his extensive writings about epistemological issues. Pervasive in his thinking is his view of "knowledge," "reality" and "truth," which he articulated in his "Dooyeweerd on Meaning and Being," published in 1958, the year Dooyeweerd lectured in Christian Reformed and Orthodox Presbyterian circles in Grand Rapids, Philadelphia and Toronto.[2] He published it in *The Reformed Journal,* six years *after* H. Evan Runner introduced reformational philosophy at CC (and, indirectly, CTS), and twenty-five years *before* he co-founded, with Wolterstorff, RE (Reformed Epistemology) as a philosophical movement. This short, and mostly forgotten, article of Plantinga reveals an ambiguity about the nature of being "Reformed," including "Christian Reformed," in especially higher education and scholarship. Does it indicate one can be a Christian *and* a philosopher, a believer *and* a thinker, or does it call for being *integrally Christian* in everything one does in society and culture, including the study of philosophy and theology?

This short article is important not because it indicates the simplicity, complexity, the depth and relevancy of Dooyeweerd's truly novel thinking, but because it reveals Plantinga's ideas about what is basic in philosophy and theology, what CC and CTS had become known for since the turn of the century. It indicates Plantinga's view of such classic terms as "Being," "being," "reality," "intelligibility," "truth," "doctrine," "fact," "meaning" and "Reformed." He complimented Dooyeweerd for not flinching from "criticizing and revising traditional ways of thinking" when they seem to have "strayed from the path of truth." He did not criticize Dooyeweerd's "system as a whole," or "any aspect of it," but only wanted to raise some "**elucidatory** questions" (emphasis mine).

The questions he raised did not indicate his desire to interact with this major Reformed philosopher active since the 1920s, but to perpetuate what he took to be the established philosophy at CC, his *alma mater*, due to an institutional osmosis of traditional Reformed thinking of L. Berkhof and S. Volbeda at CTS. The difference between the "Reformed" philosophy of W. Harry Jellema at CC and Henry J. Stob at CTS *and* the "Reformational" philosophy of H. Dooyeweerd and D. Vollenhoven at the Free University, as well as H. Evan Runner at CC, was such that A. Plantinga

---

2. As a result of H. Evan Runner's teaching since 1952 as professor of philosophy and as sponsor of the Groen van Prinsterer Club at Calvin College, and in his lecturing about *reformational* philosophy at Unionville Conferences near Toronto, Canada. For details about Dooyeweerd and Vollenhoven, see, respectively, Chapters 7 and 8 above.

did not really understand, or do justice to, Dooyeweerd's novel use of "meaning."[3]

Dooyeweerd's thinking about human "faith life" is impossible to understand without touching on what Dooyeweerd meant by, for example, "faith," "analytic life" and "knowing." One's faith life affects one's analytic life, and, *vice versa*, the latter impacts the former. This back-and-forth in one's daily life is somehow influenced by a central, *religious* stance in diverging traditions. This is evident in the difference between a "scholastic" Reform**ed** tradition and a dynamic Reform**ing**, or reformational, way of Christian living, also in one's "thinking."

This divergence calls for a scrutiny of possible reasons for such a disagreement in glocal "Christian Reformed" traditions, especially in scholarship and higher education. Why is it hard, at times impossible, for "Reformed" scholars, especially philosophers and theologians, to agree on the basic meaning of, for example, "reality," "knowledge" and "truth"? Perhaps the problem is not just philosophical, theological or logical, but something that is culturally broader and *religiously* deeper? To "walk with God" **in** any philosophical endeavor may not be equated, and confused, with being a Christian **and** a philosopher. To be "reformational" meant for Dooyeweerd (and also Vollenhoven, Runner, and others) to acknowledge specific features of created reality and their distinct sciences (*wetenschappen*), including a non-scholastic study of human faith life instead of a "scholastic" study of God (theology).

A close look at A. Plantinga's role in co-founding RE will be helpful. In a rather brief article, Plantinga responded in 1958 to Dooyeweerd's major *New Critique of Theoretical Thought (NCTT)*, I-III, 1953. In it, he stressed the importance of "metaphysics," "Aquinas/Calvin model," his own anthropology, his view of "faith-reason" and the relation between "theology and philosophy."

A core belief in Plantinga's thinking—which culminated in his *Warranted Christian Belief*, 2000—is present in his first brief reaction to Dooyeweerd's view of "meaning" and "being." In the second paragraph, and pervading throughout this short article, he commented about the nature of "truth" and "reality" in a way that is essentially the same as that of his two main mentors at CC, W. Harry Jellema and Henry J. Stob.

---

3. In a note, the editors of *The Reformed Journal* stated that this article addresses only "a single aspect" of Dooyeweerd's critique of immanence philosophy. Its intent is "not to destroy, but only to contribute to the continuing conversation going on within the Reformed community, the purpose of which is to attain to Christian philosophical clarity" (1958: 10).

Traditional Christian doctrine has held that God's creation of the world consisted in producing finite beings where there had been (if temporal language is appropriate) only one Infinite Being. After creation there were two kinds of being; and the being of creation, though finite and contingent, was nevertheless thought to be genuine being and genuinely distinct from God. Something like this, I take it, has been the root to Christian opposition to the various forms of pantheism constantly cropping up in the history of philosophy.[4]

Although the intent of this statement is to be biblical, philosophically it assumes the Platonic and Aristotelian idea that God and humans have something in common: "being" as an intellectual concept. The difference between them is that God's being is "infinite" and that of humans is "finite." This infinite-finite distinction leaves, in Plantinga's view, no room for "pantheism" and it enables humans to maintain "theism."

This view of the God-human relation is endemic, implicit in the *scholastic* mind-set of H. Bavinck, L. Berkhof, W. Harry Jellema, Henry J. Stob, Dewey J. Hoitenga Jr., N. Wolterstorff and others in traditional Reformed (and Presbyterian) thinking. Plantinga combined this way of thinking, or "method," with Anglo-American *linguistic-analytic* thinking in his first public response to *NCTT*, with respect to Dooyeweerd's anti-scholastic belief that "*Meaning* is the *being* of all that has been *created* and the nature of even our selfhood. It has a *religious* root and a *divine origin*."[5]

According to Plantinga, "meaning" usually refers to "a property of sentences, codes, problems, assertions, and (sometimes) events." It never refers to the "same thing," as in the case of any of these. Furthermore, "concepts attaching naturally to meanings do not seem to apply intelligibly to things and events, and vice versa."[6] Already the title of Plantinga's article "Dooyeweerd on Meaning *and* Being" (emphasis mine) indicates a *scholastic* view of "meaning" and "being" in his thinking. This misconception is clear in his statement "Whatever it means to say 'Meaning is the being all of that has been created,' it does not, presumably, mean to deny our basic and inevitable distinction between meanings and things."[7] It is precisely this scholastic

---

4. Plantinga (1958): 10.

5. Dooyeweerd (1953): I, Part I, (1953), 4.

6. Plantinga (1958): 11. Plantinga states that it seems "nonsense" to apply predicates such as "clear, delicate, muddy, adumbrated, concealed, esoteric, etc." to meanings, since the latter "cannot be attached intelligibly to things or events."

7. Plantinga (1958): 11.

distinction between "meanings" and "things" which Dooyeweerd opposed in all his publications on philosophy and jurisprudence.[8]

Plantinga's idea of "being" is central to his article "Necessary Being," published in *Faith and Philosophy: Philosophical Studies in Religion and Ethics*, 1964. In 1982, this article blossomed into "Reformed Epistemology."[9] The Preface of this article includes a statement that is central to Plantinga's view about

> the sense in which God can be said to be the *necessary being*. Arguing that the proposition *God exists* is neither analytic nor logically necessary, Plantinga suggests that the assertion *God is the necessary being* may be understood as the claim that some proposition referring to God is the *final* answer in a certain series of questions and answers.[10]

As "necessary being," God is "both logically proper and religiously adequate" and indispensable for Christian theism. It ascribes "*unlimited authority*" to the complex proposition of "being" and places "*absolute trust*" in it.[11] In a way "familiar since Anselm," "existence *is* one of the properties included in the concept of God." One can think of God as "a necessary being" in a way that is "faithful to the conceptual scheme of theism."[12] Since it implies a "*final* answer," the concept "necessary being" leaves no room for "why does anything exist at all?" Neither unbelievers nor believers ask *why* God does not exist: "Outside of theism, so to speak, the question is nonsensical, and inside of theism, the question is never asked."[13] Hints of pivotal implications of Plantinga's view of theism for his later philosophical and theological endeavors are evident when he writes,

8. Having audited Dooyeweerd's course in Philosophy of Jurisprudence and been an assistant of Vollenhoven at the Free University, I know that on this score Dooyeweerd and Vollenhoven are in complete agreement.

9. *Philosophical Studies in Religion and Ethics* is the subtitle of *Faith and Philosophy*. In his "Foreword," Henry Stob states in the opening paragraph: "This collection of essays is issued by his students, friends, and colleagues in honor of W. Harry Jellema, whose retirement this summer at the age of 70 closes a period of exceptional service to Calvin College, the Reformed community, and the cause of Christian philosophy" (p. v).

10. Plantinga (1964): ix–x. James F. Sennett reprinted "Necessary Being" in *The Analytic Theist: An Alvin Plantinga Reader* (1998), published—like Plantinga's book in 1964—by William B. Eerdmans, Grand Rapids, as chapter eight: 214–224.

11. Plantinga (1964): 98.

12. Plantinga (1964): 102, 104.

13. Plantinga (1964): 105, 106.

Essential to theism is an assertion to the effect that there is a connection between God and all other beings, a connection in virtue of which these others are *causally* dependent upon God. And this *proposition* is *analytic*: it is part of the Hebraic-Christian concept of God that He is "Maker of heaven and earth." But it is also a *necessary truth* that God exists. He is himself uncreated and in no way *causally* dependent upon anything else. God is a *causally necessary condition* of the existence of anything else, whereas His existence has no necessary conditions (emphasis added).[14]

To explain the notions of "dependence" and "causally necessary condition" in relation to God results in "an interesting and difficult constellation of questions about the Christian concepts of creation and divine omnipotence and timelessness." In order to explain "the conceptual system involved in Christianity," one realizes that any one of its aspects "leads to and terminates in others"—in short, Christianity involves "a conceptual *system*."[15]

"Substance"

According to Plantinga, Dooyeweerd's claim that "created reality is dependent on and refers to God" is not really a "new and startling analysis of created being," but an implausible "truism."[16] He considers Dooyeweerd's idea that "in some sense a creature is a combination of functions (or of functionings) which are themselves sometimes referred to as aspects or levels of

14. Plantinga (1964): 107. *Scholastic* thinking is evident in his argument that it is absurd to ask why God exists: "Now the absence of a necessary condition of the existence of anything is a sufficient condition of the non-existence of that thing; and if a being has no causally necessary conditions, then its non-existence has no causally sufficient conditions. And hence if God does exist, his going out of existence could have no causally sufficient conditions and is therefore causally impossible. If God has no necessary conditions, then it is analytic that His going out of existence, if it occurred, would be an uncaused event; for it is analytic that there can be no causally sufficient conditions of its occurrence. Similarly, His beginning to exist is causally impossible, for since it is analytic that God is not dependent upon anything, He has no cause; and hence His coming into existence would be an event which could have no causally sufficient conditions. So if God does exist, He cannot cease to exist; nor could He have begun to exist."

15. Plantinga (1964): 108.

16. Plantinga (1958): 10. Even Aquinas would be in "solid agreement with the doctrine that created reality is meaning rather than being, for he insisted that created reality is dependent and not self-sufficient and that it points to God" (11). Aquinas and Dooyeweerd use the same term but they do so differently.

meaning" entails a rejection of the "doctrine of substance," something "intimately connected with the doctrine that created reality is being, rather than meaning." Plantinga prefers the "traditional understanding of the dependence and referential character of creation" as expressed in the statement that "created reality *is* being and *has* meaning (instead of saying it *is* meaning)."[17]

Dooyeweerd's idea that "created things are only *the bearers of meaning*" is, in Plantinga's opinion, incorrect. It presupposes the existence of "another mode of being different from that of the dependent creaturely existence referring beyond and above itself and in no way self-sufficient." In Dooyeweerd's thinking, this implies an immanence-philosophy, which permits one to *"abstract meaning from reality."*[18] Created reality, in that case, consists of "two components," viz., "being" and "meaning," and only "meaning" would denote a "reference to God." Given his own *scholastic* concept of "Being," Plantinga thinks that Dooyeweerd's argument is "specious" and "misguided"[19] and that "created reality" must be thought of in terms of a "contingent being" that refers to "uncontingent, necessary Being."

Plantinga's view of "reality" (ontology) and "knowledge" (epistemology) is consonant with the *philosophical realism* of Thomas Reid, which N. Wolterstorff advocated, as indicated in Chapter 17 above. As an advocate of traditional scholastic philosophy, Plantinga could not do justice to Dooyeweerd's understanding of "meaning" and "being." This is clear when he writes,

> To remove the contingency of the created being is to remove the being altogether; nothing unthinkable would remain. The relation between a thing and its contingency is, if you like, an internal relation; *to remove the one in thought or in actuality is to remove the other.* In fact, the root of the whole difficulty is the propensity to think of a thing and its meaning as two things somehow conjoined.* But of course the contingency of a thing is not another thing at all. . . . The proper way to skirt that pitfall is not to deny that created reality has being, but instead to avoid thinking of a thing as another thing somehow joined to it (emphasis added).[20]

Because Dooyeweerd's use of "meaning" cannot be understood in "any sense with which we are familiar in ordinary parlance," Plantinga states

17. Plantinga (1958): 11 (emphasis is Plantinga's).

18. Dooyeweerd (1955): II, 31.

19. Plantinga (1958): 12.

20. Plantinga (1958): 12. Asterisk in this citation points to Plantinga's footnote: "Of course I am not suggesting that a creature's being and its contingency are *identical*."

that "in our attempt to discover what new sense Dooyeweerd gives to this term, we have been frustrated. . . ." Plantinga's "puzzlement" indicates that he does *not* think about "meaning" the way Dooyeweerd did (cf. "mode of being of created reality") as some abstract "doctrine." As a truly radical reformer, Dooyeweerd rejected Reformed scholasticism. Instead, he thought in a different, deeper and richer way, namely, in terms of "religious ground-motives." He rejected the Aristotelian-Thomistic speculative notion of "substance" as a "relatively independent and persistent entity."[21]

Many philosophers, including most Christian ones, used the doctrine of "substance" and "entity," Plantinga thinks. He believes it to be something truly elemental, fundamental, or basic, to understand, or explain, "freedom, causality, activity, personal identity, memory, the unity and integrity enjoyed by the things of common experience, and the like." Dooyeweerd rejects the (Greek/Aquinian) speculative notion of "substance" for three reasons.

First, since it is "purely philosophical," it is not "dependent on a Christian commitment." It violates the inherent "subject-object relation" in "naive experience" in that it breaks "the integral coherence of all the modal aspects of our experience."[22] According to Plantinga, this argument of Dooyeweerd is "extraordinary," even "very odd." He rejects it, without acknowledging Dooyeweerd's fierce *anti*-Kantian stance and rejection of Kant's subjectivist idealism.[23]

Second, Dooyeweerd's reason for rejecting the idea of "substance" is, according to Plantinga, closely "connected with Christian doctrine." For Dooyeweerd, the idea of "substance" provides "an ultimate resting point for theoretical thought within the created cosmos." Rejecting this view and defending the traditional "doctrine of substance," Plantinga thinks that the "self-sufficiency of a *created* substance is not a self-sufficiency over against God, but over against *other created* beings (emphasis added)" and that "substances are not as such parts of other created beings and have, therefore, a relative independence as contrasted with attributes and relations."[24]

---

21. Plantinga (1958): 12.

22. Plantinga (1958): 13.

23. See Dooyeweerd's public opposition in 1923 to Kantian philosophy (cf. Chapter 7 above). Dooyeweerd rejects the dilemma between "realism" and "idealism." W. Harry Jellema's opposition to idealism, not realism, is reiterated by Plantinga and other proponents of Reformed Epistemology.

24. Plantinga (1958): 13. His *scholastic* view of "substance" is obvious when he states: "All that is meant is that *substance* enjoys a mode of being more independent than that of, let us say, a color, which can exist only as a characteristic of a substance . . ."

Third, Dooyeweerd's last reason for not acknowledging "substance" as a philosophical principle is integral to his belief that "the scholastic metaphysical theory of analogical being," and its implied "concept of substance," presupposes a "dialectical religious basic motive" in pagan Greek thinking.[25] Plantinga disagrees with Dooyeweerd's interpretation of a pre-Homeric "*religion of life*" and subsequent "*cultural religion*" of Olympic gods—especially Dooyeweerd's associating these two with, respectively, "matter" and "form" in the view of Aristotle and T. Aquinas. "To chide Thomas for using a concept arising in pagan Greek thought might be like excoriating St. Augustine for writing in a language developed in pagan Rome." To develop "any Christian philosophy," Plantinga states, it is "extraordinarily difficult to draw a clear distinction between those generally human intellectual products which can be employed fruitfully in such a venture" and those which cannot; furthermore, "much of the world's treasures must be appropriated," as is evident in the case of language.[26]

Plantinga wants "an intelligible non-truistic interpretation" of Dooyeweerd's doctrine that "meaning is the mode of being of created reality." This "doctrine"[27] does not account for "action, movement, and causation," since it presuppose that some*thing* like "substance," not some "meaning or a group of meanings," acts, moves and causes. In the case of human beings, that some*thing* entails "a substantial view of the self." "Meanings" are "the *objects* of judgments; they are not themselves judgers." One cannot assert that "meaning is either free or not free" in the way "*the self*" is free. To say that "the self is being" is to imply "some sort of substantial being."[28]

The last two paragraphs of Plantinga's article reveal more about his philosophical position than it does about Dooyeweerd's distinctive stance. They indicate his inability to do justice to the scriptural intent of Dooyeweerd's *non-scholastic* (and *non-idealistic*) way of thinking. Thinking Dooyeweerd "seems to jeopardize" the "doctrine of creation," he writes the following:

> . . . the relation between God and creation is like the relation between a mind and the meanings it entertains. I am not, of course, suggesting that

---

25. Dooyeweerd (1953): III, 73.

26. Plantinga (1958): 14. Plantinga is not interested so much in "genetic connections" as in "logical connections" of ideas.

27. Dooyeweerd never called the *meaning*-character of creatureliness a "doctrine," or some intelligible belief.

28. Plantinga (1958): 14. It implies a *substance*-view of an eternal soul (apart from a temporal body) with an inherent immortality.

Dooyeweerd wishes to hold such a thing; but **if** creation is merely meaning it is hard to understand its relation to God. Now Dooyeweerd rightly rejects any dictation to philosophy on the part of theology; and where he thinks that traditional Reformed thinking deviates from the truth, he does not shrink from suggesting revisions. One of his virtues as a philosopher, I take it, is his refusal to be bound by all the formulae of past Reformed thinking. Still, however, if the total result is to be called a *Christian* philosophy and in particular a *Reformed* philosophy, it **must be consistent with the spirit and the main doctrines of the Reformed and Christian tradition**. And **if** his doctrine that meaning is the mode of being of created reality does imply that the relation between God and creation is like that between a thinker and the meanings he entertains, **then** at this point **the accusation of a really significant departure from the Reformed and Christian tradition would be justified**. For then created reality becomes constitutive of God's mind and thus of God (italics and bold added).[29]

Between God and creation an "ontological chasm" exists, and this chasm assumes "being on the part of creation as well as on the part of God." To deny this chasm makes it impossible to "conceive of sin," since not "meaning" but only an evil "*being*" can sin. Scholastically, Plantinga comments: "The Christian philosopher must steer a nice course between the Scylla of giving finite reality too much self-sufficiency and power, and the Charybdis of altogether divesting creation of distinctness and 'over-againstness' with respect to God." Neither "God's uniqueness and sovereignty" may be threatened, nor may "pantheism" be courted. Desiring to avoid the former, Dooyeweerd "steers perilously close" to the latter; although his stress on God's "transcendent uniqueness and sovereignty may end by making him the author of evil," and perhaps "by denying an ontological distinction between Creator and creation altogether."

Summarizing his difficulty with Dooyeweerd's *reformational* thinking and given his own proclivity for *scholastic* thinking,[30] Plantinga states that without "further elucidation, the dictum that meaning is the mode of being of created reality, makes it hard to see how God and creation are to be kept distinct."[31] Thinking about "Christian doctrines" in a scholastically complex

---

29. Plantinga (1958): 14–15.

30. E.g., "*relative* self-sufficiency" and "*relative* independence" presuppose the principle of "substance" (1958): 13 (emphasis added).

31. Plantinga (1958): 15.

and analytically demanding way, Plantinga created unnecessary difficulties for himself, and others, in his earliest attempt in 1958 to "discover more precisely" the thrust of Dooyeweerd's novel "dictum" about creational "being" as meaning and "meaning" as being creational.

Anthropology: *Imago Dei* and "Faculty Psychology"

Plantinga's concept of "image of God" (*imago Dei*) is based on an anthropology in which "soul" refers to something *psychic* with its own being, or essence, in distinction from what is *physical* and is called "body." The invisible soul has three distinct, though closely interrelated, capacities, or faculties, viz., thinking, willing and feeling.[32] The **first** capacity is the human "intellect," which focuses on what is *true* and avoids what is *false*. The **second** capacity is the human "will," which manifests itself in the choices humans make, or doing what is *good*, living according to the insights of the intellect, and avoiding what is evil. Unlike the *true-false* distinction of the human intellect, the *good-evil*, or *right-wrong*, difference is typical of ethical, i.e., moral, life. The **third** human "faculty" is feeling, passion, commitment, beauty, which expresses submission and devotion to what is rationally *true* and morally *good*.[33]

A *structural*[34] characteristic of Platonic-Aristotelian anthropology affected Plantinga's view of "God's image" in humans in *ontology* (cf. God, humans and their interrelation) and *epistemology* (cf. human knowledge about God). **Ontologically,** the Creator and humans share *being* and *thoughts*. The difference between them is that God is Infinite and humans are finite. The relation between them is that of *Archetype* and *ectype*, in which the former precedes the latter, and the latter reflects, mirrors, echoes, reveals or exhibits

32. For details about this classic *scholastic* anthropology, see Chapter 6 above on Faculty Psychology. For details, see Anthony A. Hoekema, *Created in God's Image* (1986) about the concept of "creature-person" that is paradoxically associated with human "creatureliness" and "personhood," and about what is (i) "unconditional" and "conditional," (ii) refers to "covenant" and "response to the gospel," (iii) consists of "work of God" and "task of man," (iv) indicates "narrow or functional" and "broad" image, (v) "sovereignty of God" and "responsibility of man," and (vi) "sovereign grace" and "personal choice" (6–10; for details, see 11–101). See also John W. Cooper, *Body, Soul and Life Everlasting: Biblical Anthropology and the Monism-Dualism Debate*, Wm. B. Eerdmans (1989).

33. See Chapter 6 above, especially Robert DeVries about "orthodoxy," "orthopraxis" and "orthopathos."

34. Used here in distinction from *religious* (for details, see Chapters 9 and 10 above).

the former. **Epistemically,** human imaging of Divine being and thoughts re-flects, and affects, human knowledge of God's *Truth* and *Goodness*. A central assumption in *scholastic* theological thinking (cf. metaphysics, philosophy) and living (cf. morality, ethics) is an anthropology based on (Platonic/Aris-totelian) "faculty psychology."

To discover truth presupposes logical rigor, airtight reasoning, an "if this, then that" way of reasoning, a suppositional manner of thinking, a defining by (re)stating propositions, eliminating contra-instances, using a "true-false" technique, meticulous delineation of words and concepts, under-standing doctrines primarily as intellectual statements, concepts or proposi-tions.[35] This scholastic thinking about the truths of Christian faith, Plantinga combines with a twentieth-century Anglo-American linguistic-analytical "doing philosophy"—in the spirit of philosophical "realism" in, for example, Anselm (tenth century), T. Aquinas (twelfth century) T. Reid (seventeenth century) and N. Wolterstorff (twentieth century). About issues related to *faith and reason*, theology and philosophy, Plantinga's thinking about "God," "humans," "reality" and "truth" is structurally, or basically, the same as that of Aquinas more than seven hundred years ago and was reaffirmed in the three famous encyclicals of the RCC in 1879, 1950 and 1998 (cf. Chapter 14 above).

This resemblance may explain, at least in part, why Plantinga moved from CC to Notre Dame University, the leading Roman Catholic University in the USA. This historic move is not surprising given the impact of *scholastic* thought-patterns at CTS by means of the *scholastic* philosophy assumed in the dogmatics of H. Bavinck,[36] as taught by L. Berkhof,[37] and S. Volbeda.

35. These features are evident in A. Plantinga's writings—less so in those of N. Wolterstorff—and in most of the articles in *Faith and Philosophy*, The Journal of the Society of Christian Philosophers. This *scholastic* tradition, reinforced by a Reformed Epistemology, in-fluenced by Anglo-American linguistic-analytical thinking, makes understanding thinkers like A. Plantinga, and cohorts, a formidable challenge, bordering on exasperating. This difficulty is not unrelated to his close contacts from 1958 to 1963 with three colleagues—Nakhnikian, Casta-neda and Gettier—at Wayne State University in Detroit, when he wrote "On Necessary Being" and, one year later, published *Faith and Philosophy*, which gave rise to Reformed Epistemology.

36. The father of A. Plantinga taught in education at CC and was keenly interested in the view of H. Bavinck.

37. Cf. Chapter 15 above.

"Aquinas/Calvin" Model

Despite his criticism of Aquinas's view of "natural theology," Plantinga introduced the novel expression (in CRC circles, as far as I know) of the "Aquinas/Calvin model" in thinking about human knowledge. The "A/C model" reflects not only Plantinga's appreciation of Thomas Aquinas's view of "faith and reason," and related disciplines of philosophy and theology, but also the significant influence on prominent ideas in the thinking of W. Harry Jellema at CC and Henry J. Stob at both CC and CTS. In fact, it reflects Plantinga's own penchant to continue a form of synthesis thinking as a Christian (Reformed) philosopher. It explains his endorsement of classical theism, interest in the medieval mind, the philosophy of Anselm (1033–1109) and T. Aquinas (1226–1274), and his appreciation of N. Wolterstorff's interest in T. Reid's "Common Sense" philosophy with respect to knowledge, reality and "faith-reason" issues.

Three years before he moved to NDU, Plantinga talked at the American Catholic Philosophical Association about "The Reformed objection to natural theology."[38] He referred to Aquinas's work as "the natural starting point for Christian philosophical reflection, Protestant as well as Catholic," and quoted a phrase of Ralph McInerny, professor at NDU, that Protestants are "Peeping Thomists."[39] He added, however, that "Reformed or Calvinist theologians" generally reject the notion that belief in God presupposes syllogistic reasoning, i.e., is based on first proving his existence. In this context, he cited from Bavinck's *The Doctrine of God* as follows:

> Of the existence of self, of the world about us, of logical and moral laws, etc., we are so deeply convinced because of the indelible impressions which all these things make upon our consciousness that we need no arguments or demonstration. Spontaneously, altogether involuntarily, without any constraint or coercion, we accept that existence. Now the same is true in regard to the existence of God. The so-called proofs are by no means the final grounds of our most certain conviction that God exists. This certainty is established only by faith, i.e., by the spontaneous testimony which forces itself upon us from every side.[40]

38. Cf. Vol. I-IV, *Proceedings of the ACPA* (1980); reprinted in *Christian Scholars Review*, XI:3 (1982) 187–198. See Plantinga, "The Reformed Objection Revisited," *Christian Scholars Review*, XII: 1 (1983), 57–61.

39. Plantinga (1982): 187.

40. Plantinga (1982): 188, cited from W. Hendriksen's translation of Bavinck, *GD*, Vol. 2 (1918), 76.

Typical of *Reformed Epistemology*, he said that "argument is not needed for *rational justification*; the believer is entirely within his epistemic right in believing that God has created the world, even if he has no argument at all for that conclusion."[41] A Christian, like Scripture, simply presupposes God's existence: it *"start[s]* from belief in God." Such belief is comparable to "belief in the existence of the *self* and of the *external world*—and, we might add, belief in *other minds* and the *past*. In none of these areas do we typically *have* proof or arguments, or *need* proofs or arguments (emphasis added)."[42]

After highlighting this epistemic principle in Bavinck's theology of the doctrine of God, and applying it to matters of epistemology, Plantinga, as *philosopher* of knowledge, appealed to what J. Calvin stated as *reformer* in his *Institutes of the Christian Religion*,

There is within the human mind, and indeed by natural instinct, an awareness of divinity." This we take to be beyond controversy. To prevent anyone from taking refuge in the pretense of ignorance, God himself has implanted in all men a certain understanding of his divine majesty. Ever renewing its memory, he repeatedly sheds fresh drops. Since men, therefore, one and all perceive that there is a God and that he is their Maker, they are condemned by their own testimony because they have failed to honor him and to consecrate their lives to his will. . . . Yet there is, as the eminent pagan says, no nation so barbarous, no people so savage, that they have not a deep-seated conviction that there is a God. So deeply does the conception occupy the minds of all, so tenaciously does it inhere in the hearts of all! Therefore, since from the beginning of the world there has been no region, no city, in short, no household, that could do without religion, there lies in this a tacit confession of a sense of deity inscribed in the hearts of all.

41. Plantinga (1982): 188. He continues: "The believer doesn't need natural theology in order to achieve rationality or epistemic propriety in believing; his belief in God can be perfectly rational even if he knows of no cogent argument, deductive or inductive, for the existence of God—indeed, even if there is *isn't* any such argument."

42. Idem. Bavinck stated in *Gereformeerde Dogmatiek*, Vol. 2: "Scripture . . . does not make God the conclusion of a syllogism, leaving it to us whether we think the argument holds or not. But it speaks with authority" (76). Plantinga comments: "Both theologically and religiously it proceeds from God as the starting point. . . . And, of course, Bavinck means to say that we must emulate Scripture here" (Plantinga 1982: 195). With this comment, Plantinga applied an epistemic principle present in H. Bavinck's nineteenth-century realist philosophy—and, earlier, T. Reid's eighteenth-century (practicalistic) rationalist "common sense" philosophy—to the two areas of "other minds and the past" (for details, see A. Plantinga's *God and Other Minds*, 1967).

Indeed, the perversity of the impious, who though they struggle furiously are unable to extricate themselves from the fear of God, is abundant testimony that this conviction, namely, that there is some God, is naturally inborn in all, and is fixed deep within, as it were in the very marrow. . . . From this we conclude that it is not the doctrine that must first be learned in school, but one of which each of us is master from his mother's womb and which nature itself permits no one to forget.[43]

These statements, in Plantinga's view, indicate "a strong inclination towards belief in [God]" that all humans have, even though this "tendency" is presently "in part overlaid or suppressed by sin," Apart from sin, humans "would believe *in God* to the *same degree* and with the *same natural spontaneity* that we believe in the existence of *other persons*, an *external world*, or of the *past* (emphasis added)."[44] In fact, "This is the natural human condition; it is because of our presently unnatural sinful condition that many of us find belief in God difficult and absurd." According to Plantinga, for Calvin anyone "who doesn't believe in God is in an epistemically substandard position— rather like a man who doesn't believe that his wife exists, or thinks she is like a cleverly constructed robot and has no thoughts, feelings, or consciousness."

Though "partly suppressed," this tendency to believe in God is "universally present." The "seed of religion" and "workmanship of the universe" are such that all who "open their eyes" are "compelled to see him" (I.v.1). Under those conditions, belief in the existence of God is "perfectly rational," even though it is not based on "any argument for justification or rationality," or "any other propositions at all." Any person is perfectly within her "epistemic rights" to hold such a belief, even in the "utter absence of any argument, deductive or inductive."[45]

Belief in God can be properly *"basic,"* or "entirely rational," even in the

43. Calvin (1960): I.iii.1 and 2. These two passages Plantinga, and other Reformed epistemologists, appealed to in their debate at an international two-day seminar of *reformational* philosophy in 1981 at the Institute for Christian Studies in Toronto.

44. Plantinga (1982): 189; from this page also the next two quotes in this paragraph are taken.

45. Plantinga (1982): 190. Plantinga thinks that Calvin's comment about the "secret testimony of the Spirit," as something higher than "human reasons, judgments, or conjectures" in relation to one's belief that God is "the author of the Scriptures," is something Calvin would affirm also about our "belief in God's existence." To believe in "the existence of God on the basis of rational argument is like believing in the existence of your spouse on the basis of the analogical argument for other minds—whimsical at best and not at all likely to delight the person concerned."

absence of an argument for such a belief, or when it is not based on any other beliefs one holds. When someone's noetic capabilities are such that one's act of believing meets the "norms or standards" for believing, such a person can be said to act rationally. To prescribe a condition, or foundation, for "*rational* noetic structures" and "proper or *rational* basicality"—in terms of what is "self-evident," "evident to the senses" or "incorrigible"—is typical of classic foundationalism, as is evident in the views of Aquinas, Descartes and others.[46] In short, the central contention of Calvin, and subsequent Reformed thinkers, is that "belief in God is properly basic" and that anyone who believes this "can also *know* that God exists."

> We may understand him [Calvin] as holding, I think, that the rational noetic structure may perfectly well contain belief in God among its foundations. Indeed, he means to go further, and in two separate directions. In the first place, he thinks that a Christian *ought* not believe in God on the basis of other propositions; a proper and well formed Christian noetic structure will *in fact* have belief in God among its foundations. And in the second place Calvin claims that one who takes belief in God as basic can nonetheless *know* that God exists. Calvin holds that one can *rationally accept* belief in God as basic; he also claims that one can *know* that God exists even if he has no argument, even if he does not believe on the basis of other propositions.[47]

While "natural theology" is not necessary for "rational justification of theistic belief" and for knowing "that God exists," such theology is useful to confirm, though not to establish, persons in their belief that God exists and to prepare them for growth in their faith.[48] The relation between *reason* and *faith*, unlike the relation between *faith* and *reason*, is such that it focuses on beliefs as propositional statements, precisely articulated doctrines. This interest in the *rational* dimension of faith reveals a propensity in Reformed faith traditions to stress careful, intellectual articulation of firmly held beliefs.[49]

It is superfluous to repeat in detail what has already been pointed out (in

46. Plantinga (1982): 191–194.

47. Plantinga (1982): 195.

48. Plantinga, "The Reformed Objection Revisited" in *Christian Scholars Review*, XII:1 (1983) 57–61, in response to three Roman Catholic critics: Joseph Boyle, Jr., J. Hubbard, and Thomas D. Sullivan.

49. See, for example, the theological tradition of G. Voetius, H. Bavinck, K. Schilder,

other parts of this book) that certain Platonic-Aristotelian anthropological ideas have had a detrimental effect on basic assumptions in Roman Catholic and mainline Protestant, especially classic Reformed, theology, about the meaning of terms like "religion," "faith," "reason," "truth" and "certainty."

Two of these philosophical assumptions, viewed as fruits of common grace, are "theism" in faith and theology and "realism" in reason and philosophy. Since the philosophical, especially epistemological, role of *faith* and *reason* are comparable in Aquinas and Calvin, Plantinga coined the concept of "Aquinas/Calvin Model." Implied in this common "model" is an ontology in which *faith* is associated with special, or divine, revelation, and *reason* with general, or natural, revelation. Furthermore, it implies (a) an anthropology in which the *soul* consist of the three standard faculties of thinking, willing and feeling, and (b) an encyclopedia of knowledge in which bodily, or physical, sciences are more *objective* and *universal* than the higher human, or psychic, disciplines which are more *subjective* and *personal*.

Rejecting "classical foundationalism" in abstract rationalism, Plantinga appreciates H. Bavinck's emphasis on Scripture's authority for "religion," "faith" and "theology." What is still inchoate, or incipient, in Bavinck's thinking, Plantinga, desiring to "emulate," or copy, in a sense Scripture's authority, states that "a proper and well-formed Christian noetic structure will in fact have belief in God among its foundations." He states,

> Calvin claims that one who takes God as basic can nonetheless *know* that God exists . . . one can *rationally accept* belief in God as basic . . . one can *know* that God exists even if he has no argument, even if he does not believe on the basis of other propositions. [For Calvin] one needs no arguments to know that God exists. Among the central contributions of these Reformed thinkers, therefore, are the claims that belief in God is properly basic, and the view that one who takes belief in God as basic can also *know* that God exists.[50]

To reject "classical foundationalism" leaves no room, however, for the irrational assumption that "anything" (God as "Great Pumpkin") can be considered "properly basic." It is not rational, but irrational, to "take as basic" denying a "proposition" that seems "self-evident." There are criteria for "mean-

---

L. Berkhof, and C. Hodge in theology, and W. Harry Jellema and Henry Stob in philosophy and ethics.

50. Plantinga (1982): 195.

ingfulness, or justified belief, or proper basicality." These criteria must have "necessary and sufficient conditions," must "be reached from below, rather than above," must be "argued to" and "tested by" the believer. Christians have their *own* criteria, or "set of examples," that makes their belief in God "entirely proper and rational."[51] God "implanted in us a natural tendency to see his hand in the world around us."

This seeing is not "inchoate," incomplete, but real, based on "examples." Essential to the "A/C model," which Plantinga applied in 2000 in his major work *Warranted Christian Belief*, is this comment: "As the Reformed thinker sees things, being self-evident, or incorrigible, or evident to the senses is not a necessary condition of proper basicality."[52] Central to the "A/C model" is the role of "natural knowledge." Aquinas raised it as a basic theme, Calvin meditated on it as "a certain general and confused knowledge of God" in most humans, and basic to *theistic* belief (*that* God exists and something is known *about* God) and to *Christian* belief (*in* God).[53]

Humans possess a faculty, a mechanism, that enables them to be aware of God (Rom. 1:18–20). This instinct, tendency, disposition, nisus, or conviction is their "sense of divinity" (*sensus divinitatis*).[54] This "cognitive mechanism" triggers in humans the disposition to form theistic beliefs. Since we do not "consciously choose" these beliefs, nor "simply decide" to have them, these beliefs are "formed in us," we "find ourselves with them, just as we find ourselves with perceptual and memory beliefs."[55] This *sensus divinitatis* is innate, "like the capacity for arithmetic knowledge." It triggers "the seed of religion sown in the minds of men" and indicates God's "glory engraved upon spectacles of the universe," as Calvin says.[56]

As to theistic belief, the "A/C model" displays a *basicality* not based on any inference, argument, proof, conclusion or evidence of other propositions. It is natural, immediate, just arises in certain circumstances a person finds oneself in. It resembles a perception in which things simply appear in,

---

51. Plantinga (1982): 196, 197.
52. Plantinga (1982): 198.
53. Plantinga (2000): 168, 172.
54. Plantinga (2000): 171, with a reference to Calvin 1960: I.iii.3.
55. Plantinga (2000): 172, 173.
56. Plantinga (2000): 173, as Calvin says in Battles 1960: I. v. 1. In footnote 9, Plantinga says that this *sensus divinitatis* can malfunction, be impeded, and sometimes be extinguished. The circumstances that occasion theistic belief can vary. Because this capacity resembles other belief-producing faculties or mechanisms, Plantinga talks about a "functional analogy," an "input-output device"; see 174.

or come to, one's mind. The *sensus divinitatis* obliges one to know something about being "guilty" and about the need to worship and obey God.[57]

One is "justified," i.e., within one's "epistemic rights," and not "irresponsible or derelict" in violating "epistemic or other duties," as evidentialists claim in rejecting "theistic belief."[58] Like perceptual memory, some *a priori*, and other beliefs, *theistic belief*—"produced by cognitive faculties functioning properly in a congenial epistemic environment according to a design plan successfully aimed at truth"—can have "*warrant.*" In the spirit of H. Bavinck, Plantinga states,

> The *sensus divinitatis* is a belief-producing faculty (or power or mechanism) that under the right conditions produces belief that isn't evidentially based on other beliefs. On this model, our cognitive faculties have been designed and created by God; the design plan, therefore, is a design plan in the literal and paradigmatic sense. It is a blueprint or plan for our ways of functioning, and it has been developed and instituted by a conscious and intelligent agent. The purpose of the *sensus divinitatis* is to have true beliefs about God; when it functions properly, it ordinarily *does* produce true beliefs about God. These beliefs therefore meet the conditions for warrant; if the beliefs are strong enough, then they constitute knowledge.[59]

The human capacity to know God is part of our "original cognitive equipment," our "fundamental epistemic establishment," our "endowment" to which were added, because of our predicament, due to sin, "incarnation and atonement" and "Scripture and the testimony of the Holy Spirit." That basic *sensus divinitatis* is not "perceptual," although it "always involves the presence of experience of some kind or other," i.e., a sense of what is "numinous," a "*doxastic experience.*"[60]

This natural knowledge (*sensus divinitatis*) has been "compromised, weakened, reduced, smothered, overlaid, or impeded by sin . . . both nar-

---

57. Plantinga (2000): 175 - 177.

58. Plantinga (2000): 177–178.

59. Plantinga (2000): 179. In footnote 15, he says that such a warranted belief is "also properly basic with respect to rationality" understood as "proper function." For details, see Plantinga, "Reason and Belief in God," (1983): 16–93 (republished in Sennett: 1998, 102–161) about which, along with his "Justification and Theism," Sennett commented that it has "come to be recognized as the cornerstone piece in the Reformed Epistemology project" ("Introduction," xvii).

60. Plantinga (2000): 180, 182, 183.

rowed in scope and partially suppressed." Not the believer, but the *unbeliever,* is the one who "displays epistemic malfunction: failing to believe in God is a result of some kind of malfunction of the *sensus divinitatis.*" As "a property or characteristic of beliefs," *warrant* is—Plantinga repeatedly reminds the reader—"formed by properly functioning cognitive faculties in a congenial epistemic environment according to a design plan successfully aimed at truth," which includes "the avoidance of error."[61]

Both rationality and irrationality have to do with proper and improper functioning of human cognitive faculties.[62] Belief formation presupposes proper functioning of all our cognitive faculties. This holds true also of belief in God in terms of the "A/C model," with its *sensus divinitatis* "damaged and corrupted by sin," and in terms of the extended model, with its *sensus divinitatis* "partly healed and restored to proper function by *faith* and the concomitant work of the Holy Spirit in one's heart." In short, a *sensus divinitatis* that functions properly can produce "theistic belief" and do so in a "basic way" that will have "warrant sufficient of knowledge."[63]

The issue of the "rationality or warrant or lack thereof for belief in God" is essentially "ontological or metaphysical or ultimately religious." Whether theistic belief is warranted depends on one's view of "what kind of beings you think humans are, what sorts of beliefs you think their noetic faculties will produce when they function properly, and which of their faculties or cognitive mechanisms are aimed at the truth." The dispute whether theistic belief is rational, or warranted, is not just epistemological, but "ontological or theological."[64] If one believes humans are "created by God in the image of God . . . with a natural tendency to see God's hand in the world around us and with a natural tendency to recognize that we . . . are beholden to our creator, owing him worship and allegiance," then "belief in God" will not be viewed as an "intellectual defect," as a "belief producing power or mechanism not aimed at the truth."

> It is instead a cognitive mechanism whereby we are put in touch with part of reality—indeed by far the most important part of reality. It is in this regard like a deliverance of sense perception, or memory, or reason, the faculty responsible for *a priori* knowledge. . . .

61. Plantinga (2000): 184.
62. Plantinga (2000): 110–111.
63. Plantinga (2000): 186.
64. Plantinga (2000): 190.

And this dependence of the question of warrant or rationality on the truth or falsehood of theism leads to a very interesting conclusion. If the *warrant* enjoyed by belief in God is related in this way to the *truth* of that belief, then the question whether theistic belief has *warrant* is not, after all, independent of the question whether theistic belief is *true*. . . . This is important: what it shows is that a successful atheological objection will have to be to the *truth* of theism, not to its rationalist justification, intellectual respectability, or whatever. . . . They can't any longer adopt the following stance: "Well, I certainly don't know whether theistic belief is *true*—who would know a thing like that?—but I do know that it is irrational, or unjustified, or not rationally justified, or contrary to reason or intellectually irresponsible or. . . ."[65]

Review of *Fides et Ratio*

Like N. Wolterstorff, A. Plantinga also reacted in 1999 to John Paul's long encyclical *Fides et Ratio* (1998). In this pastoral letter, the Pope addressed primarily bishops, but also theologians and philosophers, about the "age-old and never finished discussion of the relation between faith and reason." Although its message is a "little blurred," Plantinga believes that its rethinking, in the way of T. Aquinas, is a "most important topic for the present-day Christian community" and makes "a great deal of solid good sense."[66]

The encyclical talks about *faith* and *reason* as "two separate sources of justified or warranted belief." Knowledge "peculiar to faith" surpasses knowledge "proper to human reason," although reason can, given its nature, "discover the Creator." Reason and faith constitute the twofold structure of knowledge, and each has its own source and object. The harmony between them indicates the unity of truth. The light of philosophy and science centers on the "intelligibility and reasonableness of the natural order of things" and

---

65. Plantinga (2000): 191. See also Plantinga's revealing comments on 198: "There isn't a sensible *de jure* question or criticism that is independent of the *de facto* question. . . . This fact by itself invalidates an enormous amount of recent and contemporary atheology: for much of that atheology is devoted to *de jure* complaints that are allegedly independent of the *de facto* question." According to Paul in Romans 3:21–31, *unbelief* is a "result of dysfunction, brokenness, failure to function properly, or impedance of rational faculties."

66. Plantinga thinks the encyclical does not distinguish enough between "faith and reason" and "Christ and culture."

the light of faith, the Spirit, grace and salvation manifests the self-revelation of God the Father of the Lord Jesus Christ.

"Reason" (philosophy) focuses on the "meaning of life," figures things out for itself, does not "advert to the content of faith," has more "epistemic clout," is able to prove God's existence. "Faith" (theology) depends on something else, on "say-so," a testimony, even *God*. It deals with matters of sin, atonement and redemption; it illumines and fulfills reason—the organon for faith to understand itself—and rises to knowledge of the *triune God*.

Although reason and faith, the two sources of warranted belief, differ, they are in harmony. To counteract the spreading of "false modesty" and "*loss of confidence in reason*" in postmodern relativism, with its flouting of truth, in Western culture, the Pope advises *philosophers* to have faith in reason and to seek help from revelation, and encourages *theologians* to continue trusting reason. "Natural reason" is really "an ensemble of powers and capacities we have just by virtue of the way we were created by God." Because of the Fall, some "supernatural gifts were lost," although "natural reason was substantially unaffected."[67]

These natural powers "can take us a good way" to answer "the great questions of the meaning of life." In this regard, "ancient philosophers—perhaps, in particular, Plato and Aristotle—were able by virtue of reason to move some significant distance toward the whole Christian truth." Divine revelation, necessary for the "final steps . . . can be seen to *fulfill* reason in the sense that it is in continuity with their thought, and actually provides what they were groping for."[68]

In a way typical of Jellema, his mentor, Plantinga thinks that modern "post-Kantian and post-Humean" rejection of "Christian or even theistic belief" is "less an incomplete approach to Christian belief than arrogant apostasy" that culminated in the naturalism in "contemporary American philosophy departments" and in the nihilism of F. Nietzsche—neither of which approaches "Christian truth."

The Pope overlooks, however, the Reformed belief that non-Christian philosophy is "not merely handicapped by an 'inherent weakness of human reason,'" but is, like humanity generally, "*fallen, and in need of conversion*."[69] According to Plantinga, "Contemporary philosophy doesn't look at *all* like

---

67. Plantinga (1999): 32–33.

68. Plantinga (1999): 33. The naturalist views of Democritus and Lucretius, however, reflect the "foolishness," not wisdom, of Greek thought.

69. Plantinga (1999): 33.

an incomplete approximation to Christian truth." In fact, it is "antithetical to Christianity. . . . It is less a deliverance of reason than the articulation of a rival faith."[70]

Western contemporary philosophy is known for its three "worldviews": (i) Christian theism, (ii) ontological naturalism, especially in the *natural sciences* (no God), and (iii) nihilism, relativism, anti-realism, no "Truth," only interpretation based on human autonomy. Being neither RC, nor Christian or theistic, the third worldview is "incompatible with Christian theism."

Plantinga's **first** critical comment about *Fides et Ratio* is that humans did not merely lose "a supernatural addition to our natural faculties," which can continue to function "more or less as before." Both reason and faith "suffered substantially from the results of sin," damaging their ability "to know ourselves, others, and God." In this respect, the encyclical underestimates the place of sin and the ensuing "views of the world in explicit opposition to Christian truth." Plantinga's **second** critical comment about this *third* encyclical (in one hundred nineteen years) on the problem of "Faith and Reason,"[71] centers on the Roman Catholic lack of clarity about what "Christian philosophy" means. According to *Fides et Ratio*, before Christ's birth and untouched by the gospel, Greek *philosophy* was "an autonomous enterprise, obeying its own rules and employing the powers of reason alone." It searched "for truth within the natural order," though it was essentially open to "the supernatural" (#75).[72]

Christian philosophy points to "a Christian way of philosophizing, a philosophical speculation conceived in dynamic union with faith" (#76). This kind of philosophy has a "subjective" and an "objective" aspect. The *subjective* aspect "purifies reason" and (as a "theological virtue") "liberates reason" from "philosophical presumption," when it thinks about evil and suffering, God as person, the meaning of life, and radical metaphysical questions. The *objective* aspect explores "the rationality of certain truths"

---

70. Plantinga (1999): 34.

71. *Aeterni Patris*, (1879); *Humani Generis*, (1950); and *Fides et Ratio*, (1998). For details, see chapter 14 above.

72. The Pope continues by stating that "to argue according to rigorous rational criteria is to guarantee that the results attained are universally valid. This also *confirms the principle that grace does not destroy nature but perfects it: the assent of faith, engaging the intellect and will, does not destroy but perfects the will of each believer who deep within welcomes what has been revealed*" (emphasis added). In distinction from this original meaning of "philosophy," modern philosophy wants to be "separate," or self-sufficient, by "refusing the truth offered by divine revelation."

in Scripture and broadens "reason's scope for action" to include humans' supernatural vocation and original sin itself" (#76).[73] According to E. Gilson[74]—whom the Pope called "error detector"—faith helps reason to spot a line of thinking, arguments and propositions not incompatible with Christian faith. Furthermore, it suggests topics for philosophy, rationally proves certain items of faith, and leaves room for truths not discovered by reason, even though they are not inaccessible to reason.

Rejecting the Roman Catholic Thomistic stance of *FR*, Plantinga opts for an Augustinian (and Protestant), way of thinking by claiming that (a) "not anything one proves has more epistemic clout than anything one believes on the basis of testimony" and (b) "in philosophy one can appeal to what one knows by faith." Philosophy is essentially "faith seeking understanding."[75] It does not require purely rational proof, but focuses on "the relation of a proposition in question to other items of faith." One knows what faith entails for such philosophical questions, and answers, as to what Christian faith implies for "the nature of human beings, of knowledge of the good, of education, of natural laws, of morality, of universals, propositions, sets, possible worlds, and a thousand other topics?"[76]

In *Thomistic thinking*, premises (arguments of "Suppose . . . , then") come from reason and are rational. Premises, or "conditionals," are philosophical and require exploring, not simply asserting something to be true. In *Augus-*

73. In this case, such philosophers do not become theologians "since they have not sought to understand and expound the truths of faith on the basis of Revelation," but have worked "on their own terrain and with their own purely rational method, yet extending their research to new aspects of truth" (#76). Theology "presupposes and requires in all its research a reason formed and educated to concept and argument." Philosophy is "the *ancilla theologiae*" in the manner that Aristotle regarded "experimental sciences as 'ancillary' to '*prima philosophia*.'" In this respect, both theology and philosophy "come more directly under the authority of the Magisterium"—of the Roman Catholic Church and the Pope (#77).

74. Whose *History of Christian Philosophy in the Middle Ages* (1955) was W. Harry Jellema's favorite textbook in my course with him on Medieval Philosophy in 1957 at Calvin College. Etienne Gilson was Director of the Pontifical Institute of Medieval Studies in Toronto (where, in 1972, I met Bernard Lonergan, S.J., to talk about possibly writing a doctoral thesis—for the Free University in Amsterdam—on his reinterpretation of T. Aquinas in his *Insight*, 1957).

75. A phrase often used at CTS and CC and the subheading of *Faith and Philosophy*, the Journal of the Society of Christian Philosophers committed in support of Reformed Epistemology.

76. Plantinga (1999): 35. The pursuit of philosophical inquiry entails an "irenic compromise" in the form of "Suppose Christian faith were true," how does that affect the "conditioned result" of, for example, one's view of "causality"? Such a conclusion in an argument based on a premise of faith is neither "philosophy" nor "theology."

tinian thinking, however, all premises of faith are accepted, i.e., "If Christian faith is true, then what is the right, good, and best way of thinking?" Both traditions agree about the "antecedent" and "consequent" and are interested in the "conditionals," but they view the relation between "faith" and "reason" differently: Augustinians stress "faith seeking understanding," an essential scholastic feature in the theology and philosophy of RE.

Without distorting the intent of RE, one could say that "reason" (*philosophy* and *epistemology* of Aquinas and Augustine) can be combined with "faith" (*theology* of Augustine and Calvin) without having to "reform" the scholastic reason-faith and faith-reason tradition.

Central Issues

A brief summary of crucial issues touched on in this chapter (and indirectly already in Chapters 15–17) will highlight that in our daily life in everything we do there is a *religious* struggle, even conflict, between "accommodation" and "reformation"—also in "Reformed" thinking, teaching and everyday living. As will be indicated in Chapter 19, this difference is evident in what notably H. Evan Runner stressed in his informal contacts since 1951 with about a dozen, mainly Canadian, theology students at CTS, and in his teaching of philosophy at CC.

When Runner arrived at CC in Grand Rapids, he thanked God for the possibility of continuing what he had learned from his two main mentors in Amsterdam, Dooyeweerd and Vollenhoven, i.e., press for an ongoing reformation, which in fifteen years resulted in the ICS (Institute for Christian Studies) in Toronto, with the help of visionary persons in mainly Ontario, Alberta and British Columbia, Canada, including such *religiously* "radical" but self-effacing servants as, for example, Rev. Frans Guilluame in the CRC[77] and Gerald Vandezande[78] in Canadian Christian labor unions and national political witness.

To focus on the *religious* difference between "accommodational" and "reformational" thinking does not imply doubting the sincerity of fellow Christians whose philosophical, anthropological and epistemic methods

---

77. Cf. A prisoner in Dachau in 1944–45.

78. A simple, self-taught, powerful, fearless Canadian servant-leader in pressing regional and national labor and citizenship issues, for which he received the highest Medal of Honor from the Canadian government and an *honorary* doctorate from the ICS in Toronto.

one may disagree with and reject. Instead, we assume a common liberating commitment to God, Father/Son/Spirit, whom to serve is our intent and life-encompassing doxology.

It is not a luxury, but a necessity, for Christians, as followers of the Anointed One, to assess well-established thought-patterns of scholarship and education, research and teaching. All present and future scholars and teachers provide, locally and globally, an appropriate analytic stance which (like an invisible rudder) moves the ship of life (in society, culture and history) in an inescapably *religious* direction.

Plantinga developed his *religious* "accommodation" in philosophy. He did so by perpetuating what had, in principle, already been done for a century in "dogmatics" and "apologetics" at CTS and, for a half century, at CC in "philosophy" in terms of classic "liberal arts."[79] In the history of Reformed thinking, this initially well-intended tradition in higher education, especially theology, experienced (too) often the lure of scholastic undertows and the dangers of deadly rip-currents with respect to God, self, nature of reality, turmoil about Christian thinking, teaching and living.

In at least five ways, "scholastic" thinking has affected the Reformed mind-set in especially the disciplines of philosophy and theology. *First*, an "ontology" with respect to the nature of "being," "essence" and "existence," and to the relation between "metaphysics" and "theology." *Second*, an "anthropology" with a higher "soul" and lower "body," three faculties of "thinking, willing and feeling," "concepts, virtues and passions," "true, good and beautiful." *Third*, an "epistemology" in which (a) "intellect" influences "will" and "emotion," (b) "faith" that affects "reason" and their interrelation, and (c) nature of "logic," "concept" and "systematic." *Fourth*, meaning of "objective" and "subjective." *Fifth*, encyclopedic, or curricular, issues of (a) "liberal arts" curriculum with respect to the Greek tripod of "philosophy, ethics and religion" and (b) the distinction between "humanities" and "natural sciences."

These five scholastic issues shaped the thought-pattern of H. Bavinck's four large volumes of *Reformed Dogmatics*: Vol. I focused on philosophical issues and Vols. II-IV on dogmas to be believed. This kind of philosophy affected the scholastic theology in the thinking of L. Berkhof, S. Volbeda and Henry J. Stob at CTS, and the context for the Reformed philosophy of W. Harry Jellema, N. Wolterstorff, A. Plantinga and others at CC.

79. In the spirit of T. Beza, Calvin's close friend and colleague in Geneva, who as the keynote speaker at the official opening of Calvin's Academy in Geneva in 1559, lectured on the importance of Aristotle's philosophy, notably logic. For details, see Chapter 3 above.

Basically, these Reformed (and even many Presbyterian) professors and preachers advocated a form of "scholastic" thinking as already T. Beza did at the very start of the Academy of Geneva in 1559, and G. Voetius and others did before, during and after the Synod of Dort in 1617–18. The fifteenth-century Reformation was spiritual, i.e., *religious*, radical, a "back-to-God" movement, not explainable in terms of "scholastic" distinctions between, for example, supra-natural and natural revelation, special and common grace, spiritual and natural life, faith and reason, religion and science, and theology and philosophy.

These distinctions, prominent in Roman Catholic circles and in many Protestant traditions, function as principles, or concepts, also in a Western thinking greatly influenced by ideas and thought-patterns of Plato and his famous student, Aristotle. Those ideas were incorporated in the views of, respectively, Augustine of Hippo (fourth century) and T. Aquinas (twelfth century), J. Calvin and T. Beza (sixteenth century) and A. Kuyper and H. Bavinck (nineteenth century).

In the spirit of especially H. Bavinck, both Wolterstorff and Plantinga have advocated a philosophy of scholastic "Realism"—in the tradition of Anselm (1083–1109), T. Reid (1710–1796), John Witherspoon (1723–1794) and H. Bavinck (1854–1921). Plantinga opposes "atheism" by assuming the rational validity of "theism," a view influenced, perhaps, by his intellect-tilted anthropology, in which "God's image" in humans is more "structural" than "directional."[80]

Plantinga has not, as far as I know, commented on the important change in the title of L. Berkhof's *first* edition of *Reformed Dogmatics* (*RD*), in 1932, to *Systematic Theology* (*ST*) in the *second* edition in 1938 without changing the content of the book.[81] "*Reformed*" was replaced with "*Systematic*" and "*Dogmatics*" with "*Theology*." The reasons for this change are not clear. *First*, Berkhof wanted to stress the similarity in his views with those of his Presbyterian colleague, Charles Hodge, at PTS; *second*, S. Volbeda, L. Berkhof's colleague at CTS, who in 1914 received his Th.D. from the Free University in Amsterdam for his doctoral study of James McCosh, a prominent Presbyterian Scottish "Common Sense" philosopher and theologian, and in 1915 gave his inaugural lecture at CTS on the importance of H. Bavinck's view of

80. For details, see Chapter 10–11.

81. No one at CTS or in the excellent library of CTS/CC could explain this change but surmised that the change was made for reasons of distribution and sales in especially Presbyterian and other circles influenced by Scottish "Common Sense" thinking at PTS, particularly Charles Hodge, and WTS, especially its founder.

"Het wezen der religie,"[82] and, *third*, most likely, for primarily the publisher's ability to distribute Berkhof's (Bavinckian) book beyond CRC circles familiar with Charles Hodge's major *Systematic Theology*, I-III.[83]

82. For details, see Chapter 15 above. It is noteworthy that Hodge's theology (i.e., dogmatics) was profoundly influenced by his philosophy, anthropology and epistemology described in some detail in Volume I, something also Bavinck had done in his major study in dogmatics.

83. This outreach opened the way for CTS and CC, as well as later Dordt College, Trinity Christian College and Kuyper College in the USA, and Redeemer University, The King's University, and ICS in Canada, to reach out locally, regionally and globally. To do this in an "accommodating" way is much easier than to do it in a "reforming" and dynamic way in all areas of life and their related disciplines.

PART IV

REORIENTATION

CHAPTER NINETEEN

Reformational Worldview and Philosophy: H. Evan Runner (1916–2002)

One of the distinctive features of *reformational* philosophy is its view of the *religious* direction in which humans live, including how they think about created reality. To do this in a covenant-oriented way motivated reformers like J. Calvin (1509–1564) as a refugee in Geneva, A. Kuyper (1837–1920), a culture-oriented thinker, and philosophers such as D. H. T. Vollenhoven (1892–1977) and H. Dooyeweerd (1894–1975), who formulated a distinct *reformational* view of reality at the Free University in Amsterdam.[1] The one who introduced this tradition in the USA[2] was H. Evan Runner (1916–2002), as philosophy professor at CC for twenty-nine years (1952–1981) and main mentor of the Institute for Christian Studies (ICS) in Toronto, Canada.

Runner's passion for reformation in the academy and diverse areas of society and culture captivated a relatively small group of students, mainly from Eastern and Western Canada, at both CC and CTS. They appreciated his scriptural understanding of created reality rooted in God's love-filled

---

1. For details, see chapters 4–8 above.

2. A significant number of Dutch immigrants from the Gereformeerde Kerk had been members of the Association for Calvinistic Philosophy (Vereniging voor Calvinistische Wijsbegeerte), established by Vollenhoven and Dooyeweerd in 1936. They had studied, and financially supported, its novel way of living their faith life, thinking about education, and acting in society and culture. They shared this *reforming* way of living with their children, many of whom became servant-leaders in all four levels, or phases, of education, in labor unions, political activities, farming policies, contacts with native Canadians. Rev. F. Guilluame, a pastor in Eastern and Western Canada, played a significant role in establishing the ICS in Toronto in 1967.

covenant. This simple, profound, broad, and liberating awareness of reality he conveyed with passion, both privately and publicly.

He did this for almost three decades (a) in his unique way of teaching at CC, (b) as the sponsor of the Groen van Prinsterer Club at CC/CTS, 1953–1973, (c) as a public lecturer in Calgary, Alberta, in 1957, (d) as a public commentator in Grand Rapids, Michigan, in 1976, (e) as a primary lecturer at "Unionville Conferences," near Toronto, from 1959 to 1961, (f) as an advocate of diverse Christian organizations in terms of A. Kuyper's vision of societal "sphere sovereignty," (g) as an advocate of *integral*, not integrated, Christian thinking and teaching, and (h) as a translator (with some assistance from his wife, Elisabeth) of S. G. De Graaf, *Promise and Deliverance* (*Verbondsgeschiedenis*) I-IV,[3] with its focus on *coram Deo* living and history of revelation.[4]

Professor at Calvin College

The philosophical tradition of W. Harry Jellema and H. J. Stob, with its stress on "liberal arts," notably philosophy, theology, and ethics, differed from Runner's teaching at CC and his role, since 1954, as the sole sponsor of the "Groen Club" of mostly Canadian students at CC and CCT. Generally, Christian Reformed students from the USA were not interested in Runner's non-traditional "Christian Reformed" ideas about, for example, reality, worldview, truth, life, structure of society, culture, and history.[5]

His views were broader and deeper than what is personal, denominational, ethnic, cultural, or national. They were not primarily philosophical, logical, methodological, or theoretical. In fact, he rejected "Socratic" phil-

3. I: "From Creation to the Conquest of Canaan" ("Translator's Introduction," 10–14); II: "The Failure of Israel's Theocracy"; III: "Christ's Ministry and Death"; IV: "Christ and the Nations."

4. In addition to personal knowledge about Runner from 1954 to three weeks before he died in 2002, my main sources are: (i) Bernard Zylstra (1934–1985), (ii) Harry Van Dyke, (iii) Albert Wolters, (iv) Glenn Andreas, his roommate at Wheaton College in the 1930s, (v) speaker at his wife's funeral in 2000 and his funeral in 2002, and (vi) "Runner Legacy Conference" at Redeemer University in Ancaster, Canada, December 2002.

5. Some initial pedagogical deficiencies did not, rather oddly, undermine his charisma in articulating a worldview critical of various traditional scholastic methods and of most students and colleagues at CC not used to being challenged in their century-old Christian Reformed tradition shaped in some way by an "accommodational" way of thinking in "philosophy, anthropology and theology" at CTS and CC by perpetuating questionable *scholastic* features in especially H. Bavinck and, albeit indirectly, A. Kuyper.

osophical arm-wrestling about often discussed topics related to the nature of "reality" and of "truth." He was uneasy about *scholastic* issues at CTS and within the Christian Reformed community.[6] Conflicts within the academic community were, he believed, related to a major problem in the general "worldview" of the Christian Reformed leaders and tradition, including in its missionary endeavors with respect to the meaning of, for example, "heart" and "religion."

Having been raised in a biblical, conservative, orthodox Presbyterian faith tradition, Runner was attracted to the creedal stance of the CRC. While a graduate student in philosophy at the Free University for five years (1946–1951), he became familiar with especially four issues: (i) the views and writings of G. Groen van Prinsterer and A. Kuyper, (ii) Vollenhoven's systematic philosophy, including his logic and history of philosophy, (iii) had extensive discussions with H. Dooyeweerd, and (iv) read the publications of, and dialogued with, J. P. A. Mekkes, K. J. Popma and other neo-Kuyperian thinkers, especially about political and socio-economic areas of society and culture.[7]

Quite soon after he started to teach philosophy at CC, he became uneasy about the *religious* direction of not only "tertiary" but also "primary" and "secondary" forms of Christian education regarding the basic thrust of North American scholarship, stages of Christian education, and even general thinking in Western, including USA, culture.

At the Unionville Study Conferences, near Toronto, he challenged some one hundred students—from Canadian and USA Christian colleges and a few non-Christian Canadian universities, to be faithful to the Lord God in all their studies. He challenged inquiring pastors, various primary and secondary Christian school teachers, met with Christian labor union leaders and challenged those who were interested in public justice, art, and public communication.

His public lectures in Grand Rapids (USA) and in both Toronto and Calgary (Canada) and his sponsoring the "Groen Club" at CC/CTS resulted in the Association for Reformed Scientific Studies—in 1959 changed to Association for the Advancement of Christian Scholarship (AACS). In 1967, he gave

6. Disagreements at this time within CTS and CC are reflected in *The Banner*, the official publication of the CRC, and in two contrasting opinion-shaping papers called *Torch & Trumpet* and *The Reformed Journal*.

7. Especially Leo Oranje, a relative of Runner's spouse, Elisabeth, who was knowledgeable about Christian schools, Anti-Revolutionary Party (ARP), Christian socio-economic organizations, and the distinction between "life" and "theory." For details, see A. Van Dyke and A. Wolters, "Interview" with H. Evan Runner, in *Hearing and Doing*, (1979): 347.

the "Opening Lecture" at the Institute for Christian Studies in Toronto, and engaged in extensive correspondence with both students and colleagues in North America and Europe, and with some evangelical leaders in the USA.

Runner emphasized God's call to humans to submit to and follow Him by discovering the meaning, not just "concepts," of created reality (cf. revelation, religion, spirituality, gospel, kingdom of God, church, society, culture). He prodded young and old, Christian and even non-Christian, to renew their thinking about their calling in daily life, personally and communally. Our groping world needs a simple life-embracing, radical, invisible, firmly anchored worldview to guide our daily life by providing helpful insight into the nature, or "structure," of a reality which reflects His love and glory. Such a holistic view challenges Christians to discover more meaningful forms of education and thereby somehow make a contribution to the welfare of humans in their community and culture.

As a philosopher at CC, a guest lecturer for several years at the ICS, and as a *private tutor*—in 1981–1982, the first year of his retirement, of a CC graduate interested in Greek and Roman philosophy of law[8]—and a private adviser of former students and several colleagues, he pressed in his letters for an ongoing *religious* renewal, or "reformation," with a worldview that is deeper and broader than the Christian Reformed focus on the triad of "Church, Home, and School," but that includes also public legislation, labor unions, farming, business, industry, health care, and media.

Holistic living in everything Christians do in God's holy presence was for Runner a vision, a norm, a goal, more than a reality, as his co-workers experienced, in traditional Christian Reformed thinking and education in the USA. Inconsistencies in the worldview and way of living, especially in philosophy and (higher) education in Christian Reformed circles, made him restless. He appreciated the creedal clarity of the CRC but was saddened by the fact that the actual thinking and teaching at CC and CTS did not do justice to the full impact and blessing of being Reformed. To be reform*ed* is to be reform*ing*, i.e., to keep renewing one's way of thinking, living and witnessing, in the spirit of Kuyper's famous phrase (in his Princeton Stone Lectures in 1898) that God claims, in Christ Jesus, through the Spirit, "every square inch of life" for Himself in our love-filled obedient living, including our thinking.

Troubled by this discrepancy, Runner was surprised, and encouraged,

---

8. He was an assistant of H. Berman, an internationally famous professor of Russian law, who when he moved to Emory University in Atlanta, GA, insisted that his assistant, John Witte, Jr., would continue to be his assistant also at Emory University.

by the changes in the CRC community after the 1950s in both the USA and Canada. The **first** wave of Reformed Dutch immigrants to the USA, after 1834, had joined the established Reformed Church of America (RCA), from which they separated, however, in 1857 and established the Christian Reformed Church, the **second** wave of Reformed (*Gereformeerde*) immigrants also went to the USA. This was after A. Kuyper, with some eventual help from H. Bavinck, had functioned as a "reformer" in church, family, and educational life in The Netherlands and had pressed for renewal in government, industry, business, labor, health care, and media.

The **third** wave of Reformed (Gereformeerde) immigrants after World War II of about 45,000 went to Canada, and a smaller number to Midwest USA, i.e., Michigan, notably Grand Rapids and vicinity, Northern Illinois, and Indiana south of Chicago. The worldview of these "Reformed" immigrants differed in a significant way from the one they encountered in their new environment. That difference had to do with the relation between their so-called faith life and their daily life in society. It centered on the nature, i.e., depth and scope, of being "Reformed" in their new country and North American culture.[9]

No one sensed this problem as clearly as Runner did, despite his not being Dutch nor a member of the CRC until he started to teach at CC, the sole denominational college in the USA. As an American-born Presbyterian student, he studied for five years (1946–1951) in *post*-Bavinckian and -Kuyperian biblically directed faith life, including its unavoidable societal, political, and cultural expressions. When he started to teach at CC, he was surprised by a significant difference between the response of most USA students to his worldview and its implications and that of most Canadian students at both CC and (indirectly) CTS.

What triggered this divergence in how students responded was not always his well-prepared lectures and optimal use of pedagogical methods, but his way of challenging students to think differently about traditional ideas about such basic issues as, for example, truth *and* virtue, being a citizen *and* a Christian, culture *and* church, reason *and* faith, philosophy *and* theology, common grace *and* special grace, or natural revelation *and* special revelation. As a non-Dutch, non-Canadian and non–Christian Reformed thinker, gripped by a Christ-centered view of God's kingdom, Runner soon discovered an unanticipated reason for coming to CC. He discovered that at

9. A contributing factor may have been certain effects of World War II on the psyche of USA citizens with the horror of war and victory over a German/Italian/Japanese threat.

CC and CTS, the two official academic centers of the CRC, where pastors, teachers, and other leaders were trained, they were not aware of the *religious* depth, societal scope, and cultural importance of the novel approach of H. Dooyeweerd and D. Vollenhoven, who had pioneered in developing a "reformational" way of thinking.[10]

Sponsor of "Groen van Prinsterer Club" at Calvin College

Responding to the questions of a few local businessmen[11] and certain probing students at both CC and CTS about scriptural renewal in daily life and formal education, Runner met in 1953 with two students[12] to talk about their interests and concerns. They were eager to know more about the nature of biblical *renewal* and about the twin dangers of *biblicism* and *accommodation*. They inquired about the meaning of, for example, (i) being "Reformed," "Christian" and "Christian Reformed" in education, (ii) how to view Western society and culture, (iii) meaning of church membership, (iv) living in different countries, (v) membership in labor unions, and (vi) nature of business enterprises, etc.

10. A reformation which W. Harry Jellema and Henry Stob had not experienced and did not really understand. Cf. 1936 regarding H. Dooyeweerd, *Wijsbegeerte der Wetsidee*, I-IV, and philosophical Journal *Philosophia Reformata*, and D. Vollenhoven establishing the "Vereniging voor Calvinistische Wijsbegeerte."

11. These persons joined, somewhat hesitantly, the Reformed Fellowship—a relatively small but somewhat influential group within the Christian Reformed Church—who rejected the *Protestant* Reformed Church's opposition to "common grace" and who questioned the *Christian* Reformed Church's acceptance of "common grace" in 1924 and its importance for determining one's involvement in society and culture, especially in philosophy and higher education. The spokesman for these restless persons who consulted with Dr. Runner was Steve Harkema, a quite recent Dutch immigrant immersed in a Kuyperian tradition.

12. The spokesman for the students was Bernard Zylstra—who subsequently after (i) graduating from CTS, (ii) studied law at the University of Michigan, (iii) jurisprudence at the Free University, where he received his doctorate under H. Dooyeweerd, (iv) was professor of law at ICS in Toronto, (v) was the first president of ICS and (vi) died suddenly of cancer in 1986. For his ideas and influence, see the Center for Public Justice (CPJ) in Washington, USA, especially James W. Skillen, and Citizens for Public Justice (CPJ) in Ottawa, Canada, especially Harry Kits. Zylstra's extensive writings and correspondence moved in 2011 from Redeemer University College in Ontario to the Archives of CC in Grand Rapids, MI. One of his ICS students was Paul Marshall, who succeeded Zylstra in 1986, and moved to Washington, DC, to work for "international religious freedom." B. Zylstra and John Witte, Jr. (Emory University, Atlanta) were Runner's top students in jurisprudence.

In response to the request of a few local (Christian Reformed) busi-nessmen, who considered establishing a Calvinistic Culture Association (CCA),[13] Runner delivered his first public lecture, which he called (using a Dutch navigational expression) "Het Roer Om!" (Rudder Hard Over), in Eastern Avenue CRC, 2/5/1953. He challenged various community members, college and seminary students, and faculty members to reject American in-dividualism, establish Christian organizations, avoid rationalistic humanism, not restrict political choices to two parties, and sense that all organizations and institutions reflect a *religious* bias. Rather than uncritically accept and perpetuate misleading ways of living in society and culture, Christians must be *religiously* clear how they reveal their allegiance to the Lord of life in a secular world.

This public lecture resulted in considerable, at times heated, discus-sions in the community, especially among students and faculty members at CC/CTS. Are Runner's ideas more Dutch than biblical, or relevant for North America, perhaps undemocratic? Does his stress on a "third way" (cf. Christian organizations) not undermine the role of the church? What are the implications of Runner's views for students and their future careers as teachers, preachers, doctors, lawyers, businesspersons, workers, citizens, and political leaders?

To express their concern about these enervating questions, a group of college and seminary students asked two students to consult with Runner about what could be done to obtain clarity. One of these two students was Bernard J. Zylstra, son of a recent Dutch immigrant in Grand Rapids. Their consultation with Runner resulted in the establishing, later that year, of what became known as the "Groen Club," sponsored by H. Evan Runner and named after Guillaume Groen van Prinsterer (1801–1876), perhaps the most significant mentor of A. Kuyper as a "Reformer."[14]

Harry Van Dyke, the historian of the Groen Club—and the North American expert on G. Groen van Prinsterer's ideas and roles as a Christian leader—described the *first* meeting of this club (cf. *first* quotation) and what, twenty-three years later, Runner remembered about the club's ambitious program (cf. *second* quotation) as follows:

---

13. This small organization was started by three local immigrants who had become suc-cessful businessmen. For details, see Harry Van Dyke, "H. Evan Runner and the Groen Club" in *Comments*, Winter (2004): 27–34, esp. 27.

14. For details, see Chapter 3 above.

He [Runner] came to the expectant members with an ambitious program of study. It was designed to be a systematic approach to delving into the meaning of the Reformed or Calvinist religion in all its ramifications for the life of service that students were preparing for, whether that be in science, business, the gospel ministry, medicine, law, or education.

It involved the question of who the Puritans were, the meaning of the Enlightenment, its influence in America, the basic ideas of the Declaration of Independence and the American Constitution, the nature of Scholasticism, particularly as manifested in Reformed theology, the concept of natural law, the religious ground-motives that have successfully given order to the experience of Western man, the origins of capitalism, the rise of the labor movement, and so on and so forth.[15]

What motivated Runner as *philosopher* at CC, *sponsor* of the Groen Club, *public speaker* at certain events,[16] *adviser* to students and organizations interested in integrally Christian living, was that he was *someone* who, like his two chief philosophical mentors, stressed God's covenant promises fulfilled in Christ Jesus and sealed by the Spirit.

Assisted by various Groen Club members during the next seven years, this study program was published in 1960 as a seventy-three-page Syllabus called "The Bible and the Life of the Christian." On behalf of the Groen van Prinsterer Society, Runner, as the club's sponsor, wrote "A Prefatory Note" about the importance of this syllabus for young and old, non-academic and academic persons, and all Christians everywhere:

> The following lessons have been translated and adapted by students of Calvin College and Seminary under my general supervision in the Groen van Prinsterer Society. . . . But since such a scriptural view as these lessons present can scarcely be found in the English language elsewhere, our men's and women's societies, and even many individual persons and privately organized reading clubs, may wish to make use of the material here offered.
>
> Young people today lack *order* and *structure* in their thinking about the Bible. That is a strange thing; for the Bible is a revelation to us of *the*

15. H. Van Dyke, (2005) "The Best of Comment."

16. Runner consulted with some colleagues and several college and seminary students about whether he should accept Lester DeKoster's invitation for a *public debate* at CC about Runner's views. Given DeKoster's interest, as speech professor at CC, in "winning debates," he turned down DeKoster's request for a public debate. For details about DeKoster's inability to understand *reformational* thinking and living, see his long series of editorials in *The Banner*.

order of God in His creation. And it is the insight into this order (proper Bible-knowledge) that gives *perspective to our life-in-the-world* (kingdom service). The second flows out of the first. Thus it is not surprising that our young people also have no clear convictions about what Kingdom service is (Rom. 12:1–2). Or that they tend to shy away from people with "absolute" principles for daily Christian living. . . . Or, they do not take to reading or studying, but rather go on drifting in the given situation. What evidence have they seen that books have ever helped anyone? Do books of human words ever help here unless the Divine Word—singular, thus *structural!*— gets through, which alone is the POWER that can grip a human heart, draw it together in one and give it direction? In how many of our books, sermons, catechism classes, etc. does that happen? Or do we too often get lost in unrelated facts, individual persons in the Bible about whom we can moralize, etc.? No wonder so many of our words are POWER-less! They do not convey the WORD!

    . . . May the blessing of God accompany it [syllabus] unto the reformation of our North American life!

The nineteen chapters of this Syllabus reflect Runner's worldview, his intent with the Groen Club, the basic thrust of his public lectures, and what he believed scripturally directed living as citizens to entail. The topics dealt with in this Syllabus are: (1) Scripture as Lamp to Our Feet; (2) Office of Government; (3) National State; (4) Kingdom of God; (5) Church and Kingdom of God; (6) Confessing Church; (7) Theocracy in Israel; (8) Government and Church; (9) Freedom of Conscience; (10) Government and Law of God; (11) Culture; (12) Christian State; (13) Marriage; (14) Family; (15) School; (16)Human Society and Gospel; (17) Economic Life; (18) Industrial Organization; (19) Christian Organization.[17]

The response of the CRC in the USA to Runner's worldview and understanding of God's Word for society and culture as articulated in the *Syllabus,* was—comparable to reactions to his "Het Roer Om!" public lecture in 1953—mainly one of benign neglect, even considerable opposition from

---

17. The original syllabus "Bijbel en Staatkundige Beginselen" consisted of nineteen chapters with a specific orientation reflected in the order of the chapters. A smaller and simpler, but essentially similar, study guide was used in a Youth Club of my local Gereformeerde Church when I was *fourteen* years old and one year before my family emigrated to Canada. That study guide was also used by one of my Christian elementary school teachers during World War II. The Presbyterian and Reformed Publishing Co. published the fifth edition of this Syllabus in 1968.

certain persons at CC/CTS: he had imported not biblical but Dutch ideas and, worse, had equated them with Christian principles.

The response to Runner's views and lectures by Christian Reformed persons in Canada was generally positive, chiefly because they were familiar with central insights of especially A. Kuyper, H. Dooyeweerd, D. Vollenhoven, and other Reformed leaders. He received significant support from the Christian Labor Association of Canada (CLAC),[18] various pastors, and especially supporters of the AACS, which in 1967 opened the ICS in Toronto. Its first four professors were former "Groen Club" members. Its first students came from Trinity Christian College in Illinois, Dordt College in Iowa, and diverse Christian faith traditions in various Western and several non-Western countries.[19]

His lectures at well-attended conferences in Eastern and Western Canada emphasized the need for a new way of living and thinking in all of life. His three decades of public lecturing influenced not only Trinity Christian College and Dordt College in the USA[20] but also The Kings College in Western Canada and Redeemer University in Eastern Canada.

In his public lectures in Canada, USA, and twice the Netherlands, he stressed four themes: (i) renewal in human understanding of the "structure" of created reality, including history; (ii) the scriptural role, of the human "heart"; (iii) "religion" as something central, directional, not an option humans decide to have or not to have; (iv) God's all-encompassing, powerful Word, through whom the world was created, who became "incarnated," paid the ultimate price, and is God's gift of "love-filled-justice" which calls humans to return to God in his covenant of love here and now.

Runner's simple and culturally dynamic worldview rejects limiting "religion" to a formal agreement or some detailed "theological" study of an isolated, and insulated, faith life. *Religion* affects not only a person's "faith life" but also one's analytical life (cf. epistemology, logic) and philosophical activities (cf. ontology, anthropology, encyclopedia, and special disciplines).

He rejected being a Christian *and* a philosopher, or relying on faith *and* reason, but pressed for being a Christian thinker, philosopher, or teacher,

18. And his disagreement with the Christian Labor Association (CLA) in the USA, especially in Grand Rapids and area.

19. The *first* recipient of a M.Phil. degree was Masuo Myazaki, from Kobe, Japan, under C. Seerveld's supervision.

20. Also Kuyper College in Grand Rapids, as well as graduates of ICS in Toronto who teach at Hope College in Holland, Michigan, Calvin College and Cornerstone University in Grand Rapids, Michigan.

who (a) rejects scholastic features in Roman Catholic and Protestant, also Reformed/Presbyterian, academic thinking, (b) opposes the idols of *religious* humanism and rationalism, (c) resists the irrationalism of North American pragmatism, European phenomenology and existentialism and (d) does not rely on the "method" of linguistic-analytical philosophy in Anglo-American scholarship.

In summary, some Dutch immigrants in Grand Rapids and various students from Eastern and Western Canada at CC/CTS affected Runner's life and work in ways he had not expected in 1951/2. The general main "mind-set" in these two institutions was significantly different from what he had learned as (i) a North American Presbyterian student for a year at the Reformed Theological Seminary in Kampen, the Netherlands, just before World War II, and (ii) as a student since 1946, for five years in philosophy at the Free University regarding a faith tradition, education, society, and culture significantly shaped by **reforming** insights of G. Groen van Prinsterer, their influence on A. Kuyper as preacher, professor, author, socio-political leader, commentator, even role as prime minister, from 1880 to 1920. Philosophically, he immersed himself in the insights of H. Dooyeweerd in both philosophy and jurisprudence, and of D. Vollenhoven in philosophy, logic, and history of Western thought since the 1920s.

What compelled A. Kuyper in his practice and theory, in society and the academy, was God's overwhelming and liberating Word, something H. Evan Runner sought to convey in his teaching at CC. It was precisely at that time, that North American students,[21] with a Gereformeerde[22] background, met this North American philosopher, who challenged them in their new situation to live in terms of Romans 12:1–2.[23]

---

21. One of the first Canadian *female* Groen Club members was Wendy Helleman, who, influenced by Runner, majored in philosophy, received a Ph.D. in Greek, especially Platonic, philosophy, and who for several decades has been (with her husband, Adrian, who majored in theology) a professor of philosophy, under the aegis of IICP Russia and Africa.

22. Under the influence of A. Kuyper, and others, who seceded (Doleantie) in 1894 from the Reformed *State* Church, established in 1618/9. Also the "Christian Reformed Church" in the USA, established in 1857, had in 1834 split from the Reformed *State* Church. As a result, the worldview in "Christian Reformed" circles in North America differed from that of the older "Reformed Church" in North America (e.g., difference between CC and CTS in Grand Rapids *and* Hope College and Seminary in Holland, Michigan, and the difference between Dordt College (DC), Sioux Center *and* Central College in Pella and Northwestern College in Orange City, IA.

23. "Therefore, I urge you, brothers [and sisters], in view of God's mercy, to offer your bodies as living sacrifices, holy and pleasing to God—which is your spiritual worship. Do

After a half-century, it is understandable why the Groen Club at CC/ CTS played an important role in Runner's personal and professional life. It impacted his twenty-year sponsorship of this club, especially given the opposition to it on campus, and it stimulated many students to catch a glimpse of his emphasis on God's powerful Word, incarnated in Christ Jesus, or Anointed Savior. This Word of God may not be compromised by fusing it with Greek thinking about philosophy and anthropology through some accommodation between, for example, believing and thinking, faith and science, church and state, being a Christian and a philosopher.

Lectures in Canada and Commentary in USA

In 1957, Runner delivered a public lecture in Calgary, Alberta, for a Christian Reformed audience, on the topic "Development of Calvinism in North America and the Background of Its Development in Europe." He called attention to the importance of the Rev. John Witherspoon, a gifted Presbyterian Scottish preacher, who emigrated in 1768 to New England, USA. He became the first President of the "College of New Jersey," later known as Princeton University. He was the only Calvinist clergyman who, eight years later, signed the American Declaration of Independence.[24]

This Scottish Presbyterian preacher, and professor of philosophy, came to the USA and taught the views of Thomas Reid (1710–1796), founder of Scottish Realism, to be used as

---

not conform any longer to the patterns of this world, but be transformed by the renewing of your mind. Then you will be able to test and approve what is God's will—his good, pleasing and perfect will."

24. For details, see Varnum I. Collins, *President Witherspoon: A Biography,* I-II (Princeton: 1925) and I. H. Butterfield, *John H. Witherspoon Comes to America: A Documentary Account Based on New Materials* (Princeton, 1953). Also John C. Vander Stelt, "Philosophy and Scripture at Princeton College" in *Philosophy and Scripture: A Study in Old Princeton and Westminister Theology* (Marlton: New Jersey, 1978, republished in 2013, 65–89. In 1739, at age 16, Witherspoon received his M.A. from the University of Edinburgh for his dissertation on "Immortality of the Mind" (*De Mentis Immortalitate*). His 469 students in New England included one president of the USA, one vice-president, six members of the Continental Congress, twenty-one senators, thirty-nine members of the House of Representatives, and six cabinet members, as well as twelve governors, three members of the Supreme Court, one hundred and fourteen clergymen, nineteen presidents and professors of colleges, thirty medics, and several authors and legal scholars. As to economics and politics, he endorsed in his *Essay on Money,* 1786, the views of Adam Smith, the founder of Capitalism.

... the tool by which orthodox theology could be defended against Humean skepticism, Deism and French revolutionary ideas. In its views on reason, natural theology, conscience, the freedom of the will, and virtue Scottish realism is a kind of practical rationalism. For that reason it quickly had taken over Harvard's *new Divinity* School. . . . It also became the philosophical tool *par excellence* of the New England theology that followed upon Edwards and the Great Awakening, a movement which culminated in Nathaniel William Taylor, professor of theology in Yale Divinity School. . . . Scottish Realism accelerated the long trend toward rational theology. . . . Reformed theology was thus emptied of its most dynamic element. A kind of rationalistic *rigor mortis* set in.[25]

Later, Runner gave his second public lecture on what he cryptically called "Point, Counter-Point." In distinction from (a) his original Presbyterian theological and philosophical background and (b) certain features in W. Harry Jellema's view of what it means to be "Reformed," he talked about a *reformational* view of "reality" in the tradition of J. Calvin, G. Groen van Prinsterer, A. Kuyper, H. Dooyeweerd and D. Vollenhoven. He challenged the governors, staff, students and supporters of the Association to a "firm standing in the Truth, which is the Word of God," and called attention to A. Kuyper's emphasis in his Opening of the Free University in 1880 that "Reformed" refers to a "principle of *life*," not to something only "ecclesiastical" or "theological."

God's Word, we have come to understand, is not a collection of revealed logical propositions, conveying to us, after the natural sciences have rendered up to us a 'natural knowledge' of the 'natural world,' some additional category of 'spiritual' knowledge about a hidden world of 'supernatural' entities. We have come to see that in His Word God reveals Himself to us in the covenantal fellowship He has established with the people of His choice. The Word of God discloses and illumines this fellowship, which is at once the heart of all created reality and the central reality of our human existence. Such disclosure acts as the ordering principle of our lives. It pushes all other aspects of our lives out of this central place and makes them so many distinct expressions of what is disclosed to be central.[26]

25. Runner (1957). Speech "The Development of Calvinism in North America on the Background of its Development in Europe": 21, 22.
26. Runner (1967) "Point, Counterpoint," Address at dedication of Institute for Christian Studies.

Any created thing, or event, exists through God's Word. We must acknowledge the great power and amazing covenant love of God, the Creator. Central in Runner's work, as a reforming thinker, are the comments he made in this important public lecture:

> I say all this because it should be very clear that we are not proposing with our institute just another Bible school or theological seminary. . . . Further, it should be very clear that we are not interested at all in repristinating an older theism, philosophically reasoned in the Greek metaphysical way. We wish to have no traffic with any of those metaphysical arguments for a hidden realism or noumenal or supernatural "entities" like "God" and "soul" which the eye of reason is supposedly able to discern behind the phenomena of the physical world.
>
> By employing scientific methods men can arrive at some understanding of the functional relations of things, but meaning is never a matter of scientific analysis. Meaning has to do with a religiously perceived unity in order and coherence. In the last analysis, man is a religious being, made to live in fellowship with God and in the experience of His favour. In such fellowship he is sensitive to truth and meaning. Having alienated himself from God, he can no longer experience the meaning of creation.[27]
>
> In *this* battle as to who has the authority to determine meaning, we have not begun to fight until we have learned not to rely on our metaphysical arguments and theological systems, and to place our confidence solely in the Word of God, which is powerful to open the heart, to beget to new life. It is a matter of bringing Spirit into play against spirit, ranging Word against word. We cannot play around with symptoms.
>
> The humanist spirit has prevailed there [in science and scholarship] too, and Christians have been conspicuous either by their absence or by their silence and accommodation. There has, for example, been no general restructuring of bodies of concepts and terms that stems from an original religious understanding of the claim the Word of God makes upon such work.[28]

When, years later, Runner reflected on the "Centennial of Christian Reformed Church in North America," he warned against the widespread impact of Greek thought-patterns on Western philosophy, anthropology,

27. *Ibid.*, 7, 8.
28. *Ibid.*, 13.

epistemology, and theology. Its implied way of thinking about reality greatly affected Reformed thinking about the meaning of such common terms as "truth," "reality," "reason," "faith," "theology" and "certainty."

In his different way of thinking about human and non-human creatures, Runner stressed the need for a simpler, and richer, awareness of the intricate structure of the world which humans experience in their daily life in God's presence (*coram Deo*). Such living is not restricted to what is private, devotional, spiritual, or sacred. On the contrary, humans are by their very nature compelled to respond somehow, but always in a *religious, heart-centered*, way to God's Word and the Spirit's power. Such a way of living is not optional, nor private, but integral to what humans do in society and culture, e.g., in industry, labor, banking, sports, recreation, agriculture, and voting booth.

About a scholastic penchant in certain assumptions in "theology" at CTS and "epistemology" at CC, Runner stated in his "Some Observations on the Condition of Calvin College at the Celebration of Its Centennial"[29] that they are not appropriate. He called attention to an unreformed way of thinking in traditional Christian Reformed scholarship and higher education and to his own Presbyterian educational background influenced by Scottish "Common Sense" Realism. Perceptively and critically, he commented: "Confused by the marriage of Protestant theology and Scottish Common Sense Philosophy, we mistake the consensus that had come to be established in *such* a community for a universally *human* consensus, for what we called the commonness of rationality itself." After stating this view, he challenged the Christian Reformed educational community to rethink the *religious* direction of its "philosophical" tradition:

> In this way Calvin [College] can arrive at an answer to the question as to its identity, as to its 'being' dynamic, not Platonic-essential in the midst of a constantly changing world. [Needed is a] continual reformation [since sin's hold upon us is] often prolonged by the traditions that have formed us, particularly institutionally. [Christians should not opt for a] metaphysical enterprise [that addresses] central religious questions purely rationally. [Needed is a] different view of the task of philosophy. . . . [We have not] sufficiently and clearly broken with the Greek metaphysical tradition or attempted to develop an alternative. Today . . . a Greek exaltation of 'Mind' and the cultivation of it as opposed to bodily involvement in the world is

29. Prism (1976): 30–39.

still there. . . . [A] certain elitist smugness [is] felt in our community at times.[30]

What is inherent to the *philosophical* and *theological* tradition at CTS and CC is what he described in 1967 about the CRC as a denomination. He sensed that resistance to ongoing *reformational* thinking, also in theology, is not unrelated to a contestable view of "common grace." He writes,

> The academic interest in Common Grace was to explain that a measure of light and goodness that is allegedly found in the natural man which renders the darkness of his understanding and his unrighteousness something less absolute. . . . The emergence of this non-Kuyperian and, in my opinion, thoroughly unscriptural understanding of mammon Grace has left its mark upon the Christian Reformed Church and its college. It has reinforced the Greek views already operative in Christian circles.[31]

Although Runner studied theology for five years at WTS in Philadelphia, USA, and one year at the RTS in Kampen, the Netherlands, and received two degrees in "theology," he was never a pastor, nor a theologian, nor a professional philosopher in the way D. Vollenhoven, his chief mentor, was. He received his Ph.D. (*magna cum laude*) from the Free University for his dissertation on Aristotle's *Physics*, taught philosophy for twenty-nine years at CC, was a guest lecturer for several years at the ICS in Toronto, but never a professor of philosophy at a university.

Given the historical situation of the CRC in North America, Runner's role was that of a "pre-reformer." He saw the need to improve the *religious* direction of the CRC and the larger Christian community in North America, and elsewhere, with respect to its worldview, faith life, philosophy, education, role in society and culture, and non-Western countries and cultures. He called for a biblically *heart*-centered, not Greek intellect-focused, rethinking

---

30. "Some Observations on the Condition of Calvin College at the Celebration of Its Centennial."

31. Calvin's *Prism*, (1976). According to Runner, "Common Grace," as viewed in Christian Reformed circles during the 1920s, served as "a theological justification for their already consummated accommodation to the cultural ways of the American world." Runner was sometimes told that he was not really Christian Reformed but actually "belonged with the Hoeksema people," who seceded in 1924 from the Christian Reformed Church and established, under the leadership of Rev. H. Hoeksema, the Protestant Reformed Church, and established their own Theological Seminary and their own grade and high schools in the USA.

in traditional Reformed (Presbyterian and Evangelical) traditions.[32] He cautioned young men and women about well-intended but actually speculative thinking about basic issues like "reality," "humanity," "culture," "religion," "truth" and "love."

Traditional "theology" tends to resist *religious* renewal, perpetuate mistaken ideas, and cause misguided conflicts within, and among, theological schools. By incorporating deeply rooted "ideas" and "methods" within a rapidly changing society and culture, any "theology" that wants to be(come) popular undermines the credibility and power of biblical faith and readily appropriates what is culturally novel and more meaningful. Any *religious* synthesis gives rise, sooner or later, to unnecessary conflicts. Reading questionable think- and act-patterns "into" (eisegesis) and "out of" (exegesis) Scripture fosters futile conflicts and results in numerous truth-claiming theological seminaries, or schools of thought and, worse, even "religions."

God's powerful Word upholds the condition of created reality. This Word humans are called to acknowledge in the way they live within the covenant God established with them as his image-bearing creatures. His people, including philosophers and theologians, need not rely on "meta-physical" concepts about, for example, "reality," "substance," "essence," "truth," "body," "soul" and "faculty-psychology."[33]

A common criticism among *scholastic* thinkers, particularly in Reformed and Evangelical circles, of *reformational* thinking is that it does not allow room for atheism or theism and turns intellectual ignorance about God into some kind of virtue. Scholastics reject the notion that "integral" knowledge *precedes* "theoretic" knowledge, which is disjunctive, i.e., one-step removed from practical life. The distinction between daily faith life and general concepts violates the truth, or rational objectivity, of God's revelation.

The distinction between "practical" and "theoretical" knowledge is, unlike the scholastic one of degree, one of kind, not degree, quality, or gradation. Christian living is a "faith life," or "radical" knowing in the sense of a "heart-centered" familiarity with God's Word. Such knowing is integrally *religious*, not academic, theoretical, or theological, but hearing God's call to love.

The Creator's sustaining Word calls for constant relying on his covenant

---

32. And the larger world as well. Runner had a life-long interest in Asia, especially North Korea and China. He talked about this with me even a few minutes after his wife's burial in 2000.

33. For details, see Chapter 6 above on "Faculty Psychology," especially S. Solivan's ideas and R. C. DeVries, at CTS, about "orthodoxy, orthopraxy and orthopathy."

promises to humankind. Such constant, simple, but profound, child-like listening to God's Word enables humans, who hear his voice, to be prophetic, priestly, and royal in their everyday life. Yielding to the Spirit's power and anchored in the Anointed One, humans can be God's people again, who reveal what it means to walk in true love and loving truth as citizens of his "kingdom."[34]

Lecturer at Unionville Conferences

At the first three Unionville Conferences,[35] three presenters, from different countries, dealt with cultural issues insufficiently, if at all, discussed in Christian Reformed and other Christian academic circles. Runner was the only one who lectured at all three conferences. He explained that what motivated the Association for Reformed Scientific Studies to sponsor these conferences was the hope of establishing an academic institution, which came about in 1967 with the founding of the Institute for Christian Studies in Toronto. Central to the three Unionville Conferences was "The Relation of the Bible to Learning," which, since 1953, had been the central focus of the Groen Club at CC/CTS.

At the first Conference, in **1959**, Runner lectured on four issues: "Challenging Frontier," "Thesis," "Antithesis," and "Synthesis."[36] In **1960**, he explained the distinction between "Scientific" and "Pre-Scientific" knowledge, and described the principle of "Sphere Sovereignty" in relation to the structure of society.[37] In **1961**, he focused on "Scriptural Religion and Political

---

34. For example, "Our World Belongs to God: A Contemporary Testimony of the Christian Reformed Church in North America" (1987). Gordon J. Spykman (1926–1993), professor at Calvin College, who shared Runner's *reformational* thinking, chaired the Committee that authored this Contemporary Testimony.

35. Conferences were held in a barn on the Cherry Hill Farm of Mrs. Madsen in Unionville, a small village north of Toronto. The lectures were published as *Christian Perspectives 1960*, by Pella Publishing, Inc., Iowa, and as *Christian Perspectives 1961* and *1962*, by Guardian Publishing Company, Ltd., Hamilton, Ontario. Other lecturers in **1959**: H. Van Riessen, Free University, Amsterdam, on "The Relation of the Bible to Science," Allan Leonard Farris, Knox College, Toronto, on "The Relation of the Bible to History"; **1960**: W. Stanford Reid, McGill University, Montreal, on "Absolute Truth and the Relativism of History," and S. U. Zuidema, Free University, on "Pragmatism" and "Existentialistic Communication"; **1961**: J. J. Duyvené De Wit, Bloemfontein University, South Africa, on "Organic Life and the Evolutionistic World and Life View." H. Evan Runner also lectured at smaller conferences throughout Canada.

36. Runner, (1960): 85–158.

37. Runner, (1961): 11–87.

Task" with respect to three issues: (a) "Thesis: Its Political Articulation," (b) "Antithesis: The Forms of Its Political Expression and Their Development in Modern Times" and (c) "Synthesis: Contemporary Political Expression."[38]

In his Unionville lectures, he dealt with central issues touched on in all his speeches and writings since 1953. The *religious* depth and the *structural* scope of his worldview are evident in the terms, phrases, and expressions he used to articulate his view of created reality in a non-traditional philosophical and 'theological' way. He stressed God's power-filled Word, his central love command, the need to read Scripture in a covenant-centered way, view God's world and understand the role of humans in it, who are engrafted in the risen Lord, Jesus Christ, who is "the way, the truth, and the life." Because of a recalcitrant scholastic, pietistic, and confusing view of especially "faith" and "theology," his particular emphases were not always clearly understood, at times wrongly understood, by university students, some CRC pastors, schoolteachers, and some businesspeople.

This kind of "reformational" thinking, educating, and living was generally not known at that time in CRC circles in the USA. In Eastern and Western Canada, especially Ontario, Alberta, and British Columbia, there was a sense of the need to be distinctively Christian in, for example, farming, labor, business, and citizenship. Runner encouraged Christian students in both the USA and Canada, to be aware of two debilitating dangers, viz., scholastic accommodational and secular humanistic thinking. For this purpose, he used, sometimes coined, terms, ideas and expressions (also) in his Unionville lectures of 1959 and 1960,[39] as in the following:

> "principles of unity, order, and coherence," "Word of God as basis for knowing with confidence," "reformational awakening," "not separatism but genuine community," "synthesis diminishes both struggle and joy," "antithesis is present also in politics," "theory of functions is necessary to understand society," "distinction between modality and function," "life is religion," "religion is neither private nor optional," "integral reformation of ideas, insights

38. Runner, (1962): 135–257. Runner's Unionville lectures of 1960 and 1961 were combined in *The Relation of the Bible to Learning*, Paideia Press, Jordan Station, Canada, in 1982 and, in revised form, reprinted several times.

39. "The Relation of the Bible to Learning," (1967) edition, with Runner's five lectures at his first two Unionville Conferences. *Reformational* philosophy developed a *distinct* terminology, *not to obstruct* communication with other philosophies in Western history and culture—e.g., pagan Greek, Roman Catholic and Protestant scholastic, humanistic, rationalistic—*but to enhance* communication in our *religiously* restless world.

and actions," "accommodating established lifestyles and thought-patterns," "Reformed scholasticism perpetuates medieval scholasticism," "in ons isolement ligt onze kracht,"[40] "practice reflects awareness of Order or Structure of things," "God's Word is not an appendix, an extra, something *super*natural, but the *condition* for *all* knowledge," "either the Way of Synthesis or the Way of Antithesis," "Scripture as God's written Word and Christ as God's incarnated Word," "Word of God, not Words of God," "God's Word as Power pierces the heart of humans and converts them,"[41] "knowledge of *God, self*, and God's *Law (order)* as one insight," "knowing one's place in creation is inseparable from one's conviction of sin," "facts 'speak' to humans about God's Word for creation," "intrinsic relation between God's Word and the world of learning," "God's Word of Truth is basic to the ultimate nature of things," "metaphysical speculation is based on a purely rational analysis independent of one's religious relation to God," "metaphysics is a substitute for true religious living," "rationalism assumes that the human heart is 'rational' and all differences are ultimately conceptual," "dichotomy and trichotomy are pseudo-problems," "God **creates** the world, His Law **holds/obtains**, and creation **is**," "the Truth of God is the reality of the Covenant of Life between God and humans," "'Jesus Saves' is a republication of the creation-order centered in the covenant between humans and God," "no sphere-sovereignty without sphere-universality," "religious synthesis is combining God's Word with a pagan idea of Law," and "the effects of synthesis are devastating."[42]

In "Preface to Runner," Bernard J. Zylstra commented in 1982 on four central issues that Runner addressed: (i) liberal roots of Anglo-Saxon culture, (ii) uniqueness of Dutch "pluriform" democracy, (iii) changes in the "spirituality" of modern Western culture, and (iv) worldviews of Roman Catholic, Anabaptist, and Reformed Christianity. He ended this Preface by asking, and answering, the question "Can the Christian religion provide such

40. The phrase "in our isolation lies our strength," coined by G. Groen van Prinsterer, Runner indicates, "does not mean that we must separate ourselves from *persons*, but that in all our contacts with them we must be aware of the distinctiveness of the *rule* by which our lives are directed" (Runner, 1960: 87).

41. Resulting in *religious* renewal, not in superficial moralism in devotions, catechizing and, especially, preaching.

42. About the Great Awakening (1734–35) of J. Edwards, Runner remarked that "the apostate patterns of thought at work in the socio-economic-political life of his time had little or nothing to say" (Runner: 1960, 152). For the detrimental influence of Scottish Realism on American Presbyterianism (cf. Runner's *own* cultural and creedal background), see 152–156.

a reservoir [of new leadership] of sufficient depth and breadth to fill the cultural and societal leadership vacuum created by the decline of liberalism?"

These lectures were presented in 1959, 1960, and 1961 to future leaders of the reformed community that emigrated from Holland to Canada after the Second World War. They have shaped the leadership in that community more than any other similar statement. Their impact went far beyond the confines of that original setting. Today there is a change of potentially great significance in the spiritual foundations of North American culture. These lectures prophetically focus on the biblical direction of that change. Hence a careful, patient reading of them by a new generation will be eminently rewarding.[43]

In his Unionville lectures of 1960, Runner focused on three issues: (i) the *structural* difference between "Scientific" and "Pre-Scientific" knowledge, and the *related* principle of "Sphere Sovereignty," (ii) God's Word as "Guide or Norm or Principle of our life" and (iii) "principle" in the sense of "origin," "ultimate loyalty" or "common faith by conviction or hidden pressure."[44]

As to the subtle power of "scientism," i.e., "faith in science," Christian university students are already at the very outset lost to the need for *"integral Christianity."* What positivism thinks is "pre-scientific" is actually "unscientific" and, therefore, not "related to the Truth." It implies surrendering one's "heart to science."[45] It limits "religion" to "personal salvation" and equates (in a scholastic and pietistic way) "heart" with one's "affective life"[46] and special prayer meetings. It thinks of God's natural revelation in terms of what is "real," i.e., science, logic, and method. When "truth" is equated with "science," science will disqualify "everyday experiences" of humans. When truth is thought of in terms "T/F" (true or false), then "truth" no longer calls humans to radical obedience, or one's total life.

43. "Preface to Runner," in Runner (1982): 33, 34. B. J. Zylstra was one of the students who in 1953 talked with Runner about starting a discussion group on the campus of CC and CTS. When he died (of cancer) in 1985, he had plans to write a book entitled *Pax Americana*.
    44. Runner (1961): 15, 16.
    45. Runner (1982): 18, 19; see also 21, 22. At this conference, I heard Runner's "deep concern" about some very talented students at the conference who were drifting towards positivism. One of these students became an internationally prominent scientist and within a few years abandoned Christian faith as something "unfounded and unscientific."
    46. To associate "heart" with "affective life" presupposes Greek "faculty psychology" and equates "feeling" (in distinction from "thinking" and "willing") with faith and believing. For details, see Chapter 3 above.

To know God as the "creator of the world" is not "a logical proposition or lingual statement." It involves "*personal* knowledge, *heart*-knowledge," "immediately gained by the total person whose heart is in the grip of the Word of God." Such knowledge is "covenantal," heart-centered and life-encompassing. It is not restricted to any discipline, including theology, or a combination of disciplines.

To restrict this knowledge to a theology shaped by positivist thinking is misleading. God's covenant is not limited to a person's *faith life*, but is evident in, or basic to, all human life. Faith life is *pre*-scientific and impacts one's total, not just ecclesiastical, life. Religious knowledge is deeper and broader than any theoretic, or scientific, knowledge of a discipline. Rather than become entangled in misguided "theological" debates in organized churches and in Christian schools,[47] Runner stressed rejecting what is wrong and advocating what is right, particularly in higher, or advanced, education where future servant-leaders are educated in every area of life and society.

> Indeed, the Word of God which makes us aware of the *reality* of the covenant and of much more is the renewing Word which makes both our theology and our education new. But both you men [H. Koops and R. Geerdes] have *confused the issue by identifying our knowledge of God with theology*. If they were identical, how could our theology continue to be reformed, i.e., continue to reform itself? By what standard or norm?
>
> What we have here is an especially insidious form of *scientism which makes the knowledge of the realities of God and creation and man equivalent to a theological statement about them*. This confusion is to be found all about us. But the Reformation taught us that men are free from the theologians in understanding and interpreting the Word of God. Life precedes science, and in life God makes us aware of (reveals to us) the Truth. The theological expression, the educational expression, *all* scientific expression follows, and is informed by a deeper pre-scientific knowledge of the Truth that man does not have as a scientist but as man of God. It would seem that *our Reformed circles are often far from the Reformation* (emphases added).[48]

47. Runner's critical analysis of a misguided debate between Rev. H. Koops and Mr. R. Geerdes about the foundation for Christian schools. Koops limits "covenant" to church (not school), to theology (not education) and to recreation (not creation). This highlights a perennial problem in Christian Reformed circles in the USA about the nature of all levels of Christian education in "church-controlled" schools, including Calvin College.

48. Runner (1982): 39–40. Cf. A. Kuyper in 1895: "Just name the one name of Jesus Christ and you feel at once how the entire scientific enterprise must abandon its demand to take first

About the danger of scientism in theology, he stated:

In the Christian world a particularly striking example of the insidious working of the scientistic frame of mind is the confusion of the immediate awareness of the integral Truth of the Word of God in our hearts (God, of course, opening our hearts to believe His Word; cf. Acts 16:14) with a scientific (theological) body of propositional statements about this Truth. So much attention has been devoted to the latter that the necessary earlier possession of the former has largely been overlooked, to the great detriment, not least, of a proper understanding of theology *qua* science, of theological method in general, and in particular of the process of exegesis.

By its very nature the scientistic mind has everywhere been compelled to ignore the important role that this everyday (non- and pre-scientific) experience plays in our lives. Thus scientism fails to note something of the structure of the creation, and as a result is compelled to render a distorted account both of our experience and of the cosmos. The consequences, as we have seen, have been legion and grave.[49]

Pre-scientific experience provides "*a more integral experience of reality,*" an experience of reality's "*wholeness* of meaning," and does this "*implicitly,*" not "*explicitly.*"[50] Integral to such experiences is not merely the "wholeness" of different *universal* "ways," modes or modalities, but also the "wholeness" of *individual* "persons," "things," "events," and "institutions," together with their various forms of "*given* interwovenness." Beneath the "*coherence* of meaning" lies "a deeper *unity* of meaning," one that escapes *analytic* examination. When the "living and powerful Word of God . . . takes hold of us in our hearts and unites us to Christ," then we can "know the Truth." Only then humans "see the unity of meaning in the diversity and coherence," i.e., experience, or become aware of, their "office" as humans to act as "God's servants" in everything they do. Life is not religious (adjective), but religion (noun).[51]

Reality is . . . that wonderful covenant fellowship which God has established with man, who (now in Christ) occupies the central place in creation, who

---

place in our estimation of our life," and a distinction must be made between "the knowledge of God which every one of the Lord's children possesses and which is eternal life" and "scientific knowledge, which is practiced in our faculties of theology" Runner (1961): 40.

49. Runner (1982): 44.
50. Runner (1982): 46, 47.
51. Runner (1982): 48, 49, 50 (for the quotes in the last three sentences).

is put under the divine Law [Love command] in the three-fold office of prophet-priest-king to worship and serve God in carrying out the cultural mandate in the world in singleness of heart.[52]

Scientism is a "belief," a "faith," a "directing Principle of human life." Inasmuch as Christians, and non-Christians, are affected by this faith in science, they contribute to "revolution" and "disintegration." Its effect on Christians may seem to be innocuous, but it is debilitating, especially in theology as a discipline in Christian colleges and seminaries.

The substitution of theology for a central religious awareness of the truth is a very effective way of cutting the Christian religion down to *scientistic* size. It is just one more way of missing the central religious meaning of life. To add theological disquisitions to biological or psychological or sociological ones does not bring us one whit closer to the root-unity of life or to the Truth.

What must be rediscovered in Protestantism, if we are to survive in the gigantic cultural struggle of our time, is an awareness of the directing role in life of the Word of God, the *sense* of that Word. To a more positively articulated statement about that we shall come in the next lecture [on Sphere Sovereignty]. In the present we have had first to clear the path by discussing that *scientism which has so universally sidetracked Christians from the way to wisdom and abundant life* (emphases added).[53]

"Sphere Sovereignty" and "Christian Organizations"

At the second Unionville Conference, Runner discussed the *principle* of "sphere sovereignty" in terms of (i) Kuyper's Opening Address of the Free University in 1880, (ii) Dooyeweerd's and Vollenhoven's ontology, or philosophy of created reality, (iii) a "sacred cow" one of his colleagues at CC told students they would "do well to throw it out of the window,"[54]

---

52. Runner (1982): 50.

53. Runner (1982): 51, 52.

54. Laconically, but pointedly, Runner commented: "Now I do not know whether that professor is a practical man. But I would suggest that it is not the simplest thing in the world to throw a cow out of the window. The year before I entered my college, I have been told a number of upper classmen succeeded after much toil in placing a cow in the third floor study in one of their beloved professors. But it took pulleys and tackle and a lot of sweating firemen

and (iv) an "eminently *evangelical* principle . . . given with the Gospel itself."[55]

The principle of sphere sovereignty is a "central reality" which enables humans to "properly oversee human society in all its complexity of its functional life." The biblical notion of "life as religion" does not permit any "scientific point of view," including "theology," to provide proper "insight into the order of society." Only when God's Word takes hold of us, our "hearts have been opened to the religious root-life of the temporal world," and we take our "stand in Christ, the Truth, do we become aware of the principle of sphere sovereignty." A. Kuyper stressed in this connection the importance of *"the place of Christ within the creation-order of God*, as the new Office-bearer in Adam's stead." The "make-up of created reality" is directed by God's Word revelation. The "perilous situation of all mankind" and pervasive confusion about the order of society calls for a new "community of thought" focused on this reforming principle.[56]

The nature and boundaries of authority is "the most urgent question facing our democracies." In a society where "the people's voice is God's voice" (*vox populi vox Dei*), the nature of the "structure" of society, in relation to God as "Origin," becomes urgent. If the ultimate guide is "Reason," how does that affect societal experimentation? In their frantic search for "Guiding Lights" will people resort to a natural, or *rational*, light, appeal to an infallible *moral* conscience about right and wrong, rely on an empirical, *sensory* certainty, or rely on a combination of these three dominant attempts? Or will they lean on "supposed necessities," some pragmatist response, construct an "order" based on "last things, fruits, consequences, facts"? In other words, is there a "creation-structure or creation-order," some "command for our human life-activity"?[57]

"Structures" are not based on "human arbitrariness" but are grounded in a "divine world-order." A sense of "Order or Structure . . . comes with the (divine) opening of our heart's eye to see our whole life as religion."[58] Such seeing of "our prophetic-priestly-kingly task in the world" calls for

---

the next morning to get the cow out of that study window. Image how much more difficult the problem would have been if the cow had been sacred, i.e., untouchable." (61)

55. Runner (1821): 86.

56. Runner (1961): 54, 55, 56 (for all the quotes in this paragraph).

57. Runner (1961): 56, 57, 58, 59 (for all quotes in this paragraph).

58. Runner (1961): 60. Cf. Ps. 119:130: "The unfolding of your words gives light, it gives understanding to the simple," and Ps. 86:11: "Teach me your way, O Lord, and I will walk in your truth; give me an undivided heart, that I may fear your name."

acknowledging, not arbitrarily imposing, a life-enhancing diversity in our human tasks and responsibilities. Life and diverse human society are "there" and must be "explained." The "world" exists by virtue of "the creation fiat." To sense this, humans need to stand in "the right place."

All complex functions assume their meaningful place within the context of the whole, and that "*central* place" is "*religion.*" Humans are placed before God in covenant fellowship, in order to render to their Creator praise in "whole-hearted service of love and obedience within the length and breadth of the creation."[59] Since the principle of "sphere sovereignty" is "integral sense" to Scripture, Runner stated the following:

> I therefore regard it as highly significant that the idea of sphere-sovereignty is so closely tied up with our recovery (from the scholasticism, i.e., theologism or scientism of the theologians) of what the Word of God tells us about the central religious nature of human life and society. In Abraham Kuyper this is especially clear. Where he is dealing strictly with questions that arise in the theological tradition Kuyper is not always at his best; the traditional theological motive of the natural and the supra-natural, a dualistic motive that cannot be harmonized with the scriptural revelation of the integral religious unity of man and the world, seems often to have been too powerful even for him. But in his discussion of matters that have to do with life and society in their wholeness, matters which the theologians in their abstract study had left untouched, Kuyper is freed from the hold of traditional motives. Here he is close to the Scriptures, *and it is just in these areas of his thought that we notice the emergence of the idea of sphere-sovereignty.* As I have said, this idea is intimately bound up with the scriptural view that our life in its totality is religion.[60]

As to the scriptural meaning of "heart" and "religion," Runner regretted that in the English version of A. Kuyper's Stone Lectures on *Calvinism* (1898) "heart" is translated by "mind," reminiscent of "the persistent intellectualism of the scholastic theological tradition," a "weedy growth of useless human tradition."[61]

Central to Kuyper's view of society are "heart, office, service, adminis-

59. Runner (1961): 63, 64. Meaning of "place" is "multivocal," not "univocal"—in addition to the *modal* meanings of ethical, aesthetic, and social "place," there is the *central religious* meaning of "place" in the sense of "fullness or fulfillment of meaning."

60. Runner (1961): 65–66.

61. Runner (1961): 66. Cf. Peter S. Heslam, *Creating a Christian Worldview: Abraham*

tration" (responsibility to give and preserve order), God's sovereignty, two covenant office-bearers (Adam and Christ), and diverse sovereignties in society, each with delegated, limited, and coordinated powers. Diverse human life presupposes the "principle of sphere-sovereignty."[62] The "internal meaning of scriptural revelation" provides the "biblical proof" for this—"without sphere-sovereignty the Scriptures simply cannot be understood." As to the "general *fact* of sphere-sovereignty," he stated,

> **If** all the constantly changing states of affairs . . . can be shown to be of a *variety of kinds* . . . ; **if** only to Christ as Mediator is given all-authority, the diversity of delegated and modally limited 'authorities' in our human life being a coördinated diversity within that all-authority; **if** the Kingdom of God is the whole of re-directed human life, the diversity of spheres in our life being so many coördinate aspects of that fullness of life;—**if** these things are so, then sphere-sovereignty is indeed the expression of the very constitution of the whole creation-order, and our knowledge of it—a *religious* or heart knowledge, acquired when through the Power of the Word of God we 'see' or 'know' Christ and His Kingdom—the Directing Principle of our life in the world.[63]

When the early church fathers thought of "Church as a society additional to civil society" and did not "distinguish Church as the Body of Christ from the church as (cultic) institute," they introduced in "Western society a *second* totalitarian association." Whereas Christ's Rule "*is* total" and God's Kingdom refers to "the *total renewal*, in Christ, *of life in all its structures*," officers in the "church-institute" do not have "total authority." As a consequence, persistent tensions and "fundamental rifts in authority" developed, and "the unity of all spheres of life as aspects of a central service of God in the rule of Christ could not be achieved."[64]

To confuse "Kingdom or City of God" with "church-institute" created a tension-filled situation in which neither power permitted any "encroach-

---

Kuyper's Lectures on Calvinism, 1998; and James D. Bratt, Editor, *Abraham Kuyper: A Centennial Reader*, 1998.

62. Runner (1961): 66–69, 70.

63. Runner (1961): 73. For views of patristic and medieval theologians, reformers like J. Calvin, J. Althusius, J. Stahl, G. Groen van Prinsterer, A. Kuyper, and twentieth-century thinkers like J. Bohatec, J. Dengerink and H. van Riessen about society and diverse authorities, see 74–86.

64. Runner (1961): 82.

ment" from the other, and resulted at times in a "life-or-death" struggle between two "religiously" ultimate authorities and powers in society. The "root-
struggle between true and false religion," called "Antithesis . . . which God
graciously introduced into our history when He established the Church,"
early church fathers began to describe in terms of what is "natural" and
"supra-natural." As a result, the "civil polity" in the "natural" world does not
need to be "re-formed by the living Word of God."

Furthermore, the Body of Christ, i.e., "Church," is "reduced" to *another*
concrete, but *supra*-natural, area *alongside*, or above, what is "natural." By
denying the need for the state to be "reformed according to the Truth of the
divine word-revelation," the "Rule of Christ through His Word" is restricted
to a "supranatural 'area'" in life.[65]

This Augustinian view of "state and church as natural and supranatural
entities" and the "*civitas Dei* as the total re-creation of life in all its complexity" reflects an *accommodational* view of human life. It fails to grasp
fully "what God teaches about the central religious authority of Christ the
Mediator." Runner sought to *simplify* Christian discipleship by emphasizing
the radical character of *religion* and heart-centered *unity* of God's people. He
resisted wasting time and energy in futile "theological" (scholastic) squabbles in culturally isolated supra-natural faith communities and traditions.
Instead, he challenged his listeners to be Christian reformers,

> It is this fundamental conflict which Christians have inherited from the
> beginning of the New Testament church that explains the slow conquest in
> Christians' hearts of the scriptural teaching about sphere-sovereignty. Let
> no one here underestimate the historical forming-power of a long tradi-
> tion. Attachment to the traditional theory resulted in the *suppression* of the
> creation-motive of the Christian religion in the Christians' view of reality.
> It is the slow victory of the Word of God over a powerful accommodation
> theory that we feel in the work of Calvin, of Althusius, of Stahl, Groen and
> even Kuyper.[66]

---

65. Runner (1961): 83.

66. Runner (1961): 84. This statement is one of the, if not *the*, most succinct and clearest
expressions of Runner's role as a *reformational* thinker, educator and reformer. Cf. J. D. Dengerink's doctoral dissertation *Critisch-Historisch Onderzoek naar de sociologische ontwikkeling
van het beginsel der "souvereiniteit in eigen kring" in de 19e en 20e eeuw*, which associates
"sphere-sovereignty" with *ontology* (i.e., creation order), not just with sociology (i.e., society). Runner connects it with the *Word-revelation* (84–85) and with H. van Riessen's view of

In his **three Unionville lectures** in 1961 on "Scriptural Religion and Political Task," he basically elaborated on the content, and format, of *The Bible and the Life of the Christian*, i.e., the study guide of the "Groen Club" since 1953. As *visionary* reformer, who sponsored the "Groen Club," he lectured at all the Unionville Conferences, was the "spiritual" founder of ICS, the chief mentor of, for example, B. J. Zylstra in political theory at ICS, J. Witte, Jr., in law at Emory University, and other *reforming* thinkers in philosophy, ethics, education, art, classics, and such political pioneers as James W. Skillen in the Center for Public Justice (CPJ) in Washington, DC, and H. J. Kits in Ottawa, as well as other visionary leaders in Canada[67] and the USA.[68] Within two decades after his Unionville Conferences, Runner saw how the "principle of sphere sovereignty" was eminently practical for all who stressed *integrally* Christian living, also in their thinking and teaching, and resisted *religious* accommodational thinking in their thought-patterns, especially in their scholastic theology.[69]

The basic *direction* of a Christian culture assumes that human "life is religion" and that the *structure* of society presupposes the principle of "sphere sovereignty." He addressed this intricate and important issue in his Unionville lectures of 1961 on the topic of "Scriptural Religion and Political Task."[70] The relevance of these lectures for our study of "faith life and theology" is evident from his critical comments about both "theologism" and "pietism." About the danger of the former in political thinking, he stated,

---

creation-mandate, *central* love-commandment, humanity's *calling*, opposition to totalitarianism, and need for a Christian view of society (86–87).

67. CPJ—Toronto and Ottawa (e.g., G. Vandezande, H. Kits), Bernard Zylstra (1934–1985) at ICS, D. Koyzis at Redeemer University, John Witte Jr., at Emory University.

68. James W. Skillen, Director of CPJ (1980–2010) was influenced by B. J. Zylstra at CC and by H. Dooyeweerd at the Free University. For details, see the archives at Calvin College, in Grand Rapids, of Gordon J. Spykman, Paul G. Schrotenboer, Peter Steen, Bernard J. Zylstra and H. Evan Runner.

69. Runner has been criticized by some Christian Reformed persons in the USA for this interest in political issues, while he was commended for his views by various persons and movements in Christian Reformed circles in Canada.

70. He starts with a summary of his *first* and *second* Unionville lectures in 1959 and 1960 (136–143), the biblical basis and need for an *educational creed* (143–146), and a description of the three parts of his *third* (and longest) Unionville lecture (147–149). To illustrate his rejection of a *synthesis*-mentality, he responds to (i) an article by John T. Daling, a colleague at CC, on "A Look at the Dutch," in *The Reformed Journal* (1957), 245–250, and (ii) "Calvinism and Political Action" by William Spoelhof, president of CC, published in *God-Centered Living*, a symposium of the Calvinist Action Committee, (1951), 250–252.

The Christian religion is definitely not the formulation (and acceptance) of specifically theological propositions out of the Word of God written, which are then to be added to a body of (other kinds of scientific) knowledge that is arrived at by some other 'personal centre of experiencing' that is outside the ultimate religious situation and directedness of our lives (as e.g. Reason) and thus free from the reforming Power of the enlightening Word of God upon our *hearts*. This scholastic or theologistic perversion of the Christian religion would allow most of our life in this world to be free of the reforming POWER of the divine Word, and thus ultimately requires that we abandon that view of the Word of God that the Word of God instilled in our hearts, viz., that it is the directing Principle of our life *in its integrity. In such theologistic circles no need is felt for a Christian political action, except perhaps in the sense of dealing with certain 'immediacies'* (emphases added).[71]

The opposite danger, "pietism," also distorts Christian political life. It restricts "scriptural religion" to a "matter of God and something called the 'individual soul,'" "something separate" from a person's daily life and career. It actually fails to relate inner, personal piety to one's "external way of living" at a particular time and place.[72] "Soul," or "heart," refers to a "place apart" i.e., "religion." It is never irrelevant, but always the

concentration of my life, where I face God, hear His Word, and from out of which I am *driven*, in the totality of my bodily life-expression, in all kinds of relations and associations with my fellow-men in the world, *in a certain direction, to work in the world.*

. . . the Christian religion is not a matter of 'saved individuals' going around exercising a wholesome 'personal' influence from out of their supposed 'inner' life in Christ while the so-called 'outer' life, unreformed by the POWER of the Word of God, is permitted to go on in the accepted fashion of the time. Such a view is simply a subtle form of world-flight: our living in the world is left untouched here; . . . But a human person, according to Scripture, is quite different from an 'inner soul', conceived as something withdrawn, a thing apart. Scripture teaches that out of the inner man (heart or soul) come the 'issues' of life. Religion in its antithetical structure is also in the world round about us, not just in men's 'souls'.

71. Runner (1962): 65.
72. Runner (1962): 165. Such an approach, he adds, is typical of "accommodation or synthesis."

... Here at Unionville, we know that according to Scripture *the Christian religion is the re-direction, in Christ, the second Adam, of the whole of mankind's life in the world.* In Christ, man is profound in his Office, his God-appointed and responsible Place as ready servant of God in the whole of the creation-order.[73]

Christian Education and Scholarship: Consultation (1967)

The difference between reformational and accommodational thinking about God's Word was central to a two-day Consultation of the Association for Reformed Scientific Studies (ARSS) in Toronto and CC/CTS in Grand Rapids in 1967.[74]

In 1957, the Synod of the CRC did not act on a Minority Report of the Long Range Planning Committee of CC, which stated that the denomination has "through the years failed to face up fully to the consideration of the principle [of church- or society-control of CC] and its implications." It had allowed practical circumstances and considerations to shape her thinking about educational matters and to complicate her life and task with the maintenance and operation of an expanding venture in general education."[75]

To prepare for this Consultation in 1967, P. G. Schrotenboer, as executive director of the Association, responded in 1966 to a request of the "Graduate Studies Committee of CC and CTS" to "give serious consideration to the basic problem of church or society control" of education. He responded by indicating that basically:[76] God's Word directs how to "structure the educational institution amid other societal institutions." The control of CC has since its beginning always been "ecclesiastical." Since "university" education

73. Runner (1962): 166.

74. On Nov. 2–3, fourteen persons met in Grand Rapids: seven to represent the 'new' view (H. Hart, P. Jonker, J. Joosse, J. A. Olthuis, H. Evan Runner, C. Seerveld and J. Vander Stelt) and seven to represent the 'traditional' view (B. Van Elderen, A. Kuyvenhoven, E. Oostendorp, A. Schaafsma, W. Spoelhof, H. Stob and N. Wolterstorff).

75. *Acts* of Synod (1957) pp. 478, 479. In a very short article in 1957 in *Onward*, my local CRC in Canada, I opposed "church control" and proposed "society control" of CC. The president of CC, W. Spoelhof, questioned me about it in 1958, and in 1965 at a denominational subcommittee that interviewed me before I became a preacher in the CRC.

76. His secretary, E. Homan, copied me in on Schrotenboer's letter on April 28, 1966. All citations are from this letter.

calls for "unity of support," the issue of what "controls" Christian higher education should be addressed "frontally."

While the *organized* church must "proclaim the word, engage in worship and administer the sacraments," the "scientific enterprise" prepares men and women through "general education" for "service in each and every life relationship." The church's task centers on "redemption," the renewal of all of life in its "differentiation and specialization." History reveals an "unfolding of creation" through "variegated tasks" of humans in their response to the "created law order." To "support" Christian living in a differentiated society, it is not the (organized) church's task to carry out the "multiform tasks" of "controlling education" in business, industry, school, home, and state. In their response to the "unlimited regime of Jesus Christ," Christians present themselves as "living sacrifices" in all of life, not only in their "churchly pursuits."[77]

In response to the CRC controlling undergraduate and graduate education "as the safest way to guard the future course of the college and keep it Christian," Schrotenboer stated that safety does not lie in "church control" but in "diligent exercise by Christian believers of their responsibilities in education" and that the Graduate Studies Committee of CC should write an "educational creed" and provide education according to it.

To prepare for the Consultation in 1967 of fourteen consultants, (a) H. J. Stob provided on behalf of CTS his brief "Comments on the Educational Creed" of the Association, (b) the Graduate Studies Committee at CC submitted a lengthy "Calvin Statement" and (c) H. Hart wrote his extensive "Comments on Christian Liberal Arts Education" (Report of the Calvin College Curriculum Study Committee, Grand Rapids, 1965).

In response to the "Educational Creed" of ARSS, Stob commented briefly on: (i) God's Word and its relation to Scripture and education, (ii) the distinction between creed and principles, or non-amendable "confession" and amendable "principles"[78] based on a "viable consensus" of a community of (Reformed) scholars, (iii) the principle of "sphere sovereignty,"[79] accord-

---

77. See Ephesians 1:10, Colossians 1:18, and Romans 12:1–4.

78. These "principles should be derived from the basis" of Scripture and "shaped in accordance with the nature of the enterprise." This derivation must be done in an "intelligible" manner, one in which "all available resources of erudition, judgment, and experience resident in the community" are utilized, and representing "all responsible Reformed philosophic orientations," since the "set of principles" must reflect a "viable consensus" of "(Reformed) Scholars," not merely of some "founding committee."

79. Henry Stob continues: ". . . each of which gives its own particular organizational ex-

ing to which the "institutional church is only one of many coordinate institutions," **(iv)** the view that "life is religion," not the traditional distinction between "worship" and "service" (*ora et labora*), **(v)** the nature of "reality" in the meaning of "essence," "heart," and "covenantal communion with God in Christ," and **(vi)** the meaning of "true knowledge." In his view, the creedal articles of ARSS have "in substance controlled the Calvin enterprise these many years."

The "Statement" of CC for the "Consultation"[80] centered on the "representational" position of the College and the "exclusivistic" position of the ARSS. The former is the "Reformed Christian approach to education and learning," as stated in the "basic principles" of the "curriculum report" of CC and accordingly are all subscribers to "the Reformed creeds" and are members of the CRC. The "Reformed Christian stance on education and scholarship" permits "different points of view" in "scholarship" and in "religious matters," as a matter of "right and justice," for the benefit of the faculty and the students. However, the ARSS does not accept persons with a philosophical tradition at odds with the "philosophy of the Law-idea" on "substantial issues." It is "exclusivistic" in its "operative, governing principles" not indicated in its Creed; it acts "with less than full integrity."

The "Reformed Christian stance on education and scholarship" is basic to CC. The church as institution must be "*Christian* Reformed." The tradition of "education and scholarship" at CTS and CC is—in the spirit of L. Berkhof, W. Harry Jellema, H. J. Stob, A. Plantinga and N. Wolterstorff—"*Reformed* Christian."[81] It should be possible to "accept the Creed" and yet "reject the philosophy of the Law-idea," because the latter is not the only "Christian philosophy." The "representational" position of CC's graduate educational program is clearly stated in the last sentence of the College's Statement: "A university which aims to be representative of all genuinely Reformed viewpoints, is far less susceptible to the danger of making an idol of some philosophy, than one which systematically excludes all but adherents and likely adherents to some one philosophy."

---

pression to the body of Christ, and each of which has its own 'creed' together with appropriate 'sanctions.'" For Stob's scholastic points (iii) to (vi), see Chapter 16 above.

80. Authored by W. Spoelhof and N. Wolterstorff, who wrote the second, and final, draft in November, 1968.

81. Emphasis is added, in order to highlight the difference between "Christian Reformed" (church) and "Reformed Christian" (education and scholarship), a difference the "Association" and *reformational* thinking do not consider helpful, but superficial, confusing, and avoiding the real problem.

On behalf of the ARSS, Hart focused on "Christian Liberal Arts Education" (Report of the Calvin College Curriculum Study Committee, 1965). Against the background of a common basis in CC's "Curriculum Report" and ARSS's "Educational Creed," Hart highlighted seven issues to be addressed "openly, frankly and critically, and in brotherly love." **First**, does the notion that "the Christian has no monopoly on truth, or beauty, or goodness" reflect a "pluralism" in our culture and express a "synthesis" that ignores the "central religious antithesis of direction in life"?[82] **Second,** is Christian thinking limited only to "core," not "non-core," issues, and to "values" in the humanities and to "cultural products of mankind"? **Third**, can "alternative views" be "basically and fundamentally Christian"? Does one's "intention to train for citizenship in the Christian community" automatically make one's views "Christian," despite a prevailing spirit of pragmatism, positivism, or existentialism? **Fourth**, can "ecclesiastical control," or "reformed theology," guarantee the "Christian" character of a "curriculum" and its "foundations"? **Fifth**, does merely adding something to the "core" program make a curriculum Christian? Is a new encyclopedic understanding of reality and of the curriculum not a necessity? **Sixth,** how will CC and CTS move from having only "teaching-scholars" to having also "research-scholars," especially when all or most of them will have been trained at "secular institutions" with "secular perspectives"? **Seventh,** how can "sanctions" function in our "present climate of pluralism," when someone "does not adopt or deviates significantly" from the "foundations"?

For ARSS's delegation, Hart wrote in **February** 1968 an extensive "Position Paper for the second Consultation." He denied the Association is "exclusivistic," affirmed its "present position" and rejected the "representative" position of CC/CTS.[83] The Educational Creed of the ARSS must come to *philosophical* expression in ICS as a "provisionally accepted framework of operation" and a "provisional tool to promote unity and integration in the academic community." Not to allow persons in an academic community who reject *reformational* philosophy does *not* mean that such persons are "second class Christians," "incompetent and unbiblical thinkers" or "spiritual deviates." It does imply, however, that a "spiritual brainchild of humanism" is not allowed. Christian scholarship and education calls for "spiritual integ-

82. Regarding the Greek-based scholastic idea of "faculty psychology," see chapters 6, 14 and 15 above.

83. Because the *second* Consultation was not held, the detailed and clear analysis of what "exclusivistic" and "representative" really mean was, sad to say, never discussed in any consultation.

rity," being "integrally biblical," expressing "unity of heart commitment," an articulation in terms of one's faith, totality of life, and scientific integrity.[84]

The ICS seeks to be "reformational" in the sense of being "critically positive and positively critical." It rejects the "representative position" Henry J. Stob proposed.[85] His idea of unity is only "formal." It wants to "foster unity," but actually breaks it. It seeks to "hold together what is not unified." "Personal intentions and morally desirable attitudes" are not sufficient to evaluate "academic achievement." It produces either "painful confrontation or passive indifference." CC must guard against "characterless broadness" in its "representative" position.

In **November** 1968, the seven delegates of CC and CTS met, due to an unfortunate miscommunication, without any delegates of the Association.[86] Its final report stated two things: (a) the "basis of all scholarly effort lies in Christ, who, as revealed in Scripture, is the key to all knowledge and to whom all scholarly effort must be true"[87] and (b) it will maintain its traditional "representative" position. Since there is no agreement to establish "a single, mutually supported university," the committee (of seven) recommends that (i) CC/CTS "proceed to formulate its plan and program for a Christian university and graduate degree programs" and (ii) that the Association be "dissuaded from following a parallel program."[88]

Addressing the difference between "reformational" thinking and "scholastic" theology in Reformed Epistemology, C. Seerveld—a graduate of CC and the Free University and one of the seven delegates at the 1967 Consul-

---

84. Integrally Christian philosophy does not allow, except through a *religious* "synthesis," humanism, existentialism, pragmatism and positivism.

85. "A body of competent men representing the *widest possible spectrum* of involved insight into the meaning and thrust of the basis and representing, too, all responsible Reformed orientations . . . reflecting a viable consensus."

86. In 1967, the Association of Reformed Scientific Studies (ARSS) proposed to change its name to Association for the Advancement of Christian Scholarship (AACS).This change was adopted in 1968 for several reasons: (i)'Reformed' is more restrictive than 'Christian,' is associated with 'reformatories' and points to past, not present and future, renewal, (ii) in North America, "scientific" refers to "empirical studies" in physics, not general scholarship, and (iii) 'A.R.S.S.' *sounds* like the British slang word *arse*. Cf. Robert E. VanderVennen (2008): 11.

87. Regarding Christ, Scripture, creation, structure, total life, curriculum: cf. K. Barth, Evangelicals, Roman Catholicism, Pietism, etc.

88. Through cooperation with the Free University in Amsterdam, with the persistent efforts of ICS's President, Harry J. Fernhout, and the support of other *reformational* leaders in education, politics and media, ICS received in 2005 legal permission from the Government of Ontario to grant M.A. and Ph.D. degrees.

tation—stated in 2001, as professor emeritus of ICS, in a public lecture on "Reformational Christian Philosophy and Christian College Education" the following:

> I think that a difference I detect between 'standard Reformed theology' and 'Reformational dogmatic theology' is that 'standard Reformed theology' seems to appear with almost *ex cathedra* finality and authority to 'lead' philosophical discussion with logical certainty, while the Reformational formulation of doctrines breathes a spirit of supple, trusting certainty in offering to serve other fields of inquiry with its important limited contribution of constructing *regulae fide* (guidelines for expressing obedient faith). That difference depends upon the underlay of a general theistic 'rational realism' for 'Reformed' theology, and having 'a biblically induced Christian philosophy' underneath 'Reformational' theology.
>
> And it may be important in a Christian college to not let Reformed theology (or a Christian philosophy!) slip into taking the role of being 'the faith once for all handed down to the saints' (Jude 3). Not only functional creedal testimonies but especially the systematized theological reflection on what we (churchly) confess are structurally different from, though connected to, the fundamental matter the Bible calls faith (*pistis*), which is that existential attachment of us with certain trust at being fixed in the true God (or heart-committed to an idol) by the gift of regenerating grace in Jesus Christ (Ephesians 2:8–9). What keeps a Christian college alive in the Reformation biblical faith-tradition . . . is whether the spirit at work in the Scripturally-led philosophy, theology, history-telling, and scholarly contours of all the teaching disciplines be earthily redemptive and interdisciplinary in bearing fruit worthy of repentance (*poenitentia*) (I John 4:1, Romans 12–14, I Corinthians 12).[89]

S. G. De Graaf, *Promise and Deliverance*, I-IV

In 1975, six years before he retired in 1981, Runner sensed the need for fellow believers to read Scripture in a "more meaningful" way. He was troubled by a growing problem in Christian, including Christian Reformed, traditions, as to how to read Scripture in a life-encompassing and culture-affecting way. Brief superficial and shortsighted devotions troubled him profoundly, espe-

89. C. Seerveld (2001).

cially a rapidly spreading tradition of "moralistic" preaching and teaching. A new way of reading Scripture is needed to catch the rich meaning of the Word of God for humans in their personal and public relations and many responsibilities for fellow human and non-human creatures.

It is also a prerequisite for ongoing *reformation* in philosophy, theology, and other disciplines. Without it, Christians are handicapped in their proper behavior in society and culture. It is necessary to sense more clearly what it means to "walk with God" in whatever one does in response to God's command to love, i.e., to rely on His covenant promises. *Reformation* is impossible without *hearing* God's Word in the "Good News" of Scripture.

Shortly after the death of A. Kuyper in 1920 and of H. Bavinck in 1921, the "Gereformeerde" Reformed faith tradition was gravely weakened for three reasons: *first*, rigid scholastic thinking in the Reformed (*Gereformeerde*) dogmatics of V. Hepp (1879–1950), H. Bavinck's successor at the Free University;[90] *second*, the socio-economic effects of the great Depression; and, *third*, severe theological conflicts, widespread confusion, and a deepening uncertainty in faith life.

In response to these enfeebling forces, a small but gifted and rapidly increasing number of non-academic and academic Christians stressed the need for a radical heart-centered *renewal* in living on the cutting-edge of a restless culture and conflict-riddled higher education. They focused on Scripture reading, a Spirit-prompted "hearing"—not debating and arguing about—God's liberating Word for life and, especially, for such disciplines (*wetenschappen*) as philosophy, education, socio-economic and political studies, literature, and Bible conferences.

The cumulative effect of these initially small but soon rapidly deepening developments was a *religious* reawakening in Reformed (*Gereformeerde*) circles. To hear God's Word in a non-scholastic and exciting life-encompassing way reinvigorated many Christians in their daily life, also in their educational and academic life. In this context, D. Vollenhoven wrote *Het Calvinisme en de Reformatie der Wijsbegeerte*, in 1933, and H. Dooyeweerd his *Wijsbegeerte der Wetsidee*, I-III, in 1935/6. With these and other biblically directed *reformational* writings at a time of a crisis—at the time when W. Harry Jellema

90. V. Hepp's theology and political ideology and Christian Reformed Church view of "common grace" in the 1920s. (cf. "Valantijn Hepp" in *Christelijke Encyclopedie*, 3, p. 32 . Hepp succeeded H. Bavinck in 1922, centered his inaugural lecture on "Gereformeerde apologetiek," was editor-in-chief of *The Reformation*, a weekly Journal, from 1920–1931, and editor of the weekly *Credo* (1937–1940). For his relentless opposition to "reformational" thinking and acting, see his *Dreigende deformatie*, (1936/37).

started to teach at CC in Grand Rapids—neo-Kuyperian professors, together with other reformers,[91] relied on, and were supported by, a series of annual Bible conferences held at a resort in the (nationally central) town of Lunteren in the Netherlands.

These conferences stressed God's "covenant" (*verbond*) with all creation, especially humanity (*mensheid*). This way of reading/hearing Scripture fostered not a pietistic, or mystical, but a practical realistic, or covenant-centered, way of Scripture reading. It stressed careful listening, humble submitting to God's powerful Word, and encouraging each other to live, always and everywhere, in God's holy presence. It fostered a spirit of freedom endemic to loving obedience, and a resolve to resist living privately and publicly in a spirit of indifference.

In order to nurture a *heart*-centered renewal in reading Scripture and avoid the lure of (a) ostensibly helpful, but actually misleading, spiritualism, (b) seemingly attractive, but actually trivial moralism, and (c) philosophically searching, but in reality superficial scholasticism, Runner faced this challenge *after* 1973, when he terminated his (twenty-year) role as sponsor of the Groen Club. To encourage *reforming* all of life, not just philosophy and education, he decided to translate (with the help of his Dutch spouse, Elisabeth) S. G. De Graaf's *Verbondsgeschiedenis*, I-II, 1938.[92] His aim with this unique project was to help parents, influence schoolteachers, preachers, college and university professors, and encourage all servant-leaders to be prophetic, shun exploitation, and reflect more clearly God's life-sustaining Word in their daily life.[93]

91. For example, A. Janse (cf. Chapter 7 above on "Vollenhoven"). This information is based on Vollenhoven's accounts to me—during our several thirty-minute mid-afternoon walks on Wednesdays, at *exactly* 15:00—about the joys, challenges and strategies of "ongoing reformation" (doorgaande reformatie), guided by God's covenant promises, reading and understanding Scripture, Christ-centered and spiritual renewal in education and scholarship, society, culture, civilization and history.

92. Vol. I: *From Creation to the Conquest of Canaan* (1977); Vol. II: *The Failure of Israel's Theocracy*, (1978); Vol. III: *Christ's Ministry and Death*, (1979); Vol. IV: *Christ and the Nations*, (1981); published by Paideia Press, St. Catherines, Ontario.

93. S. G. de Graaf (1889–1955) had been involved in the Lunteren Bible Conferences, was familiar with the founders of Reformational philosophy and was on the Board of the Association for Calvinist Philosophy, and served as pastor in the Keizersgracht Gereformeerde Kerk, located near the Free University (for details, see Runner, "Translator's Introduction," *Promise and Deliverance*, I. 10–14). While a student at the Free University, de Graaf attended a class on Sunday School teaching taught by J. C. Sikkel (1855–1920), who was a gifted preacher and a close friend of A. Kuyper. For details, see Craig G. Bartholomew and Michael W. Goheen, *The*

He realized that this translation project would not enhance his standing as a Junior Fellow of the Society of Fellows at Harvard University, as author of his dissertation (*cum laude*) at the Free University on Aristotle's philosophy, or as a retired professor of philosophy for three decades.[94] In his "Translator's Introduction,"[95] he indicated his passion for *religious* renewal in how Christians read Scripture in other regions of the world familiar with the English language, and hoped that someday it might be translated into other languages—for the sake of the Christian community worldwide.[96]

Now Christians around the world will be able to read this book, study it, and reflect on it. Christians in all walks of life will benefit from it—young converts, believers of long standing, parents struggling to establish Christian homes, grandparents who tell Bible stories to their grandchildren, pastors, and even professors.[97]

Much of the literature that circulates in evangelical circles is concerned with limited topics, such as angels, demonology, the return of the Jews to Palestine as a fulfillment of prophecy, with the gifts of the Spirit, or with particular Bible books. Useful as such studies may be, in the final analysis they make little sense to minds that have not yet grasped *the divinely established order of things and the basic covenant relationship to God in terms of which this order is to be understood.* Moreover, almost all evangelical literature limits itself to a concern for the salvation of lost sinners—which concern is proper and necessary in its place—while failing to penetrate behind the drama of fall and redemption *to the order of creation and the covenantal character of religion,* which alone makes evangelism meaningful. It almost seems that we have forgotten *the significance of the revelation that God is the Creator!* (emphases added).[98]

True Story of the Whole World: Finding Your Place in the Biblical Drama, published by Faith Alive Christian Resources, Grand Rapids (2009).

94. Assistant Professor of Philosophy (1952–1959) and Professor of Philosophy (1959–1981).

95. S. G. de Graaf (1977): I, and (1979): III.

96. Runner was deeply interested in missions, especially in Korea and China. He reflected on *depth*-issues such as "heart," "religion" and "ultimate allegiance," always in connection with *"width*-issues," in different civilizations, always in terms of God's covenant with the world and coming of His kingdom.

97. S. G. de Graaf (1977): I, 10.

98. de Graaf (1978): III, 13. For translations into Spanish, Chinese, Japanese, Korean, Arabic, French and other languages in Africa, India and Indonesia, see "Translator's Introduction," III, 11–21.

Legacy

The impact of H. Evan Runner, as a *reforming* philosophy professor since 1951 at CC in Grand Rapids, and as the opening lecturer, in 1967, of ICS in Toronto, deepened and broadened the *religiously* simple, yet radical, meaning of being God's people, through Christ Jesus and the Spirit's power anywhere in the world, including USA and Canada.

Surprisingly, this originally non-Dutch and, until 1951, Presbyterian (not Christian Reformed) person shortly after his arrival at CC was questioned by CC's philosophy department about some of his views, and contacted by various students at CC/CTS to elaborate on his ideas. Several Canadian and USA students at CTS asked him to explain what he meant by the need for a "biblically directed reformation" in the USA and Canada, especially the nature and scope of a *religious* change in Western culture.

In his response, Runner indicated what he perceived to be a necessary strategy. In the **USA**, he has done this in at least seven ways: (i) his teaching at CC, (ii) his role as sponsor of the Groen van Prinsterer Club for students at CC and CTS, (iii) his assistance of several pastors in the CRC, mainly in Canada, (iv) his being a "one-year private tutor" of John Witte, Jr., a 1982 graduate of CC, with whom he read and studied (in Greek and Latin) and discussed (in English) certain classic writings about law and philosophy, and who became Professor of Law at Emory University in Atlanta, (v) his correspondence with various reformational professors at Trinity Christian College in Illinois and Dordt College in Iowa, (vi) his correspondence with Presbyterian and Evangelical educators and authors, and (vii) his emphasizing the *religious* thrust in the structure and practice of political life, which influenced Bernard J. Zylstra, whose basic perspective influenced James W. Skillen, the founder and first executive director (1981–2009) of CPJ in Washington, DC.[99]

In **Canada**, Runner's reformational stance impacted the ICS through (a) six professors, who had been influenced by Runner at CC and/or CTS, and did their doctoral work at the Free University in Amsterdam, and (b) national and international students from diverse Christian backgrounds in M.A. and Ph.D. programs, who have become servant-leaders interested in worldview- and philosophy-related issues in social relations, justice, business, education, citizenship, art, campus ministry, anthropology, etc.

---

99. Stephanie Summers—who was a student of P. Steen, whose doctoral dissertation focused on H. Dooyeweerd's anthropology—succeeded Skillen as CPJ's CEO.

Increasingly, his elementary yet complex view of created reality, encyclopedic knowledge, diversity in disciplines, relation between a curriculum and structure of society, and distinction, not separation, between *religious* direction and intricate structure of society, etc.—these insights enhance the ability of Christian thinkers, educators, and other leaders to be more effective in our broken, self-centered, and deeply hurting world.[100] This is clear in at least eleven ways.

1. The difference between, on the one hand, the "Plato Club," sponsored by W. Harry Jellema and Henry J. Stob during the 1940s at CC, and, on the other hand, the "Groen van Prinsterer Club," sponsored by H. Evan Runner for two decades (1953–1973) for students from both CC and CTS, consisted basically of an "accommodational" and a "reformational" view of the "structure" of society and the *religious* direction of culture.[101]

2. Runner's firm belief that "life is religion" permeated his thinking and lecturing. These three words capture the spirit, or intent, of especially H. Dooyeweerd and D. Vollenhoven, who since the 1920s developed a *religiously* directed view of created reality, including its structure and "spiritual" direction of human culture and its history.

3. In stressing what is unique about created reality, educating future office-bearers about it, stressing the essence of "integrally" Christian scholarship, Runner warned against scholastic accommodation, which thinks in terms of, and tries to integrate, faith and reason, Scripture and science, revelation and reality, supernatural and natural, theology and philosophy, church and college, spirituality and liberal arts, being "religious" and a citizen (employer, banker, etc.).

4. A fresh scripturally directed reform(ul)ation of philosophy, anthropology, epistemology, and any special science involves at least five basic

---

100. For details about the origin, history and challenges of ICS, especially its stance on "scripturally-directed higher learning and scholarly enterprise" and its institutional identity and relationships with other national and international institutions and agencies of higher education and scholarship, see Robert E. VanderVennen (2008) particularly 234–263 and Appendices 1–4: (1) "Institute Basis and Educational Creed," 265–266—Dirk Vollenhoven, one of Runner's two main mentors, penned the "Preamble;" (2) "Speakers for Annual Summer Student Conferences 1959–69," 267–268; (3) "Summer Academic Conferences, Workshops and Seminars," 269–271; (4) "Books Co-Published for the Institute by University Press of America between 1983 and 1997," 272–273.

101. To describe the nature of the "threefold office" of humans, Runner often referred to Proverbs 12:1–28.

assumptions, four of which are positive and one is negative: (i) the biblical *Creator-creature* distinction, (ii) *religion* as the core of being human, (iii) a holistic *worldview*, (iv) an *ontology* of a multifaceted and amazingly coherent created reality, and (v) an *encyclopedic* knowledge, curriculum, and education that is not intellect-based, shaped by "liberal arts," or compromised by an accommodated view of "common grace" and "image of God."

5. Runner's role as a non-scholastic thinker is evident in being one of the fourteen delegates at the 1967 Consultation in Grand Rapids to discuss whether the AACS in Canada should establish the ICS as a graduate school in Toronto, or should join CTS and CC in Grand Rapids to start a graduate program in scholarship and education at CTS and CC.

6. Though he was by birth neither Dutch nor Christian Reformed, Runner soon sensed, after his arrival at CC in 1951, that there was a noticeable difference between most Christian Reformed students, colleagues, preachers, and church leaders in the USA, notably Grand Rapids, and many Canadian and some USA students at both CTS and CC, whose parents, pastors, and acquaintances responded favorably to Runner's *reformational* teaching about a *religiously* simple, yet broad, even radical, view of society and culture in the spirit of notably A. Kuyper and others.

7. The principle of "sphere sovereignty" was for Runner not an abstract, Dutch, and un-American idea, but an eminently biblical idea. It is an important principle of God's Word, which enables humans to express their Christ-centered and Spirit-directed love for God and one's neighbors.[102] Being a Spirit-filled follower of God's risen Son is not just personal and private, nor is it limited to the classic CRC tripod of "church, home, and school." It affects all human endeavors, e.g., farming, legislating, constructing, banking, employing and being employed, aiding the sick, poor and widowed, and resisting idols (capitalism, communism, socialism, individualism, etc.).

8. Runner applied the all-important triad of "heart-worldview-philosophy" to his view of education, curriculum, society, culture, civilization, and history. He did this by combining Vollenhoven's distinction between "direction" and "structure" with main features in Dooyeweerd's ontology and anthropology regarding "heart" and "created reality."

---

102. Runner often referred to (the longest) Psalm 119:1–176 for its detailed description of how to respond to God in a positive (covenant-centered) way and avoid transgressing the boundaries of genuine freedom and joy.

9. Although Runner never drove a car, tended to be impractical at times, and did not always observe when to end his class lectures and public speeches, he was an acute observer of the *religious* thrust, or direction, of people, institutions, movements, and cultures. He disliked any intellectual arrogance in students, educators, and scholars. Moralistic preaching and teaching saddened and grieved him, at times even angered him.

10. Until the end of his life, he focused on (a) basic issues in Western and Eastern, including Russian, culture, (b) the impact of Scottish "Common Sense" philosophy in North American education, scholarship, business and politics, and (c) specially Reformed/Presbyterian theology and preaching. His intent throughout his life since 1951 was not to be obstinate but passionate, not to be negative but positive or "thetical," not to be self-centered but "prophetic" as a child of God in the hope that his Presbyterian, Christian Reformed, and all other followers of Christ might deepen and broaden their faith life and witness in our modern world.

11. In principle, genuine *religion* compels God's image-bearing humans to be open for, experience and celebrate an enormous array of "structural" differentiation in God's creation, including themselves as humans. The former Runner associated with God's dynamic Word, and the latter with human responses to His three-pronged revelation. God's voice (*vox Dei*) precedes the voice of the people (*vox populi*). Humans cannot respond to God's basic "law of Love" without acknowledging creation's "structural diversity" and stunning diversity in human experiences of His presence.

In the world of thinking, teaching, and scholarship in all (human and so-called natural) disciplines the difference between "reformation" and "accommodation" affects all *special* studies, including "theology" and any "natural" science, and such *general* studies as ontology, anthropology, epistemology, and perhaps history. Key to genuine renewal is the "Truth" of God's Word, guidance of the Spirit and the Anointed One, permeating all education, scholarship, and daily living as God's people, who move on his grace-filled path of light in a dark, angry, and conflict-riddled world.

Shortly after his arrival at CC in 1951, some frictions, even mini-conflicts, arose between his different worldview, manner of teaching and mentoring students, and a firmly established stance of Christian Reformed scholastic professors in especially philosophy, theology, and pedagogy. His divergence with well-established thought- and act-patterns was reflected in different views of such common terms as "creation," "being," "revelation," "religion," "grace," "philosophy," "truth," "worldview," "history," "church," "Reformed," "theology," "logic," "Bavinck," even "Kuyper."

These differences spilled over into certain classrooms, were talked about in coffee shops, touched on in certain publications at CC and CTS. Discussions often centered on the nature of non-Christian and Christian theorizing, the essence and role of logic, meaning of "facts," the idea of "common grace," Christian witness in society and culture, and the relation of the CRC as denomination to CC as a "liberal arts" academy.

CHAPTER TWENTY

Reorientation

To think of Christians as believers and non-Christians as unbelievers does not imply that the latter do not believe. To believe is not optional, but indispensable to being human. My own interest in the meaning of believing started when I attended a "secular" vocational school in the Netherlands, deepened when I studied at a Canadian "public" high school, further intrigued me for four years at Calvin College—the only Christian Reformed "liberal arts" college at that time in North America—and captivated me during my six-year graduate studies in theology and philosophy at the Free University.

This interest in the nature of "faith life," and related study of "theology," (1) *deepened* during my three years as CRC pastor in Newmarket, Ontario, one year promoting ICS in Western Canada, and lecturing and discussing with students at several universities in Ontario and at several Christian colleges in Eastern USA; (2) *broadened* during my three decades of teaching theology and philosophy at Dordt College; and (3) *climaxed* in my unforeseen long-term involvement for thirty years in what eventually became known as IAPCHE (International Association for the Promotion of Christian Higher Education).[1]

To have faith in, or believe, is a human act which under normal circumstances reveals some form of allegiance to what is important at least in this life. What this "having faith in," this "believing," entails varies from person

---

1. Office at Dordt College in Sioux Center, Iowa, and since 2008 at Calvin College in Grand Rapids, Michigan.

to person, place to place, and time to time. It is always influenced, positively and/or negatively, by one's allegiance to something central, or important, at least here and now. This is evident in the core, or *religious*, commitment of such Western thinkers as R. Descartes, A. Smith, T. Jefferson, I. Kant, A. Comte, W. James, J. Dewey, F. Nietzsche, K. Marx, B. Russell, and Eastern gurus in Buddhist, Hindu, Muslim, Confucian, Taoist, and Shintoist traditions.

How has this issue affected the *religious* thrust, the basic stance, of thinkers like Augustine, T. Aquinas, M. Luther, J. Calvin, A. Kuyper, Pope Leo XIII, H. Dooyeweerd, D. Vollenhoven, K. Barth, etc., and influenced us in what we believe, hold dear, live for? Is human faith life necessarily redemptive, i.e., Christian? Do only Christians believe in something absolute? Is non-Christian faith life really possible? Can "faith life" be formed, informed, deformed, reformed, and transformed? Do humans express their faith also in "kinematic, physical, biotic, sensitive, analytical, formative, lingual, social, economic, artistic, jural and ethical" ways? Is it possible to equate human "faith life" with "religion"? If it is possible, does that imply that non-Christians are not *religious*? In other words, how does human *faith life* express itself, privately and publicly, in distinct Christian and non-Christian ways?

This view of *human faith life,* and proper study of it, is problematic when it is done in terms of Western scholastic philosophy about "reality" (ontology), being human (anthropology) and way of thinking (methodology and epistemology). In that case, its view of "faith," "religion," "Christian," "spirituality," "theology" and "sacred" has been affected by a non-Christian Greek view of "natural" and "intellectual" truths, which humans combine with what they consider to be "supra-natural," "divine" or "sacred." Such a split mind-set does not reflect a wholehearted renewal of humans in their thinking, through the Holy Spirit, in God's living Word, the Tree of Life and Rock of salvation. It does not sense the need for a concomitant change in the study of human faith life (*pisteology*) in response to God's self-revelation.[2]

To live in a biblically redirected and reforming way entails avoiding all mind-boggling (*logically* appealing but *practically* unhelpful) scholastic impasses in most Orthodox, Roman Catholic, and Protestant theologies. Lucid discerning deepens one's awareness that "human faith life" is structurally different, encyclopedically clearer, and more practical, than traditional scholastic theology. *Directionally,* it is more distinctly Christian in three ways:

---

2. For details, see Chapters 9–13 above.

(i) it is simpler than the Greek *metaphysical* notion of "being" (ontology), (ii) recognizes that humans are not only "perceiving, reflecting, speaking, producing, befriending, etc.," but also "believing" creatures in their "human *faith* life" (anthropology), and (iii) senses the need for a non-scholastic view of "truth" and "method" (epistemology).[3]

Novel Insights

Important to the reorientation proposed in this study are six insights or reform(ul)ations: (i) the distinction between heart and functions, center and circumference, or hub and spokes; (ii) the *covenant* relation between God's revelation to humans and the *religious* response of humans to it; (iii) the *religious* direction, or "spirituality," of human behavior; (iv) human life is essentially *religious*, reflecting either a God-honoring or a God-dishonoring disposition; (v) the conflict between "Christian" and "non-Christian" living is *religious*, i.e., total, life-encompassing, not limited to what is "functional" in the sense of a specific faith tradition, denomination, or organized church; (vi) the distinction between human "faith life" and academic study of it in "pisteology" is commendable for at least three reasons: (a) it enables Christians to avoid a reason-based view of God's revelation and the related scholastic notion of, for example, religion, faith, truth, church and theology; (b) it provides a clearer sense of non-Christian knowledge and faith; and (c) it provides a deeper awareness of the power and scope of God's love for humans immersed in pseudo-faiths and groping for truth.

Being Christian implies seeking the well-being of all human and non-human creatures. God's one central law of love calls humans to hear His call to serve fellow humans, not use, hurt, or remove them. Such a love-directed disclosure of human life is, in our self-centered world, possible only by submitting to the Spirit's "gift" of faith in God's living Word, the Savior, who sealed God's covenant promises to humanity.

Such a *religious*, or heart-centered, turnaround enables humans to re-

---

3. For details, see Elaine Botha's superb and penetrating study *Metaphor and Its Moorings: Studies in the Grounding of Metaphorical Meaning* (Bern: Peter Lang AG, 2007), especially "Introduction," 1–11. In a *reformational way*, this philosophical study deals with such crucial topics as "object," "subject," "paradigm shifts," "ontology," "coherence of meaning in created reality" and the "restlessness and interdependence of meaning." This *structurally* complicated, though *religiously* simple, study encouraged me greatly to think of "theology" in terms of (Christian and non-Christian) "pisteology."

spond in a positive way to God's life-giving and -sustaining command to express the freedom of God's life-giving and -maintaining laws of life. This enables disciples of Christ, as children of God the Father, to experience genuine liberty, both personally and publicly. Such discipleship, or covenant-living, is personally liberating, culturally rejuvenating, and historically unfolding.[4]

The opposite is also true. To live outside, in ignorance, or in defiance, of God's life-sustaining Word for the world, centered in His central love-command to humanity, has resulted in much confusion, immense anger, and unimaginable cruelty. Antithetical, or negative, responses to God's life-giving Word for a conflict-filled world intensify when, through the sin of omission, Christians limit God's life-encompassing created, incarnated and written Word.

This fundamental spiritual clash affects not only the knowledge inherent in the daily faith life of Christians, but also their study of human faith life in "pisteology." While the former is *practical* in a *pistical* sense, the latter is *abstract* in an *analytical* way. These two forms of knowing are simultaneous, i.e., "structural" (cf. functional) and "*religious*" (cf. heart-centered) responses to God's powerful, or dynamic, Word for created reality. Humans are called to testify to, or express, the freedom of God's grace-filled covenant promises shown in Christ Jesus and sealed by the Spirit.

Reform(ul)ation

In a world filled with personal and cultural restlessness, private immorality, and public injustice, humanity is, to use an appropriate phrase of Martin Luther, "turned in upon itself" (*incurvatus in se*). The Christian community should not overestimate what it is for, nor underestimate what it rejects. Not just *non*-Christian but also *anti*-Christian forces are active in Western culture, notably in academic and educational centers, where, being already *religiously* confused, people cause more confusion by stressing a self-knowledge that favors "objective" truth and leans on a questionable idea of "rationality."

---

4. For example, Saul (a) was a Jew who lived his first fifteen years in the Greek-oriented culture of Tarsus; (b) studied about fifteen years in Jerusalem under Gamaliel; (c) on his way to Damascus, the risen Lord met him, and the next roughly fifteen years he learned about the importance of his *religious* turnaround; and (d) *only then*—at about age forty-five—he started his difficult and powerful 'privilege' to share the Good News of God's kingdom in Jerusalem, Corinth and Rome, in Jewish, Greek and Roman cultures, and, thus indirectly, throughout the world.

In such a world, Christians do well not to lean on certain eloquent preachers and myopic theologians. To be faddish, gain notoriety, is not an unusual temptation for preachers, professors, and theologians. In their speaking about, and on behalf of, God, professors in divinity schools, theologians in seminaries, and teachers in Religion Departments of Christian "liberal arts" colleges tend to perpetuate a questionable kind of "theology." They do so uncritically assuming that "truth" is fundamentally something "intellectual." As a result, terms like "norms," "laws," "revelation," "religion," "faith" and "belief" are thought of as "concepts," and Scripture provides systems of beliefs to be taught, and memorized as a montage, or collage, of "theologies."[5]

To develop a self-critique of Western "faith life" and "theology" is not a superfluous and irrelevant luxury. For at least four reasons, it is eminently important: *first*, its understanding of human faith life and the related study of "pisteology" is radical in its simplicity and simple in its radical implications; *second*, it enhances communication within, and among, disagreeing **Christian** faith traditions in diverse cultural and historical settings; *third*, it addresses the problem of communication between **Christian and non-Christian** faith traditions by acknowledging the distinction between the "structure" and the "*religious* direction" of human faith life; *fourth*, the benefit of fostering a biblically directed view of created reality, including human faith life, and opposing *religiously* wrong ways of private and public thinking and behaving.

The reorientation needed is for two radical reasons, namely, *religious* direction and *structural* expression. In an anthropological, societal, cultural, and civilizational way, it calls for constant awareness and discussion of a strain, even an unavoidable disagreement, between, for example, "conservatives" and "liberals." This happened already in the first Christian community, after Pentecost, and was dramatically experienced in the early Christian communities described in the writings of the New Testament. Especially in higher, or advanced, theological circles, "conservative" Christians may view my approach to be too "liberal," while "liberal" Christians may regard my views as being still "conservative."

To face this problem in a non-traditional way, without trying to immunize myself against any criticism, it is not my intent to provide a final answer

---

5. For example, the "theology" of prophets (Isaiah, Jeremiah); poets (Psalms, Job, Song of Solomon); political leaders (Moses, Daniel); Gospel writers (Matthew, Mark, Luke, and John); evangelists (Paul, Peter, Jude, James).

to an originally Western idea of "theology" as a study (logos) of God. God's profound and overwhelming, or overpowering, revelation calls for something much simpler than a Greek-based Western ontology, anthropology, and epistemology based on a speculative notion of what is "True, Good, and Beautiful." To hear, believe, proclaim, and live according to God's powerful Word—not certain ideas of speculative theological experts about God—calls for a truly heart-centered reform(ul)ation of human faith life in a world filled with experts in knowing God.

To question major thought- and act-patterns in philosophy, anthropology, methodology and "theology" does not reflect arrogance or, worse, hubris. On the contrary, my sole interest in this long study is to look for a way to be biblically positive (without becoming a biblicist), reduce false conflicts, indicate a way of loving those with whom I differ about the meaning of being *religious* in everything we do—day and night, East and West, North and South—in our fascinating, yet deeply troubled, world. What does "religion" or "being *religious*" mean? Is it something isolated, only vertical, "spiritual," "theological," crucial for the broader and complex challenges in society and culture? Given the great need for renewal in personal and public behavior, the goal of Christians is not fame or reputation but love for truth and freedom in a hurting world.

With respect to "truth," it is easier for a Christian to understand a non-Christian than it is for the latter to understand the former. Through the "gift,"[6] the human heart is turned back to God, who enables humans to walk in the "truth" again, as Saul experienced on his way to Damascus.[7] "Truth" has to do with the direction of one's life. It is total, radical, enigmatic, *religious*. It is not "structural" in the sense of some identifiable analytic,[8] psychic, social, legal, or "pistic" behavior.

To say this is not a form of Christian hubris, but a reflection of love-based freedom and liberty. Christians know what non-Christians do not know, viz., their Creator and themselves as his creatures known for their obedient love and loving obedience by living, through the Spirit, in the Anointed Savior. This knowledge is evident in humans whose lives reflect the One who endured cruelty on their behalf. The nature and power of "truth" has

---

6. In distinction from faith as act, content, and aspect, which are *structural*, not *directional*. For details, see Chapter 10 above.

7. Cf. Acts 9:1–19.

8. Cf. John 14:6: "Jesus answered: 'I am the way and the truth and the life. No one comes to the Father except through me.'"

often been more evident when forces of disintegration and death do their destructive work.[9]

Throughout human history, prophets within and outside seemingly well-established faith traditions have urged humans to acknowledge the Creator of reality and His central law(s) of love and to behave as genuine office-bearers who in freedom act justly by living in His holy presence. Refusing to bear God's image by living—as spouses, parents, farmers, judges, traders, bankers, commentators, etc.—in defiance of His single all-encompassing will for humans resulted in a lifestyle that violated God's central law to love and encouraged *self*-centered humans to use, and misuse, fellow humans.

To sense something of the nature of the *religious* conflict in how humans respond to God's all-inclusive Word, the distinction between, on the one hand, *institutional*, or *organized*, faith life—commonly, though wrongly, called "religion"—and, on the other hand, the single heart-directed spirituality of one's whole life, is significant. Comparable to any other special kind of human activity, *organized* faith life is not (necessarily) the same as the all-bracing *religious* conflict between radical obedience and disobedience. Just as any Christian marriage, home, school, labor union, hospital, political organization, credit union, recreation center, etc., can lose its *religious* anchor, even a Christian faith community can fossilize, become an end in itself, and cease to be an oasis for weary travelers on the highway of God's kingdom. Even human faith traditions can be good or evil, true or false. *Religious* renewal of *all* human life is needed, not just or primarily, organized faith life. True "reformers" challenge any self-serving, introverted community to *return* to God, *hear* the Word and be Spirit-*driven*.

A world filled with diverse, often conflicting, faith traditions needs a faith life that is sensitive to God's three-pronged revelation of creation, in-

9. One of those killed in the Second World War was Rev. J. W. Tunderman (1904–1942), whose view of God's revelation in created reality, including human history, influenced the views of D. Vollenhoven and H. Dooyeweerd, especially with regard to the distinction between "practical" and "theoretic" understanding. For his views of the meaning of being human, essence of love and truth, *anti*-thetical nature of evil, and need to reject fascism, the Gestapo seized him in 1942 and shipped him, in a cattle train, to Dachau, where he died that year. For his prophetic Catechism sermons, see his posthumous '*T Beginsel der Eeuwige Vreugde* (*The Principle of Eternal Joy*) Vol. I-II, 1949. Three other *reformational* thinkers were: (i) J. Mekkes, a friend of H. Dooyeweerd and a gifted philosopher; (ii) H. Rookmaaker, who, while in a German camp, became a Christian (through J. Mekkes's witness and philosophy lectures) philosopher of art, including "Black music and spirituality," and influenced F. A. Shaeffer at his L'Abri in Switzerland; and (iii) Rev. Fr. Guilluame, who, after emigrating to Canada, was one of the founders of ICS (Institute for Christian Studies) in Toronto in the 1960s.

carnation and inspiration, so that people surrender their hearts and listen to the Spirit's call to live a life of love, lived in the reality of the risen One. Given the *magna carta* of his kingdom, God's trustworthy promises to humanity provide humans with solid reasons to trust Him in their daily walk with Him as, for instance, Noah the ark-builder, Abraham the nomad, Saul/Paul the driven ambassador did, and countless others have done at crucial junctures in their life.[10] Such simple, yet powerful, knowledge about God does not depend on "theological" studies, degrees, abilities, skills, and astuteness.

Foundational for Christian janitors, presidents, doctors, bankers, teachers, philosophers, commentators, preachers, artists, therapists, or whatever is God's faithful upholding of created reality, His life-assuring and history-shaping covenant with humanity (Adam) and embodied in the Anointed Savior. This God is not the "God" of some theological expert or an impressive "theological system." Fundamental to *religious* renewal is a simple, but profound, *religious* reorientation about the relation between God and created reality in terms of, for example, Peter's exuberant doxology: "Praise be to the God and Father of our Lord Jesus Christ! In his great mercy he has given us new birth into a living hope through the resurrection of Jesus Christ from the dead" (1 Peter 1:3).

The reorientation needed in human *faith life*, as stressed in "pisteology," is not based on any speculative philosophy and theology. Rather, it presupposes a liberating, heart-centered awareness that to be human is not the result of an "intellectual" expertise in "scholastic" thinking or clear view of truth. Rather, it stresses that whatever humans do is always *religiously* directed. The need for, and importance of, a heart-directed simple, yet radical, *self*-awareness is a distinctive feature of "reformational" thinking.

Biblically directed and covenant-centered thinking about God, "Yahweh," is crucial not only in "theology" but also in the major studies of philosophy, anthropology, epistemology and methodology, as well as in the disciplines about the nature, or "structure," of all human and non-human creatures. A clear view of human faith life deepens our view of both Chris-

---

10. This includes someone like G. Groen van Prinsterer (1801–1876), who, though childless, founded the Christian School movement in the Netherlands and, on the verge of fame and wealth, was aware of the cultural crisis in Western Europe, especially France, and challenged fellow Christians, in particular A. Kuyper, to rethink and reform, their worldview and press for renewal in their cultural, civic, educational, socio-economic and political behavior. About **modern** "walking with God" as Christian citizens, see, for example, (1) Bernard Zylstra (1934–1985), (2) James Skillen (b. 1944), founder and thirty-year director of CPJ in Washington, DC, (3) John Witte, Jr., at Emory University, Atlanta, GA.

tian and non-Christian faith life. It reduces the danger of speculating about the nature of, for example, "truth," "love," "meaning," "reality," "knowing," "certainty" and "peace." To know what these terms really mean does not depend on combining them with some Platonic-Augustinian and Aristotelian-Aquinian mind-centered kind of logic.

Living *Coram Deo*

In light of God's threefold revelation with respect to his relation to the world He created, Christians can sense who they really are and what they are called to do in this *self*-centered, and sin-riddled, world in terms of their view of created reality (ontology), self-knowledge (anthropology) and other forms of human knowing (special disciplines).[11]

Western undergraduate and graduate education has been greatly influenced by Greek thought-patterns as is evident in the pervasiveness of "faculty psychology" thinking centered on the "mind," or "intellect." This anthropology played a prominent place, although often tacitly, in Christian thinking. It affected what they assumed to be their (lower) place in society and eventually considered this to be proper and normative. Being Christian does not imply being truly "radical" but being more relevant and more effective, especially in fostering a creative dialogue in a subtle, perhaps compromising, way. To depict the meaning of humans "walking with God," the metaphor of rest areas along a fast, busy highway may be helpful. Just as weary travelers pause at strategically placed rest areas along a busy highway, Christians pause regularly to renew their energy and prepare for the next stretch ahead. These pauses are not optional or a luxury, but necessary and indispensable, for God's image-bearers. It reminds them to be faithful in whatever they do, respond to his love by claiming his grace in the "Word-made-flesh," and depend on the sovereign guidance of the Spirit.

What rest areas are for weary travelers, that is what the houses of prayer, centers of worship, places of proclaiming, experiences of healing, and moments of embracing are for all humans—of every color, race, tribe, sex, age, vocation, and position—who latch on to God's covenant promises and are alive in the risen One.

The metaphor of a highway, with its many strategically well-placed rest

---

11. This was true also of such thinkers as Plato, Aristotle, Augustine, Aquinas, Descartes, Kant, Hegel, etc.

areas, highlights the inseparable relation between (a) living in God's presence (*coram Deo*) in all one's responsibilities and (b) celebrating His goodness with fellow-Christians to deepen their common faith in the abiding God of love and justice. For safe travel on God's highway of grace-filled love in all our tasks, with their unique responsibilities, calls for relentlessly centering our *heart* on God's love ("gift") which, through the Spirit, redirects our faith life ("act, content, aspect")[12] back to God, in our local/global world.

What is involved in genuine godly living must be(come) palpable in whatever humans do. Given their new self-awareness and role in God's world, a few comments about three distinct, yet interrelated, issues will be helpful, namely, "*calling*," "*task*" and "*culture*." To be *reformational* also in our thinking about created reality is impossible without a different, a holistic and culturally significant, anthropology.[13] This, in turn, assumes a philosophy of created reality which provides a better, or clearer, view of human faith life and study of (not theology, but) a discipline called "pisteology." Minimally, this calls for an anthropology that avoids the snare of *scholastic* thinking about such (a) *terms* as "theology," "religion," "faith," "intellect," "reason," "substance," "metaphysics," "truth," "apologetics" and "philosophy," and such (b) *problems* as "faith and reason," "sacred and secular," "religion and state," "church and culture, " "Scripture and science" or "subjective and objective."

Calling

Central to being human is the calling for people to represent God by loving Him and their fellow humans in how they live in this world as his caretakers. In the core of their being, humans bear his image. Key to their relation to God is to represent Him, reflect his love, reveal his intent in how they live. His mandate to humans is basal and clear: love your Creator and all fellow humans. This central love-command is God's central and all-encompassing *religious* law, to be distinguished, not separated, from (i) God's diverse and unchanging *structural* laws *for* created reality and (ii) human changing, or *positive*, laws in their response to God's unchanging (structural) laws.

---

12. For details, see Chapter 9 and 10 above.

13. Dr. John B. Hulst, President of Dordt College, asked me in 1985 to design a "capstone" course in General Education for upperclass students. That course, adopted in 1986, was, and still is, named "Calling, Task, and Culture." Teaching it for ten years was a joy and challenge because some colleagues and students resisted it and wanted to retain their traditional *dualistic* worldview and *pietistic* faith life.

The *structural* diversity in human behavior corresponds to a diversity in the constitution of humans. The diverse human activities are not isolated from each other, but in many ways closely interrelated, while *religiously* they are directed by how humans respond to God's single love command, viz., either for good or for evil. The distinction between different *structural* laws and one *religious* law is unique in *reformational* thinking. It may not be confused with the "scholastic" distinction between two realms related to each other as lower and higher, horizontal and vertical, temporal and eternal, natural-supernatural or material-spiritual.

This *scholastic* view of created reality, with its built-in dualistic anthropology, differs drastically from the *reformational* "structure-direction" distinction and its holistic view of being human and acting in an integral way. The two human features of "structure" and "direction" are not independent from each other. On the contrary, they are as interrelated, and interdependent, as the head and tail of a coin, or the center and periphery of a circle. They point to a distinction, not difference, between one's heart and functions, inner and outer self, commitment and behavior, *religious* stance and specific deeds. In each instance, the latter expresses, or manifests, the former, and the former directs, or guides, the latter.[14]

Humans do not have an option to respond, or not respond, to God's basic love-command. Respond they must. When they do so in loving obedience, they bear God's image in a wholesome way. To do so is not an option, but an obligation in how they live their everyday life. In all their concrete and academic, i.e., practical and theoretic, activities, humans respond to God's *structurally* diverse laws in all their vocations and duties, e.g., to be trustworthy, just, social, skilled, clear, sensitive, fair, forgiving, protective, and celebrating. In everything they do, humans must act as God's children and therein reveal they testify to God's Word. Such living is being "thetical," or positive. Not to do this is to be "anti-thetical," or negative, and violates God's covenant, His image in humans, grieves the Lord Jesus, and grieves the Holy Spirit.

To be "spiritual" is not an option for humans, a consequence of their choice. Nor is it a supernatural addition to one's nature. It is not restricted to what, especially in Western culture, is referred to as "religion" as a carefully organized and closely guarded faith tradition. Neither is it a juvenile residue of an earlier superstitious phase in human history, as "positivist"

---

14. See Chapters 9 and 10 above about, respectively, "*Many Activities— One Spirituality*" and "Structure of Reality."

philosophers, theologians, social scientists, psychologists, and historians claim in the blatantly anti-Christian spirit of the French thinker A. Comte (1798–1857).

On the contrary, to be human is to reveal what is most important in human life, namely, always rely on God's rock-solid covenant promises, reflect His image in the *religious* thrust, or direction, in all their daily tasks. To be biblically reformational is to serve the Creator, develop a culture of "love," expressed in a spirit of "freedom," acknowledging God's Word in His Son and through the Holy Spirit. If human life is viewed in terms of a "wheel," the "spokes" point to the different *tasks* of humans, the "hub" points to the human *heart* which directs humans in all their daily tasks, the "rim" refers to the circle of one's daily *routine*, and the "axle" *enables* the hub and wheel of *life* to turn and move humans from here to there, now to later, past to future, and thereby somehow affect society, culture and (ideally) history.

In terms of such a simple, but basically life-encompassing (non-biblicistic) scripturally directed anthropology, humans are called to reflect God's life-encompassing *religious* law of love in whatever they do and avoid. Such a response calls for discovering and respecting God's *structural laws* for reality. In responding wisely to God's laws for creation, humans exhibit a modicum of liberty, reflect His faithfulness, and bear his image. When humans refuse to "walk with God" in their daily tasks, their being God's image-bearers is flawed and, unless halted, may result in unimaginable misery and grief.[15]

Task(s)

For an in-depth view of what covenant-keeping and -breaking involves in how humans respond to God's central law of love, a closer look at the structure and diversity of human tasks will be helpful. Basic to being human is to reflect His image, i.e., to represent the Creator in the way(s) we interact with fellow human and non-human creatures. Living in God's presence (*coram Deo*) does not imply some mystical escape from the world, living in a sin-riddled world without hope, or succumbing to some combination of these two (unbiblical) destructive ways of living.

---

15. Humans never cease to be human. Even when they resort to terrible private and/or public perversity (e.g., gifted but deceptive educators; mesmerizing but misleading speakers; clever yet perverse entertainers), they remain human.

Given the distinction between diverse *structural* laws and one *religious* law of love, it could be said that the former laws precede the latter and that the latter indicates that humans have responded in two conflicting, or opposite, ways: an obedient and a disobedient one. To know the full meaning of being human, minimally two things are necessary, viz., first, acknowledging the diversity of different, though interrelated, tasks of humans, and, second, being aware of how humans have responded in all their tasks to God's one, central *religious* law of love.

For humans to respond to God's central law of love always involves some human task and related responsibility. Being human involves being responsible to oneself, fellow humans, and non-human creatures. It entails being commissioned or having a task to perform (e.g., being loyal, just, frugal, social, imaginative, clear, sensitive, protective). In order to respond in their tasks, humans need to be in a position, office, or situation that enables them to perform their tasks or duties: they must, for example, be a spouse, parent, lawyer, manager, child, student, senator, teacher, engineer, referee, police, doctor, journalist, pastor, or whatever.

Each task has at least two features: namely, *responsibility* **for** fellow humans and such creatures as animals, plants, soil, water and other natural things,[16] and *accountability* **to** God and other fellow humans who help each other to perform their tasks. To ignore the second feature is to be *religiously* misguided, since it ignores God's *structural* laws embedded in created reality. To disconnect human tasks from their divine Origin and to permit humans to act in lawless, or absurd, ways fosters confusion, chaos, and death.

Being faithful to His Word for creation, the Creator does not permit humans to sever the world from his life-giving Word. Life and freedom without His Word for creation, incarnated in the Anointed Savior, are phantoms, projections, of *self*-inflated egos. Humans may turn their backs on God but cannot avoid him. His revelation is too overwhelming to be ignored. The notion that humans are autonomous, self-sufficient, is a delusion. Sooner or later, they sense that freedom in any society is not unlimited, especially when they are victimized by, for example, political intrigue, military conflict, economic deception, sexual perversity, and fleeting fame.

To think of destructive forces in human behavior and history in terms of some evil spirits, demonic powers, or satanic tactics out there in society

16. E.g., environmental problems and related local and global juridical, social, agricultural, political, economic, aesthetic, and medical issues.

and culture is to ignore the *religious* nature, or essence, of humanity. Sin and guilt, repentance, and forgiveness, perseverance and sanctification are not restricted to one's personal "faith life" in some strict organized faith community. On the contrary! Like anything else in human life, "faith life" is *religious* in that it is central to everything humans do. It is not confined to what is often, misleadingly, called "spiritual," an isolated "religion" unable to address a deeply troubled society and culture.

Apart from responsibilities in our multiple tasks, such terms as sin, shame, guilt, repentance, forgiveness, reconciliation, and renewal lose their concrete and practical relevance. Detached from all one's obligations to fellow human and non-human creatures, the need for accountability to some higher authority is undermined and, as a result, the typical faith terms, mentioned above, become shallow, even hollow and meaningless. It is precisely in all their daily and diverse (not only their faith, or pistical) tasks that humans behave properly or improperly, serve others or exploit them, foster life or obstruct it, provide hope or cause misery. All human activities must reflect the scope and power of "walking with God," a *coram Deo* living.

The oases of human faith life, along God's highway in the daily life of Christians, are crucial. In these structurally *pistical* places, times, and events, humans rest, stretch, celebrate, are nourished, and prepare themselves to re-sume their journey as responsible caretakers in God's world. Christian living is not limited to be free from our daily tasks and responsibilities, but to look back, ahead, and up, to be rejuvenated, press for ongoing *religious* renewal in our private and public behavior. A *religious* regeneration is key to any truly "radical" reorientation. To develop such a human faith life is exciting and demanding. If done lovingly and concretely in food production, health care, family life, business practices, technological developments, recreational life, etc., it benefits humanity with respect to the structure of society, the direction of culture, and the course of history.

Complicating matters, however, is that the *structural* diversity in faith life is interwoven with a total, or life-encompassing, *religious* conflict be-tween obedient and disobedient responses to God's revelation. To be *refor-mational* does not reflect obstinacy or, worse, arrogance. On the contrary. To live in a *coram Deo* way is a minimum requirement of living as God's image-bearers. Named after the Risen Lord, Christians express their rad-ically, i.e., *religiously*, turned-around life by expressing their gratitude not only with their Hallelujah-songs but also in the way they reform(ulate) their daily vocational responses in the areas of their expertise. All human laws are *positive laws*, which result from earlier human (limited and perhaps fallible) responses to God's *structural laws* for all creation and *religious* law of love for humans.[17]

This view of being human rejects the myth that *faith life* is private, unaffected by the rest of life, a lingering residue of an antiquated, and outdated, superstition. It avoids the twin dangers of *over-* and *under-*estimating human *faith life* with respect to its relation to the rest of human life. It prevents human faith life from becoming myopic, turned in upon itself, being caught up in some futile *private-public* dichotomy, or getting lost in some mystical experience. To replace traditional "theology" with "pisteology" leads to a clearer understanding of how traditional faith life is affected by, and in turn affects the prayers offered, praises sung, laments expressed, and needs addressed. It enables us to (re)discover the relation between God's revelation and "human life as religion," the importance of repentance, and the need for *reform(ul)ation* in philosophy and theology.

Culture(s)

The cumulative effect of how humans respond in their central, or *religious*, responsibility to develop, and disclose, created reality is called "culture."[18] Comparable to what is described in Chapters 7–10 above (about Christ *and* Culture, Church *and* State, Christianity *and* Society), the topic of Christianity *and* World is not helpful. It is appropriate, however, to think of Christians as humans in God's kingdom, who, through the Spirit and as followers of the Way, are God's covenant-partners, called to be wise in their behavior as his graced people traveling on the busy, fast and (until the Lord's return) dangerous highway of his kingdom.

How they perform their tasks in response to God's mandates somehow influences the *religious* direction of a community and society, perhaps a culture and civilization—until, finally the full powers of "evil" are unleashed,

17. An example of this approach is the article of John Witte, Jr., "Jesus: Democratic King," in *Christianity Today*, July 2011.

18. "Culture" (Latin *colere*: to till, or cultivate, soil) can also refer to (i) improving, raising and developing plants, animals and products, and (ii) refining, training and educating humans in their habits, ideas, skills, arts, instruments, and institutions at specific times and places. When the latter are major and enduring and controlled by a strong and central power, a culture becomes a civilization. For details, see R. Niebuhr (1951) 29–39.

compelling the Risen One to return.[19] Kingdom living is not something humans do apart from, above, or beyond their daily tasks, but is a matter of whether they live in a life-enhancing or a life-threatening way. In terms of five words, each starting with the same letter, Christian living can be aptly summarized as follows: "the Lord's law of love is central to a life of liberty." To refuse to live this way violates God's covenant with humanity. Such a violation occurs in different ways: e.g., (i) replacing God with some human idol, or pseudo-god, (ii) equating God's "law of love" with a Platonic/Aristotelian *positive* law based on the scholastic tripod of "Intellect, Will, Passion," i.e., "True, Good, Beautiful," or "Philosopher, Ethicist, Theologian," and (iii) replacing genuine freedom, or liberty, with private and public misery, injustice, violence, and even death.

The immediate and long-term effects of humans who refuse to acknowledge God's *religious* "law of love" in all their activities are misery, hopelessness, enslavement, even death, unless something truly unimaginable happens. Without the latter, there is no way to escape alienation and devastation caused by humans who genuflect, or kowtow, to the pseudo-gods of, for example, absolute freedom, scientific objectivity, insatiable greed, raw power, or decadent pleasure. The reason for such misery is God's faithfulness to his *structural* laws in what He created and His one *religious* command to love in his image-bearers.

When what is normal is considered to be abnormal and what is abnormal is thought to be normal, it becomes impossible to know what to do and avoid. This impasse calls for clarity about proper human behavior. Being faithful to His covenant, the Word, through which creation came into being, became "the Son of God and the Son of Man."[20] Only through Him is it possible for humans to perform their tasks and shape a culture that celebrates life.

That "Living Word" is the backdrop, and context, of all human plans and activities. They affect the nature of office and task, sin and repentance, forgiveness and Christian living.[21] To think of Christian living in terms of, to use an escapist expression, "going to heaven" reflects an "other-worldliness" that violates a *coram Deo* living, restricts discipleship to one's "faith life," to

19. To avoid any misunderstanding, I do not believe that Revelation, the last book of Scripture, calls for any form of "dispensationalist" theory.

20. Cf. John 5:13–21.

21. Or "position-in-relationship," i.e., humans as servants, stewards or guardians of fellow humans and creatures like animals, plants, and things. For details, see Paul G. Schrotenboer, "Man in God's World: the biblical idea of office," *International Reformed Bulletin* (1967) 5–6.

something "spiritual" and tends to think of Jesus Christ as one's "personal" Savior.[22]

To stress living in God's presence here and now, before the all-seeing and -hearing God, in whatever Christians do does not imply a theocracy, in which a Christian society, denomination or church, on behalf of God, controls all human life. Humans engrafted into the Anointed Savior do not misuse, but serve and inspire fellow humans. Lovers of the Creator/Redeemer display a positive, not negative, disposition for the benefit of fellow humans.

Being Christian is *religiously* similar to and different from being Buddhist, Materialist, or Nihilist. To be *religious* is (for humans) not an either/ or option, but a necessity, a both/and affair. Rejecting God's life-giving, and -guaranteeing, Word did not reduce human history to an instant "light/ darkness" issue. Instead, a "gray" situation developed, a combination of light and darkness, gratitude and selfishness, i.e., varying between more light than dark and more dark than light. This *religious* struggle all humans have experienced, including "the Word made flesh."

This conflict between "good" and "evil" may not be isolated from, nor equated with, any "structural" difference in human life, including faith life. To equate what is *religious* with "structural" differences in a "general" way (cf. political allegiances, social customs, dress codes, kinds of entertainment) or in a "specific" way (cf. organized faith life, church, denomination, congregation, liturgy, prayers, seminaries, songs)—to do this is to equate errors with sins and sins with errors. To err, in the sense of making a mistake, is usually associated with probing, studying, testing, developing an idea about something, a relation or an event.

Unlike concrete human faith acts, an analytic, or academic, study of human faith life zeros in on the *structure* of human faith life, in its relation to other forms of human life and associated tasks. It explores how humans can, and should, develop their faith life in a way that is more holistic. Even though they do not truly know the Creator, non-Christians live in the same world Christians do, also with regard to the study of their faith life. All humans somehow express all the "structural" features of their faith life. The *religious* direction of faith is isolated from the inherent nature and diversity of creation. In terms of its "structure," human life includes faith life.

Humans revel in the way they discover their gifts and way(s) they can serve other, especially human, creatures by enabling, not hurting. What

---

22. See John Suk (2011): 140–157, chapter 6 on "Faith Is Not a Personal Relationship with Jesus," for an insightful, though not complete, analysis of this phrase.

moves them in this is something wonderful, though mysterious, viz., a sense of calling and/or destiny, a reason for being, a core, a center, something bigger and stronger that guides, directs them in their "heart." To be human is to be *"religious,"* i.e., to respond to God's central command to love Him in either a positive or negative way, obediently or disobediently. The reason for the conflict between "good" and "evil" is God's faithfulness to His Word for wayward care-takers. This clash is unique. It is not a speculative Platonic theory about a higher, and unchanging, "reality" and a lower, and changing, "shadowy" world, nor is it an Aristotelian speculative view of "truth," "four causes," "logic" or "science."[23]

Not to acknowledge God's diverse laws for the *structure* of reality and his one central "law of love" does not indicate that they are irrelevant and can be ignored, especially in philosophy. A wide range of well-established forms of "Positivism" has greatly damaged the well-being of numerous human and non-human creatures. The nature and scope of problems inherent in Positivism cannot be properly addressed in an academic tradition that associates *religion* with what is irrational, irrelevant, experiential, private, not important for a flourishing culture, nor aware of a *religious* clash between God's kingdom and Satan's lawlessness.

To sin is to deny God's central law to love Him and one's fellow humans. It is deeper, broader, and more consequential than to disagree about "theological" issues in human faith life or "ethical" issues. It ignores God's love-filled and life-sustaining laws for human economic and political life, their analytic and sensory life, marriage and family life, and concern about environmental issues.

To trample upon God's diverse "structural" laws and disavow his *religious* law of love is to cause much confusion and disarray, grief and death. The evils resulting from dishonoring and distorting God's Word(s) for creation range from subtle to blatant, peripheral to central, minor to extreme. They affect not only individual persons, but whole communities, societies, and cultures. The effect of humans violating God's law of love reveals not joy and happiness, but what is *ab*normal, a law of sin-unto-death. It does this with grave and devastating human consequences. When sin fosters wickedness, disobedience results in perversity, pride in arrogance, defiance in destruction and, finally, joy results in grief and life in death.

The difference between life and death is not parallel to being Christian

---

23. Nor some Hegelian notion of Absolute Spirit and historical dialectics, a Marxist theory of society and history, or a pragmatist idea of truth and usefulness.

and non-Christian. The difference between God's grace and human rejection of it is *religious* in two ways: resistance to God's revelation is present also in Christian persons and traditions, and God's restraining power is evident also in non-Christian persons and traditions.

Being unique (*sui generis*), the *religious* conflict is not comparable to an institutional difference between church and society, what is spiritual and secular, or vertical and horizontal, nor is it comparable to relations between church and state, faith and science, personal and public, seminary and university, or theology and philosophy.

Three *Religious* Compromises

The nature of *obedient* "human faith life," which is studied by the discipline of "pisteology," is the meaning of being Christian in everything one does and refuses to do. So to think in terms of "church *and* world," "Christ *and* culture" and "faith *and* philosophy" is mistaken, but even this approach is grounded in the fact that human life is *religious* in that it reflects an all-embracing *coram Deo* way of living, even when disobedient and thus rebellious against God. In this regard, Western thinking and daily living has become so secular that even Christians associate, even equate, "religion" with church life and associate "faith life" with something personal, spiritual, vertical, and supernatural.

In opposition to such radical "*religious* secularism," *reformational* thinkers stress a simpler, non-accommodational, dynamic, and holistic view of God's kingdom, here and now, in a world filled with arrogance, hubris, and confusion. A "reforming" disposition is not satisfied with peripherally modified "individualistic" ways of thinking, teaching, voting, Bible-reading, etc. To be "Christian" is to be grounded in the crucified and risen Word-made-flesh, to be guided by the Spirit in whatever one does as worshiper, citizen, food producer, banker, educator, researcher, entertainer, judge, soldier, spouse, child.

To live as God's "light-reflectors" in our "analytic" tasks in philosophy, anthropology, epistemology, and all related sub-disciplines is not only a privilege but also a burden. It calls for resisting *religious* compromise with fame, wealth, power, or with well-intended, but shortsighted, forms of accommodation. When early Christians, including theologians, faced countless problems about how to respond to subtle, but powerful, Greek thinking in philosophy and theology, their ways of thinking were well-intended but often actually detrimental to developing a more appropriate form of Christian thinking and living.

The incarnated Word, "the way and the truth and the life" (John 14:6), entered a world shaped by a Greek-Roman culture not familiar with God's covenant-anchored revelation, for which His Son came, lived, died, arose, returned to the Father, sent the Spirit, and to which he will return. The early Christian community was, in a sense, freed from pagan thought-patterns and, in principle, ways of living. Filled with the Spirit, they followed the Risen Lord, prayed, broke "bread," drank from the cup of thanksgiving, formed new centers of love-directed living in a culture filled with idols, pagan customs, and conflicts.

Prominent church fathers, especially preachers and educators, as theologians, attempted to be biblical in their way of thinking and living. About a millennium before the rise of medieval scholasticism,[24] some church fathers thought of God's Word in terms of Greek ideas about (a) god(s), the world, and relationships between them, and (b) the nature of "soul," what is "true, good and beautiful," the nature of "body," and ways to fuse biblical ideas with pagan ones.[25]

Any incongruity in one's thinking that intentionally, or essentially, rejects the need for any *religious* renewal is some form of compromise. Such a disposition reflects a compromise, some form of "synthesis" for three reasons: (a) the "synthesis" is intentional, i.e., by design; (b) it is not necessarily Christian, but can be, for example, Jewish and Islamic; (c) it focuses primarily on scriptural revelation, to which non-Christian ideas and ways of living are adjusted.[26]

In Western culture, the earliest **form** of Christian "compromise" in Christian thinking occurred a century before the Middle Ages, in the three classic **methods** of "eisegesis-exegesis," "paradox" and "nature-grace." Each of these forms and methods involves basic principles and ideas about the meaning of "spiritual and antithesis," "diversity in faith traditions" and "hermeneutics" (for details, see Chapters 11–13 above).

---

24. This period in Western history W. Harry Jellema and even Henry Stob considered to be Christianly normative. For details, see chapters 14 and 15 above.

25. Immersed in J. Quasten's *trilogy* on *Patrology*: (I) *The Beginnings of Patristic Literature*, (ii) *The Anti-Nicene Literature after Irenaeus* and (III) *The Golden Age of Greek Patristic Literature*, Runner obtained a new set for me and urged me to study it.

26. Jewish *synthesis* combines Old Testament ideas with pagan ones (cf. Philo of Alexandria), and Islamic *synthesis* combines both Old and New Testaments and the Qu'ran with pagan principles.

Eisegesis-Exegesis

This "method" reads basic ideas *into* Scripture and then *out of* it. The ideas of Jerusalem resemble those of Athens. The difference between them is that the latter have no biblical authority, but receive it from the former. God's written Word is not carefully listened to, but readily used to turn unbiblical ideas into divine norms for life. Such a seemingly creative, but actually superficial, use of Scripture reveals a well-intended but actually unbiblical form of world-conformity.

Such a partial, but inconsistent, conformity in Christian thinking was clear in someone like Justin Martyr, who (though killed for his faith in Jesus Christ) misread John 1:9 to claim that the phrase "coming into the world" does not refer to Christ's birth as the "true light," but to the birth of "every person."[27] Each person possesses a divine spark, an illumination of the Logos. To be a Christian makes a difference, but not a radical one. This view resulted in a form of Logos-speculation, which also in Reformed circles tended to be associated with certain notions about "common grace" and disagreements about a Christian view of philosophy, anthropology, education, theology, and political theory.

The truth of God's three-pronged revelation cannot be discovered by simply reading ideas first "into" and then "out of" Scripture. The method of "eisegesis-exegesis" assumes the validity of certain concepts and beliefs shaped by Greek and Western intellectual probing. It has no eye for the truth of God's covenant faithfulness, i.e., his incomparable dependability, reliability, and trustworthiness.

This world-conformity idea indigenous to the "eisegesis-exegesis" method is evident in some, or all, of the following: (i) mitigating the *religious* conflict by slighting Christ Jesus as the "rock of offense," (ii) succumbing to the danger of biblicism; (iii) focusing on deviant beliefs, (iv) reading Scripture in light of popular fads, (v) belittling sin, (vi) mitigating forgiveness, and (vii) questioning the triune God.

---

27. He read this text to say that Christ is "the true Light, which illumines every person who comes into the world."

Paradox

The truth of God's revelation is not merely a *paradox* between what is conceptually "objective" and experientially "subjective." Such a distinction undermines the assurance inherent in faith as the Spirit's "gift" and anchored in the truth of the Lord. Historically, the *paradox* method is the opposite of the "eisegesis-exegesis" synthesis. The relation between "Jerusalem" and "Athens" is not one of similarity, but basically one of an "either/or" contrast. As to the Logos, Christians and non-Christians have nothing in common. Non-Christians have no Logical sparks in them. As the opposite of Athens, Jerusalem breaks with all its ideas, methods, and views. Not world-*conformity*, but world-*flight* is needed. When humans open their eyes to Scripture, they close their minds to the world.

Advocates of the *religious* "paradox synthesis" focus not on what is comparable to God's revelation in the incarnated and inscripturated Word. What they consider to be distinct about "paradox synthesis" is a form of anti-cultural and anti-creational thinking. Sin and evil tend to be associated with mundane features in private and public life. Two of its first proponents, Tatian (c. 170) and Tertullian (d. 220), succumbed to the heresy of third- and seventh-century Manicheism.

The "eisegesis-exegesis" and "paradox" ways of living feed off each other in opposite ways: simultaneously, they elicit and repel each other. While the first method focuses on the "here and now," the second method centers on "there and then." In varying degrees, the second method characterized monastic, ascetic, and pietist movements, impacted Mennonite and Quaker pacifism, and has affected diverse Fundamentalist and Pentecostal faith traditions.

It encouraged ascetic and monastic leanings in Eastern Christianity. This explains, at least in part, the leaning of Eastern Orthodoxy towards (a) "monophysitism," with its stress on Christ's "divine nature" (a heresy the Council of Chalcedon rejected in 451) and (b) "monothelitism," which emphasized Christ's "divine will," a heresy the Council of Constantinople rejected in 680/1 and the Council of Nicaea in 780/1.[28]

---

28. This is a clear example of how "religious" synthesis and certain basic philosophical issues affect faith life and theology in a negative, and confusing, way. This mystical/docetic streak in Eastern Orthodoxy is still evident today and is a major obstacle in ecclesial ecumenical endeavors.

Nature-Grace

The "nature-grace" accommodation sought, and continues to seek, somehow to combine the incompatible "eisegesis-exegesis" and "paradox" forms of synthesis. To combine two errors, however, does not make a right. To avert the error inherent in the first two methods does not legitimize the third method, but only complicates it. Its long and stubborn history is rife with problems resulting from "theological" speculation, reflecting *religious* tension, bogged down by endless scholastic "faith-reason" debates and conflicts that curtail the scope and power of childlike *coram Deo* living in God's life-radiating kingdom.[29]

This third form of "synthesis" thinking and living tries to combine the two methods described above. It does not equate Jerusalem with Athens, nor does it contrast these two with each other. It assumes that Jerusalem surpasses, or transcends, Athens. One of the two realms is superior and the other one is inferior. The revelation in the higher realm supersedes that of the lower realm. In rejecting world-conformity and world-flight, it opts for a form of world-*compromise* by means of a form of, one could say, world-*colonialism*. It neither ignores, nor acknowledges, a *religious* conflict between these two realms.[30]

Equating a higher, spiritual realm (church) with Jerusalem, and a lower, or common world (nature) with Athens, prevents the former from both submerging in and avoiding the latter. It trumps, or crowns, the lower world without redirecting it. Comparable to a colonizing country, it rules another country by leaving its actual structure intact.

This kind of "synthesis" Basil of Caesarea (d. 379) and Jerome (d. 420) advocated. They taught that just as Moses and Israel robbed Egyptians of their gold and silver, and used these treasures to God's glory by transforming them into utensils for use in tabernacle rituals, so Christians may use the products of pagan culture as long as they do it "for the greater glory of God" (*ad maiorem gloriam Deo*).[31] The world's riches belong in the Temple and, after Christ's ministry and the Spirit's outpouring, in the international

---

29. This "religious synthesis" is grist for the mill of numerous conferences at which not so much everyday biblical covenant "faith life" is dealt with as complex "theological" issues which are debated in scholastically impressive, but practically irrelevant, ways. This can happen even in the tradition of A. Kuyper—for details, see chapter 5 above and VanderStelt 1978: 221, 248 and 263.

30. For details, see chapter 11 above.

31. The phrase "*soli Deo gloria*," common in Reformed circles and traditions, can be—

Roman Catholic Church.[32] This synthesis was sanctioned by the Synod of Orange (Arausio) in 529, when it stated that the human fall into sin had not drastically altered the natural, or lower, world of humans.

The classic formulation and implementation of *synthesis* thinking was developed by T. Aquinas (1225–1274) in his thinking, teaching, preaching, which then shaped the structure of society and, in a sense, shaped the direction of Western culture. It impacted sixteenth-century Protestant scholastic thinking (cf. **nature**-grace) and stimulated nineteenth- and twentieth-century neo-scholasticism (cf. **grace-*nature***). It caused the RCC to publish three encyclicals (1879, 1950, 1998)[33] about how Christians should live under the spiritual supervision and the moral guidance of the RCC.

Whereas the early "eisegesis-exegesis" synthesis was more spontaneous than intentional, the medieval "nature-grace" compromise of T. Aquinas was more deliberate, complex, and abstract. The negative effects of Aquinian thinking on integrated Christian thinking and living have been huge, especially in Western and Latin American cultures.

"Reformational" thinking resists any way of past and present thinking that reflects any form of *religious* synthesis. Since the 1920s, various neo-Kuyperian thinkers, especially Dooyeweerd and Vollenhoven, sensed the danger of advocating an ecclesiastically sanctioned view of a "nature-grace" dualism in their way of thinking in philosophy, shaping of society, and directing of culture. To be an expert in Scripture, a mesmerizing preacher, a "full-time" evangelist, or a faithful thinker is, though well-intended, perhaps actually misguided and misleading. It does injustice to the full depth and scope of God's life-giving Word. That Word is covenant-based, life embracing and renewing, for his human image-bearers.[34] Since they are

---

and often is—misused when it sanctions a compromising "grace-nature" form of "religious" synthesis.

32. A flaw in this view is the assumption that the cultural products, i.e., principles and thoughts, of non-Christians can be used by Christians in the way, for example, that natural, or physical, things can be utilized. Examples of such an approach are Christians who use J. P. Sartre's idea of "hell" and neo-positivist notions of "depravity," as if they are somehow biblical and, therefore, useful for Christians without doing justice to the reality of the "religious" conflict.

33. For details, see Chapter 14 above.

34. Cf. S. U. Zuidema, one of my philosophy professors at the Free University in Amsterdam—who in the 1940s was a missionary in Indonesia, where in 1942–3 he was separated from his family and imprisoned in a Japanese war camp. There he wrote a riveting *Ons Gebed* (Our Prayer) for his children. In 1963, as a leader of a Bible reading circle, he warned us against turning our sessions into "theological discussions that prevented us from listening to, and really hearing, God's Word." He had received his Ph.D., supervised by D. Vollenhoven, in

not theoretic, but *religious*, the three main ways of "synthesis" thinking and living are not debatable, essentially philosophically, but reflective of a *religious* accommodation. To recognize this is the reason for an unceasing "reform(ul)ation" of what it means to be human, also in one's faith life and study of "pisteology."

Conflict and Tacking

How humans live reveals what their hearts are committed to. It is broader and deeper than what they do in their "religious" or "church" life.[35] To know God as the source of life is the secret of true self-knowledge and genuine liberty. By opening their hearts to His Word, humans hear their Maker's call and reject the lure of whispering idols or screaming pseudo-gods. Only a radically *religious* reorientation enables humans to live as liberated, and liberating, children of God. It enables Christians to reflect something of the true source of well-being of both human and non-human creatures.[36]

To refuse to depend on what is reliable, or reject what should be, is essentially a *religious*, not a "structural," aberration. It reveals what is abnormal, or the mystery of iniquity, namely, humans refusing to be what they were created to be. The effect of this conflict is not something essentially private or personal, but public and communal. Why humans violate God's life-giving "structural" laws and his one and all-encompassing *religious* law of love is not something "structural" in society, e.g., a difference in gender, race, color, age, or in anything that is economic, political, social, psychic, analytical or physical.

The *religious* conflict manifests itself in numerous clashes in human history and will continue to be experienced in numerous local and global conflicts. The nature of God's revelation to humans, and how humans respond to it, is such that it is those who reject God's covenant, not Christians,

---

1930 for his study *De philosophie van Occam in zijn commentaar op de Sententien* (533 pages) and Latin Supplement (399 pages). In addition to Vollenhoven, Zuidema greatly helped me to distinguish between, not separate, faith life and theology.

35. See Minear's study of "church," especially the wide range of synonyms used in Scripture to describe this new reality at the center of human history.

36. As to the Lord's *kingdom* mandate, see Matthew 28:18–20. It is broader than evangelism done by specialists of certain organized "churches." God's people must reveal their Maker/Redeemer's image in whatever, whenever and wherever they do things differently and, therein, to be blessing for others by truly sharing the Good News.

who are "anti-thetical." As a result of "abnormal"[37] human responses to God's life-giving laws, the term "anti-thetical" indicates that to be "Christian" is, in principle, something negative, i.e., something that restricts freedom and endangers any *religiously* anti-Christian stance in society and culture. As a result, such a demonic society requires that "integral Christian living" be curtailed, or outlawed, in order to protect non-Christians in their *anti-Christian* way of living.

This anti-Christian stance is such that Christians must be wise in how they live, in what they say and do. They must avoid arrogance and complacency. Their tasks and roles in daily life must somehow indicate God's presence in their daily talk and walk. This calls for wisdom, knowing when (not) to speak, how to deal with complex situations in a town or city, a factory, hospital, sport, school, army, bank, etc., how to comfort in times of crisis, how to be angry when necessary, courageous when threatened, confident when imprisoned, and fixed on the risen One when faced with death. To write these things is easy, but to live this way is hard. It requires Spirit-filled courage.

To be *integrally* Christian in our parenting, constructing, judging, teaching, preaching, healing, banking, legislating, etc., is a privilege and a challenge. Because resistance to God's life-giving laws is often subtle and dangerous, being integrally Christian calls for being alert, trustworthy, good listeners, caring doctors, talented lawyers, clear commentators, etc. Christians must provide at least some marginal resistance to forces that mislead the *religious* direction of individuals, families, areas of society, and regions of culture.

Reformational living is not something psychic, social, ecclesiastical, philosophical, or even theological. To be Christ-centered and Spirit-directed assumes a heart-centered way of "walking with God" made possible by Christ's sacrifice and the Spirit's power. It has to do with being at home with God in everything humans do day and night. It points to a way of living in His creation with their eyes wide open and ears itching to hear God's voice about his laws, or words, *for* created reality, including human faith life, especially the "gift" of salvation, in the core of their existence, which enables humans to "walk with God" in their covenant-centered path of life and joy, not death and grief.

To walk on the road of life, illumined by the Light of the world, involves

---

37. Cf. A. Kuyper's remarkable use of "abnormal" as a synonym for "sinful." For details, see Chapter 5 above.

facing the headwinds of evil and the side winds of compromises, and it calls for an unabated reliance on God's faithfulness, confirmed by the Spirit's power on a grace-filled journey to the "Alpha and Omega," about whom John, old and imprisoned on the island of Patmos, wrote Revelation, the last book of Scripture. With their hearts focused on the risen One, who has broken Satan's backbone, Christians tack left and right, weave in and out, but essentially move in the direction of victory, especially when faced by demons.

Such "tacking" does not indicate being half-hearted, lacking love, or not hearing the voice of the Savior above the din of competing ideologies and screaming idols. Sometimes the situation of Christians may be such that the only thing they can, and will, do is thank God for His covenant love and faithfulness, especially when faced with imprisonment and death. When anti-Christian, or anti-thetical, powers force followers of Christ Jesus to tack, Christians will do so reluctantly. They will even pray for their opponents.

To determine in advance what can, and must, be done in difficult "tacking" situations is impossible. Minimally, it calls for God's covenant-centered wisdom, a Spirit-led discernment, and making a difference in terms of the nature of God's kingdom in connection with the role of humans in it and the possible implications for the form and agenda of their local faith life.

Glimpses of this kingdom are evident in such life-enhancing gifts as love, health, compassion, justice, integrity, gratitude, and peace. To be *religious* is central to being human in everything humans are called to do with their personal gifts, diverse habits, societal structures,and cultural customs.

To live in God's presence does not mean that to think about God is an option for humans to be appealed to at certain times in some "creative" way. According to Western rationalism, "reason" is its own master, subject to itself, free from conflict-causing religion, and the main "reason" for questioning, restricting, and even rejecting God's revelation(s).[38]

The inscrutable, pervasive conflict-causing difference between Christian and non-Christian responses to God's three-pronged (created, incarnated and written) revelation is a deeply *religious* one. Not only Christians but also non-Christians are profoundly *religious*. As a consequence, to think in terms of religion *and* education, faith *and* science, theology *and* philosophy, sacred *and* secular, or church *and* culture, etc., is actually misguided.

---

38. Cantwell W. Smith calls Western secularism a "religion," comparable to Judaism, Christianity, Islamism, Hinduism, Confucianism, Taoism, and Buddhism (for details, see chapter 12 above).

This thinking tries to avoid six misleading views in: (i) the Roman Catholic and Anglican/Episcopalian tradition of a "natural-supernatural" world; (ii) Fundamentalist-Evangelical circles of Jesus Christ as "personal Savior"; (iii) Christian Reformed (especially USA) thinking of Christian education in terms of "church-home-school"; (iv) a "pre-millennarian" stress on a "church now-kingdom later" paradigm; (v) the pietists' stress on creedal traditions and avoiding cultural evils; (vi) a form of proselytism in some Baptist circles regarding how to enhance "saving souls."[39]

In all these traditions, "religion" tends to be used in the sense of an institutionalized, or organized, faith community. The **content** of such faith life consists minimally of what Christ Jesus did for the salvation of sinners.[40] The **act** of such a faith life is based on God's Good News about mercy, responded to through the Holy Spirit, in joyful surrender to the Savior. Implied in such a yielding is the reality of "faith" not as "content" or "act" but as an **aspect** of created reality. This third meaning of "faith" opens the door to recognize the crucial, even indispensable, role of "metaphors" to understand the nature, or structure, of human faith life. Instead of acknowledging this facet of faith life, this thinking "spiritualizes" them through "theological" speculating about, for example, "faith," "religion," "truth," "church," "kingdom," "witnessing," "Israel," and "eschatology."

Unless humans are graced with God's goodness from their birth, nurture, and upbringing, some form of *religious* experience, often called "rebirth," involves some form of a heart-centered "experience," a bowing before, a change in the core of their being,[41] to God's gracious covenant love. Such a Spirit-guided overwhelming **gift** of faith results in a peace and assurance that affects everything one does, also in faith life. To be "at home with God" in whatever one does, including "philosophy" and "pisteology" (not scholastic theology) is to be *religious* in a Christ-centered and Spirit-driven way.

This is central to a simple, yet radical, joyful, yet demanding, way of constantly reforming, or being *reformational*, to avoid any intentional ac-

39. Some years ago, a North American evangelist showed me a large notebook with dozens of colored pictures of persons in two East Asian countries "he had converted to become Christian." At the bottom of each picture he had written the name, place, time, occasion, and moment of the conversion. The secret of his "effective evangelizing" was written, in large letters, on the cover of his notebook: "No Soul, No Supper."

40. For details about "content," "act," and "aspect" of faith, see Chapter 10.

41. Cf. The *Back to God Hour* radio program of the Christian Reformed Church in North America, in distinction from B. Graham's *Hour of Decision* and R. Schuller's famous, but now extinct, *Hour of Power.*

commodating scholastic thinking in philosophy and theology regarding basic issues in anthropology, epistemology and, for example, the discipline of (theology in the sense of) "pisteology." The aim is to help all who study, teach, and write in a rich, simple, and life-encompassing way, freed from the shackles of compromising scholasticism.

Global Positioning

Christians are called to serve the God of "heaven and earth" according to His Word for the benefit of fellow humans and non-human creatures. To live according to God's liberating covenant "with the day. . . with the night. . . with David my servant,"[42] is something humans of every race, color, age, and gender cannot avoid. Ultimately, their response is either grateful or defiant, positive or negative.

This *religious* difference affects all human teaching and learning how to live in God's world in all their tasks, here and now, as His image-bearing creatures, called to reflect his love in the way they live. This basic, simple, and all-embracing *religious* stance is what a teenager named Samuel testified to when he repeated the words of the aged and feeble Eli: "Speak, Lord, for your servant is listening."[43]

In echoing Samuel's simple, clear, and all-encompassing call of God, many minor and major prophets in the Old Testament acted as God's "covenant-centered" news commentators. They called a self-centered people to return to and acknowledge God's holy presence. In doing this, they often experienced much opposition, at times even banishment and death. That Christians and non-Christians experience a solidarity with each other at certain times in history and areas of culture does not imply that Christians need not live in a *religiously* different way. Though humans grow together the way "wheat and weeds" do, Christians, who know the *religious* difference between them, keep their eye of faith focused on the final harvest.[44]

If certain compromises are necessary, they should not be made glibly,

---

42. Cf. Jeremiah 33:20–22.

43. 1 Samuel 3:1–10. In calling God "Lord," Samuel acknowledges that he is His servant. The relation between God and Samuel is one of speaking and listening, God's revelation and Samuel responding, revelation and religion. About the depth and scope of evil in Samuel's society and pervasive in Israel, see 1 Samuel 1–2.

44. See Matthew 13:24–30, 36–43 about "good" and "bad seed," sown and harvested as "wheat" and "weeds" in the same field.

but reluctantly, not joyfully, but painfully. They do not detract from the burden of genuine discipleship, but increase the burden of cross-bearing. A not uncommon view of "common grace" in Christian Reformed circles tends to stress *structural* solidarity between Christians and non-Christians and to minimize the *religious* conflict in their daily behavior in society and culture. Such accommodational thinking in philosophy, theology, and many other disciplines is both dubious and debilitating.

The implications of an unavoidable human solidarity—in distinction from any intentional synthesis thinking, or *religious* compromises—are different for Christians than they are for non-Christians. In a "structural" sense, all humans live in the same, or common, world; however, they do so "directionally," or *religiously*, in different, if not conflicting, even possibly fatal, ways. For Christians and non-Christians to live together does not mean that Christians need not press for an ongoing reform(ul)ation of one's basic stance in life and way of thinking and living.

Humans whose hearts are moored in the Anointed One and directed by God's Spirit are directed back to God's grace in a world (a) of heartless and conflicting idols that enslave and kill them, and (b) in need of humans who, when delivered from the lure of power, wealth, strength, or fame, "walk with God" in a covenant-warranted way, also in their thinking and living in "philosophy" and "pisteology."

Scholastic thinking fosters a scholastic way of living. What is "natural" is presupposed in what is "supernatural;" the former is, in a sense, prior to the latter, human history somehow basic to redemptive history, reason a condition for faith, classic "liberal arts," especially philosophy, imperative for "theology," and "common grace" is assumed in "special grace."[45]

Christian Reformed education at CTS and CC in Grand Rapids[46] expected their professors to teach their students to think in terms of their personal and public life in terms of special grace and common grace, prophetic ministry and profitable business, giving money and making money, religion and culture, church and society, religion and a job. This life-encompassing mind-set influenced their curricular issues, pedagogical methods, ways of reading Scripture, how they related faith to reason, how they viewed the relation between theology and philosophy, the nature of religion and politics,

---

45. The notion of a "natural" and a "supernatural" realm which parallels general and special revelation, or common and redemptive grace, reflects a scholastic "nature-grace" mentality and its implied dualistic anthropology and worldview.

46. I did not study what happened at the theological seminaries and colleges of the Reformed Church of America (RCA).

being a member of a church and citizen of a nation, the role of preaching and apologetics, and the scholastic use of the Greek tripod of "thinking, willing, feeling."

It fostered a common understanding of terms like "reality," "truth," "sin," "error," "belief" and even "faith." It accounts for the impact of Plato on Augustine's view of "faith seeking understanding" (*fides quaerens intellectum*), the official motto of CTS. Some eight centuries later, it influenced T. Aquinas to incorporate in his philosophy and theology Aristotle's view of truth and "method" of logic, as something about which, three centuries later, T. Beza spoke in a positive way in his public opening lecture at the formal opening of J. Calvin's Academy in Geneva in 1559, four years before Calvin died.

The "structurally" different ways in which Christians develop, and celebrate, their faith life reflects what they believe Scripture's message to be, how it shapes their prayers, liturgies, creeds, places of worship, and offerings taken and used, but also the *"religious"* direction of their family life, agricultural and commercial endeavors, industrial and economic activities, civic and political involvement, medical and legal services.

In a rapidly shrinking world filled with major and minor Christian and non-Christian faith traditions North and South, West and East, to rethink—especially in Europe and North America—the nature of much used, and much abused, words such as *religion, faith*, and *theology* is not an option, but a necessity. Failing to do this is stereotyping what is distinct and trivializing what is significant. In his three-pronged revelation in the world He created, God calls humans to a simple and rich view of the three italicized words above.

Against the background of central issues raised in Chapters 2–8, the intent of Chapters 9–13 was not merely to be negative (e.g., rejecting "accommodational" thinking in philosophy and theology), but to be positive by exploring two things: first, a simpler, but more radical, heart-centered, *religious* reorientation, and, second, a "structurally" clearer view of the nature of human (Christian and non-Christian) faith life.

Reformational thinking also in philosophy and theology resists at least six accommodating "scholastic" ideas developed in Western culture: (i) "religion" is an option of humans or an addition to being human, (ii) the distinction between three "structural" features of faith ("act, content, aspect") and radical conversion (the "gift" of faith),[47] (iii) ignoring the *religious* con-

---

47. Cf. Ephesians 2:8–9a: "For it is by grace you have been saved, through faith—and this is not from yourselves, it is the gift of God—not by works, so that no one can boast."

flict between positive and negative responses to God's Word, (iv) justifying the immense diversity of human traditions, (v) conflicting hermeneutic methods, and (vi) denying the need for Christian discipleship in all human endeavors.

Reformational thinking and living takes place by relying on God, the Creator of "heaven and earth," whose Word, in the fullness of time, came as the Anointed Savior and, after He returned 'home,' sent the Spirit, to enable men and women, poor and rich, in every country and on all continents, to respond joyfully to God's "expensive," and "expansive," love in the incarnated Word.

May this childlike, but power-filled, vision inspire all students and educators, scholars and professors, and preachers and doctors, newscasters and authors, experts in justice and technology, entertainment and recreation, bankers and farmers, etc. The truth of God's "Wisdom, Power and Glory" calls for constant *religious* and "structural" renewal in the way we think, teach, preach, write, etc., and behave in a non-accommodational way in philosophy, so-called theology, etc., by being *religiously* humbler, and in a more radical, Christian study of "pisteology" which aims to replace speculative metaphysical thinking with a form of probing "reformational" thinking.[48]

---

48. Cf. 1 Corinthians 1:18–31 and 2:3–5 (about "Christ, the Wisdom and Power of God") and 2 Corinthians 3:7–18 (The Glory of the New Covenant). The first passage I cited in my public farewell when I retired in 1999 as professor of philosophy and theology at Dordt College, and only referred to the second passage.

Works Cited and Consulted

An apology for where gaps, omissions or errors may appear below in this list of Works Cited. As referenced in the foreword to this book, the decline of mental health due to my dad's dementia as well as lack of time and capacity to cross-verify all details have factored into our inability to finalize this section of the book with complete accuracy.

—NATE VANDER STELT

Abbing, P. J. Roscam. 1981. *Orientatie in de theologische wetenschap*. Kampen: Kok.

Abraham, William J. 1990. "Oh God, Poor God," 18–23, in *The Reformed Journal* (40:2).

Adriaanse, H. J., and H. A. Krop, eds. 1988. *Theologie en rationaliteit: Godsdienstwijsgerige bijdragen*. Kampen: Kok.

Albanese, Catherine L. 1979. "Research Needs in American Religious History," 101–105, in *Bulletin of the Council on the Study of Religion*, 10:4.

Allen, Diogenes. 1993. "Christianity and the Creed of Postmodernism," 117–126 in *Christian Scholars Review* (XXIII:2).

Alston, William P. 1991. *Perceiving God: The Epistemology of Religious Experience*. Ithaca, NY: Cornell University Press.

Althusius, J. 1964. *Politics*. Boston: Beacon Press.

Ames, William. 1979. *Technometry*. Translated and introduced by Lee W. Gibbs. Philadelphia: University of Pennsylvania Press.

Armstrong, William P. 1980. "The Reformation and Natural Law," 56–57 in *Calvin and the Reformation*. Grand Rapids: Baker.

Astley, Jeff, and Leslie J. Francis, eds. 1994. *Christian Perspectives on Faith Development.* Foreword by James W. Fowler, Grand Rapids: Eerdmans.

Augustijn, C. J., N. Prins, H. E. S. Woldring, eds. 1987. *Abraham Kuyper: Zijn volksdeel, zijn invloed.* Delft: Meinema.

Bangs, Carl. 1971. *Arminius: A Study in the Dutch Reformation.* New York: Abingdon Press.

Bavinck, Herman. 1909. *Philosophy of Revelation.* L. P. Stone Lectures. Princeton Theological Seminary. Longmans, Green, and Co. Reprint, 1979, Baker.

——.1913. *Christelijke wereldbeschouwing.* Kampen: J. H. Kok (second revised edition of original, 1904).

——.1920. *Bijbelsche en religieuze psychologie.* Kampen: Kok.

——.1921. Philosophie des geloofs, 9–16, Godgeleerdheid en Godsdienstwetenschap, 35–54, Psychologie der religie, 55–77, and Primaat van verstand of wil, 208–214, in *Verzamelde opstellen op het gebied van Godsdienst en wetenschap.* Kampen: Kok.

——.1923. *Beginselen der psychologie.* Kampen: Kok.

——.1928. *Gereformeerde Dogmatiek,* I-IV (4th print; original: 1895, 1897, 1898 and 1901). Kampen: Kok.

——.1953. *Our Reasonable Faith,* Grand Rapids, Eerdmans.

——.1955. *The Doctrine of God.* Grand Rapids: Eerdmans.

——.1956. *Our Reasonable Faith.* A popular digest of Bavinck's *Reformed Dogmatics,* I-IV, 1928, with preface by Henry Zylstra, 5–11. Grand Rapids: Eerdmans.

——.1979. The Philosophy of Revelation, Baker Book House, 1979.

——.1980. *The Certainty of Faith* (*De zekerheid des geloofs,* 1901), trans. Harry der Nederlanden. St. Catharines: Paideia Press.

——.2008. *Essays on Religion, Science, and Society.* Baker Academic, a division of Baker Publishing Group.

Bavinck, J. H. 1940. Het probleem van de pseudo-religie en de algemeene openbaring. Speech given at Reunisten-Organisatie, March 26, 1940. Publicaties van de Reunisten-Organisatie van N.D.D.D., No. 12. Amsterdam.

Bavinck, J. H., Joh. de Groot, M. J. A. de Vrijer [No date]. *Het geloof en zijn moeilijkheden.* Wageningen: Zomer en Keunings.

Bayer, Oswald. 1973. *Was ist das: Theologie?* Stuttgart: Calwer Verlag.

Beck, Lewis White. 1969. "Philip Melanchthon: The Second Praeceptor Germaniae," 101–102, in *Early German Philosophy: Kant and His Predecessors.* Cambridge: Harvard University Press.

Begeman, A. W. 1963 and 1964. De kerk in de calvinistische wijsbegeerte. *Correspondentie Bladen* (27)9–15 (28)11–21.

Berkhof, H. 1960. God, voorwerp van wetenschap? Inaugural as professor of the Nederlandse Hervormde Kerk, University of Leiden. Nijkerk: C. F. Callenbach.

——.1982a. *Inleiding tot de studie van de dogmatiek.* Kampen: Kok.

——.1982b. Commentaar: uitwisselen van vooroordelen, 84–87. *Radix,* (8:2).

Berkhof, L. 1932. *Introductory Volume to Systematic Theology,* Grand Rapids: Eerdmans.

——.1950. *Principles of Biblical Interpretation* (Sacred Hermeneutics). Grand Rapids: Baker Book House.

Berkouwer, G. C. 1950. Wat is Theologie, 7–18. *Interfacultaire Colleges, Cursus 1949–1950.* Amsterdam: Free University.

———.1953. *Modern Uncertainty and Christian Faith.* The Calvin Foundation Lectures. Grand Rapids: Eerdmans.

———.1959. Het bewijs in de theologie, 7–22. *Het Bewijs in de Wetenschap.* Interfaculty lectures. Amsterdam: Free University.

———.1977. *A Half Century of Theology: Movements and Motives,* trans. and ed. Lewis B. Smedes. Grand Rapids: Eerdmans.

———.1989. *Zoeken en vinden. Herinneringen en ervaringen* Kampen: Kok.

Berkouwer, G. C., and H. Oberman, eds. 1971. *De Dertiende apostel en het elfde gebod. Paulus in de loop der eeuwen.* Kampen: Kok.

Bernstein, Richard J. 1991. *Beyond Objectivism and Relativism: Science, Hermeneutics, and Praxis.* Philadelphia: University of Pennsylvania Press.

Bettis, Joseph Dabney, ed. 1969. *Phenomenology of Religion: Eight Modern Descriptions of the Essence of Religion.* New York: Harper & Row.

Beveridge, Henry, and Bonnet, Jules. 1983. *Selected Works of John Calvin: Tracts and Letters,* Vols 4–7: Parts 1–2, trans. D. Constable, and Parts 3–4, trans. M. R. Gilchrist. Grand Rapids: Baker.

Blackwell, Albert. 1982. *Schleiermachers' Early Philosophy of Life: Determinism, Freedom and Phantasy.* Chico, CA: Scholars Press.

Bleeker, C. J. 1930. Het begrip "ontwikkeling" in de godsdienstgeschiedenis, 2–6. *Vox Theologica* (2:1).

———.1954. *International Bibliography of the History of Religions.* Leiden: Brill.

Bloesch, Donald G. 1991. "Lost in the Mystical," 22–24, *Christianity Today* (August 19).

Blosser, Philip. 1993. "Reconnoitering Dooyeweerds' Theory of Man," 192–209, in *Philosophia Reformata* (58).

Boa, Kenneth. 1977. *Cults, World Religions, and You.* Wheaton: S. P. Publications.

Bolt, John, ed. 1986. *Orthodoxy and Orthopraxis.* Jordan Station, ON: Paideia Press.

Boonstra, Harry. 1994. Liturgy and Worship in Dutch Reformed Churches. Unpublished paper. Grand Rapids: Calvin Theological Seminary.

Bos, A. P. 1979. Oude en nieuwe discussie over de waarde van het Platonisme, 16–45. *Philosophia Reformata (44:1).*

———.1983. Aristotle on myth and philosophy, 1–18. *Philosophia Reformata* (48:1).

———.1987. *Wetenschap en zinervaring.* Amsterdam: V.U. Uitgeverij.

Bosch, David J., 1991. *Transforming Mission: Paradigm Shifts in Theology of Mission,* in *The American Society of Missiology Series,* No. 16. Maryknoll, NY: Orbis Books.

Botha, Elaine M. 1971. *Socio-kulturele metavrae,* Amsterdam: Buijten and Schipperheijn.

Bowker, John W. 1973. *The Sense of God: Sociological, Anthropological and Psychological Approaches to the Origin of the Sense of God.* Oxford: Clarendon Press.

Boyd, Malcolm. 1965. *Are You Running with Me, Jesus?* New York: Avon Books.

Bratt, James D., ed. 1998. *Abraham Kuyper: A Centennial Reader.* Grand Rapids: Eerdmans.

———.2013. *Abraham Kuyper: Modern Calvinist, Christian Democrat.* Grand Rapids: Eerdmans.

Bratt, John H., ed. 1973. *The Heritage of John Calvin.* Grand Rapids: Eerdmans.

Breems, Bradley Gene. 1991. *I Tell Them We Are a Blessed People: An Analysis of "Ethnicity" by Way of a Canadian Dutch-Calvinist Community*. Ph.D. Thesis in Department of Anthropology and Sociology, University of British Columbia, Vancouver.

Breen, Quirinus. 1986. "Twofold Truth Theory in Melanchthon," 82–84 in *Christianity and Humanism*. Grand Rapids: Eerdmans.

Bremmer, R. H. 1961. *Herman Bavinck als dogmaticus*. Kampen: Kok.

Bril, K. A. 1986. *Westerse denkstructuren*. Amsterdam: V.U. Uitgeverij.

Bruegemann-Kruijff, A. Th. and G. eds. 1982. *Geloven en denken*. Amsterdam: Philosophical Institute, Free University.

Bryant, David J. 1989. *Faith and the Play of Imagination: On the Role of Imagination in Religion*. Macon, GA: Mercer University Press.

Bultmann, R. 1968. "Pistis," 175–182. *Theologisches Wörterbuch zum Neuen Testament*, VI.

Bürki, Hans. 1971. *Tussen geloof en skepsis. Een biographisch geesteshistorische studie*. Amsterdam: Buijten & Schipperheijn.

Burnham, Frederic B., ed., 1989. *Postmodern Theology: Christian Faith in a Pluralist World*. San Francisco: Harper.

Calvin, John. 1960. *Calvin: Institutes of the Christian Religion*. Translated and indexed by Ford Lewis Battles. The Library of Christian Classics, Vol. XX, ed., John T. McNeill. Philadelphia: Westminster Press.

Campbell, James I. 1971. *The Language of Religion*. New York: Bruce Publishing.

Capps, Donald. 1987. *Deadly Sins and Saving Virtues*. Philadelphia: Fortress Press.

Caputo, John D. 1993. "The Good News about Alterity: Derrida and Theology," 453–470, in *Faith and Philosophy* (10:4).

Carter, Stephen L. 1993. *The Culture of Disbelief. How American Law and Politics Trialize Religious Devotion*. New York: Basic Books.

Chapko, John J. 1985. *Faith in Search of a Focus: An Internal Critique of the Faith Development Theory of James Fowler*. Institute for Christian Studies, Toronto.

Chapman, Colin. 1990. "The Riddle of Religions," 16–22, in *Christianity Today* (May 14).

Clapp, Rodney R. 1989. "The Ivory Tower Comes to the Windy City: In Chicago, scholars hunker down to have a look at God," 16–21. *Christianity Today*, April 7.

Clapper, Gregory S. 1987. The Practical Theology of John Wesley's Orthoaffectus. Paper at CMA Conference, Orange City, IA, September 17.

Clark, Gordon H. 1984. *In Defense of Theology*. Milford, MI: Mott. Media, Inc.

Clark, Kelly James. 1990. *Return to Reason*, Grand Rapids: Eerdmans.

Clements, Keith. 1987. *Friedrich Schleiermacher: Pioneer of Modern Theology*. San Fransisco: Collins.

Cobble, James F., Jr. 1985. *Faith and Crisis in the Stages of Life: Adult Development and Christian Growth*. Peabody, MA: Hendrickson.

Cornford, Francis MacDonald. 1953. *The Republic of Plato*, IV. 434D–441C (pp. 129–138). Translation, Introduction and Notes. Oxford and London: Oxford University Press.

Crowe, F. E., S.J. 1967. *Collection: Papers by Bernard Lonergan, S.J.* New York: Herder & Herder.

———.1980. *The Lonergan Enterprise*, Cowley.

Curtis, Michael, ed. 1961. *Hugo Gratius, Great Political Theories*, Vol. I. New York: Avon Books.

Damasio, Antonio. 1994. *Descartes's Error: Emotion, Reason, and the Human Brain*. New York: Grosset-Putnam.

Davis, John J. 1968. *Biblical Numerology: A Basic Study of the Use of Numbers in the Bible*. Grand Rapids: Baker.

Dawn, Marva J. 1995. Reaching Out Without Dumbing Down: A Theology of Worship for This Urgent Time. Grand Rapids: Eerdmans.

De Boer, P. A. H., and P. S. J. van Koningsveld, eds. 1979. *Honderd Jaar "Uit Egypte..." Leidse opstellen over de scheiding tussen kerk en staat aan de openbare theologische faculteit*. Leiden: Brill.

De Boer, Theo. 1965. Wat is Fenomenologie?, 25–28. *Correspondentie Bladen van de vereniging vor calvinistische wijsbegeerte*, 29 (April).

―――.1976. *Tussen filosofie en profetie: De wijsbegeerte van Emmanuel Levinas*. Baarn: Ambo.

―――.1989. *De God van de filosofen en de God van Pascal: Op het grensgebied van filosofie en theologie*. The Hague: Meinema.

―――.1990. Godsverduistering en godsdienstfilosofie, 170–176. *Philosophia Reformata* (55:2).

―――.1992. Transcendentie en schepping, 159–168. *Philosophia Reformata* (57).

De Graaf, A. H. 1968. *The Educational Ministry of the Church*. Philadelphia: The Craig Press.

De Graaf, A. H., and C. Seerveld. 1968. *Understanding the Scriptures*. Lectures at Study Conference, for the Association for the Advancement of Christian Scholarship, Institute for Christian Studies, Toronto.

De Graaf, S. G. 1931. *De Heilige Schrift, het Koningkrijk Gods en de oorlog*.

―――.1940. *An Introduction to Christian Dogmatics*. Grand Rapids: Eerdmans.

―――.1940. De Antithese, 2–3. *Mededelingen* (August).

De Jong, G. W. 1971. *De theologie van dr. G. C. Berkouwer. Een structurele analyse*. Kampen: Kok.

De Jonge, A. L. Janse. 1960. Enkele vragen rondom religieuze projectie, 9–15. *Sola Fide* (XIII:6).

De Kruijff, H. W., G. Dekker, J. Tennekes. 1992. *Christelijke waarden in een geseculariseerde cultuur*. Amsterdam: V. U. Uitgeverij.

De Moor, Hendrikus. 1986. *Equipping the Saints: A Church Political Study of the Controversies Surrounding Ecclesiastical Office in the Christian Reformed Church in North America, 1857–1982*. Kampen.

De Moor, Johannes. 1980. *Towards a Biblically Theological Method: A Structural Analysis and a Further Elaboration of Dr. G. C. Berkouwer's Hermeneutic-Dogmatic Method*. Kampen: Kok.

De Vries, W. G. 1966. *Een en Anders. Correspondentie tussen K. Schilder en D. H. Th. Vollenhoven*. Kampen: Kok.

De Waal Malefyt, A. 1966. *Religion and Culture. An Introduction to Anthropology of Religion*. New York: Macmillan.

Dee, Simon P. 1918. *Het Geloofsbegrip van Calvijn*. Th.D. Thesis, Free University. Kampen: Kok.

Dekker, G. 1992. *De Stille Revolutie. De ontwikkeling van de Gereformeerde kerken in Nederland tussen 1950 en 1990*. Kampen: Kok.

Den Ottolander, P. 1962. Prof. Vollenhoven, neocalvinistische wijsgeer, 70 jaar, 179–182.

Dengerink, J. D. 1948. Critisch-historisch onderzoek naar de sociologische ontwikkeling van het beginsel der "souvereiniteit in eigen kring" in de 19e en 23e eeuw. Kampen: Kok.

———.1971. Philosophari in Christo. Over grond en doel van ons wijsgerig bezig zijn, 2–10. *Mededelingen* (March).

———.1989. Mens, Kosmos, Tijdelijkheid, Eeuwigheid n.a.v. W. J. Ouweneel: *De Leer van de mens*, 83–102. *Philosophia Reformata* (54).

———.1984. "Language and the Transformation of Philosophy," 134–149. *Philosophia Reformata* (49:2).

———.Dooyeweerd, Herman. 1939. Kuyper's wetenschapsleer, 193–232, *Philosophia Reformata*, no. 4, 1942. De leer van den mensch in de wijsbegeerte der wetsidee: Stellingen voor het referaat van prof. dr. Herman Dooyeweerd, (Theory of Man in the Philosophy of the Law Idea) *Correspondentie-Bladen van de vereniging voor calvinistische wijsbegeerte* (VII:5).

———.1950. De strijd om het schriftuurlijk karakter van de wijsbegeerte der wetsidee, 3–6. *Mededelingen* (July).

———.1958. De verhouding tussen wijsbegeerte en theologie en de strijd der faculteiten, 1–21 and 49–84, *Philosophia Reformata* (23:1–2).

———.1979a. "The Problem of the Relationship of Nature and Grace in the Calvinistic Law-Idea," 13–15, translated by A. Wolters. *Anakainosis* (1:4).

———.1979b. *Roots of Western Culture: Pagan, Secular and Christian Options*, Trans. John Kraay and eds. Mark Vander Vennen and Bernard Zylstra. Toronto: Wedge Publishing Foundation.

Dusha, Ronald, and Whelan Marriellen, 1975. *Moral Development. A Guide to Piaget and Kohlberg*. New York: Paulist Press.

Dykstra, Craig, and Sharon Parks, eds. 1986. *Faith Development and Fowler*. Birmingham: Religious Education Press.

Ebeling, Gerhard. 1978. *The Study of Theology*. Trans. Duane Triebe. Philadelphia: Fortress Press.

Edwards, James R. 1985. "Faith as Noun and Verb," 21–23. *Christianity Today* (August 9).

Eigenring, A. I. 1971. *Godsdienstpedagogische opgaven in de pre-puberteit. Invloeden van godsdienstpedagogische aktiviteiten op de ontwikkeling van gevoelens van vertrouwen en zekerheid in de overgangsfase tot de puberteit*. Th.D. thesis, Free University, Amsterdam. Delft: Meinema.

Eliade, Mircea. 1959. *The Sacred and the Profane: The Nature of Religion*. Trans. Willard R. Trask. New York: Harcourt, Brace & World, Inc.

———.1969. *Images and Symbols: Studies in Religious Symbolism*, Trans. Philip Mairet. New York: Sheed and Ward.

Enroth, Ronald M., and Gordon J. Melton. 1984. "Why Cults Succeed Where the Church Fails," 14–21, in *Christianity Today* (28:5).

Evans, C. Stephen. 1982. *Subjectivity and Religious Belief: An Historical, Critical Study*. Washington: University Press of America.

Evans, Gillan R., Alister E. McGrath, Allan D. Galloway. *The Science of Theology*. In *The History of Christian Theology*, vol. I, ed. Paul Davis. Grand Rapids: Eerdmans.

Fackenheim, Emil L. 1985. "Immanuel Kant." *Nineteenth Century Religious Thought in the West*, vol. I, ed. Ninian Smart a.o. 17–40. New York: Cambridge University Press.

Farley, Edward. 1966. *Requiem for a Lost Piety in the Contemporary Search for the Christian Life*. Philadelphia: Westminster Press.

———.1975. *Ecclesial Man: A Social Phenomenology of Faith and Reality*. Philadelphia; Fortress Press.

———.1982. *Ecclesial Reflection: An Anatomy of Theological Method*. Philadelphia: Fortress Press.

———.1983a. *Theologia: The Fragmentation and Unity of Theological Education*. Philadelphia: Fortress Press.

———.1983b. "Theology and Practice outside the Clerical Paradigm," in *Practical Theology: The Emerging Field in Theology, Church and World*, 2–24, Don S. Browning, ed. San Francisco: Harper & Row.

———.1988. *The Fragility of Knowledge: Theological Education in the Church and the University*. Philadelphia: Fortress Press.

Feisser, J. J. Louet. 1950. *De huidige verhouding tussen Theologie en Wijsbegeerte. Een bijdrage tot herorientering der universitaire wetenschap*. Amsterdam: Paris.

Fernhout, Harry, J. J. 1975. There is One; One in Three. A Study in the Development of the Doctrine of the Trinity in the Late Third and the Fourth Century. Unpublished paper. Institute for Christian Studies, Toronto.

———.1978/9. Man, faith, and religion in Bavinck, Kuyper, and Dooyeweerd. *Tijdskrif vir Christelike Wetenskap*, I, 1978 (14:3–4) 74–79; II, 1979 (15:1–2) 54–71; III, 1979 (15:1–4) 119–140. [Original: Masters in Philosophical Studies, Institute for Christian Studies, 1975, Toronto.]

———.1985a. "Autonomy as Ideal: The Philosophical and Anthropological Foundations of Kohlberg's Theory," in *Christian Approaches to Learning Theory*, Vol. 2, Norm De Jong, ed., Lanham, MD: University Press of America.

———.1985b. "Faith in Autonomy: Development in Kohlberg's Perspective on Religion and Morality," 1–21, in *Religious Education* (80:2).

———.1986. "Where Is Faith? Searching for the Core of the Cube," 65–89, in *Faith Development and Fowler*, Craig Dykstra and Sharon Parks, eds. Birmingham: Religious Education Press.

———.1987. "The Metaphor of 'Development' in Moral Education," 1–41, in *Norm and Context: Proceedings of the 1987 Conference on Normativity and Contextuality in the Social Sciences*, S. Griffioen and J. Verhoogt, eds. Amsterdam: Free University Press.

Ferre, Frederick. 1961. *Language, Logic and God*. New York, Evanston, London: Harper & Row.

Feuerbach, Ludwig. 1968. *The Essence of Faith According to Luther*. Trans. Melvin Cherno. New York, Evanston, London: Harper & Row.

Firet, J. 1968. *Het agogisch moment in het pastoraal optreden*. Kampen: J. H. Kok.

———.1983. Kan bidden geleerd worden?, 29–34. *S.S.R. Congress* in Lunteren (Oct. 7–8).

———.1986. De zin van de liturgie. *Het vieren van Gods aanwezigheid*. Openbaar college ter herdenking van dr. G. N. Lammers van 1969 tot 1981 buitengewoon hoogleraar in de liturgie wetenschap en het praktisch theologish gebruik van massacommunicatiemiddelen at the Free University Boekhandel.

Flower, Elizabeth, and Murray G. Murphey. 1977. *A History of Philosophy in America*, vols. I-II. New York: C.P. Putnam's Sons.

Flynn, Thomas R. 1993. "Partial Desacralized Spaces: The Religious Availability of Foucaults's Thought," 471–485, in *Faith and Philosophy* (10:4).

Foulkes, Irene W. 1979. "Prodiadis: A New Way of Doing Theological Education in Latin America," in *Ministerial Formation*. Program on Theologial Education of WCC, January.

Fowler, James W., Tobin W. Lovin, and others. 1980. *Trajectories in Faith: Life Stories of Malcolm X, Anne Hutchinson, Blaise Pascal, Ludwig Wittgenstein, & Dietrich Bonhoeffer*. Nashville: Abingdon.

Fowler, James W. 1981. *Stages of Faith: The Psychology of Human Development and the Quest for Meaning*. San Franscisco: Harper & Row.

———.1984. *Becoming Adult, Becoming Christian: Adult Development and Christan Faith*. San Francisco: Harper & Row.

Fowler, S. 1984. "The Persistent Dualism in Calvin's Thought," 339–352, in *Our Reformational Tradition: A Rich Heritage and Lasting Vocation*. Potchefstroom University for Christian Higher Education.

———.1986. The Role of Logic in the Epistemology of Jean Piaget. M.A. Thesis, Potchefstroom University for Christian Higher Education. Potchefstroom, South Africa.

Friedman, Maurice. 1983. "The Human Way: A Dialogical Approach to Religion and Human Experience," 67–77, in *Journal of the American Academy of Religion* (LI:1).

Geertsema, H. G. 1963. De Wijsbegeerte der Wetsidee en de pistische functie, 97–130. *Lucerna* (4:3).

———.1966. Enkele opmerkingen in verband met hermeneutiek,5–11. *Correspondentie Bladen* (30, May).

———.1967. Vragen naar aanleiding van de "De realiteit van het geloof," 3–5. *Correspondentie Bladen* (31, December).

———.1971. Sola Scriptura, 4–6 and 7–10. *Mededelingen* (June) and (December).

———.1980. *Van boven naar voren. Wijsgerige achtergronden en probleem van het theologisch denken over geschiedenis by Jürgen Moltmann*. Ph.D. Thesis, Free University, Amsterdam: Kampen: Kok.

———.1981, Gereformeerde Kerken, *God met ons...over de aard van het Schriftgezag...* Speciaal Kerkinformatie van de Gereformeerde Kerken in Nederland, Leusden.

———.1982. Subjectief en objectief. N.a.v. dr. H. M. Vroom, *De Scrift Alleen? 78–90. Philosophia Reformata* (47).

———.1985. *Horen en zien. Bouwstenen voor een kentheorie*. Inaugural as special lecturer of Reformational Philosophy at the University of Groningen in the Central Interfaculty and Department of Literature. Published at the Free University.

————.1987. Higher education as service to the king, 54–78: *Critique and Challenge of Christian Higher Education*. Proceedings of international conference of the International Council for the Promotion of Christian Higher Education. Published by Kok in Kampen.

————.1988. Relationele waarheidsopvatting en Schriftgezag, 130–150. *Theologia Reformata* (XXXI:2).

————.Kan een wetenschap(per) zich bekeren? Het perspectief voor wetenschap en samenleving in het denken van Jürgen Habermas en Herman Dooyeweerd. Inaugural lecture in the Dooyeweerd Chair in Philosophy at the Free University Press.

————.1991. Contigentie als uitgangspunt. Het denken van Richard Rorty, 35–61. *Philosophia Reformata* (56:1).

————.1992a. Ik geloof in God, de vader, de almachtige, schepper van de hemel en van de aarde, 132–158. *Philosophia Reformata* (57).

————.1992b. *Het menselijk karakter van ons kennen*. Amsterdam: Buyten & Schipperheijn.

————.1993a (Christian) Faith and Science: Human Responsibility before the Face of God. Lecture, 1992, at the Pascal Centre for Advanced Studies in Faith and Science, Redeemer University College, Ancaster, Canada.

————.1993b. Alles is van beneden, maar beneden is ook niet alles. *Kuitert onder Kritiek* (wijsgerige en theologische reacties op dr. H. M. Kuitert's *Het algemeen betwijfeld christelijk geloof*). Amsterdam: Buyten & Schipperheijn.

————.1993c. "Homo Respondens: On the Historical Nature of Human Reason," 120–152, in *Philosophia Reformata* (58).

Gilkey, Langdon B. 1979a. *Message and Existence: An Introduction to Christian Theology*. New York: Seabury Press.

————.1979b. AAR and Anxiety of our Non-Being: An Analysis of our Modern Culture. Presidential speech delivered at the American Academy of Religion, November 1979.

Gilson, Etienne. 1962. *The Philosopher and Theology*. Trans. Cecile Gilson. New York: Random House.

————.1969. *God and Philosophy*. New Haven/London: Yale University Press.

Goldman, Ronald. 1968. *Religious Thinking from Childhood to Adolescence*. New York: Seabury Press.

G. Gort, H. Vroom, H. R. Fernhout and A. Wessels, eds. 1989. *Dialogue and Syncretism: An Interdisciplinary Approach*. Grand Rapids/Amsterdam: Eerdmans/Editions Rodopi.

Gravestein, A. 1963. Psychologie en geloof in wederzijdse confrontatie, 16–19. *Sola Fide* (XVII:1).

Green, Garret, ed. 1987. *Scriptural Authority and Narrative Interpretation*. Philadelphia: The Fortress Press.

————.1989. *Imaging God: Theology and Religious Imagination*. San Francisco: Harper & Row.

Greidanus, Sidney. 1982. "The Use of the Bible in Christian Scholarship," 138–147, in *Christian Scholar's Review* (XI:2).

———.1988. *The Modern Preacher and the Ancient Text. Interpreting and Preaching Biblical Literature.* Grand Rapids: Eerdmans.

Grenz, Stanley J. 1991. "Pannenberg and Evangelical Theology: Symphony and Caution," 272–285, in *Christian Scholar's Review* (XX:3).

Griffioen, S. 1982, Vooroordeel in de wetenschap, 50–68, *Radix* 8.

———.1994. Alice had gelijk: je kunt met zin niet alles doen, 23–25. *Beweging* (58:2).

Griffiths, Robert B. 1980. "Is Theology a Science?," 169–173, in *Journal of the American Scientific Association* (32:3).

Grotius, H. 1925. *The Law of War and Peace.* Indianapolis: The Bobbs-Merill Company.

Gutting, Gary, ed. 1980. *Paradigm and Revolutions: appraisals and applications of Thomas Kuhn's philosophy of science.* University of Notre Dame and Press.

Gutting, Gary. 1982. *Religious Belief and Religious Skepticism.* University of Notre Dame and Press.

———.1989. *Michel Foucault's Archeology of Scientific Reason.* Cambridge, New York: Cambridge University Press.

Haan, R. L. 1982. Gemeente-zijn in Latijns-Amerika, 33–51. *Reunisten Organisatie van SSR* (March).

Halkes, Catharine J. M. 1989. Feminisme als cultuurkritiek, en feministische theologie als religiekritiek, 4–25. *Reunisten Organisatie van SSR* (February).

Hardy, Lee. 1979. "*Angst* and Autonomy: Fundamental Ontology and the Idea of Rigorous Science," 9–13 in *Anakainosis* (2:2).

Harskamp, Anton van, editor, 1993. *Om de toekomst van een traditie: opstellen over geloofsoverdracht.* Kampen: Kok.

Hart, D. G., and R. Albert Mohler, eds., 1996. *Theological Education in the Evangelical Tradition.* Grand Rapids: Baker Book House.

Hartvelt, G. P. 1962. Over de methode der dogmatiek in de eeuw der Reformatie. Bijdrage tot de geschiedenis van de gereformeerde theologie, 97–149. *Gereformeerd Theologisch Tijdschrift* (62:4–6).

Harvey, Van A. 1979, "The Dilemma of the Unbelieving Theologian" (unpublished paper of American Academy of Religion, 1–9.

Helleman, W. E. 1991. Review of *In de greep van de Titanen: Inleiding tot een hoofdstroming van de Griekse filosofie* by A. P. Bos, 191–194. *Philosophia Reformata* (56:2).

Henderson, Robert W. 1959. The Doctoral Ministry in the Reformed Churches. Th.D. Thesis at Harvard University.

———.1962. *The Teaching Office in the Reformed Tradition: A History of Doctoral Ministry.* Philadelphia: Westminster Press.

Henderson, Roger D. 1992. "How Abraham Kuyper Became a Kuyperian," 22–35, in *Christian Scholar's Review* (XXII:1).

———.1994. *Illuminating Law: The Construction of Herman Dooyeweerd's Philosophy 1918–1928.* Ph.D. thesis at Free University in Amsterdam.

Heslam, Peter. S. 1998. *Creating a Christian Worldview: Abraham Kuyper's Lectures on Calvinism.* Grand Rapids: Eerdmans.

Hesselink, I. John. 1983. "Misunderstanding Five: Reformed Theology Is Rationalistic and Scholastic in Its Approach, 31–38, in *On Being Reformed: Distinctive Characteristics and Common Misunderstandings.* Ann Arbor.

Hexham, Irving. 1983. "Christian Politics according to Kuyper." *CRUX*, XIX:1 (March) 2–7.

Hick, John H. 1990. *An Interpretation of Religion: Philosophy of Religion,* 4th ed. Englewood Cliffs: Prentice Hall.

Hick, John, and Paul Knitter, eds. 1988. *The Myth of Christian Uniqueness: Towards a Pluralist Theology of Religion.* Maryknoll, NY: Orbis Books.

Hoekema, Anthony A. 1956a. "The Primacy of the Intellect: Greek or Christian?" 13–17, in *The Reformed Journal* (May).

———.1956b. "The Primacy of the Intellect: A Tenable Concept?" 15–16, in *The Reformed Journal.*

Holtrop, Phillip. 1977. "A Strange Language: Toward a Biblical Conception of Truth and a New Mood for Doing Reformed Theology," 9–13, in *The Reformed Journal* (February).

Honko, Laurie, ed. 1979. *Science of Religion: Studies in Methodology* (Reason and Religion: Method and Theory in the Study and Interpretation of Religion). The Hague: Mouton.

Hoogland, J. 1993. De terugkeer van het veelgodendom, 171–174. *Beweging* (57:4).

———.1993. Theologie en ervaring: 5 theses. Unpublished paper at Consultation, October 15, Nijkerk, the Netherlands.

———.1994. "Gelovend denken" 7–10. *Beweging* (58:1).

———.2000. "De Antithese," unpublished lecture, January 1, annual meeting of the Association for Reformational Philosophy, Amersfoort, The Netherlands.

Hordern, William. 1966. *New Directions in Theology Today.* Philadelphia: Westminster Press.

Horstman, Joey Earl. 1991. "Postmodern Christianity: Saussure, Derrida, and the Definition of God," 19–20, in *Perspectives* (October).

Janse, A. 1938. *Van idolen en schepselen.* Kampen: Kok.

Jelsma, Auke. 1984. *Fossielen of vruchten. Omgaan met het verleden van de kerk.* The Hague: Boekencentrum.

———.1988. *De vergeten kerk.* Kampen: Kok.

Johnson, Patricia Altenbernd, 1993. "Gadamer: Incarnation, finitude, and the Experience of Divine Infinitude, 539–552, in *Faith and Philosophy* (10:4).

Joldersma, Clarence W. 1983. Beliefs and the Scientific Enterprise: A Framework Model Based on Kuhn's Paradigms, Polanyi's Commitment Framework, and Radnitzky's Internal Steering Fields. M.A. Thesis. Toronto: Institute for Christian Studies.

Kantzer, Kenneth S. 1986. "Building Faith: How a Child Learns to Love God," 1–16. Report of Christianity Today Institute. *Christianity Today* (28:1).

Kaufman, Gordon D. 1975. *An Essay in Theological Method.* Missoula, MT: Scholars Press.

———.1981. *The Theological Imagination: Constructing the Concept of God.* Philadelphia: Westminster Press.

———.1985. *Theology for a Nuclear Age.* Philadelphia: Westminster Press.

Kelsey, David H. 1975. *The Uses of Scripture in Recent Theology*. Philadelphia: Fortress Press.

Kerr, Hugh T., and John M. Mulder, eds. 1983. *Conversions: The Christian Experience*. Grand Rapids: Eerdmans.

King, Lauren A. 1991. *The Way You Believe: Thoughts on the Nature of Faith*. Newberg, Oregon: The Barclay Press.

Klapwijk, Jacob. 1963. Ernst Troeltsch—Het historisme en zijn problemen, 14–23. *Correspondentie Bladen* (26 December) 12–24 and (27, April).

————.1970. Tussen Historisme en Relativisme. Een studie over de dynamiek van het historisime en de wijsgerige ontwikkelingsgang van Ernst Troeltsch, Ph.D. thesis at the Free University in Amsterdam, Te Assen Bij, Van Gorcum & Comp. N.V.

————.1975. Feuerbach en de nieuwere theologie, 211–220. *Radix* (1:4).

————.1980. Honderd Jaar Filosofie aan de Vrije Universiteit, 528–593. *Wetenschap en rekenschap, 1880–1980. Een eeuw wetenschapsbeoefening en wetenschapsbeschouwing aan de Vrije Universiteit*. Kampen: Kok.

————.1980. The Struggle for a Christian Philosphy: Another look at Dooyeweerd, 1–8. *The Reformed Journal*, (February-March).

————.1985a. "The Universal in Hans-George Gadamer's Hermeneutic Philosophy," in *Philosophia Reformata* (50:2).

————.1985b. "The universal in Hans-George Gadamer's Hermeneutic Philosophy, 119–129, in *Philosophia Reformata* (50:2).

————.1987a. Kritische Studie: Ernst Troeltsch en de eenheid van de geschiedenis, 73–82. *Philosophia Reformata* (43:1–2).

————.1987b. *Kijken naar kopstukken*. Amsterdam: Buyten & Schipperheijn.

————.1987c. "Reformational Philosophy on the Boundary between the Past and the Future," 101–134, in *Philosophia Reformata* (52:2).

————.1990. *Filosofische Kritik und götliche Offenbarung. Über Religionskritik im modernen Denken*. Riehen, Schweiz: Immanuel Verlag.

Klapwijk, J., S. Griffioen, and D. Groenewoud, eds. 1976. *Vrede met de rede? Over het vraagstuk van rede en religie, van autonomie en heil*. Assen/Amsterdam: Van Gorcum.

Klooster, Fred H. 1952. "Symbol and Myth in Contemporary Theology." S.T.M. Thesis, Union Theological Seminary, New York.

————.1963. The Adjective "Systematic Theology" Inaugural Address. Grand Rapids: Calvin Theological Seminary.

————.1974. "Toward a Reformed Hermeneutic," 1–12, in *Theological Bulletin of the Reformed Ecumenical Synod* (2:1).

————.1976. "Historical Method and the Resurrection in Pannenberg's Theology," 5–33, in *Calvin Theological Journal* (II:1).

————.1979. "The Uniqueness of Reformed Theology: A Preliminary Attempt at Description, 1–21 and 34–39, in *RES Theological Bullletin* (6:3–4).

Knudsen, Robert D. 1952. "Symbol and Myth in Contemporary Theology, with special reference to the thought of Paul Tillich, Reinhold Niebuhr, and Nicolas Berdyaev." S.T.M. Thesis, Union Theological Seminary, New York.

————.1969. "What evangelicals Can Learn from Abraham Kuyper and Herman Bavinck as to Theological Methodology." Unpublished lecture at the 19th Annual meeting of Evangelical Theological Society, December 27–29, at the BIBLE College of Toronto.

————.1973. "Roots of the New Theology," in *Scripture and Confession: A Book about Confessions Old and New*, John H. Skilton, ed., 247–273. Philadelphia: Presb/Reformed Publishing.

————.1979a. Enkapsis, 4–5. *Anakainosis* (1:2).

————.1979b. Transcendental Method in Dooyeweerd, 2–8. *Anakainosis* (1:3).

Kobes, W. A. 1983. "Faith Development: A View of James W. Fowler's Theory," 24–34, in *Pro Rege* (XII:1).

Kok, John H. 1988. "Vollenhoven and Scriptural Philosophy," 101–142, in *Philosophia Reformata* (53:2).

König, Adrio. 1989. *The Eclipse of Christ in Eschatology*. Grand Rapids: Eerdmans.

Kraemer, H. 1959. *De Plaats van godsdienstwetenschap en godsdienstfenomenologie in de Theologische Faculteit*. Nijkerk: Callenbach.

Kranenborg, R. 1984. *Een nieuw licht op de kerk? Bijdragn van nieuwe religieuze bewegingen voor de kerk van vandaag*. The Hague: Boekencentrum.

————.1989. *Reincarnatie en christelijk geloof*. Kampen: Kok.

————.1993. Nieuwe religiositeit en veelgodendom, 68–70. *Beweging* (57:4).

Kraus, H. J. 1958. *The People of God in the Old Testament*. New York: Association.

Kromminga, D. H. 1948. *The Millennium in the Church*. Grand Rapids: Eerdmans.

Kromminga, John H. 1963. "Teaching Theology in an Era of Change." Inaugural address as president of Calvin Theological Seminary, Grand Rapids.

Kuiper, Roel, ed. 1993. *Kuitert onder Kritiek. Wijsgerige en theologische reacties op dr. H. M. Kuiters Het algemeen betwijfeld christelijk geloof*. Amsterdam: Buyten & Schipperheijn.

Kuipers, Roland A., and Janet Catherine Wesselius, eds. 2002. *Philosophy as Responsibility: A Celebration of Hart's Contribution to the Discipline*. Lanham/New York/Oxford: University Press of America.

Kuipers, Ronald A. 2002. *Critical Faith: Toward a Renewed Understanding of Religious Life and Its Public Accountability*. In *Currents of Encounter*. Studies on the Contact Between Christianity and Other Religions, Beliefs, and Cultures, volume 19, Fernhout, R., et al., eds. Amsterdam/New York: Rodopi.

Kuitert, H. M. 1962. *De mensvormgheid Gods. Een dogmatisch-hermeneutische studie over de anthropomorphismen van de Heilige Schrift*. Kampen: Kok.

————.1972a. *Om en Om. Een bundel theologie en geloofsbezinning*. Kampen: Kok.

————.1972b. Waarheid en verificatie in de dogmatiek, 97–130. *Rondom het Woord* (14:2).

————.1974. *Zonder geloof vaart niemand wel*. Baarn: Ten Have.

————.1977. *Wat heet geloven? Structuur en herkomst van de christelijke geloofsuitspraken*. Baarn: Ten Have.

————.1980. *In rapport met de tjd. 100 jaar theologie aan de Vrije Universiteit, 1880–1980*. Kampen: Kok.

————.1986. *Everything Is Politics but Politics Is Not Everything: A Theological Perspective on Faith and Politiccs*. Trans. John Bowden. Grand Rapids: Eerdmans.

————.1988a. *Filosofie van de theologie*. Leiden: Martinus Nijhoff.

————.1988b. De theologie van G. C. Berkouwer, 9–18. *Registers op de Dogmatische Studien van Dr. G. C. Berkouwer* by M. P. van der Marel. Kampen/Amsterdam: Kok/V.U. Uitgeverij.

————.1989. Autonomie: een lastige laatkomer in de ethiek. Een kapitteltje mensbeeld en moraal. Farewell lecture in Ethics and Introduction to Dogmatics in Department of Theology, November 30, 1989. Free University, Amsterdam.

————.1990. Kerk en theologie: onheelbare tweespalt? Over de innerlijke tegenspraak van een "kirchliche Dogmatik," 109–124. In *Cultuur als partner van de theologie, Festschrift for G.E. Meuleman.*

————.1992. *Het algemeen betwijfeld christelijk geloof. Een herziening.* Baarn: Ten Have.

Kuitert, H. M., J. Veenhof, and H. M. Vroom. *Cultuur als partner van de theologie. Opstellen over de relatie tussen cultuur, theologie en godsdienstwijsbegeerte, aangeboden aan Prof. dr. G. E. Meuleman.* Kampen: Kok.

Kuitert, H. M., and H. S. Versnel. 1993. *Het kan nog erger.* Baarn: Ten Have.

Küng, Hans. 1976. *On Being a Christian.* Trans. Edward Quinn. New York: Wallaby.

Küng, H., A. van Harskamp, B. Musschenga, and W. B. Drees. 1990. *Godsdienst op een keerpunt.* Woord vooraf: Hans Tennekes. Kampen: Kok Agora.

Kuyper, Abraham. 1873–1886. *Uit het woord. Stichtelijke Bijbelstudieën,* Vols 1-VI. Amsterdam: Kruyt.

————.1890. Is er aan de Publieke Universiteit ten onzent plaats voor een Faculteit der Theologie? Pamphlet. Amsterdam: Wormser.

————.1899. *Band aan het woord. Antwoord op de vraag: Hoe is eene Universiteit aan het Woord van God te binden?* Public lecture given at a meeting in Middelberg on June 28, 1899 (translated by C. Veenstra in 1965: *Bound to the Word. Answer to the question: How is a University to be bound by the Word of God?*).

————.1901. *Drie kleine vossen.* Kampen: Kok.

————.1902–1904. *De Gemeene Gratie,* Vols I-III. Amsterdam: Höveker & Wormser.

————.1910. *Dictaten Dogmatiek,* Vols I-V. Recorded by students. Vol. II: "Locus de Sacra Scriptura, Creatione, Creaturis," Section C "Locus de Homine," 1–133. Kampen: Kok.

————.1911–1912. *Pro Rege. Het koningschap van Christus,* Vols I-III. Kampen: Kok.

————.1941. *The Work of the Holy Spirit.* Grand Rapids: Eerdmans.

————.1950. *Christianity and the Class Struggle.* Grand Rapids: Piet Hein.

————.1954. *Principles of Sacred Theology.* Trans. J. Hendrik De Vries and introd. Benjamin B. Warfield. Grand Rapids: Eerdmans.

————.1965. *Principles of Sacred Theology.* Grand Rapids: Eerdmans.

————.1970. *Lectures on Calvinism.* Grand Rapids: Eerdmans.

————.1998. *A Centennial Reader,* Grand Rapids. Eerdmans.

Ladd, George E. A. 1974. *Theology of the New Testament.* Grand Rapids: Eerdmans.

Langer, Susanne K. 1951. *Philosophy in a New Key.* Cambridge: Harvard University Press.

Laurie, S. S. 1972. *J. A. Comenius.* New York: Burt Frankling Reprints.

Lindbeck, George A.,1984. *The Nature of Doctrine: Religion and Theology in a Postliberal Age.* Philadelphia: Westminster Press.

Lints, Richard. 1992. "Two Theologies or One? Warfield and Vos on the Nature of Theology," 235–253, in *Westminster Theological Journal* (54).

————.1993. *The Fabric of Theology: A Prolegomenon to Evangelical Theology*. Grand Rapids: Eerdmans.

Loder, James E. 1989. *The Transforming Moment: Understanding Convictional Experiences*. Colorado Springs: Helmers & Howard.

Lugo, Luis E., ed. 2000. *Religion, Pluralism, and Public Life: Abraham Kuyper's Legacy for the Twenty-First Century*. Grand Rapids: Eerdmans.

Maddox, Randy L. 1984. *Toward an Ecumenical Fundamental Theology*. American Academy of Religion Series 47. Chico, CA: Scholars Press.

Maier, Gerhardt. 1977. *The End of the Historical-Critical Method*. St. Louis: Concordia.

Mann, Thomas. 1944. *Joseph the Provider*. New York: Knopf.

Maris, J. W. 1992. *Geloof en ervaring. Van Wesley tot de Pinksterbeweging*. Leiden: J. J. Groen en Zoon.

Marlet, M. F. J., S.J. 1992. *Welke God? Godsdienstwijsbegeerte in een theologische faculteit*. Afscheidscollege.

Marsden, George M. 1982. *Fundamentalism and American Culture: The Shaping of Twentieth Century Evangelicalism, 1870–1925*. Oxford University Press.

————.1997. *The Outrageous Idea of Christian Scholarship*. Oxford University Press.

Marsden, George, and Frank Roberts, eds. 1975. *A Christian View of History?* Grand Rapids: Eerdmans.

Maurice, M. A., and S. J. Noorda, eds. 1991. *De onzekere zekerheid des geloofs. Beschouwingen in het spanningsveld van geloven en denken*. Zoetermeer: Meinema.

McGoldrick, James E. 2000. *God's Renaissance Man: Abraham Kuyper*. Auburn, MA: Evangelical Press.

McIntire, C. T., ed. 1985. *The Legacy of Herman Dooyeweerd: Reflections on Critical Philosophy in the Christian Tradition*. Lanham/New York/London: University Press of America.

McKeon, R. 1973. *Introduction to Aristotle*. Chicago: University of Chicago Press.

McKim, Donald K. 1987. "Hermeneutics Today," 10–15, in *The Reformed Journal* (37:3).

————.1988. *Theological Turning Points. Major Issues in Chrisitan Thought*. Philadelphia: John Knox Press.

————.ed. 1992. *Major Themes in the Reformed Tradition*. Grand Rapids: Eerdmans.

Mekkes, J. A. P. 1949. Transcendentale critiek van het denken, 2–3. *Mededelingen* (November).

————.1952. Westeren ordinantien, 5–7. *Correspondentie Bladen* (16, May).

————.1961. Filosofie en religie, 81–91. *Philosophia Reformata* (26:1–3).

————.1965. God's Woord in de wetenschapsbeoefening, 2–16. *Lucerna* (6:1).

————.1967. Over schema's en misverstanden, 11–14. *Mededelingen* (March).

————.1970. De wijsgerige vraag over theologie, 5–8. *Mededelingen* (June).

Meuleman, G. E. 1965. De correlatie van geloof en openbaring by G. C. Berkouwer, 209–216. *Gereformeerd Theologisch Tijdschrift* (65, November).

Meyer, Hugo, A. 1986. *The Theology of Bernard Lonergan*. Atlanta: Scholars Press.

Minear, Paul S. 1960. *Images of the Church in the New Testament*. Philadelphia: Westminster Press.

Mol, Hans J. 1976. *The Identity and the Sacred: A Sketch for a New Social-Scientific Theory of Religion*. New York: Free Press.

————.1983. *Meaning and Place: An Introduction to the Social-Scientific Study of Religion*. New York: Pilgrim Press.

Mondin, Battista, S.J. 1963. *The Principle of Analogy in Protestant and Catholic Theology*. The Hague: Martinus Nijhoff.

Montsma, J. A. 1985. *De exterritoriale openbaring. De Openbaringsopvatting achter de fundamentalistische Schriftbeschouwing*. Amsterdam: Rodopi.

Mouw, Richard J. 1984. *When the Kings Come Marching In*. Grand Rapids: Eerdmans.

————.1998. "Abraham Kuyper: A Man for this Season." The surprisingly relevant advice of the Dutch statesman for engaging modern culture. In *Christianity Today* (October 26) 86–87.

Mouw, Richard J., and Griffioen, Sander, 1993. *Pluralisms and Horizons. An Essay in Christian Public Philosophy*, Grand Rapids, Eerdmans.

Mulder, D. C. 1965. *Theologie en godsdienstwetenschap*, The Hague.

————.1971. Het einde van de religie? 294–304. *Rondom het Woord* (13:3).

————.1973a. Mogelijkheden en grenzen van een fenomenologie der religie, 30–40. *Gereformeerd Theologische Tijdschrift* (February).

————.1973b. *Religie, religies, religiositeit*. Kampen: Kok.

————.1977. *Ontmoetingen van gelovigen*. Baarn: Ten Have.

————.1985. *Alle geloven op een kussen? Over de relieuze basis voor de interreligieuze dia n* Farewell lecture in history and phenomenology of non-christian religions in the Theology Department at the Free University. Amsterdam.

Muller, Richard A. 1991. *The Study of Theology*, From Biblical Interpretation to Contemporary Formulation. Grand Rapids: Zondervan.

Muller, Richard A. 1991. *The Study of Theology. From biblical interpretation to contemporary formulation*. Grand Rapids: Zondervan.

————.1993. *Post-Reformation Reformed Dogmatics, Vol. 2—Holy Scripture: The Cognitive Foundation of Theology*. Grand Rapids: Baker.

Murray, Robert. 1992. *The Cosmic Covenant: biblical themes of justice, peace and the integrity of creation*. A Heythrop Monograph. London: Sheed & Ward.

Myers, David G. 1978. *The Human Puzzle. Psychological Research and Christian Belief*. New York: Harper & Row.

Neusner, Jacob. 1979. Stranger at Home: The Task of Religious Studies, 11–10. Inaugural Lecture in the Department of Religious Studies, Arizona State University, October 25.

Newbigin, Lesslie. 1989. Religious Pluralism and the Uniqueness of Jesus Christ, 50–54. *International Bulletin of Missionary Research* (13:2).

————.1989. *The Gospel in a Pluralist Society*. Grand Rapids/Geneva: Eerdmans/WCC.

Noll, Mark A./Wells, David F, 1988. *Christian Faith & Practice in the Modern World, Theology from an Evangelical Point of View*. Grand Rapids: Eerdmans.

Norden, Rudolph F. 1985. *Symbols & Their Meaning*. St. Louis: Concordia Publishing House.

Nouwen, Henri J. M. 1975. *Reaching Out. The Three Movements of the Spiritual Life.* Garden City, NY: Doubleday.

Novak, Michael. 1978. *Ascent of the Mountain, Flight of the Dove. An Invitation to Religious Studies.* New York: Harper & Row (revised).

Nygren, Anders. 1972. *Meaning and Method in Philosophy of Religion: Prolegomena to a Scientific Philosophy of Religion and a Scientific Theology,* translated by Philip Watson. Philadelphia: Fortress Press.

Oberman, Heiko A. 1983. *Luther—mens tussen God en duivel.*

————.1988. *De erfenis van Calvijn—grootheid en grenzen.* Kampen.

Olthuis, James H. 1979. Towards a Certitudinal Hermeneutic, 65–85. *Hearing and Doing. Philosophical Essays Dedicated to H. Evan Runner,* John Kraay and Anthony Tol, eds. Toronto: Wedge Publishing Foundation.

————.1985. Dooyeweerd on Religion and Faith, 21–40. *The Legacy of Herman Dooyeweerd. Reflections on critical philosophy in the Christian tradition,* ed. C. T. McIntire. Lanham/New York/London: University Press of America.

————.1987. *A Hermeneutic of Ultimacy: Peril or Promise?* Lanham/New York/London: University Press of America.

————.1992. Be(com)ing, Humankind as Gift and Call, 153–172. *Philosophia Reformata* (58).

Olthuis, John A. and 1970. *Out of Concern for the Church.* Toronto: Wedge Publishing Foundation.

Osterhaven, Eugene. 1982. *The Faith of the Church.* Grand Rapids: Eerdmans.

Ouweneel, W. J. 1986. *Christelijke transcendetale-anthropologie. Een sympathetisch-kritische studie van de wijsgeerige anthropologie van Herman Dooyeweerd.* Ph.D. Thesis, Free University. Amsterdam: Buijten & Schipperheijn.

————.1989a. De mens als religieus wezen. 44–46. *Philosophia Reformata* (54:2).

————.1989. Is het hart tijdelijk of niet-tijdelijk? 103–108. *Philosophia Reformata* (54:3).

————.1993b. Supratemporality in the trascendental anthropology of Herman Dooyeweerd, 210–220. *Philosophia Reformata* (58).

Palmer, Richard F. 1969. *Hermeneutics. Interpretation Theory in Schleiermacher, Dilthey, Heidegger, and Gadamer.* Evanston: Northwestern University Press.

Pannenberg, Wolfhart. 1970–1971. *Basic Questions in Theology,* I-II. Trans. George H. Kehm. Philadelphia: Fortress Press.

————.1976. *Theology and Philosophy of Science.* Trans. Francis McDonagh. Philadelphia: Westminster Press.

————.1977. *Faith and Reality.* Trans. John Maxwell. Philadelphia: Westminster Press.

————.1988a. *Metaphysics and the Idea of God.* Trans. Philip Clayton. Grand Rapids: Eerdmans.

————.1988b. *Systematic Theology,* Vol. I. Trans. Geoffrey W. Bromiley. Grand Rapids: Eerdmans.

————.1991. *An Introduction to Systematic Theology.* Grand Rapids: Eerdmans.

Parker, P. H. L. 1975. John Calvin: A Biography. Philadelphia: Westminster Press.

Parks, Sharon. 1986. *The Critical Years. The Young Adult Search for a Faith to Live By.* San Francisco: Harper & Row.

Penelhum, Terrence, ed. 1984. *Faith*. New York: Macmillan.

Peterson, David. 1992. *Engaging God: A Biblical Theology of Worship*. Grand Rapids: Eerdmans.

Piaget, Jean. 1977. *Psychology and Epistemology. Towards a Theory of Knowledge*. Trans. Arnold Rosin. New York: Penguin Books. (1970).

Piet, John H. 1981. Two Ways of Doing Theology, 16–18. *Perspectives* (September).

Pinnock, Clark H. 1985 *Tracing the Maze. Finding our Way through Modern Theology from an Evangelical Perspective*. San Francisco: Harper & Row.

Plantinga, A and Wolterstorff, N, eds. 1983. *Faith and Rationality: Reason and Belief in God*. University of Notre Dame Press.

Popma, S. J. 1937. Enkele hoofdpunten bij Rudolf Otto, 107–111. *Correspondentie Bladen* (4, October).

————.1946. *De Plaats der Theologie*. Franeker: Wever.

————.*Correspondentie Bladen*: 1940. Wet en geloof, 69–72. 5, August.

————.1949. Theologie en wijsbegeerte, 23–25. 13 (February).

————.1950. De wijsheid Gods, 3–5; Het nut der wijsbegeerte, 5–7; De structuur van het geschapene, 7–9; Mythe, 9–11; Prof. Schilder's Critiek op de Calvinstische Wijsbegeerte, 30–35. 14 (May).

————.1951. Woordopenbaring en zijnsanalogie, 1–3; Schriftbeschouwing en Schriftprobleem, 23–29. 14 (January).

————.1952. Souvereiniteit in eigen kring, 7–9. 16 (May).

————.1955. De Plaats van de Theologie, 21–25. 19 (December).

————.1957. De verhouding van theologie en wijsbegeerte, 35–41. Opmerkingen n.a.v. een discussie, 41–43. 20 (June).

————.1957. Secularisatie en zichtbaarheid, 33–39. 21 (December).

————.1957. Diedrich Bonhoeffer, 40–44. 21 (December).

————.1958. De grondslagen der theologie, 24–27; Wetenschappelijke theologie, 27–30. 22 (April); Metaphysica, 13–17 and Ungegenstaendlich, 38–40. 22 (September); Threskeia, 1–4. 23 (December).

————.*Mededelingen*: 1949. Schriftgezag en wijsbegeerte, 1–2 (November) theologie, 1–4 (July).

————.1947/8. Wetenschappelijke philologie contra philosogische wetenschap, 149–179 and 1–25. *Philosophia Reformata* (12:1–2 and 13:1–2).

————.1956. *Inleiding in de wijsbegeerte*. Kampen: Kok.

————.1958. Iets over de theologie, 14–20, and Zondag 7, 155–170.

————.*Levensbeschouwing*, Vol. I. Amsterdam: Buijten & Schipperheijn.

————.1960a. Theologie en wijsbegeerte, 282–313. *Lucerna* (2:1).

————.1960b. Enige opmerkingen over het systematisch karakter van de theologische dogmatiek, 1–35. *Philosophia Reformata* (25:1–2).

————.1964. De mensvormingheid Gods, 7–12. *Sola Fide* (XVII:3).

————.1969. *De universiteit. Idee en praktijk*. Amsterdam: Buijten & Schipperheijn.

Potgieter, F. J. M. 1939. *Die verhouding tusssen die teologie en die filosofie by Calvyn*. Th.D. Thesis at Free University, Amsterdam.

Prediger, Steve. 1982. Truth and Knowledge in G. C. Berkouwer: The Contours of his

Epistemology. Unpublished paper in philosophical foundations. Toronto: Institute for Christian Studies.

Price, H. H. 1965. Some Considerations About Belief, 76–85. *Theory of Knowledge* by John W. Yolton. London: Collier Macmillan Canada Ltd.

Puchinger, G. 1980. *Ontmoetingen met theologen*. Zutphen: Terra.

————.1998. *Abraham Kuyper. His Early Journey of Faith*. Editor George Harinck and translater Simone Kennedy. Amsterdam: Free University Press.

Putnam, Hilary. 1981. *Reason, Truth, and History*. Cambridge, NY: Cambridge University Press.

Reardon, Barnard M. G. 1988. *Kant as Philosophical Theologian*. Totowa, NJ: Barnes & Noble.

Recker, Robert. 1980. *Introduction to African Traditional Religion* (Course 847). Grand Rapids: Calvin Theological Seminary.

————.ed. 1966. *Religious Thought in the Nineteenth Century*. Illustrated from writings of the period. London: Cambridge University Press.

Reformed Ecumenical Council. 1992. Hermeneutics and Ethics. Statement adopted by Reformed Ecumenical Council, Athens.

Regan, Tom, ed. 1986. *Animal Sacrifices. Religious Perspectives on the Use of Animals in Science*. Philadelphia: Temple University Press.

Reventlow, H. G. 1985. *The Authority of the Bible and the Rise of the Modern World*. Trans. J. Bowden. Phil.: Fortress Press.

Reynolds, Larry. 1983. Lawrence Kohlburg: Pursuing John Dewey's Vision, 2–13. *Pro Rege* (XII:1).

Ricoeur, Paul. 1987. *Hermeneutics and the Human Sciences. Essays on Language, Action and Interpretation*, ed., trans. and introd. John B. Thompson. London-New York-Paris: Cambridge University Press.

Ridderbos, Herman. 1962. *The Coming of the Kingdom*. Trans. H. de Jongste and ed. Raymond O. Zorn. Philadelphia: The Presbyterian and Reformed Publishing Company.

————.1968. Het liefdegebod en de "ordeningen," 4–6. *Mededelingen* (March).

————.1975. *Paul. An Outline of His Theology*. Trans. John Richard De Witt. Especially, "The New Life," "The New Man," "Faith as the Mode of Existence of the New Life" and "The Nature of Faith," 223–252. Grand Rapids: Eerdmans.

Rietkerk, W. G. 1993. *Ik wou dat ik kon geloven. Over psychische factoren die een belemmerng kunnen vormen voor het vertrouwen op God*. Kampen: Kok Voorhoeve.

Rock, Judith and Mealy, Norman. 1988. *Performer as Priest and Prophet. Restoring the Intuitive in Worship through Dance and Music*. San Francisco: Harper & Row.

Rogers, Jack B. and McKim, Donald K. 1979. *The Authority and Interpretation of the Bible. An Historical Approach*. San Francisco: Harper & Row.

Rooks, Charles Shelby. 1979. Theological Reflection in an Uncertain Age, 220–227. *Theology Today* (XXXVI: 2).

Rorty, Richard. 1979. *Philosophy and the Mirror of Nature*.

Ross, David. 1952. *The Works of Aristotle*, Vol. 12. Oxford: Clarendon Press.

Rothuizen, G. Theodoor. 1970. *Wat is Theologie? Bonhoeffers laatste woord tot zijn studenten*. Kampen: Kok.

Rowe, William. 1984. The Character and Structure of Myth, 1–9. *Anakainosis* (6:4).

———.1985. Society after the subject. Philosophy after the Worldview, 1–31. Unpublished lecture at Worldview and Social Science Conference. Grand Rapids: Calvin College.

Ray, Rusturn. 1992. An Appropriate God for a Technological Culture. Gross Memorial Lecture. Valparaiso, Indiana: Valparaiso University Press.

Rullmann, J. C. 1923, 1929, and 1940. *Kuyper Bibliographie,* Vols I-III (1860–1879; 1879–1890; and 1891–1932). Kampen: Kok.

Rümke, H. C. 1963 (19551). *Karakter en aanleg in verband met ongeloof.* Amsterdam: Ten Have.

Runia, D. T. 1989. Dooyeweerd, Bos and the *Groundmotief* of Greek Culture, 160–175. *Philosophia Reformata* (54:2).

Runia, K. 1972. Het criterium voor onze dogmatiek, 5. *Gereformeerd Weekblad* (20:41, Oct. 7).

———.1982. Op zoek naar de sleutel, 3–11. *Credo* (9:9, November).

———.1993. Küng en Kuitert. *Centraal Weekblad* (December, The Netherlands)

Runner, H. Evan. 1957. The Development of Calvinsim in North America on the Background of its Development in Europe, http://www.reformationalpublishingproject. com/

———.1976. 'Some observations on the condition of Calvin College at the celebration of its centennial' Prism 1976: 30–39

Sadler, J. E., ed. 1969. *Comenius.* London: McMillan Company.

———.1976. *Comenius and the Concept of Universal Education.* New York: Barnes and Noble.

Sauter, Gerard. 1971. *Theologie als Wissenschaft: Aufsätze und Thesen.* München: C. Kaiser

———.1993. Wissenschaftstheoretische Kritik der Theologie.

Scheiter, Robert, J.C.P.S.—Defining Syncretism: An Interim Report, 50–53. *International Bulletin of Missionary Research* (April).

Sayre, Patricia A. 1993. The dialectics of truth and suspicion, 567–584. *Faith and Philosophy* (10:4).

Scheltens, W. J. W. 1992. Geloven in God als schepper, 7–16. *Credo* (5, June).

Schilder, Aleid. 1987. *Hulpeloos maar schuldig. Het verband tussen een gereformeerde paradox en depressie.* Kampen: Kok.

Schilder, K. 1949. Zondag 7, 342–603. *Heidelbergsche Catechismus,* Vol. II. Goes: Oosterbaan en le Cointre.

Schipani, Daniel S. 1992. Theology in the Context of "A New World Order". Public lecture, Free University, October 7. Amsterdam: V.U. Boekhandel.

Schippers, K. A. 1983. De Predikant: identiteit-rol-taak, 18–39. *Gereformeerd Theologisch Tijdschrift* (83, February).

Schleiermacher, Friedrich. 1988. *Brief Outline of Theology as a Field of Study.* Trans. Terrence N. Tice. Lewiston: The Edwin Mellen Press.

Scholz Heinrich. 1971. Wie ist eine Evangelische Theologie als Wissenschaft möglich? 221–264, and Was ist unter einer Theologischer Aussage zu Verstehen?, 265–278. *Theologie als Wissenschaft* by G. Sauter. München: C. Kaiser Verlag.

Schrotenboer, Paul G. 1958. *Faith and its Problems.* Toronto: Pro Rege Publishing Co.

————.ed. 1984. Classical Confessions and Contemporary Testimony, 1–36. *REC Theological Forum* (XI:4).

————.1986. Inter-religious Dialogue, 1–12. *REC Mission Bulletin* (VI:1).

————.1988. The Many Varieties of Pluralism, 1–18. *REC Theological Forum* (XVI:4).

————.1992. *Catholicity and Secession: A Dilemma?* Kampen: Kok.

————.1993. The Bible and Myth, 1–12. *REC Theological Forum* (XXI:2).

Seerveld, Calvin. 1966. *Take Hold of God and Pull. Moments in a College Chapel.* Palos Heights, IL: Trinity Pennyasheet Press.

————.1968. *A Christian Critique of Art and Literature.* Lectures at Unionville and Banff Study Conferences of the Association for Reformed Scientific Studies, 1962 and 1963. Toronto: Association for Reformed Scientific Studies.

————.1982. Philosophy as schooled memory, 1–6. *Anakainosis* (5:1).

————.1991. Footprints in the Snow, 1–34. *Philosophia Reformata* (56:1).

————.1993. Approaching the Holy God. *Christian Courier*, Part I (March 5) 11–12; Part II (March 12) 10–11; Part III (March 19) 10.

Sell, Alan P. F. 1986. *Theology in Turmoil. The Roots, Course and Significance of the Conservative-Liberal Debate in Modern Theology.* Grand Rapids: Baker.

Sheler, Jeffrey L. 1990. From Evangelicalism to Orthodoxy. Religion: Growing numbers of churchgoers are turning to ancient ritual, 58–59. *U.S. News & World Report* (Jan. 15).

Sinnema, Donald. 1975a. The Uniqueness of Certitudinal Discourse, with Special Reference to the Language of Scripture. Unpublished paper for a course in Systematic Philosophy. Toronto: Institute for Christian Studies.

————.1979. *The Nature of Calvinist Scholasticism. A Collection of Evidence from Beza, Wollebius and Turretin.* Unpublished study *for Prof. Harry McSorley* at the University of Toronto.

————.1975b. Reflections on Theology at the University of Leyden before the Synod of Dort. M.A. Philosophical Foundations Thesis. Toronto: Institute for Christian Studies.

————.1986. Reformed Scholasticism and the Synod of Dort (1618–19), 467–506. *John Calvin's Institutes. His Opus Magnum*, Proceedings of the Second South African Congress for Calvin Research, July 31-August 3, 1984. Potchefstroom: Potchefstroom University for Christian Higher Education.

————.1990. Aristotle and Early Reformed Orthodoxy: Moments of Accommodation and Antithesis, 119–148. *Christianity and the Classics. The Acceptance of a Heritage*, Wendy Helleman, ed. Lanham, New York, London: University Press of America.

————.1994. Antoine De Chandieu's Call for a Scholastic Reformed Theology (1580), 159–190. Later Calvinism: International Perspectives, ed. W. Fred Graham. Sixteenth Century Essays & Studies 22. *Sixteenth Century Journal*. Kirksville, Missouri.

————.1999. The Distinction between Scholastic and Popular: Andreas Hyperius and Early Reformed Orthodoxy, 127–143. *Protestant Scholasticism: Essays in Reassessment*, Carl R. Trueman and R. Scott Clark, eds. Carlisle: Paternoster Press.

————.2002. Review of Willem Van Asselt and Eef Dekker, eds., *Reformation and Scholasticism: An Ecumenical Enterprise*, 157–160. *Calvin Theological Journal*, 37 (April).

Skillen, James W. 1974. Johannes Althusius, 191–217. *The Development of Calvinist Po-*

litical *Theory in the Netherlands with Special Reference to the Thought of Herman Dooyeweerd*. Ph.H. Thesis at Duke University. Ann Arbor: University Microfilms.

————.1988. Kuyper was on Time and ahead of his Time (an essay on religion as a way of life and societal differentiation). In *RES Theological Forum*, XVI:2 (June) 15–19.

————.1989. Theology, Philosophy, and the Christian Liberal Arts College, 241–251. *Christian Scholar's Review*.

Smart, Ninian. 1969. *The Religious Experience of Mankind*. New York: Scribner.

————.1970. *Philosophers and Religious Truth*. New York: Macmillan.

————.1983. *Worldviews. Crosscultural Explorations of Human Beliefs*. New York: Charles Scribner's Sons.

————.1985. *Nineteenth Century Religious Thought in the West*, Vols. 1–3.

————.1987. *Religion and the Western Mind*, Kobus, 1992 Dooyeweerd oor die hart, 159–190 and *Reformasie in Ootmoed*.

Smith, Wilfred Cantwell. C. 1978. *The Meaning and End of Religion* San Francisco: Harper & Row.

————.1979. *Faith and Belief*. Princeton: Princeton University Press.

————.1981. *Towards a World Theology. Faith and the Comparative History of Religion*. Philadelphia: Westminster Press.

Solivan, Samuel. 1990. Orthopathos: Interlocutor between Orthodoxy and Praxis, 19–25. In *Andover Newton Review*, 1 (Winter)

Sparks, Jack. 1977. *The Mind Bender. A Look at Current Cults*. Nashville/New York: Thomas Nelson Inc. Publishers.

Spiegler, Gerhard. 1967. *The Eternal Covenant. Schleiermacher's Experiment in Cultural Theology*. New York/Evanston/London: Harper & Rowe.

Spier, J. M. 1948. Wijsbegeerte en kerk, 25–39. *Wijsbegeerte en levenspraktijk. De beteknis van de wijsbegeerte der wetsidee voor veelerlei levensgebied*. Kampen: Kok.

————.1950–1951. Het veld van onderzoek voor de theologie, I, 169–178, and II, 1–15. *Philosophia Reformata* (15:4) and (16:1–2).

————.1951a. De norm voor ons geloven, 172–93. *Wetenschappelijke bijdragen door leerlingen van D. H.Th. Vollenhoven*. Franeker: Wever.

————.1951b. De huidige verhouding tussen theologie en wijsbegeerte, 29–35. *Correspondentie Bladen* (14, January).

Sprunger, Keith L. 1966. Ames, Ramus, and Method of Puritan Theology. *Harvard Theology Review*, 59:2 (April).

————.1972. *The Learned Doctor William Ames. Dutch Background of English and American Puritanism*. Chicago: University of Illinois Press.

Spykman, Gordon J. 1967. *Christian Faith in Focus*. Grand Rapids: Baker Book House.

————.1973. A Confessional Hermeneutic: alternative to the historical-critical method, 1–13. *RES Theological Bulletin* (I, December).

————.1976. *Pioneer Preacher: Albertus Christiaan Van Raalte. A Sudy of his sermon notes*. Grand Rapids: Heritage Hall Publications, No. 2. Calvin College and Seminary.

————.1992. *Reformational Theology. A New Paragigm for Doing Dogmatics*. Grand Rapids: Eerdmans.

Stackhouse, Max L. 1988. *Apologia. Contextualization. Globalization and Mission in Theological Education.* Grand Rapids: Eerdmans.

Stafleu, M. D. 1989. *De verborgen structuur. Wijsgerige beschouwingen over natuurlijke structuren en hun samenhang.* Amsterdam: Buijten & Schipperheijn.

———.1991. Being human in the cosmos, 101–131. *Philosophia Reformata* (56:2).

Stapleton, Michael. 1978. *The Illustrated Dictionary of Greek and Roman Mythology.* New York: Peter Bedrick Books.

Steen, Pete. 1964. Should Systematic Theologians Take a Vacation? *Stromata,* pages 5–7, December. Grand Rapids: Calvin Theological Seminary.

———.1965. Should Theology Go on a Vacation? 304. *Stromata* (February). Grand Rapids: Calvin Theological Seminary.

Stellingwerff, J. 1971. *Inleiding tot de Universiteit.* Amsterdam: Buijten & Schipperheijn.

———.1987a. *De Vrije Universiteit na Kuyper. De Vrije Universiteit van 1905 tot 1955, een halve eeuw geestes-geschiedenis van een civitas academica.* Kampen: Kok.

———.1987b. *Kuyper en de Vrije Universiteit.* Kampen: Kok.

———.1992. *D. H. Th. Vollenhoven (1892–1978). Reformator der Wijsbegeerte.* Baarn: Ten Have.

Stob, Henry. 1957. *The Christian Concept of Freedom.* Grand Rapids International Publications.

———.1981. *Theological Reflections.* Grand Rapids: Eerdmans.

———.2001. *Seeking Understanding,* The Stob Lectures, 1986–1998. Grand Rapids: Eerdmans.

Stoker, H. G. 1949. Is Teologie 'n Vakwetenskap? Pases 26–29. *Correspondentie Bladen* (13:1).

Stoker, W. 1980. *De christelijke godsdienst in de filosofie van de verlichting.* Assen: Van Gorcum.

Stokes, Kenneth, ed. 1983. *Faith Development in the Adult Life Cycle.* New York: W. H. Sadlier.

———.1987. *Faith Development in the Adult Life Cycle.* The Report of a Research Project, prepared for the Religious Education Association for the US and Canada and twenty-two partner organizations, sponsors of the project. Minneapolis.

Strauss, D. F. M. 1978. Woord en Wet—toegespits op die Problematiek van Biblicisme en Ontmitologisering, 95–111 and 159–178. *Tydskrif vir christelike wetenskap* (14:1–2).

———.1981a. Die Teoretiese Komponent in die Navorsingstaak, 79–97. *Tydskrif vir christelike wetenskap* (17:1–4).

———.1981b. Die Evolutionisme, 195–251. *Tydskrif vir christelike wetenskap* (17:1–4).

Stroh, Guy W. 1968. *American Philosophy from Edwards to Dewey: An Introduction.* Princeton, London, Toronto, Melbourne: Van Nostrand.

Swidler, Leonard, ed. 1987. *Toward a Universal Theology of Religion.* Maryknoll, NY: Orbis Books.

———.Tallon, Andrew. 1997. *Head and Heart: Affection, Cognition, Volition as Triune Consciousness.* New York: Fordham University Press.

Tennekes, J. 1986/7. Cultuurrelativisme in een multiculturele samenleving, 129–133. *Wijsgerig Perspectief* (27).

————.1992. Christelijk geloof en de logica van het sociale, 2–6. *In de Marge* (1:3).

————.1993. Geloofsoverdracht en religieuze ervaring: naar een nieuwe contextualisering van het christelijk geloof, 45–66. *Om de toekomst van een traditie: opstellen over geloofsoverdracht.* Kampen: Kok.

Thiselton, Anthony C. 1980. *Two Horizons. New Testament Hermeneutics and Philosophical Description.* Eerdmans.

Tieleman, Dick. 1984. *De dienst van de erk in de wereld van het hoger onderwijs.* Amsterdam: V.U. Uitgeverij.

Tillich, Paul. 1963. *Christianity and the Encounter of the World Religions.* New York/London: Columbia University Press.

Tol, Anthony. 1981. Vollenhoven, Dooyeweerd and Law, 8–10. *Anakainosis* (3:4).

————.1997. Syllabus Filosofie van de 20e eeuw, behorende bij de cursus Hedendaagse Stromingen in de Wijsbegeerte. Unpublished manuscript. Amsterdam: Free University.

Tol, A and Bril, K. A. 1992. *Vollenhoven als wijsgeer. Inleidingen en teksen.* Amsterdam: Buijten & Schipperheijn.

Torrance, T. F. 1985. *Reality and Scientific Knowledge.* Edinburgh: Scottish Academic Press.

Tracy, David. 1970. *The Achievement of Bernard Lonergan.* New York: Herder & Herder.

————.1975. *Blessed Rage for Order.* New York: Crossroad.

————.1981. *The Analogical Imagination: Christian Theology and the Culture of Pluralism.* NYork: Crossroads.

Troost, Gorden A. 1965. De eerste hoofdstukken van de Bijbel I, 2–4, II, 4–9, and III, 9–11. *Mededelingen* (April, June, December).

————.1969. De openbaring Gods en de maatschappelijke orde. Een kosmologisch en anthropologisch grondprobleem in een hedendaagse theologie der samenleving, 1–37. *Philosophia Reformata* (34:1–2).

————.1971. Bezinning over Koningkrijk Gods, 10–16. *Mededelingen* (September).

————.1976. *Geen andere macht begeren wij*

————.1977. *Theologie of filosofie? Een antwoord op "Kritische aantekeningen bij de wijsbegeerte der wetsidee," dr. J. Douma.* Kampen: Kok.

————.1978. De relatie tussen scheppingsopenbaring en woordopenbaring, 101–129. *Philosophia Reformata* (43:3–4).

————.1982/3. Theologische misverstanden inzake een reformatorische wijsbegeerte, I, 1–19, II, 179–192, and III, 19–49. *Philosophia Reformata* (47:1–2) and (48:1).

————.1989a. Kritiek van Dr. J. D. Dengerink op de Antropologie van H. Dooyeweerd, 65–82. *Philosophia Reformata* (54:1)

————.1989b. Rationalisme in de godsdienst, 414–415; Schriftgeloof, schriftbeschouwing en bijbeltheorie 431–432; van praktische schriftbeschouwing naar een theologie van de Schrift, 448–449; Theologie en de tween naturen van de Bijbel, 466–467. *Opbouw* (November 10 and 24, December 8 and 22).

————.1990. De Bijbel in de verschillende wetenschappen, 28–29; De Bijbel in de filosofie en in de theologie, 48–49. *Opbouw* (January 19 and February 2).

————.1992. Confessie en theologie, 66–67 (February 14); De vrouw en de theologie, 84–86,(February 28); Onderhoud van onze leesbril, 104–106 (March 13); Kritiek op art. 1 van de Nederlandse Geloogsbelijdenis, 147–149 (April 10); Hoe lezen of belijden wij art. 2 of the NGB, 200–201, 220–221(May 22 and June 5); Het nut van filosofie, 264–266 (July 3); Wat is scholastiek?, 284–286 (July 17); Scholastiek, een invalspoort voor secularisatie, 298–299 (July 31); Hoofdkenmerk van de scholastiek en een belangrijke bijkomstigheid, 341–343 (September 11); Over geloof en theologie, 375–377 (October 9); Begin van een noodzakelijke discussie, 391–393 (October 23); Geloofsdenken is geen theologie, 411–413 (November 6). *Opbouw*.

————.1993a: Theologie als de wetenschap van het geloofsleven en haar relaties met de filosofie. In *Reformasie in Ootmoed*, opstellen opgedragen aan Professor Pieter de Bruyn Kock, 144–158. Vereniging vir Hoer Onderwys, Studies No. 13. Potchefstroom.

————.1993b: Myth and Reason, 13–18. *Theological Forum* (XXI:2).

Tunderman, J. W. 1930. Het "object" der Theologie, 6–9. *Vox Theologica. Interacademic Theologisch Tijdschrift* (2:1).

Unger, Merril F. 1971. *Demons in the World Today. A Study of Occultism in the Light of Gods Word*. Wheaton: Tyndale House.

Valk, John. 1979. The Concept of *Coincidentia Oppositorum* in the Thought of Mircea Eliade. M.A. in Philosophical Foundations Thesis. Toronto: Institute for Christian Studies.

Van Baal, J. 1971. *Symbols for communication, an introduction to the anthropological study of religion*. Assen: Van Gorcum.

Van Buren, Paul M. 1963. *The Secular Meaning of the Gospel. Based on an Analysis of Its Language*. New York: Macmillan.

Van Dijk, M. P. 1966. *Naar een nieuwe vrijzinnigheid*. Franeker: Wever.

Van Dijk, W. K. 1955. Neurose en religie, 10–15. *Correspondentie Bladen* (December).

————.1962. Neurose en religie, 2–4. *Mededelingen* (December).

————.1968. Menselijke ontmaskwering en bijbels demasque. Over geloof en ongeloof bij Rümke (June) 10–11.

Van Dyk, John. 1985. Theology: Moulder of a Graven Image?, 3–5. *Issues—Association for Christian Scholarship in* Australia/New Zealand (February).

Van Dyke, Harry. 1988. Kuyper in Post-War Canada. An Interim Inventory. In *RES Theological Forum*, XVI:2 (June) 34–40

————.1989. *Groen van Prinsterer's Lectures on Unbelief and Revolution*. Ph.D. Thesis at the Free University in Amsterdam. Jordan Station, Ontario: Wedge Publishing Foundation [ISBN 0-88906-020-7].

————.2005. The Best of Comment (Fall 2005 | Volume 23, Issue 1), Cardus.ca

Van Es, J. J. 1976. Spreken over spreken over God, 162–171. *Gereformeerd Theologisch Tijdschrift* (August).

————.1979. *Spreken over God: letterlijk of figuurlijk? Analogie en metafoor in het spreken over God*. Th.D. Thesis at Free University. Amsterdam: Rodopi

Van Genderen, J. 1982. *Geloofskennis en geloofsverwachting*. Apeldoornse Studies. Kampen: Kok.

Van Gennep, F.O. 1989. *De terugkeer van de verloren Vader. Een theologisch essay over vaderschap en macht in cultuur en christendom*. Baarn: Ten Have.

Van Gerven, Hans and Mary Michon. 1981. *Vrijheid van Dwang. Een portret van H. M. Kuitert.* Baarn: Ten Have.

Van Hook, Jay M. 1977. Tillich on the Relation between Philosophy and Theology, 149–170. *Journal of the American Academy of Religion* (XLV:1).

————.1979. The problem of communication in Paul Tillich's philosophical theology, 87–102. *Communication and Spirituality* (4:1).

Van Huyssteen, J. W. V. 1970. *Teologie van die rede. Die funksie van die rasionele in de denke van Wolhart Pannenberg.* Th.D. Thesis at Free University. Kampen: Kok.

————.1981. Sistematiese Teologie en Wetenskapsteorie—die Vraag na Metodiesteoretiese Helderheid in die Teologie, 64–78. *Tydskrif vir christelike wetenskap* (17).

————.1989. *Theology and the Justification of Faith: Constructing Theories in Systematic Theology.* Trans. H. F. Snijders. Grand Rapids: Eerdmans.

Van Olst, E. H. 1991. Syllabus Filosofie voor studenten Psychologie en Pedagogiek. Amsterdam: Free University.

————.1992. Vieren als bestaanswijze van de mens, 14–23. *Het nodige overbodige*, Ad den Beste, ed. The Hague: Boeken Centrum.

————.1983. *Bijbel en liturgie. Een pleidooi voor het vieren.* Baarn: Ten Have.

————.1986. Het verhaal als uitnodiging tot menswording, 7–14. *Tijdschrift voor godsdienstige vorming in school en werk* (2:4).

————.1986. DE MENS: boetseersel tussen hemel en aarde—wijsgerige kanttekeningen bij het schema stof en geest, *Brein onder invloed* by P. Smelik, a.o. Kampen: Kok.

————.1987. Cultuurbeleid in christelijk perspectief. Unpublished speech given at opening of the Christelijke Hogeschool Windesheim, Zwolle, November 3.

————.1988. Abraham Joshua Heschel over viering en liturgie, 22–26; Abraham Joshua Heschel—Chassied en Geleerde, 49–55. *Werkschrift*.

————.1989a. De communicatie van het evangelie in een geseculariseerde wereld. Lecture for the Protestant Christelijke Vereniging van geestelijke verzorgers in ziekenhuizen..., September.

————.1989b. De betekenis van de liturgsche structuur van de avondmaalsviering voor een hedendaagse bijbel geinspireerde spiritualiteit. Unpublished speech given at the Theological University of Kampen.

————.1992a. Perspectieven van een christelijke spiritualiteit. Unpublished paper, October 31.

————.1992b. Godsdienstpsychologie: een noodzaak voor de Vrije Universiteit, 23–26. *In de Marge* (1:3).

Van Peursen, C. A. 1958. Schepping en lichamelijkheid. *Kerk en Theologie.*

————.1992. *De Naam die geschiedenis maakt. Het geheim van de bijbelse godsnamen.* Kampen: Kok.

————.1993. *De Verborgen Aanwezige.*

Van Riessen, H. 1966. Kiezen, 1–2. *Mededelingen* (December).

————.1967. De Bijbel, Gods Woord, 7–11. *Mededelingen* (March).

Van Teylingen, E. G. 1961. "Over terminologie in de theologie," regarding H. Berkhof's inaugural lecture in Leiden, 117–130, in *Gereformeerd Theologisch Tijdschrift* (61:4–5). Leiden), 117–130. *Gereformeerd Theologisch Tijdschrift* (6:4)

Van Woudenberg, Rene. 1991a. *J. H. Bavinck (1895-1964). Een keuze uit zijn werk.* Kampen: Kok.

———.1991b. *Transcendentle Reflecties. Een onderzoek naar transcendentale argumenten in de contemporaine filosofie, met bijzondere aandacht voor de transcendentale pragmatek van Karl-Oto Apel.* Ph.D. Thesis. Amsterdam: V.U. Uitgeverij.

———.1992. *Gelovend denken. Inleiding tot een christelijke filosofie.* Amsterdam/Kampen: Buijten & Schipperheijn/Kok.

———.1993a. *Filosofische gedachten over godsgeloof.* Kampen: Kok.

———.1993b. Is being human being rational? Otto Duintjer's critique of a philosophical tradition, 237–253. *Philosophia Reformata* (58:2)

Van Woudenberg, R. and S. Griffioen, H. G. Geertsema, eds. 1993b. *Filosofische reflecties en ontmoetingen. Opstellen van Dr. J. van der Hoeven.* Kampen: Kok Agora.

Van de Berk, A. 1982. *God kennen—met God leven. Een pleidooi voor een bevindelijk-pneumatologische fundering van kerk en theologie.* Inaugural lecture as professor in the Nederlands Hervormde Kerk at the State University of Leiden. Nijkerk: Callenbach.

Van de Velde, C., a.o. 1993. *Van werkelijkheid naar ideaal. Een praktisch boek over gemeente opbouw.* Kampen: Kok Voorhoeve.

Van den Berg van Eisinga, G.A. 1942. De waarheid van den godsdienst, 124–129. *Vox Theologica* (13:62).

Van den Beukel, A. 1990. *De dingen hebben hun geheim. Gedachten over natuurkunde, mens en God.* Baarn: Ten Have.

Van der Bruggen, J.J.G. 1986. *Verzekerde vrede or verzekerde vernietiging. Ontwikkeling van een theorie van gerechtvaardigde afschrikking.*

Vander Goot, Henry. 1979. The Modern Settlement: Religion and Culture in the Early Schleiermacher, 173–197. *Hearing and Doing. Philosophical Essays Dedicated to H. Evan Runner.* John Kraay and Anthony Tol, eds. Toronto: Wedge Publishing Foundation.

———.1984. *Interpreting the Bible in Theology and the Church.* New York/Toronto: Edwin Mellen Press.

Van der Graaf, J., W. J. Ouweneel, J. van Genderen, E. Schuurman. 1950. *Evolutie en geloof. Verleden en Toekomst.* Kampen: Kok.

Vander Hoeven, Johan. 1978. In memory of Herman Dooyeweerd: Meaning, Time and Law, 130–144. *Philosophia Reformata* (43:3–4).

———.1989. *Inademen. Oefeningen in Schriftlezen.* Baarn: Ten Have.

———.1990. Godsverduistering en godsdienstfilosofie, 152–169. *Philosophia Reformata* (55:2).

———.1991a. Vijf stellingen voor een conferentie: grondmotieven van onze beschaving (tevens hoofdlijnen van het betoog), 171–182. *Philosophia Reformata* (56:2).

———.1991b. Gadamer over "Vermittlung": De Hegeliaanse draad in zijn hermeneutiek, 81–94. *Philosophia Reformata* (56:1).

Van der Kooi, C. 1985. *De denkweg van de jonge Karl Barth. Een analyse van de ontwikkeling van zijn theologie in de jaren 1909-1927 in het licht van de vraag naar geloofsverantwoording.* Amsterdam: V.U. Uitgeverij.

Van der Leeuw, G. 1958 (19351). *Inleiding tot de theologie*. Amsterdam: Paris.
————.1978. *The Bible as Book*. St. Catherines, ON: Paideia Press.
Van der Merwe, N. T. 1982. Calvin, Augustine and Platonism. A Few Aspects of Calvin's Philosophical Background, 69–84. Calvinus Reformator. His Contribution to Theology, Church and Society. Potchefstroom: University for Christian Higher Education.
Van der Sar, H. G., ed. 1990. *Verslag Stegon-Symposium. Uitdagingen aan de theologie*. Stegon: Stichting theologisch en godsdienstwetenschappelijk onderzoek in Nederland. Kampen: Kok.
Vander Stelt, John C. 1973. Kuyper's Semi-mystical Conception, 178–190. In *The Idea of a Christian Philosophy. Essays in Honour of D. H. Th. Vollenhoven*. Introd. by H. Dooyeweerd. Toronto: Wedge Publishing Foundation.
————.1978. *Philosophy and Scripture: A Study in Old Princeton and Westminister Theology*. Marlton, NJ: Mack Publishing Company.
————.1979. Archibald Alxander: Inconsistent Empiricism and Theory of Scripture, 159–172. *Hearing and Doing. Essays Dedicated to H. Evan Runner* by John Kraay and Anthony Tol, eds. Toronto: Wedge Publishing Foundation.
————.1981. Theology or Pistology?, 115–135. *Building the House. Essays on Christian Education*, James A. De Jong and Louis Y Van Dyke, eds. Sioux Center: Dordt College Press.
————.1989. Theology as Study of Faith-Life, 15–23. *Pro Rege* (XVIII:1), Faculty Publication. Sioux Center, Iowa: Dordt College.
————.1990. Philosophical Assumptions in North American Presbyterian Theology, 9–19. *Pro Rege*, XVIII:4 (June). Faculty publication. Sioux Center: Dordt College.
————.1998. Faith-life and Theology, 71–84. In *Signposts of God's Liberating Kingdom: Perspectives for the 21 century*, Vol. 2. Potchefstroom: Institute for Reformational Studies.
Vandervelde, G. 1978. Definitive theses on the Analogy of Being. Unpublished paper. Toronto: Institute for Christan Studies.
————.1979. Theses on Analogia Entis, 3–5. *Anakainosis* (1:2).
————.ed. 1989. *The Holy Spirit. Renewing and Empowering Presence*. Winfield, British Columbia: Wood Lake Books.
Van der Walt, B. J. 1984a. *Man and Gods in Southern Africa; Religion, idolatry, church criticism, secularism, ideologies, 1–69*. Special edition of *Orientation*. International Circular of Potchefstroom University for Christian Higher Education, No.34.
————.1984b. The school that Calvin established in 1559 (in the light of the contemporary differentiation principle in education), 300–338. *Our Reformational Tradition*. Potchefstroom: University for Christian Higher Education.
Van der Walt, S. P. 1953. *Die Wysbegeerte van Dr. Herman Bavinck*. Ph.D. Thesis at University of South Africa. Potchefstroom: Pro Rege-Pers Beperk.
Vardy, Peter. 1990. *The Puzzle of God*. London: Harper Collins.
Veenhof, J. 1977. Natuur en Genade in Bavinck, 345–365. Revelatie en inspiratie: de openbarings—en schriftbeschouwing van Herman Bavinck in vergelijking met die der ethische theologie. Amsterdam: Buijten & Schipperheijn. Transl. by A. M. Wolters as *Veenhof on Grace and Nature in Bavinck*. Toronto: Institute for Christian Studies.

————.1980. Honderd Jaar Theologie aan de Vrije Universiteit. Wetenschap en reken-schap, 1880–1980, 44–104. *Een eeuw wetenschapsbeoefening en wetenschapsbeschou-wing aan de Vrije Universiteit.* Kampen: Kok.

————.1986. Heilige Geest en Hermeneutiek, 159–173. *Tussen openbaring en ervaring.* Opstellen aangeboden aan Prof. dr. G. P. Hartvelt. Kampen, Kok.

Velema, W., 1984. *Gebeden in de Bijbel.* Kampen: J. H. Kok.

Verburg, Marcel E., ed. 1986. *Herman Dooyeweerd. Grenzen van het theoretisch denken.* In *Geschiedenis van de wijsbegeerte in Nederland,* No. 20, M. J. Petry and J. Sperna Weiland, eds. Baarn: Ambo.

————.1989. *Herman Dooyeweerd. Leven en werk van een Nederlands christen-wijsgeer.* Baarn: Ten Have.

Verkuyl. J. 1989. *De New Age Beweging. Kenbegrippen, beoordeling, uitdaging.* Kampen: Kok.

Verplanke, C. J. 1963. *Subsidiering van de kerkenbouw.* Th.D. Thesis at Free University. Assen: Van Gorcum.

Visagie, P. J. 1978. Die Vraag na die Grondstruktuur. *Tydskrif vir Christelijke Wetenskap* (14:1–4).

————.1979. Humanistiese invloede in de teologie en die soeke na'n Bybelse Godsleer, 141–160. *Tydskrif vir Christelike Wetenskap* (15:3–4).

————.Dynamics of the Christian Religious Motive, 2–6. *Anakainosis* (4:1).

Vischer, Lukas, ed. 1982. *Reformed Witness Today. A Collection of Confessions and State-ments of Faith Issued by Reformed Churches.* Bern: 1982, Preface 7–9, 2.

Vitz, Paul C. 1980. *Psychology As Religion. The Cult of Self-Worship.* Grand Rapids: Eerdmans.

Vladimir, Jelinek. 1953. *The Analytic Didactic of Comenius.* Chicago: Chicago University Press.

Vlijm, J. M. 1981. *Geloofsmanieren: studies over pluraliteit in de kerk.* Kampen: Kok.

Voet, G. 1978. *De Pietate cum Scientia Coniungenda.* Edited by Aart de Groot.

Volbeda, S. 1915. Het wezen der religie. Inaugural at Calvin Theological Seminary. Grand Rapids/Kampen: Eerdmans/Kok.

Vollenhoven, Dirk H. Th. 1928. Unpublished letter of Vollenhoven to G. C. Berkouwer, in possession of A. Wolters (at Redeemer College/University), translated by John Vander Stelt, with the help of A. Tol (an expert on Vollenhoven distinct handwriting) at the Free University.

————.1932. *De noodzakelijkheid eener christelijke logica.* Amsterdam: H. J. Paris.

————.1933. *Het Calvinisme en de Reformatie van de wijsbegeerte.* Amsterdam: Paris.

————.1936a. De antithese, 5. *Mededelingen* (1:2).

————.1936b. Dogma en dogmatiek, 1–3; Zelfonderzoek bij Christenen, 7–9; Contra-Reformatie en Aufklärung. Het biblicism, speciaal van Bengel en Öttinger, *Corre-spondentie Bladen* (1:3) and (1:4).

————.1937. De nieuwe profetie. Het oude Montanism, 15–16; Bij het licht der Heilige Schrift, 7; Het Unitarism, 64–66; Philosophia Reformata, 95–97. *Correspondentieb-laden* (2:1), (2:2),(2:3), (2:4).

————.1938a. Immanentie-philosophie, 3–4; [Bijbelstudie re. L.Dürr's book], 36–39; Logos en ratio, 26. *Correspondentie—bladen* (3-1), (3-2), (3:5).

————.1938b. Objectief, 4–5. *Mededelingen* (May).

————.1939a. Positieve en negatieve theologie, 24–26; Exegese en interpretatie, *Correspondentiebladen* (4:5).

————.1939b. Karl Barth, 1–3. *Mededelingen* (4:1).

————.1942. De waarheid in de godsdienst-wijsbegeerte, 113–123. *Vox Theologica* (13:6).

————.1946. Calvinisme en Ontologie, 1–2. *Correspondentiebladen* (December).

————.1950. De souvereiniteit in eigen kring bij Kuyper en ons, 4–7. *Correspondentiebladen* (December).

————.1951. Norm en natuurwet, 3–6. *Correspondentiebladen* (July).

————.1953. Schriftgebruik en wijsbegeerte, 6–9, and Religie en geloof, 1–3. *Correspondentiebladen* (September and December).

————.1957. De wijsbegeerte van het evolutionisme 8–9. *Correspondentiebladen* (January).

————.1959. Getuigen in de wetenschap, 1–13. *Sola Fide* (XII:3).

————.1960. In memoriam Antheunis Janse, 1–2. *Correspondentie-bladen* (May).

————.1970. Historische achtergrond en toekomst, 2–3. *Correspon-dentiebladen* (December 1970).

————.2002. "Faith: Its Nature, Structure, and Significance for Science", *Vollenhoven Reader*, translated and introduced by John H. Kok. Sioux Center: Dordt College Press. [Original article Vollenhoven published in *Geloof en wetenschap: Levensbeschouwing and levenshouding van de academicus* in 1950. Utrecht-Nijmegen: Dekker & van de Vegt, N.V.]

Von Gierke, Otto F. 1966. The Development of Political Theory. New York: H. Fertig.

Vos, G. 1975 (1948). Introduction: The Nature and Method of Biblical Theology, 3–18. *Biblical Theology: Old and New Testaments*. Grand Rapids: Eerdmans.

Vriezen, T. C. 1954. *Hoofdlijnen der theologie van het Oude Testament*. Wageningen: Veenman.

————.1957. *Geloven en vertrouwen*. Nijkerk: C. F. Callenbach.

Vroom, H. M. 1978. *De Schrift alleen? Een vergelijkend onderzoek naar de toetsing van theologische uitspraken volgens de openbaringstheologische visie van Torrance en de hermeneutische-theologische opvattingen van Van Buren, Ebeling, Moltmann en Pannenberg*. Th.D. Thesis at the Free University. Kampen: Kok.

————.1980. Vast en zeker, 261–267. *In rapport me de tijd. 100 jaar theologie aan de Vrije Universiteit*. Kampen: Kok.

————.1981. Kennis in persoonlijke betrokkenheid. Een reaktie op de bespreking van *De Schrift alleen* door H. G. Geertsema, 66–73. *Philosophia Reformata* (48:1).

————.1989a. *Religions and the Truth. Philosophical Reflections and Perspectives*. In Series *Currents of Encounter: Studies on the Contrast between Christianity and Other Religions, Beliefs, and Culture*. Trans. J.W. Rebel. Grand Rapids: Eerdmans.

————.1989b. Inleiding in de theologie. Inleiding tot de studie der religie. Course 401 in Open Theologisch Onderwijs. Kampen: Kok.

———.1991. *De God van de filosofen en de God van de Bijbel. Het Christelijk Godsbeeld in discussie.* Zoetermeer: Meinema.

———.1993. Chicago 1993. The parliament of the world's religions, 114–120. *Studies in Interreligious Dialogue* (3). [Journal started in 1991 and edited by Arnulf Camps, Hendrik Vroom, Anton Wessels. Kampen: Kok Pharos.]

———.1997. Staatsvakken en kerkelijke vakken aan openbare unmiversiteiten, 210–231. *Skrif en Kerk*, 18:1.

Wallace, A. F. C. 1966. *Religion. An Anthropological View.* New York: Random House.

Walsh, Brian J. 1979. Futurity and Creation: Explorations in the Eschatological Theology of Wolfhart Pannenberg. M. A. Philosophical Foundations Thesis. Toronto: Institute for Christian Studies.

———.1982. Pannenberg's eschatological ontology, 229–249. *Christian Scholar's Review* (XI:3).

———.1986. A Critical Review of Pannenberg's *Anthropology in Theological Perspective*, 247–259. *Chr. Schol's Review* (XV).

Warfield, B. B. 1886. The Idea of Systematic Theology, 243–271. *Presbyterian and Reformed Review* (7). [Reprinted in 1932. *Studies in Theology*, 49–87. New York: Oxford University Press.]

———.1908. Herman Bavinck, 529–543. *Princeton Theological Review* (October).

Wells, David F. 1993. *No Place for Truth. Or, Whatever Happened to Evangelical Theology?* Grand Rapids: Eerdmans.

———.1991. *The Theologian's Craft* in Doing Theology in Today's World. ed. John D. Woodbridge and Thomas Edward McComiskey. Grand Rapids: Zondervan, pp. 171–194.

Wiles, Maurice. 1976. *What is Theology?* London: Oxford University Press.

World Council of Churches and Reformed Ecumenical Synod. 1975. *The nature of the church and the role of theology.* Papers from a consultation between WCC and RES, Geneva, in 1975. Geneva/Grand Rapids: WCC/RES.

Wells, David F., ed. 1985. *Reformed Theology in America. A History of its Modern Development.* Grand Rapids: Eerdmans.

———.ed. 1989. *Dutch Reformed Theology.* Grand Rapids: Baker.

———.19??. The Theologians Craft." Paper

Wiggins, James. 1979. The Department of Religion at Syracuse University, 107–110. *Bulletin of the Council of the Study of Religion* (10:4).

Wilcox, Mary M. 1979. *Developmental Journey. A Guide to the Development of Logical and Moral Reasoning and Social Perspective.* Nashville: Abingdon.

Wilson, John F. 1979. Recent Historical Studies in Western Religion, 105–107. *Bulletin of the Council on the Study of Religion* (10:4).

Wilson, John F. and Clark, W. Royce. 1989. *Religion. A Preface.* Englewood Cliffs, NJ: Prentice Hall.

Witsius, Herman, 1675. The Character of the genuine theologian, 158–170. Inaugural Oration, April 16, Franeker, 1675. Trans. Rev John Donaldson, Free Church, Ceres.

Wolters, A. 1980. The Centre and the Circumference, 2–6. *Vanguard* (10:2).

————.1979. What's in a Name?, 1–3; Theology and Philosophy, 1; Creation, 1. *Anakainosis* (1:2), (1:4) and (2:1).

————.1980. Worldview and Philosophy, 1–3 and 1–3. *Anakainosis* (3:1) and (3:2).

————.1982. Dooyeweerd commemorates Kuyper (1937), 9–13. *Anakainosis*. (5:1).

————.1983. Ground-motive, 1–4. *Anakainosis* (6:1).

————.1990. Was Aristotle committed to a cardinal tenet of Reformational philosophy?, 198–202. *Philosophia Reformata* (55:1).

Wolterstorff, N. 1969. On God Speaking, 7–11; How God Speaks 16–20; Canon and Criterion 10–15. *The Reformed Journal* (XIX:6–8).

————.1984 (19761). *Reason within the Bounds of Religion.* Grand Rapids: Eerdmans.

————.1989. Remember to remember, 11–14; Liturgy, Justice, and Holiness, 12–20. *The Reformed Journal* (XXXIX:9 and 12).

————.1988. The Project of a Christian University in a Postmodern Culture. Inaugural Lecture as professor of epistemology in the Philosophy Department at the Free University. Amsterdam: V.U. Boekhandel/Uitgeverij

Yandel, Keith. 1985. Can There Be a Science of Religion?, 28–41. *Christian Scholar's Review* (XV:1).

Zuidema, S. U. 1930. De Theologische Faculteit der Vrije Universiteit bij haar vijftig jarig bestaan, 13–16. *Vox Theologica* (2:1).

————.1950. *Van geloof tot geloof.* Franeker: Wever.

————.1951a. *Ons Gebed.* Franeker: Wever.

————.1951b. Heidegger's wijsbegeerte van het zijn, 222–243. *Dr. D. H. Th. Vollenhoven,* Franeker: Wever.

————.1964. Openbaringsinhoud en existentie in de theologische hermeneutiek van R. Bultmann. *Mededelingen* (December) 2–7.

————.1972. *Communication and Confrontation. A Philosophical Appraisal and Critique of Modern Society and Contemporary Thought.* Assen/Kampen: Van Gorcum/Kok.

Zuidervaart, Lambert. 1979. The legacy of scholarly renewal: A Response to *Anakainosis* 1:4, 1–4. *Anakainosis* (2:2).

————.2016. *Religion, Truth, and Social Transformation, Essays in Reformational Philosophy.* Montreal: McGill-Queen's University Press

CPSIA information can be obtained
at www.ICGtesting.com
Printed in the USA
BVHW070906150321
602550BV00010B/869